REREADING AMERICA

REREADING AMERICA

Cultural Contexts for Critical Thinking and Writing

TENTH EDITION

EDITED BY

Gary Colombo
Emeritus—Los Angeles City College

Robert Cullen
Emeritus—San Jose State University

Bonnie Lisle
University of California, Los Angeles

bedford/st.martin's
Macmillan Learning
Boston | New York

For Bedford/St. Martin's

Vice President, Editorial, Macmillan Learning Humanities: Edwin Hill
Editorial Director, English: Karen S. Henry
Senior Publisher for Composition, Business and Technical Writing, Developmental Writing:
   Leasa Burton
Executive Editor: John Sullivan
Developmental Editor: Regina Tavani
Editorial Assistants: Julia Domenicucci and Eliza Kritz
Production Editor: Louis C. Bruno Jr.
Publishing Services Manager: Andrea Cava
Senior Production Supervisor: Lisa McDowell
Executive Marketing Manager for Readers, Literature, and English: Joy Fisher Williams
Project Management: Books By Design, Inc.
Director of Rights and Permissions: Hilary Newman
Photo Researcher: Sheri Blaney
Text Permissions Researcher: Margaret Gorenstein
Senior Art Director: Anna Palchik
Text Design: Janis Owens
Cover Design: William Boardman
Cover Art: Painting, *Proud to Be an American*, Pat Matthews, www.patmatthewsart.com
Composition: Achorn International, Inc.
Printing and Binding: RR Donnelley and Sons

Copyright © 2016, 2013, 2010, 2007 by Bedford/St. Martin's

Manufactured in the United States of America.

1   0   9   8   7
f   e   d   c

For information, write: Bedford/St. Martin's, 75 Arlington Street, Boston, MA 02116 (617-399-4000)

ISBN 978-1-4576-9921-4 (Student Edition)
ISBN 978-1-4576-9939-9 (Instructor's Edition)

Acknowledgments
Text acknowledgments and copyrights appear at the back of the book on pages 679–81, which constitute an extension of the copyright page. Art acknowledgments and copyrights appear on the same page as the art selections they cover. It is a violation of the law to reproduce these selections by any means whatsoever without the written permission of the copyright holder.

PREFACE FOR INSTRUCTORS

ABOUT *REREADING AMERICA*

Designed for first-year writing and critical thinking courses, *Rereading America* anthologizes a diverse set of readings focused on the myths that dominate U.S. culture. This central theme brings together thought-provoking selections on a broad range of topics — family, education, technology, success, gender, and race — topics that raise controversial issues meaningful to college students of all backgrounds. We've drawn these readings from many sources, both within the academy and outside of it; the selections are both multicultural and cross-curricular and thus represent an unusual variety of voices, styles, and subjects.

The readings in this book speak directly to students' experiences and concerns. Every college student has had some brush with prejudice, and most have something to say about education, the family, or the gender stereotypes they see in films and on television. The issues raised here help students link their personal experiences with broader cultural perspectives and lead them to analyze, or "read," the cultural forces that have shaped and continue to shape their lives. By linking the personal and the cultural, students begin to recognize that they are not academic outsiders — they too have knowledge, assumptions, and intellectual frameworks that give them authority in academic culture. Connecting personal knowledge and academic discourse helps students see that they are able to think, speak, and write academically and that they don't have to absorb passively what the "experts" say.

FEATURES OF THE TENTH EDITION

A Cultural Approach to Critical Thinking   Like its predecessors, the tenth edition of *Rereading America* is committed to the premise that learning to think critically means learning to identify and see beyond dominant cultural myths — collective and often unconsciously held beliefs that influence our thinking, reading, and writing. Instead of treating cultural diversity as just another topic to be studied or "appreciated," *Rereading America* encourages students to grapple with the real differences in perspective that arise in a pluralistic society like ours. This method helps students to break through conventional assumptions and patterns of thought that hinder fresh critical responses and inhibit dialogue. It helps them recognize that even the most apparently "natural" fact or obvious idea results from a process of social construction. And it helps them to develop the intellectual independence essential to critical thinking, reading, and writing.

New Issues   This edition of *Rereading America* includes a new chapter (Chapter Three) devoted to the topic of emerging technologies. Growing up wired to cell phones, the Internet, and social media, today's students inhabit a world that embraces the promise of all things technical. Not since the 1950s has America been so infatuated with the power and promise of science and engineering. We've come to accept as a matter of faith that there is a technological fix for almost every problem — even for the problems that technology creates. In "The Wild Wired West: Myths of Progress on the Tech Frontier," students will have the opportunity to examine American attitudes toward technological innovation and to assess their own attachment to electronic media. Google executives Eric Schmidt and Jared Cohen invite readers to dream about how computers will improve our lives in coming decades. Selections by Internet critics Sherry Turkle, Charles Seife, and danah boyd challenge students to consider the personal and political costs of social media use. Contemporary feminists Laurie Penny and Emily Witt ponder what life online has meant for women and the future of long-term relationships. Selections by Lori Andrews and Henrick Karoliszyn challenge students to consider how online data mining and data-driven "predictive policing" threaten our civil liberties. The chapter's Visual Portfolio and Further Connections questions encourage students to consider how today's high-tech revolution is transforming attitudes about ourselves — and even about what it means to be human.

Timely New Readings   To keep *Rereading America* up to date, we've worked hard to bring you the best new voices speaking on issues of race, gender, class, family, education, and technological progress. As in past editions, we've retained old favorites like Gary Soto, Stephanie Coontz, John Taylor Gatto, Malcolm X, Jonathan Kozol, Mike Rose, Barbara Ehrenreich, Jamaica Kincaid, Jean Kilbourne, and Michael Kimmel. But you'll also find a host of new selections by authors such as Sarah Boxer, Diane Ravitch, William Deresiewicz, Sherry Turkle, Robert Reich, Rebecca Solnit, Ta-Nehisi Coates, and Sherman Alexie. And like earlier versions, this edition of *Rereading America* includes a healthy mix of personal and academic writing, representing a wide variety of genres, styles, and rhetorical strategies.

Visual Portfolios   In addition to frontispieces and cartoons, we've included a Visual Portfolio of myth-related images in every chapter of *Rereading America*. These collections of photographs invite students to examine how visual "texts" are constructed and how, like written texts, they are susceptible to multiple readings and rereadings. Each portfolio is accompanied by a series of questions that encourage critical analysis and connect portfolio images to ideas and themes in chapter reading selections. As in earlier editions, the visual frontispieces that open each chapter are integrated into the prereading assignments found in the chapter introductions. The cartoons, offered as a bit of comic relief and as opportunities for visual thinking, are paired with appropriate readings thoughout the text.

Focus on Media We've continued the practice of including selections focusing on the media. Chapter One includes a selection by Sarah Boxer analyzing depictions of families in animated films. In Chapter Two, Carmen Lugo-Lugo examines the ways media stereotypes shape students' assumptions about Latino/a professors. Nearly every reading in Chapter Three focuses on Internet culture and the impact of social media. Chapter Four includes a selection by Diana Kendall on the media's role in disseminating myths of material success. Chapter Five offers analyses of gender issues in the media, including Jean Kilbourne on images of women in advertising and Joan Morgan on black feminism and hip-hop culture. In Chapter Six, Cheryl I. Harris and Devon W. Carbado explore how bias shaped media reports of the aftermath of Hurricane Katrina.

Focus on Struggle and Resistance Most multicultural readers approach diversity in one of two ways: either they adopt a pluralist approach and conceive of American society as a kind of salad bowl of cultures or, in response to worries about the lack of "objectivity" in the multicultural curriculum, they take what might be called the "talk show" approach and present American culture as a series of pro-and-con debates on a number of social issues. The tenth edition of *Rereading America*, like its predecessors, follows neither of these approaches. Pluralist readers, we feel, make a promise that's impossible to keep: no single text, and no single course, can do justice to the many complex cultures that inhabit the United States. Thus the materials selected for *Rereading America* aren't meant to offer a taste of what "family" means for Native Americans or the flavor of gender relations among immigrants. Instead, we've included selections like Melvin Dixon's "Aunt Ida Pieces a Quilt" or John Taylor Gatto's "Against School" because they offer us fresh critical perspectives on the common myths that shape our ideas, values, and beliefs. Rather than seeing this anthology as a mosaic or kaleidoscope of cultural fragments that combine to form a beautiful picture, it's more accurate to think of *Rereading America* as a handbook that helps students explore the ways that the dominant culture shapes their ideas, values, and beliefs.

This notion of cultural dominance is studiously avoided in most multicultural anthologies. "Salad bowl" readers generally sidestep the issue of cultural dynamics: intent on celebrating America's cultural diversity, they offer a relatively static picture of a nation fragmented into a kind of cultural archipelago. "Talk show" readers admit the idea of conflict, but they distort the reality of cultural dynamics by presenting cultural conflicts as a matter of rational — and equally balanced — debate. All of the materials anthologized in *Rereading America* address the cultural struggles that animate American society — the tensions that result from the expectations established by our dominant cultural myths and the diverse realities that these myths often contradict.

Extensive Apparatus *Rereading America* offers a wealth of features to help students hone their analytic abilities and to aid instructors as they plan class discussions, critical thinking activities, and writing assignments. These include:

- *A Comprehensive Introductory Essay* The book begins with a comprehensive essay, "Thinking Critically, Challenging Cultural Myths," that introduces students to the relationships among thinking, cultural diversity, and the notion of dominant cultural myths, and that shows how such myths can influence their academic performance. We've also included a section devoted to active reading, which offers suggestions for prereading, prewriting, note taking, text marking, and keeping a reading journal. Another section helps students work with the many visual images included in the book.

- *"Fast Facts" Begin Each Chapter*   Several provocative statistics before each chapter introduction provide context for students and prompt discussion. For example, "60% of Americans say that they have witnessed offensive behavior online. 70% of young adults 18 to 24 say they have been threatened, harassed, or stalked online."

- *Detailed Chapter Introductions*   An introductory essay at the beginning of each chapter offers students a thorough overview of each cultural myth, placing it in historical context, raising some of the chapter's central questions, and orienting students to the chapter's internal structure.

- *Prereading Activities*   Following each chapter introduction you'll find prereading activities designed to encourage students to reflect on what they already know about the cultural myth in question. Often connected to the images that open every chapter, these prereading activities help students to engage the topic even before they begin to read.

- *Questions to Stimulate Critical Thinking*   Three groups of questions following each selection encourage students to consider the reading carefully in several contexts: "Engaging the Text" focuses on close reading of the selection itself; "Exploring Connections" puts the selection into dialogue with other selections throughout the book; "Extending the Critical Context" invites students to connect the ideas they read about here with sources of knowledge outside the anthology, including library and Internet research, personal experience, interviews, ethnographic-style observations, and so forth. As in past editions, we've included a number of questions linking readings with contemporary television shows and feature films for instructors who want to address the interplay of cultural myths and the mass media. In the tenth edition, we've increased the number of questions focusing on writers' rhetorical and stylistic strategies. These questions are now identified "Thinking Rhetorically" for easy reference; when they are included, they appear as the final question under "Engaging the Text."

- *"Further Connections" Close Each Chapter*   These questions and assignments help students make additional connections among readings. They also provide suggestions for exploring issues through research and include ideas for community projects.

ACKNOWLEDGMENTS

Critical thinking is always a collaborative activity, and the kind of critical thinking involved in the creation of a text like *Rereading America* represents collegial collaboration at its very best. Since publication of the last edition, we've heard from instructors across the country who have generously offered suggestions for new classroom activities and comments for further refinements and improvements. Among the many instructors who shared their insights with us as we reworked this edition, we'd particularly like to thank Douglas Armendarez, East Los Angeles College; Tolu Bamishigbin, University of California, Los Angeles; Sheena Boran, University of Mississippi; David Bordelon, Ocean County College; Jane Carey, Quinebaug Valley Community College; Kirsti Cole, Minnesota State University; Rachelle Costello, Indiana University, South Bend; Virginia Crisco, California State University, Fresno; Peter DeNegre, Tunxis Community College; Tiffany Denman, Sacramento City College; Peter Dorman, Central Virginia Community College; Chip Dunkin, University of Mississippi; Randa Elbih, Grand Valley State University; Maria Estrada, Mt. San Antonio College; Karen Forgette, University of Mississippi; JoAnn Foriest, Prairie State College; Kimberly Hall, Harrisburg Area Community College; Barbara Heifferon, Louisiana State University; Cristina Herrera, California State University, Fresno; Robert Imbur, University of Toledo; Danielle Lake, Grand Valley State University; Catherine Lamas, East Los Angeles College; Danielle Muller, Los Angeles City College; Pamela McGlynn, Southwestern College; Charlotte Morgan, Cleveland State University; Eduardo Munoz, East Los Angeles College; Kylie Olean, University of Hartford; Heather Seratt, University of Houston-Downtown; Phil Wagner, University of California, Los Angeles; Jessica Walsh, Harper College; Vallie Watson, University of North Carolina at Wilmington; Judith Wigdortz, Monmouth University; Mary Williams, San Jose State University.

For their help with the ninth edition, we'd like to thank the following: Janice Agee, Sacramento City College; Fredric J. Ball, Southwestern College; Chantell M. Barnhill, Indiana University, South Bend; Norka Blackman-Richards, Queens College—The City University of New York; Candace Boeck, San Diego State University; Mark Brock-Cancellieri, Stevenson University; Audrey Cameron, North Idaho College; Catheryn Cheal, Oakland University; Kirsti Cole, Minnesota State University, Mankato; Sean P. Connolly, Tulane University; Jackson Connor, Guilford College; Myrto Drizou, State University of New York at Buffalo; David Estrada, Fullerton College; Jacquelyn Lee Gardner, Western Michigan University; Rochelle Gregory, North Central Texas College; Gwyn Fallbrooke, University of Minnesota; Philip Fishman, Barry University; Naomi E. Hahn, Illinois College; Rick Hansen, California State University, Fresno; Nels P. Highberg, University of Hartford; Amy Lynn Ingalls, Three Rivers Community College; Asao B. Inoue, California State University, Fresno; Amanda Katz, Worcester State University; O. Brian Kaufman, Quinebaug Valley Community College; Barbara Kilgust, Carroll University; Carolyn Kremers, University of Alaska, Fairbanks; Catherine Lamas, East Los Angeles College; Sharon A. Lefevre, Community College of Philadelphia; Alisea Williams McLeod, Indiana University, South Bend; Tanya Millner-Harlee, Manchester Community College; Ilona Missakian, Rio Hondo College; Roxanne Munch, Joliet Junior

College; Katrina J. Pelow, Kent State University; M. Karen Powers, Kent State University at Tuscarawas; Kevin Quirk, DePaul University; Alex Reid, State University of New York at Buffalo; Brad C. Southard, Appalachian State University; Terry Spaise, University of California, Riverside; Sarah Stanley, University of Alaska, Fairbanks.

For their help with the eighth edition, we'd like to thank Lysbeth Benkert-Rasmussen, Northern State University; Harilaos Costarides, City College of San Francisco; Sharon Delmendo, St. John Fisher College; Deanne Fernandez, San Diego State University; Art Goldman, East Los Angeles College; Kim Greenfield, Lorain County Community College; Tim Gustafson, University of Minnesota; Adam Heidenreich, Joliet Junior College; Jeffrey Hillard, College of Mount St. Joseph; Robert S. Imbur, University of Toledo; Deveryle James, University at Buffalo; Kerry J. Lane, Joliet Junior College; Kristin LaTour, Joliet Junior College; Scott A. Leonard, Youngstown State University; Carol Nowotny-Young, University of Arizona; Laura Patterson, Seton Hill University; Michael Ronan, Houston Community College; Carolyn E. Rubin-Trimble, University of Houston–Downtown; Steven Wolfe, Houston Community College.

We are also grateful to those reviewers who helped shape previous editions.

As always, we'd also like to thank all the kind folks at Bedford/St. Martin's, who do their best to make the effort of producing a book like this a genuine pleasure. We're especially grateful to Edwin Hill, Leasa Burton, Karen Henry, and John Sullivan. We thank Regina Tavani, our editor, whose patience and professionalism have helped us immensely throughout the development of this new edition. We also want to thank Louis Bruno, who served as production editor; Nancy Benjamin and the team at Books By Design, who managed copyediting and composition; William Boardman, who produced our new cover; Margaret Gorenstein, for clearing text permissions; Sheri Blaney, for researching and tracking down art; and editorial assistants Eliza Kritz and Julia Domenicucci, who helped out with many of the hundreds of details that go into a project such as this. Finally, we'd like to acknowledge our spouses, Elena Barcia, Liz Silver, and Roy Weitz, for their love and support.

Gary Colombo
Robert Cullen
Bonnie Lisle

GET THE MOST OUT OF YOUR COURSE WITH *REREADING AMERICA*

Bedford/St. Martin's offers resources and format choices that help you and your students get even more out of your book and course. To learn more about or to order any of the following products, contact your Bedford/St. Martin's sales representative, e-mail sales support (**sales_support@macmillanusa.com**), or visit the Web site at **macmillanhighered.com/rereading/catalog**.

Choose from Alternative Formats of *Rereading America*

Bedford/St. Martin's offers a range of affordable formats, allowing students to choose the one that works best for them. For details, visit **macmillanhighered .com/rereading/catalog**.

- *Paperback*   To order the paperback edition, use ISBN 978-1-4576-9921-4.

- *Other popular e-book formats*   For details, visit **macmillanhighered.com /ebooks**.

Select Value Packages

Add value to your text by packaging one of the following resources with *Rereading America*. To learn more about package options for any of the following products, contact your Bedford/St. Martin's sales representative or visit **macmillanhighered.com/rereading/catalog**.

Writer's Help 2.0 is a powerful online writing resource that helps students find answers, whether they are searching for writing advice on their own or as part of an assignment.

- **Smart search**
  Built on research with more than 1,600 student writers, the smart search in *Writer's Help* provides reliable results even when students use novice terms, such as *flow* and *unstuck*.

- **Trusted content from our best-selling handbooks**
  Choose *Writer's Help 2.0, Hacker Version* or *Writer's Help 2.0, Lunsford Version* and ensure that students have clear advice and examples for all of their writing questions.

- **Adaptive exercises that engage students**
  Writer's Help 2.0 includes LearningCurve, game-like online quizzing that adapts to what students already know and helps them focus on what they need to learn.

Student access is packaged with *Rereading America* at a significant discount. Order ISBN 978-1-319-07082-3 for *Writer's Help 2.0, Hacker Version* or ISBN 978-1-319-07084-7 for *Writer's Help 2.0, Lunsford Version* to ensure your students have easy access to online writing support. Students who rent a book or buy a used book can purchase access to Writer's Help 2.0 at **macmillanhighered .com/writershelp2**.

Instructors may request free access by registering as an instructor at **macmillanhighered.com/writershelp2**.

For technical support, visit **macmillanhighered.com/getsupport**.

Portfolio Keeping, **Third Edition, by Nedra Reynolds and Elizabeth Davis**, provides all the information students need to use the portfolio method successfully in a writing course. *Portfolio Teaching*, a companion guide for instructors, provides the practical information instructors and writing program administrators need to use the portfolio method successfully in a writing course. To order *Portfolio Keeping* packaged with this text, contact your sales representative for a package ISBN.

Instructor Resources

macmillanhighered.com/rereading/catalog

You have a lot to do in your course. Bedford/St. Martin's wants to make it easy for you to find the support you need — and to get it quickly.

Resources for Teaching with **Rereading America** is available as a PDF that can be downloaded from the Bedford/St. Martin's online catalog at the URL above. In addition to chapter and reading selection overviews, the instructor's manual includes teaching tips and suggestions for classroom activities.

Join Our Community! The Macmillan English Community is now Bedford/ St. Martin's home for professional resources, featuring Bedford *Bits*, our popular blog site offering new ideas for the composition classroom and composition teachers. Connect and converse with a growing team of Bedford authors and top scholars who blog on *Bits*: Andrea Lunsford, Nancy Sommers, Steve Bernhardt, Traci Gardner, Barclay Barrios, Jack Solomon, Susan Bernstein, Elizabeth Wardle, Doug Downs, Liz Losh, Jonathan Alexander, and Donna Winchell.

In addition, you'll find an expanding collection of additional resources that support your teaching.

- Sign up for webinars

- Download resources from our professional resource series that support your teaching

- Start a discussion

- Ask a question

- Follow your favorite members

- Review projects in the pipeline

Visit **community.macmillan.com** to join the conversation with your fellow teachers.

CONTENTS

PREFACE FOR INSTRUCTORS   v

INTRODUCTION: Thinking Critically, Challenging Cultural Myths   1

①

HARMONY AT HOME   15

The Myth of the Model Family

LOOKING FOR WORK, GARY SOTO   19

> "For weeks I had drunk Kool-Aid and watched morning reruns of *Father Knows Best*, whose family was so uncomplicated in its routine that I very much wanted to imitate it. The first step was to get my brother and sister to wear shoes at dinner."

WHAT WE REALLY MISS ABOUT THE 1950s, STEPHANIE COONTZ   25

> "What most people really feel nostalgic about . . . is the belief that the 1950s provided a more family-friendly economic and social environment, an easier climate in which to keep kids on the straight and narrow, and above all, a greater feeling of hope for a family's long-term future, especially for its young."

AUNT IDA PIECES A QUILT, MELVIN DIXON   41

> "Francine say she gonna send this quilt to Washington like folks doing from all 'cross the country, so many good people gone. Babies, mothers, fathers, and boys like our Junie. . . ."

THE COLOR OF FAMILY TIES: RACE, CLASS, GENDER, AND EXTENDED FAMILY INVOLVEMENT, NAOMI GERSTEL AND NATALIA SARKISIAN   44

> "Marriage actually diminishes ties to kin."

● **VISUAL PORTFOLIO**
READING IMAGES OF AMERICAN FAMILIES 54

FROM **TO THE END OF JUNE: THE INTIMATE LIFE OF**
AMERICAN FOSTER CARE, CRIS BEAM 61

"Can the older kids, tired and traumatized by a decade or more in foster care, really jump into adoption with someone they've never met? And can parents promise to adopt a stranger without a trial run?"

FROM **MARRIAGE MARKETS: HOW INEQUALITY IS REMAKING THE**
AMERICAN FAMILY, JUNE CARBONE AND NAOMI CAHN 77

"It *is* important to see marriage and other intimate relationships as the product of markets. That is, relationships do occur as a result of an exchange, just like the purchase of the latest iPhone."

WHY ARE ALL THE CARTOON MOTHERS DEAD?, SARAH BOXER 86

"Why, when so many real families have mothers and no fathers, do so many children's movies present fathers as the only parents?"

❷

LEARNING POWER 99

The Myth of Education and Empowerment

THE ESSENTIALS OF A GOOD EDUCATION, DIANE RAVITCH 105

"We cheat children when we do not give them the chance to learn more than basic skills. We cheat them when we evaluate them by standardized tests. We undervalue them when we turn them into data points."

AGAINST SCHOOL, JOHN TAYLOR GATTO 114

"School has done a pretty good job of turning our children into addicts, but it has done a spectacular job of turning our children into children."

"I JUST WANNA BE AVERAGE," MIKE ROSE 123

"I was placed in the vocational track, a euphemism for the bottom level. Neither I nor my parents realized what this meant."

FROM **SOCIAL CLASS AND THE HIDDEN CURRICULUM**
OF WORK, JEAN ANYON 136

"Public schools in complex industrial societies like our own make available different types of educational experience and curriculum knowledge to students in different social classes."

● **VISUAL PORTFOLIO**
  READING IMAGES OF EDUCATION AND EMPOWERMENT   154

LEARNING TO READ, MALCOLM X   161

  "My homemade education gave me, with every additional book
  that I read, a little bit more sensitivity to the deafness, dumbness,
  and blindness that was afflicting the black race in America."

STILL SEPARATE, STILL UNEQUAL, JONATHAN KOZOL   170

  "'It is not fair that other kids have a garden and new things.
  But we don't have that. . . . I wish that this school was the most
  beautiful school in the whole [wide] world.'"

**A PROSTITUTE, A SERVANT, AND A CUSTOMER-SERVICE
REPRESENTATIVE: A LATINA IN ACADEMIA**, CARMEN R. LUGO-LUGO   188

  ". . . I wish my students would not dismiss me because I am not
  white and male."

DON'T SEND YOUR KIDS TO THE IVY LEAGUE, WILLIAM DERESIEWICZ   200

  "Our system of elite education manufactures young people who
  are smart and talented and driven, yes, but also anxious, timid,
  and lost, with little curiosity and a stunted sense of purpose. . . ."

THE WILD WIRED WEST   213

Myths of Progress on the Tech Frontier

OUR FUTURE SELVES, ERIC SCHMIDT AND JARED COHEN   219

  "Soon everyone on Earth will be connected. With five billion
  more people set to join the virtual world, the boom in digital
  connectivity will bring gains in productivity, health, education,
  quality of life and myriad other avenues in the physical world. . . ."

GROWING UP TETHERED, SHERRY TURKLE   236

  "Early in my study, a college senior warned me not to be fooled
  by 'anyone you interview who tells you that his Facebook page
  is "the real me." It's like being in a play. You make a character.'"

CYBERSEXISM, LAURIE PENNY   253

  "Sexist trolls, stalkers, mouth-breathing bedroom misogynists: all
  of them attack women out of hatred, in part, for the presence of
  women and girls in public space. . . ."

LOVE ME TINDER, EMILY WITT   270

  ". . . maybe Tinder will be the app for the never-ending present,
  for the idea of one's life not as culminating in a happy ending but
  a long series of encounters, sexual or otherwise."

● **VISUAL PORTFOLIO**
  READING IMAGES OF WIRED CULTURE   283

THE LONELINESS OF THE INTERCONNECTED, CHARLES SEIFE   289

"Ironically, all this interconnection is isolating us. We are all becoming solipsists, trapped in worlds of our own creation."

INEQUALITY: CAN SOCIAL MEDIA RESOLVE SOCIAL DIVISIONS?, DANAH BOYD   303

"The Internet will not inherently make the world more equal, nor will it automatically usher today's youth into a tolerant world. Instead, it lays bare existing and entrenched social divisions."

GEORGE ORWELL . . . MEET MARK ZUCKERBERG, LORI ANDREWS   322

"Everything you post on a social network or other Web site is being digested, analyzed, and monetized. In essence, a second self — a virtual interpretation of you — is being created. . . ."

PRECOGNITIVE POLICE, HENRICK KAROLISZYN   336

"What if there was an alternative to prevent these types of shootings without eradicating guns? What if predictive policing . . . were to intercept killers before they struck?"

4

MONEY AND SUCCESS   345

The Myth of Individual Opportunity

SAM WALTON / JAY Z, GEORGE PACKER   350

" 'I could just feel that stink and shame of being broke lifting off me, and it felt beautiful. The sad shit is that you never really shake it all the way off, no matter how much money you get.' "
—Jay Z

SERVING IN FLORIDA, BARBARA EHRENREICH   363

"I had gone into this venture in the spirit of science, to test a mathematical proposition, but somewhere along the line, in the tunnel vision imposed by long shifts and relentless concentration, it became a test of myself, and clearly I have failed."

CLASS IN AMERICA — 2012, GREGORY MANTSIOS   377

"From cradle to grave, class position has a significant impact on our well-being."

FROM BEYOND OUTRAGE, ROBERT B. REICH   399

"Those at the top get giant rewards no matter how badly they screw up while the rest of us get screwed no matter how hard we work."

● **VISUAL PORTFOLIO**
  READING IMAGES OF INDIVIDUAL OPPORTUNITY   409

FROM A TANGLE OF PATHOLOGY TO A RACE-FAIR AMERICA,
ALAN AJA, DANIEL BUSTILLO, WILLIAM DARITY JR., AND
DARRICK HAMILTON   415

  "What explains the marked and persistent racial gaps in
  employment and wealth? Is discrimination genuinely of only
  marginal importance in America today?"

**FRAMING CLASS, VICARIOUS LIVING, AND CONSPICUOUS
CONSUMPTION,** DIANA KENDALL   424

  "The poor do not fare well on television entertainment shows,
  where writers typically represent them with one-dimensional,
  bedraggled characters standing on a street corner holding
  cardboard signs that read 'Need money for food.'"

SLAVERY IN THE LAND OF THE FREE, KEVIN BALES AND
RON SOODALTER   443

  "We do know that slaves in America are found—or rather
  not found—in nearly all fifty states, working as commercial
  sex slaves, fruit pickers, construction workers, gardeners, and
  domestics."

5

TRUE WOMEN AND REAL MEN   463

Myths of Gender

GIRL, JAMAICA KINCAID   469

  "Try to walk like a lady and not like the slut you are so bent on
  becoming."

**BECOMING MEMBERS OF SOCIETY: LEARNING THE SOCIAL
MEANINGS OF GENDER,** AARON H. DEVOR   471

  "It seems most likely that gender roles are the result of systematic
  power imbalances based on gender discrimination."

QUANDARIES OF REPRESENTATION, MONA EL-GHOBASHY 481

  "Real Muslim and Arab women are extraordinarily diverse. . . .
  Like other human beings, they are fraught with ambiguity,
  contradiction, and inconsistency."

**"TWO WAYS A WOMAN CAN GET HURT": ADVERTISING
AND VIOLENCE,** JEAN KILBOURNE   488

  "Ads don't directly cause violence, of course. But the violent
  images contribute to the state of terror . . . a climate in which
  there is widespread and increasing violence."

● **VISUAL PORTFOLIO**
  READING IMAGES OF GENDER   515

THE LONGEST WAR, REBECCA SOLNIT   522

  "Violence doesn't have a race, a class, a religion, or a nationality,
  but it does have a gender."

FROM FLY-GIRLS TO BITCHES AND HOS, JOAN MORGAN   533

  "The seemingly impenetrable wall of sexism in rap music is really
  the complex mask African Americans often wear both to hide and
  express the pain."

"BROS BEFORE HOS": THE GUY CODE, MICHAEL KIMMEL   540

  "Masculinity is a constant test—always up for grabs, always
  needing to be proved. And the testing starts early."

SISTERHOOD IS COMPLICATED, RUTH PADAWER   550

  "Where . . . should Wellesley draw a line, if a line should even
  be drawn? At trans men? At transmasculine students? What about
  students who are simply questioning their gender?"

6

CREATED EQUAL

                                                              567

The Myth of the Melting Pot

THE CASE FOR REPARATIONS, TA-NEHISI COATES   572

  "An America that asks what it owes its most vulnerable citizens
  is improved and humane. An America that looks away is
  ignoring not just the sins of the past but the sins of the present
  and the certain sins of the future."

THEORIES AND CONSTRUCTS OF RACE, LINDA HOLTZMAN AND
LEON SHARPE   599

  "While race itself is a fiction, the consequences of racism
  are a historical and contemporary fact of American life."

GENTRIFICATION, SHERMAN ALEXIE   615

  "I waved to them but they didn't wave back. I pretended they
  hadn't noticed me and waved again. They stared at me. They
  knew what I had done."

LOOT OR FIND: FACT OR FRAME?, CHERYL I. HARRIS AND
DEVON W. CARBADO   620

  "Frames are not static. Epic events like Katrina push up against
  and can temporarily displace them. All those people. All that
  suffering. This can't be America."

● **VISUAL PORTFOLIO**
   READING IMAGES OF THE MELTING POT   637

LAND OF THE GIANTS, ALEX TIZON   645
   "Americans did seem to me at times like a different species, one
   that had evolved over generations into supreme behemoths."

**FROM REZ LIFE: AN INDIAN'S JOURNEY THROUGH RESERVATION
LIFE**, DAVID TREUER   651
   "To claim that Indian cultures can continue without Indian
   languages only hastens our end . . . because if the culture dies,
   we will have lost the chance not only to live on our own terms
   (something for which our ancestors fought long and hard) but also
   to live in our own terms."

HOW IMMIGRANTS BECOME "OTHER," MARCELO M. SUÁREZ-OROZCO
AND CAROLA SUÁREZ-OROZCO   666
   "Unauthorized immigrants live in a parallel universe. Their lives
   are shaped by forces and habits that are unimaginable to many
   American citizens."

INDEX OF AUTHORS AND TITLES   683

THINKING CRITICALLY, CHALLENGING CULTURAL MYTHS

BECOMING A COLLEGE STUDENT

Beginning college can be a disconcerting experience. It may be the first time you've lived away from home and had to deal with the stresses and pleasures of independence. There's increased academic competition, increased temptation, and a whole new set of peer pressures. In the dorms you may find yourself among people whose backgrounds make them seem foreign and unapproachable. If you commute, you may be struggling against a feeling of isolation that you've never faced before. And then there are increased expectations. For an introductory history class you may read as many books as you covered in a year of high school coursework. In anthropology, you might be asked to conduct ethnographic research — when you've barely heard of an ethnography before, much less written one. In English, you may tackle more formal analytic writing in a single semester than you've ever done in your life.

College typically imposes fewer rules than high school, but also gives you less guidance and makes greater demands — demands that affect the quality as well as the quantity of your work. By your first midterm exam, you may suspect that your previous academic experience is irrelevant, that nothing you've done in school has prepared you to think, read, or write in the ways your professors expect. Your sociology instructor says she doesn't care whether you can remember all the examples in the textbook as long as you can apply the theoretical concepts to real situations. In your composition class, the perfect five-paragraph essay you turn in for your first assignment is dismissed as "superficial, mechanical, and dull." Meanwhile, the lecturer in your political science or psychology course is rejecting ideas about country, religion, family, and self that have always been a part of your deepest beliefs. How can you cope with these new expectations and challenges?

There is no simple solution, no infallible five-step method that works for everyone. As you meet the personal challenges of college, you'll grow as a human being. You'll begin to look critically at your old habits, beliefs, and values, to see them in relation to the new world you're entering. You may have to re-examine your relationships to family, friends, neighborhood, and heritage. You'll have to sort out your strengths from your weaknesses and make tough choices about who you are and who you want to become. Your academic work demands the same process of serious self-examination. To excel in college work you need to grow intellectually — to become a critical thinker.

WHAT IS CRITICAL THINKING?

What do instructors mean when they tell you to think critically? Most would say that it involves asking questions rather than memorizing information. Instead of simply collecting the "facts," a critical thinker probes them, looking for underlying assumptions and ideas. Instead of focusing on dates and events in history or symptoms in psychology, she probes for motives, causes — an explanation of how these things came to be. A critical thinker cultivates the ability to imagine and value points of view different from her own — then strengthens, refines, enlarges, or reshapes her ideas in light of those other perspectives. She is at once open and skeptical: receptive to new ideas yet careful to test them against previous experience and knowledge. In short, a critical thinker is an active learner, someone with the ability to shape, not merely absorb, knowledge.

All this is difficult to put into practice, because it requires getting outside your own skin and seeing the world from multiple perspectives. To see why critical thinking doesn't come naturally, take another look at the cover of this book. Many would scan the title, *Rereading America,* take in the surface meaning — to reconsider America — and go on to page one. There isn't much to question here; it just "makes sense." But what happens with the student who brings a different perspective? For example, a student from El Salvador might justly complain that the title reflects an ethnocentric view of what it means to be an American. After all, since America encompasses all the countries of North, South, and Central America, he lived in "America" long before arriving in the United States. When this student reads the title, then, he actually does *reread* it; he reads it once in the "commonsense" way but also from the perspective of someone who has lived in a country dominated by U.S. intervention and interests. This double vision or double perspective frees him to look beyond the "obvious" meaning of the book and to question its assumptions.

Of course you don't have to be bicultural to become a proficient critical thinker. You can develop a genuine sensitivity to alternative perspectives even if you've never lived outside your hometown. But to do so you need to recognize that there are no "obvious meanings." The automatic equation that the native-born student makes between "America" and the United States seems to make sense only because our culture has traditionally endorsed the idea that the United States *is* America and, by implication, that other countries in this hemisphere are somehow inferior — not the genuine article. We tend to accept this equation and its unfortunate implications because we are products of our culture.

THE POWER OF CULTURAL MYTHS

Culture shapes the way we think; it tells us what "makes sense." It holds people together by providing us with a shared set of customs, values, ideas, and beliefs, as well as a common language. We live enmeshed in this cultural web: it influences the way we relate to others, the way we look, our tastes, our habits; it enters our dreams and desires. But as culture binds us together it also selectively blinds us. As we grow up, we accept ways of looking at the world, ways of thinking and being that might best be characterized as cultural frames of reference or cultural myths. These myths help us understand our place in the world — our place as prescribed by our culture. They define our relationships to friends and lovers, to the past and future, to nature, to power, and to nation. Becoming a critical thinker means learning how to look beyond these cultural myths and the assumptions embedded in them.

You may associate the word "myth" primarily with the myths of the ancient Greeks. The legends of gods and heroes like Athena, Zeus, and Oedipus embodied the central ideals and values of Greek civilization — notions like civic responsibility, the primacy of male authority, and humility before the gods. The stories were "true" not in a literal sense but as reflections of important cultural beliefs. These myths assured the Greeks of the nobility of their origins; they provided models for the roles that Greeks would play in their public and private lives; they justified inequities in Greek society; they helped the Greeks understand human life and destiny in terms that "made sense" within the framework of that culture.

Our cultural myths do much the same. Take, for example, the American dream of success. Since the first European colonists came to the "New World" some four centuries ago, America has been synonymous with the idea of individual opportunity. For generations, immigrants have been lured across the ocean to make their fortunes in a land where the streets were said to be paved with gold. Of course we don't always agree on what success means or how it should be measured. Some calculate the meaning of success in terms of six-figure salaries or the acreage of their country estates. Others discover success in the attainment of a dream — whether it's graduating from college, achieving excellence on the playing field, or winning new rights and opportunities for less fortunate fellow citizens. For some Americans, the dream of success is the very foundation of everything that's right about life in the United States. For others, the American dream is a cultural mirage that keeps workers happy in low-paying jobs while their bosses pocket the profits of an unfair system. But whether you embrace or reject the dream of success, you can't escape its influence. As Americans, we are steeped in a culture that prizes individual achievement; growing up in the United States, we are told again and again by parents, teachers, advertisers, Hollywood writers, politicians, and opinion makers that we, too, can achieve our dream — that we, too, can "Just Do It" if we try. You might aspire to become an Internet tycoon, or you might rebel and opt for a simple life, but you can't ignore the impact of the myth. We each define success in our own way, but ultimately, the myth of success defines who we are and what we think, feel, and believe.

Cultural myths gain such enormous power over us by insinuating themselves into our thinking before we're aware of them. Most are learned at a deep, even unconscious level. Gender roles are a good example. As children we get gender role models from our families, our schools, our churches, and other important institutions. We see them acted out in the relationships between family members or portrayed on television, in the movies, or in song lyrics. Before long, the culturally determined roles we see for women and men appear to us as "self-evident": it seems "natural" for a man to be strong, responsible, competitive, and heterosexual, just as it may seem "unnatural" for a man to shun competitive activity or to take a romantic interest in other men. Our most dominant cultural myths shape the way we perceive the world and blind us to alternative ways of seeing and being. When something violates the expectations that such myths create, it may even be called unnatural, immoral, or perverse.

CULTURAL MYTHS AS OBSTACLES TO CRITICAL THINKING

Cultural myths can have more subtle effects as well. In academic work they can reduce the complexity of our reading and thinking. A few years ago, for example, a professor at Los Angeles City College noted that he and his students couldn't agree in their interpretations of the following poem by Theodore Roethke:

My Papa's Waltz

The whiskey on your breath
Could make a small boy dizzy;
But I hung on like death:
Such waltzing was not easy.

We romped until the pans
Slid from the kitchen shelf;
My mother's countenance
Could not unfrown itself.

The hand that held my wrist
Was battered on one knuckle;
At every step you missed
My right ear scraped a buckle.

You beat time on my head
With a palm caked hard by dirt,
Then waltzed me off to bed
Still clinging to your shirt.

The instructor read this poem as a clear expression of a child's love for his blue-collar father, a rough-and-tumble man who had worked hard all his life ("a palm caked hard by dirt"), who was not above taking a drink of whiskey to ease his mind, but who also found the time to "waltz" his son off to bed. The students didn't see this at all. They saw the poem as a story about an abusive father and heavy drinker. They seemed unwilling to look beyond the father's roughness and the whiskey on his breath, equating these with drunken violence. Although the poem does suggest an element of fear mingled with the boy's excitement ("I hung on like death"), the class ignored its complexity — the mixture of fear, love, and boisterous fun that colors the son's memory of his father. It's possible that some students might overlook the positive traits in the father in this poem because they have suffered child abuse themselves. But this couldn't be true for all the students in the class. The difference between these interpretations lies, instead, in the influence of cultural myths. After all, in a culture now dominated by images of the family that emphasize "positive" parenting, middle-class values, and sensitive fathers, it's no wonder that students refused to see this father sympathetically. Our culture simply doesn't associate good, loving families with drinking or with even the suggestion of physical roughness.

Years of acculturation — the process of internalizing cultural values — leave us with a set of rigid categories for "good" and "bad" parents, narrow conceptions of how parents should look, talk, and behave toward their children. These cultural categories work like mental pigeonholes: they help us sort out and evaluate our experiences rapidly, almost before we're consciously aware of them. They give us a helpful shorthand for interpreting the world; after all, we can't stop to ponder every new situation we meet as if it were a puzzle or a philosophical problem. But while cultural categories help us make practical decisions in everyday life, they also impose their inherent rigidity on our thinking and thus limit our ability to understand the complexity of our experience. They reduce the world to dichotomies — simplified either/or choices: either women or men, either heterosexuals or homosexuals, either nature or culture, either animal or human, either "alien" or American, either them or us.

Rigid cultural beliefs can present serious obstacles to success for first-year college students. In a psychology class, for example, students' cultural myths may so color their thinking that they find it nearly impossible to comprehend Freud's ideas about infant sexuality. Ingrained assumptions about childhood innocence and sexual guilt may make it impossible for them to see children as sexual beings — a concept absolutely basic to an understanding of the history of psychoanalytic theory. Yet college-level critical inquiry thrives on exactly this kind of revision of common sense: academics prize the unusual, the subtle, the ambiguous, the complex — and expect students to appreciate them as well. Good critical thinkers in all academic disciplines welcome the opportunity to challenge conventional ways of seeing the world; they seem to take delight in questioning everything that appears clear and self-evident.

QUESTIONING: THE BASIS OF CRITICAL THINKING

By questioning the myths that dominate our culture, we can begin to resist the limits they impose on our vision. In fact, they invite such questioning. Often our personal experience fails to fit the images the myths project: a young woman's ambition to be a test pilot may clash with the ideal of femininity our culture promotes; a Cambodian immigrant who has suffered from racism in the United States may question our professed commitment to equality; a student in the vocational track may not see education as the road to success that we assume it is; and few of our families these days fit the mythic model of husband, wife, two kids, a dog, and a house in the suburbs.

Moreover, because cultural myths serve such large and varied needs, they're not always coherent or consistent. Powerful contradictory myths coexist in our society and our own minds. For example, while the myth of "the melting pot" celebrates equality, the myth of individual success pushes us to strive for inequality — to "get ahead" of everyone else. Likewise, our attitudes toward education are deeply paradoxical: on one level, Americans tend to see schooling as a valuable experience that unites us in a common culture and helps us bring out the best in ourselves; yet at the same time, we suspect that formal classroom instruction stifles creativity and chokes off natural intelligence and enthusiasm. These contradictions infuse our history, literature, and popular culture; they're so much a part of our thinking that we tend to take them for granted, unaware of their inconsistencies.

Learning to recognize contradictions lies at the very heart of critical thinking, for intellectual conflict inevitably generates questions. Can both (or all) perspectives be true? What evidence do I have for the validity of each? Is there some way to reconcile them? Are there still other alternatives? Questions like these represent the beginning of serious academic analysis. They stimulate the reflection, discussion, and research that are the essence of good scholarship. Thus whether we find contradictions between myth and lived experience, or between opposing myths, the wealth of powerful, conflicting material generated by our cultural mythology offers a particularly rich context for critical inquiry.

THE STRUCTURE OF *REREADING AMERICA*

We've designed this book to help you develop the habits of mind you'll need to become a critical thinker — someone who recognizes the way that cultural myths shape thinking and can move beyond them to evaluate issues from multiple perspectives. Each of the book's six chapters addresses one of the dominant myths of American culture. We begin with the myth that's literally closest to home — the myth of the model family. In Chapter One, "Harmony at Home," we begin with readings that show what makes the mythical nuclear family so appealing and yet so elusive. Subsequent readings and visual images dissect the myth, exploring and explaining working-class families, flexible kinship structures, multiracial families, and foster parenting. The chapter also explores the economic underpinnings of marriage and examines representations of families in animated films. Next we turn to a topic that every student should have a lot to say about — the myth of educational empowerment. Chapter Two, "Learning Power," gives you the chance to reflect on how the "hidden curriculum" of schooling has shaped your own attitudes toward learning. We begin our exploration of American cultural myths by focusing on home and education because most students find it easy to make personal connections with these topics and because they both involve institutions — families and schools — that are surrounded by a rich legacy of cultural stories and myths. These two introductory chapters are followed by consideration of one of the most durable American myths — our national belief in progress. In Chapter Three, "The Wild Wired West: Myths of Progress on the Tech Frontier," you'll have the chance to explore how technologies like the Internet and social media are reshaping American lives. You'll also be invited to consider how our instinctive faith in technology may blind us to threats to privacy, personal liberty, and civility as we join in the silicon revolution.

The second portion of the book focuses on three cultural myths that offer greater intellectual and emotional challenges because they touch on highly charged social issues. Chapter Four introduces what is perhaps the most famous of all American myths, the American Dream. "Money and Success" addresses the idea of unlimited personal opportunity that brought millions of immigrants to our shores and set the story of America in motion. It invites you to weigh some of the human costs of the dream and to reconsider your own definition of a successful life. The next chapter, "True Women and Real Men," considers the socially constructed categories of gender — the traditional roles that enforce differences between women and men. This chapter also explores the perspectives of Americans who defy conventional gender boundaries. Chapter Six, "Created Equal," examines two myths that have powerfully shaped racial and ethnic relations in the United States: the myth of the melting pot, which celebrates cultural homogenization, and the myth of racial and ethnic superiority, which promotes separateness and inequality. This chapter probes the nature of prejudice, explores the ways that prejudicial attitudes are created, and examines ethnic identities within a race-divided society. Each of these two chapters questions how our culture divides and defines our world, how it artificially channels our experience into oppositions like black and white, male and female, straight and gay.

THE SELECTIONS

Our identities — who we are and how we relate to others — are deeply entangled with the cultural values we have internalized since infancy. Cultural myths become so closely identified with our personal beliefs that rereading them actually means rereading ourselves, rethinking the way we see the world. Questioning long-held assumptions can be an exhilarating experience, but it can be distressing too. Thus you may find certain selections in *Rereading America* difficult, controversial, or even downright offensive. They are meant to challenge you and to provoke classroom debate. But as you discuss the ideas you encounter in this book, remind yourself that your classmates may bring with them very different, and equally profound, beliefs. Keep an open mind, listen carefully, and treat other perspectives with the same respect you'd expect other people to show for your own. It's by encountering new ideas and engaging with others in open dialogue that we learn to grow.

Because *Rereading America* explores cultural myths that shape our thinking, it doesn't focus on the kind of well-defined public issues you might expect to find in a traditional composition anthology. You won't be reading arguments for and against affirmative action, bilingual education, or the death penalty here. We've deliberately avoided the traditional pro-and-con approach because we want you to aim deeper than that; we want you to focus on the subtle cultural beliefs that underlie, and frequently determine, the debates that are waged on public issues. We've also steered clear of the "issues approach" because we feel it reinforces simplistic either/or thinking. Polarizing American culture into a series of debates doesn't encourage you to examine your own beliefs or explore how they've been shaped by the cultures you're part of. To begin to appreciate the influence of your own cultural myths, you need new perspectives: you need to stand outside the ideological machinery that makes American culture run to begin to appreciate its power. That's why we've included many strongly dissenting views: there are works by community activists, gay-rights activists, socialists, libertarians, and more. You may find that their views confirm your own experience of what it means to be an American, or you may find that you bitterly disagree with them. We only hope that you will use the materials here to gain some insight into the values and beliefs that shape our thinking and our national identity. This book is meant to complicate the mental categories that our cultural myths have established for us. Our intention is not to present a new "truth" to replace the old but to expand the range of ideas you bring to all your reading and writing in college. We believe that learning to see and value other perspectives will enable you to think more critically — to question, for yourself, the truth of any statement.

You may also note that several selections in *Rereading America* challenge the way you think writing is supposed to look or sound. You won't find many "classic" essays in this book, the finely crafted reflective essays on general topics that are often held up as models of "good writing." It's not that we reject this type of essay in principle. It's just that most writers who stand outside mainstream culture seem to have little use for it.

Our selections, instead, come from a wide variety of sources: professional books and journals from many disciplines, popular magazines, college textbooks, autobiographies, oral histories, and literary works. We've included this variety partly for the very practical reason that you're likely to encounter texts like these in your college coursework. But we also see textual diversity, like ethnic and political diversity, as a way to multiply perspectives and stimulate critical analysis. For example, an academic article like Jean Anyon's study of social class and school curriculum might give you a new way of understanding Mike Rose's personal narrative about his classroom experiences. On the other hand, you may find that some of the teachers Rose encounters don't neatly fit Anyon's theoretical model. Do such discrepancies mean that Anyon's argument is invalid? That her analysis needs to be modified to account for these teachers? That the teachers are simply exceptions to the rule? You'll probably want to consider your own classroom experience as you wrestle with such questions. Throughout the book, we've chosen readings that "talk to each other" in this way and that draw on the cultural knowledge you bring with you. These readings invite you to join the conversation; we hope they raise difficult questions, prompt lively discussion, and stimulate critical inquiry.

THE POWER OF DIALOGUE

Good thinking, like good writing and good reading, is an intensely social activity. Thinking, reading, and writing are all forms of relationship — when you read, you enter into dialogue with an author about the subject at hand; when you write, you address an imaginary reader, testing your ideas against probable responses, reservations, and arguments. Thus you can't become an accomplished writer simply by declaring your right to speak or by criticizing as an act of principle: real authority comes when you enter into the discipline of an active exchange of opinions and interpretations. Critical thinking, then, is always a matter of dialogue and debate — discovering relationships between apparently unrelated ideas, finding parallels between your own experiences and the ideas you read about, exploring points of agreement and conflict between yourself and other people.

We've designed the readings and questions in this text to encourage you to make just these kinds of connections. You'll notice, for example, that we often ask you to divide into small groups to discuss readings, and we frequently suggest that you take part in projects that require you to collaborate with your classmates. We're convinced that the only way you can learn critical reading, thinking, and writing is by actively engaging others in an intellectual exchange. So we've built into the text many opportunities for listening, discussion, and debate.

The questions that follow each selection should guide you in critical thinking. Like the readings, they're intended to get you started, not to set limits; we strongly recommend that you also devise your own questions and pursue them either individually or in study groups. We've divided our questions into three categories. Here's what to expect from each:

- Those labeled "Engaging the Text" focus on the individual selection they follow. They're designed to highlight important issues in the reading, to help you begin questioning and evaluating what you've read, and sometimes to remind you to consider the author's choices of language, evidence, structure, and style. Questions in the latter category are now helpfully labeled "Thinking Rhetorically," and we've included more of them in this edition.

- The questions labeled "Exploring Connections" will lead you from the selection you've just finished to one or more other readings in this book. When you think critically about these connecting questions, though, you'll see some real collisions of ideas and perspectives, not just polite and predictable "differences of opinion."

- The final questions for each reading, "Extending the Critical Context," invite you to extend your thinking beyond the book — to your family, your community, your college, the media, the Internet, or the more traditional research environment of the library. The emphasis here is on creating new knowledge by applying ideas from this book to the world around you and by testing these ideas in your world.

ACTIVE READING

You've undoubtedly read many textbooks, but it's unlikely that you've had to deal with the kind of analytic, argumentative, and scholarly writing you'll find in college and in *Rereading America*. These different writing styles require a different approach to reading as well. In high school you probably read to "take in" information, often for the sole purpose of reproducing it later on a test. In college you'll also be expected to recognize larger issues, such as the author's theoretical slant, her goals and methods, her assumptions, and her relationship to other writers and researchers. These expectations can be especially difficult in the first two years of college, when you take introductory courses that survey large, complex fields of knowledge. With all these demands on your attention, you'll need to read actively to keep your bearings. Think of active reading as a conversation between you and the text: instead of listening passively as the writer talks, respond to what she says with questions and comments of your own. Here are some specific techniques you can practice to become a more active reader.

Prereading and Prewriting

It's best with most college reading to "preread" the text. In prereading, you briefly look over whatever information you have on the author and the selection itself. Reading chapter introductions and headnotes like those provided in this book can save you time and effort by giving you information about the author's background and concerns, the subject or thesis of the selection, and its place in the chapter as a whole. Also take a look at the title and at any headings or subheadings in the piece. These will give you further clues about an article's general scope and organization. Next, quickly skim the entire selection, paying a bit more attention to the first few paragraphs and the conclusion. Now you should have a pretty good sense of the author's position — what she's trying to say in this piece of writing.

At this point you may do one of several things before you settle down to in-depth reading. You may want to jot down in a few lines what you think the author is doing. Or you may want to make a list of questions you can ask about this topic based on your prereading. Or you may want to freewrite a page or so on the subject. Informally writing out your own ideas will prepare you for more in-depth reading by recalling what you already know about the topic.

We emphasize writing about what you've read because reading and writing are complementary activities: being an avid reader will help you as a writer by familiarizing you with a wide range of ideas and styles to draw on; likewise, writing about what you've read will give you a deeper understanding of your reading. In fact, the more actively you "process" or reshape what you've read, the better you'll comprehend and remember it. So you'll learn more effectively by marking a text as you read than by simply reading; taking notes as you read is even more effective than marking, and writing about the material for your own purposes (putting it in your own words and connecting it with what you already know) is better still.

Marking the Text and Taking Notes

After prereading and prewriting, you're ready to begin critical reading in earnest. As you read, be sure to highlight ideas and phrases that strike you as especially significant — those that seem to capture the gist of a particular paragraph or section, or those that relate directly to the author's purpose or argument. While prereading can help you identify central ideas, you may find that you need to reread difficult sections or flip back and skim an earlier passage if you feel yourself getting lost. Many students think of themselves as poor readers if they can't whip through an article at high speed without pausing. However, the best readers read recursively — that is, they shuttle back and forth, browsing, skimming, and rereading as necessary, depending on their interest, their familiarity with the subject, and the difficulty of the material. This shuttling actually parallels what goes on in your mind when you read actively, as you alternately recall prior knowledge or experience and predict or look for clues about where the writer is going next.

Keep a record of your mental shuttling by writing comments in the margins as you read. It's often useful to gloss the contents of each paragraph or section, to summarize it in a word or two written alongside the text. This note will serve as a reminder or key to the section when you return to it for further thinking, discussion, or writing. You may also want to note passages that puzzled you. Or you may want to write down personal reactions or questions stimulated by the reading. Take time to ponder why you felt confused or annoyed or affirmed by a particular passage. Let yourself wonder "out loud" in the margins as you read.

The following section illustrates one student's notes on a passage from Mike Rose's "I Just Wanna Be Average" (p. 124). In this example, you can see that the reader puts glosses or summary comments to the left of the passage and questions or personal responses to the right. You should experiment and create your own system of note taking, one that works best for the way you read. Just remember that your main goals in taking notes are to help you understand the author's over-all position, to deepen and refine your responses to the selection, and to create a permanent record of those responses.

"I JUST WANNA BE AVERAGE"
MIKE ROSE

Who says this?

A **professor** in the **UCLA Graduate School of Education and Information Studies**, Mike Rose (b. 1944) has won awards from the National Academy of Education, the National Council of Teachers of English, and the John Simon Guggenheim Memorial Foundation. Below you'll read the story of how this highly successful teacher and writer **started high school in the vocational education track**, learning dead-end skills from teachers who were often underprepared or incompetent.

Like tech-ed or woodshop?

Not public school

Intro: Trip to school

IT TOOK TWO BUSES TO GET TO Our Lady of Mercy. The first started deep in South Los Angeles and caught me at midpoint. The second drifted through neighborhoods with trees, parks, big lawns, and lots of flowers. The rides were long but were livened up by a group of South L.A. veterans whose parents also thought that Hope had set up shop in the west end of the county. There was Christy Biggars, who, at sixteen, was dealing and was, according to rumor, a pimp as well. There were Bill Cobb and Johnny Gonzales, grease-pencil artists extraordinaire, who left Nembutal-enhanced[1] swirls of "Cobb" and "Johnny" on the corrugated walls of the bus. And then there was Tyrrell Wilson. Tyrrell was the coolest kid I knew. He ran the dozens[2] like a

Goes from inner city to suburbs?

Friends = his street cred?

---

[1]**Nembutal:** Trade name for pentobarbital, a sedative drug. [All notes are the editors'.]
[2]**the dozens:** A verbal game of African origin in which competitors try to top each other's insults.

metric halfback, laid down a rap that outrhymed and outpointed Cobb, whose rap was good but not great—the curse of a moderately soulful kid trapped in white skin. But it was Cobb who would sneak a radio onto the bus, and thus underwrote his patter with Little Richard, Fats Domino, Chuck Berry, the Coasters, and Ernie K. Doe's[3] mother-in-law, an awful woman who was "sent from down below." . . .

My homeroom was supervised by <u>Brother Dill</u>, a troubled and unstable man who also taught freshman English. When his class drifted away from him, which was often, his voice would rise in paranoid accusations, and occasionally he would lose control and <u>shake or smack us</u>. I hadn't been there two months when one of his brisk, face-turning slaps had my glasses sliding down the aisle. <u>Physical education</u> was also pretty harsh. Our teacher was a stubby ex-lineman who had played old-time pro ball in the Midwest. He routinely had us grabbing our ankles to <u>receive his stinging paddle across our butts</u>. He did that, he said, to make men of us. "Rose," he bellowed on our first encounter; me standing geeky in line in my baggy shorts. "'Rose'? What the hell kind of name is that?"

Abuse, sexism, prejudice (Not my H.S.!)

Classes + Teachers

"Italian, sir," I squeaked.

"Italian! Ho. Rose, do you know the sound a bag of shit makes when it hits the wall?"

"No, sir."

"Wop!"[4]

Keeping a Reading Journal

You may also want (or be required) to keep a reading journal in response to the selections you cover in *Rereading America*. In such a journal you'd keep all the freewriting that you do either before or after reading. Some students find it helpful to keep a double-entry journal, writing initial responses on the left side of the page and adding later reflections and reconsiderations on the right. You may want to use your journal as a place to explore personal reactions to your reading. For example, you might make notes about ideas or lines in the reading that surprise you. Or you might want to note how the selection connects to your own experiences or why you found it particularly interesting or dull. You can do this by writing out imaginary dialogues — between two writers who address the same subject, between yourself and the writer of the selection, or between two parts of yourself. You can use the journal as a place to rewrite passages from a poem or an essay in your own voice and from your own point of view. You can write letters to an author you particularly like or dislike or to a character in a story or poem. You might even draw a cartoon that comments on one of the reading selections.

Many students don't write as well as they could because they're afraid to take risks. They may have been repeatedly penalized for breaking "rules" of grammar or

[3]**Little Richard . . . and Ernie K. Doe:** Popular black musicians of the 1950s.
[4]**Wop:** Derogatory term for Italian.

essay form; their main concern becomes avoiding trouble rather than exploring ideas or experimenting with style. But without risk and experimentation, there's little possibility of growth. One of the benefits of journal writing is that it gives you a place to experiment with ideas, free from worries about "correctness." Here are two examples of student journal entries, in response to Mike Rose's "I Just Wanna Be Average" (we reprint the entries as they were written):

Entry 1: Personal Response to Rose

It's interesting that Rose describes how school can label you and stifle your dreams and also how it can empower you and open doors in your life. When he goes to Our Lady, they put him in a crappy Voc-Ed. track by mistake — incredible because this could mess up his entire life. I knew lots of kids who were forced into ESL back in middle school just because they spoke Spanish. What a waste! Still, when Rose meets Mr. MacFarland, his whole life changes cause the guy makes learning exciting and he knows how to hook the kids on ideas. Mr. Moore was my Mr. Mac. He used to push us to read stuff way beyond grade level, things like Fight Club and Malcolm X. He was also like MacFarland because he made everything personal. We used to spend weeks doing research on big issues like police brutality — and then we'd hold day-long debates that'd get really heated. But then there were a-hole teachers too — the ones who didn't care and would just sit there and read the paper while we did homework drills in our books. We had some nut-jobs like Brother Dill, but nobody'd dare hit us or call us names. All that's changed since Rose was in school — or maybe it's changed at least in public school. Maybe the nuns still can get away with it?

Entry 2: Dialogue Between Rose and Ken Harvey

Rose: I never really understood why you said that you just wanted to be average. It always seemed to me that you were just buying into the bull that the Voc-Ed teachers were handing out about us. Why would you give up when you were obviously smarter than most of them?

Harvey: You wouldn't understand 'cause you were one of McFarland's favorites. You were a hipster-nerd and that was the ID that got you through school. Mine was different. I was a jock and a rebel—and both seemed better than being a brain. We thought you guys were just kissing up— and that you read books because you couldn't make it on the field.

Rose: But you just threw your future away. We all knew you were a leader and that you could've done anything if you tried.

Harvey: Yeah, but why try? I wasn't interested in postponing my life the way you were. I had girlfriends and people thought I was cool. My parents didn't expect much out of me except sports. So why not just do the minimum in school and enjoy my life? Reading a lot of weird books on religion and philosophy didn't make me particularly happy. Maybe we just wanted different things. Have you thought about that?

Rose: I just figured you were protecting yourself against being classified as a Voc-Ed. Protecting yourself against being seen as working class.

Harvey: Maybe I wasn't. Maybe I was happy being who I was and I didn't need school to change me the way you did. School just isn't for everybody.

You'll notice that in the first entry the writer uses Rose's memoir as a point of departure for her own reflections on school and education. She also uses the journal as a place to pose questions about Rose's essay and about schooling in general. In the second entry she explores how a shift in perspective might challenge Rose's conclusions about Ken Harvey and his attitude toward education. Rose sees the damage schooling can do, but he ultimately accepts the idea that education can empower us. That's why he assumes that Harvey has given up on himself when he won't try to be more than just average. But what if Harvey's choice isn't just a matter of self-protection? What if it's a rational expression of who he is? Here, the writer uses an imaginary dialogue to explore alternatives to Rose's own thinking about school as a means of self-transformation.

WORKING WITH VISUAL IMAGES

The myths we examine in *Rereading America* make their presence felt not only in the world of print — essays, stories, poems, memoirs — but in every aspect of our culture. Consider, for example, the myth of "the American family." If you want to design a minivan, a restaurant, a cineplex, a park, a synagogue, a personal computer, or a tax code, you had better have some idea of what families are like and how they behave. Most important, you need a good grasp of what Americans *believe* about families, about the mythology of the American family. The Visual Portfolio in each chapter, while it maintains our focus on myths, also carries you beyond the medium of print and thus lets you practice your analytic skills in a different arena.

Although we are all surrounded by visual stimuli, we don't always think critically about what we see. Perhaps we are numbed by constant exposure to a barrage of images on TV, in films, and in social media and other Web sites. In any case, here are a few tips on how to get the most out of the images we have collected for this book. Take the time to look at the images carefully; first impressions are important, but many of the photographs contain details that might not strike you immediately. Once you have noted the immediate impact of an image, try focusing on separate elements such as background, foreground, facial expressions, and body language. Read any text that appears in the photograph, even if it's on a T-shirt or a belt buckle. Remember that many photographs are carefully *constructed*, no matter how "natural" they may look. In a photo for a magazine advertisement, for example, everything is meticulously chosen and arranged: certain actors or models are cast for their roles; they wear makeup; their clothes are really costumes; the location or setting of the ad is designed to reinforce its message; lighting is artificial; and someone is trying to sell you something.

Also be sure to consider the visual images contextually, not in isolation. How does each resemble or differ from its neighbors in the portfolio? How does it reinforce or challenge cultural beliefs or stereotypes? Put another way, how can it be understood in the context of the myths examined in *Rereading America*? Each portfolio is accompanied by a few questions to help you begin this type of analysis. You can also build a broader context for our visual images by collecting your own, then working in small groups to create a portfolio or collage.

Finally, remember that both readings and visual images are just starting points for discussion. You have access to a wealth of other perspectives and ideas among your family, friends, classmates; in your college library; in your personal experience; and in your imagination. We urge you to consult them all as you grapple with the perspectives you encounter in this text.

HARMONY AT HOME
The Myth of the Model Family

The Donna Reed Show.

FAST FACTS

1. Only 46% of American kids now live in a "traditional family"—defined as a home with two married heterosexual parents in their first marriage. In 1973, 73% of U.S. children lived in such families.

2. Roughly one in four young adults now lives in a multigenerational family household.

3. More than 400,000 American children live in some form of foster care.

4. Among "millennials"—those born after 1980—only 30% say having a successful marriage is "one of the most important things" in life.

5. In 1960, there were 87 employed African American men per 100 black women, and in 2012, only 51.

6. Approximately 22% of Americans ages 25 to 34 have used an online dating site or mobile dating app, as have 10% of those ages 18 to 24.

7. In the months after the U.S. Supreme Court legalized same-sex marriage nationwide, Texas issued approximately 2,500 marriage licenses to same-sex couples—nearly 6% of the statewide total.

Data from (1), (2), (4), (6) Pew Research Center; (3) U.S. Department of Health and Human Services; (5) *The Wall Street Journal*, September 24, 2014; (7) Associated Press, September 13, 2015.

THE FAMILY MAY BE THE ORIGINAL CULTURAL INSTITUTION; people lived in families long before they invented the wheel, began farming, or founded cities. You might think that by now we would have clear and stable ideas about what defines a family, how families form and dissolve, what forms they can take, and how they can best raise their children. But such absolutely fundamental elements of family life have shifted dramatically through the centuries and continue to change today—perhaps faster than ever before. The most dramatic recent change in the United States is the groundswell of support for same-sex marriage: marriage equality, a concept almost unheard of thirty years ago, is now being claimed as a fundamental human right. Other changes are garnering fewer headlines but nonetheless are reshaping the values and behaviors we associate with family life. Both divorce and cohabitation have become more common and less stigmatized, and "singlehood" has gained traction as a perfectly normal alternative to marriage. An increasing number of adult Americans are now living in multigenerational families, whose larger households help them economize in tough times as well as provide for elderly members. Meanwhile, birth control, reproductive technologies, surrogacy, and genetic screening for heritable diseases are giving people more choices about whether, when, and how to have children.

Although experts agree that family and marriage are changing, there is little consensus about what these changes mean. Are we witnessing the collapse of family values, or a welcome evolution beyond restrictive and discriminatory models of family life? Central to this cultural debate is the traditional nuclear family — Dad, Mom, a couple of kids, maybe a dog, and a spacious suburban home. Millions of Americans aspire to this middle-class "model family," while others see it as limiting, unattainable, or simply outdated. Whatever value you, your family, or your community may place on the nuclear family, it's important to recognize that it's been around a short time, especially compared with the long history of the family itself.

In fact, what we call the "traditional" family, headed by a breadwinner-father and a housewife-mother, has existed for little more than two hundred years, and the suburbs only came into being in the 1950s. But the family as a social institution was legally recognized in Western culture at least as far back as the Code of Hammurabi, created in ancient Mesopotamia some four thousand years ago. To appreciate how profoundly concepts of family life have changed, consider the absolute power of the Mesopotamian father, the patriarch: the law allowed him to use any of his dependents, including his wife, as collateral for loans or even to sell family members outright to pay his debts.

Although patriarchal authority was less absolute in Puritan America, fathers remained the undisputed heads of families. Seventeenth-century Connecticut, Massachusetts, and New Hampshire enacted laws condemning rebellious children to severe punishment and, in extreme cases, to death. In the early years of the American colonies, as in Western culture stretching back to Hammurabi's time, unquestioned authority within the family served as both the model for and the basis of state authority. Just as family members owed complete obedience to the father, so all citizens owed unquestioned loyalty to the king and his legal representatives. In his influential volume *Democracy in America* (1835), French aristocrat Alexis de Tocqueville describes the relationship between the traditional European family and the old political order:

> Among aristocratic nations, social institutions recognize, in truth, no one in the family but the father; children are received by society at his hands; society governs him, he governs them. Thus, the parent not only has a natural right, but acquires a political right to command them; he is the author and the support of his family; but he is also its constituted ruler.

By the mid-eighteenth century, however, new ideas about individual freedom and democracy were stirring the colonies. And by the time Tocqueville visited the United States in 1831, they had evidently worked a revolution in the family as well as in the nation's political structure: he observes, "When the condition of society becomes democratic, and men adopt as their general principle that it is good and lawful to judge of all things for one's self, . . . the power which the opinions of a father exercise over those of his sons diminishes, as well as his legal power." To Tocqueville, this shift away from strict patriarchal rule signaled a change in the emotional climate of families: "as manners and laws become more democratic, the relation of father and son becomes more intimate and more affectionate; rules and authority are less talked of, confidence and tenderness are oftentimes increased, and it would seem that the natural bond is drawn closer." In his view, the American family heralded a new era in human relations. Freed from the rigid hierarchy of the past, parents and children could meet as near equals, joined by "filial love and fraternal affection."

This vision of the democratic family — a harmonious association of parents and children united by love and trust — has mesmerized popular culture in the United States. From the nineteenth century to the present, popular novels, magazines, music, and advertising images have glorified the comforts of loving domesticity. The mythical American family — happy, healthy, and modestly affluent — is well portrayed in the frontispiece to this chapter (*The Donna Reed Show*, p. 15). For several decades we have absorbed our strongest impressions of the family from television. In the 1950s we watched the Andersons on *Father Knows Best*, the Stones on *The Donna Reed Show*, and the real-life Nelson family on *The Adventures of Ozzie & Harriet*. Over the next three decades the model stretched to include single parents, second marriages, and interracial adoptions on *My Three Sons*, *The Brady Bunch*, and *Diff 'rent Strokes*, but the underlying ideal of wise, loving parents and harmonious happy families remained unchanged. Over the last twenty-five years our collective vision of the family has grown darker; prominent television families have included gangsters on *The Sopranos*, a drug-dealing mother on *Weeds*, drug abusers on *Nurse Jackie*, a drunk deadbeat dad on *Shameless*, and innumerable nontraditional family structures, including the four-wife, one-husband household on *Sister Wives*. Clearly the 1950s myth of the happy nuclear family scarcely reflects the complexities of current American life. Just as clearly, our never-ending fascination with television families underscores the cultural importance of family dynamics and family boundaries.

This chapter examines the myths and realities surrounding the American family. The myths' origins are explored in the chapter's first reading selection, "Looking for Work," in which Gary Soto recalls his boyhood desire to transform his working-class Chicano family into a facsimile of the Cleavers on *Leave It to Beaver*. Stephanie Coontz, in "What We Really Miss About the 1950s," then takes a close analytical look at the 1950s family, explaining its lasting appeal to some Americans but also documenting its dark side.

The next selections use literary, sociological, and visual approaches to explore the meanings of family. "Aunt Ida Pieces a Quilt," a short poem by Melvin Dixon, tells the story of an extended African American family helping one another cope with the loss of Ida's nephew to AIDS. "The Color of Family Ties: Race, Class, Gender, and Extended Family Involvement," by Naomi Gerstel and Natalia Sarkisian, moves us from individual experience to sociological analysis, as the authors challenge common misconceptions by carefully examining how ethnicity and social class shape the behaviors of American families. Next, the chapter's Visual Portfolio offers you a chance to practice interpreting images; the photographs in this collection suggest some of the complex ways the contemporary American family intersects with gender, ethnicity, and social class.

After the Visual Portfolio, the chapter investigates three diverse arenas of American family life. In an excerpt from *To the End of June: The Intimate Life of American Foster Care*, Cris Beam tells the story of "Oneida," a girl attempting to transition from a foster care facility to life with a married middle-class couple. Next, family law experts June Carbone and Naomi Cahn explain the profound influence of economics in people's decisions about marriage; the selection comes from their 2014 book *Marriage Markets: How Inequality Is Remaking the American Family*. The chapter concludes with a lively essay by Sarah Boxer, answering a question that perhaps haunted your childhood: "Why Are All the Cartoon Mothers Dead?"

Sources

Lerner, Gerda. *The Creation of Patriarchy*. New York: Oxford University Press, 1986. Print.

Mintz, Steven, and Susan Kellogg. *Domestic Revolutions: A Social History of American Life*. New York: Free Press, 1988. Print.

Tocqueville, Alexis de. *Democracy in America*. 1835. New York: Vintage Books, 1990. Print.

BEFORE READING

- Spend ten minutes or so jotting down every word, phrase, or image you associate with the idea of "family." Write as freely as possible, without censoring your thoughts or worrying about grammatical correctness. Working in small groups, compare lists and try to categorize your responses. What assumptions about families do they reveal?

- Draw a visual representation of your family. This could take the form of a graph, chart, diagram, map, cartoon, symbolic picture, or literal portrait. Don't worry if you're not a skillful artist: the main point is to convey an idea, and even stick figures can speak eloquently. When you're finished, write a journal entry about your drawing. Was it easier to depict some feelings or ideas visually than it would have been to describe them in words? Did you find some things about your family difficult or impossible to convey visually? Does your drawing "say" anything that surprises you?

- Write a journal entry about how you think attending college has changed, or will change, your relationship to your family.

LOOKING FOR WORK
GARY SOTO

"Looking for Work" is the narrative of a nine-year-old Mexican American boy who wants his family to imitate the "perfect families" he sees on TV. Much of the humor in this essay comes from the author's perspective as an adult looking back at his childhood self, but Soto also respects the child's point of view. In the marvelous details of this mid-summer day, Soto captures the interplay of seductive myth and complex reality. Gary Soto (b. 1952) grew up "on the industrial side of Fresno, right smack against a junkyard and the junkyard's cross-eyed German shepherd." Having discovered poetry almost by chance in a city college library, he has now published eleven volumes of his own for adult readers, in addition to many volumes of fiction, nonfiction, and poetry for children and young adult readers. His *New and Selected Poems* (1995) was a finalist for both the *Los Angeles Times* Book Award and the National Book Award. Recent publications include a book of poems entitled *Sudden Loss of Dignity* and a memoir, *What Poets Are Like: Up and Down with the Writing Life* (both 2013).

ONE JULY, WHILE KILLING ANTS ON THE KITCHEN SINK with a rolled newspaper, I had a nine-year-old's vision of wealth that would save us from ourselves. For weeks I had drunk Kool-Aid and watched morning reruns of *Father Knows Best*, whose family was so uncomplicated in its routine that I very much wanted to imitate it. The first step was to get my brother and sister to wear shoes at dinner.

"Come on, Rick—come on, Deb," I whined. But Rick mimicked me and the same day that I asked him to wear shoes he came to the dinner table in only his swim trunks. My mother didn't notice, nor did my sister, as we sat to eat our beans and tortillas in the stifling heat of our kitchen. We all gleamed like cellophane, wiping the sweat from our brows with the backs of our hands as we talked about the day: Frankie our neighbor was beat up by Faustino; the swimming pool at the playground would be closed for a day because the pump was broken.

Such was our life. So that morning, while doing-in the train of ants which arrived each day, I decided to become wealthy, and right away! After downing a bowl of cereal, I took a rake from the garage and started up the block to look for work.

We lived on an ordinary block of mostly working class people: warehousemen, egg candlers,[1] welders, mechanics, and a union plumber. And there were many retired people who kept their lawns green and the gutters uncluttered of the chewing gum wrappers we dropped as we rode by on our bikes. They bent down to gather our litter, muttering at our evilness.

At the corner house I rapped the screen door and a very large woman in a muu-muu answered. She sized me up and then asked what I could do.

"Rake leaves," I answered smiling.

"It's summer, and there ain't no leaves," she countered. Her face was pinched with lines; fat jiggled under her chin. She pointed to the lawn, then the flower bed, and said: "You see any leaves there—or there?" I followed her pointing arm, stupidly. But she had a job for me and that was to get her a Coke at the liquor store. She gave me twenty cents, and after ditching my rake in a bush, off I ran. I returned with an unbagged Pepsi, for which she thanked me and gave me a nickel from her apron.

[1]**egg candler:** One who inspects eggs by holding them up to a light. [All notes are the editors'.]

I skipped off her porch, fetched my rake, and crossed the street to the next block where Mrs. Moore, mother of Earl the retarded man, let me weed a flower bed. She handed me a trowel and for a good part of the morning my fingers dipped into the moist dirt, ripping up runners of Bermuda grass. Worms surfaced in my search for deep roots, and I cut them in halves, tossing them to Mrs. Moore's cat who pawed them playfully as they dried in the sun. I made out Earl whose face was pressed to the back window of the house, and although he was calling to me I couldn't understand what he was trying to say. Embarrassed, I worked without looking up, but I imagined his contorted mouth and the ring of keys attached to his belt — keys that jingled with each palsied step. He scared me and I worked quickly to finish the flower bed. When I did finish Mrs. Moore gave me a quarter and two peaches from her tree, which I washed there but ate in the alley behind my house.

I was sucking on the second one, a bit of juice staining the front of my T-shirt, when Little John, my best friend, came walking down the alley with a baseball bat over his shoulder, knocking over trash cans as he made his way toward me.

Little John and I went to St. John's Catholic School, where we sat among the "stupids." Miss Marino, our teacher, alternated the rows of good students with the bad, hoping that by sitting side-by-side with the bright students the stupids might become more intelligent, as though intelligence were contagious. But we didn't progress as she had hoped. She grew frustrated when one day, while dismissing class for recess, Little John couldn't get up because his arms were stuck in the slats of the chair's backrest. She scolded us with a shaking finger when we knocked over the globe, denting the already troubled Africa. She muttered curses when Leroy White, a real stupid but a great softball player with the gift to hit to all fields, openly chewed his host[2] when he made his First Communion; his hands swung at his sides as he returned to the pew looking around with a big smile.

Little John asked what I was doing, and I told him that I was taking a break from work, as I sat comfortably among high weeds. He wanted to join me, but I reminded him that the last time he'd gone door-to-door asking for work his mother had whipped him. I was with him when his mother, a New Jersey Italian who could rise up in anger one moment and love the next, told me in a polite but matter-of-fact voice that I had to leave because she was going to beat her son. She gave me a homemade popsicle, ushered me to the door, and said that I could see Little John the next day. But it was sooner than that. I went around to his bedroom window to suck my popsicle and watch Little John dodge his mother's blows, a few hitting their mark but many whirring air.

It was midday when Little John and I converged in the alley, the sun blazing in the high nineties, and he suggested that we go to Roosevelt

[2]**his host:** The wafer that embodies, in the Catholic sacrament of Communion, the bread of the Last Supper and the body of Christ.

High School to swim. He needed five cents to make fifteen, the cost of admission, and I lent him a nickel. We ran home for my bike and when my sister found out that we were going swimming, she started to cry because she didn't have the fifteen cents but only an empty Coke bottle. I waved for her to come and three of us mounted the bike—Debra on the cross bar, Little John on the handle bars and holding the Coke bottle which we would cash for a nickel and make up the difference that would allow all of us to get in, and me pumping up the crooked streets, dodging cars and pot holes. We spent the day swimming under the afternoon sun, so that when we got home our mom asked us what was darker, the floor or us? She feigned a stern posture, her hands on her hips and her mouth puckered. We played along. Looking down, Debbie and I said in unison, "Us."

That evening at dinner we all sat down in our bathing suits to eat our beans, laughing and chewing loudly. Our mom was in a good mood, so I took a risk and asked her if sometime we could have turtle soup. A few days before I had watched a television program in which a Polynesian tribe killed a large turtle, gutted it, and then stewed it over an open fire. The turtle, basted in a sugary sauce, looked delicious as I ate an afternoon bowl of cereal, but my sister, who was watching the program with a glass of Kool-Aid between her knees, said, "Caca."

My mother looked at me in bewilderment. "Boy, are you a crazy Mexican. Where did you get the idea that people eat turtles?"

"On television," I said, explaining the program. Then I took it a step 15 further. "Mom, do you think we could get dressed up for dinner one of these days? David King does."

"Ay, Dios," my mother laughed. She started collecting the dinner plates, but my brother wouldn't let go of his. He was still drawing a picture in the bean sauce. Giggling, he said it was me, but I didn't want to listen because I wanted an answer from Mom. This was the summer when I spent the mornings in front of the television that showed the comfortable lives of white kids. There were no beatings, no rifts in the family. They wore bright clothes; toys tumbled from their closets. They hopped into bed with kisses and woke to glasses of fresh orange juice, and to a father sitting before his morning coffee while the mother buttered his toast. They hurried through the day making friends and gobs of money, returning home to a warmly lit living room, and then dinner. *Leave It to Beaver* was the program I replayed in my mind:

"May I have the mashed potatoes?" asks Beaver with a smile.

"Sure, Beav," replies Wally as he taps the corners of his mouth with a starched napkin.

The father looks on in his suit. The mother, decked out in earrings and a pearl necklace, cuts into her steak and blushes. Their conversation is politely clipped.

"Swell," says Beaver, his cheeks puffed with food. 20

Our own talk at dinner was loud with belly laughs and marked by our pointing forks at one another. The subjects were commonplace.

"Gary, let's go to the ditch tomorrow," my brother suggests. He explains that he has made a life preserver out of four empty detergent bottles strung together with twine and that he will make me one if I can find more bottles. "No way are we going to drown."

"Yeah, then we could have a dirt clod fight," I reply, so happy to be alive.

Whereas the Beaver's family enjoyed dessert in dishes at the table, our mom sent us outside, and more often than not I went into the alley to peek over the neighbor's fences and spy out fruit, apricots or peaches.

I had asked my mom and again she laughed that I was a crazy *chavalo*[3] as she stood in front of the sink, her arms rising and falling with suds, face glistening from the heat. She sent me outside where my brother and sister were sitting in the shade that the fence threw out like a blanket. They were talking about me when I plopped down next to them. They looked at one another and then Debbie, my eight-year-old sister, started in.

"What's this crap about getting dressed up?"

She had entered her *profanity* stage. A year later she would give up such words and slip into her Catholic uniform, and into squealing on my brother and me when we "cussed this" and "cussed that."

I tried to convince them that if we improved the way we looked we might get along better in life. White people would like us more. They might invite us to places, like their homes or front yards. They might not hate us so much.

My sister called me a "craphead," and got up to leave with a stalk of grass dangling from her mouth. "They'll never like us."

My brother's mood lightened as he talked about the ditch—the white water, the broken pieces of glass, and the rusted car fenders that awaited our knees. There would be toads, and rocks to smash them.

David King, the only person we knew who resembled the middle class, called from over the fence. David was Catholic, of Armenian and French descent, and his closet was filled with toys. A bear-shaped cookie jar, like the ones on television, sat on the kitchen counter. His mother was remarkably kind while she put up with the racket we made on the street. Evenings, she often watered the front yard and it must have upset her to see us—my brother and I and others—jump from trees laughing, the unkillable kids of the very poor, who got up unshaken, brushed off, and climbed into another one to try again.

David called again. Rick got up and slapped grass from his pants. When I asked if I could come along he said no. David said no. They were two years older so their affairs were different from mine. They greeted one another with foul names and took off down the alley to look for trouble.

I went inside the house, turned on the television, and was about to sit down with a glass of Kool-Aid when Mom shooed me outside.

[3]**chavalo:** Kid.

"It's still light," she said. "Later you'll bug me to let you stay out longer. So go on."

I downed my Kool-Aid and went outside to the front yard. No $_{35}$ one was around. The day had cooled and a breeze rustled the trees. Mr. Jackson, the plumber, was watering his lawn and when he saw me he turned away to wash off his front steps. There was more than an hour of light left, so I took advantage of it and decided to look for work. I felt suddenly alive as I skipped down the block in search of an over-grown flower bed and the dime that would end the day right.

ENGAGING THE TEXT

1. Why is the narrator attracted to the kind of family life depicted on TV? What, if anything, does he think is wrong with his life? Why do his desires apparently have so little impact on his family?

2. Why does the narrator first go looking for work? How has the meaning of work changed by the end of the story, when he goes out again "in search of an over-grown flower bed and the dime that would end the day right"? Explain.

3. As Soto looks back on his nine-year-old self, he has a different perspective on things than he had as a child. How would you characterize the mature Soto's thoughts about his childhood family life? (Was it "a good family"? What was wrong with Soto's thinking as a nine-year-old?) Back up your remarks with spe-cific references to the narrative.

4. Review the story to find each mention of food or drink. Explain the role these references play.

5. Review the cast of "supporting characters" in this narrative — the mother, sis-ter, brother, friends, and neighbors. What does each contribute to the story and in particular to the meaning of family within the story?

EXPLORING CONNECTIONS

6. Look ahead to the selection from *To the End of June* by Cris Beam (p. 61). Compare Soto's family to Mindy and Glenn's family, being sure to consider issues like parental expectations, the differing neighborhoods, the food, gender roles, and levels of affluence. What would it be like to live in each of these families? Can you imagine Oneida's view of her Staten Island experience gradually changing as she matures?

7. Compare and contrast the relationship of school and family in this narrative to that described by Mike Rose in "I Just Wanna Be Average" (p. 123).

EXTENDING THE CRITICAL CONTEXT

8. Write a journal entry about a time when you wished your family were some-how different. What caused your dissatisfaction? What did you want your fam-ily to be like? Was your dissatisfaction ever resolved?

9. "Looking for Work" is essentially the story of a single day. Write a narrative of one day when you were eight or nine or ten; use details as Soto does to give the events of the day broader significance.

WHAT WE REALLY MISS ABOUT THE 1950s

STEPHANIE COONTZ

Popular myth has it that the 1950s were the ideal decade for the American family. In this example of academic writing at its best, Stephanie Coontz (b. 1944) provides a clear, well-documented, and insightful analysis of what was really going on and suggests that our nostalgia for the 1950s could mislead us today. Stephanie Coontz teaches family studies and history at the Evergreen State College in Olympia, Washington. An award-winning writer and internationally recognized expert on the family, she has testified before a House Select Committee on families, appeared in several television documentaries, and published extensively for both general and scholarly audiences. Her latest book is *A Strange Stirring: The Feminine Mystique and American Women at the Dawn of the 1960s* (2011); the selection below is excerpted from her earlier study *The Way We Really Are: Coming to Terms with America's Changing Families* (1997).

IN A 1996 POLL BY THE KNIGHT-RIDDER NEWS AGENCY, more Americans chose the 1950s than any other single decade as the best time for children to grow up.[1] And despite the research I've done on the underside of 1950s families, I don't think it's crazy for people to feel nostalgic about the period. For one thing, it's easy to see why people might look back fondly to a decade when real wages grew more in any single year than in the entire ten years of the 1980s combined, a time when the average 30-year-old man could buy a median-priced home on only 15–18 percent of his salary.[2]

But it's more than just a financial issue. When I talk with modern parents, even ones who grew up in unhappy families, they associate the 1950s with a yearning they feel for a time when there were fewer complicated choices for kids or parents to grapple with, when there was more predictability in how people formed and maintained families, and when there was a coherent "moral order" in their community to serve as a reference point for family norms. Even people who found that moral

---

[1]Steven Thomma, "Nostalgia for '50s Surfaces," *Philadelphia Inquirer*, February 4, 1996. [All notes are Coontz's.]

[2]Frank Levy, *Dollars and Dreams: The Changing American Income Distribution* (New York: Russell Sage, 1987), p. 6; Frank Levy, "Incomes and Income Inequality," in Reynolds Farley, ed., *State of the Union: America in the 1990s*, vol. 1 (New York: Russell Sage, 1995), pp. 1–57; Richard May and Kathryn Porter, "Poverty and Income Trends, 1994," Washington, DC: Center on Budget and Policy Priorities, March 1996; Rob Nelson and Jon Cowan, "Buster Power," *USA Weekend*, October 14–16, 1994, p. 10.

order grossly unfair or repressive often say that its presence provided them with something concrete to push against.

I can sympathize entirely. One of my most empowering moments occurred the summer I turned 12, when my mother marched down to the library with me to confront a librarian who'd curtly refused to let me check out a book that was "not appropriate" for my age. "Don't you *ever* tell my daughter what she can and can't read," fumed my mom. "She's a mature young lady and she can make her own choices." In recent years I've often thought back to the gratitude I felt toward my mother for that act of trust in me. I wish I had some way of earning similar points from my own son. But much as I've always respected his values, I certainly wouldn't have walked into my local video store when he was 12 and demanded that he be allowed to check out absolutely anything he wanted!

Still, I have no illusions that I'd actually like to go back to the 1950s, and neither do most people who express such occasional nostalgia. For example, although the 1950s got more votes than any other decade in the Knight-Ridder poll, it did not win an outright majority: 38 percent of respondents picked the 1950s; 27 percent picked the 1960s or the 1970s. Voters between the ages of 50 and 64 were most likely to choose the 1950s, the decade in which they themselves came of age, as the best time for kids; voters under 30 were more likely to choose the 1970s. African Americans differed over whether the 1960s, 1970s, or 1980s were best, but all age groups of blacks agreed that later decades were definitely preferable to the 1950s.

Nostalgia for the 1950s is real and deserves to be taken seriously, 5 but it usually shouldn't be taken literally. Even people who *do* pick the 1950s as the best decade generally end up saying, once they start discussing their feelings in depth, that it's not the family arrangements in and of themselves that they want to revive. They don't miss the way women used to be treated, they sure wouldn't want to live with most of the fathers they knew in their neighborhoods, and "come to think of it" —I don't know how many times I've recorded these exact words— "I communicate with my kids *much* better than my parents or grandparents did." When Judith Wallerstein recently interviewed 100 spouses in "happy" marriages, she found that only five "wanted a marriage like their parents'." The husbands "consciously rejected the role models provided by their fathers. The women said they could never be happy living as their mothers did."[3]

People today understandably feel that their lives are out of balance, but they yearn for something totally *new*—a more equal distribution of work, family, and community time for both men and women, children and adults. If the 1990s are lopsided in one direction, the 1950s were equally lopsided in the opposite direction.

---

[3]Judith Wallerstein and Sandra Blakeslee, *The Good Marriage: How and Why Love Lasts* (Boston: Houghton Mifflin, 1995), p. 15.

What most people really feel nostalgic about has little to do with the internal structure of 1950s families. It is the belief that the 1950s provided a more family-friendly economic and social environment, an easier climate in which to keep kids on the straight and narrow, and above all, a greater feeling of hope for a family's long-term future, especially for its young. The contrast between the perceived hopefulness of the fifties and our own misgivings about the future is key to contemporary nostalgia for the period. Greater optimism *did* exist then, even among many individuals and groups who were in terrible circumstances. But if we are to take people's sense of loss seriously, rather than merely to capitalize on it for a hidden political agenda, we need to develop a historical perspective on where that hope came from.

Part of it came from families comparing their prospects in the 1950s to their unstable, often grindingly uncomfortable pasts, especially the two horrible decades just before. In the 1920s, after two centuries of child labor and income insecurity, and for the first time in American history, a bare majority of children had come to live in a family with a male breadwinner, a female homemaker, and a chance at a high school education. Yet no sooner did the ideals associated with such a family begin to blossom than they were buried by the stock market crash of 1929 and the Great Depression of the 1930s. During the 1930s domestic violence soared; divorce rates fell, but informal separations jumped; fertility plummeted. Murder rates were higher in 1933 than they were in the 1980s. Families were uprooted or torn apart. Thousands of young people left home to seek work, often riding the rails across the country.[4]

World War II brought the beginning of economic recovery, and people's renewed interest in forming families resulted in a marriage and childbearing boom, but stability was still beyond most people's grasp. Postwar communities were rocked by racial tensions, labor strife, and a right-wing backlash against the radical union movement of the 1930s. Many women resented being fired from wartime jobs they had grown to enjoy. Veterans often came home to find that they had to elbow their way back into their families, with wives and children resisting their attempts to reassert domestic authority. In one recent study of fathers who returned from the war, four times as many reported painful, even traumatic, reunions as remembered happy ones.[5]

By 1946 one in every three marriages was ending in divorce. Even 10 couples who stayed together went through rough times, as an acute housing shortage forced families to double up with relatives or friends.

[4]Donald Hernandez, *America's Children: Resources from Family, Government and the Economy* (New York: Russell Sage, 1993), pp. 99, 102; James Morone, "The Corrosive Politics of Virtue," *American Prospect* 26 (May–June 1996), p. 37; "Study Finds U.S. No. 1 in Violence," *Olympian*, November 13, 1992. See also Stephen Mintz and Susan Kellogg, *Domestic Revolutions: A Social History of American Family Life* (New York: The Free Press, 1988).

[5]William Tuttle Jr., *"Daddy's Gone to War": The Second World War in the Lives of America's Children* (New York: Oxford University Press, 1993).

Tempers frayed and generational relations grew strained. "No home is big enough to house two families, particularly two of different generations, with opposite theories on child training," warned a 1948 film on the problems of modern marriage.[6]

So after the widespread domestic strife, family disruptions, and violence of the 1930s and the instability of the World War II period, people were ready to try something new. The postwar economic boom gave them the chance. The 1950s was the first time that a majority of Americans could even *dream* of creating a secure oasis in their immediate nuclear families. There they could focus their emotional and financial investments, reduce obligations to others that might keep them from seizing their own chance at a new start, and escape the interference of an older generation of neighbors or relatives who tried to tell them how to run their lives and raise their kids. Oral histories of the postwar period resound with the theme of escaping from in-laws, maiden aunts, older parents, even needy siblings.

The private family also provided a refuge from the anxieties of the new nuclear age and the cold war, as well as a place to get away from the political witch hunts led by Senator Joe McCarthy and his allies. When having the wrong friends at the wrong time or belonging to any "suspicious" organization could ruin your career and reputation, it was safer to pull out of groups you might have joined earlier and to focus on your family. On a more positive note, the nuclear family was where people could try to satisfy their long-pent-up desires for a more stable marriage, a decent home, and the chance to really enjoy their children.

The 1950s Family Experiment

The key to understanding the successes, failures, and comparatively short life of 1950s family forms and values is to understand the period as one of *experimentation* with the possibilities of a new kind of family, not as the expression of some longstanding tradition. At the end of the 1940s, the divorce rate, which had been rising steadily since the 1890s, dropped sharply; the age of marriage fell to a 100-year low; and the birth rate soared. Women who had worked during the Depression or World War II quit their jobs as soon as they became pregnant, which meant quite a few women were specializing in child raising; fewer women remained childless during the 1950s than in any decade since the late nineteenth century. The timing and spacing of childbearing became far more compressed, so that young mothers were likely to have two or more children in diapers at once, with no older sibling to help in their care. At the same time, again for the first time in 100 years, the educational gap between young middle-class women and men increased, while job segregation for working men and women seems to

---

[6]"Marriage and Divorce," *March of Time*, film series 14 (1948).

have peaked. These demographic changes increased the dependence of women on marriage, in contrast to gradual trends in the opposite direction since the early twentieth century.[7]

The result was that family life and gender roles became much more predictable, orderly, and settled in the 1950s than they were either twenty years earlier or would be twenty years later. Only slightly more than one in four marriages ended in divorce during the 1950s. Very few young people spent any extended period of time in a nonfamily setting: They moved from their parents' family into their own family, after just a brief experience with independent living, and they started having children soon after marriage. Whereas two-thirds of women aged 20 to 24 were not yet married in 1990, only 28 percent of women this age were still single in 1960.[8]

Ninety percent of all the households in the country were families in the 1950s, in comparison with only 71 percent by 1990. Eighty-six percent of all children lived in two-parent homes in 1950, as opposed to just 72 percent in 1990. And the percentage living with both biological parents—rather than, say, a parent and stepparent—was dramatically higher than it had been at the turn of the century or is today: seventy percent in 1950, compared with only 50 percent in 1990. Nearly 60 percent of kids—an all-time high—were born into male breadwinner–female homemaker families; only a minority of the rest had mothers who worked in the paid labor force.[9]

If the organization and uniformity of family life in the 1950s were new, so were the values, especially the emphasis on putting all one's emotional and financial eggs in the small basket of the immediate nuclear family. Right up through the 1940s, ties of work, friendship, neighborhood, ethnicity, extended kin, and voluntary organizations were as important a source of identity for most Americans, and sometimes a *more* important source of obligation, than marriage and the nuclear family. All this changed in the postwar era. The spread of suburbs and automobiles, combined with the destruction of older ethnic neighborhoods in many cities, led to the decline of the neighborhood social club. Young

---

[7]Arlene Skolnick and Stacey Rosencrantz, "The New Crusade for the Old Family," *American Prospect*, Summer 1994, p. 65; Hernandez, *America's Children*, pp. 128–32; Andrew Cherlin, "Changing Family and Household: Contemporary Lessons from Historical Research," *Annual Review of Sociology* 9 (1983), pp. 54–58; Sam Roberts, *Who We Are: A Portrait of America Based on the Latest Census* (New York: Times Books, 1995), p. 45.

[8]Levy, "Incomes and Income Inequality," p. 20; Arthur Norton and Louisa Miller, *Marriage, Divorce, and Remarriage in the 1990s*, Current Population Reports Series P23-180 (Washington, DC: Bureau of the Census, October 1992); Roberts, *Who We Are* (1995 ed.), pp. 50–53.

[9]Dennis Hogan and Daniel Lichter, "Children and Youth: Living Arrangements and Welfare," in Farley, ed., *State of the Union*, vol. 2, p. 99; Richard Gelles, *Contemporary Families: A Sociological View* (Thousand Oaks, Calif.: Sage, 1995), p. 115; Hernandez, *America's Children*, p. 102. The fact that only a small percentage of children had mothers in the paid labor force, though a full 40 percent did not live in male breadwinner–female homemaker families, was because some children had mothers who worked, unpaid, in farms or family businesses, or fathers who were unemployed, or the children were not living with both parents.

couples moved away from parents and kin, cutting ties with traditional extrafamilial networks that might compete for their attention. A critical factor in this trend was the emergence of a group of family sociologists and marriage counselors who followed Talcott Parsons in claiming that the nuclear family, built on a sharp division of labor between husband and wife, was the cornerstone of modern society.

The new family experts tended to advocate views such as those first raised in a 1946 book, *Their Mothers' Sons*, by psychiatrist Edward Strecker. Strecker and his followers argued that American boys were infantilized and emasculated by women who were old-fashioned "moms" instead of modern "mothers." One sign that you might be that dreaded "mom," Strecker warned women, was if you felt you should take your aging parents into your own home, rather than putting them in "a good institution . . . where they will receive adequate care and comfort." Modern "mothers" placed their parents in nursing homes and poured all their energies into their nuclear family. They were discouraged from diluting their wifely and maternal commitments by maintaining "competing" interests in friends, jobs, or extended family networks, yet they were also supposed to cheerfully grant early independence to their (male) children—an emotional double bind that may explain why so many women who took this advice to heart ended up abusing alcohol or tranquilizers over the course of the decade.[10]

The call for young couples to break from their parents and youthful friends was a consistent theme in 1950s popular culture. In *Marty*, one of the most highly praised TV plays and movies of the 1950s, the hero almost loses his chance at love by listening to the carping of his mother and aunt and letting himself be influenced by old friends who resent the time he spends with his new girlfriend. In the end, he turns his back on mother, aunt, and friends to get his new marriage and a little business of his own off to a good start. Other movies, novels, and popular psychology tracts portrayed the dreadful things that happened when women became more interested in careers than marriage or men resisted domestic conformity.

Yet many people felt guilty about moving away from older parents and relatives; "modern mothers" worried that fostering independence in their kids could lead to defiance or even juvenile delinquency (the recurring nightmare of the age); there was considerable confusion about how men and women could maintain clear breadwinner-homemaker distinctions in a period of expanding education, job openings, and consumer aspirations. People clamored for advice. They got it from the new family education specialists and marriage counselors, from columns in women's magazines, from government pamphlets, and above all from television. While 1950s TV melodramas warned against letting anything dilute the commitment to getting married and having kids, the new family sitcoms gave people nightly lessons on how to make their marriage

[10]Edward Strecker, *Their Mothers' Sons: The Psychiatrist Examines an American Problem* (Philadelphia: J. B. Lippincott, 1946), p. 209.

or rapidly expanding family work—or, in the case of *I Love Lucy*, probably the most popular show of the era, how *not* to make their marriage and family work. Lucy and Ricky gave weekly comic reminders of how much trouble a woman could get into by wanting a career or hatching some hare-brained scheme behind her husband's back.

At the time, everyone knew that shows such as *Donna Reed, Ozzie and Harriet, Leave It to Beaver,* and *Father Knows Best* were not the way families really were. People didn't watch those shows to see their own lives reflected back at them. They watched them to see how families were *supposed* to live—and also to get a little reassurance that they were headed in the right direction. The sitcoms were simultaneously advertisements, etiquette manuals, and how-to lessons for a new way of organizing marriage and child raising. I have studied the scripts of these shows for years, since I often use them in my classes on family history, but it wasn't until I became a parent that I felt their extraordinary pull. The secret of their appeal, I suddenly realized, was that they offered 1950s viewers, wracked with the same feelings of parental inadequacy as was I, the promise that there were easy answers and surefire techniques for raising kids.

Ever since, I have found it useful to think of the sitcoms as the 1950s equivalent of today's beer ads. As most people know, beer ads are consciously aimed at men who *aren't* as strong and sexy as the models in the commercials, guys who are uneasily aware of the gap between the ideal masculine pursuits and their own achievements. The promise is that if the viewers on the couch will just drink brand X, they too will be able to run 10 miles without gasping for breath. Their bodies will firm up, their complexions will clear up, and maybe the Swedish bikini team will come over and hang out at their place.

Similarly, the 1950s sitcoms were aimed at young couples who had married in haste, women who had tasted new freedoms during World War II and given up their jobs with regret, veterans whose children resented their attempts to reassert paternal authority, and individuals disturbed by the changing racial and ethnic mix of postwar America. The message was clear: Buy these ranch houses, Hotpoint appliances, and child-raising ideals; relate to your spouse like this; get a new car to wash with your kids on Sunday afternoons; organize your dinners like that— and you too can escape from the conflicts of race, class, and political witch hunts into harmonious families where father knows best, mothers are never bored or irritated, and teenagers rush to the dinner table each night, eager to get their latest dose of parental wisdom.

Many families found it possible to put together a good imitation of this way of living during the 1950s and 1960s. Couples were often able to construct marriages that were much more harmonious than those in which they had grown up, and to devote far more time to their children. Even when marriages were deeply unhappy, as many were, the new stability, economic security, and educational advantages parents were able to offer their kids counted for a lot in people's assessment of their life satisfaction. And in some matters, ignorance could be bliss:

The lack of media coverage of problems such as abuse or incest was terribly hard on the casualties, but it protected more fortunate families from knowledge and fear of many social ills.[11]

There was tremendous hostility to people who could be defined as "others": Jews, African Americans, Puerto Ricans, the poor, gays or lesbians, and "the red menace." Yet on a day-to-day basis, the civility that prevailed in homogeneous neighborhoods allowed people to ignore larger patterns of racial and political repression. Racial clashes were ever-present in the 1950s, sometimes escalating into full-scale antiblack riots, but individual homicide rates fell to almost half the levels of the 1930s. As nuclear families moved into the suburbs, they retreated from social activism but entered voluntary relationships with people who had children the same age; they became involved in PTAs together, joined bridge clubs, went bowling. There does seem to have been a stronger sense of neighborly commonalities than many of us feel today. Even though this local community was often the product of exclusion or repression, it sometimes looks attractive to modern Americans whose commutes are getting longer and whose family or work patterns give them little in common with their neighbors.[12]

The optimism that allowed many families to rise above their internal difficulties and to put limits on their individualistic values during the 1950s came from the sense that America was on a dramatically different trajectory than it had been in the past, an upward and expansionary path that had already taken people to better places than they had ever seen before and would certainly take their children even further. This confidence that almost everyone could look forward to a better future stands in sharp contrast to how most contemporary Americans feel, and it explains why a period in which many people were much worse off than today sometimes still looks like a better period for families than our own.

Throughout the 1950s, poverty was higher than it is today, but it was less concentrated in pockets of blight existing side-by-side with extremes of wealth, and, unlike today, it was falling rather than rising. At the end of the 1930s, almost two-thirds of the population had

[11]For discussion of the discontents, and often searing misery, that were considered normal in a "good-enough" marriage in the 1950s and 1960s, see Lillian Rubin, *Worlds of Pain: Life in the Working-Class Family* (New York: Basic Books, 1976); Mirra Komarovsky, *Blue Collar Marriage* (New Haven, Conn.: Vintage, 1962); Elaine Tyler May, *Homeward Bound: American Families in the Cold War Era* (New York: Basic Books, 1988).

[12]See Robert Putnam, "The Strange Disappearance of Civic America," *American Prospect,* Winter 1996. For a glowing if somewhat lopsided picture of 1950s community solidarities, see Alan Ehrenhalt, *The Lost City: Discovering the Forgotten Virtues of Community in the Chicago of the 1950s* (New York: Basic Books, 1995). For a chilling account of communities uniting against perceived outsiders, in the same city, see Arnold Hirsch, *Making the Second Ghetto: Race and Housing in Chicago, 1940–1960* (Cambridge, Mass.: Harvard University Press, 1983). On homicide rates, see "Study Finds United States No. 1 in Violence," *Olympian,* November 13, 1992; *New York Times,* November 13, 1992, p. A9; and Douglas Lee Eckberg, "Estimates of Early Twentieth-Century U.S. Homicide Rates: An Econometric Forecasting Approach," *Demography* 32 (1995), p. 14. On lengthening commutes, see "It's Taking Longer to Get to Work," *Olympian,* December 6, 1995.

incomes below the poverty standards of the day, while only one in eight had a middle-class income (defined as two to five times the poverty line). By 1960, a majority of the population had climbed into the middle-income range.[13]

Unmarried people were hardly sexually abstinent in the 1950s, but the age of first intercourse was somewhat higher than it is now, and despite a tripling of nonmarital birth rates between 1940 and 1958, more than 70 percent of nonmarital pregnancies led to weddings before the child was born. Teenage birth rates were almost twice as high in 1957 as in the 1990s, but most teen births were to married couples, and the effect of teen pregnancy in reducing further schooling for young people did not hurt their life prospects the way it does today. High school graduation rates were lower in the 1950s than they are today, and minority students had far worse test scores, but there were jobs for people who dropped out of high school or graduated without good reading skills—jobs that actually had a future. People entering the job market in the 1950s had no way of knowing that they would be the last generation to have a good shot at reaching middle-class status without the benefit of postsecondary schooling.

Millions of men from impoverished, rural, unemployed, or poorly educated family backgrounds found steady jobs in the steel, auto, appliance, construction, and shipping industries. Lower-middle-class men went further on in college during the 1950s than they would have been able to expect in earlier decades, enabling them to make the transition to secure white-collar work. The experience of shared sacrifices in the Depression and war, reinforced by a New Deal–inspired belief in the ability of government to make life better, gave people a sense of hope for the future. Confidence in government, business, education, and other institutions was on the rise. This general optimism affected people's experience and assessment of family life. It is no wonder modern Americans yearn for a similar sense of hope.

But before we sign on to any attempts to turn the family clock back to the 1950s we should note that the family successes and community solidarities of the 1950s rested on a totally different set of political and economic conditions than we have today. Contrary to widespread belief, the 1950s was not an age of laissez-faire government and free market competition. A major cause of the social mobility of young families in the 1950s was that federal assistance programs were much more generous and widespread than they are today.

[13]The figures in this and the following paragraph come from Levy, "Incomes and Income Inequality," pp. 1–57; May and Porter, "Poverty and Income Trends, 1994"; Reynolds Farley, *The New American Reality: Who We Are, How We Got Here, Where We Are Going* (New York: Russell Sage, 1996), pp. 83–85; Gelles, *Contemporary Families*, p. 115; David Grissmer, Sheila Nataraj Kirby, Mark Berends, and Stephanie Williamson, *Student Achievement and the Changing American Family*, Rand Institute on Education and Training (Santa Monica, Calif.: Rand, 1994), p. 106.

In the most ambitious and successful affirmative action program ever adopted in America, 40 percent of young men were eligible for veterans' benefits, and these benefits were far more extensive than those available to Vietnam-era vets. Financed in part by a federal income tax on the rich that went up to 87 percent and a corporate tax rate of 52 percent, such benefits provided quite a jump start for a generation of young families. The GI Bill paid most tuition costs for vets who attended college, doubling the percentage of college students from prewar levels. At the other end of the life span, Social Security began to build up a significant safety net for the elderly, formerly the poorest segment of the population. Starting in 1950, the federal government regularly mandated raises in the minimum wage to keep pace with inflation. The minimum wage may have been only $1.40 as late as 1968, but a person who worked for that amount full-time, year-round, earned 118 percent of the poverty figure for a family of three. By 1995, a full-time minimum-wage worker could earn only 72 percent of the poverty level.[14]

30

[14]William Chafe, *The Unfinished Journey: America Since World War II* (New York: Oxford University Press, 1986), pp. 113, 143; Marc Linder, "Eisenhower-Era Marxist-Confiscatory Taxation: Requiem for the Rhetoric of Rate Reduction for the Rich," *Tulane Law Review* 70 (1996), p. 917; Barry Bluestone and Teresa Ghilarducci, "Rewarding Work: Feasible Antipoverty Policy," *American Prospect* 28 (1996), p. 42; Theda Skocpol, "Delivering for Young Families," *American Prospect* 28 (1996), p. 67.

An important source of the economic expansion of the 1950s was that public works spending at all levels of government comprised nearly 20 percent of total expenditures in 1950, as compared to less than 7 percent in 1984. Between 1950 and 1960, nonmilitary, nonresidential public construction rose by 58 percent. Construction expenditures for new schools (in dollar amounts adjusted for inflation) rose by 72 percent; funding on sewers and waterworks rose by 46 percent. Government paid 90 percent of the costs of building the new Interstate Highway System. These programs opened up suburbia to growing numbers of middle-class Americans and created secure, well-paying jobs for blue-collar workers.[15]

Government also reorganized home financing, underwriting low down payments and long-term mortgages that had been rejected as bad business by private industry. To do this, government put public assets behind housing lending programs, created two new national financial institutions to facilitate home loans, allowed veterans to put down payments as low as a dollar on a house, and offered tax breaks to people who bought homes. The National Education Defense Act funded the socioeconomic mobility of thousands of young men who trained themselves for well-paying jobs in such fields as engineering.[16]

Unlike contemporary welfare programs, government investment in 1950s families was not just for immediate subsistence but encouraged long-term asset development, rewarding people for increasing their investment in homes and education. Thus it was far less likely that such families or individuals would ever fall back to where they started, even after a string of bad luck. Subsidies for higher education were greater the longer people stayed in school and the more expensive the school they selected. Mortgage deductions got bigger as people traded up to better houses.[17]

These social and political support systems magnified the impact of the postwar economic boom. "In the years between 1947 and 1973," reports economist Robert Kuttner, "the median paycheck more than doubled, and the bottom 20 percent enjoyed the greatest gains." High rates of unionization meant that blue-collar workers were making much more financial progress than most of their counterparts today. In 1952, when eager home buyers flocked to the opening of Levittown, Pennsylvania, the largest planned community yet constructed, "it took a factory

[15]Joel Tarr, "The Evolution of the Urban Infrastructure in the Nineteenth and Twentieth Centuries," in Royce Hanson, ed., *Perspectives on Urban Infrastructure* (Washington, DC: National Academy Press, 1984); Mark Aldrich, *A History of Public Works Investment in the United States*, report prepared by the CPNSAD Research Corporation for the U.S. Department of Commerce, April 1980.

[16]For more information on this government financing, see Kenneth Jackson, *Crabgrass Frontier: The Suburbanization of the United States* (New York: Oxford University Press, 1985); and *The Way We Never Were*, chapter 4.

[17]John Cook and Laura Sherman, "Economic Security Among America's Poor: The Impact of State Welfare Waivers on Asset Accumulation," Center on Hunger, Poverty, and Nutrition Policy, Tufts University, May 1996.

worker one day to earn enough money to pay the closing costs on a new Levittown house, then selling for $10,000." By 1991, such a home was selling for $100,000 or more, and it took a factory worker *eighteen weeks* to earn enough money for just the closing costs.[18]

The legacy of the union struggle of the 1930s and 1940s, combined with government support for raising people's living standards, set limits on corporations that have disappeared in recent decades. Corporations paid 23 percent of federal income taxes in the 1950s, as compared to just 9.2 percent in 1991. Big companies earned higher profit margins than smaller firms, partly due to their dominance of the market, partly to America's postwar economic advantage. They chose (or were forced) to share these extra earnings, which economists call "rents," with employees. Economists at the Brookings Institution and Harvard University estimate that 70 percent of such corporate rents were passed on to workers at all levels of the firm, benefiting secretaries and janitors as well as CEOs. Corporations routinely retained workers even in slack periods, as a way of ensuring workplace stability. Although they often received more generous tax breaks from communities than they gave back in investment, at least they kept their plants and employment offices in the same place. AT&T, for example, received much of the technology it used to finance its postwar expansion from publicly funded communications research conducted as part of the war effort, and, as current AT&T Chairman Robert Allen puts it, there "used to be a lifelong commitment on the employee's part and on our part." Today, however, he admits, "the contract doesn't exist anymore."[19]

Television trivia experts still argue over exactly what the fathers in many 1950s sitcoms did for a living. Whatever it was, though, they obviously didn't have to worry about downsizing. If most married people stayed in long-term relationships during the 1950s, so did most corporations, sticking with the communities they grew up in and the employees they originally hired. Corporations were not constantly relocating in search of cheap labor during the 1950s; unlike today, increases in worker productivity usually led to increases in wages. The number of workers covered by corporate pension plans and health benefits increased steadily. So did limits on the work week. There is good reason that people look back to the 1950s as a less hurried age: The average American was working a shorter workday in the 1950s than his or her

---

[18]Robert Kuttner, "The Incredible Shrinking American Paycheck," *Washington Post National Weekly Edition*, November 6–12, 1995, p. 23; Donald Bartlett and James Steele, *America: What Went Wrong?* (Kansas City: Andrews McMeel, 1992), p. 20.

[19]Richard Barnet, "Lords of the Global Economy," *Nation*, December 19, 1994, p. 756; Clay Chandler, "U.S. Corporations: Good Citizens or Bad?" *Washington Post National Weekly Edition*, May 20–26, 1996, p. 16; Steven Pearlstein, "No More Mr. Nice Guy: Corporate America Has Done an About-Face in How It Pays and Treats Employees," *Washington Post National Weekly Edition*, December 18–24, 1995, p. 10; Robert Kuttner, "Ducking Class Warfare," *Washington Post National Weekly Edition*, March 11–17, 1996, p. 5; Henry Allen, "Ha! So Much for Loyalty," *Washington Post National Weekly Edition*, March 4–10, 1996, p. 11.

counterpart today, when a quarter of the workforce puts in 49 or more hours a week.[20]

So politicians are practicing quite a double standard when they tell us to return to the family forms of the 1950s while they do nothing to restore the job programs and family subsidies of that era, the limits on corporate relocation and financial wheeling-dealing, the much higher share of taxes paid by corporations then, the availability of union jobs for noncollege youth, and the subsidies for higher education such as the National Defense Education Act loans. Furthermore, they're not telling the whole story when they claim that the 1950s was the most prosperous time for families and the most secure decade for children. Instead, playing to our understandable nostalgia for a time when things seemed to be getting better, not worse, they engage in a tricky chronological shell game with their figures, diverting our attention from two important points. First, many individuals, families, and groups were excluded from the economic prosperity, family optimism, and social civility of the 1950s. Second, the all-time high point of child well-being and family economic security came not during the 1950s but *at the end of the 1960s*.

We now know that 1950s family culture was not only nontraditional; it was also not idyllic. In important ways, the stability of family and community life during the 1950s rested on pervasive discrimination against women, gays, political dissidents, non-Christians, and racial or ethnic minorities, as well as on a systematic cover-up of the underside of many families. Families that were harmonious and fair of their own free will may have been able to function more easily in the fifties, but few alternatives existed for members of discordant or oppressive families. Victims of child abuse, incest, alcoholism, spousal rape, and wife battering had no recourse, no place to go, until well into the 1960s.[21]

At the end of the 1950s, despite ten years of economic growth, 27.3 percent of the nation's children were poor, including those in white "underclass" communities such as Appalachia. Almost 50 percent of married-couple African American families were impoverished—a figure far higher than today. It's no wonder African Americans are not likely to pick the 1950s as a golden age, even in comparison with the setbacks they experienced in the 1980s. When blacks moved north to find jobs in the postwar urban manufacturing boom they met vicious harassment and violence, first to prevent them from moving out of the central cities, then to exclude them from public space such as parks or beaches.

---

[20]Ehrenhalt, *The Lost City*, pp. 11–12; Jeremy Rifken, *The End of Work: The Decline of the Global Labor Force and the Dawn of the Post-Market Era* (New York: G. P. Putnam's Sons, 1995), pp. 169, 170, 231; Juliet Schorr, *The Overworked American: The Unexpected Decline of Leisure* (New York: Basic Books, 1991).

[21]For documentation that these problems existed, see chapter 2 of *The Way We Never Were*.

In Philadelphia, for example, the City of Brotherly Love, there were more than 200 racial incidents over housing in the first six months of 1955 alone. The Federal Housing Authority, such a boon to white working-class families, refused to insure homes in all-black or in racially mixed neighborhoods. Two-thirds of the city dwellers evicted by the urban renewal projects of the decade were African Americans and Latinos; government did almost nothing to help such displaced families find substitute housing.[22]

Women were unable to take out loans or even credit cards in their own names. They were excluded from juries in many states. A lack of options outside marriage led some women to remain in desperately unhappy unions that were often not in the best interests of their children or themselves. Even women in happy marriages often felt humiliated by the constant messages they received that their whole lives had to revolve around a man. "You are not ready when he calls—miss one turn," was a rule in the Barbie game marketed to 1950s girls; "he criticizes your hairdo—go to the beauty shop." Episodes of *Father Knows Best* advised young women: "The worst thing you can do is to try to beat a man at his own game. You just beat the women at theirs." One character on the show told women to always ask themselves, "Are you after a job or a man? You can't have both."[23]

The Fifties Experiment Comes to an End

The social stability of the 1950s, then, was a response to the stick of racism, sexism, and repression as well as to the carrot of economic opportunity and government aid. Because social protest mounted in the 1960s and unsettling challenges were posed to the gender roles and sexual mores of the previous decade, many people forget that families continued to make gains throughout the 1960s and into the first few years of the 1970s. By 1969, child poverty was down to 14 percent, its lowest level ever; it hovered just above that marker until 1975, when it began its steady climb up to contemporary figures (22 percent in 1993; 21.2 percent in 1994). The high point of health and nutrition for poor children was reached in the early 1970s.[24]

So commentators are being misleading when they claim that the 1950s was the golden age of American families. They are disregarding

---

[22]The poverty figures come from census data collected in *The State of America's Children Yearbook, 1996* (Washington, DC: Children's Defense Fund, 1996), p. 77. See also Hirsch, *Making the Second Ghetto*; Raymond Mohl, "Making the Second Ghetto in Metropolitan Miami, 1940–1960," *Journal of Urban History* 25 (1995), p. 396; Micaela di Leonardo, "Boys on the Hood," *Nation*, August 17–24, 1992, p. 180; Jackson, *Crabgrass Frontier*, pp. 226–27.

[23]Susan Douglas, *Where the Girls Are: Growing Up Female with the Mass Media* (New York: Times Books, 1994), pp. 25, 37.

[24]*The State of America's Children Yearbook, 1966*, p. 77; May and Porter, "Poverty and Income Trends: 1994," p. 23; Sara McLanahan et al., *Losing Ground: A Critique*, University of Wisconsin Institute for Research on Poverty, Special Report No. 38, 1985.

the number of people who were excluded during that decade and ignoring the socioeconomic gains that continued to be made through the 1960s. But they are quite right to note that the improvements of the 1950s and 1960s came to an end at some point in the 1970s (though not for the elderly, who continued to make progress).

Ironically, it was the children of those stable, enduring, supposedly idyllic 1950s families, the recipients of so much maternal time and attention, that pioneered the sharp break with their parents' family forms and gender roles in the 1970s. This was not because they were led astray by some youthful Murphy Brown in her student rebel days or inadvertently spoiled by parents who read too many of Dr. Spock's child-raising manuals.

Partly, the departure from 1950s family arrangements was a logical extension of trends and beliefs pioneered in the 1950s, or of inherent contradictions in those patterns. For example, early and close-spaced childbearing freed more wives up to join the labor force, and married women began to flock to work. By 1960, more than 40 percent of women over the age of 16 held a job, and working mothers were the fastest growing component of the labor force. The educational aspirations and opportunities that opened up for kids of the baby boom could not be confined to males, and many tight-knit, male-breadwinner, nuclear families in the 1950s instilled in their daughters the ambition to be something other than a homemaker.[25]

Another part of the transformation was a shift in values. Most people would probably agree that some changes in values were urgently needed: the extension of civil rights to racial minorities and to women; a rejection of property rights in children by parents and in women by husbands; a reaction against the political intolerance and the wasteful materialism of 1950s culture. Other changes in values remain more controversial: opposition to American intervention abroad; repudiation of the traditional sexual double standard; rebellion against what many young people saw as the hypocrisy of parents who preached sexual morality but ignored social immorality such as racism and militarism.

Still other developments, such as the growth of me-first individualism, are widely regarded as problematic by people on all points along the political spectrum. It's worth noting, though, that the origins of antisocial individualism and self-indulgent consumerism lay at least as much in the family values of the 1950s as in the youth rebellion of the 1960s. The marketing experts who never allowed the kids in *Ozzie and Harriet* sitcoms to be shown drinking milk, for fear of offending soft-drink companies that might sponsor the show in syndication, were ultimately the same people who slightly later invested billions of dollars

---

[25]For studies of how both middle-class and working-class women in the 1950s quickly departed from, or never quite accepted, the predominant image of women, see Joanne Meyerowitz, ed., *Not June Cleaver: Women and Gender in Postwar America, 1945–1960* (Philadelphia: Temple University Press, 1994).

to channel sexual rebelliousness and a depoliticized individualism into mainstream culture.

There were big cultural changes brewing by the beginning of the 1970s, and tremendous upheavals in social, sexual, and family values. And yes, there were sometimes reckless or simply laughable excesses in some of the early experiments with new gender roles, family forms, and personal expression. But the excesses of 1950s gender roles and family forms were every bit as repellent and stupid as the excesses of the sixties: Just watch a dating etiquette film of the time period, or recall that therapists of the day often told victims of incest that they were merely having unconscious oedipal fantasies.

Ultimately, though, changes in values were not what brought the 1950s family experiment to an end. The postwar family compacts between husbands and wives, parents and children, young and old, were based on the postwar social compact between government, corporations, and workers. While there was some discontent with those family bargains among women and youth, the old relations did not really start to unravel until people began to face the erosion of the corporate wage bargain and government broke its tacit societal bargain that it would continue to invest in jobs and education for the younger generation.

In the 1970s, new economic trends began to clash with all the social expectations that 1950s families had instilled in their children. That clash, not the willful abandonment of responsibility and commitment, has been the primary cause of both family rearrangements and the growing social problems that are usually attributed to such family changes, but in fact have *separate* origins.

ENGAGING THE TEXT

1. According to Coontz, what do we really miss about the 1950s? In addition, what *don't* we miss?

2. In Coontz's view, what was the role of the government in making the 1950s in America what they were? What part did broader historical forces or other circumstances play?

3. Although she concentrates on the 1950s, Coontz also describes the other decades from the 1920s to the 1990s, when she wrote this piece. Use her information to create a brief chart naming the key characteristics of each decade. Then consider your own family history and see how well it fits the pattern Coontz outlines. Discuss the results with classmates or write a journal entry reflecting on what you learn.

4. Consider the most recent ten years of American history. What events or trends (for example, same-sex marriage legislation, financial crises, the Obama presidency) do you think a sociologist or cultural historian might consider important for understanding our current mythologies of family? How do you think our ideas about family have changed in this decade?

EXPLORING CONNECTIONS

5. Compare the photo from *The Donna Reed Show* (p. 15) to the accounts of 1950s families Coontz provides. How does Coontz help us understand such an iconic image in a cultural context? If the image seems like a quaint artifact, do you think the values it projects still appeal to Americans?

6. Review "Looking for Work" by Gary Soto (p. 19). How does this narrative evoke nostalgia for a simpler, better era for families? Does it reveal any of the problems with the 1950s that Coontz describes?

EXTENDING THE CRITICAL CONTEXT

7. Coontz suggests that an uninformed nostalgia for the 1950s could promote harmful political agendas. (See, for example, paras. 7 and 37.) Do you see any evidence in contemporary media of nostalgia for the 1950s? Do you agree with Coontz that such nostalgia can be dangerous? Why or why not?

8. Watch an episode of a 1950s sitcom such as *Father Knows Best*, *The Donna Reed Show*, *Leave It to Beaver*, or *I Love Lucy*. Analyze the extent to which it reveals both positive and negative aspects of the 1950s that Coontz discusses (for example, an authoritarian father figure, limited roles for wives, economic prosperity, or a sense of a secure community).

AUNT IDA PIECES A QUILT
MELVIN DIXON

This is an extraordinary poem about AIDS, love, and family life. Its author, Melvin Dixon (1950–1992), received his Ph.D. from Brown University; in addition to teaching English at Queens College in New York, he published poetry, literary criticism, translations, and two novels. "Aunt Ida" appeared in *Brother to Brother: New Writings by Black Gay Men* (1991). Dixon died of complications from AIDS in 1992.

You are right, but your patch isn't big enough. —JESSE JACKSON

When a cure is found and the last panel is sewn into place, the Quilt will be displayed in a permanent home as a national monument to the individual, irreplaceable people lost to AIDS—and the people who knew and loved them most.

—CLEVE JONES, *founder,* THE NAMES PROJECT

They brought me some of his clothes. The hospital gown,
those too-tight dungarees, his blue choir robe
with the gold sash. How that boy could sing!
His favorite color in a necktie. A Sunday shirt.
What I'm gonna do with all this stuff?   5
I can remember Junie without this business.
My niece Francine say they quilting all over the country.
So many good boys like her boy, gone.

At my age I ain't studying no needle and thread.
My eyes ain't so good now and my fingers lock in a fist,   10
they so eaten up with arthritis. This old back
don't take kindly to bending over a frame no more.
Francine say ain't I a mess carrying on like this.
I could make two quilts the time I spend running my mouth.

Just cut his name out the cloths, stitch something nice   15
about him. Something to bring him back. You can do it,
Francine say. Best sewing our family ever had.
Quilting ain't that easy, I say. Never was easy.
Y'all got to help me remember him good.

Most of my quilts was made down South. My mama   20
And my mama's mama taught me. Popped me on the tail
if I missed a stitch or threw the pattern out of line.
I did "Bright Star" and "Lonesome Square" and "Rally Round,"
what many folks don't bother with nowadays. Then Elmo and me
married and came North where the cold in Connecticut   25
cuts you like a knife. We was warm, though.
We had sackcloth and calico and cotton, 100% pure.
What they got now but polyester rayon. Factory made.

Let me tell you something. In all my quilts there's a secret
nobody knows. Every last one of them got my name Ida   30
stitched on the back side in red thread.
That's where Junie got his flair. Don't let nobody fool you.
When he got the Youth Choir standing up and singing
the whole church would rock. He'd throw up his hands
from them wide blue sleeves and the church would hush   35
right down to the funeral parlor fans whisking the air.
He'd toss his head back and holler and we'd all cry holy.

And nevermind his too-tight dungarees.
I caught him switching down the street one Saturday night,
and I seen him more than once. I said, Junie,   40
you ain't got to let the world know all your business.
Who cared where he went when he wanted to have fun.
He'd be singing his heart out come Sunday morning.

When Francine say she gonna hang this quilt in the church
I like to fall out. A quilt ain't no showpiece,   45

it's to keep you warm. Francine say it can do both.
Now I ain't so old-fashioned I can't change,
but I made Francine come over and bring her daughter
Belinda. We cut and tacked his name, *JUNIE.*
Just plain and simple, *"JUNIE, our boy."*   50
Cut the *J* in blue, the *U* in gold. *N* in dungarees
just as tight as you please. The *I* from the hospital gown
and the white shirt he wore First Sunday. Belinda
put the necktie in *E* in the cross stitch I showed her.

Wouldn't you know we got to talking about Junie.   55
We could smell him in the cloth.
Underarm. Afro Sheen pomade.[1] Gravy stains.
I forgot all about my arthritis.
When Francine left me to finish up, I swear
I heard Junie giggling right along with me   60
as I stitched Ida on the back side in red thread.

Francine say she gonna send this quilt to Washington
like folks doing from all 'cross the country,
so many good people gone. Babies, mothers, fathers
and boys like our Junie. Francine say   65
they gonna piece this quilt to another one,
another name and another patch
all in a larger quilt getting larger and larger.

Maybe we all like that, patches waiting to be pieced.
Well, I don't know about Washington.   70
We need Junie here with us. And Maxine,
she cousin May's husband's sister's people,
she having a baby and here comes winter already.
The cold cutting like knives. Now where did I put that needle?

ENGAGING THE TEXT

1. Identify all of the characters and their relationships in the poem. Then retell the story of the poem in your own words.

2. Discuss the movement of Aunt Ida's mind and her emotions as we move from stanza to stanza. What happens to Aunt Ida in the poem? What is the dominant feeling at the end of the poem?

3. Junie's clothes take on symbolic weight in the quilt and, of course, in the poem as well. What do the hospital gown, the dungarees, the choir robe, and the white shirt and necktie represent?

4. What is Aunt Ida about to make at the end of the poem, and what is its significance?

[1]**Afro Sheen pomade:** Hair-care product for African Americans. [Eds.]

EXPLORING CONNECTIONS

5. Look at the images in this chapter's Visual Portfolio (p. 54). Discuss how you might tell the story of "Aunt Ida Pieces a Quilt" visually instead of verbally — for example, as a painting, a mural, a photograph, or a photo essay. Sketch or draw an image based on the poem and share it with classmates.

6. What roles do women play in "Aunt Ida Pieces a Quilt"? Compare these roles to those played by women in Gary Soto's "Looking for Work" (p. 19), and "What We Really Miss About the 1950s" by Stephanie Coontz (p. 25). Based on these examples, would it be fair to conclude that Americans see "the family" as predominantly a woman's responsibility?

EXTENDING THE CRITICAL CONTEXT

7. Write a screenplay or dramatic script to "translate" the story of "Aunt Ida Pieces a Quilt" into dramatic form. Time permitting, organize a group to read or perform the piece for the class.

8. Watch the documentary *Common Threads: Stories from the Quilt* and write a poem based on the life of one of the people profiled in this film.

THE COLOR OF FAMILY TIES: RACE, CLASS, GENDER, AND EXTENDED FAMILY INVOLVEMENT

NAOMI GERSTEL AND NATALIA SARKISIAN

The myth of the nuclear family is not just a harmless cliché; rather, it can lock us into fundamental misunderstandings of how American families live, misunderstandings that can divide groups and promote simplistic public policy. In this study, sociologists Naomi Gerstel and Natalia Sarkisian examine data on black, white, and Latino/a families to challenge the popular notion that minority families have weaker ties and are more fragmented than white families. They find that social class is more important than ethnicity; moreover, while differences between ethnic groups do exist, each group has developed ways to cope with the practical, emotional, and financial challenges they face and to maintain family solidarity. Gerstel and Sarkisian are professors of sociology, Gerstel at the University of Massachusetts Amherst and Sarkisian at Boston College. Their coauthored article on gender, employment, and help given to parents (in *Journal of Marriage and the Family*, 2004) won the

2005 Rosabeth Moss Kanter International Award for Research Excellence in Families and Work. "The Color of Family Ties" appeared in *American Families: A Multicultural Reader*, edited by Stephanie Coontz (see p. 25) with Maya Parson and Gabrielle Raley (2008).

WHEN TALKING ABOUT FAMILY OBLIGATIONS and solidarities, politicians and social commentators typically focus on the ties between married couples and their children. We often hear that Black and Latino/a, especially Puerto Rican, families are more disorganized than White families, and that their family ties are weaker, because rates of non-marriage and single parenthood are higher among these minority groups. But this focus on the nuclear family ignores extended family solidarities and caregiving activities. Here we examine these often overlooked extended kinship ties.[1]

Taking this broader perspective on family relations refutes the myth that Blacks and Latinos/as lack strong families. Minority individuals are more likely to live in extended family homes than Whites and in many ways more likely to help out their aging parents, grandparents, adult children, brothers, sisters, cousins, aunts, uncles, and other kin.

According to our research using the second wave of the National Survey of Families and Households, as Figures 1 and 2 show, Blacks and Latinos/as, both women and men, are much more likely than Whites to share a home with extended kin: 42 percent of Blacks and 37 percent of Latinos/as, but only 20 percent of Whites, live with relatives. Similar patterns exist for living near relatives: 54 percent of Blacks and 51 percent of Latinos/as, but only 37 percent of Whites, live within two miles of kin. Blacks and Latinos/as are also more likely than Whites to frequently visit kin. For example, 76 percent of Blacks, 71 percent of Latinos/as, but just 63 percent of Whites see their relatives once a week or more.

[1]For the extensive analysis underlying this discussion, see: (1) Natalia Sarkisian, Mariana Gerena, and Naomi Gerstel, "Extended Family Integration Among Mexican and Euro Americans: Ethnicity, Gender, and Class," *Journal of Marriage and Family*, 69 (2007), 1 (February), 40–54. (2) Natalia Sarkisian, Mariana Gerena, and Naomi Gerstel, "Extended Family Ties Among Mexicans, Puerto Ricans and Whites: Superintegration or Disintegration?," *Family Relations*, 55 (2006), 3 (July), 331–344. (3) Natalia Sarkisian and Naomi Gerstel, "Kin Support Among Blacks and Whites: Race and Family Organization," *American Sociological Review*, 69 (2004), 4 (December), 812–837. (4) Amy Armenia and Naomi Gerstel, "Family Leaves, The FMLA, and Gender Neutrality: The Intersection of Race and Gender," *Social Science Research*, 35 (2006), 871–891. (5) Naomi Gerstel and Natalia Sarkisian, "A Sociological Perspective on Families and Work: The Import of Gender, Class, and Race," in Marcie Pitt Catsouphes, Ellen Kossek, and Steven Sweet (eds.), *The Work and Family Handbook: Multi-disciplinary Perspectives, Methods, and Approaches* (Mahwah, NJ: Lawrence Erlbaum, 2006), pp. 237–266. (6) Naomi Gerstel and Natalia Sarkisian, "Marriage: The Good, the Bad, and the Greedy," *Contexts*, 5 (2006) 4 (November), 16–21. (7) Naomi Gerstel and Natalia Sarkisian, "Intergenerational Care and the Greediness of Adult Children's Marriages," in J. Suitor and T. Owens (eds.), *Interpersonal Relations Across the Life Course. Advances in the Life Course Research*, Volume 12 (Greenwich, CT: Elsevier/JAI Press, 2007). [Gerstel and Sarkisian's note.]

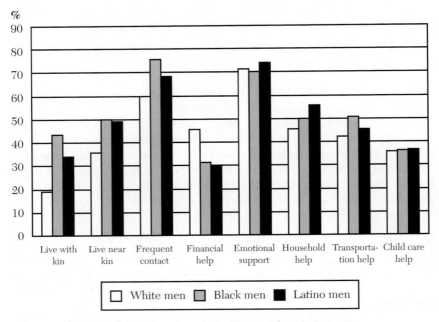

Figure 1. Ethnicity and extended kin involvement among men.
Data from National Survey of Families and Households, 1992–1994.

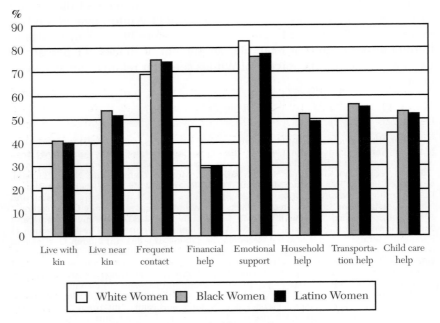

Figure 2. Ethnicity and extended kin involvement among women.
Data from National Survey of Families and Households, 1992–1994.

Even if they don't live together, Blacks and Latinos/as are as likely as Whites—and in some ways more likely—to be supportive family members. But there are important racial and ethnic differences in the type of support family members give each other. Whites are more likely than ethnic minorities to give and receive large sums of money, and White women are more likely than minority women to give and receive emotional support, such as discussing personal problems and giving each other advice. When it comes to help with practical tasks, however, we find that Black and Latino/a relatives are more likely than Whites to be supportive: they are more likely to give each other help with household work and child care, as well as with providing rides and running errands. These differences are especially pronounced among women.

This is not to say that Black and Latino men are not involved with kin, as is implied in popular images of minority men hanging out on street corners rather than attending to family ties. In fact, Black and Latino men are more likely than White men to live near relatives and to stay in touch with them. White men, however, are more likely to give and receive large-scale financial help. Moreover, the three groups of men are very similar when it comes to giving and getting practical help and emotional support.

These data suggest that if we only consider married couples or parents and their young children, we are missing much of what families in general and families of color in particular do for each other. A focus on nuclear families in discussions of race differences in family life creates a biased portrait of families of color.

Explaining Race Differences: Is It Culture or Class?

When discussing differences in family experiences of various racial and ethnic groups, commentators often assume that these differences can be traced to cultural differences or competing "family values." Sometimes these are expressed in a positive way, as in the stereotype that Latino families have more extended ties because of their historical traditions and religious values. Other times these are expressed in a negative way, as when Blacks are said to lack family values because of the cultural legacy of slavery and subsequent years of oppression. Either way, differences in family behaviors are often explained by differences in cultural heritage.

In contrast, in our research, we find that social class rather than culture is the key to understanding the differences in extended family ties and behaviors between Whites and ethnic minorities. To be sure, differences in cultural values do exist. Blacks and Latinos/as are more likely than Whites to say they believe that extended family is important; both groups are also more likely to attend religious services. Blacks tend to hold more egalitarian beliefs about gender than Whites, while

TABLE 1 Education, Income, and Poverty Rates by Race			
	WHITES	BLACKS	LATINOS/AS
Median household income	$50,784	$30,858	$35,967
Percentage below poverty line	8.4%	24.7%	22.0%
Education:			
Less than high school	14.5%	27.6%	47.6%
High school graduate	58.5%	58.1%	42.0%
Bachelor's degree or higher	27.0%	14.3%	10.4%

Data from U.S. Census Bureau, 2005.

Latinos/as, especially Mexican Americans, tend to hold more "traditional" views. But these differences in values do not explain racial differences in actual involvement with relatives. It is, instead, social class that matters most in explaining these differences.

It is widely known (and confirmed by U.S. Census data presented in Table 1) that Blacks and Latinos/as tend to have far less income and education than Whites. Families of color are also much more likely than White families to be below the official poverty line. In our research, we find that the differences in extended family ties and behaviors between Whites and ethnic minorities are primarily the result of these social class disparities.

Simply put, White, Black, and Latino/a individuals with the same amount of income and education have similar patterns of involvement with their extended families. Just like poor minorities, impoverished Whites are more likely to exchange practical aid and visit with extended kin than are their wealthier counterparts. Just like middle-class Whites, middle-class Blacks and Latinos/as are more likely to talk about their personal concerns or share money with relatives than are their poorer counterparts. 10

More specifically, it is because Whites tend to have more income than Blacks and Latinos/as that they are more likely to give money to their relatives or get it from them. And the higher levels of emotional support among White women can be at least in part traced to their higher levels of education, perhaps because schooling encourages women to talk out their problems and makes them more likely to give (and get) advice.

Conversely, we find that the relative economic deprivation of racial/ethnic minorities leads in many ways to higher levels of extended family involvement. Individuals' lack of economic resources increases their need for help from kin and boosts their willingness to give help in return. Because Blacks and Latinos/as typically have less income and education than Whites, they come to rely more on their relatives for daily needs such as child care, household tasks, or rides. The tendency of Blacks and Latinos/as to live with or near kin may also reflect their greater need for kin cooperation, as well as their decreased opportunities and pressures to move away, including moving for college.

Social Class and Familial Trade-Offs

How do our findings on race, social class, and familial involvement challenge common understandings of minority families? They show that poor minority families do not necessarily lead lives of social isolation or lack strong family solidarities. The lower rates of marriage among impoverished groups may reflect not a rejection of family values but a realistic assessment of how little a woman (and her children) may be able to depend upon marriage. Sociologists Kathryn Edin and Maria Kefalas (2007) recently found that because disadvantaged men are often unable to offer women the kind of economic security that advantaged men provide, poor women are less likely to marry. Instead, these women create support networks beyond the nuclear family, regularly turning to extended kin for practical support.

Reliance on extended kin and lack of marital ties are linked. In another analysis of the National Survey of Families and Households, we found that, contrary to much rhetoric about marriage as a key source of adult social ties, marriage actually diminishes ties to kin. Married people—women as well as men—are less involved with their parents and siblings than those never married or previously married. These findings indicate a trade-off between commitments to nuclear and extended family ties. Marriage, we have found, is a "greedy" institution: it has a tendency to consume the bulk of people's energies and emotions and to dilute their commitments beyond the nuclear family.

On the one hand, then, support given to spouses and intimate partners sometimes comes at the expense of broader kin and community ties. Indeed, married adult children take care of elderly parents less often than their unmarried siblings. Marriage can also cut people off from networks of mutual aid. Married mothers, for example, whether Black, Latina, or White, are often unable to obtain help from kin in the way that their single counterparts can. Although the "greedy" nature of marriage may pose a problem across social class, it is especially problematic for those less well off economically, as these individuals most need to cultivate wider circles of obligation, mutual aid, and reciprocity.

On the other hand, support to relatives sometimes comes at the expense of care for partners, and can interfere with nuclear family formation or stability. Indeed, individuals who are deeply immersed in relationships with extended families may be less likely to get married or, if they marry, may be less likely to put the marital ties first in their loyalties. Several decades ago in her observations of a poor Black community, anthropologist Carol Stack (1974) found that the reciprocal patterns

15

MORE NONTRADITIONAL FAMILY UNITS

Guy, Chair, Three-Way Lamp

A Woman, Her Daughter, Forty-four My Little Ponies

The Troy Triplets and Their Personal Trainer

Two Guys, Two Gals, Two Phones, a Fax, and a Blender

R. Chast

of sharing with kin and "fictive kin" forged in order to survive hardship often made it difficult for poor Blacks either to move up economically or to marry. To prevent the dilution of their social support networks, some extended families may even discourage their members from getting married, or unconsciously sabotage relationships that threaten to pull someone out of the family orbit. As sociologists Domínguez and

Watkins (2003) argue, the ties of mutual aid that help impoverished individuals survive on a day-to-day basis may also prevent them from saying "no" to requests that sap their ability to get ahead or pursue individual opportunities.

Overall, we should avoid either denigrating or glorifying the survival strategies of the poor. Although social class disparities are key to understanding racial and ethnic variation in familial involvement, it is too simple to say that class differences create "more" involvement with relatives in one group and "less" in another. In some ways economic deprivation increases ties to kin (e.g., in terms of living nearby or exchanging practical help) and in other ways it reduces them (e.g., in terms of financial help or emotional support). These findings remind us that love and family connections are expressed both through talk and action. Equally important, focusing solely on the positive or on the negative aspects of either minority or White families is problematic. Instead, we need to think in terms of trade-offs — among different kinds of care and between the bonds of kinship and the bonds of marriage. Both trade-offs are linked to social class.

Why Do These Differences in Family Life Matter?

Commentators often emphasize the disorganization and dysfunction of Black and Latino/a family life. They suggest that if we could "fix" family values in minority communities and get them to form married-couple households, all their problems would be solved. This argument misunderstands causal connections by focusing on the family as the source of problems. Specifically, it ignores the link between race and class and attributes racial or ethnic differences to cultural values. Instead, we argue, it is important to understand that family strategies and behaviors often emerge in response to the challenges of living in economic deprivation or constant economic insecurity. Therefore, social policies should not focus on changing family behaviors, but rather aim to support a range of existing family arrangements and improve economic conditions for the poor.

Social policies that overlook extended family obligations may introduce, reproduce, or even increase ethnic inequalities. For example, the relatives of Blacks and Latinos/as are more likely than those of Whites to provide various kinds of support that policymakers tend to assume is only provided by husbands and wives. Such relatives may need the rights and support systems that we usually reserve for spouses. For instance, the Family and Medical Leave Act is an important social policy, but it only guarantees unpaid leave from jobs to provide care to spouses, children, or elderly parents requiring medical attention. Our findings suggest that, if we really want to support families, such policies must be broadened to include adult children, needy grown-up brothers and sisters, cousins, aunts and uncles. Similarly, Medicaid regulations that only pay for non-familial care of ill, injured, or disabled individuals implicitly discriminate against Blacks and Latinos/as who provide significant amounts of care to extended kin. "Pro-marriage" policies that give special incentives to impoverished women for getting married may penalize other women who turn down marriage to a risky mate and rely instead on grandparents or other relatives to help raise their children.

Extended family obligations should be recognized and accommo- ₂₀ dated where possible. But they should not be counted on as a substitute for antipoverty measures, nor should marriage promotion be used in this way. Policymakers must recognize that support from family — whether extended or nuclear — cannot fully compensate for the disadvantages of being poor, or minority, or both. Neither marital ties nor extended family ties can substitute for educational opportunities, jobs with decent wages, health insurance, and affordable child care. Instead of hoping that poor families pull themselves out of poverty by their own bootstraps, social policy should explicitly aim to rectify economic disadvantages. In turn, improvements in economic opportunities and resources will likely shape families.

References

Domínguez, Silvia, and Celeste Watkins. "Creating Networks for Survival and Mobility: Examining Social Capital Amongst Low-Income African-American and Latin-American Mothers." *Social Problems*, 50 (2003), 1 (February), 111–135.

Edin, Kathryn, and Maria Kefalas. *Promises I Can Keep: Why Poor Women Put Motherhood Before Marriage* (Berkeley, CA: University of California Press, 2007).

Stack, Carol B. *All Our Kin: Strategies for Survival in a Black Community* (New York: Harper and Row, 1974).

ENGAGING THE TEXT

1. In paragraph 1, what might politicians and social commentators mean when they describe black and Latino/a families as "more disorganized" than white families? How accurate is this label in Gerstel and Sarkisian's view? Why might a politician find the term "disorganized" useful?

2. What evidence do Gerstel and Sarkisian give that social class is even more important than ethnicity in understanding differences among families? Why is this a critical distinction to the authors?

3. What examples of "extended family solidarities and caregiving activities" (para. 1) do the authors provide? How common or uncommon are these in your own family or community? Do your personal experiences and those of your classmates tend to support, refute, or complicate Gerstel and Sarkisian's analysis?

4. Explain why you agree or disagree with the claim that "social policy should explicitly aim to rectify economic disadvantages" (para. 20). What would this abstract language mean in practice?

EXPLORING CONNECTIONS

5. Review the selections listed below. To what extent could these families be described as "disorganized" (para. 1) and to what extent do they exhibit "extended family solidarities and caregiving activities" (para. 1)? Review Gary Soto's "Looking for Work" (p. 19) and Melvin Dixon's "Aunt Ida Pieces a Quilt" (p. 41).

6. Carefully study the frontispiece to Chapter Four on page 345. What symbols of affluence does the photograph contain? How might Gerstel and Sarkisian read the importance of family background in the man's level of economic achievement?

7. How might Gerstel and Sarkisian read the cartoon on page 50?

EXTENDING THE CRITICAL CONTEXT

8. In this article, Gerstel and Sarkisian focus on just three groups — blacks, Latinos/as, and whites. What do you think the data would look like for other groups such as Asian Americans, Pacific Islanders, Native Americans, or recent immigrants? Find data to support or refute your guesses.

9. Study the footnote on page 45, which lists seven articles by Gerstel, Sarkisian, and others. Based on the journal and article titles in the footnote, what can you say about the scope, purpose, and methodologies of Gerstel and Sarkisian's research? To extend the assignment, read one of the articles and report its key findings to the class.

VISUAL PORTFOLIO
READING IMAGES OF AMERICAN FAMILIES

Freedom from What (2014), by Pops Peterson.

Image Source/Getty Images

AP Photo/Paul Sancya

Reuters/Anthony Bolante/Landov

VISUAL PORTFOLIO

READING IMAGES OF AMERICAN FAMILIES

1. The illustration on page 54 by artist Pops Peterson closely mirrors *Freedom from Fear*, an iconic painting by Norman Rockwell (1894–1978) that depicts two American children being safely tucked into bed while World War II rages in Europe. Find *Freedom from Fear* online and list all the similarities and differences you can see between the original painting and Peterson's re-creation. Then explain how you read the relationship between the two pieces, accounting not only for Peterson's switch to showing an African American family but also for details like the dolls, the facial expressions, the body language, and the newspaper headlines (the partially visible headline "Bombings Ki . . . Horror Hit" in *Freedom from Fear* and "I Can't Breathe!" in Peterson's reinterpretation). What is Peterson saying about freedom, fear, and race in America?

2. The family pictured on page 55 is gathered at an Eid al-Fitr celebration to mark the end of the Ramadan month of fasting. Read the image through cultural lenses: What does it suggest about American diversity, about family values, about generations, about gender, about faith, and about tradition? Finally, compare it to the preceding photo by Pops Peterson or Norman Rockwell's *Freedom from Want*, which you can find online.

3. The young women pictured on page 56 are Lucy and Maria Aylmer; they are sisters — in fact *twin* sisters born to a white father and half-Jamaican mother. Explain how this image of biracial twins may complicate our understanding of racial and family identity. Do you think Maria and Lucy's divergent appearances are likely to impact their life experiences? Why or why not?

4. The image on page 57 was taken in April 2015 during demonstrations after Freddie Gray Jr., a twenty-five-year-old African American, died while in Baltimore Police custody. What emotions can you read in the faces pictured? How do you read the signs and symbols in the image — the children's hands, the father's Baltimore Orioles T-shirt, and the photograph itself in its racially charged context? Finally, compare this image to the portrait of Lucy and Maria Aylmer, who are also members of a multi-ethnic family (p. 56).

5. Compare the photo of the DeBoer-Rowse family on page 58 to the frontispiece for this chapter (p. 15). How was each family formed, for example? What elements do the images have in common, and how do the striking differences reflect how ideas of family have evolved over the past half century? To extend the discussion, research and report on the legal case *DeBoer v. Snyder*, one of the cases settled by the U.S. Supreme Court's ruling of June 2015 recognizing same-sex marriage as a fundamental right.

6. The custom bicycle on page 59 is being prepared to make a delivery. Who is delivering what to whom? What does the photo say about technology and the contemporary American family?

FROM TO THE END OF JUNE: THE INTIMATE LIFE OF AMERICAN FOSTER CARE

CRIS BEAM

According to data from the U.S. Department of Health and Human Services, more than 400,000 American youth live in some form of foster care at any given time, with more than 20,000 "aging out" each year — moving from foster care to independent living when they turn eighteen or twenty-one. Youth who age out fare poorly compared to youth with permanent families, with lower educational achievement and dramatically increased risks of homelessness, early pregnancy, low wages, and incarceration.[1] In this excerpt from her book on foster care, Cris Beam tells the story of "Oneida," a seventeen-year-old who moves from a foster care institution to live with prospective adoptive parents. Although the narrative focuses on a single foster placement, it vividly illustrates the formidable challenges faced by foster kids, adoptive / foster parents, and social service organizations and agencies across the nation. Cris Beam, herself a foster parent, teaches creative writing at Columbia University and New York University; she is the author of *Transparent: Love, Family, and Living the T with Transgender Teenagers* (Harcourt 2007) and the young-adult novel *I am J* (Little, Brown 2011). *To the End of June: The Intimate Life of American Foster Care* was named a *New York Times* Notable Book in 2013.

MARY WORKS FOR AN IMPROBABLE ORGANIZATION with an improbable name. It's not a foster care agency, though it does train and license foster parents. It is not an adoption agency, though it does connect around sixty hard-to-place teenagers with permanent families each year. It's called You Gotta Believe! and what it is, is a kind of bridge: You Gotta Believe! pulls hard-to-place kids from their group homes or RTCs[2] and connects them with adoptive parents their agencies said didn't exist. It calls itself a homelessness prevention program, and according to the founder, Pat O'Brien, it's the first and only organization of its kind in the country.

What Mary and YGB do is find other people like her to adopt the kids the way she's adopted. In a way, YGB has had to create something

---

[1]Teresa Wiltz, "States Tackle 'Aging Out' of Foster Care." March 25, 2015, The Pew Charitable Trusts at pewtrusts.org. Web. [All notes are Beam's, except 2, 3, 7, 8, 9, 10.]

[2]**RTCs:** Residential Treatment Centers. Beam describes these centers as "the last stop on the foster care train . . . places for kids who have behavior, psychiatric, or substance problems but don't merit psychiatric hospitals or correctional facilities."

entirely outside of the system because it's the system that's damaged the kids; it's the system that claimed teenagers would be fine on their own.

I visited You Gotta Believe! on a cold winter morning, stepping off the train to the smell of the ocean and the view of Coney Island's carnival rides, shut down for the season. The headquarters are located a few blocks off the boardwalk, near a Golden Krust, a Mexican deli, and a place called Hair For U. The office was cluttered with file cabinets and file boxes; a box of Raisin Bran perched on the front counter next to a bucket of salt for melting sidewalk ice. The front door advertised the organization's services. "Adopt a Teen!" a poster read, alongside prices for faxing, copying, and enlisting a notary public.

"The whole system is cockamamie," YGB founder Pat O'Brien said by way of introduction. Pat is a gregarious white guy in his forties, with curly hair and a mustache, who spent his early career at a foster agency working to get older kids adopted. "We placed mostly preteens at that agency; the average age was eleven because everybody thought nobody wanted older kids."

These older kids—both then and now—could legally decide at age fourteen that they no longer wanted to find an adoptive family, getting themselves placed on the independent living track and aging out on their own. Because ACS[3] and the Department of Homeless Services are entirely different governmental branches, it's hard to get accurate statistics about the flow from one into the other, but Pat, along with several credible studies, estimates that about 50 percent of the current homeless population were once in foster care.[4] This is why Pat describes YGB, above all else, as homeless prevention.

"The system comes up with all these crazy programs for teenagers— shared parents, bridge parents, lifetime connections, resources, mentors— all this crap that's not going to keep the kids from being homeless when they age out of care. They come up with every cockamamie answer under the sun, except the only answer," Pat said, describing various adolescent programming offered around the country. "And the only answer is to get a kid a family."

---

[3] **ACS:** Administration for Children's Services, the New York City agency that handles child welfare, juvenile justice, and early care and education services.

[4] The Coalition for the Homeless in its 1989 *Blueprint for Solving New York's Homeless Crisis, New York City: A Report to Mayor David Dinkins*, claimed that 60 percent of the homeless in New York City municipal shelters had some history of foster care (101). In a study called *Runaway and Homeless Youth in New York City: A Report to the Ittleson Foundation, NYC* (New York: New York State Psychiatric Institute and Columbia University College of Physicians and Surgeons, Division of Child Psychiatry, 1984), David Shaffer and Carl Caton found that 50 percent of the young people came to shelters from a group home, foster home, or other foster institution. Nationally, according to the Child Welfare League of America, 58 percent of all young adults who access federally funded youth shelters had previously been part of the foster care system in 1997 (Child Welfare League of America's data page, "The Links Between Child Welfare and Homelessness," http://www.cwla.org/programs/housing/homelessnesslinks.htm#note13). In California, the Department of Social Services estimated in 2004 that 65 percent of the kids who age out of foster care face homelessness and up to 50 percent end up sleeping on the streets. See Ken Fagan, "Saving Foster Kids from the Streets," *San Francisco Chronicle*, April 11, 2004.

"The secret to our approach is to find out who cares about this kid," said Chester Jackson, the associate executive director of YGB. Chester, a tall, broad African American man with an intelligent face and a slight limp, joined Pat when he started the organization in 1995. He explained that YGB staff reach out to group homes and RTCs to identify the teenagers who need and want permanent parents; they contract with every foster agency in New York City and several upstate. Once they have a teenager, Chester said, the YGB staff interview her and then conduct simple detective work to locate one person from her present or past who might want to take on a more prominent role. "We'll say, 'Who visits you? Who's in your life?' We'll talk to the kid's social worker and say, 'Who comes to see her?'"

Pat and Chester have been friends since college, and they tumble and barge into one another's sentences constantly. "We've placed kids with everybody. Professionals from their lives—teachers, therapists, lawyers," Pat said. "And family members! I mean, you terminate a kid's rights, you'd think you've killed the whole family. But it often happens there are loads of family members who were too young to take a kid when he came into care, but are old enough now—including older siblings and cousins and . . ."

"Neighbors!" Chester interrupted. "Even if you're living in foster care, you're living somewhere. Sometimes you live in a lot of somewheres. You're next to people—you may go next door and watch TV every day at the same person's house," Chester said, nodding to Pat.

"And we've placed with those people," Pat interrupted back. 10

Finding people that the child has loved wouldn't be so hard, I thought, but the next step, getting them to commit, was tougher to picture. I imagined Pat and Chester, both so eager and assured, calling up some kid's former teacher, his bus driver, his older sister, and saying, "Guess what? You're pregnant! With a teenager!"

So they take it in steps. They first explain the teenager's need, and his chances for falling into trouble or homelessness, and then they encourage the potential parent to "take a learning experience," or enroll in the ten-week licensing classes required by the state to become a foster parent. Technically, You Gotta Believe! parents *do* become foster parents, except in the classes that YGB offers, they're encouraged—or mandated, really, if they do house the child—to become "forever parents." Whether they eventually legally adopt or "morally adopt" is up to the kids and the parents. But they're in it for life.

"We don't have all the answers, because family life is hard, but we happen to have the only answer, which is this: You need somebody that'll say, 'I'm that kid's parent,'" Pat said, an old Brooklyn accent flattening his vowels. He offers YGB classes eleven times a week all over the five boroughs, and unlike the standard classes elsewhere where parents have to wait for a start date, they can jump in at any part of the ten-week cycle. Once YGB has identified a potential parent, they want to catch him fast. "All we've got to do is get one. If we hit the jackpot, there's two. But that's all you've got to do."

Pat and Chester and their staff find last-minute families for around sixty kids a year. It's undoubtedly beautiful work, but it's also triage; they're saving the kids teetering at the edge of crisis, and without better system intervention earlier on in their lives, the teenagers will just keep coming. Over time, though, YGB may be expanding awareness about foster care, by expanding the onus of accountability. Rather than continuing the legacy of treating foster kids as other people's children, or as the state's problem to be institutionalized and hidden away, they're connecting deeply with the community. Like the old-time outdoor relief, they're asking the kids, "Who do you know?" and bringing the help to them.

Still, a commitment to lifetime parenthood can be a tough sell, and even after all the sleuthing and mining of contacts, some kids end up without a single prospect. Sometimes YGB teenagers don't know anyone at all who will take them in. For such cases, Chester produces a weekly cable-access television show, where kids can tell their individual stories and ask flat-out for families.

In general, I've always felt uncomfortable with these kinds of public displays: they're a little too close to human auctions, where minors advertise their attributes and hawk their cuteness, their vulnerability, their need. Children aren't products, and they shouldn't be featured on commercials as such. I worry that the clips raise false hopes, but I also know that exhibitionism like the Heart Gallery project, wherein professional portraits of foster kids are displayed in malls or galleries along with their adoption information, has led to some five thousand adoptions.[5] "Wednesday's Child" is a weekly clip of a hard-to-place foster child, featured on the evening news in five major cities. More than 1,500 kids have been adopted through "Wednesday's Child," and forty-two thousand viewers have called up with questions about becoming a parent.[6]

But does this really work? Can the older kids, tired and traumatized by a decade or more in foster care, really jump into adoption with someone they've never met? And can parents promise to adopt a stranger without a trial run? When I talked with Pat and Chester, I worried that the expectations were too high, the damage too deep.

And then I met a couple who were willing to take the risk. Their names were Glenn and Mindy, and they lived in Staten Island. Glenn and Mindy saw a sixteen-year-old girl named Oneida on "Wednesday's Child," and they were intrigued. On the news, Oneida was taking a salsa lesson in a fancy red dress and informing the newscaster that she "wants a family that's hardworking and understanding that will be there and support me and make me smile when I don't have nothing to worry

[5]The Heart Gallery was launched in New Mexico in 2001 and is now nationwide. Matthew Straeb, "A Message from Our President," *Heart Gallery of America Newsletter*, Inaugural Edition, January 2010. http://www.heartgalleryofamerica.org/Newsletter/2010 _Jan.htm.

[6] "Freddie Mac Foundation's Wednesday's Child: Finding Adoptive Homes for Children," retrieved from the Freddie Mac Foundation Web site: http://www.freddiemacfoundation .org/ourwork/founwedn.html.

about. That would be the happiest thing in my life, if I was to receive a family."

We could do this, Glenn and Mindy thought when they saw the news. Glenn's biological daughter had just left home for college; her room was empty and Oneida seemed so great, if terribly unlucky. On TV, Oneida's social worker boasted that Oneida "tries to reach the highest goal she can within everything." Oneida, wearing her curly dark hair pinned back with a red flower and big hoop earrings, backed her up. "I want to become a professional dancer, I want to work in movies," she said, grinning. "I want to become a foster parent, a social worker, and a lawyer."

By the time I met Glenn and Mindy, they had completed their classes at You Gotta Believe! and they trusted the program. They believed that teenagers needed "forever families," that no one was too old for adoption. Glenn and Mindy had attended support groups for adoptive parents, had completed their home study and been approved by the city, had swapped survivor stories with other foster kids to better understand their bruises and fears. They were ready to adopt a kid like Oneida. They were ready, in fact, for Oneida. The only thing left was to meet her.

In her regular life, which didn't ever include salsa dancing (that was set up for the television broadcast), Oneida lived at Graham Windham—[7]. . . . In her regular life, Oneida preferred Spanish pop to salsa, and, although she really was a foster kid, she had come to Graham Windham through the courts: for partying too much, staying out late, and spray-painting a heart onto a bodega wall.

Her primary advocate at Graham Windham was a woman named Doris Laurenceau, whose job title was Director of Family and Permanency Planning Services, which meant that she guided the older kids toward a final, or permanent, goal. Unlike many executives in congregate care, who deem group homes or RTCs the last stop for teenagers, Doris still believed in finding them lifelong families.

Doris thought that Glenn and Mindy would be a good match for Oneida. She hadn't met them in person yet, but she'd read their file, and she reasoned they were fit for a challenge. Oneida had been acting out, but she had a conscience and she could be saved; what she needed was someone to pay attention to her. Glenn and Mindy had family dinners at home every night, and their quiet suburban block could be a welcome respite from the urban distractions that were getting Oneida in trouble. Plus, while Glenn and Mindy were waiting for all the paperwork on Oneida to go through, they had started weekend visits with another foster child, a quiet honor roll student named Nayelly. A smart, bookish sister, Doris thought, could be a good influence. Doris knew how adoption, even later in life, solidifies one's sense of self and belonging, because she herself was adopted at thirty-eight. . . . Having a mother had changed everything for Doris. When I saw her again at

---

[7]**Graham Windham:** A residential treatment center roughly twenty miles north of Manhattan.

her office at Graham Windham, she was hoping to carve a similar path for Oneida.

Glenn and Mindy drove the forty-five miles from Staten Island to Graham Windham after work one Friday in April of 2009. They were excited, but both dressed casually, in jeans and black T-shirts, though Mindy's was studded with rhinestones. Diamond rings glinted from each of her ring fingers, and her jet-black hair was cut in a shag to her shoulders. Glenn and Mindy were scheduled to talk with Doris first, in her office, to discuss Oneida's background and the steps to adoption. Then Oneida would be brought in, to meet them.

"I always tell the kids that *they're* the ones in charge at these meetings, *they're* the ones interviewing the parents," Doris said, after Glenn and Mindy shook her hand and we all settled around a small conference table in her office. "This isn't a pet shop where parents get to pick out a kid. And it's not a guarantee on either side."

Glenn and Mindy smiled and nodded: of course. They said they had seen Oneida on "Wednesday's Child"; they expected to like her, and they were ready to answer any of her questions. Doris relaxed her face and gave one of her characteristic dimpled grins. "You seem like a happy couple," she said.

Despite Doris's introduction, I knew the pressure was on: Oneida was seventeen and scheduled to be released from Graham Windham in a month. After that, Doris wouldn't have any jurisdiction over her anymore, and she could be sent anywhere. Oneida didn't have any other prospects for permanent parents, and without Glenn and Mindy, Oneida would most likely age out of the system on her own. Privately, Doris had told me she had to make this adoption work.

"OK," Doris said with a sigh, "I'm going to tell you everything that's been written in Oneida's file—some of which may be true." Behind her, giant windows revealed the first pink streaks of a sunset, reflecting off three jars of honey on the sill. "She's half Italian, half Cuban and Dominican, with a lot of domestic abuse before the age of five. She has two brothers, both in care, but she was separated from them. The older brother is quite high-functioning. She was first placed in one home, then removed to go into a paraprofessional home, funded through the Office of Mental Health—which is supposed to be for kids going in and out of mental hospitals, because she was labeled depressed. She did well there—"

Suddenly, in the middle of Doris's speech, the office door burst open. There stood Oneida, her eyes wide and expectant, taking in the scene at the table. She grinned and looked down at her hand. She was clutching an umbrella. "Um, is this anyone's umbrella?" she asked quickly. "I thought maybe someone forgot it."

"Oneida!" Doris quickly reprimanded, her tone low and stern. "You know you have to wait outside! We'll ask you in soon."

Oneida popped back out the door, still grinning, and once she closed it, we all laughed. Clearly, she had just wanted to check Glenn and Mindy out. "After that, she had another four or five foster homes,"

Doris whispered. "And she got into stuff, like partying. She did admit to drinking, and she tried marijuana. She stopped going to school, and she got caught writing on a wall. She also ran away. Maybe I'm minimizing this, but in foster care, two or three days running away is not so bad."

Mindy, who had been nodding along with Doris's story, stepped in. "OK, but you know what? It's all understandable."

Doris looked relieved. "Yes. She's not an angel, but she doesn't deny anything," she said. She told them that Oneida had also forged signatures to get out of work and had once stolen her boyfriend's credit card. "She's a very loving child, and she's excellent at taking her consequences. And if she's connected to you, she won't want to disappoint you."

As Oneida was welcomed back for her official introduction, I felt a   35
terrible anxiety strike my heart. Glenn and Mindy wanted a teenager, they wanted to give her hope and new roots. But they had never fostered before, and they were expecting to love and adopt Oneida, sight unseen. I worried that they were enacting what Francine Cournos[8] at Columbia warned about: jumping into the marriage without the courtship. And yet, I knew YGB was right—a kid like Oneida also needs adoption, needs parents like Glenn and Mindy to say, "I want you, forever."

After her second entrance, Oneida was shyer. She'd abandoned the umbrella and sat quietly at the table, fiddling with a set of pink headphones. She wore jeans, a white sweatshirt, and rectangular glasses festooned with pink and purple geometric designs. She was still smiling, but she glanced around nervously. Doris touched her arm. "What would you like to say?" she asked.

"Ummm, I eat Italian food," Oneida said hopefully. Doris nodded for her to continue. "I like music. My favorite stations are 103.5 and 105.1, the Spanish music, obviously. I like having different types of friends. I like to cook different kinds of food, Spanish food . . ." Oneida trailed off. What can a kid say to people who might, if she played her cards right, want to be her parents?

Glenn smiled at her. He was more soft-spoken than Mindy and had a gentle, reserved demeanor. He was somebody who could be alone for hours a day, as he had delivered mail his entire adult life and was now the postmaster for his region. Mindy was chattier; she worked in sales for a T-shirt manufacturer. "When you cook Spanish food," Glenn asked, "is it spicy?"

"No," Oneida said, uncertain, searching Glenn's face for the correct answer. The she reconsidered. "Well, maybe only the meat."

"Dinner is very important to us," Mindy said earnestly.   40

"My favorite thing to eat is cheesecake," Oneida answered.

---

[8]**Francine Cournos:** Dr. Francine Cournos, professor of clinical psychiatry at Columbia University Medical Center, an expert on the mental health needs of foster children and author of *City of One* (1999), an autobiography that recounts her struggles after losing her parents and being placed in foster care.

"Well, there are two ways to make it," Mindy said, happily steering the conversation onto baking—a pastime she hoped to share with a daughter. Her accent, like Glenn's, was thick, old-school Brooklyn. "The easy way and the hard way."

This seemed to stump Oneida, so she started chatting about the people who were important to her: her brothers and her boyfriend. Her boyfriend, she said, was a poet, and he drove a car and had parents. Her gaze flicked quickly from Mindy to Glenn and back again, gauging their reactions. "I also like to read," she said. "I'm reading a book right now called *The Dirty Truth*. It's about a murderer and people who sleep with a lot of people. Oh, and in the morning, I just eat cereal."

"Breakfast is very important. Even if it's just a Pop Tart," said Mindy.

"Yeah, and I do my homework. I like to be home on the weekends, and I like to shop," Oneida said, sitting up straighter in her chair. 45

Mindy's eyes widened in pleasure. "Oh, I *hate* shopping," she said sarcastically. "But I guess I could do it for you."

Oneida grinned; the meeting was going well. Mindy asked her what she was looking for in her life. "A permanent home," she said quickly. "I mean, throughout the years, I've been through some hard times in all the homes. And then I wrote a heart on a wall and got paroled to some Jamaican lady who wouldn't let me eat the same food her own kids ate, and after that there were no more homes for me. Now that I'm getting old, I really don't want to move anymore."

Glenn asked Oneida how she would feel about a sister, and she said she would love to have someone to go shopping with. Oneida asked about house rules, and Glenn told her that honesty was the major directive in the household. "All the rules we have are based on love," Glenn said.

Oneida considered this and squeezed her eyebrows together; love wasn't something she was used to talking about, at least not right away. "I'll probably watch the news with you, every night, while you cook," she said.

Her enthusiasm was catching, as Glenn and Mindy's descriptions 50 grew more concrete and Oneida clung to the idea that she just might go home with them. "Do you like to swim?" Glenn asked. "We live in a development with two Olympic-size pools."

"Cool!" Oneida gushed. "I used to swim a lot. But it was only in the bathtub, and then I got too big. I've never been in a pool."

Pity, or something like it, flickered briefly across Mindy's face. If Oneida caught it, she didn't show it. "Do you like to travel?" Oneida asked.

"Well, I *love* cruises," Mindy said, conspiratorially, leaning in. "I've been on forty-two of them. And we're about to go on my forty-third—to Italy and Greece!"

"Oh," Oneida said. She looked at Doris; this might be a snag in the plans. Parents can't just go off on cruises—or admit it to officials like Doris—with teenagers living in the house. But Doris saved the moment:

maybe Oneida could finish out the school year at Graham Windham, she suggested, so Glenn and Mindy could have their vacation, and then, she'd make the move to Staten Island. The trick would be getting ACS to approve the cost of an extended stay; if they didn't, they would send Oneida to another foster home and Doris would lose her, when the court order that sent Oneida to the RTC was up in May.

"Or . . . maybe I could come visit?" Oneida asked, her voice suddenly small and shy.

"Of *course* we want you to visit!" both Glenn and Mindy said, practically in unison.

Oneida grinned, relieved, and there was an awkward silence. Doris prodded her. "Is there anything else you want to say?"

"Um," Oneida said, looking at Doris for backup, "could I come this weekend?"

Glenn and Mindy exchanged glances; this was happening awfully fast. In the parent training, they tell you to expect a certain process: first you'll meet a child in a neutral setting, then maybe the child will come to visit you at your home. This could lead to an overnight, and then to a weekend visit, and then maybe a longer weekend, and if all goes well, you decide to permanently welcome her into your family. On paper, this gives parents time to adjust (and squeeze in a final cruise) and helps the child smoothly transition from one placement to another. In reality, there often isn't such wiggle room. Kids need to leave unsafe or, as with Oneida, expensive placements when the state says it's time.

Everybody knew adoption was on the line; it's what Glenn and Mindy signed up for. . . . I felt as if I was about to witness a grand experiment, or duel. On one side was Oneida, embodying Cournos's idea that trauma blocks attachment, even if she didn't know it. On the other were Glenn and Mindy, . . . chanting, "You've got to rock with a kid, all the way." And everybody wanted to win, together.

Mindy turned her chair toward Glenn and started brainstorming. This weekend wasn't a possibility. There was the barbecue, and the other foster daughter coming to visit; they would need to prepare her. But maybe next Friday—couldn't Glenn leave work early and pick Oneida up from school? Oneida whispered to Doris, "This is like a fantasy. Make them take me."

And then, suddenly, it was decided: Oneida would come the next weekend, for a full three days; Doris would get her excused from school. Glenn and Mindy would take their cruise, and then, after that, Oneida would move in. For good.

● ● ●

Glenn and Mindy had to jump so fast with Oneida because foster care and juvenile justice were separate divisions at that time. When Oneida painted the heart on the bodega wall, she was removed from ACS and handed over to the state as a juvenile delinquent. Doris worked for the state and couldn't advocate for Oneida once she completed her sentence—at which point she would be returned to ACS and sent to any number of agencies and any family, rather than to Glenn and Mindy, who wanted her. There are problems with merging foster care and juvenile justice, but one united agency would have benefited someone like Oneida. She could have had one social worker, one judge, one set of files following her through her many transitions and buying her the time to ease into Glenn and Mindy's life slowly. Instead, the trio had to close their eyes to the less savory details (Oneida's history of lying and abuse; Glenn and Mindy's lack of experience). They all wanted a family and believed it could work. They jumped. . . .

To get to Manhattan's leafiest and least-populated borough without a car, you have to take a ferry. Then there's one subway line, timed with the ferry's landing, which runs tip to tip along Staten Island. If you're a kid, you take a bus to get to a strip mall or the movies. If you want to get to Brooklyn, it takes about two hours.

This was Oneida's first big beef with the place, Glenn told me as he picked me up from the train station in his white Toyota. "Oneida used to call it *carajo*-land," he said, waving his hand toward the white houses with trim lawns tucked along the quiet streets. "She missed the bodegas in Brooklyn."

Mindy understood this stance, at first. She grew up in Bensonhurst in Brooklyn, and her accent still betrayed her roots. The kitchen and living room were festooned with Saint Patrick's Day decorations when I came to visit; green garland chains hung from the ceiling and leprechauns peeped from the cupboards. Mindy said these were a throwback to her childhood. "My mom died when I was ten, and my dad thought that holidays were a way to bring the family together," she explained, but even without the decorations, the 1,500-square-foot house was packed with sentiment. Pictures of the family covered walls and tabletops, but there were none of Oneida. When Mindy pulled out her bulging floral scrapbook so she could trace back the whole arduous demise, she found one, of Oneida curled up on the couch. "Well, she looked cute when she was sleeping," she said hopefully. Glenn shuddered; he wouldn't even look at the photo. "Brings back too many terrible memories," he said.

When Oneida first came to the house, there was a short honeymoon phase, they both told me, finishing each other's sentences. Right at the beginning, they'd splurged on a weekend at Disney World for Oneida, the foster daughter, Nayelly, and the biological daughter, Kristine; Oneida had screamed dramatically and clutched Mindy's hand on the plane, as she'd never flown before. They both admitted that the trip was fun; aside from Oneida wanting to parade herself at the hotel pool, Mindy said, everyone was on good behavior.

When they got home, Glenn said, the agency was frantic: Oneida was classified as "therapeutic" and Glenn and Mindy weren't certified to house a child with therapeutic needs. (Because Oneida had shifted from

65

the state's jurisdiction and back to a city agency, she fell back under her old foster requirements. Doris worked for the state and likely hadn't noticed this stipulation; besides, Doris had landed the much larger prize— a married couple willing to adopt.) The agency argued that Glenn and Mindy had to drop everything for the next three weekends and attend the requisite classes up in the Bronx if they wanted to keep her. So they took the classes.

"That's the way the agencies are. When they need you to do something, they need it done tomorrow. When you need something for the kid, you get nothing," Glenn said, shaking his head. What Glenn and Mindy needed, for the therapeutically classified teenager, was therapy. Within a few weeks of her arrival, Oneida started acting out. At first, she just lied: she'd say she was going to Brooklyn, but she'd end up in the Bronx. Or she'd promise to be home at a certain time and trot in hours later. But then she started disappearing for nights at a time, which later morphed into weeks. Glenn and Mindy would talk to her, ground her, take away her privileges, but they wanted some backup from the agency. They felt that some of this behavior was rooted in Oneida's early traumas and her years in foster care; she was authorized for free therapy, but for the entire summer she lived with them, no one returned Glenn's phone calls to set it up.

"We'd call and they wouldn't call back. When Oneida was in the RTC, she was in therapy all the time. What changed? Just because she's in Staten Island, she doesn't need therapy anymore?" Glenn fumed. He also said they didn't receive an agency check for Oneida's care until August, though she moved in with them in June, and their water and electric bills doubled due to her hour-long showers and her inattention to lights. Arguments in the home escalated; Oneida believed Glenn and Mindy were hoarding her allowance money, and she disappeared for longer and longer stretches. "Even when she was AWOL and she ran away, we'd call the agency and they wouldn't follow up on it. They're useless, totally useless."

The crisis peaked in September, three months after Oneida's arrival. Glenn got a call from someone who knew Oneida, who also made Glenn promise never to reveal his or her identity. Glenn agreed, and the person told Glenn that Oneida wanted out of the house, but she was afraid the agency wouldn't allow it without cause. So Oneida had hatched a plan: she was going to peg Glenn with an accusation of sexual abuse.

"I panicked," Glenn said. "The postmaster is the second most powerful governmental official, and in the little towns like where we are, everybody knows you. If this would have gotten back to my job, I would have been fired, like that." Glenn snapped his fingers. "Once the allegation's been made, even if it's disproved, there are still people who'll believe it. I didn't work twenty-three years to get fired, just because I'm trying to help a kid."

This time, when Glenn called the agency, he got a response. He located a director and said, "When I go home today, I'm packing up all her stuff and leaving it in front of my house. You need to come pick it up, because she's never coming back. We're done with her."

Suddenly, Glenn and Mindy were the terrible stereotype: foster parents who hurl a foster kid's belongings to the curb, in garbage bags.

"We were petrified," Mindy said. "This was our life."   75

But the agency fought back. Glenn said they told him, "You're not done with her; she's in your house and she's staying there. Otherwise, we will shut down your house as a foster home."

Glenn relented; after all, they had Nayelly, and Nayelly was still a foster child. They couldn't, and wouldn't, lose her. They agreed to have a meeting—with Oneida, with the agency, and with ACS.

Mindy interrupted, her dark eyes blazing: "We had to say we were going to have Oneida removed before they would even think about helping us. And we'd been asking for help all along!"

It was clear at the meeting, both Glenn and Mindy asserted, that Oneida was happy to leave Staten Island. They believe she originally wanted any escape from the residential treatment center, and once Glenn and Mindy had provided that, Oneida could think only of Brooklyn.

"She uses people," Glenn said bitterly.   80

Mindy nodded, watching her husband carefully. "She uses people, but that's how she's gotten through her life."

At the meeting, despite Glenn's impatience, the agency said Oneida had to stay one more night; then they'd find her another placement.

Oneida stayed, but once everyone was sleeping she used a knife to cut all the cords to the house computer. In the morning she left for Brooklyn.

It took me several months to track down Oneida, so I could get her side of the story. I finally found her online, promoting some dance at a club in the Bronx.

"Ya this is me," Oneida texted when I landed her phone number.   85
"How r u?"

We met on a sunny afternoon in the Bronx, on the corner of 180th and Morris Park, across from the transit police station. She was about half an hour late, giving me plenty of time to peruse the real estate listings tacked onto a sandwich board, offering Section 8[9] apartments. Little kids bought popsicles from the bodega, and a drug dealer eyed me suspiciously; I was standing there too long.

Oneida looked the same as she had the day of her adoption meeting with Glenn and Mindy some eighteen months before, though she was missing her glasses and squinted a bit to see. Her curly hair was crimped with gel, her bangs crispy straight lines down her forehead. Her puffy upper lip makes her look as if she's been either crying or kissing, though that day it was neither; Oneida had just been relaxing at home— her fifth since she'd left Staten Island.

---

[9]**Section 8:** A rental subsidy program for low- and moderate-income families in New York City.

"Them white people?" Oneida answered, when I asked her what happened with Glenn and Mindy. She made a face as if she had swallowed something bitter, and also as if she was remembering something very long ago. "They was racist."

We were walking toward East Tremont, looking for someplace to eat. McDonald's was out, because Oneida had just been fired from there, for "getting into an altercation with a customer." Oneida waved her hand vaguely down the block. "My biological dad lives not too far from here, just a couple blocks away," she said. I asked if she had seen him. "Not for a long time, maybe a few weeks before the summer. I don't really like seeing him; he lives in this bummy basement apartment. He's a junkie. I mean, I don't mind if people ask me for money, but every time?"

We settled on a Chinese place, with a $6 all-you-can-eat buffet. "I'm a very picky eater," Oneida said, piling her plate with bright red sweet-and-sour pork and cheesecake from the end of the table. She ate only meat and cheese and bread; no rice, no vegetables, no fruits. And cheesecake, when she could get it.

At the beginning, Oneida admitted while chewing thoughtfully on her pork, she liked being a part of the Staten Island family. But shortly after she moved in, Oneida said, Glenn and Mindy became "judgmental." One time her boyfriend stopped by when she wasn't home, and Glenn wouldn't let him in, "not even to use the bathroom!" Oneida was outraged. "And then they were judgmental of my music. The guy was Catholic and the lady was Jewish. If you that way, why take me? I'm Hispanic, you know I'm going to listen to Hispanic music."

The stated issue was one of noise control, but Oneida felt racism was underneath. "I'd only play my music on the computer, and you know that can't get that loud," she explained. "And then one day I came home and they'd put Krazy Glue on the volume!"

Oneida agreed that she took off for Brooklyn a lot, but that was only to visit her best friend, and to get a break from Staten Island, which she described as "too much of a suburb. All you see is bushes and trees." The high school, too, was a difficult adjustment. "The school was huge, like four thousand children, and it was nothing but Chinese and white. I didn't mind being at that school, but it was how the kids looked at me— like I was some ghetto Spanish girl."

Glenn, she told me, was more troubling than Mindy because he had a temper. They had their biggest argument right before their final meeting with the agency. "I wanted to go into my room and he was in there watching TV," Oneida said. Oneida's bedroom was in the basement, where the sixty-four-inch flat-screen TV was mounted to the wall and where Glenn had always watched sports—long before any kids arrived. I saw this room when I visited Staten Island; despite the girly bedspread it still looked like a sports fan's room: team pennants were pegged all over the walls. "I was like, 'Can you get out? I want to get my things for a shower.'"

Glenn told her to wait; he was at an important part of the game. Or she could simply get her clothes and go. Oneida was horrified, and furious. "I said, 'You want to watch me get my bra and panties? Have some type of respect—I'm a female, I sleep here!' I called him a pervert."

Oneida knew from past experience that she had to be extra-vigilant to protect herself. She told me she'd been raped twice, in her teens, by two different men, and she was molested repeatedly as a young child. She never confessed to these early incidents, but she was examined at three different hospitals and the doctors figured it out; she remembers these exams distinctly. Oneida knows these experiences have sometimes made it difficult for her to assess true danger. "Like one night, Glenn stood in my room while I was sleeping because somebody called the house at three in the morning," she said, by way of example. "I was scared. I didn't know what that was about. I didn't know if he was being inappropriate."

So were these incidents the reason that Glenn got a phone call about Oneida's idea of charging him with sexual misconduct? I told her that in Glenn's version of events, she was planning to file an accusation of abuse.

Oneida didn't blink. "Not at all. I guess they just felt like that."

In Oneida's memory, the reason she was removed from Staten Island was that Glenn believed she was going to set fire to the house. It was an apt metaphor, but one I'd never heard from Glenn. In the end it didn't matter much to Oneida what anyone thought she was plotting; all she wanted at that time was out.

Unfortunately for Oneida, she didn't like any of her next placements better. After Staten Island, Oneida was moved to a home where, Oneida claimed, the foster mother hit her children with spatulas and her foster sister stole her sneakers.

Oneida was removed and sent to "a Trinidadian lady who was cool." But she lived in the neighborhood where Oneida had been raped, and Oneida didn't want to leave the house to go to school. "The guys in that neighborhood is all on top of me, on top of me, and the lady is calling me lazy. I kind of messed it up for myself; I got in an altercation," she said. "Horrible."

In the next house, Oneida was alone—too alone. There were no other foster kids, and the mother made Oneida stay home by herself whenever she left. "It was horrible. There was no phone reception there; I had to go to the bathroom and talk through the window, that's how bad the connection was. And there was no cable!"

The next place had kids, but the mom was stingy, Oneida said. She wouldn't give Oneida her allowance money, and she never did the laundry. "She was an elderly lady and all she do is talk about you to the other foster girl. Horrible."

The long string of horrible seemed to have hit pause recently, Oneida said. She liked her new foster family, just a few blocks away from the Chinese restaurant. There was a mom and a dad, and a few foster kids, and the parents had even let Oneida's ex-boyfriend sleep over, on the couch. She had her own room with a queen-size bed, and the family watched movies together, on cable.

Oneida had lived with her latest family for only two weeks, and she knew all about the deceptive promise of a honeymoon period. Still, this short reprieve from upheavals had allowed her to think again about her long-term plans. Oneida was almost eighteen and figured she had about one year of high school left to graduate. She'd attended three different high schools in the past academic year alone, and all of those infrequently, so it was hard to tell where her credits really lined up. She knew she wasn't prepared to take the Regents exams,[10] and the new high school she was thinking of attending didn't even offer a Regents diploma, which was a requisite for college.

"With the diploma that I'll get, I'll be better off with a GED. I can only go to a vocational school, like a cooking school. Or dancing, I love dancing," Oneida said, tapping at her cell phone. "I want to do something professional, where you get up in the morning and wear a suit. Like a lawyer, or a security guard. I want to have high income, but I don't know how to do that with my diploma."

Oneida's real dream, she said, was to move into her own apartment in Bushwick, Brooklyn, near Knickerbocker and DeKalb, where she was born. Ideally, she'd work for the Special Victims Unit. "I want to be a detective, like on *Law and Order*," she added, finally putting down her phone and widening her small brown eyes. "The only thing is it may not be possible because I'm too emotional. I'm emotional when I see dead people, or kids getting raped."

ENGAGING THE TEXT

1. Characterize each step in the placement process Beam describes, including the *Wednesday's Child* program, Mindy and Glenn's training, and the briefing and interview at Graham Windham. What problems do you see, and what improvements can you imagine?

2. What distinguishes "You Gotta Believe!" from other programs promoting the welfare of foster children? Debate Pat O'Brien's contention that in the struggle to minimize homelessness as a likely outcome of foster care, "the only answer is to get a kid a family" (para. 6).

3. The first half of Oneida's story is filled with descriptions of hope, hard work, dedication, and optimism. What goes wrong, and why? Why doesn't Oneida's placement work out, and what personal and bureaucratic shortcomings are most responsible? In particular, compare Glenn and Mindy's version of what went wrong with Oneida's.

[10]**Regents exams:** Standardized statewide exams in New York in core areas of the high school curriculum such as English, math, and science.

4. What roles do race or ethnicity play in this narrative, and what roles, if any, do you think they should play in foster child placements? Should agencies try to match kids to adoptive parents of the same race?

5. In paragraph 19 Oneida expresses her interests in dancing professionally, working in movies, and becoming "a foster parent, a social worker, and a lawyer." In paragraphs 106 and 107 she mentions that she would perhaps like to be a lawyer, a security guard, or a detective. Which of these ambitions seem most and least likely? Are any of them clearly out of reach?

6. **Thinking Rhetorically** Do you think Beam's account is neutral, or is it slanted in favor of the adults or Oneida? Point to specific passages that reveal Beam's position. Is it possible to critique Oneida without falling into the trap of "blaming the victim"?

EXPLORING CONNECTIONS

7. Review "Looking for Work" by Gary Soto (p. 19) to see how he uses the story of a single day to portray his childhood sense of family. Then, adopting the point of view of Oneida, Mindy, or Glenn, tell the story of one important day — perhaps the day they all met, the day Oneida came to live with her foster parents, or the day she left. You may freely mix information from the reading with imagined events and conversations.

8. Look ahead to "Theories and Constructs of Race" by Linda Holtzman and Leon Sharpe (p. 599). First, apply their definition of "assimilation" to Oneida's placement with Mindy and Glenn: How does Oneida's movement from a foster-care facility to a private home present challenges similar to those faced by immigrants to the United States? Second, think about the distinction Holtzman and Sharpe draw between viewing racism as "interpersonal and episodic" versus "structural and systemic" (para. 5). How does the meaning of Oneida's story shift when viewed through these different interpretive lenses?

EXTENDING THE CRITICAL CONTEXT

9. Watch *Short Term 12*, an award-winning 2013 film written and directed by Destin Cretton whose protagonist runs a group facility for troubled teens, or *Aging Out*, a 2004 documentary directed by Roger Weisberg, Maria Finitzo, and Vanessa Roth that focuses on the stories of three foster children transitioning to independent life with little in the way of resources or support. How do these films extend and complicate the perspective on foster care provided by Oneida's story?

10. Foster care populations, programs, and facilities vary widely across the United States. Research how foster care works in your city or county. For a group project, choose specific areas to investigate — the demographics of populations served; placement policies for institutions and foster families; mandatory training, regulations, licensing, and oversight; government and community resources; and support for youth "aging out" of foster care.

11. Search the Web to find print and video interviews with Cris Beam; consult one or more of these to learn about *To the End of June*, Beam's other books, or the author herself, and report to the class.

FROM MARRIAGE MARKETS: HOW INEQUALITY IS REMAKING THE AMERICAN FAMILY

JUNE CARBONE AND NAOMI CAHN

What words come to mind when someone says "marriage"? Maybe "love," "soul mate," "bridal gown," "romance," "honeymoon," "children," or "commitment"? For the cynic, perhaps "trap" or "divorce" or "alimony"? In any case, few of us link marriage to "markets" or "supply and demand," but this selection asks you to do exactly that. June Carbone and Naomi Cahn explain the strong role class plays in shaping marriage choices and argue that the institution itself now holds different meanings for rich, middle-class, and poor Americans. June Carbone is an expert on family law and holds the Robina Chair of Law, Science and Technology at the University of Minnesota. Naomi Cahn is the Harold H. Greene Professor at George Washington University Law School. In addition to their numerous individual publications, Professors Carbone and Cahn are coauthors of *Red Families v. Blue Families: Legal Polarization and the Creation of Culture* (2010); this selection comes from their second book together, *Marriage Markets: How Inequality Is Remaking the American Family* (2014).

THE AMERICAN FAMILY IS CHANGING—and the changes guarantee that inequality will be greater in the next generation. For the first time, America's children will almost certainly not be as well educated, healthy, or wealthy as their parents, and the result stems from the growing disconnect between the resources available to adults and those invested in children. The time to address the *real* explanation for the changing American family is now.

The changes themselves, of course, have been the subject of endless commentary, both positive and negative. The age of marriage is going up, the rate of marriage is falling, and almost half of all marriages fail. An increasing number of states allow women to marry women, and men to marry men. The number of children born outside of marriage is drawing equal with the number of children born within marriage. And, the percentage of children growing up in single-parent households is the highest in the developed world. These changes, however, do not affect everyone equally. Describing how the "average" family has changed hides what is really going on: economic inequality is remaking the American family along class lines, and families are not going through the same changes together. To understand what is happening to the American family—and how family law locks in the growing class divisions—requires examining the links between family change along the continuum from the top to the bottom of the American economy.

In the process, many of the existing explanations for why the American family today is so radically different from the American family of fifty years ago will prove hollow. The right blames declining moral values, the pill, welfare as we knew it, the rise of "soulmate" marriage, and a host of other social ills without providing a convincing explanation of why these changes affect one group more than another. The left celebrates individual choice, sexual liberation, and women's equality without acknowledging that not all sources of change are benign and that the consequences of some of the changes they support contribute to the growing inequality they oppose. Neither group provides a complete explanation of these changes, and without a better explanation of why the top and bottom of American families are moving in opposite directions, efforts at family reform will remain futile.

A complete explanation of family change requires taking seriously the role of class in scripting our lives as well as the effect of greater economic inequality in remaking the terms of marriage, divorce, and child-rearing. Such an explanation needs to address not just why marriage has disappeared from the poorest communities, but also why, in a reversal of historical trends, elite women have become the *most* likely to marry. It requires the ability to explain why divorce rates, which for decades moved in the same direction for the country as a whole, are now diverging, falling back to the levels that existed before no-fault divorce for the most educated while continuing to rise for everyone else. A comprehensive analysis must also be able to make sense of the decisions of working-class women, who often describe themselves as religious or conservative, to have children on their own even when the fathers of their children are willing to propose.

In short, a full explanation cannot look at the family in isolation from economic forces. Any attempt to respond to family change must include reconstruction of the script for the college educated, prompting investment in careers and marriages that can withstand the stresses of career changes, children's illness, and geographic mobility. It also must address the destruction of the pathways that helped the working class aspire to the same combination of financial and family security.

The story accordingly starts with the greater inequality that characterizes the American economy. Rising inequality has affected men more than women, increasing both the number of men at the top who are eager to pair with high-status women and the number of men at the bottom who no longer play productive roles. These changes fundamentally alter the "gender bargain," that is, the terms on which men and women find it worthwhile to forge lasting relationships, and they do so in ways that push the top and the bottom of the socioeconomic system in different directions. At the top, increasing disparities among men and among women have made both pickier about potential mates and wary of early commitments that might limit future opportunities. Women used to "shop around" for successful men. Male executives used to marry their secretaries, who would take care of them at home the way they did in the office. Now both look for mates who reflect (and enhance) their own expectations about the ability to enjoy the good life. Two substantial incomes rather than one make the difference between the home overlooking the golf course and the modest tract house in the less tony school district, and even if money is not at issue, the stay-at-home spouse with the Ph.D. possesses much more social status than does a high school graduate playing the same domestic role. College graduates still largely forge lasting relationships and they typically will do so with one another, but they hedge their bets by delaying marriage and childbearing until they have a better idea of where they (and the partners to whom they commit) are likely to end up—concentrating elite advantage in the process as overwhelming numbers of them raise their children in financially secure, two-parent families.

For those whose incomes place them in the bottom third of the population, increasing disparities between men and women have made both more likely to give up on each other. International and interstate comparisons demonstrate that higher rates of inequality tend to be associated with chronic unemployment, high rates of imprisonment, and substance abuse—factors that disproportionately affect men.[1] Women in these communities view commitment to a man who runs up the credit card bill, cycles in and out of jobs, or deals drugs on the side as more of a threat than an asset to the ability to care for children. Men view women who take their money when they have it but do not stand by them when they flounder with distrust. These patterns encourage women to invest in their own resources rather than in the men in their lives and men to move on to new relationships when their current ones hit rough patches. Family stability is an inevitable casualty.

The hardest patterns to analyze are those of the middle—the group clustered around the fiftieth percentile of family income in the United States. This group, which used to be called the "white working class," is now more racially diverse than both its comparable cohort of fifty years ago and the college-educated upper third of today. This group was once associated with well-paying blue-collar manufacturing jobs, but manufacturing jobs are no longer numerous or distinct enough to define the group. Education is perhaps the best proxy. Members of this group are high school graduates but lack a B.A. Many start at a university but do

---

[1]Richard Wilkinson & Kat Pickett, *The Spirit Level: Why Greater Equality Makes Societies Stronger* (New York: Bloomsbury, 2009). [All notes are Carbone and Cahn's.]

not finish, or they earn a community college or vocational degree. The women from these families in the middle have done well. Unlike those in the top group, where sons are more likely than daughters to graduate from college and where the gender gap in income has widened, the women in this middle group have outpaced the men. They earn higher grades, stay in school longer, and are more likely to return to complete an unfinished degree later in life. When they have the same level of education and work the same number of hours as the men, the income gender gap narrows. With these changing fortunes, this larger group of successful women in the center seeks to pair with a shrinking group of comparable men. Female high school graduates used to be able to marry men with a college education; today they are much less likely to get married at all. And sociologists find that women in this center group, particularly among whites, cohabit more than American women in any other group; they live with a partner, marry, divorce, and cohabit with someone else to a greater degree than in any other group.[2] We are providing a portrait of the changes that remade the country in the years 1990–2007. But the jury is still out as to whether the family patterns of the center, which used to look more like the family patterns at the top, will eventually resemble those of the poor.

These economic changes, which have increased the dominance of high-income men at the top, marginalized a large number of men at the bottom, and reduced the number of men in the middle, have unsettled the foundations of family life. To be sure, the family does not change with the stock market ticker or the seasonal adjustments in the unemployment rate. Instead, shifts in the economy change the way men and women match up, and, over time, they alter young people's expectations about each other and about their prospects in newly reconstituted marriage markets. These expectations go to the core of what many see as a shift in values. The ambitious college students, who are said to have mastered the "hook-up," know that attending to their studies pays off in terms of both marriage and career prospects and that too early a commitment to a partner or to childbearing may derail both. Yet, they still largely believe that when they are ready, a suitable partner—male, female, or the product of a sperm bank—will be there for them. Women who do not graduate from college are more likely to see childbearing as the event that will most give meaning to their lives, and they are more likely to respond to experiences with unreliable and unfaithful partners by giving up on men and investing in themselves and their children. These differing expectations, treated as the subject of moral failings, women's liberation, and cultural clashes, are a predictable consequence of the remaking of marriage markets. At the top, there are more successful men seeking to pair

[2]Andrew J. Cherlin, *The Marriage-Go-Round: The State of Marriage and the Family in America Today* (New York: Vintage, 2009), 168–69; Andrew J. Cherlin, "Between Poor and Prosperous: Do the Family Patterns of Moderately-Educated Americans Deserve a Closer Look?" in *Social Class and Changing Families in an Unequal Society*, ed. Marcia J. Carlson and Paula England (Stanford, CA: Stanford University Press, 2011), 68–84.

with a smaller pool of similarly successful women. In the middle and the bottom, there are more competent and stable women seeking to pair with a shrinking pool of reliable men. What we are watching as the shift in marriage markets rewrites family scripts and increases gender distrust is the re-creation of class—of harder edged boundaries that separate the winners and losers in the new American economy.

These developments and their connections to growing economic inequality do more to explain changing marriage patterns than does any discussion of shifting social mores taken in isolation. The class dimension means that all of the previous explanations for family change—women's independence, welfare, changing moral values, the embrace of soulmate marriage—ring hollow.

If we want to understand why our lives have changed, why our children's marriages are shaky, and why our grandchildren cannot count on the resources their parents enjoyed, we must be willing to confront the consequences of greater inequality. Although the story of what has happened to the American family is at times complex, the conclusion is short and simple: it's the economy, stupid. And any analysis or proposed solution that does not take growing inequality into account is based on a lie. Inequality matters to overall social health, and it matters to the well-being of future generations.[3]

● ● ●

In attempting to link family change to inequality and class, we start with two conundrums: Just what does *class* mean in American society, and isn't a marriage market an oxymoron? Americans often reject the very idea of class—of social constructions that separate families on one part of the economic spectrum from others—as an "un-American" concept. They are more likely to see divisions in racial or ethnic terms, and they are more likely to identify with religious, cultural, or ideological categories. Yet, whether we acknowledge it or not, class is critical to the understanding of contemporary families. It is critical because it shapes the attitudes and expectations that underlie culture as well as the practical consequences that channel resources to the next generation. We therefore use class as a functional category that explains the structure of marriage markets, educational expectations, and the possibilities for movement up and down the socioeconomic ladder.

Marx, of course, defined class in terms of antagonism between the interests of the "capitalists," who owned the means of production, and the workers, who depended on wages for their labor but had little ability to shape the terms of employment. Yet, Marxian notions do not apply directly to a post-industrial economy, and Marx himself did not anticipate the development of a "middle class" independent of the capitalists.

---

[3]Wilkinson and Pickett, *Spirit Level.*

Since Marx's time, much of the discussion of class has largely been relegated to those who chart the course of financial progress in Asia, Latin America, and the rest of the developing world. While this literature treats the size and health of the middle class as a primary subject of attention, it pays little attention to the re-emergence of class divisions in countries such as the United States. Accordingly, we recognize that our efforts to describe class do not piggyback on existing definitions. . . .

For our purposes, class is a social construct that is often—but not always—correlated with income. It is a term designed to make more visible the way that society creates expectations about behavior and/or channels societal resources, such as wealth and income, parental time and attention, and human capital acquisition. We use the idea of class most critically to describe who is likely to marry whom, who is willing to live with whom, and how prospective parents view the appropriate family structures for raising children. The most voluminous, consistent, and reliable data on these issues are from the census and distinguish among three groups. First, college graduates are a group constituting roughly one-third of today's young adults though a smaller percentage of the overall population.[4] Every recent study of marriage indicates that college graduates have become more likely to marry fellow graduates.

The second group, which is harder to define precisely, is the "middle" of the American population, including those who graduated from high school, but not college, and those who, while perhaps struggling economically, are not poor. The group can be defined demographically: a household at the fiftieth percentile of the American population in 2011 earned a little over $42,000,[5] and the average American adult graduated from high school and attended college but did not complete a four-year degree.[6] This group has lost ground over the past twenty years, with shrinking income distinctions between those with some skills and those without, and while this group continues to differ from the bottom group, distinctions between them, in terms of both income and marriage, have become less pronounced than they were in the middle of the twentieth century.

The third group is the poor or the marginalized. This group includes high school dropouts, but it is certainly broader than the 7.4 percent of those between the ages of sixteen and twenty-four who lack a high

15

[4]The *New York Times* indicates that 30.4 percent of those over the age of 25 held a college degree in 2012, an all-time high. Richard Pérez-Peña, "U.S. Bachelor Degree Rate Passes Milestone," Feb. 23, 2012, *New York Times*, www.nytimes.com/2012/02/24 /education/census-finds-bachelors-degrees-at-record-level.html. That figure rose to 33.5 percent of Americans ages 25 to 29, up 24.7 percent in 1995. National Center for Education Statistics. Catherine Rampell, "Data Reveal a Rise Among College Degrees Among Americans," June 12, 2013, www.nytimes.com/2013/06/13/education/a-sharp-rise-in-americans -with-college-degrees.html (citing National Center for Education Statistics).

[5]Catherine Rampell, "Where Do You Fall on the Income Curve?" Economix blog, *New York Times*, May 24, 2011.

[6]Nicole Stoops, "Educational Attainment in the United States: 2003," Current Population Reports P20-550 (Washington, DC: U.S. Census Bureau, June 2004), www.census.gov /prod/2004pubs/p20-550.pdf.

school degree.[7] It includes most of the 15 percent of Americans below the poverty line.[8] In terms of family characteristics, it is a group for whom marriage is rapidly disappearing. . . .

We use these class-based groups to construct "marriage markets" or, more accurately, to explain how mate choice occurs in the twenty-first century. In so doing, we are very aware that many from all political and philosophical persuasions object to the very idea of treating intimate relationships as something that should ever be the product of exchange. We believe, however, that to explain why the family has become a marker of class requires looking at the mechanisms that connect a changing society to what takes place in the family. We believe that the way men and women, gays and lesbians, and intimate partners of all kinds match up in a given community has a lot to do with the resulting understanding of family values. To understand how the shift in the organization of the economy has affected the assumptions that underlie family behavior for the rich, the poor, and the middle, it *is* important to see marriage and other intimate relationships as the product of markets. That is, relationships do occur as a result of an exchange, just like the purchase of the latest iPhone. Intimate markets, however, are special ones. They depend on trust, they incorporate assumptions about gender, and they reflect community reinforcement (or obstruction in the case of same-sex couples) of institutions like marriage. These exchanges, like other kinds of human interactions, also reflect supply and demand.

In all societies, marriage declines if there is an imbalance in the number of willing partners. Yet the impact of market changes is not simply a shift in marginal price, a few more men who have to work harder to find the right woman, and a few more women who will end up alone. Instead, changes in supply and demand affect the factors that underlie trust—can a partner, for example, be expected to be faithful and dependable? And trust in turn affects a host of other decisions: Is it important to stay in school to land the right type of partner? Is staying in school a realistic possibility? Is one better able to provide for children by investing in oneself or one's mate? Are intimate relationships likely to be temporary or long-term? These considerations are part of what we think of as "values," and they in fact reflect mundane changes in supply that reverberate through communities in predictable ways.

We have a rich literature that looks at the way men and women match up across different countries, time periods, and neighborhoods. That literature finds that when the marriageable men outnumber marriageable women, community norms look a lot like those of college graduates. The women can be picky about their choice of intimate partners, and

---

[7]National Center for Education Statistics, "Fast Facts: Dropout Rates" (Washington, DC: National Center for Education Statistics, 2012), www.nces.ed.gov/fastfacts/display.asp ?id=16; Statistic Brain, "High School Dropout Statistics," www.statisticbrain.com/high-school -dropout-statistics (last viewed May 17, 2013).

[8]U.S. Census Bureau, "Income, Poverty and Health Insurance in the United States: 2011— Highlights, www.census.gov/hhes/www/poverty/data/incpovhlth/2011/highlights.html.

"He was a rescue."

the men find that they have to shape up, work hard, and be respectful to win over the women they desire. Where the women outnumber the men, however, family understandings look more like the behavior of those losing out on the American dream. The most desirable men (the ones with jobs) find that they can play the field rather than commit. They disappoint enough women that the women invest in themselves rather than their partners. Over time, family stability increases in one community and declines in the other; investment in children increases in one community and declines in the other.

The stakes, like the facts themselves, are now impossible to deny. 20 Increasing inequality has remade the pathways into the middle class, secured class advantages for those who are winning the "rugrat race," and pulled up the ladders that once allowed the diligent working class to find ways to a better life.

ENGAGING THE TEXT

1. How could information and data about the "average" family (para. 2) be misleading? Explain why you agree or disagree with the authors' basic assertion that to understand the changing American family we need to examine "the continuum from the top to the bottom of the American economy."

2. Carbone and Cahn define the "gender bargain" (para. 6) as "the terms on which men and women find it worthwhile to forge lasting relationships." Brainstorm

with classmates to identify several contemporary movies or television series that feature marriages or long-term relationships. What examples can you find of characters reaching a gender bargain? What specific benefits such as income, education, career opportunities, or family connections does each partner contribute to the bargain?

3. The authors write that "a complete explanation of family change requires taking seriously the role of class in scripting our lives" (para. 4). What does the metaphor of a "script" mean in this context? How free or constrained are our choices concerning partners, marriage, and child-rearing if we are somehow following a script?

4. Review the definitions and descriptions of class that Carbone and Cahn provide in paragraphs 12–16. Then summarize the authors' claims about how social class shapes people's choices as they consider marriage and negotiate "gender bargains." What evidence do you find in the lives of friends, family, or community members to support or contradict the authors' claims?

5. Write a journal entry or reflective essay about marriage and money matters. How much do you consider wealth, income, career prospects, and other economic issues when you think about marriage? Overall, do you think marriage facilitates social mobility? Do you expect a college education to help you maintain or advance your social class?

6. Is it possible to accept Carbone and Cahn's analysis of marriage markets and still save a place for romantic love or even "soulmate marriage"? Explain.

EXPLORING CONNECTIONS

7. Look at the cartoon on page 84. Why is it funny, and how might Carbone or Cahn read it a little differently than other people do?

8. Read the profiles of "Harold Browning," "Bob Farrell," and "Cheryl Mitchell" in "Class in America — 2012" by Gregory Mantsios (p. 377). Using these three fictitious characters as representatives of the upper, middle, and working classes, sketch a brief narrative in which Harold or Bob meets Cheryl, falls in love with her, marries her, and raises children with her. Can you construct a plausible story of cross-class marriage that doesn't rely on some unlikely plot twist like winning the lottery?

9. In "Love Me Tinder" (p. 270), Emily Witt writes that "to think about marriage is to completely miss the point of Tinder. The app is about the world around you, the people in your immediate vicinity, and the desires of a particular moment." Do you agree? To what extent might marriage markets be influenced by online dating sites, phone apps like Tinder or Grindr, or other social media? What roles do you think technology will play in your generation's decisions about marriage?

EXTENDING THE CRITICAL CONTEXT

10. This reading selection comes from the introduction to Carbone and Cahn's book *Marriage Markets*. Subsequent chapters in the book extend their

analysis to such topics as shared parenting, children and achievement, family law, and rewriting the marital script. Read and report on one chapter of *Marriage Markets* that particularly interests you.

11. Use Carbone and Cahn's overview of social class, markets, supply and demand, and gender bargains to analyze one or more dating apps such as Tinder, OKCupid, Grindr, Hinge, Down, Hot Or Not, Skout, and Pure. Are markers of social class on such apps invisible, readily apparent, or perhaps "coded"—signaled, for example, by a casual reference to an upscale brand or a popular club? Are users exchanging explicit or implied economic information along with pictures, likes, and locations?

WHY ARE ALL THE CARTOON MOTHERS DEAD?

SARAH BOXER

As the title of this essay suggests, an astounding number of mothers in animated films are killed off early—or before the movie even begins. Their kids are then raised by "plucky fathers," or perhaps a wooly mammoth. This erasure of the mother figures is no accident, Boxer claims, and her essay provides a disturbing answer to the question she poses in her title. Sarah Boxer, formerly a staff writer and editor for the *New York Times*, has published widely on the arts and photography in such venues as *The Atlantic, Slate, Artforum, The Comics Journal*, and the *Los Angeles Review of Books*. Her books include the cartoon novel *In the Floyd Archives: A Psycho-Bestiary* (2001) and an anthology of blogs, *Ultimate Blogs: Masterworks from the Wild Web* (2008). "Why Are All the Cartoon Mothers Dead?" appeared in *The Atlantic* (July / August 2014).

BAMBI'S MOTHER, SHOT. Nemo's mother, eaten by a barracuda. Lilo's mother, killed in a car crash. Koda's mother in *Brother Bear*, speared. Po's mother in *Kung Fu Panda 2*, done in by a power-crazed peacock. Ariel's mother in the third *Little Mermaid*, crushed by a pirate ship. Human baby's mother in *Ice Age*, chased by a saber-toothed tiger over a waterfall.

I used to take the Peter Pan bus between Washington, D.C., and New York City. The ride was terrifying but the price was right, and you could count on watching a movie on the screen mounted behind the driver's seat. *Mrs. Doubtfire*, *The Man Without a Face*, that kind of thing. After a few trips, I noticed a curious pattern. All the movies on board seemed somehow to feature children lost or adrift, kids who had meta-phorically fallen out of their prams. Gee, I thought, Peter Pan Bus Lines sure is keen to reinforce its brand identity. The mothers in the movies were either gone or useless. And the father figures? To die for!

A decade after my Peter Pan years, I began watching a lot of ani-mated children's movies, both new and old, with my son. The same pat-tern held, but with a deadly twist. Either the mothers died onscreen, or they were mysteriously disposed of before the movie began: *Chicken Little, Aladdin, The Fox and the Hound, Pocahontas, Beauty and the Beast, The Emperor's New Groove, The Great Mouse Detective, Ratatouille, Barn-yard, Despicable Me, Cloudy With a Chance of Meatballs*, and, this year, *Mr. Peabody and Sherman*. So many animated movies. Not a mother in sight.

The cartoonist Alison Bechdel once issued a challenge to the film industry with her now-famous test: show me a movie with at least two women in it who talk to each other about something besides a man. Here's another challenge: show me an animated kids' movie that has a named mother in it who lives until the credits roll. Guess what? Not many pass the test. And when I see a movie that does (*Brave, Coraline, A Bug's Life, Antz, The Incredibles, The Lion King, Fantastic Mr. Fox*), I have to admit that I am shocked . . . and, well, just a tad wary.

But I'm getting ahead of myself. The dead-mother plot has a long and storied history, going back past *Bambi* and *Snow White*, past the mystical motherless world of Luke Skywalker and Princess Leia, past Dickens's orphans, past Hans Christian Andersen's Little Mermaid, past the Brothers Grimm's stepmothers, and past Charles Perrault's Sleeping Beauty and Cinderella. As Marina Warner notes in her book *From the Beast to the Blonde*, one of the first Cinderella stories, that of Yeh-hsien, comes from ninth-century China. The dead-mother plot is a fixture of fiction, so deeply woven into our storytelling fabric that it seems impos-sible to unravel or explain.

But some have tried. In *Death and the Mother from Dickens to Freud: Victorian Fiction and the Anxiety of Origins* (1998), Carolyn Dever, a pro-fessor of English, noted that character development begins "in the space of the missing mother." The unfolding of plot and personality, she sug-gests, depends on the dead mother. In *The Uses of Enchantment* (1976), Bruno Bettelheim, the child psychologist, saw the dead mother as a psy-chological boon for kids:

> The typical fairy-tale splitting of the mother into a good (usually dead) mother and an evil stepmother . . . is not only a means of preserving an internal all-good mother when the real mother is not all-good, but it also permits anger at this bad "stepmother" without endangering the goodwill of the true mother.

You may notice that these thoughts about dead mothers share a notable feature: they don't bother at all with the dead mother herself, only with the person, force, or thing that sweeps in and benefits from her death.

Bettelheim focuses on the child's internal sense of himself, Dever on sub-jectivity[1] itself. Have we missed something here? Indeed. I present door No. 3, the newest beneficiary of the dead mother: the good father.

Take *Finding Nemo* (Disney/Pixar, 2003), the mother of all modern motherless movies. Before the title sequence, Nemo's mother, Coral, is eaten by a barracuda, so Nemo's father, Marlin, has to raise their kid alone. He starts out as an overprotective, humorless wreck, but in the course of the movie he faces down everything—whales, sharks, currents, surfer turtles, an amnesiac lady-fish, hungry seagulls—to save Nemo from the clutches of the evil stepmother-in-waiting Darla, a human monster-girl with hideous braces (vagina dentata,[2] anyone?). Thus Marlin not only replaces the dead mother but becomes the dependable yet adventurous parent Nemo always wanted, one who can both hold him close and let him go. He is protector and playmate, comforter and buddy, mother and father.

In the parlance of Helen Gurley Brown,[3] he has it all! He's not only the perfect parent but a lovely catch, too. (Usually when a widowed father is shown onscreen mooning over his dead wife's portrait or some other relic, it's to establish not how wonderful she was but rather how wonderful he is.) To quote Emily Yoffe in *The New York Times*, writing about the perfection of the widowed father in *Sleepless in Seattle*, "He is charming, wry, sensitive, successful, handsome, a great father, and, most of all, he absolutely adores his wife. Oh, the perfect part? She's dead." Dad's magic depends on Mom's death. Boohoo, and then yay!

In a striking number of animated kids' movies of the past couple of decades (coincidental with the resurgence of Disney and the rise of Pixar and DreamWorks), the dead mother is replaced not by an evil stepmother but by a good father. He may start out hypercritical (*Chicken Little*) or reluctant (*Ice Age*). He may be a tyrant (*The Little Mermaid*) or a ne'er-do-well (*Despicable Me*). He may be of the wrong species (*Kung Fu Panda*). He may even be the killer of the child's mother (*Brother Bear*). No matter how bad he starts out, though, he always ends up good.

He doesn't just do the job, he's fabulous at it. In *Brother Bear* (Disney, 2003) when the orphaned Koda tries to engage the older Kenai as a father figure (not knowing Kenai killed his mom), Kenai (who also doesn't know) refuses: "There is no 'we,' okay? I'm not taking you to any salmon run . . . Keep all that cuddly-bear stuff to a minimum." In the end, though, Kenai turns out to be quite the father figure. And they both live happily ever after in a world without mothers.

10

---

[1]**subjectivity:** The ability to act as a subject rather than be acted upon as an object; in the narratives Boxer is critiquing, the development of a child's subjectivity seems to require the death of the mother. [All notes are the editors'.]

[2]**vagina dentata:** Latin: "toothed vagina," a neurosis in which a male imagines a woman's vagina containing teeth, thus threatening injury or castration.

[3]**Helen Gurley Brown:** Author (1922–2012) of *Having It All* (1982) and *Sex and the Single Girl* (1962) and longtime editor-in-chief of *Cosmopolitan* magazine.

So desperate are these kids' movies to get rid of the mother that occasionally they wind up in some pretty weird waters. Near the beginning of *Ice Age* (Blue Sky/20th Century Fox, 2002), the human mother jumps into a waterfall to save herself and her infant, drags herself to shore, and holds on long enough to hand her child to a woolly mammoth. To quote an online review by C. L. Hanson, "She has the strength to push her baby up onto a rock and look sadly into the eyes of the mammoth, imploring him to steady her baby with his trunk," but—hold on— she doesn't have the strength to save herself? And by the way, if Manny the woolly mammoth is such a stand-up guy, why doesn't he "put his trunk around *both of them* and *save them both*" rather than watching her float downriver with a weary sigh? Because, as the reviewer noted, "the only purpose of her life was to set up their buddy adventure." Her work is done. Time to dispose of the body.

Many movies don't even bother with the mother; her death is simply assumed from the outset. In *Despicable Me* (Universal/Illumination, 2010), three orphaned girls, Margo, Edith, and Agnes, are adopted from an orphanage by Gru, a supervillain. Gru adopts them not because he wants children but because he plans to use them in his evil plot. He wants to shrink the moon and steal it. (Hey, wait, isn't the moon a symbol of female fertility?) But by the end of the movie, Gru discovers that his girls are more dear to him than the moon itself. And, as if this delicious father-cake needed some sticky icing, Gru gets to hear his own hyper-critical mother—remember, it was *her* negativity that turned him evil in the first place!—admit that Gru's a better parent than she ever was. The supervillain becomes a superfather, redeemer of all bad mothers.

Quite simply, mothers are killed in today's kids' movies so the fathers can take over. (Of course, there are exceptions; in *Lilo and Stitch*, for instance, both of Lilo's parents die and it's her big sister who becomes the surrogate parent.) The old fairy-tale, family-romance movies that pitted poor motherless children against horrible vengeful stepmothers are a thing of the past. Now plucky children and their plucky fathers join forces to make their way in a motherless world. The orphan plot of yore seems to have morphed, over the past decade, into the buddy plot of today. Roll over, Freud: in a neat reversal of the Oedipus complex,[4] the *mother* is killed so that the children can have the *father* to themselves. Sure, women and girls may come and go, even participate in the adventure, but mothers? Not allowed. And you know what? It looks like fun!

Dear reader, I hear your objection: So what? Hollywood has always been a fantasyland. Or, to quote the cat in *Bolt* (Disney, 2008), a kids'

[4]**Oedipus complex:** In Freudian psychology, a young child's unconscious sexual desire for the parent of the opposite sex (named after the Greek king in Sophocles' tragedy *Oedipus Rex*, who kills his father and marries his mother). Freud linked this desire to "castration anxiety" in boys and "penis envy" in girls.

movie about a dog who thinks he's actually a superhero because he plays one on TV: "Look, genius . . . It's entertainment for people. It's fake! Nothing you think is real is real!" Get over it. It's just a movie. Or, to quote the empowerment anthem from *Frozen* (in which both parents die), "Let it go."

Okay, I will. But first, a brief dip into reality. Did you know that 67 percent of U.S. households with kids are headed by married couples, 25 percent by single mothers, and only 8 percent by single fathers (almost half of whom live with their partners)? In other words, the fantasy of the fabulous single father that's being served up in a theater near you isn't just any fantasy; it's close to the opposite of reality. And so I wonder: Why, when so many real families have mothers and no fathers, do so many children's movies present fathers as the only parents?

Is the unconscious goal of these motherless movies to paper over reality? Is it to encourage more men to be maternal? To suggest that fathers would be better than mothers if only they had the chance? To hint that the world would be better without mothers? Or perhaps we're just seeing a bad case of what the psychoanalyst Karen Horney[5] called "womb envy." Or maybe an expression of the primal rage that the psychoanalyst Melanie Klein described as the infant's "uncontrollable greedy and destructive phantasies and impulses against his mother's breasts."

Consider *Barnyard* (Paramount/Nickelodeon, 2006), a deeply lame reworking of the *Lion King* plot, in which the father bull, Ben, teaches his reckless, motherless, goof-off son, Otis, how to be a man. ("A strong man stands up for himself; a stronger man stands up for others.") As pathetic as *Barnyard* is, there's something truly staggering in it. Whenever the bulls stand up on two hooves, they reveal pink udders right where their male equipment should be—rubbery teats that resemble, as Manohla Dargis described them in *The New York Times*, "chubby little fingers waving toodle-oo."

In the whacked-out, reality-denying world of animated movies, these chubby, wiggly four-fingered udders, which appear on both females and males, are my favorite counterfactuals, bar none. I love, love, love them. The first time I laid eyes on those honkers, my jaw dropped. Even Walt Disney himself, who cooked up pink elephants on parade, never tried *this*. It was as if the comical leather phalluses of ancient Greek theater had come back to life. As if the directors' very ids were plastered on the screen. Not only do *Barnyard*'s bulls have bizarre phallic teats, but Otis rudely swings his out the window of a speeding stolen car while drinking a six-pack of milk—yes, *milk*—and, as the police chase him, shouts, "Milk me!" Is he saying what I think he's saying? In a kids' movie? Could udder envy be any more naked?

---

[5]**Karen Horney:** Neo-Freudian psychoanalyst (1885–1952) who critiqued Freud's theory of penis envy and postulated that a parallel neurosis, womb envy, may exist in men who are jealous of women's ability to bear children.

When I finally shut my jaw, I realized that *Barnyard* isn't the only kids' movie with a case of udder confusion. (In the third *Ice Age*, Sid the Sloth, while trying to feed the three baby dinosaurs he's adopted, starts to milk a musk ox before discovering that it's a guy—ack!) But as far as I know, the *Barnyard* scene is the most violent instance; when the teated bull yells "Milk me!" it's like he's shouting at women everywhere: "You think you're so hot with your tits and your babies. Well, suck on this! (And then die.)"

That's how I see it, anyway, and I don't think I'm alone.

In *How to Read Donald Duck* (1975), Ariel Dorfman, the Chilean American activist and writer, and Armand Mattelart, a Belgian sociologist, discuss the insidiousness of "the absence of woman as *mother* in Disney." Rather than presenting any really maternal figure, they say, Disney offers up only "the captive and ultimately frivolous woman," who lacks any tie to "the natural cycle of life itself"—Cinderella, Sleeping Beauty, Snow White. And in the natural mother's place, they note, Disney erects a "false mother Mickey," a creature of "chivalrous generosity" and "fair play" whose authority looks benign and cheery. The absence of a real mother thus makes way for a new authority, a new "natural" order. The road to social repression, in other words, is paved with Mickey Mouse.

In today's movie fathers, there's plenty of Mickey Mouse. They're magnanimous, caring, and fun. And I imagine these animated fathers look great to most kids. But let's call a spade a spade. The ineluctable regularity of the dead-mother, fun-father pattern is not just womb envy at work, and not just aggression against the breast; it's Mickey's glove displacing the maternal teat. It's misogyny made cute.

Dear reader, I hear you objecting again. Perhaps you're getting irritated. Perhaps you like Pixar. Perhaps you'd like to remind me of some living mothers in a few animated movies: Isn't that a single mother raising two kids in *Toy Story*? (Yes, she's the one who keeps trying to give away the toys.) And isn't that a mother at the end of *The Lego Movie*? (Yes, she's the one who cuts short the nascent father-son bonding moment in the basement by announcing that supper is ready.)

What about Fiona, the ogre-princess in *Shrek* (DreamWorks, 2001)? She certainly seems to be someone's caricature of a feminist—tough, competent, belching earthily with the boys. By *Shrek the Third* (2007), she's pregnant. At her baby shower, she makes all her beautiful, single friends—Snow White, Sleeping Beauty, Cinderella, and Rapunzel—seem like spoiled, materialistic wimps. But when it comes time for Fiona's own father, a frog king, to pass down the crown, he offers it not to *her* but to her ogre-husband, Shrek—who eventually turns it down because he has "something much more important in mind." (He's going to be a father!) That's right: the male gallantly refuses all that power (sweet old Mickey) while the female, who should have been next in line for the throne, isn't asked, and doesn't complain.

Patriarchy is slyly served. We've been slipped a Mickey!

A similar thing happens in *Ice Age: Dawn of the Dinosaurs* (2009). When Ellie, a sassy woolly mammoth, goes into labor, she's stuck on a cliff and her man, Manny, is off fighting predators. This leaves Diego, the saber-toothed tiger, to play birth coach. At one puzzling point, Ellie, the very picture of strength, yells to Diego, "You can do it! Push, push!" as if he were the one giving birth. He snaps back: "You have no idea what I'm going through!" (He's fending off vicious blue dinosaurs—more work than childbirth, from the looks of it.)

It's funny! The filmmakers, after all, don't *really* think Diego is working harder than Ellie. (Sexism always slides down better with a self-ironizing wink and giggle.) But once the baby pops out, we get patriarchy in earnest: the father, Manny, fresh from his own heroics, reenters the scene. Ellie hands him the baby, which he secures with his trunk and declares "perfect."

This cozy family scene reprises the original *Ice Age*, when Manny the woolly mammoth saved the human baby—and not the mother—with his trunk. This time, though, the mother is allowed to live. Why? Because she never upstaged the buddy plot. Her death would have been, well, overkill.

Have we moved beyond killing mothers, to a place where it no longer matters whether they live or die? From the newest crop of kids' animated movies, which are mostly buddy movies—*Planes*, *Turbo*, *Cloudy With a Chance of Meatballs 2*, *Monsters University*, *Free Birds*, *The Lego Movie*—it sure looks that way. It seems as if we have entered, at least in movie theaters, a post-mother world.

In March, when I took my son to see *Mr. Peabody and Sherman* (DreamWorks, 2014), I suspected that we'd be watching a buddy movie, pure and simple, in which the presence or absence of mothers was immaterial. I was wrong.

Apparently, it was finally time to blast mothers out of history. At the start of the movie, Mr. Peabody—a dog, a Harvard graduate, a Nobel laureate, and the inventor of Zumba, the fist bump, and the WABAC (pronounced "wayback") machine—says his dearest dream is to be a father. He adopts a human boy, Sherman; vows "to be the best father"; and is wildly successful at it. (He uses the WABAC to teach his son history by introducing him to figures like Benjamin Franklin, Vincent van Gogh, and William Shakespeare.)

The movie thus begins where other kids' movies end, with the perfect father-son relationship. Nothing can threaten them—except, alas, two gals, Ms. Grunion, an ugly social worker (the evil-stepmother figure), who wants to tear dog and boy apart, and Penny, a bratty girl who is jealous of Sherman's knowledge and gets him to take her on a trip in the WABAC. And there the adventure begins.

They go to Leonardo's Italy. (Why won't the Mona Lisa smile?) They go to ancient Troy. ("Don't even get me started about Oedipus. Let's just say that you do *not* want to be at his house over the holidays! It's awkward.") And they go to ancient Egypt, where Penny herself is inserted into history. Tellingly, she's not given the obvious, powerful role — Cleopatra — but instead becomes the bride of King Tut, who's destined to die early. (Her reaction to learning this bit of history? Vintage Valley Girl with a hint of gold digger: "Oh, trust me, I've thought it through. I'm getting everything!")

But the key moment comes at the end of the movie, when we get to see George Washington muttering about changing the Declaration of Independence. I held my breath. Would the Founding Father (yes, Father) correct one of the most famous, glaring faults of the document? I listened for the magic words, and this is what I heard: "We hold these truths to be self-evident, that all men — and *some dogs* — are created equal." What?!?! (Insert spit take.)[6] Given the chance to rewrite history, the filmmakers give rights to *some dogs*? But not to the bitches (I mean to the women)? Sure, it's funny. Funny like udders on male cows. Funny sad. Funny infuriating. Funny painful.

The power of the WABAC to rewrite history, if only in fantasy, made me remember why I like animation so much. Just as time travel imagines the way things might have been, so does animation give the creator total omnipotence. With animation you can suspend the laws of physics and the laws of society and the laws of reason and the laws of biology and the laws of family. You can have a dog adopt a boy. You can turn a rat into a French chef. You can make male cows with big pink udders. You can change the Declaration of Independence. You can have a family in which every member is a doggone superhero.

As the Soviet film director and theorist Sergei Eisenstein wrote of Disney's early work, you can have "a family of octopuses on four legs, with a fifth serving as a tail, and a sixth — a trunk." You can do anything. Eisenstein marveled, "How much (imaginary!) divine omnipotence there is in this! What magic of reconstructing the world according to one's fantasy and will!"

And yet, in this medium where the creators have total control, we keep getting the same damned world — a world without mothers. Is this really the dearest wish of animation? Can mothers really be so threatening?

I'd like to end on a hopeful note, with a movie that passes my test with flying colors — *The Incredibles* (Disney/Pixar, 2004), which happens to feature not only three major female characters, including a great mother figure, Elastigirl (a k a Helen Parr), who lives for the whole movie, but also a pretty credible father figure, Mr. Incredible (a k a Bob Parr). Unlike just about every other movie dad, Mr. Incredible is far from perfect. He daydreams during dinner. He is more interested in getting back to hero-work (he has been forcibly retired, along with all the other heroes) than in how his kids are doing at school. He even lies to his wife about where he's going and what he's doing. He is super-angry. When his car door won't shut, he slams it so hard that the window shatters.

---

[6]**spit take:** The gag in which an actor spews a liquid from his mouth as a comic expression of surprise.

The hero of the movie isn't Mr. Incredible, but the mother, who turns back into Elastigirl, a really flexible, sexy, and strong superhero, in order to save her husband. ("Either he's in trouble or he's going to be!") At one point during the rescue mission, the plane that the mother is flying is hit by missiles and she and the kids have to eject. The mother uses her elasticity to reach out and grab her children and parachute them, with herself as the chute, to the ocean below. Then she transforms her body into a speedboat (her son, who has super-speed, is the motor) to reach the shore. It's a view of what animated movies could be — not another desperate attempt to assert the inalienable rights of men, but an incredible world where everyone has rights and powers, even the mothers.

I should point out that Elastigirl's superpower — flexibility, stretchi- 40 ness, or what Eisenstein, back in the 1940s, termed "plasmaticness" — happens to be the very attribute he singled out as the most attractive imaginable in art, a universal sign of the ability to assume any form. He found this elasticity not only in his beloved Mickey Mouse but also in Lewis Carroll's long-necked Alice, in the eighteenth-century Japanese etchings of "the many-metred arms of geishas," in the rubber-armed snake dancers of New York's black nightclubs, in Balzac's[7] *La Peau de Chagrin*, in Wilhelm Busch's *Max und Moritz*, and in the stretched noses of the Tengu.[8] Elastigirl, then, is not only a great character and a great mother, but the very picture of protoplasmic freedom.

For some reason, though, what really sticks in my mind is not Elastigirl stretching the limits of plasticity but rather a scene from *Ratatouille* (Disney/Pixar, 2007). Colette, the sole female in the kitchen of Gusteau's restaurant, is trying to teach the basics of cooking to Linguini, the bumbling orphan boy who gets a job in Gusteau's kitchen only because his mother slept with the great chef before she (yes) died.

As Colette chops away frenetically at some celery stalks, she shouts: "You think cooking is a cute job, eh? Like Mommy in the kitchen? Well, Mommy never had to face the dinner rush, when the orders come flooding in . . . Every second counts — and *you cannot be Mommy*!" Who is she shouting at? Linguini the lucky orphan? Herself? Men in general? Men who want to have it all? Women who want to have it all? Animators? Fathers? I really don't know, but it's a fantastic moment of pure rage. And it sure rings true.

[7]**Balzac:** French novelist and playwright Honoré de Balzac (1799–1850), author of *La Peau de Chagrin* (*The Wild Ass's Skin*) among many other works.
[8]**Tengu:** Legendary creatures in Japanese folklore characterized by long noses (or large beaks in their earlier, birdlike forms).

"Skip to the part where the princess climbs to the top of the corporate ladder."

ENGAGING THE TEXT

1. Which of the animated films Boxer mentions have you seen? Do you generally agree with her assessment of how they treat mothers and motherhood? Do you think anything has changed since 2014, when this article appeared? What animated films can you name that pass Boxer's test of having "a named mother in it who lives until the credits roll" (para. 4)?

2. Boxer anticipates some readers saying "Get over it. It's just a movie. . . . Let it go" (para. 15), but the last emotion she mentions — and seemingly endorses — is "pure rage" (para. 42). Where along the spectrum from indifference to rage would you situate yourself, and why?

3. Boxer writes that "sexism always slides down better with a self-ironizing wink and giggle" (para. 27). Brainstorm with classmates to identify areas outside television and film where sexism or misogyny are sometimes masked by humor — as in "dumb blonde" jokes, for example.

4. How and when should parents begin to educate their children about potentially noxious media messages? How difficult would it be for a family with young children to "boycott" a brand like Disney or Pixar?

5. **Thinking Rhetorically** List the various ways Boxer establishes her credibility as a critic of animated films. Where does she anticipate resistance to her ideas, and how does she attempt to win readers over? Where does she present her thesis, and why do you think it is delayed? Finally, look at several examples of Boxer's boldest and funniest sentences: Do her tone and humor in these instances enhance her argument, or possibly undermine its seriousness?

EXPLORING CONNECTIONS

6. Read or review the excerpt from Cris Beam's *To the End of June: The Intimate Life of American Foster Care* (p. 61). How do you think Beam or "Oneida" might characterize some of the frequent plot elements in animated films, such as orphaned children, absent mothers, and super-fathers?

7. In "'Two Ways a Woman Can Get Hurt': Advertising and Violence" (p. 488), Jean Kilbourne takes the advertising industry to task for condoning and normalizing violence against women; near the end of her essay she writes that "this pervasive harassment of and contempt for girls and women constitute a kind of abuse" (para. 48). To what extent do you think animated films are another way girls and women can get hurt? What similarities and differences do you see between misogynistic ads and the films Boxer describes, and do you think the films "constitute a kind of abuse"?

EXTENDING THE CRITICAL CONTEXT

8. Boxer praises *The Incredibles* for having three important female characters, including Elastigirl — a "really flexible, sexy, and strong superhero" (para. 39). Can you think of any equivalents to Elastigirl in other media arenas like gaming, comics, Manga, or anime? Do these media, like animated films, tend to ignore or kill off mothers?

9. Watch a recent animated film, paying particular attention to its representation of mothers and fathers. Using Boxer's essay as a model, write a paragraph or two analyzing the film's portrayals of these characters. Compare notes with classmates and discuss the extent to which your observations support Boxer's thesis.

FURTHER CONNECTIONS

1. Family relationships are a frequent subject for novels and films, per-haps because these extended forms can take the time to explore the complexities of family dynamics. Keeping in mind the issues raised in this chapter, write an essay analyzing the portrayal of family in a single contemporary novel or film.

2. Writers and analysts routinely use data from the U.S. Census Bureau to get a "snapshot" of the American population as a whole or to track national trends over time. However, the bureau also provides a wealth of information at the state and county levels. Choose two counties in your state that you think are substantially different demographically; explore the Census Bureau Web site (www.census.gov) and gather statistical data on items like size of households, their median income, the number of households headed by women, and so on. Report your findings to the class, or collaborate with classmates to build an overview of your state.

3. Tolstoy wrote that all happy families are alike, but that each unhappy family is unhappy in its own way. Taking into account your own experi-ence and the readings in this chapter, write a journal entry or an essay articulating your views of what makes families happy or unhappy, and assessing your own experiences of family up to this point in your life.

LEARNING POWER
The Myth of Education and Empowerment

FAST FACTS

1. In 2014, U.S. workers over the age of 25 without a high school diploma had an expected annual income of $25,376 and an unemployment rate of 9%. Those with a bachelor's degree had an annual income of $57,252 and an unemployment rate of 3.5%.

2. Public school students spend from 60 to 110 hours a year preparing for accountability testing. The estimated annual cost of testing per pupil ranges from $700 to $1,000.

3. In 2012, the average white U.S. student attended a school with 27% black or Latino/a enrollment; by contrast, the average black and Latino/a student attended a school where approximately 66% of the student body was made up of blacks and Latinos/as. In these "intensely segregated" schools, most students live near or below the poverty line.

4. Between 1970 and 2013, the percentage of students from low-income families (with annual incomes less than $34,160) attaining a bachelor's degree increased from 6% to 9% while the percentage of students from the wealthiest families (with annual incomes greater than $108,650) earning a degree increased from 44% to 77%.

5. Over the past 40 years, the percentage of undergraduates majoring in business has nearly doubled while the percentage of those studying English, foreign languages, and education has declined significantly. Since 1986, the percentage of students in computer science has also declined to less than 3%.

6. According to a 2014 White House report, one in five women is sexually assaulted while in college, and 75% to 80% of those suffering an assault know their attacker.

7. According to the *Wall Street Journal*, total student loan debt grew from $509 billion in 2006 to $1.31 trillion as of 2014. More than 40 million Americans now have at least one student loan and carry an average debt of $33,000 after graduation.

Data from (1) U.S. Bureau of Labor Statistics; (2) *Testing More, Teaching Less: What America's Obsession with Student Testing Costs in Money and Lost Instructional Time*, the American Federation of Teachers; (3) *Brown at 60: Great Progress, a Long Retreat and an Uncertain Future*, the Civil Rights Project at UCLA; (4) *Indicators of Higher Education Equity in the United States*, the Pell Institute for the Study of Opportunity in Higher Education; (5) *College Majors and Degrees*, Benjamin M. Schmidt, Northwestern University; (6) *Not Alone: The First Report of the White House Task Force to Protect Students from Sexual Assault*; (7) "Lenders Shift to Help Struggling Student Borrowers," the *Wall Street Journal*.

MOST AMERICANS TEND TO SEE EDUCATION as something intrinsically valuable or important. After all, education is the engine that drives the American Dream. The chance to learn, better oneself, and gain the skills that pay off in upward mobility has sustained the hope of millions of Americans. As a nation we look up to figures like Abraham Lincoln and Frederick Douglass, who learned to see beyond poverty and slavery by learning to read. Education tells us that the American Dream can work for everyone. It reassures us that we are, in fact, "created equal" and that the path to achievement lies through individual effort and hard work, not blind luck or birth.

But American attitudes toward teachers and teaching haven't always been overwhelmingly positive. The Puritans who established the Massachusetts Bay Colony viewed education with respectful skepticism. Schooling in Puritan society was a force for spiritual rather than worldly advancement. Lessons were designed to reinforce moral and religious training and to teach children to read the Bible for themselves. Education was important to the Puritan "Divines" because it was a source of order, control, and discipline. But when education aimed at more worldly goals or was undertaken for self-improvement, it was seen as a menacing, sinful luxury. Little wonder, then, that the Puritans often viewed teaching as something less than an ennobling profession. In fact, teachers in the early colonies were commonly treated as menial employees by the families and communities they served, performing duties like serving summonses, ringing bells for church service, and digging graves. Frequently, they came to the New World as indentured servants. Once here, they drilled their masters' children in spiritual exercises until they earned their freedom — or escaped.

The reputation of education in America began to improve with the onset of the Revolutionary War. Following the overthrow of British rule, leaders sought to create a spirit of nationalism that would unify the former colonies. Differences were to be set aside, for, as George Washington pointed out, "the more homogeneous our citizens can be made . . . the greater will be our prospect of permanent union." The goal of schooling became the creation of uniformly loyal, patriotic Americans. In the words of Benjamin Rush, one of the signers of the Declaration of Independence, "Our schools of learning, by producing one general and uniform system of educa- tion, will render the mass of people more homogeneous and thereby fit them more easily for uniform and peaceable government."

Thomas Jefferson saw school as a training ground for citizenship and demo- cratic leadership. Recognizing that an illiterate and ill-informed population would be unable to assume the responsibilities of self-government, Jefferson laid out a comprehensive plan in 1781 for public education in the state of Virginia. According to Jefferson's blueprint, all children would be eligible for three years of free public instruction. Of those who could not afford further schooling, one promising "genius" from each school was to be "raked from the rubbish" and given six more years of free education. At the end of that time, ten boys would be selected to attend college at public expense. Jeffersonian Virginia may have been the first place in the United States where education so clearly offered the penniless boy a path to self-improvement. However, this path was open to very few, and Jefferson, like Washington and Rush, was more concerned with benefiting the state than serving the individual student: "We hope to avail the state of those talents which nature has sown as liberally among the poor as the rich, but which perish without use, if not sought for and cultivated." For leaders of the American Revolution, education was seen as a tool for nation-building, not personal development.

In the nineteenth century two great historical forces — industrialization and immigration — combined to exert pressure for the "homogenization" of young Americans. Massive immigration from Ireland and Eastern and Central Europe led to fears that "non-native" peoples would undermine the cultural identity of the United States. Many saw school as the first line of defense against this perceived threat, a place where the children of "foreigners" could become Americanized. In a meeting of educators in 1836, one college professor stated the problem as bluntly as possible:

> Let us now be reminded, that unless we educate our immigrants, they will be our ruin. It is no longer a mere question of benevolence, of duty, or of enlightened self-interest, but the intellectual and religious training of our foreign population has become essential to our own safety; we are prompted to it by the instinct of self-preservation.

Industrialization gave rise to another kind of uniformity in nineteenth-century public education. Factory work didn't require the kind of educational preparation needed to transform a child into a craftsman or merchant. So, for the first time in American history, school systems began to categorize students into different educational "tracks" that offered qualitatively different kinds of education to different groups. Some — typically students from well-to-do homes — were prepared for professional and managerial positions. But most were consigned to education for life "on the line." Increasing demand for factory workers put a premium on young people who were obedient and able to work in large groups according to fixed schedules. As a result, leading educators in 1874 proposed a system of schooling that would meet the needs of the "modern industrial community" by stressing "punctuality, regularity, attention, and silence, as habits necessary through life." History complicates the myth of education as a source of personal empowerment. School can bind as effectively as it can liberate; it can enforce conformity and limit life chances as well as foster individual talent.

But history also supplies examples of education serving the idealistic goals of democracy, equality, and self-improvement. Nineteenth-century educator and reformer Horace Mann worked to expand educational opportunity for all. Perhaps more than any other American, Mann helped fashion the myth of personal empowerment through education. Born on a farm in Franklin, Massachusetts, in 1796, Mann raised himself from poverty to a position of national importance through study and hard work. His own early educational experiences left an indelible imprint: the ill-trained and often brutal schoolmasters he encountered in rural Massachusetts made rote memorization and the power of the rod the hallmarks of their classroom practice. After graduating from Brown University and a successful career in politics, Mann became Secretary of the Massachusetts Board of Education in 1837, a role that gave him the opportunity to design what he called the "common school," the model of the first comprehensive public school in the United States.

Mann sketched his vision of democratic public education in the "Report of the Massachusetts Board of Education, 1848." In this famous document, he claimed that if the people were to govern themselves, every citizen had to be sufficiently educated to make independent judgments about the issues of the day. Education, according to Mann, "must prepare our citizens to become municipal officers, intelligent jurors, honest witnesses, legislators, or competent judges of legislation — in fine, to fill all the manifold relations of life." Mann saw the school as "the most effective and benignant of all the forces of civilization." In his view, schooling fulfills an almost sacred social mission:

> In teaching the blind and the deaf and dumb, in kindling the latent spark of intelligence that lurks in an idiot's mind, and in the more holy work of reforming abandoned and outcast children, education has proved what it can do by glorious experiments. These wonders it has done in its infancy, and with the lights of a limited experience; but when its faculties shall be fully developed, when it shall be trained to wield its mighty energies for the protection of society against the giant vices which now invade and torment it,— against intemperance, avarice, war, slavery, bigotry, the woes of want, and the wickedness of waste,—then there will not be a height to which these enemies of the race can escape which it will not scale, nor a Titan among them all whom it will not slay.

The common school, according to Mann, would empower students by providing them with the physical, moral, intellectual, and political tools they would need to lead socially productive lives. Compulsory public education would target every major social ill — including what Mann saw as a dangerous, growing division between the classes:

> Now, surely nothing but universal education can counterwork this tendency to the domination of capital and servility of labor. If one class possesses all the wealth and the education, while the residue of society is ignorant and poor, it matters not by what name the relation between them may be called: the latter, in fact and in truth, will be the servile dependants and subjects of the former. But, if education be equally diffused, it will draw property after it by the strongest of all attractions, for such a thing never did happen, and never can happen, as that an intelligent and practical body of men should be permanently poor ... Education, then, beyond all other devices of human origin, is the great equalizer of the conditions of men,—the balance-wheel of the social machinery ... I mean that it gives each man the independence and the means by which he can resist the selfishness of other men. It does better than to disarm the poor of their hostility towards the rich: it prevents being poor.

At the turn of the century, philosopher and educational theorist John Dewey made even greater claims for educational empowerment. A fierce opponent of the kind of "tracking" associated with industrial education, Dewey proposed that schools should strive to produce thinking citizens rather than obedient workers. As members of a democracy, all men and women, according to Dewey, are entitled to an education that helps them make the best of their natural talents and enables them to participate as fully as possible in the life of their community: "only by being true to the full growth of the individuals who make it up, can society by any chance be true to itself." Most of our current myths of education echo the optimism of Mann and Dewey. Guided by their ideas, most Americans still believe that education leads to self-improvement and can help us empower ourselves — and perhaps even transform our society.

In recent decades, however, the reputation of schools has again been questioned. In 1983, a special commission appointed by President Ronald Reagan published *A Nation at Risk*, an assessment of public education that portrayed our schools as failing students and their families at every level. Since then, the nation has experienced more than thirty years of federal and state educational reform efforts aimed at improving the "mediocre" performance of our public schools and teachers. Interventions like the 2001 No Child Left Behind Act, the 2009 Race to the Top grant program, and the recent Common Core Standards Initiative have invested billions of taxpayer dollars to "fix" our educational system. Charter schools have proliferated, and high-stakes testing has become a staple of American education, often taking up time that once was dedicated to art, music, and physical education.

Today, then, we find ourselves still asking the central question: Does education empower us, or does it stifle personal growth? This chapter takes a critical look at what American education does and how it shapes or enhances our identities. We begin with a meditation on "The Essentials of a Good Education" by educational historian and policy analyst Diane Ravitch. An outspoken critic of public schools in the 1980s who has today become one of their most ardent supporters, Ravitch invites us to rethink our assumptions about the goals of schooling and challenges us to imagine the possibility of educational excellence for all Americans. Next, in "Against School," award-winning teacher and libertarian John Taylor Gatto offers his own provocative analysis of how public education "cripples our kids" by training them to be "employees and consumers." In "I Just Wanna Be Average," Mike Rose provides a moving personal account of the dream of educational success and pays tribute to an inner-city teacher who never loses sight of what can be achieved in a classroom. An excerpt from Jean Anyon's "Social Class and the Hidden Curriculum of Work" rounds off the section by suggesting that schools virtually program students for success or failure according to their socioeconomic status.

Following these initial readings, the chapter's Visual Portfolio opens with the image of a 1950s classroom that echoes both the idyllic and nightmarish aspects of the school experience. The photographs that follow raise questions about our national and personal educational priorities and about whether higher education itself hasn't become a dangerous proposition for students who leave school in debt or suffer sexual assault.

The next pair of readings offers you the chance to explore the complex interaction of education, race, and power in American society. In "Learning to Read," Malcolm X describes how his own self-education in prison liberated him from the "whitened" accounts of history he learned in school. In "Still Separate, Still Unequal," educational activist Jonathan Kozol examines the resegregation of America's urban schools and the negative impact of the school reform movement.

The chapter concludes with two selections focusing on the goals of higher education. First, Carmen Lugo-Lugo offers her perspective as a Latina on what it's like to teach today's market-savvy students at a typical American college. In "Don't Send Your Kids to the Ivy League," William Deresiewicz rounds off our examination of schooling in America by suggesting that today's parents and students are placing social status and vocational training above the true purpose of college education.

Sources

Best, John Hardin, and Robert T. Sidwell, eds. *The American Legacy of Learning: Readings in the History of Education*. Philadelphia: J. B. Lippincott Co., 1966. Print.

Dewey, John. "The School and Society" (1899) and "My Pedagogic Creed" (1897). *John Dewey on Education*. New York: Modern Library, 1964. Print.

Jefferson, Thomas. *Notes on the State of Virginia*. Chapel Hill: University of North Carolina Press, 1955. Print.

Mann, Horace, "Report of the Massachusetts Board of Education, 1848." *An American Primer*. Ed. Daniel Boorstein. New York: Penguin Books, 1966. Print.

Pangle, Lorraine Smith, and Thomas L. Prangle. *The Learning of Liberty: The Educational Ideas of the American Founders*. Lawrence: University Press of Kansas, 1993. Print.

Stevens, Edward, and George H. Wood. *Justice, Ideology, and Education: An Introduction to the Social Foundations of Education*. New York: Random House, 1987. Print.

Vallance, Elizabeth. "Hiding the Hidden Curriculum: An Interpretation of the Language of Justification in Nineteenth-Century Educational Reform." *Curriculum Theory Network*, Vol. 4, No. 1. Toronto: Ontario Institute for Studies in Education, 1973–1974. 5–21. Print.

Westbrook, Robert B. "Public Schooling and American Democracy." *Democracy, Education, and the Schools*. Ed. Roger Soder. San Francisco: Jossey-Bass Publishers, 1996. Print.

BEFORE READING

- Freewrite for fifteen or twenty minutes about your best and worst educational experiences. Then, working in groups, compare notes to see if you can find recurring themes or ideas in what you've written. What aspects of school seem to stand out most clearly in your memories? Do the best experiences have anything in common? How about the worst? What aspects of your school experience didn't show up in the freewriting?

- Work in small groups to draw a collective picture that expresses your experi- ence of high school or college. Don't worry about your drawing skill — just load the page with imagery, feelings, and ideas. Then show your work to other class members and let them try to interpret it.

- Write a journal entry about the first graders reciting the Pledge of Allegiance back in 1955 on the title page of this chapter (p. 99). What does this photo suggest about the role of education in American society? How realistic is this depiction of public schooling?

THE ESSENTIALS OF A GOOD EDUCATION

DIANE RAVITCH

In 1983, President Ronald Reagan's National Commission on Excellence in Education published the first of a series of reports that would spark more than thirty years of school reform efforts. *A Nation at Risk* painted a bleak picture of our public schools, describing the state of teaching and learning in the United States as a self-inflicted "act of war" — "an act of unthink- ing, unilateral educational disarmament." Back in the 1980s, educational historian and policy analyst Diane Ravitch initially embraced the report's findings and championed school reforms that called for more standardized testing and linked test outcomes to school funding. But by 2010 Ravitch had changed her mind. Since then, she has emerged as a leading critic of standardized testing, charter schools, and what she sees as a deliberately orchestrated assault on public education. In this excerpt from her 2014 book *Reign of Error: The Hoax of the Privatization Movement and the Danger to America's Public Schools*, Ravitch pauses to reflect on the goals of education and challenges us to reconsider what schools should do for American kids. Diane Ravitch (b. 1938) is a research professor at New York University's Steinhardt School of Culture, Education, and Human Development. She has published more than twenty books and 500 articles on education and school reform, including *The Death and Life of the Great American School System: How Testing and Choice Are Undermining Education* (2010) and *The Language Police: How Pressure Groups Restrict What Students Learn* (2003).

SINCE THE ADVENT OF NO CHILD LEFT BEHIND,[1] many schools have cut back on every subject that was not tested. The federal law demanded that all students be proficient in mathematics and reading by 2014, and every state was required to test those subjects. Nothing counted other than mathematics and reading. Schools expanded the time available to teach these subjects, which determined whether they would be honored or humiliated, whether they would live or die. More time was allotted to take practice tests in mathematics and reading. Because there are only so many hours in a day, there was less time for subjects that were not tested. When the economic recession of 2008 began, many schools experienced budget cuts. The combination of budget cuts and high-stakes testing meant that something had to go. When cutbacks were necessary, it was in the nontested subjects. When teachers were laid off, they were usually those who did not teach the tested subjects.

Our policy makers today think that what matters most is getting high test scores in reading and mathematics. They don't show any regrets if a school spends inordinate amounts of time and money on test preparation materials. They will pin an A label on a school that gets high scores, even if its students spend all day every day practicing to take tests in mathematics and reading. But such a school is really not a good school, even if it gets high scores and the state awards it an A.

So we must look for other indicators, not just test scores, and not the official grade offered by the state or the district, which is unduly tied to test scores.

Let us consider two other ways of evaluating schools. One is to ask what the most demanding families seek in a school. The other is to consider the school in relation to the purposes of public education.

---

[1]**No Child Left Behind:** A 2001 act of Congress that requires states to test children's basic skills to qualify for federal funding. [All notes are the editors', except 4.]

What do the most demanding families seek in a school? Whether they are parents in an affluent suburb or parents whose children attend an expensive private school, they expect their children to have much, much more than training in basic skills. They expect their children to study history and literature, science and mathematics, the arts and foreign languages. They would never tolerate a school that did not have dramatics, art, music, and science laboratories. They would insist that the school have up-to-date technology that their children could use every day. They would expect excellent athletic facilities and daily physical education. If their child is unusually bright, they would expect advanced courses to keep her curiosity and zest for learning alive. If their child has disabilities of any kind, they would expect the school to have appropriately trained personnel to offer the help and support the child needs. They would correctly anticipate small classes, projects, and frequent writing assignments. They would want a full range of student activities, including student government, a newspaper, clubs, after-school activities, and plays.

In affluent communities today, such schools are the norm in the public sector, not just the private sector. They were once the norm in ordinary American public schools. Today, however, the No Child Left Behind law and the Race to the Top[2] program have undermined this ideal curriculum and restricted it to only the most affluent communities. Because federal policies value only test scores, they have unleashed an almost fanatical obsession with data based on test scores. Today, almost every state has received federal funding to create a data "warehouse," where information about all students and teachers will be stored for future retrieval. What is the purpose of the data warehouse? No one knows for sure, but it will enable all students to be tracked throughout their lifetimes in relation to their test scores, graduation dates, future earnings, and who knows what else. Even now, the Gates Foundation and Rupert Murdoch's Amplify division[3] have joined to create a $100 million database called inBloom to collect confidential student information from several states and districts and put it on an electronic "cloud" managed by Amazon.com. This data will include students' names, birthdates, addresses, social security numbers, grades, test scores, disability status, attendance, and other confidential information. The database may be made available to vendors for marketing purposes. Why the modern state should collect and share so much confidential information about its citizens is baffling.[4]

---

[2]**Race to the Top:** A $4.35 billion Department of Education competitive grant initiated in 2009 that rewards states adopting certain educational policies, including performance-based evaluations of teachers and implementation of common educational standards and assessments.

[3]**Rupert Murdoch's Amplify division:** A division of conservative entrepreneur Rupert Murdoch's News Corp, dedicated to the sale of educational technology and software and testing services.

[4]Stephanie Simon, "K–12 Student Database Jazzes Tech Startups, Spooks Parents," Reuters, March 2, 2013. [Ravitch's note.]

In contrast to federal policy, which is obsessed with test-based data, educated consumers of schooling want their children to have a full, balanced, and rich curriculum. They may look into outcome data about a school (for example, how many of its students graduate, how many go to college, which colleges admit its graduates), but their first concern is "inputs": What educational experiences will my child have? How experienced are the teachers? How small are classes? Are there a variety of athletic programs that are right for my child? Will my child have a broad curriculum? If she needs extra help, will she get it? Does the school have a warm and welcoming climate? Will this school take good care of my child?

An educated parent would not accept a school where many weeks of every school year were spent preparing for state tests. An educated parent would not tolerate a school that cut back or eliminated the arts to spend more time preparing for state tests. If you want to know what an educated parent-consumer would insist upon, go online and look at the curricula in schools such as Sidwell Friends in the District of Columbia; Lakeside School in Seattle; Deerfield Academy in Deerfield, Massachusetts; Phillips Academy in Andover, Massachusetts; and Maumee Valley Country Day School in Toledo, Ohio. Every one of these schools has a curriculum with extensive offerings in the arts, languages, world cultures, history, sciences, mathematics, and athletics.

A similar curriculum may be found in affluent suburban communities, richly endowed by their strong tax bases and committed parents. Families in communities like Plano, Texas; Deerfield, Illinois; and Scarsdale, New York, would accept nothing less for their children.

The typical public school today cannot afford the same offerings. It cannot afford the small classes and rich curriculum available only to the richest citizens. And yet I can personally attest that in the past American public schools routinely offered a varied curriculum, even if the class sizes were not 1:15 as they are in many elite private schools. Why today are public schools unable to afford the curriculum they once offered? Why is the richest nation in the world unable to provide a full curriculum for all students in public schools? Why are budget cuts in the wake of the Great Recession of 2008 falling so heavily on the public schools? Why are states willing to spend hundreds of millions on testing and test preparation materials even as they cut back on teachers of the arts and foreign languages and on librarians and counselors?

We cannot provide equal educational opportunity if some children get access to a full and balanced curriculum while others get a heavy dose of basic skills. This is one instance where no research is needed. The fact of inequality is undeniable, self-evident, and unjustifiable. This inequality of opportunity may damage the hearts and minds of the children who are shortchanged in ways that may never be undone.

We know that those who can afford the best for their children demand a full curriculum. Another way to judge the importance of a high-value curriculum is to consider what it should be in light of the purposes of public education. Communities and states established public education as a public responsibility in the nineteenth century to educate future citizens and to sustain our democracy. The essential purpose of the public schools, the reason they receive public funding, is to teach young people the rights and responsibilities of citizens. As citizens, they will be expected to discuss and deliberate issues, to choose our leaders, to take an active role in their communities, and to participate in civic affairs. A secondary purpose was to strengthen our economy and our culture by raising the intelligence of our people and preparing them to lead independent lives as managers, workers, producers, consumers, and creators of ideas, products, and services. A third purpose is to endow every individual with the intellectual and ethical power to pursue his or her own interests and to develop the judgment and character to survive life's vicissitudes.

Today, policy makers think of education solely in terms of its secondary purposes. They speak of children as future global competitors. They sometimes refer to children in rather ugly terms as "human assets," forgetting that they are unique people and they are not fungible. They want all students to be "college and career ready." They tend to speak only of preparation for the workforce, not education for citizenship. But this is misguided. Workforce training may take place in schools; it may take place in the workplace. It is not unimportant. Nor is college preparation unimportant. But getting ready for college is not the central purpose of education. Nor is workforce training. The central purpose of education is to prepare everyone to assume the rights and responsibilities of citizenship in a democracy.

What does this mean for schooling?

It means first of all that all citizens need the essential tools of learn- 15 ing, which are reading and mathematics. Knowing how to read and knowing how numbers are used (and misused) to characterize almost everything are basic necessities for citizens.

Basic skills are necessary, but they are not enough to prepare the citizen.

A citizen of a democratic society must be able to read critically, listen carefully, evaluate competing claims, weigh evidence, and come to a thoughtful judgment. In their hands will be the most important responsibilities of citizenship: choosing our leaders and serving on juries. One determines the fate of our nation and the other determines the fate of other humans.

To come to a thoughtful judgment about political affairs, citizens need a solid grounding in history, economics, and statistics. They will hear candidates make conflicting claims about what history proves and what the economy needs. Citizens need to understand the great issues in American and world history. They should know about Jim Crow, the Progressive movement, Prohibition, the Great Depression, the McCarthy era, the *Brown* decision,[5] the Cold War, and the other events and issues that shaped our world today. They need to understand the measures that have helped or harmed the economy. They need to recognize how conflicts have started and ended. They need to know and understand enough to reach their own judgments about candidates and issues and proposed legislation.

To know the evil and the goodness of which men are capable, they must study history. To know the mechanisms that have been created to protect our rights and freedoms, they must study the Constitution and other founding documents. To learn about the many struggles that others have waged to improve our imperfect democracy, they must study history.

To be prepared for their weighty responsibilities, they need to study government, economics, and civics. These studies teach them how their society functions and how it may be changed. To be prepared to judge issues on the world scene, they need to study world history and world geography to learn about other forms of government and other ways of organizing society than the one that is most familiar to us.

As citizens, our students will be expected to come to judgments about complex scientific issues. They need to understand science and to bring their critical judgment to bear on questions such as global warming, cloning, evolution, the effects of smoking or sugar, regulation of drilling for natural gas and oil, and debates about maintaining clean air and clean water. As candidates debate these issues, voters must be informed and ready to make their own judgments. They must know how to research the issues and assess contesting claims. As advocates for industry advance their interests, citizens must be able to weigh their assertions. Their knowledge of science and their understanding of scientific method will prepare them to reach their own judgments in matters of public dispute.

As citizens, our students will be called upon to judge the character of those who seek to persuade them. They will need that judgment when casting a vote, when serving on a jury, when deciding whom to

---

[5]**Jim Crow, the Progressive movement, Prohibition, . . . the McCarthy era, the *Brown* decision:** Jim Crow refers to the period of legally enforced segregation that existed in southern states between 1865 and the civil rights movement; the Progressive movement is the name given to a number of late nineteenth-century social and political efforts that fought against social problems related to rapid industrialization, such as child labor and public corruption; Prohibition refers to the ban on the production, importation, sale, and consumption of alcoholic beverages in the United States between 1920 and 1933; the Great Depression was a serious, decade-long economic decline that began with the stock market crash of 1929; the McCarthy era refers to the period between 1950 and 1956 when Republican senator Joseph McCarthy led the House Un-American Activities Committee in the public repression of citizens who had been affiliated with the American Communist Party; the *Brown* decision refers to the U.S. Supreme Court's landmark 1954 decision in the case of *Brown v. Board of Education Topeka*, which declared segregated schools unconstitutional.

trust. They will gain insight into character through the study of litera-ture. By reading good and great works of fiction, students learn about character, motivation, kindness, greatness of spirit, imagination, the depths of evil, chicanery, and other aspects of human nature. Literature provides students with the opportunity to experience life through the eyes of other people in other times and other places. Literature, like history, is a superb way to travel through time, to be transported into another world. A good education steps outside the world of textbooks and work sheets and introduces students to worlds that they never dreamed of and to ideas that change their way of thinking. It introduces them to authors who use language imaginatively and beautifully and to cultural experiences that they can enjoy and share.

To function effectively in the world of the twenty-first century, stu-dents should learn a foreign language. They should use their language skills to learn about the culture, literature, history, and arts of other soci-eties. They should broaden their knowledge of the world so that they recognize that other people think differently; by doing so, they may abandon narrow provincialism and get a clearer understanding of other cultures.

All of these studies are important parts of a rich and balanced cur-riculum. They may be taught separately, or they may be taught as inte-grated studies of society. There is no single right way. Teachers are best equipped to judge how to teach, how to inspire young minds with a thirst to learn more.

None of these studies should be subject to budget cuts. They are [25] fundamental ingredients of a liberal education.

All are enriched and enhanced by the arts. The arts are essential for everyone. Life is enhanced by the arts. No student should be denied the opportunity to participate in the arts or to learn about the arts as prac-ticed here and in other cultures. All students should have the chance to sing, dance, draw, and paint in school. They should have the resources for video production and for chorus, band, orchestra, and dramatics. The arts are a source of joy, a means of self-expression and group expression. To master a musical instrument or to participate in choral music requires self-discipline and practice; no one can do it for you. Every school should have the resources to enable students to express their individuality or to take pleasure in joyful communal activity.

The ancients spoke of a healthy mind in a healthy body, and in our time we have forgotten the wisdom of that maxim. Children and adolescents need physical activity. They need recess during the day, to relax and run and shout and play. They need structured play and games where they can learn physical discipline, whether in gymnastics or sports. Their youthful energy should be channeled into track and field, basket-ball, cycling, swimming, volleyball, and other activities.

School provides a place for mental, physical, and ethical develop-ment. Character is taught and learned in many settings: in the classroom, in the hallways, in the lunchroom, and on the sports field. One of the reasons that online schools do not succeed is that children and youths need social interaction to develop the soft skills that are needed in life and work. They must learn the skills of democratic society, the give-and-take of participation in shared activities. They learn together to put on a play, to organize a game, to collaborate on a science project or a mock trial. All of these activities prepare them for life in ways unmeasured by standardized tests. These skills of interaction cannot be learned on a computer. They are learned together with others in shared tasks.

For the past two decades, even before No Child Left Behind, the U.S. educational system has had an unhealthy focus on testing and accountability—unhealthy because it has driven public policy to concentrate on standardized tests of uneven quality at the expense of the more important goals of education, like character and love of learning. Sadly, the growing obsession with data has shoved aside these important goals. Consequently, children are tested again and again, compelled to select a box on a multiple-choice test, which is then turned into a definitive judgment about their value and their intelligence. Today, we accord to standardized test scores the same power that was once granted to intelligence tests. They are taken to be a measure of the worth of boys and girls and ultimately a measure of their teachers as well.

Anyone who truly cares about children must be repelled by the 30 insistence on ranking them, rating them, and labeling them. Whatever the tests measure is not the sum and substance of any child. The tests do not measure character, spirit, heart, soul, potential. When overused and misused, when attached to high stakes, the tests stifle the very creativity and ingenuity that our society needs most. Creativity and ingenuity stubbornly resist standardization. Tests should be used sparingly to help students and teachers, not to allocate rewards and punishments and not to label children and adults by their scores.

We cheat children when we do not give them the chance to learn more than basic skills. We cheat them when we evaluate them by standardized tests. We undervalue them when we turn them into data points.

If we mean to educate them, we must recognize that all children deserve a full liberal arts curriculum. All children need the chance to develop their individual talents. And all need the opportunity to learn the skills of working and playing and singing with others. Whatever the careers of the twenty-first century may be, they are likely to require creativity, thoughtfulness, and the capacity for social interaction and personal initiative, not simply routine skills. All children need to be prepared as citizens to participate in a democratic society. A democratic society cannot afford to limit the skills and knowledge of a liberal education only to children of privilege and good fortune.

ENGAGING THE TEXT

1. What, according to Ravitch, do affluent parents expect from schools? To what extent did the schools you attended provide these features? How many hours per week, for example, did you spend on art, music, drama, science labs, advanced courses, and extracurricular activities when you were in middle school and high school?

2. Why might students and parents be concerned about the government collecting and tracking student school achievement data throughout their educational careers? How might the cloud-based learning databank Ravitch describes be abused by colleges, future employers, and others?

3. What, according to Ravitch, was the purpose of public education when it emerged during the nineteenth century? In Ravitch's opinion, how do policy makers see the purpose of public education today? Should schools do more than offer students preparation for college or work-force training? Why or why not?

4. How well did your own K–12 education prepare you to "assume the rights and responsibilities of citizenship in a democracy"? Did you study topics like world history, geography, global warming, cloning, evolution, and the regulation of gas and oil? To what extent were you exposed to "new worlds" or new ideas that challenged your way of thinking?

5. How could you explain why "the richest nation in the world" can't provide all students with a full curriculum or why states cut education budgets while spending "hundreds of millions" on standardized tests?

6. **Thinking Rhetorically** Ravitch makes a number of critical assumptions about what "educated parents" expect from schools (para. 8) and about the original purposes of public schooling (para. 5). How accurate are these assumptions in your view? Does she need to substantiate these claims?

EXPLORING CONNECTIONS

7. Review the cartoon "21st Century Public Education" that appears on page 135. Freewrite for a few minutes about what the student in this cartoon is probably thinking. Then share your ideas in class. What sorts of things would he be doing if he attended the kind of public school Ravitch might design?

8. What concerns might Lori Andrews (p. 322) raise about the creation of extensive cloud-based data warehouses dedicated to tracking achievement test scores during a student's entire educational career? How might such information be misused by colleges, employers, law enforcement, and other institutions?

EXTENDING THE CRITICAL CONTEXT

9. Do some research to learn more about No Child Left Behind, Race to the Top, the Common Core, and other educational reform initiatives. How effective do these reform efforts appear to have been? Would you agree with Ravitch that the U.S. educational system places too much emphasis on standardized testing

and accountability? If real learning can't be measured by standardized tests, as Ravitch claims, how should it be measured?

10. As Ravitch suggests, go online to explore the academic and extracurricular offerings of elite private schools like Sidwell Friends, Lakeside School, Deerfield Academy, and Philips Academy. How do the opportunities provided by these schools compare with your own experiences in high school?

AGAINST SCHOOL

JOHN TAYLOR GATTO

The official mission statements of most American schools brim with good intentions. On paper, schools exist to help students realize their full potential, to equip them with the skills they'll need to achieve success and contribute to society, or to foster the development of independence, critical thinking, and strong ethical values. But as John Taylor Gatto (b. 1935) sees it, public schools actually exist to fulfill six covert functions meant to "cripple our kids." The frightening thing is that Gatto might know what he's talking about. An award-winning educator and ardent libertarian, Gatto has taught in New York public schools for more than two decades. In 1989, 1990, and 1991, he was named New York City Teacher of the Year, and in 1991 he was also honored as New York State Teacher of the Year. His publications include *Dumbing Us Down: The Hidden Curriculum of Compulsory Schooling* (1992), *A Different Kind of Teacher* (2000), *The Underground History of American Education* (2001), and *Weapons of Mass Instruction: A Schoolteacher's Journey through the Dark World of Compulsory Schooling* (2008). This selection originally appeared in *Harper's* magazine in 2003.

I TAUGHT FOR THIRTY YEARS in some of the worst schools in Manhattan, and in some of the best, and during that time I became an expert in boredom. Boredom was everywhere in my world, and if you asked the kids, as I often did, why they felt so bored, they always gave the same answers: They said the work was stupid, that it made no sense, that they already knew it. They said they wanted to be doing something real, not just sitting around. They said teachers didn't seem to know much about their subjects and clearly weren't interested in learning more. And the kids were right: their teachers were every bit as bored as they were.

Boredom is the common condition of schoolteachers, and anyone who has spent time in a teachers' lounge can vouch for the low energy, the whining, the dispirited attitudes, to be found there. When asked why *they* feel bored, the teachers tend to blame the kids, as you might expect. Who wouldn't get bored teaching students who are rude and interested only in grades? If even that. Of course, teachers are themselves products of the same twelve-year compulsory school programs that so thoroughly bore their students, and as school personnel they are trapped inside structures even more rigid than those imposed upon the children. Who, then, is to blame?

We all are. My grandfather taught me that. One afternoon when I was seven I complained to him of boredom, and he batted me hard on the head. He told me that I was never to use that term in his presence again, that if I was bored it was my fault and no one else's. The obligation to amuse and instruct myself was entirely my own, and people who didn't know that were childish people, to be avoided if possible. Certainly not to be trusted. That episode cured me of boredom forever, and here and there over the years I was able to pass on the lesson to some remarkable student. For the most part, however, I found it futile to challenge the official notion that boredom and childishness were the natural state of affairs in the classroom. Often I had to defy custom, and even bend the law, to help kids break out of this trap.

The empire struck back, of course; childish adults regularly conflate opposition with disloyalty. I once returned from a medical leave to discover that all evidence of my having been granted the leave had been purposely destroyed, that my job had been terminated, and that I no longer possessed even a teaching license. After nine months of tormented effort I was able to retrieve the license when a school secretary testified to witnessing the plot unfold. In the meantime my family suffered more than I care to remember. By the time I finally retired in 1991, I had more than enough reason to think of our schools—with their long-term, cell-block-style, forced confinement of both students and teachers—as virtual factories of childishness. Yet I honestly could not see *why* they had to be that way. My own experience had revealed to me what many other teachers must learn along the way, too, yet keep to themselves for fear of reprisal: if we wanted to we could easily and inexpensively jettison the old, stupid structures and help kids *take* an education rather than merely *receive* a schooling. We could encourage the best qualities of youthfulness—curiosity, adventure, resilience, the capacity for surprising insight—simply by being more flexible about time, texts, and tests, by introducing kids to truly competent adults, and by giving each student what autonomy he or she needs in order to take a risk every now and then.

But we don't do that. And the more I asked why not, and persisted in thinking about the "problem" of schooling as an engineer might, the more I missed the point: What if there is no "problem" with our schools? What if they are the way they are, so expensively flying in the face of common sense and long experience in how children learn things, not because they are doing something wrong but because they are doing something right?

5

Is it possible that George W. Bush accidentally spoke the truth when he said we would "leave no child behind"? Could it be that our schools are designed to make sure not one of them ever really grows up?

Do we really need school? I don't mean education, just forced schooling: six classes a day, five days a week, nine months a year, for twelve years. Is this deadly routine really necessary? And if so, for what? Don't hide behind reading, writing, and arithmetic as a rationale, because 2 million happy homeschoolers have surely put that banal justification to rest. Even if they hadn't, a considerable number of well-known Americans never went through the twelve-year wringer our kids currently go through, and they turned out all right. George Washington, Benjamin Franklin, Thomas Jefferson, Abraham Lincoln? Someone taught them, to be sure, but they were not products of a school *system,* and not one of them was ever "graduated" from a secondary school. Throughout most of American history, kids generally didn't go to high school, yet the unschooled rose to be admirals, like Farragut;[1] inventors, like Edison; captains of industry, like Carnegie[2] and Rockefeller;[3] writers, like Melville and Twain and Conrad;[4] and even scholars, like Margaret Mead.[5] In fact, until pretty recently people who reached the age of thirteen weren't looked upon as children at all. Ariel Durant, who cowrote an enormous, and very good, multivolume history of the world with her husband, Will, was happily married at fifteen, and who could reasonably claim that Ariel Durant[6] was an uneducated person? Unschooled, perhaps, but not uneducated.

We have been taught (that is, schooled) in this country to think of "success" as synonymous with, or at least dependent upon, "schooling," but historically that isn't true in either an intellectual or a financial sense. And plenty of people throughout the world today find a way to educate themselves without resorting to a system of compulsory secondary schools that all too often resemble prisons. Why, then, do Americans confuse education with just such a system? What exactly is the purpose of our public schools?

[1] **Farragut:** Admiral David Glasgow Farragut (1801–1870), American naval officer who won several important victories for the North in the Civil War, including the capture of the port of New Orleans in 1862. [All notes are the editors'.]

[2] **Carnegie:** Andrew Carnegie (1835–1919), American businessman and philanthropist who made his enormous fortune in the steel industry.

[3] **Rockefeller:** John D. Rockefeller (1839–1937), American industrialist who founded Standard Oil and who was for a time the richest man in the world.

[4] **Melville and Twain and Conrad:** Herman Melville (1819–1891), American novelist best known as the author of *Moby-Dick* (1851); Mark Twain, the pen name of American writer Samuel Langhorne Clemens (1835–1910), author of *Adventures of Huckleberry Finn* (1884); and Polish-born writer Joseph Conrad (1857–1924), best known for the novella "Heart of Darkness" (1899).

[5] **Margaret Mead:** American anthropologist (1901–1978) and author of the groundbreaking book *Coming of Age in Samoa* (1928).

[6] **Ariel Durant:** With husband Will (1885–1981), Ariel (1898–1981) won the Pulitzer Prize for literature for volume ten of their eleven-volume *The Story of Civilization,* published from 1935 to 1975.

Mass schooling of a compulsory nature really got its teeth into the United States between 1905 and 1915, though it was conceived of much earlier and pushed for throughout most of the nineteenth century. The reason given for this enormous upheaval of family life and cultural traditions was, roughly speaking, threefold:

1. To make good people.

2. To make good citizens.

3. To make each person his or her personal best.

These goals are still trotted out today on a regular basis, and most of us accept them in one form or another as a decent definition of public education's mission, however short schools actually fall in achieving them. But we are dead wrong. Compounding our error is the fact that the national literature holds numerous and surprisingly consistent statements of compulsory schooling's true purpose. We have, for example, the great H. L. Mencken,[7] who wrote in *The American Mercury* for April 1924 that the aim of public education is not

> to fill the young of the species with knowledge and awaken their intelligence....Nothing could be further from the truth. The aim...is simply to reduce as many individuals as possible to the same safe level, to breed and train a standardized citizenry, to put down dissent and originality. That is its aim in the United States...and that is its aim everywhere else.

Because of Mencken's reputation as a satirist, we might be tempted to dismiss this passage as a bit of hyperbolic sarcasm. His article, however, goes on to trace the template for our own educational system back to the now vanished, though never to be forgotten, military state of Prussia. And although he was certainly aware of the irony that we had recently been at war with Germany, the heir to Prussian thought and culture, Mencken was being perfectly serious here. Our educational system really is Prussian in origin, and that really is cause for concern.

The odd fact of a Prussian provenance for our schools pops up again and again once you know to look for it. William James[8] alluded to it many times at the turn of the century. Orestes Brownson,[9] the hero of Christopher Lasch's[10] 1991 book, *The True and Only Heaven*, was publicly denouncing the Prussianization of American schools back in the 1840s. Horace Mann's[11] "Seventh Annual Report" to the Massachusetts State Board of Education in 1843 is essentially a paean to the land of

---

[7] **H. L. Mencken:** American social critic and commentator known for his satiric wit (1880–1956).

[8] **William James:** American psychologist and philosopher (1842–1910).

[9] **Orestes Brownson:** American philosopher and essayist (1803–1876).

[10] **Christopher Lasch:** American historian and social critic (1932–1994), probably best known for *The Culture of Narcissism: American Life in an Age of Diminished Expectations* (1979) and *The Revolt of the Elites: And the Betrayal of Democracy* (1994).

[11] **Horace Mann:** U.S. politician and Secretary of the Massachusetts State Board of Education from 1837 to 1847.

Frederick the Great[12] and a call for its schooling to be brought here. That Prussian culture loomed large in America is hardly surprising given our early association with that utopian state. A Prussian served as Washington's aide during the Revolutionary War, and so many German-speaking people had settled here by 1795 that Congress considered publishing a German-language edition of the federal laws. But what shocks is that we should so eagerly have adopted one of the very worst aspects of Prussian culture: an educational system deliberately designed to produce mediocre intellects, to hamstring the inner life, to deny students appreciable leadership skills, and to ensure docile and incomplete citizens—all in order to render the populace "manageable."

It was from James Bryant Conant—president of Harvard for twenty years, World War I poison-gas specialist, World War II executive on the atomic-bomb project, high commissioner of the American zone in Germany after World War II, and truly one of the most influential figures of the twentieth century—that I first got wind of the real purposes of American schooling. Without Conant, we would probably not have the same style and degree of standardized testing that we enjoy today, nor would we be blessed with gargantuan high schools that warehouse 2,000 to 4,000 students at a time, like the famous Columbine High[13] in Littleton, Colorado. Shortly after I retired from teaching I picked up Conant's 1959 book-length essay, *The Child, the Parent, and the State*, and was more than a little intrigued to see him mention in passing that the modern schools we attend were the result of a "revolution" engineered between 1905 and 1930. A revolution? He declines to elaborate, but he does direct the curious and the uninformed to Alexander Inglis's 1918 book, *Principles of Secondary Education*, in which "one saw this revolution through the eyes of a revolutionary."

Inglis, for whom a lecture in education at Harvard is named, makes it perfectly clear that compulsory schooling on this continent was intended to be just what it had been for Prussia in the 1820s: a fifth column[14] into the burgeoning democratic movement that threatened to give the peasants and the proletarians a voice at the bargaining table. Modern, industrialized, compulsory schooling was to make a sort of surgical incision into the prospective unity of these underclasses. Divide children by subject, by age-grading, by constant rankings on tests, and by many other more subtle means, and it was unlikely that the ignorant mass of mankind, separated in childhood, would ever re-integrate into a dangerous whole.

Inglis breaks down the purpose—the *actual* purpose—of modern schooling into six basic functions, any one of which is enough to curl

---

[12] **Frederick the Great:** King of Prussia (now part of present-day Germany), who reigned from 1740 to 1786.

[13] **Columbine High:** Site of April 20, 1999, massacre by students Eric Harris and Dylan Klebold, who killed twelve and wounded twenty-four others before killing themselves.

[14] **a fifth column:** Secret group of infiltrators who undermine a nation's defenses.

the hair of those innocent enough to believe the three traditional goals listed earlier:

1. The *adjustive* or *adaptive* function. Schools are to establish fixed habits of reaction to authority. This, of course, precludes critical judgment completely. It also pretty much destroys the idea that useful or interesting material should be taught, because you can't test for *reflexive* obedience until you know whether you can make kids learn, and do, foolish and boring things.

2. The *integrating* function. This might well be called "the conformity function," because its intention is to make children as alike as possible. People who conform are predictable, and this is of great use to those who wish to harness and manipulate a large labor force.

3. The *diagnostic and directive* function. School is meant to determine each student's proper social role. This is done by logging evidence mathematically and anecdotally on cumulative records. As in "your permanent record." Yes, you do have one.

4. The *differentiating* function. Once their social role has been "diagnosed," children are to be sorted by role and trained only so far as their destination in the social machine merits — and not one step further. So much for making kids their personal best.

5. The *selective* function. This refers not to human choice at all but to Darwin's theory of natural selection as applied to what he called "the favored races." In short, the idea is to help things along by consciously attempting to improve the breeding stock. Schools are meant to tag the unfit — with poor grades, remedial placement, and other punishments — clearly enough that their peers will accept them as inferior and effectively bar them from the reproductive sweepstakes. That's what all those little humiliations from first grade onward were intended to do: wash the dirt down the drain.

6. The *propaedeutic* function. The societal system implied by these rules will require an elite group of caretakers. To that end, a small fraction of the kids will quietly be taught how to manage this continuing project, how to watch over and control a population deliberately dumbed down and declawed in order that government might proceed unchallenged and corporations might never want for obedient labor.

That, unfortunately, is the purpose of mandatory public education in this country. And lest you take Inglis for an isolated crank with a rather too cynical take on the educational enterprise, you should know that he was hardly alone in championing these ideas. Conant himself, building on the ideas of Horace Mann and others, campaigned tirelessly for an American school system designed along the same lines. Men like George Peabody, who funded the cause of mandatory schooling throughout the South, surely understood that the Prussian system was useful in creating not only a harmless electorate and a servile labor force but also a virtual herd of mindless consumers. In time a great number of industrial titans came to recognize the enormous profits to be had by cultivating and tending just such a herd via public education, among them Andrew Carnegie and John D. Rockefeller.

There you have it. Now you know. We don't need Karl Marx's conception of a grand warfare between the classes to see that it is in the interest of complex management, economic or political, to dumb people down, to demoralize them, to divide them from one another, and to discard them if they don't conform. Class may frame the proposition, as when Woodrow Wilson, then president of Princeton University, said the following to the New York City School Teachers Association in 1909: "We want one class of persons to have a liberal education, and we want another class of persons, a very much larger class, of necessity, in every society, to forgo the privileges of a liberal education and fit themselves to perform specific difficult manual tasks." But the motives behind the disgusting decisions that bring about these ends need not be class-based at all. They can stem purely from fear, or from the by now familiar belief that "efficiency" is the paramount virtue, rather than love, liberty, laughter, or hope. Above all, they can stem from simple greed.

There were vast fortunes to be made, after all, in an economy based on mass production and organized to favor the large corporation rather than the small business or the family farm. But mass production required mass consumption, and at the turn of the twentieth century most Americans considered it both unnatural and unwise to buy things they didn't actually need. Mandatory schooling was a godsend on that count. School didn't have to train kids in any direct sense to think they should consume nonstop, because it did something even better: it encouraged them not to think at all. And that left them sitting ducks for another great invention of the modern era—marketing.

Now, you needn't have studied marketing to know that there are two groups of people who can always be convinced to consume more than they need to: addicts and children. School has done a pretty good job of turning our children into addicts, but it has done a spectacular job of turning our children into children. Again, this is no accident. Theorists from Plato to Rousseau[15] to our own Dr. Inglis knew that if children could be cloistered with other children, stripped of responsibility and independence, encouraged to develop only the trivializing emotions of greed, envy, jealousy, and fear, they would grow older but never truly grow up. In the 1934 edition of his once well-known book *Public Education in the United States,* Ellwood P. Cubberley detailed and praised the way the strategy of successive school enlargements had extended childhood by two to six years, and forced schooling was at that point still quite new. This same Cubberley—who was dean of Stanford's School

---

[15]**Plato to Rousseau:** Plato (c. 427–c. 347 B.C.E.), extraordinarily influential Greek philosopher. Jean-Jacques Rousseau, Swiss philosopher and writer (1712–1778).

of Education, a textbook editor at Houghton Mifflin, and Conant's friend and correspondent at Harvard—had written the following in the 1922 edition of his book *Public School Administration:* "Our schools are...factories in which the raw products (children) are to be shaped and fashioned.... And it is the business of the school to build its pupils according to the specifications laid down."

It's perfectly obvious from our society today what those specifications were. Maturity has by now been banished from nearly every aspect of our lives. Easy divorce laws have removed the need to work at relationships; easy credit has removed the need for fiscal self-control; easy entertainment has removed the need to learn to entertain oneself; easy answers have removed the need to ask questions. We have become a nation of children, happy to surrender our judgments and our wills to political exhortations and commercial blandishments that would insult actual adults. We buy televisions, and then we buy the things we see on the television. We buy computers, and then we buy the things we see on the computer. We buy $150 sneakers whether we need them or not, and when they fall apart too soon we buy another pair. We drive SUVs and believe the lie that they constitute a kind of life insurance, even when we're upside-down in them. And, worst of all, we don't bat an eye when Ari Fleischer[16] tells us to "be careful what you say," even if we remember having been told somewhere back in school that America is the land of the free. We simply buy that one too. Our schooling, as intended, has seen to it.

Now for the good news. Once you understand the logic behind modern schooling, its tricks and traps are fairly easy to avoid. School trains children to be employees and consumers; teach your own to be leaders and adventurers. School trains children to obey reflexively; teach your own to think critically and independently. Well-schooled kids have a low threshold for boredom; help your own to develop an inner life so that they'll never be bored. Urge them to take on the serious material, the *grown-up* material, in history, literature, philosophy, music, art, economics, theology—all the stuff schoolteachers know well enough to avoid. Challenge your kids with plenty of solitude so that they can learn to enjoy their own company, to conduct inner dialogues. Well-schooled people are conditioned to dread being alone, and they seek constant companionship through the TV, the computer, the cell phone, and through shallow friendships quickly acquired and quickly abandoned. Your children should have a more meaningful life, and they can.

First, though, we must wake up to what our schools really are: laboratories of experimentation on young minds, drill centers for the habits and attitudes that corporate society demands. Mandatory education serves children only incidentally; its real purpose is to turn them into servants. Don't let your own have their childhoods extended, not even

20

---

[16] **Ari Fleischer:** Press secretary for George W. Bush from 2001 to 2003 (b. 1960).

for a day. If David Farragut could take command of a captured British warship as a preteen, if Thomas Edison could publish a broadsheet at the age of twelve, if Ben Franklin could apprentice himself to a printer at the same age (then put himself through a course of study that would choke a Yale senior today), there's no telling what your own kids could do. After a long life, and thirty years in the public school trenches, I've concluded that genius is as common as dirt. We suppress our genius only because we haven't yet figured out how to manage a population of educated men and women. The solution, I think, is simple and glorious. Let them manage themselves.

ENGAGING THE TEXT

1. Why does Gatto think that school is boring and childish? How does Gatto's depiction of school compare with your own elementary and secondary school experience?

2. What, according to Gatto, are the six unstated purposes of public schooling? To what extent does your own prior educational experience support this bleak view of American education?

3. To what extent would you agree that we really don't need to go to school? Given the current state of technology and a globalizing economy, do you think most people would gain the abilities they need to survive and thrive through homeschooling?

4. How would you go about teaching your own children to be "leaders and adventurers," to think "critically and independently," and to "develop an inner life so that they'll never be bored" (para. 19)? How many parents, in your estimation, have the time, experience, and resources to make Gatto's ideal education a reality?

5. **Thinking Rhetorically** When does Gatto introduce his thesis in this essay, and why does he postpone it so long? What kinds of evidence does he offer to support his thesis, and how effective is this support? For example, how persuasive are his allusions to the Prussian approach to education or the influence of James Conant and Alexander Inglis? What other types of evidence could he have used to support his critique of American education?

EXPLORING CONNECTIONS

6. Review the Calvin and Hobbes cartoon on page 123. What does Bill Waterson seem to be saying about the effects of schooling? To what extent does Calvin appear to confirm or challenge Gatto's bleak assessment of what school does to students? Did your own education turn you into a "mindless consumer," "a servant," a Calvin, or a critical thinker and adventurer? How?

7. Compare Gatto's view of the state and purpose of public school with that of Diane Ravitch (p. 105). To what extent do Gatto and Ravitch appear to agree on the limitations of the current educational system and on the purposes of a genuine education?

8. Look ahead to Jean Anyon's excerpt from *Social Class and the Hidden Curriculum of Work* (p. 136) and compare Anyon's analysis of the real agenda of American public education with that described by Gatto. To what extent does Anyon's class-based analysis of education in America support Gatto's description of the unspoken purposes of public schooling?

EXTENDING THE CRITICAL CONTEXT

9. Working in groups, write a proposal for a school that wouldn't be boring or childish and that would create the kind of independent, critical, active thinkers that Gatto prizes. What would a day in such a school be like? What would the students do? What would they learn? Who would teach them?

10. Research the state of Prussia and Frederick the Great to learn more about Prussian history and culture. How might your findings change your response to Gatto's argument? Would you agree that the Prussian influence on American schooling is really a "cause for concern"? Why? What other nineteenth-century nation might have offered a better model?

"I JUST WANNA BE AVERAGE"

MIKE ROSE

Mike Rose is anything but average: he has published poetry, scholarly research, a textbook, and several widely praised books on education in America. A professor in the UCLA Graduate School of Education and Information Studies, Rose (b. 1944) has won awards from the National Academy of Education, the National Council of Teachers of English, and the John Simon Guggenheim Memorial Foundation. Below you'll read the story of how this highly successful teacher and writer started high school in the vocational education track, learning dead-end skills from

teachers who were often underprepared or incompetent. Rose shows that students whom the system has written off can have tremendous unrealized potential, and his critique of the school system specifies several reasons for the failure of students who go through high school belligerent, fearful, stoned, frustrated, or just plain bored. This selection comes from *Lives on the Boundary* (1989), Rose's exploration of America's educationally under-privileged. His publications also include *Possible Lives* (1996), an explana-tion of nationwide educational innovation; *The Mind at Work* (2006), a study of the complex thinking involved in common labor; *Back to School: Why Everyone Deserves a Second Chance at Education* (2012); and, with Michael B. Katz, *Public Education Under Siege* (2013).

IT TOOK TWO BUSES TO GET TO Our Lady of Mercy. The first started deep in South Los Angeles and caught me at midpoint. The second drifted through neighborhoods with trees, parks, big lawns, and lots of flowers. The rides were long but were livened up by a group of South L.A. veterans whose parents also thought that Hope had set up shop in the west end of the county. There was Christy Biggars, who, at sixteen, was dealing and was, according to rumor, a pimp as well. There were Bill Cobb and Johnny Gonzales, grease-pencil artists extraordinaire, who left Nembutal-enhanced[1] swirls of "Cobb" and "Johnny" on the corrugated walls of the bus. And then there was Tyrrell Wilson. Tyr-rell was the coolest kid I knew. He ran the dozens[2] like a metric half-back, laid down a rap that outrhymed and outpointed Cobb, whose rap was good but not great—the curse of a moderately soulful kid trapped in white skin. But it was Cobb who would sneak a radio onto the bus, and thus underwrote his patter with Little Richard, Fats Domino, Chuck Berry, the Coasters, and Ernie K. Doe's[3] mother-in-law, an awful woman who was "sent from down below." And so it was that Christy and Cobb and Johnny G. and Tyrrell and I and assorted others picked up along the way passed our days in the back of the bus, a funny mix brought together by geography and parental desire.

Entrance to school brings with it forms and releases and assessments. Mercy relied on a series of tests, mostly the Stanford-Binet,[4] for place-ment, and somehow the results of my tests got confused with those of another student named Rose. The other Rose apparently didn't do very well, for I was placed in the vocational track, a euphemism for the bottom level. Neither I nor my parents realized what this meant. We had no sense that Business Math, Typing, and English-Level D were dead ends. The

---

[1] **Nembutal:** Trade name for pentobarbital, a sedative drug. [All notes are the editors'.]
[2] **the dozens:** A verbal game of African origin in which competitors try to top each other's insults.
[3] **Little Richard, Fats Domino, Chuck Berry, the Coasters, and Ernie K. Doe:** Popular black musicians of the 1950s.
[4] **Stanford-Binet:** An IQ test.

current spate of reports on the schools criticizes parents for not involving themselves in the education of their children. But how would someone like Tommy Rose, with his two years of Italian schooling, know what to ask? And what sort of pressure could an exhausted waitress apply? The error went undetected, and I remained in the vocational track for two years. What a place.

My homeroom was supervised by Brother Dill, a troubled and unstable man who also taught freshman English. When his class drifted away from him, which was often, his voice would rise in paranoid accusations, and occasionally he would lose control and shake or smack us. I hadn't been there two months when one of his brisk, face-turning slaps had my glasses sliding down the aisle. Physical education was also pretty harsh. Our teacher was a stubby ex-lineman who had played old-time pro ball in the Midwest. He routinely had us grabbing our ankles to receive his stinging paddle across our butts. He did that, he said, to make men of us. "Rose," he bellowed on our first encounter; me standing geeky in line in my baggy shorts. " 'Rose'? What the hell kind of name is that?"

"Italian, sir," I squeaked.

"Italian! Ho. Rose, do you know the sound a bag of shit makes   5
when it hits the wall?"

"No, sir."

"Wop!"[5]

Sophomore English was taught by Mr. Mitropetros. He was a large, bejeweled man who managed the parking lot at the Shrine Auditorium. He would crow and preen and list for us the stars he'd brushed against. We'd ask questions and glance knowingly and snicker, and all that fueled the poor guy to brag some more. Parking cars was his night job. He had little training in English, so his lesson plan for his day work had us reading the district's required text, *Julius Caesar,* aloud for the semester. We'd finished the play way before the twenty weeks was up, so he'd have us switch parts again and again and start again: Dave Snyder, the fastest guy at Mercy, muscling through Caesar to the breathless squeals of Calpurnia, as interpreted by Steve Fusco, a surfer who owned the school's most envied paneled wagon. Week ten and Dave and Steve would take on new roles, as would we all, and render a water-logged Cassius and a Brutus that are beyond my powers of description.

Spanish I—taken in the second year—fell into the hands of a new recruit. Mr. Montez was a tiny man, slight, five foot six at the most, soft-spoken and delicate. Spanish was a particularly rowdy class, and Mr. Montez was as prepared for it as a doily maker at a hammer throw. He would tap his pencil to a room in which Steve Fusco was propelling spitballs from his heavy lips, in which Mike Dweetz was taunting Billy Hawk, a half-Indian, half-Spanish, reed-thin, quietly explosive boy. The vocational track at Our Lady of Mercy mixed kids traveling in from South

[5] **Wop:** Derogatory term for Italian.

L.A. with South Bay surfers and a few Slavs and Chicanos from the harbors of San Pedro. This was a dangerous miscellany: surfers and hodads[6] and South-Central blacks all ablaze to the metronomic tapping of Hector Montez's pencil.

One day Billy lost it. Out of the corner of my eye I saw him strike   10 out with his right arm and catch Dweetz across the neck. Quick as a spasm, Dweetz was out of his seat, scattering desks, cracking Billy on the side of the head, right behind the eye. Snyder and Fusco and others broke it up, but the room felt hot and close and naked. Mr. Montez's tenuous authority was finally ripped to shreds, and I think everyone felt a little strange about that. The charade was over, and when it came down to it, I don't think any of the kids really wanted it to end this way. They had pushed and pushed and bullied their way into a freedom that both scared and embarrassed them.

Students will float to the mark you set. I and the others in the vocational classes were bobbing in pretty shallow water. Vocational education has aimed at increasing the economic opportunities of students who do not do well in our schools. Some serious programs succeed in doing that, and through exceptional teachers—like Mr. Gross in *Horace's Compromise*[7]—students learn to develop hypotheses and troubleshoot, reason through a problem, and communicate effectively—the true job skills. The vocational track, however, is most often a place for those who are just not making it, a dumping ground for the disaffected. There were a few teachers who worked hard at education; young Brother Slattery, for example, combined a stern voice with weekly quizzes to try to pass along to us a skeletal outline of world history. But mostly the teachers had no idea of how to engage the imaginations of us kids who were scuttling along at the bottom of the pond.

And the teachers would have needed some inventiveness, for none of us was groomed for the classroom. It wasn't just that I didn't know things—didn't know how to simplify algebraic fractions, couldn't identify different kinds of clauses, bungled Spanish translations—but that I had developed various faulty and inadequate ways of doing algebra and making sense of Spanish. Worse yet, the years of defensive tuning out in elementary school had given me a way to escape quickly while seeming at least half alert. During my time in Voc. Ed., I developed further into a mediocre student and a somnambulant problem solver, and that affected the subjects I did have the wherewithal to handle: I detested Shakespeare; I got bored with history. My attention flitted here and there. I fooled around in class and read my books indifferently—the intellectual equivalent of playing with your food. I did what I had to do to get by, and I did it with half a mind.

But I did learn things about people and eventually came into my own socially. I liked the guys in Voc. Ed. Growing up where I did, I understood

---

[6] **hodads:** Nonsurfers.
[7] ***Horace's Compromise:*** A 1984 book on American education by Theodore Sizer.

and admired physical prowess, and there was an abundance of muscle here. There was Dave Snyder, a sprinter and halfback of true quality. Dave's ability and his quick wit gave him a natural appeal, and he was welcome in any clique, though he always kept a little independent. He enjoyed acting the fool and could care less about studies, but he possessed a certain maturity and never caused the faculty much trouble. It was a testament to his independence that he included me among his friends—I eventually went out for track, but I was no jock. Owing to the Latin alphabet and a dearth of *R*s and *S*s, Snyder sat behind Rose, and we started exchanging one-liners and became friends.

There was Ted Richard, a much-touted Little League pitcher. He was chunky and had a baby face and came to Our Lady of Mercy as a seasoned street fighter. Ted was quick to laugh and he had a loud, jolly laugh, but when he got angry he'd smile a little smile, the kind that simply raises the corner of the mouth a quarter of an inch. For those who knew, it was an eerie signal. Those who didn't found themselves in big trouble, for Ted was very quick. He loved to carry on what we would come to call philosophical discussions: What is courage? Does God exist? He also loved words, enjoyed picking up big ones like *salubrious* and *equivocal* and using them in our conversations—laughing at himself as the word hit a chuckhole rolling off his tongue. Ted didn't do all that well in school—baseball and parties and testing the courage he'd speculated about took up his time. His textbooks were *Argosy* and *Field and Stream,* whatever newspapers he'd find on the bus stop—from the *Daily Worker* to pornography—conversations with uncles or hobos or businessmen he'd meet in a coffee shop, *The Old Man and the Sea.* With hindsight, I can see that Ted was developing into one of those rough-hewn intellectuals whose sources are a mix of the learned and the apocryphal, whose discussions are both assured and sad.

And then there was Ken Harvey. Ken was good-looking in a puffy way and had a full and oily ducktail and was a car enthusiast...a hodad. 15 One day in religion class, he said the sentence that turned out to be one of the most memorable of the hundreds of thousands I heard in those Voc. Ed. years. We were talking about the parable of the talents, about achievement, working hard, doing the best you can do, blah-blah-blah, when the teacher called on the restive Ken Harvey for an opinion. Ken thought about it, but just for a second, and said (with studied, minimal affect), "I just wanna be average." That woke me up. Average? Who wants to be average? Then the athletes chimed in with the clichés that make you want to laryngectomize them, and the exchange became a platitudinous melee. At the time, I thought Ken's assertion was stupid, and I wrote him off. But his sentence has stayed with me all these years, and I think I am finally coming to understand it.

Ken Harvey was gasping for air. School can be a tremendously disorienting place. No matter how bad the school, you're going to encounter notions that don't fit with the assumptions and beliefs that you grew up with—maybe you'll hear these dissonant notions from teachers, maybe from the other students, and maybe you'll read them. You'll also be thrown in with all kinds of kids from all kinds of backgrounds, and that can be unsettling—this is especially true in places of rich ethnic and linguistic mix, like the L.A. basin. You'll see a handful of students far excel you in courses that sound exotic and that are only in the curriculum of the elite: French, physics, trigonometry. And all this is happening while you're trying to shape an identity, your body is changing, and your emotions are running wild. If you're a working-class kid in the vocational track, the options you'll have to deal with this will be constrained in certain ways: you're defined by your school as "slow"; you're placed in a curriculum that isn't designed to liberate you but to occupy you, or, if you're lucky, train you, though the training is for work the society does not esteem; other students are picking up the cues from your school and your curriculum and interacting with you in particular ways. If you're a kid like Ted Richard, you turn your back on all this and let your mind roam where it may. But youngsters like Ted are rare. What Ken and so many others do is protect themselves from such suffocating madness by taking on with a vengeance the identity implied in the vocational track. Reject the confusion and frustration by openly defining yourself as the Common Joe. Champion the average. Rely on your own good sense. Fuck this bullshit. Bullshit, of course, is everything you—and the others—fear is beyond you: books, essays, tests, academic scrambling, complexity, scientific reasoning, philosophical inquiry.

The tragedy is that you have to twist the knife in your own gray matter to make this defense work. You'll have to shut down, have to reject intellectual stimuli or diffuse them with sarcasm, have to cultivate stupidity, have to convert boredom from a malady into a way of confronting the world. Keep your vocabulary simple, act stoned when you're not or act more stoned than you are, flaunt ignorance, materialize your dreams. It is a powerful and effective defense—it neutralizes the insult and the frustration of being a vocational kid and, when perfected, it drives teachers up the wall, a delightful secondary effect. But like all strong magic, it exacts a price.

My own deliverance from the Voc. Ed. world began with sophomore biology. Every student, college prep to vocational, had to take biology, and unlike the other courses, the same person taught all sections. When teaching the vocational group, Brother Clint probably slowed down a bit or omitted a little of the fundamental biochemistry, but he used the same book and more or less the same syllabus across the board. If one class got tough, he could get tougher. He was young and powerful and very handsome, and looks and physical strength were high currency. No one gave him any trouble.

I was pretty bad at the dissecting table, but the lectures and the textbook were interesting: plastic overlays that, with each turned page, peeled away skin, then veins and muscle, then organs, down to the very bones that Brother Clint, pointer in hand, would tap out on our hanging skeleton. Dave Snyder was in big trouble, for the study of life—versus the living of it—was sticking in his craw. We worked out a code for our multiple-choice exams. He'd poke me in the back: once for the answer under *A,* twice for *B,* and so on; and when he'd hit the right one, I'd look up to the ceiling as though I were lost in thought. Poke: cytoplasm. Poke, poke: methane. Poke, poke, poke: William Harvey. Poke, poke, poke, poke: islets of Langerhans. This didn't work out perfectly, but Dave passed the course, and I mastered the dreamy look of a guy on a record jacket. And something else happened. Brother Clint puzzled over this Voc. Ed. kid who was racking up 98s and 99s on his tests. He checked the school's records and discovered the error. He recommended that I begin my junior year in the College Prep program. According to all I've read since, such a shift, as one report put it, is virtually impossible. Kids at that level rarely cross tracks. The telling thing is how chancy both my placement into and exit from Voc. Ed. was; neither I nor my parents had anything to do with it. I lived in one world during spring semester, and when I came back to school in the fall, I was living in another.

Switching to College Prep was a mixed blessing. I was an erratic   20
student. I was undisciplined. And I hadn't caught onto the rules of the game: why work hard in a class that didn't grab my fancy? I was also hopelessly behind in math. Chemistry was hard; toying with my chemistry set years before hadn't prepared me for the chemist's equations. Fortunately, the priest who taught both chemistry and second-year algebra was also the school's athletic director. Membership on the track team covered me; I knew I wouldn't get lower than a C. U.S. history was taught pretty well, and I did okay. But civics was taken over by a football coach who had trouble reading the textbook aloud—and reading aloud was the centerpiece of his pedagogy. College Prep at Mercy was certainly an improvement over the vocational program—at least it carried some status—but the social science curriculum was weak, and the mathematics and physical sciences were simply beyond me. I had a miserable quantitative background and ended up copying some assignments and finessing the rest as best I could. Let me try to explain how it feels to see again and again material you should once have learned but didn't.

You are given a problem. It requires you to simplify algebraic fractions or to multiply expressions containing square roots. You know this is pretty basic material because you've seen it for years. Once a teacher took some time with you, and you learned how to carry out these operations. Simple versions, anyway. But that was a year or two or more in the past, and these are more complex versions, and now you're not sure. And this, you keep telling yourself, is ninth- or even eighth-grade stuff.

Next it's a word problem. This is also old hat. The basic elements are as familiar as story characters: trains speeding so many miles per hour or shadows of buildings angling so many degrees. Maybe you know enough, have sat through enough explanations, to be able to begin setting up the problem: "If one train is going this fast..." or "This shadow is really one line of a triangle..." Then: "Let's see..." "How did Jones do this?" "Hmmmm." "No." "No, that won't work." Your attention wavers. You wonder about other things: a football game, a dance, that cute new checker at the market. You try to focus on the problem again. You scribble on paper for a while, but the tension wins out and your attention flits elsewhere. You crumple the paper and begin daydreaming to ease the frustration.

The particulars will vary, but in essence this is what a number of students go through, especially those in so-called remedial classes. They open their textbooks and see once again the familiar and impenetrable formulas and diagrams and terms that have stumped them for years. There is no excitement here. *No* excitement. Regardless of what the teacher says, this is not a new challenge. There is, rather, embarrassment and frustration and, not surprisingly, some anger in being reminded once again of long-standing inadequacies. No wonder so many students finally attribute their difficulties to something inborn, organic: "That part of my brain just doesn't work." Given the troubling histories many of these students have, it's miraculous that any of them can lift the shroud of hopelessness sufficiently to make deliverance from these classes possible.

Through this entire period, my father's health was deteriorating with cruel momentum. His arteriosclerosis progressed to the point where a simple nick on his shin wouldn't heal. Eventually it ulcerated and widened. Lou Minton would come by daily to change the dressing. We tried renting an oscillating bed—which we placed in the front room—to force blood through the constricted arteries in my father's legs. The bed hummed through the night, moving in place to ward off the inevitable. The ulcer continued to spread, and the doctors finally had to amputate. My grandfather had lost his leg in a stockyard accident. Now my father too was crippled. His convalescence was slow but steady, and the doctors placed him in the Santa Monica Rehabilitation Center, a sun-bleached building that opened out onto the warm spray of the Pacific. The place gave him some strength and some color and some training in walking with an artificial leg. He did pretty well for a year or so until he slipped and broke his hip. He was confined to a wheelchair after that, and the confinement contributed to the diminishing of his body and spirit.

I am holding a picture of him. He is sitting in his wheelchair and 25 smiling at the camera. The smile appears forced, unsteady, seems to quaver, though it is frozen in silver nitrate. He is in his mid-sixties and looks eighty. Late in my junior year, he had a stroke and never came out of the resulting coma. After that, I would see him only in dreams, and to this day that is how I join him. Sometimes the dreams are sad and grisly and primal: my father lying in a bed soaked with his suppuration,[8] holding me, rocking me. But sometimes the dreams bring him back to me healthy: him talking to me on an empty street, or buying some pictures to decorate our old house, or transformed somehow into someone strong and adept with tools and the physical.

Jack MacFarland couldn't have come into my life at a better time. My father was dead, and I had logged up too many years of scholastic indifference. Mr. MacFarland had a master's degree from Columbia and decided, at twenty-six, to find a little school and teach his heart out. He never took any credentialing courses, couldn't bear to, he said, so he had to find employment in a private system. He ended up at Our Lady of Mercy teaching five sections of senior English. He was a beatnik who was born too late. His teeth were stained, he tucked his sorry tie in between the third and fourth buttons of his shirt, and his pants were chronically wrinkled. At first, we couldn't believe this guy, thought he slept in his car. But within no time, he had us so startled with work that we didn't much worry about where he slept or if he slept at all. We wrote three or four essays a month. We read a book every two to three weeks, starting with the *Iliad* and ending up with Hemingway. He gave us a quiz on the reading every other day. He brought a prep school curriculum to Mercy High.

MacFarland's lectures were crafted, and as he delivered them he would pace the room jiggling a piece of chalk in his cupped hand, using it to scribble on the board the names of all the writers and philosophers and plays and novels he was weaving into his discussion. He asked questions often, raised everything from Zeno's paradox to the repeated last line of Frost's "Stopping by Woods on a Snowy Evening." He slowly and carefully built up our knowledge of Western intellectual history — with facts, with connections, with speculations. We learned about Greek philosophy, about Dante, the Elizabethan world view, the Age of Reason, existentialism. He analyzed poems with us, had us reading sections from John Ciardi's *How Does a Poem Mean?*, making a potentially difficult book accessible with his own explanations. We gave oral reports on poems Ciardi didn't cover. We imitated the styles of Conrad, Hemingway, and *Time* magazine. We wrote and talked, wrote and talked. The man immersed us in language.

Even MacFarland's barbs were literary. If Jim Fitzsimmons, hung over and irritable, tried to smart-ass him, he'd rejoin with a flourish that would spark the indomitable Skip Madison — who'd lost his front teeth in a hapless tackle — to flick his tongue through the gap and opine, "good chop," drawing out the single "o" in stinging indictment. Jack Mac-Farland, this tobacco-stained intellectual, brandished linguistic weapons of a kind I hadn't encountered before. Here was this *egghead*, for God's sake, keeping some pretty difficult people in line. And from what

---

[8]**suppuration:** Discharge from wounds.

I heard, Mike Dweetz and Steve Fusco and all the notorious Voc. Ed. crowd settled down as well when MacFarland took the podium. Though a lot of guys groused in the schoolyard, it just seemed that giving trouble to this particular teacher was a silly thing to do. Tomfoolery, not to mention assault, had no place in the world he was trying to create for us, and instinctively everyone knew that. If nothing else, we all recognized MacFarland's considerable intelligence and respected the hours he put into his work. It came to this: the troublemaker would look foolish rather than daring. Even Jim Fitzsimmons was reading *On the Road* and turning his incipient alcoholism to literary ends.

There were some lives that were already beyond Jack MacFarland's ministrations, but mine was not. I started reading again as I hadn't since elementary school. I would go into our gloomy little bedroom or sit at the dinner table while, on the television, Danny McShane was paralyzing Mr. Moto with the atomic drop, and work slowly back through *Heart of Darkness*, trying to catch the words in Conrad's sentences. I certainly was not MacFarland's best student; most of the other guys in College Prep, even my fellow slackers, had better backgrounds than I did. But I worked very hard, for MacFarland had hooked me. He tapped my old interest in reading and creating stories. He gave me a way to feel special by using my mind. And he provided a role model that wasn't shaped on physical prowess alone, and something inside me that I wasn't quite aware of responded to that. Jack MacFarland established a literacy club, to borrow a phrase of Frank Smith's, and invited me — invited all of us — to join.

There's been a good deal of research and speculation suggesting that the acknowledgment of school performance with extrinsic rewards — smiling faces, stars, numbers, grades — diminishes the intrinsic satisfaction children experience by engaging in reading or writing or problem solving. While it's certainly true that we've created an educational system that encourages our best and brightest to become cynical grade collectors and, in general, have developed an obsession with evaluation and assessment, I must tell you that venal though it may have been, I loved getting good grades from MacFarland. I now know how subjective grades can be, but then they came tucked in the back of essays like bits of scientific data, some sort of spectroscopic readout that said, objectively and publicly, that I had made something of value. I suppose I'd been mediocre for too long and enjoyed a public redefinition. And I suppose the workings of my mind, such as they were, had been private for too long. My linguistic play moved into the world; ... these papers with their circled, red B-pluses and A-minuses linked my mind to something outside it. I carried them around like a club emblem.

One day in the December of my senior year, Mr. MacFarland asked me where I was going to go to college. I hadn't thought much about it. Many of the students I teach today spent their last year in high school with a physics text in one hand and the Stanford catalog in the other, but I wasn't even aware of what "entrance requirements" were. My folks would say that they wanted me to go to college and be a doctor, but I don't know how seriously I ever took that; it seemed a sweet thing to say, a bit of supportive family chatter, like telling a gangly daughter she's graceful. The reality of higher education wasn't in my scheme of things: no one in the family had gone to college; only two of my uncles had completed high school. I figured I'd get a night job and go to the local junior college because I knew that Snyder and Company were going there to play ball. But I hadn't even prepared for that. When I finally said, "I don't know," MacFarland looked down at me—I was seated in his office—and said, "Listen, you can write."

My grades stank. I had A's in biology and a handful of B's in a few English and social science classes. All the rest were C's—or worse. MacFarland said I would do well in his class and laid down the law about doing well in the others. Still, the record for my first three years wouldn't have been acceptable to any four-year school. To nobody's surprise, I was turned down flat by USC and UCLA. But Jack MacFarland was on the case. He had received his bachelor's degree from Loyola University, so he made calls to old professors and talked to somebody in admissions and wrote me a strong letter. Loyola finally accepted me as a probationary student. I would be on trial for the first year, and if I did okay, I would be granted regular status. MacFarland also intervened to get me a loan, for I could never have afforded a private college without it. Four more years of religion classes and four more years of boys at one school, girls at another. But at least I was going to college. Amazing.

In my last semester of high school, I elected a special English course fashioned by Mr. MacFarland, and it was through this elective that there arose at Mercy a fledgling literati. Art Mitz, the editor of the school newspaper and a very smart guy, was the kingpin. He was joined by me and by Mark Dever, a quiet boy who wrote beautifully and who would die before he was forty. MacFarland occasionally invited us to his apartment, and those visits became the high point of our apprenticeship: we'd clamp on our training wheels and drive to his salon.

He lived in a cramped and cluttered place near the airport, tucked away in the kind of building that architectural critic Reyner Banham calls a *dingbat*. Books were all over: stacked, piled, tossed, and crated, underlined and dog eared, well worn and new. Cigarette ashes crusted with coffee in saucers or spilling over the sides of motel ashtrays. The little bedroom had, along two of its walls, bricks and boards loaded with notes, magazines, and oversized books. The kitchen joined the living room, and there was a stack of German newspapers under the sink. I had never seen anything like it: a great flophouse of language furnished by City Lights and Café le Metro. I read every title. I flipped through paperbacks and scanned jackets and memorized names: Gogol, *Finnegans Wake*, Djuna Barnes, Jackson Pollock, *A Coney Island of the Mind*, F. O. Matthiessen's *American Renaissance*, all sorts of Freud, *Troubled Sleep*, Man Ray, *The Education of Henry Adams*, Richard Wright, *Film as Art*, William Butler Yeats, Marguerite Duras, *Redburn*,

A Season in Hell, Kapital. On the cover of Alain-Fournier's *The Wanderer* was an Edward Gorey drawing of a young man on a road winding into dark trees. By the hotplate sat a strange Kafka novel called *Amerika,* in which an adolescent hero crosses the Atlantic to find the Nature Theater of Oklahoma. Art and Mark would be talking about a movie or the school newspaper, and I would be consuming my English teacher's library. It was heady stuff. I felt like a Pop Warner[9] athlete on steroids.

Art, Mark, and I would buy stogies and triangulate from MacFarland's apartment to the Cinema, which now shows X-rated films but was then L.A.'s premier art theater, and then to the musty Cherokee Bookstore in Hollywood to hobnob with beatnik homosexuals — smoking, drinking bourbon and coffee, and trying out awkward phrases we'd gleaned from our mentor's bookshelves. I was happy and precocious and a little scared as well, for Hollywood Boulevard was thick with a kind of decadence that was foreign to the South Side. After the Cherokee, we would head back to the security of MacFarland's apartment, slaphappy with hipness.

Let me be the first to admit that there was a good deal of adolescent passion in this embrace of the avant-garde: self-absorption, sexually charged pedantry, an elevation of the odd and abandoned. Still it was a time during which I absorbed an awful lot of information: long lists of titles, images from expressionist paintings, new wave shibboleths,[10] snippets of philosophy, and names that read like Steve Fusco's misspellings — Goethe, Nietzsche, Kierkegaard. Now this is hardly the stuff of deep understanding. But it was an introduction, a phrase book, a Baedeker[11] to a vocabulary of ideas, and it felt good at the time to know all these words. With hindsight I realize how layered and important that knowledge was.

It enabled me to do things in the world. I could browse bohemian bookstores in far-off, mysterious Hollywood; I could go to the Cinema and see events through the lenses of European directors; and, most of all, I could share an evening, talk that talk, with Jack MacFarland, the man I most admired at the time. Knowledge was becoming a bonding agent. Within a year or two, the persona of the disaffected hipster would prove too cynical, too alienated to last. But for a time it was new and exciting: it provided a critical perspective on society, and it allowed me to act as though I were living beyond the limiting boundaries of South Vermont.[12]

[9] **Pop Warner:** A nationwide youth athletics organization.
[10] **new wave shibboleths:** Trendy phrases or jargon.
[11] **Baedeker:** Travel guide.
[12] **South Vermont:** A street in an economically depressed area of Los Angeles.

35

ENGAGING THE TEXT

1. Describe Rose's life in Voc. Ed. What were his teachers like? Have you ever had experience with teachers like these?

2. What did Voc. Ed. do to Rose and his fellow students? How did it affect them intellectually, emotionally, and socially? Why was it subsequently so hard for Rose to catch up in math?

3. Why is high school so disorienting to students like Ken Harvey? How does he cope with it? What other strategies do students use to cope with the pressures and judgments they encounter in school?

4. What does Jack MacFarland offer Rose that finally helps him learn? Do you think it was inevitable that someone with Rose's intelligence would eventually succeed?

EXPLORING CONNECTIONS

5. To what extent do Rose's experiences challenge or confirm John Taylor Gatto's critique of public education in "Against School" (p. 114)? How might Gatto account for the existence of truly remarkable teachers like Rose's Jack MacFarland?

6. Read Gregory Mantsios's "Class in America — 2012" (p. 377) and write an imaginary dialogue between Rose and Mantsios about why some students, like Rose, seem to be able to break through social class barriers and others, like Dave Snyder, Ted Richard, and Ken Harvey, do not.

EXTENDING THE CRITICAL CONTEXT

7. Rose explains that high school can be a "tremendously disorienting place" (para. 16). What, if anything, do you find disorienting about college? What steps can students at your school take to lessen feelings of disorientation? What could the college do to help them?

8. Review one or more of Rose's descriptions of his high school classmates; then write a description of one of your own high school classmates, trying to capture in a nutshell how that person coped or failed to cope with the educational system.

9. Watch any one of the many films that have been made about charismatic teachers (for example, *Dangerous Minds, Renaissance Man, Stand and Deliver*, or *Dead Poets Society*) and compare Hollywood's depiction of a dynamic teacher to Rose's portrayal of Jack MacFarland. What do such charismatic teachers offer their students personally and intellectually? Do you see any disadvantages to classes taught by teachers like these?

FROM SOCIAL CLASS AND THE HIDDEN CURRICULUM OF WORK

JEAN ANYON

It's no surprise that schools in wealthy communities are better than those in poor communities, or that they better prepare their students for desirable jobs. It may be shocking, however, to learn how vast the differences in schools are—not so much in resources as in teaching methods and philosophies of education. Jean Anyon observed five elementary schools over the course of a full school year and concluded that fifth graders of different economic backgrounds are already being prepared to occupy particular rungs on the social ladder. In a sense, some whole schools are on the vocational education track, while others are geared to produce future doctors, lawyers, and business leaders. Anyon's main audience is professional educators, so you may find her style and vocabulary challenging, but, once you've read her descriptions of specific classroom activities, the more analytic parts of the essay should prove easier to understand. Anyon (1941–2013) was a social activist and professor of educational policy in the Ph.D. Program in Urban Education at The City University of New York. Her publications include *Radical Possibilities: Public Policy, Urban Education and a New Social Movement* (2005) and *Theory and Educational Research: Toward Critical Social Explanation* (2009). This essay first appeared in the *Journal of Education* in 1980.

SCHOLARS IN POLITICAL ECONOMY and the sociology of knowledge have recently argued that public schools in complex industrial societies like our own make available different types of educational experience and curriculum knowledge to students in different social classes. Bowles and Gintis,[1] for example, have argued that students in different social-class backgrounds are rewarded for classroom behaviors that correspond to personality traits allegedly rewarded in the different occupational strata—the working classes for docility and obedience, the managerial classes for initiative and personal assertiveness. Basil Bernstein, Pierre Bourdieu, and Michael W. Apple,[2] focusing on school knowledge, have argued that knowledge and skills leading to social power and regard (medical, legal, managerial) are made available to the advantaged social groups but are withheld from the working classes, to whom a more "practical" curriculum is offered (manual skills, clerical knowledge). While there has been considerable argumentation of these points regarding education in England, France, and North America, there has been little or no attempt to investigate these ideas empirically in elementary or secondary schools and classrooms in this country.[3]

[1] S. Bowles and H. Gintis, *Schooling in Capitalist America: Educational Reform and the Contradictions of Economic Life* (New York: Basic Books, 1976). [All notes are Anyon's, except 4 and 11.]

[2] B. Bernstein, *Class, Codes and Control*, Vol. 3. *Towards a Theory of Educational Transmission*, 2d ed. (London: Routledge & Kegan Paul, 1977); P. Bourdieu and J. Passeron, *Reproduction in Education, Society and Culture* (Beverly Hills, Calif.: Sage, 1977); M. W. Apple, *Ideology and Curriculum* (Boston: Routledge & Kegan Paul, 1979).

[3] But see, in a related vein, M. W. Apple and N. King, "What Do Schools Teach?" *Curriculum Inquiry* 6 (1977): 341–58; R. C. Rist, *The Urban School: A Factory for Failure* (Cambridge, MA: MIT Press, 1973).

This article offers tentative empirical support (and qualification) of the above arguments by providing illustrative examples of differences in student *work* in classrooms in contrasting social-class communities. The examples were gathered as part of an ethnographical[4] study of curricular, pedagogical, and pupil evaluation practices in five elementary schools. The article attempts a theoretical contribution as well and assesses student work in the light of a theoretical approach to social-class analysis.... It will be suggested that there is a "hidden curriculum" in schoolwork that has profound implications for the theory—and consequence—of everyday activity in education....

The Sample of Schools

...The social-class designation of each of the five schools will be identified, and the income, occupation, and other relevant available social characteristics of the students and their parents will be described. The first three schools are in a medium-sized city district in northern New Jersey, and the other two are in a nearby New Jersey suburb.

The first two schools I will call *working-class schools.* Most of the parents have blue-collar jobs. Less than a third of the fathers are skilled, while the majority are in unskilled or semiskilled jobs. During the period of the study (1978–1979), approximately 15 percent of the fathers were unemployed. The large majority (85 percent) of the families are white. The following occupations are typical: platform, storeroom, and stockroom workers; foundrymen, pipe welders, and boilermakers; semiskilled and unskilled assemblyline operatives; gas station attendants, auto mechanics, maintenance workers, and security guards. Less than 30 percent of the women work, some part-time and some full-time, on assembly lines, in storerooms and stockrooms, as waitresses, barmaids, or sales clerks. Of the fifth-grade parents, none of the wives of the skilled workers had jobs. Approximately 15 percent of the families in each school are at or below the federal "poverty" level;[5] most of the rest of the family incomes are at or below $12,000, except some of the skilled workers whose incomes are higher. The incomes of the majority of the families in these two schools (at or below $12,000) are typical of 38.6 percent of the families in the United States.[6]

The third school is called the *middle-class school*, although because of neighborhood residence patterns, the population is a mixture of several social classes. The parents' occupations can be divided into three

[4] **ethnographical:** Based on an anthropological study of cultures or subcultures—the "cultures" in this case being the five schools observed. [Eds.]

[5] The U.S. Bureau of the Census defines *poverty* for a nonfarm family of four as a yearly income of $6,191 a year or less. U.S. Bureau of the Census, *Statistical Abstract of the United States: 1978* (Washington, DC: U.S. Government Printing Office, 1978), 465, table 754.

[6] U.S. Bureau of the Census, "Money Income in 1977 of Families and Persons in the United States," *Current Population Reports* Series P-60, no. 118 (Washington, DC: U.S. Government Printing Office, 1979), p. 2, table A.

groups: a small group of blue-collar "rich," who are skilled, well-paid workers such as printers, carpenters, plumbers, and construction workers. The second group is composed of parents in working-class and middle-class white-collar jobs: women in office jobs, technicians, supervisors in industry, and parents employed by the city (such as firemen, policemen, and several of the school's teachers). The third group is composed of occupations such as personnel directors in local firms, accountants, "middle management," and a few small capitalists (owners of shops in the area). The children of several local doctors attend this school. Most family incomes are between $13,000 and $25,000, with a few higher. This income range is typical of 38.9 percent of the families in the United States.[7]

The fourth school has a parent population that is at the upper income level of the upper middle class and is predominantly professional. This school will be called the *affluent professional school.* Typical jobs are: cardiologist, interior designer, corporate lawyer or engineer, executive in advertising or television. There are some families who are not as affluent as the majority (the family of the superintendent of the district's schools, and the one or two families in which the fathers are skilled workers). In addition, a few of the families are more affluent than the majority and can be classified in the capitalist class (a partner in a prestigious Wall Street stock brokerage firm). Approximately 90 percent of the children in this school are white. Most family incomes are between $40,000 and $80,000. This income span represents approximately 7 percent of the families in the United States.[8]

In the fifth school the majority of the families belong to the capitalist class. This school will be called the *executive elite school* because most of the fathers are top executives (for example, presidents and vice-presidents) in major United States–based multinational corporations— for example, AT&T, RCA, Citibank, American Express, U.S. Steel. A sizable group of fathers are top executives in financial firms on Wall Street. There are also a number of fathers who list their occupations as "general counsel" to a particular corporation, and these corporations are also among the large multinationals. Many of the mothers do volunteer work in the Junior League, Junior Fortnightly, or other service groups; some are intricately involved in town politics; and some are themselves in well-paid occupations. There are no minority children in the school. Almost all the family incomes are over $100,000, with some in the $500,000 range. The incomes in this school represent less than 1 percent of the families in the United States.[9]

[7] Ibid.
[8] This figure is an estimate. According to the Bureau of the Census, only 2.6 percent of families in the United States have money income of $50,000 or over. U.S. Bureau of the Census, *Current Population Reports* Series P-60. For figures on income at these higher levels, see J. D. Smith and S. Franklin, "The Concentration of Personal Wealth, 1922–1969," *American Economic Review* 64 (1974): 162–67.
[9] Smith and Franklin, "The Concentration of Personal Wealth."

Since each of the five schools is only one instance of elementary education in a particular social-class context, I will not generalize beyond the sample. However, the examples of schoolwork which follow will suggest characteristics of education in each social setting that appear to have theoretical and social significance and to be worth investigation in a larger number of schools. . . .

The Working-Class Schools

In the two working-class schools, work is following the steps of a procedure. The procedure is usually mechanical, involving rote behavior and very little decision making or choice. The teachers rarely explain why the work is being assigned, how it might connect to other assignments, or what the idea is that lies behind the procedure or gives it coherence and perhaps meaning or significance. Available textbooks are not always used, and the teachers often prepare their own dittos or put work examples on the board. Most of the rules regarding work are designations of what the children are to do; the rules are steps to follow. These steps are told to the children by the teachers and are often written on the board. The children are usually told to copy the steps as notes. These notes are to be studied. Work is often evaluated not according to whether it is right or wrong but according to whether the children followed the right steps.

The following examples illustrate these points. In math, when two-digit division was introduced, the teacher in one school gave a four-minute lecture on what the terms are called (which number is the divisor, dividend, quotient, and remainder). The children were told to copy these names in their notebooks. Then the teacher told them the steps to follow to do the problems, saying, "This is how you do them." The teacher listed the steps on the board, and they appeared several days later as a chart hung in the middle of the front wall: "Divide, Multiply, Subtract, Bring Down." The children often did examples of two-digit division. When the teacher went over the examples with them, he told them what the procedure was for each problem, rarely asking them to conceptualize or explain it themselves: "Three into twenty-two is seven; do your subtraction and one is left over." During the week that two-digit division was introduced (or at any other time), the investigator did not observe any discussion of the idea of grouping involved in division, any use of manipulables, or any attempt to relate two-digit division to any other mathematical process. Nor was there any attempt to relate the steps to an actual or possible thought process of the children. The observer did not hear the terms *dividend*, *quotient*, and so on, used again. The math teacher in the other working-class school followed similar procedures regarding two-digit division and at one point her class seemed confused. She said, "You're confusing yourselves. You're tensing up. Remember, when you do this, it's the same steps over and over again—and that's the way division always is." Several weeks later, after a test, a group of her children "still didn't get it," and she made no attempt to explain the concept of dividing things into groups or to give them manipulables for their own investigation. Rather, she went over the steps with them again and told them that they "needed more practice."

In other areas of math, work is also carrying out often unexplained fragmented procedures. For example, one of the teachers led the children through a series of steps to make a 1-inch grid on their paper *without* telling them that they were making a 1-inch grid or that it would be used to study scale. She said, "Take your ruler. Put it across the top. Make a mark at every number. Then move your ruler down to the bottom. No, put it across the bottom. Now make a mark on top of every number. Now draw a line from..." At this point a girl said that she had a faster way to do it and the teacher said, "No, you don't; you don't even know what I'm making yet. Do it this way or it's wrong." After they had made the lines up and down and across, the teacher told them she wanted them to make a figure by connecting some dots and to measure that, using the scale of 1 inch equals 1 mile. Then they were to cut it out. She said, "Don't cut it until I check it."

In both working-class schools, work in language arts is mechanics of punctuation (commas, periods, question marks, exclamation points), capitalization, and the four kinds of sentences. One teacher explained to me, "Simple punctuation is all they'll ever use." Regarding punctuation, either a teacher or a ditto stated the rules for where, for example, to put commas. The investigator heard no classroom discussion of the aural context of punctuation (which, of course, is what gives each mark its meaning). Nor did the investigator hear any statement or inference that placing a punctuation mark could be a decision-making process, depending, for example, on one's intended meaning. Rather, the children were told to follow the rules. Language arts did not involve creative writing. There were several writing assignments throughout the year, but in each instance the children were given a ditto, and they wrote answers to questions on the sheet. For example, they wrote their "autobiography" by answering such questions as "Where were you born?" "What is your favorite animal?" on a sheet entitled "All About Me."

In one of the working-class schools, the class had a science period several times a week. On the three occasions observed, the children were not called upon to set up experiments or to give explanations for facts or concepts. Rather, on each occasion the teacher told them in his own words what the book said. The children copied the teacher's sentences from the board. Each day that preceded the day they were to do a science experiment, the teacher told them to copy the directions from the book for the procedure they would carry out the next day and to study the list at home that night. The day after each experiment, the teacher went over what they had "found" (they did the experiments as a class, and each was actually a class demonstration led by the teacher). Then the teacher wrote what they "found" on the board, and the children copied that in their notebooks. Once or twice a year there are science projects. The project is chosen and assigned by the teacher from a box of 3-by-5-inch cards. On the card the teacher has written the question to be answered, the books to use, and how much to write. Explaining the cards to the observer, the teacher said, "It tells them exactly what to do, or they couldn't do it."

Social studies in the working-class schools is also largely mechanical, rote work that was given little explanation or connection to larger contexts. In one school, for example, although there was a book available, social studies work was to copy the teacher's notes from the board. Several times a week for a period of several months the children copied these notes. The fifth grades in the district were to study United States history. The teacher used a booklet she had purchased called "The Fabulous Fifty States." Each day she put information from the booklet in outline form on the board and the children copied it. The type of information did not vary: the name of the state, its abbreviation, state capital, nickname of the state, its main products, main business, and a "Fabulous Fact" ("Idaho grew twenty-seven billion potatoes in one year. That's enough potatoes for each man, woman, and..."). As the children finished copying the sentences, the teacher erased them and wrote more. Children would occasionally go to the front to pull down the wall map in order to locate the states they were copying, and the teacher did not dissuade them. But the observer never saw her refer to the map; nor did the observer ever hear her make other than perfunctory remarks concerning the information the children were copying. Occasionally the children colored in a ditto and cut it out to make a stand-up figure (representing, for example, a man roping a cow in the Southwest). These were referred to by the teacher as their social studies "projects."

Rote behavior was often called for in classroom work. When going over math and language arts skills sheets, for example, as the teacher asked for the answer to each problem, he fired the questions rapidly, staccato, and the scene reminded the observer of a sergeant drilling recruits: above all, the questions demanded that you stay at attention: "The next one? What do I put here?...Here? Give us the next." Or "How many commas in this sentence? Where do I put them...The next one?"

The four fifth-grade teachers observed in the working-class schools attempted to control classroom time and space by making decisions without consulting the children and without explaining the basis for their decisions. The teacher's control thus often seemed capricious. Teachers, for instance, very often ignored the bells to switch classes—deciding among themselves to keep the children after the period was officially over to continue with the work or for disciplinary reasons or so they (the teachers) could stand in the hall and talk. There were no clocks in the rooms in either school, and the children often asked, "What period is this?" "When do we go to gym?" The children had no access to materials.

15

These were handed out by teachers and closely guarded. Things in the room "belonged" to the teacher: "Bob, bring me my garbage can." The teachers continually gave the children orders. Only three times did the investigator hear a teacher in either working-class school preface a directive with an unsarcastic "please," or "let's," or "would you." Instead, the teachers said, "Shut up," "Shut your mouth," "Open your books," "Throw your gum away—if you want to rot your teeth, do it on your own time." Teachers made every effort to control the movement of the children, and often shouted, "Why are you out of your seat??!!" If the children got permission to leave the room, they had to take a written pass with the date and time....

Middle-Class School

In the middle-class school, work is getting the right answer. If one accumulates enough right answers, one gets a good grade. One must follow the directions in order to get the right answers, but the directions often call for some figuring, some choice, some decision making. For example, the children must often figure out by themselves what the directions ask them to do and how to get the answer: what do you do first, second, and perhaps third? Answers are usually found in books or by listening to the teacher. Answers are usually words, sentences, numbers, or facts and dates; one writes them on paper, and one should be neat. Answers must be given in the right order, and one cannot make them up.

The following activities are illustrative. Math involves some choice: one may do two-digit division the long way or the short way, and there are some math problems that can be done "in your head." When the teacher explains how to do two-digit division, there is recognition that a cognitive process is involved; she gives you several ways and says, "I want to make sure you understand what you're doing—so you get it right"; and, when they go over the homework, she asks the *children* to tell how they did the problem and what answer they got.

In social studies the daily work is to read the assigned pages in the textbook and to answer the teacher's questions. The questions are almost always designed to check on whether the students have read the assignment and understood it: who did so-and-so; what happened after that; when did it happen, where, and sometimes, why did it happen? The answers are in the book and in one's understanding of the book; the teacher's hints when one doesn't know the answers are to "read it again" or to look at the picture or at the rest of the paragraph. One is to search for the answer in the "context," in what is given.

Language arts is "simple grammar, what they need for everyday life." The language arts teacher says, "They should learn to speak properly, to write business letters and thank-you letters, and to understand what nouns and verbs and simple subjects are." Here, as well, actual work is to choose the right answers, to understand what is given. The teacher often says, "Please read the next sentence and then I'll question

20

you about it." One teacher said in some exasperation to a boy who was fooling around in class, "If you don't know the answers to the questions I ask, then you can't stay in this *class!* [pause] You *never* know the answers to the questions I ask, and it's not fair to me—and certainly not to you!"

Most lessons are based on the textbook. This does not involve a critical perspective on what is given there. For example, a critical perspective in social studies is perceived as dangerous by these teachers because it may lead to controversial topics; the parents might complain. The children, however, are often curious, especially in social studies. Their questions are tolerated and usually answered perfunctorily. But after a few minutes the teacher will say, "All right, we're not going any farther. Please open your social studies workbook." While the teachers spend a lot of time explaining and expanding on what the textbooks say, there is little attempt to analyze how or why things happen, or to give thought to how pieces of a culture, or, say, a system of numbers or elements of a language fit together or can be analyzed. What has happened in the past and what exists now may not be equitable or fair, but (shrug) that is the way things are and one does not confront such matters in school. For example, in social studies after a child is called on to read a passage about the pilgrims, the teacher summarizes the paragraph and then says, "So you can see how strict they were about everything." A child asks, "Why?" "Well, because they felt that if you weren't busy you'd get into trouble." Another child asks, "Is it true that they burned women at the stake?" The teacher says, "Yes, if a woman did anything strange, they hanged them. [*sic*] What would a woman do, do you think, to make them burn them? [*sic*] See if you can come up with better answers than my other [social studies] class." Several children offer suggestions, to which the teacher nods but does not comment. Then she says, "Okay, good," and calls on the next child to read.

Work tasks do not usually request creativity. Serious attention is rarely given in school work on *how* the children develop or express their own feelings and ideas, either linguistically or in graphic form. On the occasions when creativity or self-expression is requested, it is peripheral to the main activity or it is "enrichment" or "for fun." During a lesson on what similes are, for example, the teacher explains what they are, puts several on the board, gives some other examples herself, and then asks the children if they can "make some up." She calls on three children who give similes, two of which are actually in the book they have open before them. The teacher does not comment on this and then asks several others to choose similes from the list of phrases in the book. Several do so correctly, and she says, "Oh good! You're picking them out! See how good we are?" Their homework is to pick out the rest of the similes from the list.

Creativity is not often requested in social studies and science projects, either. Social studies projects, for example, are given with directions to "find information on your topic" and write it up. The children are not supposed to copy but to "put it in your own words." Although a number of the projects subsequently went beyond the teacher's direction to find information and had quite expressive covers and inside illustrations, the teacher's evaluative comments had to do with the amount of information, whether they had "copied," and if their work was neat.

The style of control of the three fifth-grade teachers observed in this school varied from somewhat easygoing to strict, but in contrast to the working-class schools, the teachers' decisions were usually based on external rules and regulations—for example, on criteria that were known or available to the children. Thus, the teachers always honor the bells for changing classes, and they usually evaluate children's work by what is in the textbooks and answer booklets.

There is little excitement in schoolwork for the children, and the assignments are perceived as having little to do with their interests and feelings. As one child said, what you do is "store facts up in your head like cold storage—until you need it later for a test or your job." Thus, doing well is important because there are thought to be *other*, likely rewards: a good job or college.[10]

Affluent Professional School

In the affluent professional school, work is creative activity carried out independently. The students are continually asked to express and apply ideas and concepts. Work involves individual thought and expressiveness, expansion and illustration of ideas, and choice of appropriate method and material. (The class is not considered an open classroom, and the principal explained that because of the large number of discipline problems in the fifth grade this year they did not departmentalize. The teacher who agreed to take part in the study said she is "more structured" this year than she usually is.) The products of work in this class are often written stories, editorials and essays, or representations of ideas in mural, graph, or craft form. The products of work should not be like everybody else's and should show individuality. They should exhibit good design, and (this is important) they must also fit empirical reality. Moreover, one's work should attempt to interpret or "make sense" of reality. The relatively few rules to be followed regarding work are usually criteria for, or limits on, individual activity. One's product is usually evaluated for the quality of its expression and for the appropriateness of its conception to the task. In many cases, one's own satisfaction with the product is an important criterion for its evaluation. When right answers are called for, as in commercial materials like SRA (Science Research Associates) and math, it is important that the children decide on an answer as a result of thinking about the idea involved in

[10] A dominant feeling, expressed directly and indirectly by teachers in this school, was boredom with their work. They did, however, in contrast to the working-class schools, almost always carry out lessons during class times.

what they're being asked to do. Teacher's hints are to "think about it some more."

The following activities are illustrative. The class takes home a sheet requesting each child's parents to fill in the number of cars they have, the number of television sets, refrigerators, games, or rooms in the house, and so on. Each child is to figure the average number of a type of possession owned by the fifth grade. Each child must compile the "data" from all the sheets. A calculator is available in the class-room to do the mechanics of finding the average. Some children decide to send sheets to the fourth-grade families for comparison. Their work should be "verified" by a classmate before it is handed in.

Each child and his or her family has made a geoboard. The teacher asks the class to get their geoboards from the side cabinet, to take a handful of rubber bands, and then to listen to what she would like them to do. She says, "I would like you to design a figure and then find the perimeter and area. When you have it, check with your neighbor. After you've done that, please transfer it to graph paper and tomorrow I'll ask you to make up a question about it for someone. When you hand it in, please let me know whose it is and who verified it. Then I have some-thing else for you to do that's really fun. [pause] Find the average num-ber of chocolate chips in three cookies. I'll give you three cookies, and you'll have to *eat* your way through, I'm afraid!" Then she goes around the room and gives help, suggestions, praise, and admonitions that they are getting noisy. They work sitting, or standing up at their desks, at benches in the back, or on the floor. A child hands the teacher his paper and she comments, "I'm not accepting this paper. Do a better design." To another child she says, "That's fantastic! But you'll never find the area. Why don't you draw a figure inside [the big one] and subtract to get the area?"

The school district requires the fifth grade to study ancient civili-zation (in particular, Egypt, Athens, and Sumer). In this classroom, the emphasis is on illustrating and re-creating the culture of the people of ancient times. The following are typical activities: the children made an 8mm film on Egypt, which one of the parents edited. A girl in the class wrote the script, and the class acted it out. They put the sound on themselves. They read stories of those days. They wrote essays and stories depicting the lives of the people and the societal and occupa-tional divisions. They chose from a list of projects, all of which involved graphic representations of ideas: for example, "Make a mural depicting the division of labor in Egyptian society."

Each child wrote and exchanged a letter in hieroglyphics with a fifth grader in another class, and they also exchanged stories they wrote in cuneiform. They made a scroll and singed the edges so it looked authen-tic. They each chose an occupation and made an Egyptian plaque rep-resenting that occupation, simulating the appropriate Egyptian design. They carved their design on a cylinder of wax, pressed the wax into clay, and then baked the clay. Although one girl did not choose an occupation but carved instead a series of gods and slaves, the teacher said, "That's all right, Amber, it's beautiful." As they were working the teacher said, "Don't cut into your clay until you're satisfied with your design."

Social studies also involves almost daily presentation by the children of some event from the news. The teacher's questions ask the children to expand what they say, to give more details, and to be more specific. Occasionally she adds some remarks to help them see connections between events.

The emphasis on expressing and illustrating ideas in social studies is accompanied in language arts by an emphasis on creative writing. Each child wrote a rebus story for a first grader whom they had interviewed to see what kind of story the child liked best. They wrote editorials on pending decisions by the school board and radio plays, some of which were read over the school intercom from the office and one of which was performed in the auditorium. There is no language arts textbook because, the teacher said, "The principal wants us to be creative." There is not much grammar, but there is punctuation. One morning when the observer arrived, the class was doing a punctuation ditto. The teacher later apologized for using the ditto. "It's just for review," she said. "I don't teach punctuation that way. We use their language." The ditto had three unambiguous rules for where to put commas in a sentence. As the teacher was going around to help the children with the ditto, she repeated several times, "Where you put commas depends on how you say the sentence; it depends on the situation and what you want to say." Several weeks later the observer saw another punctuation activity. The teacher had printed a five-paragraph story on an oak tag and then cut it into phrases. She read the whole story to the class from the book, then passed out the phrases. The group had to decide how the phrases could best be put together again. (They arranged the phrases on the floor.) The point was not to replicate the story, although that was not irrelevant, but to "decide what you think the best way is." Punctuation marks on cardboard pieces were then handed out, and the children discussed and then decided what mark was best at each place they thought one was needed. At the end of each paragraph the teacher asked, "Are you satisfied with the way the paragraphs are now? Read it to yourself and see how it sounds." Then she read the original story again, and they compared the two.

Describing her goals in science to the investigator, the teacher said, "We use ESS (Elementary Science Study). It's very good because it gives a hands-on experience—so they can make *sense* out of it. It doesn't matter whether it [what they find] is right or wrong. I bring them together and there's value in discussing their ideas."

The products of work in this class are often highly valued by the children and the teacher. In fact, this was the only school in which the investigator was not allowed to take original pieces of the children's work for her files. If the work was small enough, however, and was on paper, the investigator could duplicate it on the copying machine in the office.

The teacher's attempt to control the class involves constant negotia- 35 tion. She does not give direct orders unless she is angry because the children have been too noisy. Normally, she tries to get them to foresee the consequences of their actions and to decide accordingly. For example, lining them up to go see a play written by the sixth graders, she says, "I presume you're lined up by someone with whom you want to sit. I hope you're lined up by someone you won't get in trouble with." . . .

One of the few rules governing the children's movement is that no more than three children may be out of the room at once. There is a school rule that anyone can go to the library at any time to get a book. In the fifth grade I observed, they sign their name on the chalkboard and leave. There are no passes. Finally, the children have a fair amount of officially sanctioned say over what happens in the class. For example, they often negotiate what work is to be done. If the teacher wants to move on to the next subject, but the children say they are not ready, they want to work on their present projects some more, she very often lets them do it.

Executive Elite School

In the executive elite school, work is developing one's analytical intellectual powers. Children are continually asked to reason through a problem, to produce intellectual products that are both logically sound and of top academic quality. A primary goal of thought is to conceptualize rules by which elements may fit together in systems and then to apply these rules in solving a problem. Schoolwork helps one to achieve, to excel, to prepare for life.

The following are illustrative. The math teacher teaches area and perimeter by having the children derive formulas for each. First she helps them, through discussion at the board, to arrive at $A = W \times L$ as a formula (not *the* formula) for area. After discussing several, she says, "Can anyone make up a formula for perimeter? Can you figure that out yourselves? [pause] Knowing what we know, can we think of a formula?" She works out three children's suggestions at the board, saying to two, "Yes, that's a good one," and then asks the class if they can think of any more. No one volunteers. To prod them, she says, "If you use rules and good reasoning, you get many ways. Chris, can you think up a formula?"

She discusses two-digit division with the children as a decision-making process. Presenting a new type of problem to them, she asks, "What's the *first* decision you'd make if presented with this kind of example? What is the first thing you'd *think*? Craig?" Craig says, "To find my first partial quotient." She responds, "Yes, that would be your first decision. How would you do that?" Craig explains, and then the teacher says, "OK, we'll see how that works for you." The class tries his way. Subsequently, she comments on the merits and shortcomings of several other children's decisions. Later, she tells the investigator that her goals in math are to develop their reasoning and mathematical thinking and that, unfortunately, "there's no *time* for manipulables."

While right answers are important in math, they are not "given" by the book or by the teacher but may be challenged by the children. Going over some problems in late September the teacher says, "Raise your hand if you do not agree." A child says, "I don't agree with sixty-four." The teacher responds, "OK, there's a question about sixty-four. [to class] Please check it. Owen, they're disagreeing with you. Kristen, they're checking yours." The teacher emphasized this repeatedly during September and October with statements like "Don't be afraid to say you disagree. In the last [math] class, somebody disagreed, and they were right. Before you disagree, check yours, and if you still think we're wrong, then we'll check it out." By Thanksgiving, the children did not often speak in terms of right and wrong math problems but of whether they agreed with the answer that had been given.

There are complicated math mimeos with many word problems. Whenever they go over the examples, they discuss how each child has set up the problem. The children must explain it precisely. On one occasion the teacher said, "I'm more—just as interested in *how* you set up the problem as in what answer you find. If you set up a problem in a good way, the answer is *easy* to find."

Social studies work is most often reading and discussion of concepts and independent research. There are only occasional artistic, expressive, or illustrative projects. Ancient Athens and Sumer are, rather, societies to analyze. The following questions are typical of those that guide the children's independent research. "What mistakes did Pericles make after the war?" "What mistakes did the citizens of Athens make?" "What are the elements of a civilization?" "How did Greece build an economic empire?" "Compare the way Athens chose its leaders with the way we choose ours." Occasionally the children are asked to make up sample questions for their social studies tests. On an occasion when the investigator was present, the social studies teacher rejected a child's question by saying, "That's just fact. If I asked you that question on a test, you'd complain it was just memory! Good questions ask for concepts."

In social studies—but also in reading, science, and health—the teachers initiate classroom discussions of current social issues and problems. These discussions occurred on every one of the investigator's visits, and a teacher told me, "These children's opinions are important—it's important that they learn to reason things through." The classroom discussions always struck the observer as quite realistic and analytical, dealing with concrete social issues like the following: "Why do workers strike?" "Is that right or wrong?" "Why do we have inflation, and what can be done to stop it?" "Why do companies put chemicals in food when the natural ingredients are available?" and so on. Usually the children did not have to be prodded to give their opinions. In fact, their statements and the interchanges between them struck the observer as quite sophisticated conceptually and verbally, and well-informed. Occasionally the teachers would prod with statements such as, "Even if you don't know [the answers], if you think logically about it, you can figure it out." And "I'm asking you [these] questions to help you think this through."

Language arts emphasizes language as a complex system, one that should be mastered. The children are asked to diagram sentences of complex grammatical construction, to memorize irregular verb conjugations (he lay, he has lain, and so on...), and to use the proper participles, conjunctions, and interjections in their speech. The teacher (the same one who teaches social studies) told them, "It is not enough to get these right on tests; you must use what you learn [in grammar classes] in your written and oral work. I will grade you on that."

Most writing assignments are either research reports and essays for social studies or experiment analyses and write-ups for science. There is only an occasional story or other "creative writing" assignment. On the occasion observed by the investigator (the writing of a Halloween story), the points the teacher stressed in preparing the children to write involved the structural aspects of a story rather than the expression of feelings or other ideas. The teacher showed them a filmstrip, "The Seven Parts of a Story," and lectured them on plot development, mood setting, character development, consistency, and the use of a logical or appropriate ending. The stories they subsequently wrote were, in fact, well-structured, but many were also personal and expressive. The teacher's evaluative comments, however, did not refer to the expressiveness or artistry but were all directed toward whether they had "developed" the story well.

Language arts work also involved a large amount of practice in presentation of the self and in managing situations where the child was expected to be in charge. For example, there was a series of assignments in which each child had to be a "student teacher." The child had to plan a lesson in grammar, outlining, punctuation, or other language arts topic and explain the concept to the class. Each child was to prepare a worksheet or game and a homework assignment as well. After each presentation, the teacher and other children gave a critical appraisal of the "student teacher's" performance. Their criteria were: whether the student spoke clearly, whether the lesson was interesting, whether the student made any mistakes, and whether he or she kept control of the class. On an occasion when a child did not maintain control, the teacher said, "When you're up there, you have authority and you have to use it. I'll back you up." ...

The executive elite school is the only school where bells do not demarcate the periods of time. The two fifth-grade teachers were very strict about changing classes on schedule, however, as specific plans for each session had been made. The teachers attempted to keep tight control over the children during lessons, and the children were sometimes flippant, boisterous, and occasionally rude. However, the children may be brought into line by reminding them that "It is up to you," "You must control yourself," "You are responsible for your work," you must "set your own priorities." One teacher told a child, "You are the only driver of your car—and only you can regulate your speed." A new teacher complained to the observer that she had thought "these children" would have more control.

While strict attention to the lesson at hand is required, the teachers make relatively little attempt to regulate the movement of the children at other times. For example, except for the kindergartners the children in this school do not have to wait for the bell to ring in the morning; they may go to their classroom when they arrive at school. Fifth graders often came early to read, to finish work, or to catch up. After the first two months of school, the fifth-grade teachers did not line the children up to change classes or to go to gym, and so on, but, when the children were ready and quiet, they were told they could go—sometimes without the teachers.

In the classroom, the children could get materials when they needed them and took what they needed from closets and from the teacher's desk. They were in charge of the office at lunchtime. During class they did not have to sign out or ask permission to leave the room; they just got up and left. Because of the pressure to get work done, however, they did not leave the room very often. The teachers were very polite to the children, and the investigator heard no sarcasm, no nasty remarks, and few direct orders. The teachers never called the children "honey" or "dear" but always called them by name. The teachers were expected to be available before school, after school, and for part of their lunchtime to provide extra help if needed....

The foregoing analysis of differences in schoolwork in contrasting social-class contexts suggests the following conclusion: the "hidden curriculum" of schoolwork is tacit preparation for relating to the process of production in a particular way. Differing curricular, pedagogical, and pupil evaluation practices emphasize different cognitive and behavioral skills in each social setting and thus contribute to the development in the children of certain potential relationships to physical and symbolic capital,[11] to authority, and to the process of work. School experience, in the sample of schools discussed here, differed qualitatively by social class. These differences may not only contribute to the development in

[11]**physical and symbolic capital:** Elsewhere Anyon defines *capital* as "property that is used to produce profit, interest, or rent"; she defines *symbolic capital* as the knowledge and skills that "may yield social and cultural power." [Eds.]

the children in each social class of certain types of economically signifi-cant relationships and not others but would thereby help to *reproduce* this system of relations in society. In the contribution to the reproduc-tion of unequal social relations lies a theoretical meaning and social consequence of classroom practice.

The identification of different emphases in classrooms in a sample of contrasting social-class contexts implies that further research should be conducted in a large number of schools to investigate the types of work tasks and interactions in each to see if they differ in the ways dis-cussed here and to see if similar potential relationships are uncovered. Such research could have as a product the further elucidation of com-plex but not readily apparent connections between everyday activity in schools and classrooms and the unequal structure of economic relation-ships in which we work and live.

ENGAGING THE TEXT

1. Examine the ways any single subject is taught in the four types of schools Anyon describes. What differences in teaching methods and in the student-teacher relationship do they reflect? What other differences do you note in the schools? What schools in your geographic region would closely approxi-mate the working-class, middle-class, affluent professional, and executive elite schools of her article?

2. What attitudes toward knowledge and work are the four types of schools teaching their students? What kinds of jobs are students being prepared to do? Do you see any evidence that the schools in your community are produc-ing particular kinds of workers?

3. What is the "hidden curriculum" of Anyon's title? How is this curriculum taught, and what social, cultural, or political purposes does it serve?

EXPLORING CONNECTIONS

4. How does Anyon's analysis of the impact of economic class on education compli-cate Diane Ravitch's claim (p. 105) that schools today no longer share the common goal of preparing students to become citizens in a democracy? What do you think would happen if, as Ravitch suggests, all students were given the kind of educa-tion that Anyon associates with executive elite schools?

5. How might Anyon explain the boredom, absurdity, and childishness that John Taylor Gatto (p. 114) associates with compulsory public education? To what extent do Anyon and Gatto seem to agree about the relationship between school and social class?

6. Analyze the teaching styles that Mike Rose (p. 123) encounters at Our Lady of Mercy. Which of Anyon's categories would they fit best? Do Rose's experiences at his high school tend to confirm or complicate Anyon's analysis?

EXTENDING THE CRITICAL CONTEXT

7. Should all schools be run like professional or elite schools? What would be the advantages of making these schools models for all social classes? Do you see any possible disadvantages?

8. Choose a common elementary school task or skill that Anyon does not mention. Outline four ways it might be taught in the four types of schools.

VISUAL PORTFOLIO
READING IMAGES OF EDUCATION AND EMPOWERMENT

Aaron Rubino/San Francisco Chronicle/Polaris

Jon Chase/Harvard Public Affairs

Liv Gjestvang, Office of Distance Education and eLearning, The Ohio State University

AP Photo/Jacquelyn Martin

VISUAL PORTFOLIO

READING IMAGES OF EDUCATION AND EMPOWERMENT

1. Compare the image of the 1950s San Francisco classroom on page 154 with the 1955 photograph of first graders reciting the Pledge of Allegiance on the opening page of this chapter (p. 99). What does each of these images of mid-twentieth century classrooms tell us about the role and importance of education in the lives of young Americans? What does the Portfolio image suggest about the nature of schooling and the experience of learning? Which of these images do you identify with more, and why?

2. What, do you imagine, is the Native American high school student in the photo on page 155 thinking as she leafs through a brochure during a Harvard University college day at her reservation high school? Why might she want to go to Harvard? What challenges do you think she might face there as an undergrad? Overall, what are images like this, taken from Harvard's online newsletter, designed to suggest about educational opportunity and personal empowerment in America?

3. What does the sign on page 156 suggest about the real priorities of the North Georgia Falcons? How might John Taylor Gatto (p. 114) assess the sign and interpret what it says about contemporary American secondary education? Make a similar sign stating the priorities of the high school you attended. Share these in class and discuss what they reveal.

4. How many of the students in the college pictured on page 157, in your view, are actually taking notes? What do you think the rest of the students are doing? How common are laptops and cell phones in the classes at your college or university? In general, do you think they enhance or disrupt the classroom experience? Should colleges prohibit or limit their use? Why or why not?

5. What does the photo of an Occupy Wall Street protester on page 158 suggest about the myth of personal empowerment through educational success? Why do you think he calls himself a "superhero"? Go online to learn more about recent increases in college tuition and the debt accrued by college students as the result of student loans. How much debt would you be willing to assume to get your degree? How might being "shackled by debt" affect the values, attitudes, and choices of future American college grads? Would students and society benefit if public colleges were tuition-free for all qualified students?

6. The photograph on page 159 shows students at Dickinson College protesting sexual assault in 2011. Since it was taken, a number of states and college campuses have adopted "affirmative consent" policies that require that both parties get unambiguous, clear consent before and while engaging in sexual activity. Working in groups, discuss the issue of sexual assault at your college. Do you agree that sexual assault is a serious problem in higher education? Do you think that the adoption of affirmative consent policies will make U.S. colleges safer places for all students? Why or why not?

LEARNING TO READ
MALCOLM X

Born Malcolm Little on May 19, 1925, Malcolm X was one of the most articulate and powerful leaders of black America during the 1960s. A street hustler convicted of robbery in 1946, he spent seven years in prison, where he educated himself and became a disciple of Elijah Muhammad, founder of the Nation of Islam. In the days of the civil rights movement, Malcolm X emerged as the leading spokesman for black separatism, a philosophy that urged black Americans to cut political, social, and economic ties with the white community. After a pilgrimage to Mecca, the capital of the Muslim world, in 1964, he became an orthodox Muslim, adopted the Muslim name El Hajj Malik El-Shabazz, and distanced himself from the teachings of the black Muslims. He was assassinated in 1965. In the following excerpt from his autobiography, coauthored with Alex Haley and published the year of his death, Malcolm X describes his self-education.

IT WAS BECAUSE OF MY LETTERS that I happened to stumble upon starting to acquire some kind of a homemade education.

I became increasingly frustrated at not being able to express what I wanted to convey in letters that I wrote, especially those to Mr. Elijah Muhammad.[1] In the street, I had been the most articulate hustler out there—I had commanded attention when I said something. But now, trying to write simple English, I not only wasn't articulate, I wasn't even functional. How would I sound writing in slang, the way I would *say* it, something such as, "Look, daddy, let me pull your coat about a cat, Elijah Muhammad—"

Many who today hear me somewhere in person, or on television, or those who read something I've said, will think I went to school far beyond the eighth grade. This impression is due entirely to my prison studies.

It had really begun back in the Charlestown Prison, when Bimbi[2] first made me feel envy of his stock of knowledge. Bimbi had always taken charge of any conversations he was in, and I had tried to emulate him. But every book I picked up had few sentences which didn't contain anywhere from one to nearly all of the words that might as well have been in Chinese. When I just skipped those words, of course, I really ended up with little idea of what the book said. So I had come to the

---

[1]**Elijah Muhammad:** American clergyman (1897–1975); leader of the Nation of Islam, 1935–1975. [All notes are the editors'.]
[2]**Bimbi:** A fellow inmate whose encyclopedic learning and verbal facility greatly impressed Malcolm X.

Norfolk Prison Colony still going through only book-reading motions. Pretty soon, I would have quit even these motions, unless I had received the motivation that I did.

I saw that the best thing I could do was get hold of a dictionary—to ⁵ study, to learn some words. I was lucky enough to reason also that I should try to improve my penmanship. It was sad. I couldn't even write in a straight line. It was both ideas together that moved me to request a dictionary along with some tablets and pencils from the Norfolk Prison Colony school.

I spent two days just riffling uncertainly through the dictionary's pages. I'd never realized so many words existed! I didn't know *which* words I needed to learn. Finally, just to start some kind of action, I began copying.

In my slow, painstaking, ragged handwriting, I copied into my tablet everything printed on that first page, down to the punctuation marks.

I believe it took me a day. Then, aloud, I read back, to myself, everything I'd written on the tablet. Over and over, aloud, to myself, I read my own handwriting.

I woke up the next morning, thinking about those words— immensely proud to realize that not only had I written so much at one time, but I'd written words that I never knew were in the world. Moreover, with a little effort, I also could remember what many of these words meant. I reviewed the words whose meanings I didn't remember. Funny thing, from the dictionary first page right now, that "aardvark" springs to my mind. The dictionary had a picture of it, a long-tailed, long-eared, burrowing African mammal, which lives off termites caught by sticking out its tongue as an anteater does for ants.

I was so fascinated that I went on—I copied the dictionary's next ¹⁰ page. And the same experience came when I studied that. With every succeeding page, I also learned of people and places and events from history. Actually the dictionary is like a miniature encyclopedia. Finally the dictionary's A section had filled a whole tablet—and I went on into the B's. That was the way I started copying what eventually became the entire dictionary. It went a lot faster after so much practice helped me to pick up handwriting speed. Between what I wrote in my tablet, and writing letters, during the rest of my time in prison I would guess I wrote a million words.

I suppose it was inevitable that as my word-base broadened, I could for the first time pick up a book and read and now begin to understand what the book was saying. Anyone who has read a great deal can imagine the new world that opened. Let me tell you something: from then until I left that prison, in every free moment I had, if I was not reading in the library, I was reading on my bunk. You couldn't have gotten me out of books with a wedge. Between Mr. Muhammad's teachings, my correspondence, my visitors, ... and my reading of books, months passed without my even thinking about being imprisoned. In fact, up to then, I never had been so truly free in my life.

The Norfolk Prison Colony's library was in the school building. A variety of classes was taught there by instructors who came from such places as Harvard and Boston universities. The weekly debates between inmate teams were also held in the school building. You would be astonished to know how worked up convict debaters and audiences would get over subjects like "Should Babies Be Fed Milk?"

Available on the prison library's shelves were books on just about every general subject. Much of the big private collection that Parkhurst[3] had willed to the prison was still in crates and boxes in the back of the library—thousands of old books. Some of them looked ancient: covers faded, old-time parchment-looking binding. Parkhurst . . . seemed to have been principally interested in history and religion. He had the money and the special interest to have a lot of books that you wouldn't have in a general circulation. Any college library would have been lucky to get that collection.

As you can imagine, especially in a prison where there was heavy emphasis on rehabilitation, an inmate was smiled upon if he demonstrated an unusually intense interest in books. There was a sizable number of well-read inmates, especially the popular debaters. Some were said by many to be practically walking encyclopedias. They were almost celebrities. No university would ask any student to devour literature as I did when this new world opened to me, of being able to read and *understand.*

I read more in my room than in the library itself. An inmate who   15
was known to read a lot could check out more than the permitted maximum number of books. I preferred reading in the total isolation of my own room.

When I had progressed to really serious reading, every night at about ten P.M. I would be outraged with the "lights out." It always seemed to catch me right in the middle of something engrossing.

Fortunately, right outside my door was a corridor light that cast a glow into my room. The glow was enough to read by, once my eyes adjusted to it. So when "lights out" came, I would sit on the floor where I could continue reading in that glow.

At one-hour intervals at night guards paced past every room. Each time I heard the approaching footsteps, I jumped into bed and feigned sleep. And as soon as the guard passed, I got back out of bed onto the floor area of that light-glow, where I would read for another fifty-eight minutes until the guard approached again. That went on until three or four every morning. Three or four hours of sleep a night was enough for me. Often in the years in the streets I had slept less than that.

The teachings of Mr. Muhammad stressed how history had been "whitened"—when white men had written history books, the black

---

[3]**Parkhurst:** Charles Henry Parkhurst (1842–1933); American clergyman, reformer, and president of the Society for the Prevention of Crime.

man simply had been left out. Mr. Muhammad couldn't have said anything that would have struck me much harder. I had never forgotten how when my class, me and all of those whites, had studied seventh-grade United States history back in Mason, the history of the Negro had been covered in one paragraph, and the teacher had gotten a big laugh with his joke, "Negroes' feet are so big that when they walk, they leave a hole in the ground."

This is one reason why Mr. Muhammad's teachings spread so 20 swiftly all over the United States, among *all* Negroes, whether or not they became followers of Mr. Muhammad. The teachings ring true—to every Negro. You can hardly show me a black adult in America—or a white one, for that matter—who knows from the history books anything like the truth about the black man's role. In my own case, once I heard of the "glorious history of the black man," I took special pains to hunt in the library for books that would inform me on details about black history.

I can remember accurately the very first set of books that really impressed me. I have since bought that set of books and I have it at home for my children to read as they grow up. It's called *Wonders of the World*. It's full of pictures of archeological finds, statues that depict, usually, non-European people.

I found books like Will Durant's[4] *Story of Civilization*. I read H. G. Wells'[5] *Outline of History*. *Souls of Black Folk* by W. E. B. Du Bois[6] gave me a glimpse into the black people's history before they came to this country. Carter G. Woodson's[7] *Negro History* opened my eyes about black empires before the black slave was brought to the United States, and the early Negro struggles for freedom.

J. A. Rogers'[8] three volumes of *Sex and Race* told about race-mixing before Christ's time; and Aesop being a black man who told fables; about Egypt's Pharaohs; about the great Coptic Christian Empire;[9] about Ethiopia, the earth's oldest continuous black civilization, as China is the oldest continuous civilization.

Mr. Muhammad's teaching about how the white man had been created led me to *Findings in Genetics*, by Gregor Mendel.[10] (The dictionary's G section was where I had learned what "genetics" meant.) I

[4]**Will Durant:** American author and historian (1885–1981). Durant, with his wife Ariel (1898–1981), won the Pulitzer Prize for literature for volume ten of their eleven-volume *The Story of Civilization*, published from 1935 to 1975.

[5]**H. G. Wells:** English novelist and historian (1866–1946).

[6]**W. E. B. Du Bois:** William Edward Burghardt Du Bois, distinguished black scholar, author, and activist (1868–1963). Du Bois was the first director of the NAACP and was an important figure in the Harlem Renaissance; his best-known book is *The Souls of Black Folk*.

[7]**Carter G. Woodson:** Distinguished African American historian (1875–1950); considered the father of black history.

[8]**J. A. Rogers:** African American historian and journalist (1883–1965).

[9]**Coptic Christian Empire:** The domain of the Coptic Church, a native Egyptian Christian church that retains elements of its African origins.

[10]**Gregor Mendel:** Austrian monk, botanist, and pioneer in genetic research (1822–1884).

really studied this book by the Austrian monk. Reading it over and over, especially certain sections, helped me to understand that if you started with a black man, a white man could be produced; but starting with a white man, you never could produce a black man—because the white chromosome is recessive. And since no one disputes that there was but one Original Man, the conclusion is clear.

During the last year or so, in the *New York Times*, Arnold Toynbee[11] used the word "bleached" in describing the white man. His words were: "White (i.e., bleached) human beings of North European origin...." Toynbee also referred to the European geographic area as only a peninsula of Asia. He said there was no such thing as Europe. And if you look at the globe, you will see for yourself that America is only an extension of Asia. (But at the same time Toynbee is among those who have helped to bleach history. He has written that Africa was the only continent that produced no history. He won't write that again. Every day now, the truth is coming to light.)

I never will forget how shocked I was when I began reading about slavery's total horror. It made such an impact upon me that it later became one of my favorite subjects when I became a minister of Mr. Muhammad's. The world's most monstrous crime, the sin and the blood on the white man's hands, are almost impossible to believe. Books like the one by Frederick Olmsted[12] opened my eyes to the horrors suffered when the slave was landed in the United States. The European woman, Fanny Kemble,[13] who had married a Southern white slaveowner, described how human beings were degraded. Of course I read *Uncle Tom's Cabin*.[14] In fact, I believe that's the only novel I have ever read since I started serious reading.

Parkhurst's collection also contained some bound pamphlets of the Abolitionist[15] Anti-Slavery Society of New England. I read descriptions of atrocities, saw those illustrations of black slave women tied up and flogged with whips; of black mothers watching their babies being dragged off, never to be seen by their mothers again; of dogs after slaves, and of the fugitive slave catchers, evil white men with whips and clubs and chains and guns. I read about the slave preacher Nat Turner, who put the fear of God into the white slavemaster. Nat Turner wasn't going around preaching pie-in-the-sky and "non-violent" freedom for the black man. There in Virginia one night in 1831, Nat and seven other slaves started out at his master's home and through the night they went from one plantation "big house" to the next, killing, until by the next morning 57 white people were dead and Nat had about 70 slaves

---

[11]**Arnold Toynbee:** English historian (1889–1975).

[12]**Frederick Olmsted:** Frederick Law Olmsted (1822–1903), American landscape architect, city planner, and opponent of slavery.

[13]**Fanny Kemble:** Frances Anne Kemble, English actress and author (1809–1893); best known for her autobiographical *Journal of a Residence on a Georgia Plantation*, published in 1863 to win support in Britain for the abolitionist cause.

[14]***Uncle Tom's Cabin:*** Harriet Beecher Stowe's 1852 antislavery novel.

[15]**Abolitionist:** Advocating the prohibition of slavery.

following him. White people, terrified for their lives, fled from their homes, locked themselves up in public buildings, hid in the woods, and some even left the state. A small army of soldiers took two months to catch and hang Nat Turner. Somewhere I have read where Nat Turner's example is said to have inspired John Brown[16] to invade Virginia and attack Harpers Ferry nearly thirty years later, with thirteen white men and five Negroes.

I read Herodotus,[17] "the father of History," or, rather, I read about him. And I read the histories of various nations, which opened my eyes gradually, then wider and wider, to how the whole world's white men had indeed acted like devils, pillaging and raping and bleeding and draining the whole world's non-white people. I remember, for instance, books such as Will Durant's *The Story of Oriental Civilization,* and Mahatma Gandhi's[18] accounts of the struggle to drive the British out of India.

Book after book showed me how the white man had brought upon the world's black, brown, red, and yellow peoples every variety of the suffering of exploitation. I saw how since the sixteenth century, the so-called "Christian trader" white man began to ply the seas in his lust for Asian and African empires, and plunder, and power. I read, I saw, how the white man never has gone among the non-white peoples bearing the Cross in the true manner and spirit of Christ's teachings — meek, humble, and Christlike.

I perceived, as I read, how the collective white man had been actually nothing but a piratical opportunist who used Faustian machinations[19] to make his own Christianity his initial wedge in criminal conquests. First, always "religiously," he branded "heathen" and "pagan" labels upon ancient non-white cultures and civilizations. The stage thus set, he then turned upon his non-white victims his weapons of war.

I read how, entering India — half a *billion* deeply religious brown people — the British white man, by 1759, through promises, trickery, and manipulations, controlled much of India through Great Britain's East India Company. The parasitical British administration kept tentacling out to half of the sub-continent. In 1857, some of the desperate people of India finally mutinied — and, excepting the African slave trade, nowhere has history recorded any more unnecessary bestial and ruthless human carnage than the British suppression of the non-white Indian people.

Over 115 million African blacks — close to the 1930s population of the United States — were murdered or enslaved during the slave trade. And I read how when the slave market was glutted, the cannibalistic

[16]**John Brown:** American abolitionist (1800–1859); leader of an attack on Harpers Ferry, West Virginia, in 1859.
[17]**Herodotus:** Early Greek historian (484?–425? B.C.E.).
[18]**Mahatma Gandhi:** Hindu religious leader, social reformer, and advocate of nonviolence (1869–1948).
[19]**Faustian machinations:** Evil plots or schemes. Faust was a legendary character who sold his soul to the devil for knowledge and power.

white powers of Europe next carved up, as their colonies, the richest areas of the black continent. And Europe's chancelleries for the next century played a chess game of naked exploitation and power from Cape Horn to Cairo.

Ten guards and the warden couldn't have torn me out of those books. Not even Elijah Muhammad could have been more eloquent than those books were in providing indisputable proof that the collective white man had acted like a devil in virtually every contact he had with the world's collective non-white man. I listen today to the radio, and watch television, and read the headlines about the collective white man's fear and tension concerning China. When the white man professes ignorance about why the Chinese hate him so, my mind can't help flashing back to what I read, there in prison, about how the blood forebears of this same white man raped China at a time when China was trusting and helpless. Those original white "Christian traders" sent into China millions of pounds of opium. By 1839, so many of the Chinese were addicts that China's desperate government destroyed twenty thousand chests of opium. The first Opium War[20] was promptly declared by the white man. Imagine! Declaring *war* upon someone who objects to being narcotized! The Chinese were severely beaten, with Chinese-invented gunpowder.

The Treaty of Nanking made China pay the British white man for the destroyed opium; forced open China's major ports to British trade; forced China to abandon Hong Kong; fixed China's import tariffs so low that cheap British articles soon flooded in, maiming China's industrial development.

After a second Opium War, the Tientsin Treaties legalized the ravaging opium trade, legalized a British-French-American control of China's customs. China tried delaying that Treaty's ratification; Peking was looted and burned.

"Kill the foreign white devils!" was the 1901 Chinese war cry in the Boxer Rebellion.[21] Losing again, this time the Chinese were driven from Peking's choicest areas. The vicious, arrogant white man put up the famous signs, "Chinese and dogs not allowed."

Red China after World War II closed its doors to the Western white world. Massive Chinese agricultural, scientific, and industrial efforts are described in a book that *Life* magazine recently published. Some observers inside Red China have reported that the world never has known such a hate-white campaign as is now going on in this non-white country where, present birth-rates continuing, in fifty more years Chinese will be half the earth's population. And it seems that some Chinese chickens will soon come home to roost, with China's recent successful nuclear tests.

[20]**Opium War:** 1839–1842 war between Britain and China that ended with China's cession of Hong Kong to British rule.
[21]**Boxer Rebellion:** The 1898–1900 uprising by members of a secret Chinese society who opposed foreign influence in Chinese affairs.

Let us face reality. We can see in the United Nations a new world order being shaped, along color lines—an alliance among the non-white nations. America's U.N. Ambassador Adlai Stevenson[22] complained not long ago that in the United Nations "a skin game"[23] was being played. He was right. He was facing reality. A "skin game" *is* being played. But Ambassador Stevenson sounded like Jesse James accusing the marshal of carrying a gun. Because who in the world's history ever has played a worse "skin game" than the white man?

Mr. Muhammad, to whom I was writing daily, had no idea of what a new world had opened up to me through my efforts to document his teachings in books.

When I discovered philosophy, I tried to touch all the landmarks of philosophical development. Gradually, I read most of the old philosophers, Occidental and Oriental. The Oriental philosophers were the ones I came to prefer; finally, my impression was that most Occidental philosophy had largely been borrowed from the Oriental thinkers. Socrates, for instance, traveled in Egypt. Some sources even say that Socrates was initiated into some of the Egyptian mysteries. Obviously Socrates got some of his wisdom among the East's wise men.

I have often reflected upon the new vistas that reading opened to me. I knew right there in prison that reading had changed forever the course of my life. As I see it today, the ability to read awoke inside me some long dormant craving to be mentally alive. I certainly wasn't seeking any degree, the way a college confers a status symbol upon its students. My homemade education gave me, with every additional book that I read, a little bit more sensitivity to the deafness, dumbness, and blindness that was afflicting the black race in America. Not long ago, an English writer telephoned me from London, asking questions. One was, "What's your alma mater?" I told him, "Books." You will never catch me with a free fifteen minutes in which I'm not studying something I feel might be able to help the black man.

Yesterday I spoke in London, and both ways on the plane across the Atlantic I was studying a document about how the United Nations proposes to insure the human rights of the oppressed minorities of the world. The American black man is the world's most shameful case of minority oppression. What makes the black man think of himself as only an internal United States issue is just a catch-phrase, two words, "civil rights." How is the black man going to get "civil rights" before first he wins his *human* rights? If the American black man will start thinking about his *human* rights, and then start thinking of himself as part of one of the world's great peoples, he will see he has a case for the United Nations.

40

[22]**Adlai Stevenson:** American politician (1900–1965); Democratic candidate for the presidency in 1952 and 1956.

[23]**skin game:** A dishonest or fraudulent scheme, business operation, or trick, with the added reference in this instance to skin color.

I can't think of a better case! Four hundred years of black blood and sweat invested here in America, and the white man still has the black man begging for what every immigrant fresh off the ship can take for granted the minute he walks down the gangplank.

But I'm digressing. I told the Englishman that my alma mater was books, a good library. Every time I catch a plane, I have with me a book that I want to read—and that's a lot of books these days. If I weren't out here every day battling the white man, I could spend the rest of my life reading, just satisfying my curiosity—because you can hardly mention anything I'm not curious about. I don't think anybody ever got more out of going to prison than I did. In fact, prison enabled me to study far more intensively than I would have if my life had gone differently and I had attended some college. I imagine that one of the biggest troubles with colleges is there are too many distractions, too much panty-raiding, fraternities, and boola-boola and all of that. Where else but in a prison could I have attacked my ignorance by being able to study intensely sometimes as much as fifteen hours a day?

ENGAGING THE TEXT

1. What motivated Malcolm X to educate himself?

2. What kind of knowledge did Malcolm X gain by learning to read? How did this knowledge free or empower him?

3. Would it be possible for public schools to empower students in the way that Malcolm X's self-education empowered him? If so, how? If not, why not?

4. **Thinking Rhetorically** Some readers are offended by the strength of Malcolm X's accusations and by his grouping of all members of a given race into "collectives." Who, in your view, was the intended audience of this excerpt? How do you think Malcolm X expected non–African American readers to react to it? Given the history of racial injustice he recounts, do you feel he is justified in making such claims and assumptions?

THE BOONDOCKS   by AARON MCGRUDER

THE BOONDOCKS © 2000 Aaron McGruder. Dist. By UNIVERSAL UCLICK. Reprinted with permission. All rights reserved.

EXPLORING CONNECTIONS

5. Imagine that John Taylor Gatto (p. 114), Mike Rose (p. 123), and Malcolm X have been appointed to redesign American education. Working in groups, role-play a meeting in which the committee attempts to reach consensus on its recommendations. Report to the class the results of the committee's deliberations and discuss them.

6. What does the *Boondocks* cartoon (p. 169) suggest about the possibility of teaching and learning "revolutionary" ideas within the setting of a public school system?

EXTENDING THE CRITICAL CONTEXT

7. Survey some typical elementary or secondary school textbooks to test the currency of Malcolm X's charge that the educational establishment presents a "whitened" view of America. What view of America is presently being projected in public school history and social science texts?

8. Go to the library and read one page of a dictionary chosen at random. Study the meanings of any unfamiliar words and follow up on the information on your page by consulting encyclopedias, books, or articles. Let yourself be guided by chance and by your interests. After you've tried this experiment, discuss in class the benefits and drawbacks of an unsystematic self-education like Malcolm X's.

STILL SEPARATE, STILL UNEQUAL
JONATHAN KOZOL

In *Brown v. Board of Education* (1954), the U.S. Supreme Court overturned its ruling in *Plessy v. Ferguson* (1896), which had sanctioned "separate but equal" facilities for blacks and whites throughout the South for more than half a century. The Court's decision in *Brown* ended the deliberate segregation of U.S. schools and promised to usher in a new era of equality in American education. But according to longtime educational critic Jonathan Kozol, American schools today may be more segregated than at any time since 1954. And the "educational apartheid" that Kozol sees in U.S. schools isn't just about color. Kozol associates the "resegregation" of public education with a deterioration of classroom conditions and teaching practices that threatens an entire generation of Americans.

After graduating from Harvard with a degree in literature and studying as a Rhodes Scholar at Oxford University, Kozol (b. 1936) took his first job teaching in an inner-city elementary school near Boston. His account of that experience, *Death at an Early Age: The Destruction of the Hearts and Minds of Negro Children in the Boston Public Schools* (1967) **won national acclaim and established him as one of the country's foremost educational activists and social reformers. Since then, his work with poor children and their families has resulted in a dozen books, including** *Illiterate America* (1980), *On Being a Teacher* (1981), *Rachel and Her Children: Homeless Families in America* (1988), *Savage Inequalities: Children in America's Schools* (1991), **and** *The Shame of the Nation: The Restoration of Apartheid Schooling in America* (2005), **the source of this selection. His most recent book is** *Fire in the Ashes: Twenty-Five Years Among the Poorest Children in America* (2012).

MANY AMERICANS who live far from our major cities and who have no firsthand knowledge of the realities to be found in urban public schools seem to have the rather vague and general impression that the great extremes of racial isolation that were matters of grave national significance some thirty-five or forty years ago have gradually but steadily diminished in more recent years. The truth, unhappily, is that the trend, for well over a decade now, has been precisely the reverse. Schools that were already deeply segregated twenty-five or thirty years ago are no less segregated now, while thousands of other schools around the country that had been integrated either voluntarily or by the force of law have since been rapidly resegregating.

In Chicago, by the academic year 2002–2003, 87 percent of public-school enrollment was black or Hispanic; less than 10 percent of children in the schools were white. In Washington, D.C., 94 percent of children were black or Hispanic; less than 5 percent were white. In St. Louis, 82 percent of the student population were black or Hispanic; in Philadelphia and Cleveland, 79 percent; in Los Angeles, 84 percent; in Detroit, 96 percent; in Baltimore, 89 percent. In New York City, nearly three quarters of the students were black or Hispanic.

Even these statistics, as stark as they are, cannot begin to convey how deeply isolated children in the poorest and most segregated sections of these cities have become. In the typically colossal high schools of the Bronx, for instance, more than 90 percent of students (in most cases, more than 95 percent) are black or Hispanic. At John F. Kennedy High School in 2003, 93 percent of the enrollment of more than 4,000 students were black and Hispanic; only 3.5 percent of students at the school were white. At Harry S. Truman High School, black and Hispanic students represented 96 percent of the enrollment of 2,700 students; 2 percent were white. At Adlai Stevenson High School, which enrolls 3,400 students, blacks and Hispanics made up 97 percent of the student population; a mere eight-tenths of one percent were white.

A teacher at P.S. 65 in the South Bronx once pointed out to me one of the two white children I had ever seen there. His presence in her class was something of a wonderment to the teacher and to the other pupils. I asked how many white kids she had taught in the South Bronx in her career. "I've been at this school for eighteen years," she said. "This is the first white student I have ever taught."

One of the most disheartening experiences for those who grew up   5
in the years when Martin Luther King Jr. and Thurgood Marshall[1] were
alive is to visit public schools today that bear their names, or names
of other honored leaders of the integration struggles that produced the
temporary progress that took place in the three decades after *Brown v.
Board of Education*,[2] and to find out how many of these schools are
bastions of contemporary segregation. It is even more disheartening
when schools like these are not in deeply segregated inner-city neighborhoods but in racially mixed areas where the integration of a public
school would seem to be most natural, and where, indeed, it takes a
conscious effort on the part of parents or school officials in these districts to avoid the integration option that is often right at their front door.

In a Seattle neighborhood that I visited in 2002, for instance, where
approximately half the families were Caucasian, 95 percent of students
at the Thurgood Marshall Elementary School were black, Hispanic,
Native American, or of Asian origin. An African American teacher at
the school told me—not with bitterness but wistfully—of seeing clusters of white parents and their children each morning on the corner of
a street close to the school, waiting for a bus that took the children to a
predominantly white school.

"At Thurgood Marshall," according to a big wall poster in the school's
lobby, "the dream is alive." But school-assignment practices and federal
court decisions that have countermanded long-established policies that
previously fostered integration in Seattle's schools make the realization
of the dream identified with Justice Marshall all but unattainable today.
In San Diego there is a school that bears the name of Rosa Parks in which
86 percent of students are black and Hispanic and only some 2 percent are white. In Los Angeles there is a school that bears the name of
Dr. King that is 99 percent black and Hispanic, and another in Milwaukee in which black and Hispanic children also make up 99 percent of
the enrollment. There is a high school in Cleveland that is named for
Dr. King in which black students make up 97 percent of the student body,
and the graduation rate is only 35 percent. In Philadelphia, 98 percent
of children at a high school named for Dr. King are black. At a middle
school named for Dr. King in Boston, black and Hispanic children make
up 98 percent of the enrollment....

There is a well-known high school named for Martin Luther King Jr.
in New York City too. This school, which I've visited repeatedly in
recent years, is located in an upper-middle-class white neighborhood,
where it was built in the belief—or hope—that it would draw large
numbers of white students by permitting them to walk to school, while

---

[1]**Thurgood Marshall:** First African American justice on the Supreme Court (1908–
1993). [All notes are the editors', except 3, 6, and 8.]

[2]***Brown v. Board of Education:*** 1954 Supreme Court case outlawing public school segregation. The court ruled, "Separate educational facilities are inherently unequal."

only their black and Hispanic classmates would be asked to ride the bus or come by train. When the school was opened in 1975, less than a block from Lincoln Center in Manhattan, "it was seen," according to the *New York Times*, "as a promising effort to integrate white, black and Hispanic students in a thriving neighborhood that held one of the city's cultural gems." Even from the start, however, parents in the neighborhood showed great reluctance to permit their children to enroll at Martin Luther King, and, despite "its prime location and its name, which itself creates the highest of expectations," notes the *Times*, the school before long came to be a destination for black and Hispanic students who could not obtain admission into more successful schools. It stands today as one of the nation's most visible and problematic symbols of an expectation rapidly receding and a legacy substantially betrayed.

Perhaps most damaging to any serious effort to address racial segregation openly is the refusal of most of the major arbiters of culture in our northern cities to confront or even clearly name an obvious reality they would have castigated with a passionate determination in another section of the nation fifty years before—and which, moreover, they still castigate today in retrospective writings that assign it to a comfortably distant and allegedly concluded era of the past. There is, indeed, a seemingly agreed-upon convention in much of the media today not even to use an accurate descriptor like "racial segregation" in a narrative description of a segregated school. Linguistic sweeteners, semantic somersaults, and surrogate vocabularies are repeatedly employed. Schools in which as few as 3 or 4 percent of students may be white or Southeast Asian or of Middle Eastern origin, for instance—and where *every other child* in the building is black or Hispanic—are referred to as "diverse." Visitors to schools like these discover quickly the eviscerated meaning of the word, which is no longer a proper adjective but a euphemism for a plainer word that has apparently become unspeakable.

School systems themselves repeatedly employ this euphemism in describing the composition of their student populations. In a school I visited in the fall of 2004 in Kansas City, Missouri, for example, a document distributed to visitors reports that the school's curriculum "addresses the needs of children from diverse backgrounds." But as I went from class to class, I did not encounter any children who were white or Asian—or Hispanic, for that matter—and when I was later provided with precise statistics for the demographics of the school, I learned that 99.6 percent of students there were African American. In a similar document, the school board of another district, this one in New York State, referred to "the diversity" of its student population and "the rich variations of ethnic backgrounds." But when I looked at the racial numbers that the district had reported to the state, I learned that there were 2,800 black and Hispanic children in the system, 1 Asian child, and 3 whites. Words, in these cases, cease to have real meaning; or, rather, they mean the opposite of what they say.

High school students whom I talk with in deeply segregated neighborhoods and public schools seem far less circumspect than their elders and far more open in their willingness to confront these issues. "It's more like being hidden," said a fifteen-year-old girl named Isabel[3] I met some years ago in Harlem, in attempting to explain to me the ways in which she and her classmates understood the racial segregation of their neighborhoods and schools. "It's as if you have been put in a garage where, if they don't have room for something but aren't sure if they should throw it out, they put it there where they don't need to think of it again."

I asked her if she thought America truly did not "have room" for her or other children of her race. "Think of it this way," said a sixteen-year-old girl sitting beside her. "If people in New York woke up one day and learned that we were gone, that we had simply died or left for somewhere else, how would they feel?"

"How do you think they'd feel?" I asked.

"I think they'd be relieved," this very solemn girl replied.

Many educators make the argument today that given the demographics of large cities like New York and their suburban areas, our only realistic goal should be the nurturing of strong, empowered, and well-funded schools in segregated neighborhoods. Black school officials in these situations have sometimes conveyed to me a bitter and clear-sighted recognition that they're being asked, essentially, to mediate and render functional an uncontested separation between children of their race and children of white people living sometimes in a distant section of their town and sometimes in almost their own immediate communities. Implicit in this mediation is a willingness to set aside the promises of *Brown* and—though never stating this or even thinking of it clearly in these terms—to settle for the promise made more than a century ago in *Plessy v. Ferguson*, the 1896 Supreme Court ruling in which "separate but equal" was accepted as a tolerable rationale for the perpetuation of a dual system in American society.

Equality itself—equality alone—is now, it seems, the article of faith to which most of the principals of inner-city public schools subscribe. And some who are perhaps most realistic do not even dare to ask for, or expect, complete equality, which seems beyond the realm of probability for many years to come, but look instead for only a sufficiency of means—"adequacy" is the legal term most often used today—by which to win those practical and finite victories that appear to be within their reach. Higher standards, higher expectations, are repeatedly demanded of these urban principals, and of the teachers and students in their schools, but far lower standards—certainly in ethical

[3]The names of children mentioned in this article have been changed to protect their privacy. [Kozol's note]

respects—appear to be expected of the dominant society that isolates these children in unequal institutions.

"Dear Mr. Kozol," wrote the eight-year-old, "we do not have the things you have. You have Clean things. We do not have. You have a clean bathroom. We do not have that. You have Parks and we do not have Parks. You have all the thing and we do not have all the thing. Can you help us?"

The letter, from a child named Alliyah, came in a fat envelope of twenty-seven letters from a class of third-grade children in the Bronx. Other letters that the students in Alliyah's classroom sent me registered some of the same complaints. "We don't have no gardens," "no Music or Art," and "no fun places to play," one child said. "Is there a way to fix this Problem?" Another noted a concern one hears from many children in such overcrowded schools: "We have a gym but it is for lining up. I think it is not fair." Yet another of Alliyah's classmates asked me, with a sweet misspelling, if I knew the way to make her school into a "good" school— "like the other kings have" —and ended with the hope that I would do my best to make it possible for "all the kings" to have good schools.

The letter that affected me the most, however, had been written by a child named Elizabeth. "It is not fair that other kids have a garden and new things. But we don't have that," said Elizabeth. "I wish that this school was the most beautiful school in the whole why world."

"The whole why world" stayed in my thoughts for days. When I later met Elizabeth, I brought her letter with me, thinking I might see whether, in reading it aloud, she'd change the "why" to "wide" or leave it as it was. My visit to her class, however, proved to be so pleasant, and the children seemed so eager to bombard me with their questions about where I lived, and why I lived there rather than in New York, and who I lived with, and how many dogs I had, and other interesting questions of that sort, that I decided not to interrupt the nice reception they had given me with questions about usages and spelling. I left "the whole why world" to float around unedited and unrevised in my mind. The letter itself soon found a resting place on the wall above my desk.

In the years before I met Elizabeth, I had visited many other schools in the South Bronx and in one northern district of the Bronx as well. I had made repeated visits to a high school where a stream of water flowed down one of the main stairwells on a rainy afternoon and where green fungus molds were growing in the office where the students went for counseling. A large blue barrel was positioned to collect rainwater coming through the ceiling. In one makeshift elementary school housed in a former skating rink next to a funeral establishment in yet another nearly all-black-and-Hispanic section of the Bronx, class size rose to thirty-four and more; four kindergarten classes and a sixth-grade class were packed into a single room that had no windows. The air was stifling in many rooms, and the children had no place for recess because there was no outdoor playground and no indoor gym.

In another elementary school, which had been built to hold 1,000 children but was packed to bursting with some 1,500, the principal poured out his feelings to me in a room in which a plastic garbage bag had been attached somehow to cover part of the collapsing ceiling. "This," he told me, pointing to the garbage bag, then gesturing around him at the other indications of decay and disrepair one sees in ghetto schools much like it elsewhere, "would not happen to white children."

Libraries, once one of the glories of the New York City school system, were either nonexistent or, at best, vestigial in large numbers of the elementary schools. Art and music programs had also for the most part disappeared. "When I began to teach in 1969," the principal of an elementary school in the South Bronx reported to me, "every school had a full-time licensed art and music teacher and librarian." During the subsequent decades, he recalled, "I saw all of that destroyed."

School physicians also were removed from elementary schools during these years. In 1970, when substantial numbers of white children still attended New York City's public schools, 400 doctors had been present to address the health needs of the children. By 1993 the number of doctors had been cut to 23, most of them part-time—a cutback that affected most severely children in the city's poorest neighborhoods, where medical facilities were most deficient and health problems faced by children most extreme. Teachers told me of asthmatic children who came into class with chronic wheezing and who at any moment of the day might undergo more serious attacks, but in the schools I visited there were no doctors to attend to them.

In explaining these steep declines in services, political leaders in New York tended to point to shifting economic factors, like a serious budget crisis in the middle 1970s, rather than to the changing racial demographics of the student population. But the fact of economic ups and downs from year to year, or from one decade to the next, could not convincingly explain the permanent shortchanging of the city's students, which took place routinely in good economic times and bad. The bad times were seized upon politically to justify the cuts, and the money was never restored once the crisis years were past.

"If you close your eyes to the changing racial composition of the schools and look only at budget actions and political events," says Noreen Connell, the director of the nonprofit Educational Priorities Panel in New York, "you're missing the assumptions that are underlying these decisions." When minority parents ask for something better for their kids, she says, "the assumption is that these are parents who can be discounted. These are kids who just don't count—children we don't value."

This, then, is the accusation that Alliyah and her classmates send our way: "You have...We do not have." Are they right or are they wrong? Is this a case of naive and simplistic juvenile exaggeration? What does a third-grader know about these big-time questions of fairness and justice? Physical appearances apart, how in any case do you begin to measure something so diffuse and vast and seemingly abstract as having more, or having less, or not having at all?

Around the time I met Alliyah in the school year 1997–1998, New York's Board of Education spent about $8,000 yearly on the education of a third-grade child in a New York City public school. If you could have scooped Alliyah up out of the neighborhood where she was born and plunked her down in a fairly typical white suburb of New York, she would have received a public education worth about $12,000 a year. If you were to lift her up once more and set her down in one of the wealthiest white suburbs of New York, she would have received as much as $18,000 worth of public education every year and would likely have had a third-grade teacher paid approximately $30,000 more than her teacher in the Bronx was paid.

The dollars on both sides of the equation have increased since then, but the discrepancies between them have remained. The present per-pupil spending level in the New York City schools is $11,700, which may be compared with a per-pupil spending level in excess of $22,000 in the well-to-do suburban district of Manhasset, Long Island. The present New York City level is, indeed, almost exactly what Manhasset spent per pupil eighteen years ago, in 1987, when that sum of money bought a great deal more in services and salaries than it can buy today. In dollars adjusted for inflation, New York City has not yet caught up to where its wealthiest suburbs were a quarter-century ago....

As racial isolation deepens and the inequalities of education finance remain unabated and take on new and more innovative forms, the principals of many inner-city schools are making choices that few principals in public schools that serve white children in the mainstream of the nation ever need to contemplate. Many have been dedicating vast amounts of time and effort to create an architecture of adaptive strategies that promise incremental gains within the limits inequality allows.

New vocabularies of stentorian determination, new systems of incentive, and new modes of castigation, which are termed "rewards and sanctions," have emerged. Curriculum materials that are alleged to be aligned with governmentally established goals and standards and particularly suited to what are regarded as "the special needs and learning styles" of low-income urban children have been introduced. Relentless emphasis on raising test scores, rigid policies of nonpromotion and nongraduation, a new empiricism and the imposition of unusually detailed lists of named and numbered "outcomes" for each isolated parcel of instruction, an oftentimes fanatical insistence upon uniformity of teachers in their management of time, an openly conceded emulation of the rigorous approaches of the military and a frequent use of terminology that comes out of the world of industry and commerce—these are just a few of the familiar aspects of these new adaptive strategies.

Although generically described as "school reform," most of these practices and policies are targeted primarily at poor children of color; and although most educators speak of these agendas in broad language that sounds applicable to all, it is understood that they are valued chiefly as responses to perceived catastrophe in deeply segregated and unequal schools.

"If you do what I tell you to do, how I tell you to do it, when I tell you to do it, you'll get it right," said a determined South Bronx principal observed by a reporter for the *New York Times.* She was laying out a memorizing rule for math to an assembly of her students. "If you don't, you'll get it wrong." This is the voice, this is the tone, this is the rhythm and didactic certitude one hears today in inner-city schools that have embraced a pedagogy of direct command and absolute control. "Taking their inspiration from the ideas of B. F. Skinner[4]..." says the *Times,* proponents of scripted rote-and-drill curricula articulate their aim as the establishment of "faultless communication" between "the teacher, who is the stimulus," and "the students, who respond."

The introduction of Skinnerian approaches (which are commonly employed in penal institutions and drug-rehabilitation programs), as a way of altering the attitudes and learning styles of black and Hispanic children, is provocative, and it has stirred some outcries from respected scholars. To actually go into a school where you know some of the children very, very well and see the way that these approaches can affect their daily lives and thinking processes is even more provocative.

On a chilly November day four years ago in the South Bronx, I entered P.S. 65, a school I had been visiting since 1993. There had been major changes since I'd been there last. Silent lunches had been instituted in the cafeteria, and on days when children misbehaved, silent recess had been introduced as well. On those days the students were obliged to sit in rows and maintain perfect silence on the floor of a small indoor room instead of going out to play. The words SUCCESS FOR ALL, the brand name of a scripted curriculum—better known by its acronym, SFA—were prominently posted at the top of the main stairway and, as I would later find, in almost every room. Also frequently displayed within the halls and classrooms were a number of administrative memos that were worded with unusual didactic absoluteness. "Authentic Writing," read a document called "Principles of Learning" that was posted in the corridor close to the principal's office, "is driven by curriculum and instruction." I didn't know what this expression meant. Like many other undefined and arbitrary phrases posted in the school, it seemed to be a dictum that invited no interrogation.

I entered the fourth grade of a teacher I will call Mr. Endicott, a man in his mid-thirties who had arrived here without training as a teacher, one of about a dozen teachers in the building who were sent into this

35

---

[4]**B. F. Skinner:** American psychologist (1904–1990) known for his theories on stimulus and response.

school after a single summer of short-order preparation. Now in his second year, he had developed a considerable sense of confidence and held the class under a tight control.

As I found a place to sit in a far corner of the room, the teacher and his young assistant, who was in her first year as a teacher, were beginning a math lesson about building airport runways, a lesson that provided children with an opportunity for measuring perimeters. On the wall behind the teacher, in large letters, was written: "Portfolio Protocols: 1. You are responsible for the selection of [your] work that enters your portfolio. 2. As your skills become more sophisticated this year, you will want to revise, amend, supplement, and possibly replace items in your portfolio to reflect your intellectual growth." On the left side of the room: "Performance Standards Mathematics Curriculum: M-5 Problem Solving and Reasoning. M-6 Mathematical Skills and Tools..."

My attention was distracted by some whispering among the children sitting to the right of me. The teacher's response to this distraction was immediate: his arm shot out and up in a diagonal in front of him, his hand straight up, his fingers flat. The young co-teacher did this, too. When they saw their teachers do this, all the children in the classroom did it, too.

"Zero noise," the teacher said, but this instruction proved to be unneeded. The strange salute the class and teachers gave each other, which turned out to be one of a number of such silent signals teachers in the school were trained to use, and children to obey, had done the job of silencing the class.

"Active listening!" said Mr. Endicott. "Heads up! Tractor beams!" 40 which meant, "Every eye on me."

On the front wall of the classroom, in handwritten words that must have taken Mr. Endicott long hours to transcribe, was a list of terms that could be used to praise or criticize a student's work in mathematics. At Level Four, the highest of four levels of success, a child's "problem-solving strategies" could be described, according to this list, as "systematic, complete, efficient, and possibly elegant," while the student's capability to draw conclusions from the work she had completed could be termed "insightful" or "comprehensive." At Level Two, the child's capability to draw conclusions was to be described as "logically unsound"; at Level One, "not present." Approximately 50 separate categories of proficiency, or lack of such, were detailed in this wall-sized tabulation.

A well-educated man, Mr. Endicott later spoke to me about the form of classroom management that he was using as an adaptation from a model of industrial efficiency. "It's a kind of 'Taylorism'[5] in the classroom," he explained, referring to a set of theories about the management of factory employees introduced by Frederick Taylor in the early

---

[5]**Taylorism:** Approach to management named after American engineer and business school professor Frederick Taylor. His *Principles of Scientific Management* (1911) sought to increase efficiency and productivity.

1900s. "Primitive utilitarianism" is another term he used when we met some months later to discuss these management techniques with other teachers from the school. His reservations were, however, not apparent in the classroom. Within the terms of what he had been asked to do, he had, indeed, become a master of control. It is one of the few classrooms I had visited up to that time in which almost nothing even hinting at spontaneous emotion in the children or the teacher surfaced while I was there.

The teacher gave the "zero noise" salute again when someone whispered to another child at his table. "In two minutes you will have a chance to talk and share this with your partner." Communication between children in the class was not prohibited but was afforded time slots and, remarkably enough, was formalized in an expression that I found included in a memo that was posted on the wall beside the door. "An opportunity...to engage in Accountable Talk."

Even the teacher's words of praise were framed in terms consistent with the lists that had been posted on the wall. "That's a Level Four suggestion," said the teacher when a child made an observation other teachers might have praised as simply "pretty good" or "interesting" or "mature."

There was, it seemed, a formal name for every cognitive event within this school: "Authentic Writing," "Active Listening," "Accountable Talk." The ardor to assign all items of instruction or behavior a specific name was unsettling me. The adjectives had the odd effect of hyping every item of endeavor. "Authentic Writing" was, it seemed, a more important act than what the children in a writing class in any ordinary school might try to do. "Accountable Talk" was something more self-conscious and significant than merely useful conversation.

Since that day at P.S. 65, I have visited nine other schools in six different cities where the same Skinnerian curriculum is used. The signs on the walls, the silent signals, the curious salute, the same insistent naming of all cognitive particulars, became familiar as I went from one school to the next.

"Meaningful Sentences," began one of the many listings of proficiencies expected of the children in the fourth grade of an inner-city elementary school in Hartford (90 percent black, 10 percent Hispanic) that I visited a short time later. "Noteworthy Questions," "Active Listening," and other designations like these had been posted elsewhere in the room. Here, too, the teacher gave the kids her outstretched arm, with hand held up, to reestablish order when they grew a little noisy, but I noticed that she tried to soften the effect of this by opening her fingers and bending her elbow slightly so it did not look quite as forbidding as the gesture Mr. Endicott had used. A warm and interesting woman, she later told me she disliked the regimen intensely.

Over her desk, I read a "Mission Statement," which established the priorities and values for the school. Among the missions of the school, according to the printed statement, which was posted also in some other classrooms of the school, was "to develop productive citizens" who have the skills that will be needed "for successful global competition," a message that was reinforced by other posters in the room. Over the heads of a group of children at their desks, a sign anointed them BEST WORKERS OF 2002.

Another signal now was given by the teacher, this one not for silence but in order to achieve some other form of class behavior, which I could not quite identify. The students gave exactly the same signal in response. Whatever the function of this signal, it was done as I had seen it done in the South Bronx and would see it done in other schools in months to come. Suddenly, with a seeming surge of restlessness and irritation—with herself, as it appeared, and with her own effective use of all the tricks that she had learned—she turned to me and said, "I can do this with my dog." ...

In some inner-city districts, even the most pleasant and old-fashioned class activities of elementary schools have now been over-taken by these ordering requirements. A student teacher in California, for example, wanted to bring a pumpkin to her class on Halloween but knew it had no ascertainable connection to the California standards. She therefore had developed what she called "The Multi-Modal Pumpkin Unit" to teach science (seeds), arithmetic (the size and shape of pumpkins, I believe—this detail wasn't clear), and certain items she adapted out of language arts, in order to position "pumpkins" in a frame of state proficiencies. Even with her multi-modal pumpkin, as her faculty adviser told me, she was still afraid she would be criticized because she knew the pumpkin would not really help her children to achieve expected goals on state exams.

Why, I asked a group of educators at a seminar in Sacramento, was a teacher being placed in a position where she'd need to do preposterous curricular gymnastics to enjoy a bit of seasonal amusement with her kids on Halloween? How much injury to state-determined "purpose" would it do to let the children of poor people have a pumpkin party once a year for no other reason than because it's something fun that other children get to do on autumn days in public schools across most of America?

"Forcing an absurdity on teachers does teach something," said an African-American professor. "It teaches acquiescence. It breaks down the will to thumb your nose at pointless protocols—to call absurdity 'absurd.'" Writing out the standards with the proper numbers on the chalkboard has a similar effect, he said; and doing this is "terribly important" to the principals in many of these schools. "You *have* to post the standards, and the way you know the children know the standards is by asking them to *state* the standards. And they *do* it—and you want to be quite certain that they do it if you want to keep on working at that school."

In speaking of the drill-based program in effect at P.S. 65, Mr. Endi-cott told me he tended to be sympathetic to the school administrators, more so at least than the other teachers I had talked with seemed to be. He said he believed his principal had little choice about the implemen-tation of this program, which had been mandated for all elementary schools in New York City that had had rock-bottom academic records over a long period of time. "This puts me into a dilemma," he went on, "because I love the kids at P.S. 65." And even while, he said, "I know that my teaching SFA is a charade...if I don't do it I won't be permitted to teach these children."

Mr. Endicott, like all but two of the new recruits at P.S. 65—there were about fifteen in all—was a white person, as were the principal and most of the administrators at the school. As a result, most of these neo-phyte instructors had had little or no prior contact with the children of an inner-city neighborhood; but, like the others I met, and despite the distancing between the children and their teachers that resulted from the scripted method of instruction, he had developed close attachments to his students and did not want to abandon them. At the same time, the class- and race-specific implementation of this program obviously troubled him. "There's an expression now," he said. "'The rich get richer, and the poor get SFA.'" He said he was still trying to figure out his "professional ethics" on the problem that this posed for him.

White children made up "only about one percent" of students 55 in the New York City schools in which this scripted teaching system was imposed,[6] according to the *New York Times*, which also said that "the prepackaged lessons" were intended "to ensure that all teachers— even novices or the most inept"—would be able to teach reading. As seemingly pragmatic and hardheaded as such arguments may be, they are desperation strategies that come out of the acceptance of inequity. If we did not have a deeply segregated system in which more expe-rienced instructors teach the children of the privileged and the least experienced are sent to teach the children of minorities, these prac-tices would not be needed and could not be so convincingly defended. They are confections of apartheid,[7] and no matter by what arguments of urgency or practicality they have been justified, they cannot fail to further deepen the divisions of society.

There is no misery index for the children of apartheid education. There ought to be; we measure almost everything else that happens to them in their schools. Do kids who go to schools like these enjoy the days they spend in them? Is school, for most of them, a happy place

[6]SFA has since been discontinued in the New York City public schools, though it is still being used in 1,300 U.S. schools, serving as many as 650,000 children. Similar scripted systems are used in schools (overwhelmingly minority in population) serving several mil-lion children. [Kozol's note]

[7]**apartheid:** Literally "apartness," the policy of racial segregation and discrimination in South Africa, restricting the rights of nonwhites, which ended in 1990.

to be? You do not find the answers to these questions in reports about achievement levels, scientific methods of accountability, or structural revisions in the modes of governance. Documents like these don't speak of happiness. You have to go back to the schools themselves to find an answer to these questions. You have to sit down in the little chairs in first and second grade, or on the reading rug with kindergarten kids, and listen to the things they actually say to one another and the dialogue between them and their teachers. You have to go down to the basement with the children when it's time for lunch and to the playground with them, if they have a playground, when it's time for recess, if they still have recess at their school. You have to walk into the children's bathrooms in these buildings. You have to do what children do and breathe the air the children breathe. I don't think that there is any other way to find out what the lives that children lead in school are really like.

High school students, when I first meet them, are often more reluctant than the younger children to open up and express their personal concerns; but hesitation on the part of students did not prove to be a problem when I visited a tenth-grade class at Fremont High School in Los Angeles. The students were told that I was a writer, and they took no time in getting down to matters that were on their minds.

"Can we talk about the bathrooms?" asked a soft-spoken student named Mireya.

In almost any classroom there are certain students who, by the force of their directness or the unusual sophistication of their way of speaking, tend to capture your attention from the start. Mireya later spoke insightfully about some of the serious academic problems that were common in the school, but her observations on the physical and personal embarrassments she and her schoolmates had to undergo cut to the heart of questions of essential dignity that kids in squalid schools like this one have to deal with all over the nation.

Fremont High School, as court papers filed in a lawsuit against the 60 state of California document, has fifteen fewer bathrooms than the law requires. Of the limited number of bathrooms that are working in the school, "only one or two...are open and unlocked for girls to use." Long lines of girls are "waiting to use the bathrooms," which are generally "unclean" and "lack basic supplies," including toilet paper. Some of the classrooms, as court papers also document, "do not have air conditioning," so that students, who attend school on a three-track schedule that runs year-round, "become red-faced and unable to concentrate" during "the extreme heat of summer." The school's maintenance records report that rats were found in eleven classrooms. Rat droppings were found "in the bins and drawers" of the high school's kitchen, and school records note that "hamburger buns" were being "eaten off [the] bread-delivery rack."

No matter how many tawdry details like these I've read in legal briefs or depositions through the years, I'm always shocked again to learn how often these unsanitary physical conditions are permitted to continue in the schools that serve our poorest students—even after they have been vividly described in the media. But hearing of these conditions in Mireya's words was even more unsettling, in part because this student seemed so fragile and because the need even to speak of these indignities in front of me and all the other students was an additional indignity.

"The problem is this," she carefully explained. "You're not allowed to use the bathroom during lunch, which is a thirty-minute period. The only time that you're allowed to use it is between your classes." But "this is a huge building," she went on. "It has long corridors. If you have one class at one end of the building and your next class happens to be way down at the other end, you don't have time to use the bathroom and still get to class before it starts. So you go to your class and then you ask permission from your teacher to go to the bathroom and the teacher tells you, 'No. You had your chance between the periods...'

"I feel embarrassed when I have to stand there and explain it to a teacher."

"This is the question," said a wiry-looking boy named Edward, leaning forward in his chair. "Students are not animals, but even animals need to relieve themselves sometimes. We're here for eight hours. What do they think we're supposed to do?"

"It humiliates you," said Mireya, who went on to make the interesting statement that "the school provides solutions that don't actually work," and this idea was taken up by several other students in describing course requirements within the school. A tall black student, for example, told me that she hoped to be a social worker or a doctor but was programmed into "Sewing Class" this year. She also had to take another course, called "Life Skills," which she told me was a very basic course—"a retarded class," to use her words—that "teaches things like the six continents," which she said she'd learned in elementary school. 65

When I asked her why she had to take these courses, she replied that she'd been told they were required, which as I later learned was not exactly so. What was required was that high school students take two courses in an area of study called "The Technical Arts," and which the Los Angeles Board of Education terms "Applied Technology." At schools that served the middle class or upper-middle class, this requirement was likely to be met by courses that had academic substance and, perhaps, some relevance to college preparation. At Beverly Hills High School, for example, the technical-arts requirement could be fulfilled by taking subjects like residential architecture, the designing of commercial structures, broadcast journalism, advanced computer graphics, a sophisticated course in furniture design, carving and sculpture, or an honors course in engineering research and design. At Fremont High, in contrast, this requirement was far more often met by courses that were basically vocational and also obviously keyed to low-paying levels of employment.

Mireya, for example, who had plans to go to college, told me that she had to take a sewing class last year and now was told she'd been assigned to take a class in hairdressing as well. When I asked her teacher why Mireya could not skip these subjects and enroll in classes that would help her to pursue her college aspirations, she replied, "It isn't a question of what students want. It's what the school may have available. If all the other elective classes that a student wants to take are full, she has to take one of these classes if she wants to graduate."

A very small girl named Obie, who had big blue-tinted glasses tilted up across her hair, interrupted then to tell me with a kind of wild gusto that she'd taken hairdressing *twice*! When I expressed surprise that this was possible, she said there were two levels of hairdressing offered here at Fremont High. "One is in hairstyling," she said. "The other is in braiding."

Mireya stared hard at this student for a moment and then suddenly began to cry. "I don't *want* to take hairdressing. I did not need sewing either. I knew how to sew. My mother is a seamstress in a factory. I'm trying to go to college. I don't need to sew to go to college. My mother sews. I hoped for something else."

"What would you rather take?" I asked.   70

"I wanted to take an AP class," she answered.

Mireya's sudden tears elicited a strong reaction from one of the boys who had been silent up till now: a thin, dark-eyed student named Fortino, who had long hair down to his shoulders. He suddenly turned directly to Mireya and spoke into the silence that followed her last words.

"Listen to me," he said. "The owners of the sewing factories need laborers. Correct?"

"I guess they do," Mireya said.

"It's not going to be their own kids. Right?"   75

"Why not?" another student said.

"So they can grow beyond themselves," Mireya answered quietly. "But we remain the same."

"You're ghetto," said Fortino, "so we send you to the factory." He sat low in his desk chair, leaning on one elbow, his voice and dark eyes loaded with a cynical intelligence. "You're ghetto—so you sew!"

"There are higher positions than these," said a student named Samantha.

"You're ghetto," said Fortino unrelentingly, "So sew!"   80

Admittedly, the economic needs of a society are bound to be reflected to some rational degree within the policies and purposes of public schools. But, even so, there must be *something* more to life as it is lived by six-year-olds or ten-year-olds, or by teenagers, for that matter, than concerns about "successful global competition." Childhood is not merely basic training for utilitarian adulthood. It should have some claims upon our mercy, not for its future value to the economic interests of competitive societies but for its present value as a perishable piece of life itself.

Very few people who are not involved with inner-city schools have any real idea of the extremes to which the mercantile distortion of the purposes and character of education have been taken or how unabashedly proponents of these practices are willing to defend them. The head of a Chicago school, for instance, who was criticized by some for emphasizing rote instruction that, his critics said, was turning children into "robots," found no reason to dispute the charge. "Did you ever stop to think that these robots will never burglarize your home?" he asked, and "will never snatch your pocketbooks.... These robots are going to be producing taxes."

Corporate leaders, when they speak of education, sometimes pay lip-service to the notion of "good critical and analytic skills," but it is reasonable to ask whether they have in mind the critical analysis of *their* priorities. In principle, perhaps some do; but, if so, this is not a principle that seems to have been honored widely in the schools I have been visiting. In all the various business-driven inner-city classrooms I have observed in the past five years, plastered as they are with corporation brand names and managerial vocabularies, I have yet to see the two words "labor unions." Is this an oversight? How is that possible? Teachers and principals themselves, who are almost always members of a union, seem to be so beaten down that they rarely even question this omission.

It is not at all unusual these days to come into an urban school in which the principal prefers to call himself or herself "building CEO" or "building manager." In some of the same schools teachers are described as "classroom managers."[8] I have never been in a suburban district in which principals were asked to view themselves or teachers in this way. These terminologies remind us of how wide the distance has become between two very separate worlds of education....

[8]A school I visited three years ago in Columbus, Ohio, was littered with "Help Wanted" signs. Starting in kindergarten, children in the school were being asked to think about the jobs that they might choose when they grew up. In one classroom there was a poster that displayed the names of several retail stores: J. C. Penney, Wal-Mart, Kmart, Sears, and a few others. "It's like working in a store," a classroom aide explained. "The children are learning to pretend they're cashiers." At another school in the same district, children were encouraged to apply for jobs in their classrooms. Among the job positions open to the children in this school, there was an "Absence Manager" and a "Behavior Chart Manager," a "Form Collector Manager," a "Paper Passer Outer Manager," a "Paper Collecting Manager," a "Paper Returning Manager," an "Exit Ticket Manager," even a "Learning Manager," a "Reading Corner Manager," and a "Score Keeper Manager." I asked the principal if there was a special reason why those two words "management" and "manager" kept popping up throughout the school. "We want every child to be working as a manager while he or she is in this school," the principal explained. "We want to make them understand that, in this country, companies will give you opportunities to work, to prove yourself, no matter what you've done." I wasn't sure what she meant by "no matter what you've done," and asked her if she could explain it. "Even if you have a felony arrest," she said, "we want you to understand that you can be a manager someday." [Kozol's note]

© Bendib, LLC.

ENGAGING THE TEXT

1. Compare notes in class on your own elementary and secondary school experiences. How do the schools you attended compare with the public schools Kozol describes, both in terms of physical condition and teaching approach?

2. What evidence have you seen of reluctance on the part of politicians, educators, and the media to talk about the segregated state of America's public schools? Would you agree that the current state of public education in the United States amounts to "resegregation" and is, in fact, evidence of "apartheid" in American society?

3. Who is to blame for the current resegregation of American public schools, according to Kozol? Whom — or what — would you blame? To what extent would you agree that the state of inner-city schools represents a "moral failure" in America? Why might it be so important to Kozol to see this issue in moral — and not simply in political or social — terms?

4. **Thinking Rhetorically** Kozol includes a variety of facts, statistics, illustrations, and personal anecdotes in his examination of segregated schools. Review the passages that you found particularly convincing or powerful. In class, discuss the strengths and limitations of the various types of evidence Kozol uses to advance his claims. What, for example, do you find more persuasive — personal anecdotes about the students he meets, his own detailed classroom observations, or the statistics and studies he cites? Why?

EXPLORING CONNECTIONS

5. Compare Mike Rose's account of his own school experience during the 1950s and 1960s (p. 123) with the contemporary urban classrooms described by Kozol in this selection. How might Rose assess the teaching methods that dominate the school reforms Kozol describes? Do you think a Jack MacFarland would succeed in today's inner-city schools? Why or why not?

6. Compare what Kozol and John Taylor Gatto (p. 114) have to say about the impact of corporate America on U.S. schools. To what extent does your own prior educational experience suggest that corporate influence is undermining American education?

7. How well do the schools that Kozol describes fit any of the four categories of schools presented by Jean Anyon (p. 136)? To what extent do you think it would be possible to adapt the approaches and methods used in Anyon's professional or elite schools more broadly?

EXTENDING THE CRITICAL CONTEXT

8. Working in groups, sample news and magazine stories published in the last year to determine if Kozol is correct when he says that the media are reluctant to discuss the "segregation" of American public education. How many of the articles you identify address the idea of segregation? Of the inequalities of public education?

9. Over the past few years, a number of states have begun requiring high school students to take standardized "exit exams" to guarantee that they meet minimum academic standards before graduation. Research the use of testing in your state to find out more about its impact on students, and then debate its merits in class. Would you support recent proposals that would require a standardized nationwide test for college students before they receive their degrees? Why or why not?

A PROSTITUTE, A SERVANT, AND A CUSTOMER-SERVICE REPRESENTATIVE: A LATINA IN ACADEMIA

CARMEN R. LUGO-LUGO

Students and teachers live along fault lines of intimacy and authority. Teachers often have enormous impact on students' lives, one that's sometimes as potent and enduring as that of a parent. Yet we rarely think — let alone talk — about the assumptions that teachers and students bring to the classroom about one another. In this selection, Carmen R. Lugo-Lugo explores what she believes her students assume about her as a Latina professor of Ethnic Studies and examines what those assumptions suggest about their attitudes toward education. Lugo-Lugo's awareness of herself as a woman of color and as a professor with a political agenda challenges us to consider our own "archetypal" expectations of who a college professor should be and what a college education should do for us. Lugo-Lugo was born and grew up in Puerto Rico. Today, she is an associate professor in the Department of Critical Culture, Gender, and Race Studies at Washington State University. Along with her wife, Mary K. Bloodsworth-Lugo, she has published a number of books and articles on race, sexuality, and culture. This selection originally appeared in *Presumed Incompetent: The Intersections of Race and Class for Women in Academia* (2012), edited by Gabriella Gutiérrez y Muhs, Yolanda Flores Niemann, Carmen G. González, and Angela P. Harris.

Introduction: Or, Allow Me to Illustrate the Title of My Essay

During my first time teaching introduction to comparative ethnic studies as a newly hired, tenure-track faculty member, I was about to begin class one day when a white male student raised his hand. I acknowledged him, and the following exchange ensued:

> Student: Can we cancel class today?
> Me: Why should we cancel class?
> Student: I don't feel like being in the classroom today, and since my parents pay for your salary, I think it is only fair you do what I say.

Though I was momentarily taken aback, I also chuckled at his reasoning (and audacity) a bit, after which I explained to him that by paying his tuition (which is what I suspected he meant), his parents were actually paying for his SEAT in my classroom, not my salary, since that is actually paid by the Washington state legislature. Up to this point, the other students in the class were following this exchange very closely, like a tennis match. Perhaps interested in seeing how I handled their classmate's request, and thus how seriously they should take me, the students were as attentive as I had ever seen them, some on the edge of their seats looking anxious, others wearing a horrified look on their faces. I finally concluded the exchange with the following statement: "and, regardless of who pays for my services, I am your professor, not your personal prostitute." The class let out a collective, sizable gasp, followed by uproarious laughter, which helped dissipate the tension somewhat.

My admittedly awkward final comment was an attempt at highlighting the fact that although I might have been there to provide a service for them (I was there to teach him and his classmates about race relations), I was not at their disposal, so they could not dismiss me whenever they weren't in the mood for class. I then proceeded to preempt the material for that day to have a discussion about entitlement and white privilege, even though I am fairly certain we had covered those topics before (nothing like a real-life, just-happened example to provide insight and drive a point home).

As I reflect back on that encounter and the class discussion that followed, I can identify three elements that were operating in that one request: (1) I was a woman of color; (2) I was teaching a subject that many consider unnecessary (I keep hearing that racism is now a thing of the past) or academically flawed (meaning too critical of whites); and (3) I was teaching at a historical juncture marked by the relentless corporatization of the university, a process that has turned teaching into a marketplace (or shopping mall of sorts), where students feel like self-entitled customers and faculty and staff are forced to play the roles of either clerks, checkout cashiers, or customer-service representatives. Something to keep in mind is that although these three elements may have had different origins, as I discovered in the conversation that ensued afterward with the entire class, they were operating simultaneously in that one exchange.

As I recall, our class discussion that day was pretty fruitful, and after much processing and back-and-forth analysis by the students, a female student of color — still baffled by the incident — challenged her classmates to "just think of the kind of nerve that it takes" for any student not only to think that he owns his teacher but to feel free and secure enough to tell her in front of forty-nine classmates that he, in fact, does. Aha! Exactly. After that comment, I let the class go an entire five minutes before the bell rang, not because I wanted to honor in any way the original request that class be dismissed early, but because I did not want any other comment to taint that final insightful observation. I wanted it to linger in their minds (haunt them perhaps) until the next class period. The important thing is that the sense of entitlement the female student of color was talking about is the result of the three elements I listed. And because I believe they still inform many of my interactions with students (for I still teach that class at the same institution), I shall spend the rest of this essay discussing these elements in detail.

A Latina in the Ivory Tower

Although the university is often seen as a space detached from the rest of society (hence the term "ivory tower"), as a trained sociologist I know full well that the same ideas we find in society at large operate within the confines of the university, because it is part of and develops from that very society. That is why my position within both U.S. society and academia is an important component of this discussion, a position that is described something like this: I am a woman. A woman who is of color. A woman of color who is a Puerto Rican (which means I am viewed as a Latina). And those markers mean something at the beginning of the twenty-first century in and outside the U.S. academy. As identities, they inform the way I position myself in relation to other gendered and racial subjects, but as markers, they provide my students with a lens through which to look at, interpret, and treat me. This lens, of course, is created by the current understanding that our society has about Latinos/as at this historical juncture.

Since the United States is such a segregated society, it is fair to assume that its mainstream culture does not derive any understanding of Latinos/as from daily interactions. According to the last census, Americans tend to live in neighborhoods with people who are like them in both race and social class. Moreover, according to a data-analysis report released by the U.S. Bureau of the Census, the national index of residential segregation for Latinos/as rose 1.5 percent between 1980 and 2000 (U.S. Bureau of the Census 2008). It is then only fair to conclude that mainstream (white) Americans obtain their understanding of Latinos/as not from personal experience or face-to-face encounters but from social institutions, including, of course, pervasive and omnipresent ones such as the media and popular culture.

What does it mean, then, for mainstream white America to understand Latinos/as through an institution like the media? Since the Latino/a explosion of the 1990s, U.S. popular culture has systematically sold specific images of Latinos/as. According to music, film, television, and other venues, Latino males are hot, dark, handsome womanizing law enforcement officers or criminals (see, for instance, most of the characters played by Jimmy Smits, Benjamin Bratt, or Benicio del Toro), while Latinas are just hot and sexy (see, for instance, most of the characters played by Eva Longoria, Jennifer Lopez, or Eva Mendez). Magazine covers are full of phrases like "sizzling hot" and "hot tamale" or the word "sexy" when describing Latinos/as. When I wrote this essay in September 2009, a general search on Amazon.com under the keyword "Latina" produced hundreds of results. What's really telling is that of the first ten, nine were DVDs with the following titles: *Sizzling Latinas*, vol. 2; *Joe Pusher's Latinas*, vol. 1; *Joe Pusher's Latinas*, vol. 5; *Latina Pole Queens; Muy Caliente: Nude Latinas; Joe Pusher's Latinas*, vol. 4; *Latina Party; Sexy Latinas del Reggaeton*, vol. 2; and *Latina Girls Going Bananas*, vol. 2. I assume I don't have to describe the pictures on the covers of these DVDs, but I will say that they match the titles beautifully.

Similarly the first two hits in a Google search under the keyword "Latinas" produced the following: "Sizzling Latinas" and "Sexy Latinas, Spanish Girls, Hot Latin." I can't say for sure—because I dared not go to those sites—but I suspect they were pornographic, giving us a good idea of the forceful ways that Latinas and their supposed hotness are sexualized and turned into commodities. Similarly, an advanced Google search with the keywords "handsome Latinos" produced more than two hundred hits, most of them related to gay porn. These results are important, because they tell us a story of the commodification (by way of sexuality) of Latinos/as at the beginning of the twenty-first century. Though some may be skeptical about my using pornographic Web sites to show or measure Latino/a commodification, I would like to point out that just like academia, the porn industry reflects the society from which it emerges.

For more than ten years now, these views on Latinos/as have permeated U.S. mainstream society and culture, creating archetypes of these groups. These archetypal images are then superimposed on the bodies of flesh-and-blood Latinos/as, like a cloak of expectations. In fact, these portrayals and descriptions have become ingrained in people's minds to the point where they are part of the collective understanding of Latinos/as in the United States and create a reality. The results of my hasty searches in Amazon and Google ring true to that collective understanding and reality. As a white female student once told me when I was talking about stereotypical representations of Latinas in popular culture, "But Latinas *are* hot."

Mainstream understandings of Latinos/as affect the way they are treated and thus, the way they live their lives. Though this may seem like a simplistic conclusion, its simplicity should not be mistaken for banality. After all, with that statement, I am suggesting that mainstream understandings of Latinos/as (as flawed, inaccurate, and even misguided as they may be) have a direct impact on their material existence. That is why when looking back at some experiences I have had over the years, I must remember that this society sees me through a specific lens. For instance, as a graduate student in the 1990s, I had to contend with being viewed as a hot commodity by some of my professors, including one who once intimated in a hopeful tone that he had never been with a "hot Latin lover." As a graduate instructor close in age to the students I was teaching, I also had to deal with similar comments from my students, along with invitations to hang out or have a few drinks or fun in town. For better or worse, I learned to deal with all that as part of who I was within the academy and the well-rounded education I was getting.

Now that I am a professor—dealing with both my identity and the perceptions that others have of me—dealing with who I am within the academic setting has a great deal to do with who I am not: a white male, the archetypical expectation for a college professor. This white male is supposed to be knowledgeable, wise, and capable. And it is clear to my students—from the moment they step foot in my classroom for the first time—that I am neither white nor male. Being a college professor is difficult enough for any woman because women are still, to this day, not seen as prone to reason or even possessing intelligence; in fact, many people continue to regard them as volatile creatures dominated by their feelings, their "hearts." If you think I am exaggerating, a female white student said just this semester in class that as she understands it (that is, as she's been told), women "do not have the brain capability to understand engineering." If this society can get a white woman to believe she does not have the brain to do engineering, I can only imagine what things you can get her to believe about other people, especially those with whom she has only a few, if any, interactions.

Given all this, a Latina in the classroom is sure to evoke a different set of images, many of which, I would imagine, led the student in the original story I told to think he could command me to stop class without any repercussions. After all—as he admitted in the postexchange discussion—he would not have thought about asking his math professor (who he conveyed was male and white) to dismiss class. That is why it is difficult not to cringe when students write in the course evaluations at the end of the semester things like "she is really knowledgeable," "she knows what she is talking about," "she's really smart," or the one I got last semester: "Carmen is the woman of my dreams; she is intelligent and funny." I know that they mean those accolades as compliments, but I also know that in many cases, they say these things because those were not their expectations when they walked into the classroom and saw me (a Latina) on the first day of class. They did not expect an intelligent, knowledgeable person, which is why I suspect they feel the need to write those comments, as if implying "she is not what I expected," or "I was pleasantly surprised with the way things turned out." But regardless of the way things ended up, I am still teaching classes that many of my students think (at least when they enroll in them because they must so they can get their diversity credits) are not necessary (at best) or a waste of their time (at worst).

A Latina in the Ivory Tower
Teaching Ethnic Studies

Racism and racial inequalities are alive and well. That is the basic tenet of the classes I teach and the discipline of ethnic studies in general. As simple and intuitive as that statement may seem to some, however, it goes against contemporary understandings of race relations that are ingrained in our students' minds, namely, that racism is a thing of the past. Apparently, somewhere among the march in Washington, the Freedom Summer, the urban riots, the assassination of Dr. Martin Luther King Jr., the war against Vietnam, the war on drugs, the continual reelection of staunch segregationist Strom Thurman to the U.S. Congress, the Rodney King incident, the voracious expansion of the prison industrial complex, the welfare reform, the lynching of James Byrd, No Child Left Behind, the creation of the Department of Homeland Security, the Patriot Act, the invasions of and wars against Afghanistan and Iraq, Abu Ghraib and Guantanamo, the three nooses hanging from a tree in Jena's high school, and the Secure Fence Act, we overcame racism.

And, if there is a problem, it is an individual one (i.e., a few bad apples), which means it is definitely smaller than it was before, which means things will work themselves out with time. Students are quick to declare (as if it were a badge of honor) that they learned not to see color (the

15

color-blind mentality Eduardo Bonilla-Silva[1] [2009] talks about in his work), and that we actually live in a society where race does not matter anymore (the so-called postracial society, also addressed by Bonilla-Silva [2009]). After all, we have a black president (one whom many suspect was not born in the United States because his father is Kenyan, is a Muslim, and hates America, but a black president nonetheless). So when I actually tell them, as I stated in the sentence opening this section, that racism and racial inequalities are alive and well, their understanding of the world where they live is threatened. By me. A woman. Of color.

The color-blind mentality leads them to conclude, then, that ethnic studies classes are unnecessary and a squandering of time, energy and resources. The translation: my job is a waste of their (parents') money. What can an ethnic studies professor teach them about racial inequality when that problem has basically evaporated from our society? Those of us working on ethnic studies and calling students to reflect on racism, they often argue, are stuck in history—because for students, history is something that happened a long time ago and has no relevance today. From their perspective, we just need to let go of the past, stop bitching about it, and move on. As a student so expressively (if inaccurately) put it in an introductory class when trying to respond to an author's point that racism affects people's livelihoods, "Slavery ended like hundreds of years ago. We need to like forget about it and like move on."

At the same time that they trumpet the complete elimination of racism and racial inequality, however, students also talk about *reverse racism*: "immigrants who can't even speak English" taking American jobs, people of color playing "the race card" to get their way, and, of course, hot Latinas. The fact that they can parrot the nonsense that conservative pundits rehearse daily in the media is, of course, not surprising. We do have to put this in a context, though, because this is the generation that came of age with a color-coded terror alert and a government telling them to be vigilant about threats. The words of former President Bush following the September 11, 2001, attacks— "either you are with us, or you are with the terrorists"—resonated for seven years and informed the way these students understand their position in the world. As this message made it clear, not only was there an "us" and a "them," but obviously, more importantly, the "them" was always and without question a threat to the security and safety of "us."

Ethnic studies turns all those concepts upside down by forcing students to understand the genesis of an us/them binary and analyze its consequences. In addition, ethnic studies is different from disciplines like sociology, political science, and anthropology, which tend to hide behind the curtain of scientific objectivity and present issues by discussing numbers and an array of calculated theories designed to provide some explanation for the numbers. In fact, listening to my colleagues

---

[1]E. Bonilla-Silva, 2009. *Racism without racists: Colorblind racism and the persistence of racial inequality in the United States.* Lanham, MD: Rowman & Littlefield Publishers, Inc. [All notes are Lugo-Lugo's, except 2.]

and friends in those disciplines discuss their student evaluations, it appears that if professors in any of these (and related) disciplines try to move beyond mere presentation of facts, they are told to "shut up and teach." Because of its transdisciplinary methodology, ethnic studies is not a shut-up-and-teach kind of discipline. Ethnic studies does not hide behind the veil of objectivity, and in fact, to be effective, it has to advocate and strive for a fundamental transformation of race relations. Stating that there is inequality is not enough. And here is where I come in: I am Latina telling my mostly white students that racism, discrimination, and inequality still exist and affect all our lives (theirs included), both in ways that can be measured and ones that cannot. I also tell them that they are implicated in those things, that they must do something about them, and that their comforts come at the expense of others. And, of course, they do not want to hear that. Especially not from me.

A Latina in the Corporatized Ivory Tower

The global market forces that have shaped and characterized our contemporary society spare no one and nothing. That includes the academy. Seeking a corporate model of efficiency, universities are restructuring academic and administrative units and running them like departments within a corporation. This is why the last two presidents at our university have proclaimed without raising many eyebrows that they are the CEOs. In addition, the devaluing of education and the resulting lack of funding recently experienced by universities in the United States have turned places of higher learning into symbolic (and sometimes even literal) shopping centers. For instance, Barnes & Noble owns the bookstore at our university, and it has its own Starbucks stand. Starbucks also owns (or its coffee is sold in) most coffee stands on campus, and the food court at the Student Union Building features fast-food chains like Subway and Panda Express, among others. As in any shopping center, customers need currency, and at our institution, students can use their identification badges as debit cards in any of these establishments. Also the gear sold by the athletic department is sponsored by Nike, turning athletes and students wearing the school clothing into walking billboards for their company. It is then no surprise that college students behave not like people seeking a higher form of knowledge but like customers of academia. They walk into the bookstore as customers, and they walk into my classroom, latte in hand, as customers as well. Why should they behave any differently when my classroom is only a few steps away from the bookstore?

Within this new structuring of the academic institution as a corporate marketplace, students begin to treat their professors and other university workers as clerks or cashiers at a department store, who are there to serve and satisfy their every need. Because of this, professors must accommodate their preferences: "Can we have more discussion? I learn better when I talk things out." Or, "Can we have less discussion?

I like it better when you lecture." Trying to accommodate the "I like it better this way" or "I like it better that way" turns professors into customer-service representatives, kowtowing to the demands made by customers and making sure they are satisfied with the product. As the business cliché goes, "The customer is always right."

In the marketplace academy, students shop for classes that suit their schedules, professors that they like, and experiences that satisfy them. Asking to be added to my class two weeks after the semester started last spring, a student told me that for that time period, she had been "shopping for a class" that fit her schedule and available time, and mine would be "just perfect." When I told her it was too late to add my class, her response was quite telling: "But I want this class." Students also, as illustrated in the opening story, think they are paying for all that with their (or their parents') tuition money.

As customer-service representatives with email addresses and office phone numbers, we are also supposed to be available always (at all times and any time) to satisfy our students' demands and appease their concerns. I can't even begin to count the number of times a student has told me, "I sent you an email last night, and I never heard back from you." This usually means the person sent the electronic message around 10:00 P.M., and it is 10:00 A.M., and I still have not replied to the message. I have also had many instances where a student seriously expected me to reply to a message he or she sent on Sunday evening asking me to give him or her ideas for a paper that was due the next morning. And they seem genuinely baffled when I tell them that I am not on call twenty-four hours a day and that I do not check my messages on Sundays. In fact, I said just that to a male student once, and his response was this: "What do you mean you don't check your messages on Sundays?" Even JCPenneys gets to have store hours.

The Classroom as a Stage

As Jim Farrell[2] tells us, shopping is "the great American pastime" [Gage 2003].[3] Moreover, consumerism has turned into entertainment. It is only logical to assume, then, that if students are learning to treat the university as a marketplace, they also want to regard it as a place to satisfy their entertainment needs. That may be why, a few years ago, a white female student told me that according to her boyfriend's calculations, each class period was costing them the same as a ticket to the movies (full price, not matinee). In a similar fashion to the student who asked me to cancel class, she made her observation as I was getting ready to start class, perhaps commanding me (in a more subtle way than the male student did) to be entertaining. By turning the academy

---

[2]**Jim Farrell:** Farrell (1949–2013) was a professor of history, American studies, and environmetal studies at St. Olaf College. [Eds.]

[3]A. Gage. 2003. "The great American pastime" is shopping says history professor in new book. *St. Olaf College News*, December 5. Available online at http://www.stolaf.edu /news/index.cfm?fuseaction=NewsDetails&id=1871.

into a marketplace (a shopping mall), universities have (inadvertently perhaps) turned professors into clerks. In addition, because of the relationship between consumerism and entertainment, coupled with the performative aspect of teaching, the academy as marketplace has also transformed into the academy as Hollywood. And as we know, within our celebritydom, not all performers are created equal. That is to say, a white performer is not treated in the same way as a nonwhite one. I will use two Hollywood actors to illustrate this point.

Let us analyze the expectations our society has of actress Angelina Jolie and those it has of actress Penélope Cruz. Even though they are approximately the same age, and both are Academy Award winners, it seems fair to argue that we expect different things from them, and those differences are (at least in part) the result of Jolie being perceived as white and Cruz as nonwhite. And before anyone raises the point that as a Spaniard, Cruz is a white European, I would like to remind everyone that because of her dark looks, name, and accent, and the weird ethnic classifications involving Hispanics and Latinos/as in the United States, she is, in fact, considered a Latina, and thus nonwhite. Although Jolie and Cruz are both sex symbols, if we look at media reports about both of them, Jolie is consistently portrayed as a human being with depth, whereas Cruz is consistently described only in relation to her perceived ethnicity: within this context, she is another hot Latina (who may be a good actress but who is definitely, and first and foremost, hot). The mainstream, online magazine AskMen.com provides the perfect means of analysis.

Let us begin with Jolie. According to AskMen.com,

> When she's not busy adopting third-world children and making the world a better place, Angelina Jolie is making the world a prettier place . . . [and] when both men and women consistently rate you as the woman they'd most like to sleep with, you know you're sexy, possibly even the sexiest woman alive. *Esquire* at least thinks so, and *People* magazine once voted her the Sexiest Person Alive. Whether she's a blonde [or] a brunette . . . , Angelina Jolie always looks hot, even when she's not trying. . . . She is the epitome of beauty whether she's wearing a headscarf in an African refugee camp or she's donning a designer gown on the red carpet. And those lips. . . . [Ask Men.com 2009][4]

And here is what the magazine says about Penélope Cruz:

> Able to jump from Spanish to English with ease, Penélope is the ultimate Hollywood Latin beauty, with oodles of talent to boot. . . . Cruz's status as a bona fide sex symbol has been firmly in place for well over a decade now, as the actress established herself early on as the textbook definition of a sultry Spaniard. Her willingness to doff her top has certainly won her a legion of male fans across the globe, though there's little doubt it's her genuine abilities as an actress that's

25

---

[4]Askmen.com. Angelina Jolie. Available online at http://www.askmen.com/celebs /women/actress/8_angelina_jolie.html.

ensured the endurance of her career. . . . It's just as clear that, no matter what her future holds, Penélope Cruz has earned a permanent place in our hearts as one of Hollywood's most indelible, exotic beauties. [AskMen.com 2008][5]

As we can gather from these two accounts, while Jolie is hot, Cruz is Latina hot (i.e., an exotic beauty). In addition, and perhaps more importantly, Jolie is granted a humanity to which Cruz does not have access. We can find that humanity in AskMen.com's descriptions of Jolie's humanitarian work. Statements such as "when she's not busy adopting third-world children and making the world a better place," and "she is the epitome of beauty whether she's wearing a headscarf in an African refugee camp or she's donning a designer gown on the red carpet" present Jolie as something more human than a sex symbol. Cruz, who has also done humanitarian work in Africa, publicly supported organizations seeking to eliminate poverty, AIDS, and weapons of mass destruction, and provide clean and fresh water is obviously not granted the same courtesy.

It follows, then, that if students see the classroom as a stage and their professors as performers, they have different expectations for their professors, based not only on the classes they teach but also on their race and gender. Thus, the performance of a white male professor teaching ethnic studies will be received differently than that of a Puerto Rican female with an accent.

A Few Concluding Remarks

Regardless of all the things I have discussed and the complicated interactions I may have with my students, I love being a college professor. I see it as a contribution to improving this most incomprehensible society. I also see it as my way of helping leave this place in a better condition than I found it. I take racism and racial inequalities seriously, and because I do, I spend an inordinate amount of time providing my students with the tools they need to understand what those things are, the shapes they take, and the impact they have on all of us, regardless of our racial background.

Still, I wish I did not have to pleasantly surprise my students by showing them I have a brain because after they walked in my class and saw me, they were expecting me not to have one. Relatedly, I wish my students would not dismiss me because I am not white and male. And I sure as hell wish they would not tell me they think I am the woman of their dreams. But I know that—in the light of the reality of race relations in our country—my wishes will remain only that. After all, dealing with all that is part of the reason why I have to teach my classes in the

---

[5]Askmen.com. Penélope Cruz. Available online at http://www.askmen.com/celebs/women/actress/56_penelope_cruz.html.

first place. As I already said, I have accepted my reality, and I can live with it. I also know I am not the only professor in the United States who has had to deal with these situations. Because of conversations I have had with colleagues and the literature I have read, I know my experiences are similar to those of other faculty of color and white female faculty members teaching unconventional disciplines.

What I have not accepted yet, still troubles me tremendously, and will continue to peeve me for as long as it is a reality in my life, is the rampant and unabashed corporatization of higher learning and its effects on students. I resolutely refuse to be my students' personal assistant. I will not be their brown-faced entertainer. And I will not check them out like a cashier as they make their way to the rest of their lives. I do understand that the corporate mentality is also part of our society, and since, as I discussed earlier, what happens in society at large also operates within the confines of the university, I can only expect the corporatization of society to be part of academia. 30

However, I also know that the university (especially a state, land-grant university such as the one where I teach) can resist the pressure to become another corporation. I believe it should have the moral imperative to do so. Instead of advancing marketplace ideologies, as a place of higher learning, the university can privilege learning over money, students over corporation, and people over profit. The university can become a place where people go to seek knowledge, not one where they go to buy their diploma. In the end, it would be just a tad easier to be able to talk to students about race relations, racial inequality, and racism without having to contend with an institution that puts a price tag on me, my class, and my lectures.

ENGAGING THE TEXT

1. What do you think Lugo-Lugo means when she says that white male college students often seem to feel a sense of entitlement? Do you think that white male students at your college act entitled, or see themselves that way? Entitled to what, and why?

2. To what extent do you think that students view professors differently based on their age, gender, ethnicity, or nationality? Would you agree that students tend to view white male professors as being "knowledgeable, wise, [and] capable" while female professors of color are seen as "volatile" or less capable "creatures"? Have you ever found yourself making assumptions about a professor based solely on his or her gender, race, or age?

3. Why does Lugo-Lugo believe that Ethnic Studies is important for all students? To what extent would you agree, and why? In your opinion, should colleges include or require subjects where professors don't simply "shut up and teach"? Why or why not?

4. Would you agree that today's students think of college as a kind of academic "shopping center" and view professors as "clerks and cashiers at a department

store" or "entertainers"? What's wrong with expecting "customer service" from your teachers? How should professors be viewed by their students, and why?

5. **Thinking Rhetorically** Who is the intended audience of this essay? Is Lugo-Lugo addressing a group of college administrators, her fellow faculty, her students, or a general audience? Which specific lines or passages in the essay help you answer this question? If Lugo-Lugo were writing this piece as an open letter to students in the college newspaper, what changes do you think she might make in the essay's content, structure, and tone? Why?

EXPLORING CONNECTIONS

6. In your journal, write an imaginary dialogue between Lugo-Lugo and Malcolm X (p. 161) in response to the ideas that racism died with slavery and that study of race history is a waste of time. How might Malcolm X be expected to respond to the notion that professors should "shut up and teach"? Why?

7. How might Jonathan Kozol (p. 170) respond to the idea that we now live in a post-racial society? To what extent does his discussion of the resegregation of American schools challenge the idea that "race doesn't matter anymore"?

EXTENDING THE CRITICAL CONTEXT

8. Lugo-Lugo identifies a number of possible sources for mainstream America's understanding of what it means to be Latino and Latina, including pop culture figures like Benjamin Bratt, Benicio del Toro, Eva Longoria, and Jennifer Lopez. Who would you identify as America's current models of Latino- and Latina-ness? How much have media images of Latinos and Latinas changed since 2009 when Lugo-Lugo wrote this essay?

9. Working in groups, try to identify the examples of racism that Lugo-Lugo mentions in paragraph 14. Later, look up the references that you can't identify and discuss what additional examples of contemporary racism and racial conflict Lugo-Lugo might include if she were writing her essay today. Do you agree that students today often think that "racism is a thing of the past"? Why or why not?

DON'T SEND YOUR KIDS TO THE IVY LEAGUE

WILLIAM DERESIEWICZ

Every spring, millions of high school students and their families look forward to the *U.S. News and World Report*'s ranking of America's top colleges. While admission to elite institutions like Yale, Harvard, Brown, or Princeton has long been seen as a badge of privilege and success, in today's highly competitive educational market, getting into the Ivy

League has become an obsession for many ambitious students. But, as William Deresiewicz suggests in this selection, an elite education may actually harm students by turning them into people who are "anxious, timid, lost, with little curiosity and a stunted sense of purpose." The problem, according to Deresiewicz — himself once a Yale professor — is that many students today enter college for the wrong reasons and with the wrong goals. As he sees it, if you come to college thinking only about getting a good "return" on your investment, you just might end up turning into "an out-of-touch, entitled little shit." Deresiewicz (b. 1964) attended Columbia University before teaching at Yale from 1998 to 2008. Today he is an author, an essayist, and a literary critic. His publications include *The Death of Friendship* (2011), *A Jane Austen Education: How Six Novels Taught Me About Love, Friendship, and the Things That Really Matter* (2012), and *Excellent Sheep: The Miseducation of the American Elite and the Way to a Meaningful Life* (2014). This selection originally appeared in the *New Republic*.

IN THE SPRING OF 2008, I did a daylong stint on the Yale admissions committee. We—that is, three admissions staff, a member of the college dean's office, and me, the faculty representative—were going through submissions from eastern Pennsylvania. The applicants had been assigned a score from one to four, calculated from a string of figures and codes—SATs, GPA, class rank, numerical scores to which the letters of recommendation had been converted, special notations for legacies[1] and diversity cases. The ones had already been admitted, and the threes and fours could get in only under special conditions—if they were a nationally ranked athlete, for instance, or a "DevA" (an applicant in the highest category of "development" cases, which means a child of very rich donors). Our task for the day was to adjudicate among the twos. Huge bowls of junk food were stationed at the side of the room to keep our energy up.

The junior officer in charge, a young man who looked to be about 30, presented each case, rat-a-tat-tat, in a blizzard of admissions jargon that I had to pick up on the fly. "Good rig": the transcript exhibits a good degree of academic rigor. "Ed level 1": parents have an educational level no higher than high school, indicating a genuine hardship case. "MUSD": a musician in the highest category of promise. Kids who had five or six items on their list of extracurriculars—the "brag"—were already in trouble, because that wasn't nearly enough. We listened, asked questions, dove into a letter or two, then voted up or down.

With so many accomplished applicants to choose from, we were looking for kids with something special, "PQs"—personal qualities—that were often revealed by the letters or essays. Kids who only had the

---

[1]**legacies:** Students who receive special consideration when applying to a college because of family ties to the institution. [All notes are the editors'.]

numbers and the résumé were usually rejected: "no spark," "not a team-builder," "this is pretty much in the middle of the fairway for us." One young person, who had piled up a truly insane quantity of extracurriculars and who submitted nine letters of recommendation, was felt to be "too intense." On the other hand, the numbers and the résumé were clearly indispensable. I'd been told that successful applicants could either be "well-rounded" or "pointy"—outstanding in one particular way—but if they were pointy, they had to be *really* pointy: a musician whose audition tape had impressed the music department, a scientist who had won a national award.

"Super People," the writer James Atlas has called them—the stereotypical ultra-high-achieving elite college students of today. A double major, a sport, a musical instrument, a couple of foreign languages, service work in distant corners of the globe, a few hobbies thrown in for good measure: They have mastered them all, and with a serene self-assurance that leaves adults and peers alike in awe. A friend who teaches at a top university once asked her class to memorize thirty lines of the eighteenth-century poet Alexander Pope. Nearly every single kid got every single line correct. It was a thing of wonder, she said, like watching thoroughbreds circle a track.

These enviable youngsters appear to be the winners in the race we 5
have made of childhood. But the reality is very different, as I have witnessed in many of my own students and heard from the hundreds of young people whom I have spoken with on campuses or who have written to me over the last few years. Our system of elite education manufactures young people who are smart and talented and driven, yes, but also anxious, timid, and lost, with little intellectual curiosity and a stunted sense of purpose: trapped in a bubble of privilege, heading meekly in the same direction, great at what they're doing but with no idea why they're doing it.

When I speak of elite education, I mean prestigious institutions like Harvard or Stanford or Williams as well as the larger universe of second-tier selective schools, but I also mean everything that leads up to and away from them—the private and affluent public high schools; the ever-growing industry of tutors and consultants and test-prep courses; the admissions process itself, squatting like a dragon at the entrance to adulthood; the brand-name graduate schools and employment opportunities that come after the B.A.; and the parents and communities, largely upper-middle class, who push their children into the maw of this machine. In short, our entire system of elite education.

I should say that this subject is very personal for me. Like so many kids today, I went off to college like a sleepwalker. You chose the most prestigious place that let you in; up ahead were vaguely understood objectives: status, wealth—"success." What it meant to actually get an education and why you might want one—all this was off the table. It was only after twenty-four years in the Ivy League—college and a Ph.D. at Columbia, ten years on the faculty at Yale—that I started to think about what this system does to kids and how they can escape from it, what it does to our society and how we can dismantle it.

A young woman from another school wrote me this about her boyfriend at Yale:

> Before he started college, he spent most of his time reading and writing short stories. Three years later, he's painfully insecure, worrying about things my public-educated friends don't give a second thought to, like the stigma of eating lunch alone and whether he's "networking" enough. No one but me knows he fakes being well-read by thumbing through the first and last chapters of any book he hears about and obsessively devouring reviews in lieu of the real thing. He does this not because he's incurious, but because there's a bigger social reward for being able to talk about books than for actually reading them.

I taught many wonderful young people during my years in the Ivy League—bright, thoughtful, creative kids whom it was a pleasure to talk with and learn from. But most of them seemed content to color within the lines that their education had marked out for them. Very few were passionate about ideas. Very few saw college as part of a larger project of intellectual discovery and development. Everyone dressed as if they were ready to be interviewed at a moment's notice.

Look beneath the façade of seamless well-adjustment, and what you often find are toxic levels of fear, anxiety, and depression, of emptiness and aimlessness and isolation. A large-scale survey of college freshmen recently found that self-reports of emotional well-being have fallen to their lowest level in the study's twenty-five-year history.

So extreme are the admission standards now that kids who manage to get into elite colleges have, by definition, never experienced anything but success. The prospect of *not* being successful terrifies them, disorients them. The cost of falling short, even temporarily, becomes not merely practical, but existential. The result is a violent aversion to risk. You have no margin for error, so you avoid the possibility that you will ever make an error. Once, a student at Pomona told me that she'd love to have a chance to think about the things she's studying, only she doesn't have the time. I asked her if she had ever considered not trying to get an A in every class. She looked at me as if I had made an indecent suggestion.

There are exceptions, kids who insist, against all odds, on trying to get a real education. But their experience tends to make them feel like freaks. One student told me that a friend of hers had left Yale because she found the school "stifling to the parts of yourself that you'd call a soul."

"Return on investment": that's the phrase you often hear today when people talk about college. What no one seems to ask is what the "return" is supposed to be. Is it just about earning more money? Is the only purpose of an education to enable you to get a job? What, in short, is college for?

The first thing that college is for is to teach you to think. That doesn't simply mean developing the mental skills particular to individual disciplines. College is an opportunity to stand outside the world for a few years, between the orthodoxy of your family and the exigencies of career, and contemplate things from a distance.

Learning how to think is only the beginning, though. There's something in particular you need to think about: building a self. The notion may sound strange. "We've taught them," David Foster Wallace[2] once said, "that a self is something you just have." But it is only through the act of establishing communication between the mind and the heart, the mind and experience, that you become an individual, a unique being—a soul. The job of college is to assist you to begin to do that. Books, ideas, works of art and thought, the pressure of the minds around you that are looking for their own answers in their own ways.

College is not the only chance to learn to think, but it is the best. One thing is certain: If you haven't started by the time you finish your B.A., there's little likelihood you'll do it later. That is why an undergraduate experience devoted exclusively to career preparation is four years largely wasted.

Elite schools like to boast that they teach their students how to think, but all they mean is that they train them in the analytic and rhetorical skills that are necessary for success in business and the professions. Everything is technocratic—the development of expertise—and everything is ultimately justified in technocratic terms.

Religious colleges—even obscure, regional schools that no one has ever heard of on the coasts—often do a much better job in that respect. What an indictment of the Ivy League and its peers: that colleges four levels down on the academic totem pole, enrolling students whose SAT scores are hundreds of points lower than theirs, deliver a better education, in the highest sense of the word.

At least the classes at elite schools are academically rigorous, demanding on their own terms, no? Not necessarily. In the sciences, usually; in other disciplines, not so much. There are exceptions, of course, but professors and students have largely entered into what one observer called a "nonaggression pact." Students are regarded by the institution as "customers," people to be pandered to instead of challenged. Professors are rewarded for research, so they want to spend as little time on their classes as they can. The profession's whole incentive structure is biased against teaching, and the more prestigious the school, the stronger the bias is likely to be. The result is higher marks for shoddier work.

It is true that today's young people appear to be more socially engaged than kids have been for several decades and that they are more apt to harbor creative or entrepreneurial impulses. But it is also true, at least at the most selective schools, that even if those aspirations make it out of college—a big "if"—they tend to be played out within the same

15

20

---

[2]**David Foster Wallace:** American writer and novelist (1962–2008).

narrow conception of what constitutes a valid life: affluence, credentials, prestige.

Experience itself has been reduced to instrumental function, via the college essay. From learning to commodify your experiences for the application, the next step has been to seek out experiences in order to have them to commodify. The *New York Times* reports that there is now a thriving sector devoted to producing essay-ready summers, but what strikes one is the superficiality of the activities involved: a month traveling around Italy studying the Renaissance, "a whole day" with a band of renegade artists. A whole day!

I've noticed something similar when it comes to service. Why is it that people feel the need to go to places like Guatemala to do their projects of rescue or documentation, instead of Milwaukee or Arkansas? When students do stay in the States, why is it that so many head for New Orleans? Perhaps it's no surprise, when kids are trained to think of service as something they are ultimately doing for themselves—that is, for their résumés. "Do well by doing good," goes the slogan. How about just doing good?

If there is one idea, above all, through which the concept of social responsibility is communicated at the most prestigious schools, it is "leadership." "Harvard is for leaders," goes the Cambridge cliché. To be a high-achieving student is to constantly be urged to think of yourself as a future leader of society. But what these institutions mean by leadership is nothing more than getting to the top. Making partner at a major law firm or becoming a chief executive, climbing the greasy pole of whatever hierarchy you decide to attach yourself to. I don't think it occurs to the people in charge of elite colleges that the concept of leadership ought to have a higher meaning, or, really, any meaning.

The irony is that elite students are told that they can be whatever they want, but most of them end up choosing to be one of a few very similar things. As of 2010, about a third of graduates went into financing or consulting at a number of top schools, including Harvard, Princeton, and Cornell. Whole fields have disappeared from view: the clergy, the military, electoral politics, even academia itself, for the most part, including basic science. It's considered glamorous to drop out of a selective college if you want to become the next Mark Zuckerberg, but ludicrous to stay in to become a social worker. "What Wall Street figured out," as Ezra Klein[3] has put it, "is that colleges are producing a large number of very smart, completely confused graduates. Kids who have ample mental horsepower, an incredible work ethic and no idea what to do next."

For the most selective colleges, this system is working very well indeed. Application numbers continue to swell, endowments are robust, tuition hikes bring ritual complaints but no decline in business. Whether it is working for anyone else is a different question.

[3]**Ezra Klein:** American blogger and liberal columnist (b. 1985).

It almost feels ridiculous to have to insist that colleges like Harvard are bastions of privilege, where the rich send their children to learn to walk, talk, and think like the rich. Don't we already know this? They aren't called elite colleges for nothing. But apparently we like pretending otherwise. We live in a meritocracy, after all.

The sign of the system's alleged fairness is the set of policies that travel under the banner of "diversity." And that diversity does indeed represent nothing less than a social revolution. Princeton, which didn't even admit its first woman graduate student until 1961—a year in which a grand total of one (no doubt very lonely) African American matriculated at its college—is now half female and only about half white. But diversity of sex and race has become a cover for increasing economic resegregation. Elite colleges are still living off the moral capital they earned in the 1960s, when they took the genuinely courageous step of dismantling the mechanisms of the WASP[4] aristocracy.

The truth is that the meritocracy was never more than partial. Visit any elite campus across our great nation, and you can thrill to the heartwarming spectacle of the children of white businesspeople and professionals studying and playing alongside the children of black, Asian, and Latino businesspeople and professionals. Kids at schools like Stanford think that their environment is diverse if one comes from Missouri and another from Pakistan, or if one plays the cello and the other lacrosse. Never mind that all of their parents are doctors or bankers.

That doesn't mean there aren't a few exceptions, but that is all they are. In fact, the group that is most disadvantaged by our current admissions policies are working-class and rural whites, who are hardly present on selective campuses at all. The only way to think these places are diverse is if that's all you've ever seen.

Let's not kid ourselves: The college admissions game is not primarily about the lower and middle classes seeking to rise, or even about the upper-middle class attempting to maintain its position. It is about determining the exact hierarchy of status within the upper-middle class itself. In the affluent suburbs and well-heeled urban enclaves where this game is principally played, it is not about whether you go to an elite school. It's about which one you go to. It is Penn versus Tufts, not Penn versus Penn State. It doesn't matter that a bright young person can go to Ohio State, become a doctor, settle in Dayton, and make a very good living. Such an outcome is simply too horrible to contemplate. [30]

This system is exacerbating inequality, retarding social mobility, perpetuating privilege, and creating an elite that is isolated from the society that it's supposed to lead. The numbers are undeniable. In 1985, 46 percent of incoming freshmen at the 250 most selective colleges came from the top quarter of the income distribution. By 2000, it was 55 percent. As of 2006, only about 15 percent of students at the most competitive

---

[4] **WASP:** Acronym for White Anglo-Saxon Protestant.

schools came from the bottom half. The more prestigious the school, the more unequal its student body is apt to be. And public institutions are not much better than private ones. As of 2004, 40 percent of first-year students at the most selective state campuses came from families with incomes of more than $100,000, up from 32 percent just five years earlier.

The major reason for the trend is clear. Not increasing tuition, though that is a factor, but the ever-growing cost of manufacturing children who are fit to compete in the college admissions game. The more hurdles there are, the more expensive it is to catapult your kid across them. Wealthy families start buying their children's way into elite colleges almost from the moment they are born: music lessons, sports equipment, foreign travel ("enrichment" programs, to use the all-too-perfect term)—most important, of course, private-school tuition or the costs of living in a place with top-tier public schools. The SAT is supposed to measure aptitude, but what it actually measures is parental income, which it tracks quite closely. Today, fewer than half of high-scoring students from low-income families even *enroll* at four-year schools.

The problem isn't that there aren't more qualified lower-income kids from which to choose. Elite private colleges will never allow their students' economic profile to mirror that of society as a whole. They can't afford to—they need a critical mass of full payers and they need to tend to their donor base—and it's not even clear that they'd want to.

And so it is hardly a coincidence that income inequality is higher than it has been since before the Great Depression, or that social mobility is lower in the United States than in almost every other developed country. Elite colleges are not just powerless to reverse the movement toward a more unequal society; their policies actively promote it.

Is there anything that I can do, a lot of young people have written to ask me, to avoid becoming an out-of-touch, entitled little shit? I don't have a satisfying answer, short of telling them to transfer to a public university. You cannot cogitate your way to sympathy with people of different backgrounds, still less to knowledge of them. You need to interact with them directly, and it has to be on an equal footing: not in the context of "service," and not in the spirit of "making an effort," either—swooping down on a member of the college support staff and offering to "buy them a coffee," as a former Yalie once suggested, in order to "ask them about themselves."

Instead of service, how about service *work*? That'll really give you insight into other people. How about waiting tables so that you can see how hard it is, physically and mentally? You really aren't as smart as everyone has been telling you; you're only smarter in a certain way. There are smart people who do not go to a prestigious college, or to any college—often precisely for reasons of class. There are smart people who are not "smart."

I am under no illusion that it doesn't matter where you go to college. But there are options. There are still very good public universities in every region of the country. The education is often impersonal, but the student body is usually genuinely diverse in terms of socioeconomic background, with all of the invaluable experiential learning that implies.

U.S. News and World Report[5] supplies the percentage of freshmen at each college who finished in the highest 10 percent of their high school class. Among the top 20 universities, the number is usually above 90 percent. I'd be wary of attending schools like that. Students determine the level of classroom discussion; they shape your values and expectations, for good and ill. It's partly because of the students that I'd warn kids away from the Ivies and their ilk. Kids at less prestigious schools are apt to be more interesting, more curious, more open, and far less entitled and competitive.

If there is anywhere that college is still college—anywhere that teaching and the humanities are still accorded pride of place—it is the liberal arts college. Such places are small, which is not for everyone, and they're often fairly isolated, which is also not for everyone. The best option of all may be the second-tier—not second-rate—colleges, like Reed, Kenyon, Wesleyan, Sewanee, Mount Holyoke, and others. Instead of trying to compete with Harvard and Yale, these schools have retained their allegiance to real educational values.

Not being an entitled little shit is an admirable goal. But in the end, the deeper issue is the situation that makes it so hard to be anything else. The time has come, not simply to reform that system top to bottom, but to plot our exit to another kind of society altogether.   40

The education system has to act to mitigate the class system, not reproduce it. Affirmative action should be based on class instead of race, a change that many have been advocating for years. Preferences for legacies and athletes ought to be discarded. SAT scores should be weighted to account for socioeconomic factors. Colleges should put an end to résumé-stuffing by imposing a limit on the number of extracurriculars that kids can list on their applications. They ought to place more value on the kind of service jobs that lower-income students often take in high school and that high achievers almost never do. They should refuse to be impressed by any opportunity that was enabled by parental wealth. Of course, they have to stop cooperating with *U.S. News*.

More broadly, they need to rethink their conception of merit. If schools are going to train a better class of leaders than the ones we have today, they're going to have to ask themselves what kinds of qualities they need to promote. Selecting students by GPA or the number of extracurriculars more often benefits the faithful drudge than the original mind.

The changes must go deeper, though, than reforming the admissions process. That might address the problem of mediocrity, but it won't address the greater one of inequality. The problem is the Ivy League itself. We have contracted the training of our leadership class to a set

[5] ***U.S. News and World Report:*** A magazine famous for its annual ranking of institutions of higher education.

of private institutions. However much they claim to act for the common good, they will always place their interests first. The arrangement is great for the schools, but is Harvard's desire for alumni donations a sufficient reason to perpetuate the class system?

I used to think that we needed to create a world where every child had an equal chance to get to the Ivy League. I've come to see that what we really need is to create one where you don't have to go to the Ivy League, or any private college, to get a first-rate education.

High-quality public education, financed with public money, for the benefit of all: the exact commitment that drove the growth of public higher education in the postwar years. Everybody gets an equal chance to go as far as their hard work and talent will take them—you know, the American Dream. Everyone who wants it gets to have the kind of mind-expanding, soul-enriching experience that a liberal arts education provides. We recognize that free, quality K–12 education is a right of citizenship. We also need to recognize—as we once did and as many countries still do—that the same is true of higher education. We have tried aristocracy. We have tried meritocracy. Now it's time to try democracy.

Candorville

Candorville used with the permission of Darrin Bell, the Washington Post Writers Group, and the Cartoonist Group. All rights reserved.

ENGAGING THE TEXT

1. Do you agree with Deresiewicz that today's college students are prone to "toxic levels of fear, anxiety, and depression, of emptiness and aimlessness and isolation" (para. 10)? To what extent have you experienced similar feelings as a college student? Would you agree that such feelings are caused by fear of failure? What other factors might cause students to feel depressed or anxious?

2. How did you choose the college you're currently attending? What kind of research did you do, and what were your reasons for selecting it? To what extent were you a "sleepwalker" like Deresiewicz when it came to making this important life decision?

3. How, according to Deresiewicz, do most students today view the purpose of higher education? Do you think he's right when he says that the purpose of college is to "teach you to think" and to "build a self"? How much of the time you spend in college should focus on preparation for a career?

4. Deresiewicz says that for most students today, leadership means "getting to the top." How do you think members of your generation define leadership? What role does "doing good" play in your own idea of what it means to be a leader?

5. What changes would Deresiewicz make in American colleges in order to "plot our exit to another kind of society altogether"? How advisable and feasible do his ideas seem to you? How, for example, could a college distinguish between the "faithful drudge" and the "original mind" during the admissions process? What changes would we have to make in the current structure of higher education to give everyone "an equal chance to go as far as their hard work and talent will take them"?

EXPLORING CONNECTIONS

6. How might Mike Rose (p. 123) and Malcolm X (p. 161) respond to Deresiewicz's claims that college offers students the opportunity to "stand outside the world for a few years . . . and contemplate things from a distance" (para. 14), and that the ultimate goal of college is "building a self"?

7. Drawing on the ideas of Deresiewicz, Diane Ravitch (p. 105), and Carmen Lugo-Lugo (p. 188), write a journal entry or an essay on the commercialization of education. Do you think that we are placing too much emphasis on education as a form of career training today or that college culture has been infected by corporate culture? Why or why not?

8. Review Jean Anyon's analysis of the "hidden curriculum" of social class (p. 136), Jonathan Kozol's examination of "apartheid" schools (p. 170), and Deresiewicz's discussion of the "economic re-segregation" of higher education. How does each of these writers challenge the idea that education is a powerful means of social mobility and individual empowerment? To what extent do you agree with them?

EXTENDING THE CRITICAL CONTEXT

9. Working in groups, research the demographics of the students admitted to your college over the last thirty years. How has the racial, socioeconomic, and gender profile of incoming students changed? What do these statistics say about your college's commitment to diversity? To what extent is the student body of your college representative of society at large?

10. Review the general education requirements at your college. How heavily does your college appear to emphasize "technocratic training" and "career preparation"? What does your college do to encourage you to "become an individual, a unique being — a soul"? What kind of class or experience would it take to do that?

FURTHER CONNECTIONS

1. In the United States, the notion of schooling as the road to success has always been balanced by a pervasive distrust of education. This phenomenon, known as "American anti-intellectualism," grew out of the first settlers' suspicion of anything that reminded them of the "corrupting" influences of European sophistication. American anti-intellectualism often shows up most vividly in pop-cultural portrayals of school, students, and educators. It also emerges in recent attacks on the value of formal schooling and the college degree. Working in groups, survey recent portrayals of school on television, in films, and on Internet blogs and Web sites. How is schooling treated in the mass media and by popular bloggers on the left and the right of the political spectrum? Overall, how powerful does anti-intellectualism seem to be in American culture today?

2. Go online to review the latest results of the Program for International Student Assessment (PISA), the most respected worldwide comparative evaluation of student learning (http://www.oecd.org/pisa/keyfindings/pisa-2012-results.htm). Where does the United States stand in relation to other nations in terms of student performance in mathematics, reading, and science? How can you explain the fact that despite thirty years of educational reform efforts, U.S. scores trail those of nations like Slovenia, Vietnam, Italy, Spain, and Russia?

3. Educational researchers estimate that 25 percent to 60 percent of the ninth graders in America's urban public schools will drop out before graduation. Do additional research on the "dropout crisis" to learn more about the scope and causes of this problem. Why are so many Americans opting out of school today? Which groups are most in danger of leaving school before graduation? What can be done to encourage young Americans to stay in school?

4. Over the past few years, educational critics across the political spectrum have voiced concern about declining success rates for males in America's schools and colleges. During the last decade, for example, the number of women in America's colleges and universities has steadily increased until, today, women outnumber men in almost every academic field outside the so-called hard sciences. Research this issue to learn more about how males are faring in America's schools. Do you think, as some critics claim, that school is particularly hostile to boys? What other reasons might explain declines in male educational achievement over the past two decades?

THE WILD WIRED WEST
Myths of Progress on the Tech Frontier

FAST FACTS

1. 59% of Americans believe that technology will make life better in the future. 39% think that technology will eventually make teletransportation possible, and 33% believe that we will someday have long-term colonies in space.

2. 60% of Americans say that they have witnessed offensive behavior online. 70% of young adults 18 to 24 say they have been threatened, harassed, or stalked online.

3. According to a Drexel University study, more than 50% of American teens have engaged in sexting; nearly 30% say they have included nude photos in their sexts.

4. 91% of adults agree that consumers have lost control over how personal information is collected by companies online. 80% agree that Americans should be concerned about government monitoring of phone calls and Internet communications.

5. According to National Security Agency documents leaked to the press by Edward Snowden in 2013, the government routinely accesses consumer data on the servers of Microsoft, Google, Apple, Facebook, YouTube, Instagram, and other Internet companies.

6. As the result of changes in photographic technologies, Eastman Kodak Corporation, which once employed over 145,000 people and had annual earnings of nearly $16 billion, applied for bankruptcy in 2012. When Instagram was sold to Facebook for $1 billion the same year, it had 30 million customers and 13 employees.

Data from (1–2, 4) Pew Research Center: Internet, Science, and Tech; (3) "Majority of Minors Now Engage in Sexting," DrexelNow.com; (5) "NSA Slides Explain the PRISM Data-Collection Program," washingtonpost.com; (6) "Coming to an Office Near You," *The Economist*.

A LITTLE OVER A CENTURY AGO, two of America's most powerful cultural myths crossed paths at the Chicago World's Fair. Officially known as the World's Columbian Exposition, the fair celebrated the 400th anniversary of Christopher Columbus's "discovery" of the Americas and served as a showcase for the cultural and economic achievements of the United States. By any measure, it was an astonishing event. The exposition included 200 temporary buildings spread over 635 acres on Chicago's South Side, and during its brief six-month run it attracted over 27 million visitors — more than half the U.S. population in 1893. Dubbed the "White City" because of the elaborate stucco buildings that lined its central court, the exposition featured 65,000 exhibits. It also witnessed a number of notable firsts. Americans drank their first carbonated sodas and ate their first hamburgers at the fair; they also got their first taste of Aunt Jemima's Pancake Mix and Pabst Blue Ribbon beer. Visitors lined up to take rides on the world's first Ferris wheel, a 265-foot-high behemoth that accommodated 2,160 passengers in 36 closed gondolas. They also had the chance to stroll along the "Midway Plaisance," the nation's first modern amusement park, which included rides along with food concessions, sideshow attractions, and corporate-sponsored exhibits. Over the next century, the World's Exposition would have an enduring influence on American pop culture. The "Midway" would inspire a series of theme parks across the country, from Coney Island to Disneyland, and the charms of the White City itself would echo in Chicagoan L. Frank Baum's depiction of the Emerald City in his 1899 classic *The Wonderful Wizard of Oz*.

© PF-(bygone1)/Alamy

But the fair had a more telling legacy. During a meeting of the American Historical Association held on fair grounds, a young University of Wisconsin professor delivered a scholarly paper that would influence American politics and culture for decades to come. In "The Significance of the Frontier in American History," Frederick Jackson Turner argued that life on the western frontier — and not the influence of Europe — had left an indelible impression on American society. According to Turner's famous "Frontier Thesis," life on the untamed, ever-advancing western edge of the United States had freed Americans from the old subservient traditions and authoritarian ways of Europe's feudal past. The western frontier had transformed Americans into fiercely independent, freedom-loving individualists who had a "practical, inventive turn of mind" and who were "full of restless nervous energy." According to Turner, the demands of frontier life had toughened American settlers and endowed them with the kind of self-reliance citizens needed in a democratic society. Turner's optimistic vision of the West as a purifying and liberating force reassured generations of Americans that their nation was indeed the "land of the free and the home of the brave." It also provided a ready-made explanation for America's growing sense of its superiority and national destiny as it moved into the new century.

Ironically, while Turner was explaining that the real American Frontier had "closed," or ceased to exist, because civilization had finally overwhelmed the last

traces of open prairie in 1890, the myth of the "Old West" was just getting started. As Turner finished delivering his paper, William Frederick Cody was selling tickets to the first "Buffalo Bill's Wild West Show" just outside the Exposition's gates. The frontier may have "closed" in 1890, but the national fantasy of cowboy independence and heroism was just taking hold of America. Buffalo Bill's traveling Wild West show offered melodramatic dime-novel reenactments of famous Western scenes and cowboy exploits, from the "Great Train Robbery" to "Custer's Last Stand" at the Battle of Little Bighorn. It popularized mythic American figures like Annie Oakley, Calamity Jane, Wild Bill Hickok, and Sitting Bull. Thanks to Buffalo Bill's theatrics, the glamor of the untamed Old West and the rough virtues of the cowboy hero would have a lasting impact on American culture.

Yet, as we know today, the future didn't belong to the cowboy. Technology was the real star of the 1893 World Exposition. Almost every exhibit featured some type of technological innovation calculated to awe the visiting public. At night, the fair's main buildings were illuminated by 100,000 incandescent lights in a stunning demonstration of how electrification would transform American cities in the coming century. The Machinery Hall proudly displayed the 127 dynamos that powered the fair's exhibits and mechanical attractions. In the Electricity Hall, Thomas Edison demonstrated his newly invented phonograph, gave rides in electric

horseless carriages, and introduced visitors to the kinetoscope and the prospect of moving pictures. There was even an exhibit showcasing the "Kitchen of the Future," complete with electric stove, refrigerator, and dishwasher.

Since then, Americans have never stopped dreaming about the promise of technology. After the turn of the twentieth century, it seemed as if electricity and the innovations it made possible would solve every problem and satisfy every need. In his book *The Big Switch*, author Nicholas Carr describes the impact of the American cult of technology in the early twentieth century:

> Electrification, people were told, would cleanse the earth of disease and strife, turning it into a pristine new Eden. "We are soon to have everywhere," wrote one futurist, "smoke annihilators, dust absorbers, ozonators, sterilizers of water, air, food, and clothing, and accident preventers on the streets, elevated roads, and subways. It will become next to impossible to contract disease germs or get hurt in the city.
>
> People expected emerging technologies to "eliminate blizzards, droughts, and other climatic extremes." They believed that new forms of transportation would "practically eliminate distances" and that under the sway of technical expertise, we would all live in harmony like "cogs" in a "wonderful mechanism . . . acting in response to the will of a corporate mind . . .

Technology, then, and not the Wild West, fueled the myths of progress and perfection that drove American dreams in the twentieth century. For our models of heroism and the promise of a better life, we began to look forward to the frontier of technological innovation and not backward to the dusty past of buffalo hunters and cowboy roundups. And modern science didn't disappoint. The incandescent light was followed by the automobile, the airplane, television, antibiotics, the X-ray, space flight, nuclear power, the laser, and the digital computer. Every new technology spawned a new batch of inflated expectations. Television would put an end to ignorance. Antibiotics would eliminate disease. Nuclear energy would free us from dependence on coal and oil. Space travel would lead to colonies on the moon by the year 2001.

Of course, the myth of technology also has its dark side. Every dream of technological utopia has inspired a corresponding nightmare vision of tech-driven apocalypse. Today, in the new digital age of social media and increasingly intelligent machines, most of us are well-versed in high-tech fantasies and fears. We all know how scientists can accidentally unleash deadly microbes — or resurrected dinosaurs — and how computers designed to help us do the impossible might someday turn a glowing eye against us when the chips are down. Yet, as a nation, we're still hooked on the idea that technology can solve our problems and that innovations like the cell phone and the Internet have changed our lives for the better.

In this chapter, you'll have the chance to explore the myth of technological progress and reflect on how emerging technologies are changing our society and our sense of self. The chapter opens with a selection by two committed technodreamers. In "Our Future Selves," Google's Eric Schmidt and Jared Cohen invite us to contemplate what life will be like in a "connected" world of super smart phones, household robots, and intelligent apartments that anticipate your every need. Next, a trio of selections highlights the impact of social media and the Internet on our current lives. In "Growing Up Tethered," MIT sociologist Sherry Turkle explores how living online has robbed teens of their independence and their willingness to express dissent. "Cybersexism" by blogger, journalist, and Internet activist Laurie Penny expands on Turkle's analysis by assessing the Internet's growing influence — both positive and negative — on the lives of tech-savvy women. Emily Witt's "Love Me Tinder" rounds off the first half of the chapter by exploring how Internet dating is transforming American attitudes toward sex, love, and long-term relationships.

Next, the chapter's Visual Portfolio presents images that invite further think-ing about American attitudes toward technology. The section begins with a pair of photos that raise questions about the impact of smart phones on children and social relationships. The portfolio also features two screen shots from Anita Sarkeesian's "Feminist Frequency" Web site, which was involved in the misogynist Gamergate controversy of 2014. The final Portfolio image features the home page of the Westboro Baptist Church, infamous for its homophobic assaults on families during military funerals. Like thousands of hate group sites on the Web, the West-boro home page challenges us to consider the balance between liberty and bigotry in the new Wild Wired West.

The second half of the chapter begins by questioning the notion that the Internet enhances our "connectivity" and expands our world. In "The Loneliness of the Interconnected," Charles Seife argues that life online actually discourages critical thinking and reinforces our personal biases. Next, danah boyd expands on this idea in "Inequality: Can Social Media Resolve Social Divisions?" According to boyd's research on the Internet habits of American teens, life in the virtual world looks a lot like life in reality: segregated by race and class. The chapter concludes with two readings on the topic of technology, surveillance, and individual rights. In "George Orwell . . . Meet Mark Zuckerberg," Lori Andrews investigates the world of data aggregators, companies that secretly track every move you make online and then sell your virtual profile to the highest bidder. Henrick Karoliszyn's "Precogni-tive Police" draws our examination of the myth of technological progress to a close by raising questions about what it might mean for our civil liberties when police begin to predict crimes before they happen.

In the chapter's Further Connections section you'll find more ideas for research projects on the impact of the Internet and issues related to the development of artificial intelligence, robotics, and automation. This section also includes proj-ects related to government surveillance and "transhumanism"—the idea of using emerging technologies to transcend normal human limitations.

Sources

Carr, Nicholas. *The Big Switch: Rewiring the World from Edison to Google*. New York: W. W. Norton & Company, 2008. Print.

Hine, Robert H., and John Mack Faragher. *The American West: A New Interpretive History*. New Haven, CT: Yale University Press, 2000. Print.

Turner, Frederick Jackson. "The Significance of the Frontier in American History." *An Amer-ican Primer*, edited by Daniel Boorstin. Chicago: University of Chicago Press, 1966. Print.

"The World's Columbian Exposition: Idea, Experience, Aftermath." American Studies at the University of Virginia Hypertexts. 1 August 1996. 24 June 2015.

BEFORE READING

- In groups, discuss your own expectations about technology and the future. How, in your view, will technology change your life in the next twenty years? How will expanding access to the Internet and emerging technolo-gies affect the way we learn, work, and socialize? What inventions or tech-nological breakthroughs are you looking forward to, and why?

- Inventory the different types of technology you use every day. What kinds of technology do you use most frequently? Which technologies could you live without if you had to? On a scale of 1 to 10, how would you rate your technology dependence?

OUR FUTURE SELVES

ERIC SCHMIDT AND JARED COHEN

What will the technological future look like? It may come as no surprise that to former Google CEO Eric Schmidt it seems pretty bright. Since Thomas Edison ushered in the age of electricity from his lab in Menlo Park, Americans have dreamed of future technological utopias where all material needs are satisfied and all social problems solved. Today, the invention of the computer and the development of the Internet have inspired a new generation of high-tech dreamers. In this selection from their best-selling 2013 book, *The New Digital Age: Reshaping the Future of People, Nations, and Business*, Eric Schmidt and Jared Cohen offer their vision of how technology will change the world and revolutionize our lives. Trained as an electrical engineer, Eric Schmidt (b. 1955) joined Google founders Sergey Brin and Larry Page in 2001 as the company's CEO. In 2011 he left that position to become Google's first Executive Chairman. Jared Cohen (b. 1981) has served as an adviser to former Secretaries of State Condoleezza Rice and Hillary Clinton. Currently, he is the director of Google Ideas, a think tank dedicated to finding technological solutions to global problems. He is also an adjunct senior fellow at the Council on Foreign Relations. Eric Schmidt's most recent publication, coauthored with Jonathan Rosenberg, is *How Google Works* (2014).

SOON EVERYONE ON EARTH WILL BE CONNECTED. With five billion more people[1] set to join the virtual world, the boom in digital connectivity will bring gains in productivity, health, education, quality of life and myriad other avenues in the physical world—and this will be true for everyone, from the most elite users to those at the base of the economic pyramid. But being "connected" will mean very different things to different people, largely because the problems they have to solve differ

---

[1] *The World in 2011: ICT Facts and Figures,* International Telecommunication Union (ITU), accessed October 10, 2012, http://www.itu.int/ITUD/ict/facts/2011/material/ICTFacts Figures2011.pdf. The above source shows that as of 2011 35 percent of the world's population is online. We factored in population increase projections to estimate five billion set to join the virtual world. [All notes are Schmidt and Cohen's, except 13 and 17.]

so dramatically. What might seem like a small jump forward for some—like a smart phone priced under $20—may be as profound for one group as commuting to work in a driverless car is for another. People will find that being connected virtually makes us feel more equal—with access to the same basic platforms, information and online resources—while significant differences persist in the physical world. Connectivity will not solve income inequality, though it will alleviate some of its more intractable causes, like lack of available education and economic opportunity. So we must recognize and celebrate innovation in its own context. Everyone will benefit from connectivity, but not equally, and how those differences manifest themselves in the daily lives of people is our focus here.

Increased Efficiency

Being able to do more in the virtual world will make the mechanics of our physical world more efficient. As digital connectivity reaches the far corners of the globe, new users will employ it to improve a wide range of inefficient markets, systems and behaviors, in both the most and least advanced societies. The resulting gains in efficiency and productivity will be profound, particularly in developing countries where technological isolation and bad policies have stymied growth and progress for years, and people will do more with less.

The accessibility of affordable smart devices, including phones and tablets, will be transformative in these countries. Consider the impact of basic mobile phones[2] for a group of Congolese fisherwomen today. Whereas they used to bring their daily catch to the market and watch it slowly spoil as the day progressed, now they keep it on the line, in the river, and wait for calls from customers. Once an order is placed, a fish is brought out of the water and prepared for the buyer. There is no need for an expensive refrigerator, no need for someone to guard it at night, no danger of spoiled fish losing their value (or poisoning customers), and there is no unnecessary overfishing. The size of these women's market can even expand as other fishermen in surrounding areas coordinate with them over their own phones. As a substitute for a formal market economy (which would take years to develop), that's not a bad work-around, for these women or the community at large.

Mobile phones are transforming how people in the developing world access and use information, and adoption rates are soaring. There are already more than 650 million mobile-phone users in Africa,[3] and close to 3 billion across Asia.[4] The majority of these people are using basic-

[2]This fisherwomen thought experiment came out of a conversation with Rebecca Cohen, and while we put it in the context of the Congo, the example belongs to her.
[3] "Africa's Mobile Phone Industry 'Booming,'" BBC, November 9, 2011, http://www.bbc .co.uk/news/world-africa-15659983.
[4]See mobile cellular subscriptions, Asia & Pacific, year 2011, in "Key ICT Indicators for the ITU/BDT Regions (Totals and Penetration Rates)," International Telecommunication Union (ITU), ICT Data and Statistics (IDS), updated November 16, 2011, http://www.itu.int /ITU-D/ict/statistics/at_glance/KeyTelecom.html.

feature phones[5]—voice calls and text messages only—because the cost of data service in their countries is often prohibitively expensive, so that even those who can buy Web-enabled phones or smart phones cannot use them affordably. This will change, and when it does, the smart-phone revolution will profoundly benefit these populations.

Hundreds of millions of people today are living the lives of their grandparents, in countries where life expectancy is less than sixty years, or even fifty in some places,[6] and there is no guarantee that their political and macroeconomic circumstances will improve dramatically anytime soon. What is new in their lives and their futures is connectivity. Critically, they have the chance to bypass earlier technologies, like dial-up modems, and go directly to high-speed wireless connections, which means the transformations that connectivity brings will occur even more quickly than they did in the developed world. The introduction of mobile phones is far more transformative than most people in modern countries realize. As people come online, they will quite suddenly have access to almost all the world's information in one place in their own language. This will even be true for an illiterate Maasai cattle herder in the Serengeti, whose native tongue, Maa, is not written[7]—he'll be able to verbally inquire about the day's market prices and crowd-source the whereabouts of any nearby predators, receiving a spoken answer from his device in reply. Mobile phones will allow formerly isolated people to connect with others very far away and very different from themselves. On the economic front, they'll find ways to use the new tools at their disposal to enlarge their businesses, make them more efficient and maximize their profits, as the fisherwomen did much more locally with their basic phones.

What connectivity also brings, beyond mobile phones, is the ability to collect and use data. Data itself is a tool, and in places where unreliable statistics about health, education, economics and the population's needs have stalled growth and development, the chance to gather data effectively is a game-changer. Everyone in society benefits from digital data, as governments can better measure the success of their programs, and media and other nongovernmental organizations can use data to support their work and check facts. For example, Amazon is able to take its data on merchants and, using algorithms, develop customized bank loans to offer them—in some cases when traditional banks have completely shut their doors. Larger markets and better metrics can help create healthier and more productive economies.

[5]Ibid. Compare mobile cellular subscriptions to active mobile broadband subscriptions for 2011.

[6]"Country Comparison: Life Expectancy at Birth," CIA, World Fact Book, accessed October 11, 2012, https://www.cia.gov/library/publications/the-world-factbook/rankorder /2102rank.html#top.

[7]One of the authors spent the summer of 2001 in this remote village, without electricity, running water, or a single cell phone or landline. During a return trip in the fall of 2010, many of the Maasai women had crafted beautiful beaded pouches to store their cell phones in.

And the developing world will not be left out of the advances in gadgetry and other high-tech machinery. Even if the prices for sophisticated smart phones and robots to perform household tasks like vacuuming remain high, illicit markets like China's expansive *"shanzhai"* network[8] for knock-off consumer electronics will produce and distribute imitations that bridge the gap. And technologies that emerged in first-world contexts will find renewed purpose in developing countries. In "additive manufacturing," or 3-D printing, machines can actually "print" physical objects by taking three-dimensional data about an object and tracing the contours of its shape, ultra-thin layer by ultra-thin layer, with liquid plastic or other material, until the whole object materializes.[9] Such printers have produced a huge range of objects, including customized mobile phones, machine parts and a full-sized replica motorcycle.[10] These machines will definitely have an impact on the developing world. Communal 3-D printers in poor countries would allow people to make whatever tool or item they require from open-source templates—digital information that is freely available in its edited source—rather than waiting on laborious or iffy delivery routes for higher-priced premade goods.

In wealthier countries 3-D printing will be the perfect partner for advanced manufacturing. New materials and products will all be built uniquely to a specification from the Internet and on demand by a machine run by a sophisticated, trained operator. This will not replace the acres of high-volume, lowest-cost manufacturing present in many industries, but it will bring an unprecedented variety to the products used in the developed world.

As for life's small daily tasks, information systems will streamline many of them for people living in those countries, such as integrated clothing machines (washing, drying, folding, pressing and sorting) that keep an inventory of clean clothes and algorithmically suggest outfits based on the user's daily schedule. Haircuts will finally be automated and machine-precise. And cell phones, tablets and laptops will have wireless recharging capabilities, rendering the need to fiddle with charging cables an obsolete nuisance. Centralizing the many moving parts of one's life into an easy-to-use, almost intuitive system of information management and decision making will give our interactions with technology an effortless feel. As long as safeguards are in place to protect privacy and prevent data loss, these systems will free us of many small burdens—including errands, to-do lists and assorted "monitoring" tasks—that today

[8]Nicholas Schmidle, "Inside the Knockoff-Tennis-Shoe Factory," *New York Times Magazine,* August 19, 2010, Global edition, http://www.nytimes.com/2010/08 /22/magazine/22fake -t.html?pagewanted=all.

[9]"The Printed World: Three-Dimensional Printing from Digital Designs Will Transform Manufacturing and Allow More People to Start Making Things," *Economist,* February 10, 2011, http://www.economist.com/node/18114221.

[10]Patrick Collinson, "Hi-Tech Shares Take US for a Walk on the High Side," *Guardian* (Manchester), March 16, 2012, http://www.guardian.co.uk/money/2012/mar/16/hi-tech -shares-us.

add stress and chip away at our mental focus throughout the day. Our own neurological limits, which lead us to forgetfulness and oversights, will be supplemented by information systems designed to support our needs. Two such examples are memory prosthetics—calendar reminders and to-do lists—and social prosthetics, which instantly connect you with your friend who has relevant expertise in whatever task you are facing.

By relying on these integrated systems, which will encompass both the professional and the personal sides of our lives, we'll be able to use our time more effectively each day—whether that means having the time to have a "deep think," spending more time preparing for an important presentation or guaranteeing that a parent can attend his or her child's soccer game without distraction. Suggestion engines that offer alternative terms to help a user find what she is looking for will be a particularly useful aid in efficiency by consistently stimulating our thinking processes, ultimately enhancing our creativity, not pre-empting it. Of course, the world will be filled with gadgets, holograms that allow a virtual version of you to be somewhere else, and endless amounts of content, so there will be plenty of ways to procrastinate, too—but the point is that when you choose to be productive, you can do so with greater capacity.

Other advances in the pipeline in areas like robotics, artificial intelligence and voice recognition will introduce efficiency into our lives by providing more seamless forms of engagement with the technology in our daily routines. Fully automated human-like robots with superb AI [artificial intelligence] abilities will probably be out of most people's price range for some time, but the average American consumer will find it affordable to own a handful of different multipurpose robots fairly soon. The technology in iRobot's Roomba vacuum cleaner, the progenitor of this field of consumer "home" robots (first introduced in 2002), will only become more sophisticated and multipurpose in time. Future varieties of home robots should be able to handle other household duties, electrical work and even plumbing issues with relative ease.

We also can't discount the impact that superior voice-recognition software will have on our daily lives. Beyond searching for information online and issuing commands to your robots (both of which are possible today), better voice recognition will mean instant transcription of anything you produce: e-mails, notes, speeches, term papers. Most people speak much faster than they type, so this technology will surely save many of us time in our daily affairs—not to mention helping us avoid cases of carpal tunnel syndrome. A shift toward voice-initiated writing may well change our world of written material. Will we learn to speak in paragraphs, or will our writing begin to mirror speech patterns?

Everyday use of gesture-recognition technology is also closer than we think. Microsoft's Kinect, a hands-free sensor device for the Xbox 360 video-game console that captures and integrates a player's motion, set a world record in 2011 as the fastest selling consumer-electronics device in history, with more than eight million devices sold in the first sixty days on the market. Gestural interfaces will soon move beyond gaming and entertainment into more functional areas; the futuristic information screens displayed so prominently in the film *Minority Report*—in which Tom Cruise used gesture technology and holographic images to solve crimes on a computer—are just the beginning. In fact, we've already moved beyond that—the really interesting work today is building "social robots" that can recognize human gestures and respond to them in kind, such as a toy dog that sits when a child makes a command gesture.[11]

And, looking further down the line, we might not need to move physically to manipulate those robots. There have been a series of exciting breakthroughs in thought-controlled motion technology—directing motion by thinking alone—in the past few years. In 2012, a team at a robotics laboratory in Japan demonstrated successfully that a person lying in an fMRI machine (which takes continuous scans of the brain to measure changes in blood flow) could control a robot hundreds of miles away just by imagining moving different parts of his body.[12] The subject could see from the robot's perspective, thanks to a camera on its head, and when he thought about moving his arm or his legs, the robot would move correspondingly almost instantaneously. The possibilities of thought-controlled motion, not only for "surrogates" like separate robots but also for prosthetic limbs, are particularly exciting in what they portend for mobility-challenged or "locked in" individuals—spinal-cord-injury patients, amputees and others who cannot communicate or move in their current physical state.

More Innovation, More Opportunity

That the steady march of globalization will continue apace, even accelerate, as connectivity spreads will come as no surprise. But what might surprise you is how small some of the advances in technology, when paired with increased connection and interdependence across countries, will make your world feel. Instant language translation, virtual-reality interactions and real-time collective editing—most easily understood today as wikis—will reshape how firms and organizations interact with partners, clients and employees in other places. While certain differences will perhaps never be fully overcome—like cultural nuance and time zones—the ability to engage with people in disparate locations, with near-total comprehension and on shared platforms, will make such interactions feel incredibly familiar.

Supply chains for corporations and other organizations will become increasingly disaggregated, not just on the production side but also with respect to people. More effective communication across borders and lan-

15

[11]Sarah Constantin, "Gesture Recognition, Mind-Reading Machines, and Social Robotics," *H+ Magazine*, February 8, 2011, http://hplusmagazine.com/2011/02/08/gesture-recognition-mind-reading-machines-and-social-robotics/.

[12]Helen Thomson, "Robot Avatar Body Controlled by Thought Alone," *New Scientist*, July 2012, 19–20.

guages will build trust and create opportunities for hardworking and talented individuals around the world. It will not be unusual for a French technology company to operate its sales team from Southeast Asia, while locating its human-resources people in Canada and its engineers in Israel. Bureaucratic obstacles that prevent this level of decentralized operation today, like visa restrictions and regulations around money transfers, will either become irrelevant or be circumvented as digital solutions are discovered. Perhaps a human-rights organization with staff living in a country under heavy diplomatic sanctions will pay its employees in mobile money credits, or in an entirely digital currency.

As fewer jobs require a physical presence, talented individuals will have more options available to them. Skilled young adults in Uruguay will find themselves competing for certain types of jobs against their counterparts in Orange County. Of course, just as not all jobs can or will be automated in the future, not every job can be conducted from a distance—but more can than you might think. And for those living on a few dollars per day, there will be endless opportunities to increase their earnings. In fact, Amazon Mechanical Turk,[13] which is a digital task-distribution platform, offers a present-day example of a company outsourcing small tasks that can be performed for a few cents by anyone with an Internet connection. As the quality of virtual interactions continues to improve, a range of vocations can expand the platform's client base; you might retain a lawyer from one continent and use a Realtor from another. Globalization's critics will decry this erosion of local monopolies, but it should be embraced, because this is how our societies will move forward and continue to innovate. Indeed, rising connectivity should *help* countries discover their competitive advantage—it could be that the world's best graphic designers come from Botswana, and the world just doesn't know it yet.

This leveling of the playing field for talent extends to the world of ideas, and innovation will increasingly come from the margins, outside traditional bastions of growth, as people begin to make new connections and apply unique perspectives to difficult problems, driving change. New levels of collaboration and cross-pollination across different sectors internationally will ensure that many of the best ideas and solutions will have a chance to rise to the top and be seen, considered, explored, funded, adopted and celebrated. Perhaps an aspiring Russian programmer currently working as a teacher in Novosibirsk will discover a new application of the technology behind the popular mobile game Angry Birds, realizing how its game framework could be used to improve the educational tools he is building to teach physics to local students. He finds

---

[13]**Amazon Mechanical Turk:** A crowd-sourcing Internet marketplace that allows individuals to earn money doing tasks inside computer applications that computers are currently unable to do by themselves. The original Mechanical Turk was a chess-playing "robot" that created a sensation when it toured Europe in the eighteenth century defeating famous opponents like Napoleon Bonaparte and Benjamin Franklin. Not really a robot at all, the "Turk" actually contained a live chess master hidden behind a mechanical façade. [Eds.]

similar gaming software that is open source and then he builds on it. As the open-source movement around the world continues to gain speed (for governments and companies it is low cost, and for contributors the benefits are in recognition and economic opportunities to improve and enlarge the support ecosystems), the Russian teacher-programmer will have an enormous cache of technical plans to learn from and use in his own work. In a fully connected world, he is increasingly likely to catch the eyes of the right people, to be offered jobs or fellowships, or to sell his creation to a major multinational company. At a minimum, he can get his foot in the door.

Innovation can come from the ground up, but not all local innovation will work on a larger scale, because some entrepreneurs and inventors will be building for different audiences, solving very specific problems. This is true today as well. Consider the twenty-four-year-old Kenyan inventor Anthony Mutua, who unveiled at a 2012 Nairobi science fair an ultrathin crystal chip he developed that can generate electricity when put under pressure.[14] He placed the chip in the sole of a tennis shoe and demonstrated how, just by walking, a person can charge his mobile phone.[15] (It's a reminder of how bad the problems of reliable and affordable electricity, and to a lesser extent short battery life, are for many people—and how some governments are not rushing to fix the electricity grids—that innovators like Mutua are designing microchips that turn people into portable charging stations.) Mutua's chip is now set to go into mass production,[16] and if that successfully brings down the cost, he will have invented one of the cleverest designs that no one outside the developing world will ever use, simply because they'll never need to. Unfortunately, the level of a population's access to technology is often determined by external factors, and even if power and electricity problems are eventually solved (by the government or by citizens), there is no telling what new roadblocks will prevent certain groups from reaching the same level of connectivity and opportunity as others.

The most important pillar behind innovation and opportunity—education—will see tremendous positive change in the coming decades as rising connectivity reshapes traditional routines and offers new paths for learning. Most students will be highly technologically literate, as schools continue to integrate technology into lesson plans and, in some cases, replace traditional lessons with more interactive workshops. Education will be a more flexible experience, adapting itself to children's learning styles and pace instead of the other way around. Kids will still go to physical schools, to socialize and be guided by teachers, but as much, if not more, learning will take place employing carefully designed educational

20

---

[14] "Shoe Technology to Charge Cell Phones," *Daily Nation*, May 2012, http://www.nation.co.ke/News/Shoe+technology+to+charge+cell+phones++/-/1056/1401998/-/view/printVersion/-/sur34lz/-/index.html.
[15] Ibid.
[16] Ibid.

tools in the spirit of today's Khan Academy,[17] a nonprofit organization that produces thousands of short videos (the majority in science and math) and shares them online for free. With hundreds of millions of views on the Khan Academy's YouTube channel already, educators in the United States are increasingly adopting its materials and integrating the approach of its founder, Salman Khan—modular learning tailored to a student's needs. Some are even "flipping" their classrooms, replacing lectures with videos watched at home (as homework) and using school time for traditional homework, such as filling out a problem set for math class.[18] Critical thinking and problem-solving skills will become the focus in many school systems as ubiquitous digital-knowledge tools, like the more accurate sections of Wikipedia, reduce the importance of rote memorization.

For children in poor countries, future connectivity promises new access to educational tools, though clearly not at the level described above. Physical classrooms will remain dilapidated; teachers will continue to take paychecks and not show up for class; and books and supplies will still be scarce. But what's new in this equation—connectivity—promises that kids with access to mobile devices and the Internet will be able to experience school physically *and* virtually, even if the latter is informal and on their own time.

In places where basic needs are poorly met by the government, or in insecure areas, basic digital technologies like mobile phones will offer safe and inexpensive options for families looking to educate their children. A child who cannot attend school due to distance, lack of security or school fees will have a lifeline to the world of learning if she has access to a mobile phone. Even for those children without access to data plans or the mobile Web, basic mobile services, like text messages and IVR (interactive voice response, a form of voice-recognition technology), can provide educational outlets. Loading tablets and mobile phones with high-quality education applications and entertainment content before they are sold will ensure that the "bandwidth poor," who lack reliable connectivity, will still benefit from access to these devices. And for children whose classrooms are overcrowded or understaffed, or whose national curriculum is dubiously narrow, connectivity through mobile devices will supplement their education and help them reach their full potential, regardless of their origins. Today numerous pilot projects exist in developing countries that leverage mobile technology to teach a wide range of topics and skills, including basic literacy for children and adults, second languages and advanced courses from universities. In 2012, the

[17]**Khan Academy:** A nonprofit, online educational organization that provides micro lectures on thousands of academic topics via YouTube videos. [Eds.]

[18]Clive Thompson, "How Khan Academy Is Changing the Rules of Education," *Wired Magazine,* August 2011, posted online July 15, 2011, http://www.wired.com/magazine /2011/07/ff_khan/.

MIT Media Lab tested this approach in Ethiopia[19] by distributing pre-loaded tablets to primary-age kids without instructions or accompanying teachers.[20] The results were extraordinary: within months the kids were reciting the entire alphabet and writing complete sentences in English. Without the connectivity that will be ubiquitous in the future, there are limits to what any of these efforts can accomplish today.

Just imagine the implications of these burgeoning mobile or tablet-based learning platforms for a country like Afghanistan, which has one of the lowest rates of literacy in the world.[21] Digital platforms, whether presented in simple mobile form or in more sophisticated ways online, will eventually be able to withstand any environmental turbulence (political instability, economic collapse, perhaps even bad weather) and continue to serve the needs of users. So while the educational experience in the physical world will remain volatile for many, the virtual experience will increasingly become the more important and predictable option. And students stuck in school systems that teach narrow curriculums or only rote memorization will have access to a virtual world that encourages independent exploration and critical thinking.

A Better Quality of Life

In tandem with the wide variety of functional improvements in your daily life, future connectivity promises a dazzling array of "quality of life" improvements: things that make you healthier, safer and more engaged. As with other gains, there remains a sliding scale of access here, but that doesn't make them any less meaningful.

The devices, screens and various machines in your future apartment will serve a purpose beyond utility—they will offer entertainment, wanted distraction, intellectual and cultural enrichment, relaxation and opportunities to share things with others. The key advance ahead is personalization. You'll be able to customize your devices—indeed, much of the technology around you—to fit your needs, so that your environment reflects your preferences. People will have a better way to curate their life stories and will no longer have to rely on physical or online photo albums, although both will still exist. Future videography and photography will allow you to project any still or moving image you've captured as a three-dimensional holograph. Even more remarkable, you will be able to integrate any photos, videos and geographic settings that you choose to save into a single holographic device that you will place on the

[19]Nicholas Negroponte, "EmTech Preview: Another Way to Think About Learning," *Technology Review*, September 13, 2012, http://www.technologyreview.com/view/429206/emtech-preview-another-way-to-think-about/.

[20]David Talbot, "Given Tablets but No Teachers, Ethiopian Children Teach Themselves," *Technology Review*, October 29, 2012, http://www.technologyreview.com/news/506466/given-tablets-but-no-teachers-ethiopian-children-teach-themselves/.

[21]"Field Listing: Literacy," CIA, World Fact Book, accessed October 11, 2012, https://www.cia.gov/library/publications/the-world-factbook/fields/2103.html#af.

floor of your living room, instantaneously transforming the space into a memory room. A couple will be able to re-create their wedding ceremony for grandparents who were too ill to attend.

What you can watch on your various displays (high-quality LCD—liquid crystal display—screens, holographic projections or a handheld mobile device) will be determined by you, not by network-television schedules. At your fingertips will be an entire world's worth of digital content, constantly updated, ranked and categorized to help you find the music, movies, shows, books, magazines, blogs and art you like. Individual agency over entertainment and information channels will be greater than ever, as content producers shift from balkanized protectiveness to more unified and open models, since a different business model will be necessary in order to keep the audience. Contemporary services like Spotify, which offers a large catalog of live-streaming music for free, give us a sense of what the future will look like: an endless amount of content, available anytime, on almost any device, and at little or no cost to users, with copyrights and revenue streams preserved. Long-standing barriers to entry for content creators are being flattened as well; just as YouTube can be said to launch careers today[22] (or at least offer fleeting fame), in the future, even more platforms will offer artists, writers, directors, musicians and others in every country the chance to reach a wider audience. It will still require skill to create quality content, but it will also be easier to assemble a team with the requisite skills to do this—say, an animator from South Korea, a voice actor from the Philippines, a storyboarder from Mexico and a musician from Kenya—and the finished product may have the potential to reach as wide an audience as any Hollywood blockbuster.

Entertainment will become a more immersive and personalized experience in the future. Integrated tie-ins will make today's product placements seem passive and even clumsy. If while watching a television show you spot a sweater you want or a dish you think you'd like to cook, information including recipes or purchasing details will be readily available, as will every other fact about the show, its story lines, actors and locations. If you're feeling bored and want to take an hour-long holiday, why not turn on your holograph box and visit Carnival in Rio? Stressed? Go spend some time on a beach in the Maldives. Worried your kids are becoming spoiled? Have them spend some time wandering around the Dharavi slum in Mumbai. Frustrated by the media's coverage of the Olympics in a different time zone? Purchase a holographic pass for a reasonable price and watch the women's gymnastics team compete right in front of you, live. Through virtual-reality interfaces and holographic-projection capabilities, you'll be able to "join" these activities as they happen and experience them as if you were truly there. Nothing beats the real thing, but this will be a very close second. And if nothing else,

---

[22]The Korean K-pop star Psy's fame reached global proportions almost overnight as the video he created for his song "Gangnam Style" became the most-watched YouTube video ever within a span of three months.

it will certainly be more affordable. Thanks to these new technologies, you can be more stimulated, or more relaxed, than ever before.

You'll be safer, too, at least on the road. While some of the very exciting new possibilities in transportation, like supersonic tube commutes and suborbital space travel, are still far in the distance, ubiquitous self-driving cars are imminent. Google's fleet of driverless cars, built by a team of Google and Stanford University engineers, has logged hundreds of thousands of miles without incident, and other models will soon join it on the road. Rather than replacing drivers altogether, the liminal step will be a "driver-assist" approach, where the self-driving option can be turned on, just as an airline captain turns on the autopilot. Government authorities are already well versed on self-driving cars and their potential—in 2012, Nevada became the first state to issue licenses to driverless cars,[23] and later that same year California also affirmed their legality.[24] Imagine the possibilities for long-haul truck-driving. Rather than testing the biological limits of human drivers with thirty-hour trips, the computer can take over primary responsibility and drive the truck for stretches as the driver rests.

The advances in health and medicine in our near future will be among the most significant of all the new game-changing developments. And thanks to rising connectivity, an even wider range of people will benefit than at any other time in history. Improvements in disease detection and treatment, the management of medical records and personal-health monitoring promise more equitable access to health care and health information for potentially billions more people when we factor in the spread of digital technology.

The diagnostic capability of your mobile phone will be old news. (*Of course* you will be able to scan body parts the way you do bar codes.) But soon you will be benefiting from a slew of physical augmentations designed to monitor your well-being, such as microscopic robots in your circulatory system that keep track of your blood pressure, detect nascent heart disease and identify early-stage cancer. Inside your grandfather's new titanium hip there will be a chip that can act as a pedometer, monitor his insulin levels to check for the early stages of diabetes, and even trigger an automated phone call to an emergency contact if he takes a particularly hard fall and might need assistance. A tiny nasal implant will be available to you that will alert you to airborne toxins and early signs of a cold.

30

[23]Chris Gaylord, "Ready for a Self-Driving Car? Check Your Driveway," *Christian Science Monitor*, June 25, 2012, http://www.csmonitor.com/Innovation/Tech/2012/0625/Ready -for-a-self-driving-car-Check-your-driveway.

[24]James Temple, "California Affirms Legality of Driverless Cars," *The Tech Chronicles* (blog), *San Francisco Chronicle*, September 25, 2012, http://blog.sfgate.com/techron /2012/09/25/california-legalizes-driverless-cars/; Florida has passed a similar law. See Joann Muller, "With Driverless Cars, Once Again It Is California Leading the Way," *Forbes*, September 26, 2012, http://www.forbes.com/sites/joannmuller/2012/09/26/with-driverless-cars -once-again-it-is-california-leading-the-way/.

Eventually these accoutrements will be as uncontroversial as artificial pacemakers (the first of which was implanted in the 1950s). They are the logical extensions of today's personal-health-tracking applications, which allow people to use their smart phones to log their exercise, track their metabolic rates and chart their cholesterol levels. Indeed, ingestible health technology already exists—the Food and Drug Administration (FDA) approved the first electronic pill in 2012. Made by a California-based biomedical firm called Proteus Digital Health, the pill carries a tiny sensor one square millimeter in size, and once the pill is swallowed, stomach acid activates the circuit and sends a signal to a small patch worn outside the body (which then sends its data to a mobile phone). The patch can collect information about a patient's response to a drug (monitoring body temperature, heart rate and other indicators), relay data about regular usage to doctors and even track what a person eats. For sufferers of chronic illnesses and the elderly particularly, this technology will allow for significant improvements: automatic reminders to take various medications, the ability to measure directly how drugs are reacting in a person's body and the creation of an instant digital feedback loop with doctors that is personalized and data-driven. Not everyone will want to actively oversee their health to this degree, let alone the even more detailed version of the future, but they probably will want their doctor to have access to such data. "Intelligent pills" and nasal implants will be sufficiently affordable so as to be as accessible as vitamins and supplements. In short order, we will have access to personal health-care systems run off of our mobile devices that will automatically detect if something is wrong with us based on data collected from some of the above-mentioned augmentations, prompt us with appointment options for a nearby doctor and subsequently (with consent) send all of the relevant data about our symptoms and health indicators to the doctor being consulted.

Tissue engineers will be able to grow new organs to replace patients' old or diseased ones, using either synthetic materials or a person's own cells. At the outset, affordability will limit the use. Synthetic skin grafts, which exist today, will give way to grafts made from burn victims' own cells. Inside hospitals, robots will take on more responsibilities, as surgeons increasingly let sophisticated machines handle difficult parts of certain procedures, where delicate or tedious work is involved or a wider range of motion is required.[25]

Advances in genetic testing will usher in the era of personalized medicine. Through targeted tests and genome sequencing (decoding a person's full DNA), doctors and disease specialists will have more information about patients, and what might help them, than ever before. Despite steady scientific progress, severe negative reactions to prescribed drugs remain a leading cause of hospitalization and death. Pharmaceutical

---

[25]Robotic surgical suites are already in operation in hospitals in the United States and Europe.

companies traditionally pursue a "one-size-fits-all" approach to drug development, but this is due to change as the burgeoning field of pharmacogenetics continues to develop. Better genetic testing will reduce the likelihood of negative reactions, improve patients' chances and provide doctors and medical researchers with more data to analyze and use. Eventually, and initially only for the wealthy, it will be possible to design pharmaceutical drugs tailored to an individual's genetic structure. But this too will change as the cost of DNA sequencing drops below $100 and almost everything biological is sequenced, making it possible for a much broader segment of the world's population to benefit from highly specific, personalized diagnoses. . . .

The Upper Band

Connectivity benefits everyone. Those who have none will have some, and those who have a lot will have even more. To demonstrate that, imagine you are a young urban professional living in an American city a few decades from now. An average morning might look something like this:

There will be no alarm clock in your wake-up routine — at least, not in the traditional sense. Instead, you'll be roused by the aroma of freshly brewed coffee, by light entering your room as curtains open automatically, and by a gentle back massage administered by your high-tech bed. You're more likely to awake refreshed, because inside your mattress there's a special sensor that monitors your sleeping rhythms, determining precisely when to wake you so as not to interrupt a REM cycle.

Your apartment is an electronic orchestra, and you are the conductor. With simple flicks of the wrist and spoken instructions, you can control temperature, humidity, ambient music and lighting. You are able to skim through the day's news on translucent screens while a freshly cleaned suit is retrieved from your automated closet because your calendar indicates an important meeting today. You head to the kitchen for breakfast and the translucent news display follows, as a projected hologram hovering just in front of you, using motion detection, as you walk down the hallway. You grab a mug of coffee and a fresh pastry, cooked to perfection in your humidity-controlled oven — and skim new e-mails on a holographic "tablet" projected in front of you. Your central computer system suggests a list of chores your housekeeping robots should tackle today, all of which you approve. It further suggests that, since your coffee supply is projected to run out next Wednesday, you consider purchasing a certain larger-size container that it noticed currently on sale online. Alternatively, it offers a few recent reviews of other coffee blends your friends enjoy.

As you mull this over, you pull up your notes for a presentation you'll give later that day to important new clients abroad. All of your data — from your personal and professional life — is accessible through all of your various devices, as it's stored in the cloud, a remote digital-storage system with near limitless capacity. You own a few different and inter-changeable digital devices; one is the size of a tablet, another the size of a pocket watch, while others might be flexible or wearable. All will be lightweight, incredibly fast and will use more powerful processors than anything available today.

You take another sip of coffee, feeling confident that you'll impress your clients. You already feel as if you know them, though you've never met in person, since your meetings have been conducted in a virtual-reality interface. You interact with holographic "avatars" that exactly capture your clients' movements and speech. You understand them and their needs well, not least because autonomous language-translation software reproduces the speech of both parties in perfect translations almost instantly. Real-time virtual interactions like these, as well as the ability to edit and collaborate on documents and other projects, makes the actual distance between you seem negligible.

As you move about your kitchen, you stub your toe, hard, on the edge of a cabinet—ouch! You grab your mobile device and open the diagnostics app. Inside your device there is a tiny microchip that uses low-radiation submillimeter waves to scan your body, like an X-ray. A quick scan reveals that your toe is just bruised, not broken. You decline the invitation your device suggests to get a second opinion at a nearby doctor's office.

There's a bit of time left before you need to leave for work—which you'll get to by driverless car, of course. Your car knows what time you need to be in the office each morning based on your calendar and, after factoring in traffic data, it communicates with your wristwatch to give you a sixty-minute countdown to when you need to leave the house. Your commute will be as productive or relaxing as you desire.

Before you head out, your device reminds you to buy a gift for your nephew's upcoming birthday. You scan the system's proposed gift ideas, derived from anonymous, aggregated data on other nine-year-old boys with his profile and interests, but none of the suggestions inspire you. Then you remember a story his parents told you that had everyone forty and older laughing: Your nephew hadn't understood a reference to the old excuse "A dog ate my homework"; how could a dog eat his cloud storage drive? He had never gone to school before digital textbooks and online lesson plans, and he had used paper to do his homework so rarely—and used cloud storage so routinely—that the notion that he would somehow "forget" his homework *and* come up with an excuse like that struck him as absurd. You do a quick search for a robotic dog and buy one with a single click, after adding a few special touches he might like, such as a reinforced titanium skeleton so that he can ride on it. In the card input, you type: "Just in case." It will arrive at his house within a five-minute window of your selected delivery time.

You think about having another cup of coffee, but then a haptic device ("haptic" refers to technology that involves touch and feeling) that is embedded in the heel of your shoe gives you a gentle pinch—a signal that you'll be late for your morning meeting if you linger any longer. Perhaps you grab an apple on the way out, to eat in the backseat of your car as it chauffeurs you to your office.

If you are a part of the world's upper band of income earners (as most residents of wealthy Western countries are), you will have access to many of these new technologies directly, as owners or as friends of those who own them. You probably recognize from this morning routine a few things you have already imagined or experienced. Of course, there will always be the super-wealthy people whose access to technology will be even greater—they'll probably eschew cars altogether and travel to work in motion-stabilized automated helicopters, for example.

We will continue to encounter challenges in the physical world, but the expansion of the virtual world and what is possible online—as well as the inclusion of five billion more minds—means we will have new ways of getting information and moving resources to solve those problems, even if the solutions are imperfect. While there will remain significant differences between us, more opportunities to interact and better policy can help blur the edges.

ENGAGING THE TEXT

1. How do Schmidt and Cohen portray the impact of technology on the future? Which of the innovations they mention would you particularly look forward to, and why? Which of their predictions seem problematic or overly optimistic?

2. How do the authors see technology changing global human relations? Do you think that greater "connectivity" will necessarily make the world politically, cul- turally, and economically a better place? What other effects might it have?

3. What role has technology played in your own education? For example, how much experience have you had with technological "tools" like the Kahn Academy or concepts like the "flipped classroom"? Do you agree with Schmidt and Cohen that more technology in the classroom will increase critical thinking and problem solving?

4. How do you think new technologies like personalized devices, immersive virtual reality, holographic TV, driverless cars, genetic testing, and electronic memory aids will change human beings in the future? Would you like to live in the "upper band" world Schmidt and Cohen envision at the end of this selection?

EXPLORING CONNECTIONS

5. How might Diane Ravitch (p. 105) and Jonathan Kozol (p. 170) respond to Schmidt and Cohen's predictions about the impact of technology on the classroom? Why might they be less than optimistic about Schmidt and Cohen's vision of a coming educational revolution?

6. Schmidt and Cohen conclude this selection by imagining what a day will be like in the future for someone who is in the "upper band" of technology users. How do you think technology will change the worlds of poor or working-class people, like those described by Barbara Ehrenreich (p. 363) or Gregory Mantsios (p. 377)? Explain why you think technology will equalize or exacerbate class divisions.

EXTENDING THE CRITICAL CONTEXT

7. Research the impact of new technologies on the developing world today. How, for example, are things like inexpensive cell phones, tablet computers, and alternative energy sources changing lives in Africa and Latin America? For more information, browse the Web sites of Kopernick and other nongovernmental organizations dedicated to bringing modern technologies to developing nations.

8. As a class, watch a film about artificial intelligence, like *Ex Machina*, *Chappie*, or *Her*, or view an episode of the 2015 television series *Humans*, and then discuss what it suggests about the future of human–robot relations. How is the impact of artificial intelligence on humans portrayed, and what questions are raised about the ethics of artificial intelligence? Do you think that in the future people and machines will have "relationships"?

GROWING UP TETHERED

SHERRY TURKLE

In the past decade and a half, the invention of the cell phone and the development of social media have revolutionized the American way of life. Smart phones and social networks have changed the way we work, the way we relate to our friends — even the way we fall in love. In fact, as sociologist Sherry Turkle indicates in this selection, life online may be altering our sense of self. A clinical psychologist and early critic of the impact of computer technology, Turkle worries that spending too much time online is undermining the spirit of self-reliance that has traditionally been associated with American identity. As she sees it, "growing up tethered" to the Internet is also a major source of stress in our modern lives. Turkle (b. 1948) holds an endowed chair at the Massachusetts Institute of Technology. She is also the founder of the MIT Initiative on Technology and the Self. Her many books include *The Second Self: Computers and the Human Spirit* (1984), *Life on the Screen: Identity in the Age of the Internet* (1995), and *Alone Together: Why We Expect More from Technology and Less from Each Other* (2011), the source of this selection.

ROMAN, EIGHTEEN, ADMITS THAT HE TEXTS while driving and he is not going to stop. "I know I should, but it's not going to happen. If I get a Facebook message or something posted on my wall . . . I have to see it. I have to." I am speaking with him and ten of his senior classmates at the Cranston School, a private urban coeducational high school in Connecticut. His friends admonish him, but then several admit to the same behavior. Why do they text while driving? Their reasons are not reasons; they simply express a need to connect. "I interrupt a call even if the new call says 'unknown' as an identifier—I just have to know who it is. So I'll cut off a friend for an 'unknown,'" says Maury. "I need to know who wanted to connect. . . . And if I hear my phone, I have to answer it. I don't have a choice. I have to know who it is, what they are calling for." Marilyn adds, "I keep the sound on when I drive. When a text comes in, I have to look. No matter what. Fortunately, my phone shows me the text as a pop up right up front . . . so I don't have to do too much looking while I'm driving." These young people live in a state of waiting for connection. And they are willing to take risks, to put themselves on the line. Several admit that tethered to their phones, they get into accidents when walking. One chipped a front tooth. Another shows a recent bruise on his arm. "I went right into the handle of the refrigerator."

I ask the group a question: "When was the last time you felt that you didn't want to be interrupted?" I expect to hear many stories. There are none. Silence. "I'm waiting to be interrupted right now," one says. For him, what I would term "interruption" is the beginning of a connection.

Today's young people have grown up with robot pets and on the network in a fully tethered life. In their views of robots, they are pioneers, the first generation that does not necessarily take simulation to be second best. As for online life, they see its power—they are, after all risking their lives to check their messages—but they also view it as one might the weather: to be taken for granted, enjoyed, and sometimes endured. They've gotten used to this weather but there are signs of weather fatigue. There are so many performances; it takes energy to keep things up; and it takes time, a lot of time: "Sometimes you don't have time for your friends except if they're online," is a common complaint. And then there are the compulsions of the networked life—the ones that lead to dangerous driving and chipped teeth.

Today's adolescents have no less need than those of previous generations to learn empathic skills, to think about their values and identity, and to manage and express feelings. They need time to discover themselves, time to think. But technology, put in the service of always-on communication and telegraphic speed and brevity, has changed the rules of engagement with all of this. When is downtime, when is stillness? The text-driven world of rapid response does not make self-reflection impossible but does little to cultivate it. When interchanges are reformatted for the small screen and reduced to the emotional shorthand of emoticons, there are necessary simplifications. And what of adolescents' need for secrets, for marking out what is theirs alone?

I wonder about this as I watch cell phones passed around high school ⁵ cafeterias. Photos and messages are being shared and compared. I cannot help but identify with the people who sent the messages to these wandering phones. Do they all assume that their words and photographs are on public display? Perhaps. Traditionally, the development of intimacy required privacy. Intimacy without privacy reinvents what intimacy means. Separation, too, is being reinvented. Tethered children know they have a parent on tap—a text or a call away.

Degrees of Separation

Mark Twain mythologized the adolescent's search for identity in the Huck Finn story, the on-the-Mississippi moment, a time of escape from an adult world. Of course, the time on the river is emblematic not of a moment but of an ongoing process through which children separate from their parents. That rite of passage is now transformed by technology. In the traditional variant, the child internalizes the adults in his or her world before crossing the threshold of independence. In the modern, technologically tethered variant, parents can be brought along in an intermediate space, such as that created by the cell phone, where everyone important is on speed dial. In this sense, the generations sail down the river together, and adolescents don't face the same pressure to develop the independence we have associated with moving forward into young adulthood.

When parents give children cell phones—most of the teenagers I spoke with were given a phone between the ages of nine and thirteen—the gift typically comes with a contract: children are expected to answer their parents' calls. This arrangement makes it possible for the child to engage in activities—see friends, attend movies, go shopping, spend time at the beach—that would not be permitted without the phone. Yet, the tethered child does not have the experience of being alone with only him- or herself to count on. For example, there used to be a point for an urban child, an important moment, when there was a first time to navigate the city alone. It was a rite of passage that communicated to children that they were on their own and responsible. If they were frightened, they had to experience those feelings. The cell phone buffers this moment.

Parents want their children to answer their phones, but adolescents need to separate. With a group of seniors at Fillmore, a boys' preparatory school in New York City, the topic of parents and cell phones elicits strong emotions. The young men consider, "If it is always possible to be in touch, when does one have the right to be alone?"

Some of the boys are defiant. For one, "It should be my decision about whether I pick up the phone. People can call me, but I don't have to talk to them." For another, "To stay free from parents, I don't take my cell. Then they can't reach me. My mother tells me to take my cell, but I just don't." Some appeal to history to justify ignoring parents' calls. Harlan, a distinguished student and athlete, thinks he has earned the right to greater independence. He talks about older siblings who grew up before cell phones and enjoyed greater freedom: "My mother makes me take my phone, but I never answer it when my parents call, and they get mad at me. I don't feel I should have to. Cell phones are recent. In the last ten years, everyone started getting them. Before, you couldn't just call someone whenever. I don't see why I have to answer when my mom calls me. My older sisters didn't have to do that." Harlan's mother, unmoved by this argument from precedent, checks that he has his phone when he leaves for school in the morning; Harlan does not answer her calls. Things are at an unhappy stalemate.

Several boys refer to the "mistake" of having taught their parents how to text and send instant messages (IMs), which they now equate with letting the genie out of the bottle. For one, "I made the mistake of teaching my parents how to text-message recently, so now if I don't call them when they ask me to call, I get an urgent text message." For another, "I taught my parents to IM. They didn't know how. It was the stupidest thing I could do. Now my parents IM me all the time. It is really annoying. My parents are upsetting me. I feel trapped and less independent."

Teenagers argue that they should be allowed time when they are not "on call." Parents say that they, too, feel trapped. For if you know your child is carrying a cell phone, it is frightening to call or text and get no response. "I didn't ask for this new worry," says the mother of two high school girls. Another, a mother of three teenagers, "tries not to call them if it's not important." But if she calls and gets no response, she panics:

> I've sent a text. Nothing back. And I know they have their phones. Intellectually, I know there is little reason to worry. But there is something about this unanswered text. Sometimes, it made me a bit nutty. One time, I kept sending texts, over and over. I envy my mother. We left for school in the morning. We came home. She worked. She came back, say at six. She didn't worry. I end up imploring my children to answer my every message. Not because I feel I have a right to their instant response. Just out of compassion.

Adolescent autonomy is not just about separation from parents. Adolescents also need to separate from each other. They experience their friendships as both sustaining and constraining. Connectivity brings complications. Online life provides plenty of room for individual experimentation, but it can be hard to escape from new group demands. It is common for friends to expect that their friends will stay available—a technology-enabled social contract demands continual peer presence. And the tethered self becomes accustomed to its support.

Traditional views of adolescent development take autonomy and strong personal boundaries as reliable signs of a successfully maturing self. In this view of development, we work toward an independent self capable of having a feeling, considering it, and deciding whether to share it. Sharing a feeling is a deliberate act, a movement toward intimacy. This description was always a fiction in several ways. For one thing, the "gold standard" of autonomy validated a style that was culturally "male." Women (and indeed, many men) have an emotional style that defines itself not by boundaries but through relationships.[1] Furthermore, adolescent conversations are by nature exploratory, and this in healthy ways. Just as some writers learn what they think by looking at what they write, the years of identity formation can be a time of learning what you think by hearing what you say to others. But given these caveats, when we think about maturation, the notion of a bounded self has its virtues, if only as a metaphor. It suggests, sensibly, that before we forge successful life partnerships, it is helpful to have a sense of who we are.[2]

But the gold standard tarnishes if a phone is always in hand. You touch a screen and reach someone presumed ready to respond, someone who also has a phone in hand. Now, technology makes it easy to express emotions while they are being formed. It supports an emotional style in which feelings are not fully experienced until they are communicated. Put otherwise, there is every opportunity to form a thought by sending out for comments.

---

[1]Carol Gilligan, *In a Different Voice: Psychological Theory and Women's Development* (1982; Cambridge, MA: Harvard University Press, 1993). [All notes are Turkle's, except 8, 10, 15, 16, and 19.]

[2]Erik Erikson, *Identity and the Life Cycle* (1952; New York: W. W. Norton, 1980) and *Childhood and Society* (New York: Norton, 1950).

The Collaborative Self

Julia, sixteen, a sophomore at Branscomb, an urban public high school in   15
New Jersey, turns texting into a kind of polling. Julia has an outgoing and
warm presence, with smiling, always-alert eyes. When a feeling bubbles
up, Julia texts it. Where things go next is guided by what she hears next.
Julia says,

> If I'm upset, right as I feel upset, I text a couple of my friends . . . just
> because I know that they'll be there and they can comfort me. If some-
> thing exciting happens, I know that they'll be there to be excited with
> me, and stuff like that. So I definitely feel emotions when I'm text-
> ing, as I'm texting. . . . Even before I get upset and I know that I have
> that feeling that I'm gonna start crying, yeah, I'll pull up my friend . . .
> uh, my phone . . . and say like . . . I'll tell them what I'm feeling, and,
> like, I need to talk to them, or see them.

"I'll pull up my friend . . . uh, my phone." Julia's language slips tellingly. When Julia thinks about strong feelings, her thoughts go both to her
phone and her friends. She mixes together "pulling up" a friend's name
on her phone and "pulling out" her phone, but she does not really correct herself so much as imply that the phone is her friend and that friends
take on identities through her phone.

After Julia sends out a text, she is uncomfortable until she gets one
back: "I am always looking for a text that says, 'Oh, I'm sorry,' or 'Oh, that's
great.'" Without this feedback, she says, "It's hard to calm down." Julia
describes how painful it is to text about "feelings" and get no response:
"I get mad. Even if I e-mail someone, I want the response, like, right
away.[3] I want them to be, like, right there answering me. And sometimes
I'm like, 'Uh! Why can't you just answer me?'. . . I wait, like, depending
on what it is, I wait like an hour if they don't answer me, and I'll text
them again. 'Are you mad? Are you there? Is everything okay?'" Her anxiety is palpable. Julia must have a response. She says of those she texts,
"You want them there, because you need them." When they are not there,
she moves on with her nascent feelings, but she does not move on alone:
"I go to another friend and tell them."

Claudia, seventeen, a junior at Cranston, describes a similar progression. "I start to have some happy feelings as soon as I start to text." As
with Julia, things move from "I have a feeling, I want to make a call" to
"I want to have a feeling, I need to make a call," or in her case, send a
text. What is not being cultivated here is the ability to be alone and reflect
on one's emotions in private. On the contrary, teenagers report discomfort

[3]In Julia's world, e-mail is considered "slow" and rarely used because texting has greater
immediacy.

when they are without their cell phones.[4] They need to be connected in order to feel like themselves. Put in a more positive way, both Claudia and Julia share feelings as part of discovering them. They cultivate a collaborative self.

Estranged from her father, Julia has lost her close attachments to his relatives and was traumatized by being unable to reach her mother during the day of the September 11 attacks on the Twin Towers. Her story illustrates how digital connectivity—particularly texting—can be used to manage specific anxieties about loss and separation. But what Julia does—her continual texting, her way of feeling her feelings only as she shares them—is not unusual. The particularities of every individual case express personal history, but Julia's individual "symptom" comes close to being a generational style.[5]

Sociologist David Riesman, writing in the mid-1950s, remarked on the American turn from an inner- to an other-directed sense of self.[6] Without a firm inner sense of purpose, people looked to their neighbors for validation. Today, cell phone in hand, other-directedness is raised to a higher power. At the moment of beginning to have a thought or feeling, we can have it validated, almost prevalidated. Exchanges may be brief, but more is not necessarily desired. The necessity is to have someone be there.

Ricki, fifteen, a freshman at Richelieu, a private high school for girls in New York City, describes that necessity: "I have a lot of people on my contact list. If one friend doesn't 'get it,' I call another." This marks a turn to a hyper-other-directedness. This young woman's contact or buddy list has become something like a list of "spare parts" for her fragile adolescent self. When she uses the expression "get it," I think she means "pick up the phone." I check with her if I have gotten this right. She says, "'Get it,' yeah, 'pick up,' but also 'get it,' 'get *me*.'" Ricki counts on her friends to finish her thoughts. Technology does not cause but encourages a sensibility in which the validation of a feeling becomes part of establishing it, even part of the feeling itself.

I have said that in the psychoanalytic tradition, one speaks about narcissism not to indicate people who love themselves, but a personality

[4]It is so common to see teenagers (and others) attending to their mobiles rather than what is around them, that it was possible for a fake news story to gain traction in Britain. Taken up by the media, the story went out that there was a trial program to pad lampposts in major cities. Although it was a hoax, I fell for it when it was presented online as news. In fact, in the year prior to the hoax, one in five Britons did walk into a lamppost or other obstruction while attending to a mobile device. This is not surprising because research reported that "62 per cent of Britons concentrate so hard on their mobile phone when texting they lose peripheral vision." See Charlie Sorrel, "Padded Lampposts Cause Fuss in London," *Wired*, March 10, 2008, www.wired.com/gadgetlab/2008/03/padded-lampposts (accessed October 5, 2009).

[5]New communications technology makes it easier to serve up people as slivers of self, providing a sense that to get what you need from others you have multiple and inexhaustible options. On the psychology that needs these "slivers," see Paul H. Ornstein, ed., *The Search for Self: Selected Writings of Heinz Kohut (1950–1978)*, vol. 2 (New York: International Universities Press, 1978).

[6]David Riesman, Nathan Glazer, and Reuel Denney, *The Lonely Crowd: A Study of the Changing American Character* (1950; New Haven, CT: Yale University Press, 2001).

so fragile that it needs constant support.[7] It cannot tolerate the complex demands of other people but tries to relate to them by distorting who they are and splitting off what it needs, what it can use. So, the narcissistic self gets on with others by dealing only with their made-to-measure representations. These representations (some analytic traditions refer to them as "part objects," others as "self-objects") are all that the fragile self can handle. We can easily imagine the utility of inanimate companions to such a self because a robot or a computational agent can be sculpted to meet one's needs. But a fragile person can also be supported by selected and limited contact with people (say, the people on a cell phone "favorites" list). In a life of texting and messaging, those on that contact list can be made to appear almost on demand. You can take what you need and move on. And, if not gratified, you can try someone else.

Again, technology, on its own, does not cause this new way of relating to our emotions and other people. But it does make it easy. Over time, a new style of being with each other becomes socially sanctioned. In every era, certain ways of relating come to feel natural. In our time, if we can be continually in touch, needing to be continually in touch does not seem a problem or a pathology but an accommodation to what technology affords. It becomes the norm.

The history of what we think of as psychopathology is dynamic. If in a particular time and place, certain behaviors seem disruptive, they are labeled pathological. In the nineteenth century, for example, sexual repression was considered a good and moral thing, but when women lost sensation or the ability to speak, these troubling symptoms were considered a disease, hysteria. With more outlets for women's sexuality, hysterical symptoms declined, and others took their place. So, the much-prescribed tranquilizers of the 1950s spoke to women's new anxieties when marginalized in the home after a fuller civic participation during World War II.

Now, we have symptoms born of fears of isolation and abandonment. In my study of growing up in the networked culture, I meet many children and teenagers who feel cast off. Some have parents with good intentions who simply work several jobs and have little time for their children. Some have endured divorce — sometimes multiple divorces — and float from one parent to another, not confident of their true home. Those lucky children who have intact families with stable incomes can experience other forms of abandonment. Busy parents are preoccupied, often by what is on their cell phones. When children come home, it is often to a house that is empty until a parent returns from work.

---

[7]Ornstein, *The Search for Self*. For an earlier work, of a very different time, that linked cultural change and narcissistic personality style, see Christopher Lasch, *The Culture of Narcissism* (New York: Norton, 1979). Lasch said that "pathology represents a heightened version of normality." This formulation is helpful in thinking about the "normal" self in a tethered society and those who suffer more acutely from its discontents. From a psychodynamic perspective, we all suffer from the same things, some of us more acutely than others.

For young people in all of these circumstances, computers and mobile devices offer communities when families are absent. In this context, it is not surprising to find troubling patterns of connection and disconnection: teenagers who will only "speak" online, who rigorously avoid face-to-face encounters, who are in text contact with their parents fifteen or twenty times a day, who deem even a telephone call "too much" exposure and say that they will "text, not talk." But are we to think of these as pathologies? For as social mores change, what once seemed "ill" can come to seem normal. Twenty years ago, as a practicing clinical psychologist, if I had met a college junior who called her mother fifteen times a day, checking in about what shoes to buy and what dress to wear, extolling a new kind of decaffeinated tea, and complaining about the difficulty of a physics problem set, I would have thought her behavior problematic. I would have encouraged her to explore difficulties with separation. I would have assumed that these had to be addressed for her to proceed to successful adulthood. But these days, a college student who texts home fifteen times a day is not unusual.

High school and college students are always texting—while waiting in line at the cafeteria, while eating, while waiting for the campus shuttle. Not surprisingly, many of these texts are to parents. What once we might have seen as a problem becomes how we do things. But a behavior that has become typical may still express the problems that once caused us to see it as pathological. Even a typical behavior may not be in an adolescent's developmental interest.

Consider Leo, a college sophomore far from home, who feels crippling loneliness. He tells me that he "handles" this problem by texting and calling his mother up to twenty times a day. He remarks that this behavior does not make him stand out; everyone he knows is on a phone all day. But even if invisible, he considers his behavior a symptom all the same.

These days, our relationship to the idea of psychological autonomy is evolving. I have said that central to Erik Erikson's thinking[8] about adolescents is the idea that they need a moratorium, a "time out," a relatively consequence-free space for experimentation. But in Erikson's thinking, the self, once mature, is relatively stable. Though embedded in relationships, in the end it is bounded and autonomous.[9] One of Erikson's students, psychiatrist Robert Jay Lifton, has an alternative vision of the mature self. He calls it *protean*[10] and emphasizes its multiple aspects.[11] Thinking of the self as protean accents connection and reinvention. This self, as Lifton puts it, "fluid and many-sided," can embrace and modify

[8]**Erik Erikson:** German-born American psychologist (1902–1994) known for his theory on the psychosocial development of human beings. [Eds.]

[9]See Erik Erikson, *Identity and the Life Cycle* and *Childhood and Society; Young Man Luther: A Study in Psychoanalysis and History* (New York: W. W. Norton and Company, 1958).

[10]**protean:** In Greek mythology, Proteus was a sea-god who could change shape at will; hence, something protean is mutable or able to assume different forms. [Eds.]

[11]Robert Jay Lifton, *The Protean Self: Human Resilience in an Age of Fragmentation* (New York: Basic Books, 1993).

ideas and ideologies. It flourishes when provided with things diverse, disconnected, and global.

Publicly, Erikson expressed approval for Lifton's work, but after Erikson's death in 1994, Lifton asked the Erikson family if he might have the books he had personally inscribed and presented to his teacher. The family agreed; the books were returned. In his personal copy of Lifton's *The Protean Self*, Erikson had written extensive marginal notes. When he came to the phrase "protean man," Erikson had scrawled "protean boy?"[12] Erikson could not accept that successful maturation would not result in something solid. By Erikson's standards, the selves formed in the cacophony of online spaces are not protean but juvenile. Now I suggest that the culture in which they develop tempts them into narcissistic ways of relating to the world.

The Avatar of Me

Erikson said that identity play is the work of adolescence. And these days adolescents use the rich materials of online life to do that work. For example, in a game such as The Sims Online (think of this as a very junior version of Second Life), you can create an avatar that expresses aspects of yourself, build a house, and furnish it to your taste. Thus provisioned, you can set about reworking in the virtual aspects of life that may not have gone so well in the real.

Trish, a timid and anxious thirteen-year-old, has been harshly beaten by her alcoholic father. She creates an abusive family on The Sims Online, but in the game her character, also thirteen, is physically and emotionally strong. In simulation, she plays and replays the experience of fighting off her aggressor. A sexually experienced girl of sixteen, Katherine, creates an online innocent. "I want to have a rest," she says. Beyond rest, Katherine tells me she can get "practice at being a different kind of person. That's what Sims is for me. Practice."

Katherine "practices" on the game at breakfast, during school recess, and after dinner. She says she feels comforted by her virtual life. I ask her if her activities in the game have led her to do anything differently in her life away from it. She replies, "Not really," but then goes on to describe how her life is in fact beginning to change: "I'm thinking about breaking up with my boyfriend. I don't want to have sex anymore, but I would like to have a boyfriend. My character on Sims has boyfriends but doesn't have sex. They [the boyfriends of her Sims avatar] help her with her job. I think to start fresh I would have to break up with my boyfriend." Katherine does not completely identify with her online character and refers to her avatar in the third person. Yet, The Sims Online is a place where she can see her life anew.

---

[12]Lifton shared this story at a meeting of the Wellfleet Seminar in October 2009, an annual gathering that began as a forum for Erikson and his students as they turned their attention to psychohistory.

This kind of identity work can take place wherever you create an avatar. And it can take place on social-networking sites as well, where one's profile becomes an avatar of sorts, a statement not only about who you are but who you want to be. Teenagers make it clear that games, worlds, and social networking (on the surface, rather different) have much in common. They all ask you to compose and project an identity. Audrey, sixteen, a junior at Roosevelt, a suburban public high school near New York City, is explicit about the connection between avatars and profiles. She calls her Facebook profile "my Internet twin" and "the avatar of me."

Mona, a freshman at Roosevelt, has recently joined Facebook. Her parents made her wait until her fourteenth birthday, and I meet her shortly after this long-awaited day. Mona tells me that as soon as she got on the site, "Immediately, I felt power." I ask her what she means. She says, "The first thing I thought was, 'I am going to broadcast the real me.'" But when Mona sat down to write her profile, things were not so straightforward. Whenever one has time to write, edit, and delete, there is room for performance. The "real me" turns out to be elusive. Mona wrote and rewrote her profile. She put it away for two days and tweaked it again. Which pictures to add? Which facts to include? How much of her personal life to reveal? Should she give any sign that things at home were troubled? Or was this a place to look good?

Mona worries that she does not have enough of a social life to make herself sound interesting: "What kind of personal life should I *say* I have?" Similar questions plague other young women in her class. They are starting to have boyfriends. Should they list themselves as single if they are just starting to date someone new? What if they consider themselves in a relationship, but their boyfriends do not? Mona tells me that "it's common sense" to check with a boy before listing yourself as connected to him, but "that could be a very awkward conversation." So there are misunderstandings and recriminations. Facebook at fourteen can be a tearful place. For many, it remains tearful well through college and graduate school. Much that might seem straightforward is fraught. For example, when asked by Facebook to confirm someone as a friend or ignore the request, Helen, a Roosevelt senior, says, "I always feel a bit of panic. . . . Who should I friend? . . . I really want to only have my cool friends listed, but I'm nice to a lot of other kids at school. So I include the more unpopular ones, but then I'm unhappy." It is not how she wants to be seen. . . .

Presentation Anxiety

What are the truth claims in a Facebook profile? How much can you lie? And what is at stake if you do? Nancy, an eighteen-year-old senior at Roosevelt, answers this question. "On the one hand, low stakes, because no one is really checking." Then, with a grimace, she says, "No, high stakes. Everyone is checking." A few minutes later, Nancy comes back to the question: "Only my best friends will know if I lie a little bit, and they will totally understand." Then she laughs. "All of this, it is, I guess, a bit of stress."[13]

At Cranston, a group of seniors describe that stress. One says, "Thirteen to eighteen are the years of profile writing." The years of identity construction are recast in terms of profile production. These private school students had to write one profile for their applications to middle school, another to get into high school, and then another for Facebook. Now they are beginning to construct personae for college applications. And here, says Tom, "You have to have a slightly different persona for the different colleges to which you are applying: one for Dartmouth, a different one, say, for Wesleyan." For this aficionado of profile writing, every application needs a different approach. "By the time you get to the questions for the college application, you are a professional profile writer," he says. His classmate Stan describes his online profiles in great detail. Each serves a different purpose, but they must overlap, or questions of authenticity will arise. Creating the illusion of authenticity demands virtuosity. Presenting a self in these circumstances, with multiple media and multiple goals, is not easy work. The trick, says Stan, is in "weaving profiles together . . . so that people can see you are not too crazy. . . . What I learned in high school was profiles, profiles, profiles, how to make a me."

Early in my study, a college senior warned me not to be fooled by "anyone you interview who tells you that his Facebook page is 'the real me.' It's like being in a play. You make a character." Eric, a college-bound senior at Hadley, a boys' preparatory school in rural New Jersey, describes himself as savvy about how you can "mold a Facebook page." Yet, even he is shocked when he finds evidence of girls using "shrinking" software to appear thinner on their profile photographs. "You can't see that they do it when you look at the little version of the picture, but when you look at a big picture, you can see how the background is distorted." By eighteen, he has become an identity detective. The Facebook profile is a particular source of stress because it is so important to high school social life. Some students feel so in its thrall that they drop out of Facebook, if only for a while, to collect themselves.

Brad, eighteen, a senior at Hadley, is about to take a gap year[14] to do community service before attending a small liberal arts college in the Midwest. His parents are architects; his passion is biology and swimming. Brad wants to be part of the social scene at Hadley, but he doesn't like texting or instant messaging. He is careful to make sure I know he is

40

---

[13]The performances of everyday life—playing the roles of father, mother, child, wife, husband, life partner, worker—also provide "a bit of stress." There is room for considerable debate about how much online life really shares with our performances of self in "real life." Some look to the sociology of "self-presentation" to argue that online and off, we are always onstage. Erving Goffman, *The Presentation of Self in Everyday Life* (Garden City, NY: Doubleday Anchor, 1959).

[14]**gap year:** A year between high school and college during which students typically work, travel, or engage in extracurricular studies. [Eds.]

"no Luddite."[15] He has plenty of good things to say about the Net. He is sure that it makes it easier for insecure people to function. Sometimes the ability to compose his thoughts online "can be reassuring," he says, because there is a chance to "think through, calculate, edit, and make sure you're as clear and concise as possible." But as our conversation continues, Brad switches gears. Even as some are able to better function because they feel in control, online communication also offers an opportunity to ignore other people's feelings. You can avoid eye contact. You can elect not to hear how "hurt or angry they sound in their voice." He says, "Online, people miss your body language, tone of voice. You are not really you." And worst of all, online life has led him to mistrust his friends. He has had his instant messages "recorded" without his knowledge and forwarded on "in a cut-and-paste world."

In fact, when I meet Brad in the spring of his senior year, he tells me he has "dropped out" of online life. "I'm off the Net," he says, "at least for the summer, maybe for my year off until I go to college." He explains that it is hard to drop out because all his friends are on Facebook. A few weeks before our conversation, he had made a step toward rejoining but immediately he felt that he was not doing enough to satisfy its demands. He says that within a day he felt "rude" and couldn't keep up. He felt guilty because he didn't have the time to answer all the people who wrote to him. He says that he couldn't find a way to be "a little bit" on Facebook — it does not easily tolerate a partial buy-in. Just doing the minimum was "pure exhaustion."

In the world of Facebook, Brad says, "your minute movie preferences matter. And what groups you join. Are they the right ones?" Everything is a token, a marker for who you are:

> When you have to represent yourself on Facebook to convey to anyone who doesn't know you what and who you are, it leads to a kind of obsession about minute details about yourself. Like, "Oh, if I like the band State Radio and the band Spoon, what does it mean if I put State Radio first or Spoon first on my list of favorite musical artists? What will people think about me?" I know for girls, trying to figure out, "Oh, is this picture too revealing to put? Is it prudish if I don't put it?" You have to think carefully for good reason, given how much people will look at your profile and obsess over it. You have to know that everything you put up will be perused very carefully. And that makes it necessary for you to obsess over what you do put up and how you portray yourself. . . . And when you have to think that much about what you come across as, that's just another way that. . . you're thinking of yourself in a bad way.

For Brad, "thinking of yourself in a bad way" means thinking of yourself in reduced terms, in "short smoke signals" that are easy to read. To

---

[15]**Luddite:** During the nineteenth century, English textile workers, supposedly led by a youth named Nedd Lud, rebelled against the introduction of the power loom; hence, a person opposed to new technologies. [Eds.]

me, the smoke signals suggest a kind of reduction and betrayal. Social media ask us to represent ourselves in simplified ways. And then, faced with an audience, we feel pressure to conform to these simplifications. On Facebook, Brad represents himself as cool and in the know—both qualities are certainly part of who he is. But he hesitates to show people online other parts of himself (like how much he likes Harry Potter). He spends more and more time perfecting his online Mr. Cool. And he feels pressure to perform him all the time because that is who he is on Facebook.

At first Brad thought that both his Facebook profile and his college essays had gotten him into this "bad way" of thinking, in which he reduces himself to fit a stereotype. Writing his Facebook profile felt to him like assembling cultural references to shape how others would see him. The college essay demanded a victory narrative and seemed equally unhelpful: he had to brag, and he wasn't happy. But Brad had a change of heart about the value of writing his college essays. "In the end I learned a lot about how I write and think—what I know how to think about and some things, you know, I really can't think about them well at all." I ask him if Facebook might offer these kinds of opportunities. He is adamant that it does not: "You get reduced to a list of favorite things. 'List your favorite music'—that gives you no liberty at all about how to say it." Brad says that "in a conversation, it might be interesting that on a trip to Europe with my parents, I got interested in the political mural art in Belfast. But on a Facebook page, this is too much information. It would be the kiss of death. Too much, too soon, too weird. And yet . . . it is part of who I am, isn't it? . . . You are asked to make a lot of lists. You have to worry that you put down the 'right' band or that you *don't* put down some Polish novel that nobody's read." And in the end, for Brad, it is too easy to lose track of what is important:

> What does it matter to anyone that I prefer the band Spoon over State Radio? Or State Radio over Cake? But things like Facebook . . . make you think that it really does matter. . . . I look at someone's profile and I say, "Oh, they like these bands." I'm like, "Oh, they're a poser," or "they're really deep, and they're into good music." We all do that, I think. And then I think it doesn't matter, but . . . the thing is, in the world of Facebook it *does* matter. Those minute details *do* matter.

Brad, like many of his peers, worries that if he is modest and doesn't put down all of his interests and accomplishments, he will be passed over. But he also fears that to talk about his strengths will be unseemly. None of these conflicts about self presentation are new to adolescence or to Facebook. What is new is living them out in public, sharing every mistake and false step. Brad, attractive and accomplished, sums it up with the same word Nancy uses: "Stress. That's what it comes down to for me. It's just worry and stressing out about it." Now Brad only wants to see friends in person or talk to them on the telephone. "I can just act how I want to act, and it's a much freer way." But who will answer the phone?

• • •

Privacy Has a Politics

It has become commonplace to talk about all the good the Web has done for politics. We have new sources of information, such as news of political events from all over the world that comes to us via photographs and videos taken by the cameras on cell phones. There is organizing and fund-raising; ever since the 2004 primary run of Howard Dean, online connections have been used as a first step in bringing people together physically. The Barack Obama campaign transformed the Dean-era idea of the "meet up" into a tool for bringing supporters out of the virtual and into each other's homes or onto the streets. We diminish none of these very positive developments if we attend to the troubling realities of the Internet when it comes to questions of privacy. Beyond passivity and resignation, there is a chilling effect on political speech.

When they talk about the Internet, young people make a disturbing distinction between embarrassing behavior that will be forgiven and political behavior that might get you into trouble. For high school and college students, stalking and anything else they do *to each other* fall into the first category. Code such antics as embarrassing. They believe that you can apologize for embarrassing behavior and then move on. Celebrity culture, after all, is all about transgression and rehabilitation. (These young people's comfort with "bullying" their peers is part of this pattern — something for which they believe they will be forgiven.) But you can't "take back" political behavior, like signing a petition or being at a demonstration. One eighteen-year-old puts it this way: "It [the Internet] definitely makes you think about going to a protest or something. There would be so many cameras. You can't tell where the pictures could show up."

Privacy has a politics. For many, the idea "we're all being observed all the time anyway, so who needs privacy?" has become a commonplace. But this state of mind has a cost. At a Webby Awards ceremony, an event to recognize the best and most influential Web sites, I was reminded of just how costly it is. The year I attended the Webbies, the ceremonies took place just as a government wiretapping scandal dominated the press. When the question of illegal eavesdropping arose, a common reaction among the gathered "Weberati" was to turn the issue into a nonissue. There was much talk about "all information being good information," "information wanting to be free," and "if you have nothing to hide, you have nothing to fear." At a pre-awards cocktail party, one Web luminary spoke to me with animation about the wiretapping controversy. To my surprise, he cited Michel Foucault[16] on the panopticon to explain why he was not worried about privacy on the Internet.

---

[16]**Michel Foucault:** French philosopher and literary critic (1926–1984) who wrote extensively about the concept of the panopticon in his book *Discipline and Punish: The Birth of the Prison*. [Eds.]

For Foucault, the task of the modern state is to reduce its need for actual surveillance by creating a citizenry that will watch itself. A disciplined citizen minds the rules. Foucault wrote about Jeremy Bentham's design for a panopticon because it captured how such a citizenry is shaped.[17] In the panopticon, a wheel-like structure with an observer at its hub, one develops the sense of always being watched, whether or not the observer is actually present. If the structure is a prison, inmates know that a guard can potentially always see them. In the end, the architecture encourages self-surveillance.[18]

The panopticon serves as a metaphor for how, in the modern state, 50 every citizen becomes his or her own policeman. Force becomes unnecessary because the state creates its own obedient citizenry. Always available for scrutiny, all turn their eyes on themselves. By analogy, said my Webby conversation partner, on the Internet, someone might always be watching, so it doesn't matter if, from time to time, someone actually is. As long as you are not doing anything wrong, you are safe. Foucault's critical take on disciplinary society had, in the hands of this technology guru, become a justification for the U.S. government to use the Internet to spy on its citizens. All around us at the cocktail party, there were nods of assent. We have seen that variants of this way of thinking, very common in the technology community, are gaining popularity among high school and college students.

If you relinquish your privacy on MySpace or Facebook about everything from your musical preferences to your sexual hang-ups, you are less likely to be troubled by an anonymous government agency knowing whom you call or what Web sites you frequent. Some are even gratified by a certain public exposure; it feels like validation, not violation. Being seen means that they are not insignificant or alone. For all the talk of a generation empowered by the Net, any discussion of online privacy generates claims of resignation and impotence. When I talk to teenagers about the certainty that their privacy will be invaded, I think of my very different experience growing up in Brooklyn in the 1950s.

[17]Michel Foucault, *Discipline and Punish: The Birth of the Prison*, trans. Alan Sheridan (1979; New York: Vintage Books, 1995).

[18]Foucault, *Discipline and Punish*, 195–228. Here is one example of Foucault on the relationship between remembrance and the constitution of a new kind of self: "First, to bring out a certain number of historical facts which are often glossed over when posing this problem of writing, we must look into the famous question of the hypomnemata. . . . Now, in fact, hypomnemata has a very precise meaning. It is a copybook, a notebook. Precisely this type of notebook was coming into vogue in Plato's time for personal and administrative use. This new technology was as disrupting as the introduction of the computer into private life today. It seems to me the question of writing and the self must be posed in terms of the technical and material framework in which it arose. . . . What seems remarkable to me is that these new instruments were immediately used for the constitution of a permanent relationship to oneself—one must manage oneself as a governor manages the governed, as a head of an enterprise manages his enterprise, a head of household manages his household." See Paul Rabinow, "An Interview with Michel Foucault," in *The Foucault Reader*, ed. Paul Rabinow (New York: Pantheon, 1984), 363–65.

As the McCarthy era[19] swirled about them, my grandparents were frightened. From Eastern-European backgrounds, they saw the McCarthy hearings not as a defense of patriotism but as an attack on people's rights. Joseph McCarthy was spying on Americans, and having the government spy on its citizens was familiar from the old world. There, you assumed that the government read your mail, which never led to good. In America, things were different. I lived with my grandparents as a young child in a large apartment building. Every morning, my grandmother took me downstairs to the mailboxes. Looking at the gleaming brass doors, on which she noted, "people were not afraid to have their names listed, for all to see," my grandmother would tell me, as if it had never come up before, "In America, no one can look at your mail. It's a federal offense. That's the beauty of this country." From the earliest age, my civics lessons at the mailbox linked privacy and civil liberties. I think of how different things are today for children who learn to live with the idea that their e-mail and messages are shareable and unprotected. And I think of the Internet guru at the Webby awards who, citing Foucault with no apparent irony, accepted the idea that the Internet has fulfilled the dream of the panopticon and summed up his political position about the Net as follows: "The way to deal is to just be good."

But sometimes a citizenry should not simply "be good." You have to leave space for dissent, real dissent. There needs to be technical space (a sacrosanct mailbox) and mental space. The two are intertwined. We make our technologies, and they, in turn, make and shape us. My grandmother made me an American citizen, a civil libertarian, a defender of individual rights in an apartment lobby in Brooklyn. I am not sure where to take my eighteen-year-old daughter, who still thinks that Loopt (the application that uses the GPS capability of the iPhone to show her where her friends are) seems "creepy" but notes that it would be hard to keep it off her phone if all her friends had it. "They would think I had something to hide."

In [a] democracy, perhaps we all need to begin with the assumption that everyone has something to hide, a zone of private action and reflection, one that must be protected no matter what our techno-enthusiasms. I am haunted by the sixteen-year-old boy who told me that when he needs to make a private call, he uses a pay phone that takes coins and complains how hard it is to find one in Boston. And I am haunted by the girl who summed up her reaction to losing online privacy by asking, "Who would care about me and my little life?"

I learned to be a citizen at the Brooklyn mailboxes. To me, opening up a conversation about technology, privacy, and civil society is not romantically nostalgic, not Luddite in the least. It seems like part of democracy defining its sacred spaces.

[19]**the McCarthy era:** During the 1950s, Wisconsin senator Joseph McCarthy (1908–1957) became infamous for chairing a series of Senate investigations of Americans accused of supporting the Communist Party. [Eds.]

ENGAGING THE TEXT

1. Discuss whether young people today generally feel as compelled to "connect" as do Roman and the other teens Turkle describes. For example, to what extent do you and your friends text while driving or look forward to being interrupted?

2. According to Turkle, how has life online changed the way people grow up today? How, for example, has it changed the meaning of intimacy? To what extent have you experienced the feeling of being "tethered"?

3. What does Turkle mean when she says that today's teens have become "other directed" and that they are developing a "collaborative sense of self"? What evidence have you seen online to support the claim that narcissism has become a "generational style"?

4. How, according to Turkle, does the Internet operate like a "panopticon" to undermine freedom and shrink "space for dissent"? Discuss whether members of your generation are less concerned about personal privacy than were past generations of Americans. What evidence do you see to suggest that most young Americans view their lack of privacy online with "resignation and impotence"? Why might it be important in a democracy for us to assume that "everyone has something to hide" (para. 54)?

5. Turkle notes that life online can be a significant source of stress. What situations do you find particularly stressful when you text or use social media? Have you ever "dropped out" of life online or considered dropping out? If so, why, and what was the experience like?

EXPLORING CONNECTIONS

6. Review "Don't Send Your Kids to the Ivy League" in Chapter Two (p. 200), and then write a dialogue in your journal between Turkle and William Deresiewicz about the stresses Americans face while growing up today. How might they assess a kid's chances for "building a self" in contemporary American culture? What solutions would they offer to the problem?

7. How might Turkle respond to the portrayal of the high-tech future offered by Eric Schmidt and Jared Cohen in the previous selection (p. 219)? What questions does her analysis of being "tethered" raise about how "our future selves" might be affected by emerging technologies?

EXTENDING THE CRITICAL CONTEXT

8. Survey students outside your class to learn about their early experiences with the Internet. How many of them found life online to be a source of stress and anxiety? Share your results in class and then work together to create a list of guidelines for parents who are thinking about giving their children a cell phone and Internet access. What tips would you include to help kids avoid some of the negative experiences Turkle describes?

9. Turkle claims that social media and online avatars represent a kind of "identity work," a statement less of who you are than of "who you want to be" (para. 34). Working in groups, go online and examine the social media home pages of your fellow students and discuss how they represent themselves. How does your evidence support or challenge Turkle's claim that most people "reduce" their online identities by portraying themselves in simplified or stereotypical ways?

CYBERSEXISM

LAURIE PENNY

As Laurie Penny suggests at the start of this selection, electronic pioneers once believed that gender wouldn't exist on the Internet. Back in the 1980s when bulletin boards, chat rooms, and early "virtual communities" like The Well fueled utopian visions of how the Internet would change the world, cyber-evangelists dreamt that no one would care about race, class, and gender in cyberspace. But recent history has demonstrated that sexism is alive and well online. Over the past few years, incidents like the 2014 Gamergate controversy, which involved vicious attacks on female video game developers and critics, have shown that the Internet world of "sexist trolls" and "mouth-breathing bedroom misogynists" can be a dangerous place for a woman. As someone who credits the Internet with saving her life, Penny, however, isn't about to abandon the Internet to men. Instead, she argues that it's time to rein in online violence against women so that the cybersphere can live up to its original promise. Having grown up online, she's also clearly not afraid to express herself in language that Internet misogynists will understand. Penny was born in London, England, in 1986. She launched her blog, *Penny Red*, in

2007. Today she is a writer and regular columnist for publications like *The Guardian* and the *New Statesman*. In 2014 she became a Nieman Fellow in journalism at Harvard University. Her books include *Meat Market: Female Flesh Under Capitalism* (2011) and *Unspeakable Things: Sex, Lies, and Revolution* (2014), the source of this selection.

> *Information wants nothing. People want to be free.*
>
> —CORY DOCTOROW

> *There are no girls on the Internet.*—4CHAN

"THIS IS FOR EVERYONE." The Internet is a godless place, but that's as close to an in-the-beginning-was-the-word as it gets. The phrase was coined by Tim Berners-Lee,[1] the inventor of the World Wide Web, in time for the London Olympics Opening ceremony, but the principle that the Internet should be socially, economically and politically free, and that anyone anywhere should be able to use it to build new interactive platforms, extend the frontiers of human knowledge or just surf dating forums for cute redheads is basically sound. This is for everyone. Or at least, it was supposed to be.

There was a time, not so long ago, when nerds, theorists and hackers, the first real colonizers of cyberspace, believed that the Internet would liberate us from gender. Science-fiction writers imagined a near future just on the edge of imagination where people's physical bodies would become immaterial as we travelled beyond space and distance and made friends and connections and business deals all over the planet in the space of a split second. Why would it matter, in this brave new networked world, what sort of body you had? And if your body didn't matter, why would it matter if you were a man or a woman, a boy or a girl, or something else entirely?

1998. I'm twelve years old and I've started hanging out in the type of chat forums where everyone will pretend to believe you're a forty-five-year-old history teacher called George. At the same time, the other half of the Internet seems intent on pretending that they are thirteen-year-old schoolgirls from the south coast of England. Amid growing moral panic about pedophiles and teen sluts preying on one another in the murky, unpoliced backwaters of MySpace, I feel something a little akin to freedom. Here, my body, with all of its weight and anxiety, its blood and grease and embarrassing eruptions, is not important; only my words are important. I don't want to be just a girl, because I already knew from experience that girls weren't understood. I want to be what Web theorist Donna Haraway calls a cyborg: "A cyborg is a cybernetic

---

[1]**Tim Berners-Lee:** English computer scientist (b. 1955) known as the inventor of the Internet. [Eds.]

PENNY · CYBERSEXISM

organism, a hybrid of machine and organism, a creature of social reality as well as a creature of fiction. By the late twentieth century, our time, a mythic time, we are all chimeras, theorized and fabricated hybrids of machine and organism . . . I'd rather be a cyborg than a goddess."[2]

At the turn of the twenty-first century my tits were coming in and I wasn't at all impressed with the messy biopolitics of approaching adolescence. The Internet became part of my life early enough to be the coolest thing ever and late enough that I have memories of Geocities before it became a howling desert rolling with tumbleweed and pixels that don't have the decency to decay, and it seemed like a place where all of the bullshit, the boys and dress codes and harassment and the way grown-up guys were starting to look at me, didn't matter. It was a place where I could be my "real" self, rather than the self imposed upon me by the ravening maw of girl-world that wanted to swallow me up. It turned out, though, as more and more of our daily lives migrated online, that it did matter if you were a boy or a girl on the Internet. It mattered a very great deal.

Users of the sprawling 4chan forum—a vast, anarchic, nameless playground of the id inhabited mainly but not exclusively by angry young men, which spawned the Anonymous activist network as well as half the stupid cat memes you used to giggle at at work—declared early on that there were "no girls on the Internet." That idea sounded like sweet freedom for a lot of us, but it turned out to be a threat.

"In ye olden tymes of 1987, the rhetoric was that we would change genders the way we change underwear," says Clay Shirky, media theorist and author of *Here Comes Everybody*, "[but] a lot of it assumed that everyone would be happy passing as people like me—white, straight, male, middle class and at least culturally Christian."[3] Shirky calls this "the gender closet" — "people like me saying to people like you, 'you can be treated just like a regular normal person and not like a woman at all, as long as we don't know you're a woman.'"[4]

It turned out that the Internet wasn't for everyone. Not really. Not yet. It was for boys, and if you weren't one, you had to pretend to be, or you'd be dismissed. "I'm fine with people deciding individually that they don't want to identify as female on the Internet—in the same way I'm fine with people deciding not to wear a short skirt if they feel afraid or uncomfortable—but no one should tell you to do that, and imply that if you don't comply you are somehow the one at fault," says journalist Helen Lewis, who was among the first to speak out against online misogyny in the mainstream press.[5] She says that such advice translates to "duck, so that the shits abuse someone else."

---

[2]Donna Haraway. See Interview with Donna J. Haraway, *Cyborg Manifesto*, 1987. [All notes are Penny's, except 1, 6, 7, 8, 9, and 15.]

[3]Ibid.

[4]Ibid.

[5]http://www.newstatesman.com/blogs/helen-lewis-hasteley/2013/11/comments-rape-abuse-women.

I'm seventeen and I'm not allowed on the Internet and it feels like being gagged and blindfolded. During the nine months I spent in a women's ward for the mentally interesting, the Internet was deemed a bad influence, possibly the worst influence, on young girls trying to become healthy, well-behaved women: all that porn, all that trash, all those poisonous pictures of very thin models shared on "pro-ana"[6] sites where we had encouraged each other to starve down to ecstatic skeletons before we were hospitalized.

The Internet was bad for us. It could only ever be bad for us. So were books and magazines, although television and clothing catalogues were allowed. We needed to be "contained." That was the word they used: "contained." This was precisely the sort of thinking that I'd tried to get away from by getting sick in the first place, but I wanted to be given a clean certificate of health so I could get out of that terrible place and get on with my life. And so I did what girls have always done in desperate situations, in order to survive when the body is contained. I wrote.

I began to write compulsively in paper notebooks, because computers and smart phones were forbidden. I wrote late into the night and just for myself in a messy, spidery hand that I never showed to anyone, because it was purely mine. Years later when I saw *Girl, Interrupted,* the film of Susanna Kaysen's account of being treated in a women's mental hospital in the 1960s, I was startled that the protagonist does the same, writing frantically in longhand like the pen was a shovel digging her out of the shallow grave of social mores where she'd been buried alive. I wonder if this is why many women write, because it allows us to breathe.

Writing was always freedom for me. I'm aware that that's the sort of observation that belongs in my personal journal, which is why I kept them. By the time I was certified sane enough to walk the streets I had filled twenty volumes, and I continued to do so in the mad years that followed, years of homeless, precarious teenage dicking about and hanging on to a college place with my fingernails while I wrote, learned to be human, wrote, learned to take care of myself, and wrote. And then, sometime after my nineteenth birthday, I discovered LiveJournal, and everything changed.

It was my housemate, who I'd met in a cabaret audition, who turned me on to it. Specifically, she told me that this vast Web site full of teenage fan fiction, nerdy sub-groups and threaded comments of excitable strangers discussing politics and philosophy and the best place to get coffee in cities we'd never even heard of was where she spent most of her time, and that if I ever wanted to talk to her, despite her being in the next room, I was going to have to join, and post. And so I picked a username out of a hat, this being the year before Facebook, when one's

10

---

[6]**pro-ana:** Refers to online organizations that promote the eating disorder anorexia nervosa. [Eds.]

online handle was still a pseudonymous statement of identity, and started writing little blog entries. And that's how I learned to write in public, in a way far more immediate, far more enticing and personal, than the blank, limited audience of the college newspaper could ever be.

I wrote to survive, but I learned how to be a writer online, and so did millions of other women all over the world. And not just how to write, but how to speak and listen, how to understand my own experience and raise my voice. I educated myself online. Grew up online. And on blogs and journals and, later, in the pages of digital magazines, I discovered that I wasn't the only pissed-off girl out there. The Internet made misogyny routine and sexual bullying easy, but first it did something else. It gave women, girls and queer people space to speak to each other without limits, across borders, sharing stories and changing our reality.

The fact that so many women were spending so much time talking to one another online without oversight or policing was part of what led to the feminist revival of the mid-2000s. Suddenly, those of us who had nursed our rage in private realized that we were not alone: there were many thousands of others, all over the world, who felt that there was work still to be done. Young women. Women of color. Older women. Weird women. Queer women. Mothers. Transgender people of every denomination. To be in such a lightly policed space, to be able to make connections, voice opinions and acquire information without fear of punishment continues empowering when mainstream culture still punishes women who speak up except explicitly to claim victimhood. This is the story of how the Net became a universe of infinite possibilities which women are often excluded from building or influencing. You can open your browser and stare into an exhilarating terrain of information exchange and creativity and silly film clips in which women and girls still know, as we know offline, that to participate fully is to risk violence and sexual harassment. The Internet is not monolithic. There are many Internets, and some of them have facilitated new conversations and communities dedicated to raising awareness of women's liberation, gender issues, and there is still so much more to do. But we have a brave new world that looks far too much like the cruel old world. It doesn't have to be that way. Women, girls and everyone who believes that the future of human society should include women and girls as active agents are conspiring to reclaim the Internet for all of us.

Ceiling Patriarchy Is Watching You Operate

The biggest thing we now learn about sex from the Internet is this: it happens in front of a camera. Welcome to the world of your tits on screen the next day. At nineteen years old, I was one of the first users of Facebook in its first few weeks of viral expansion in Europe, and that means I was among the first cohort to experience the cultural phenomenon of frantic next-day detagging. The lesson you learn, the lesson you have to learn, is that you are always potentially being watched and you must adjust your behavior accordingly.

Nineteen and getting my picture taken. A warm October night in the front room of a student house where we still hadn't understood the potential pitfalls of prancing around in our pants girls-gone-wild style, snogging and fumbling and demanding pictures to prove it, like any kids excited by mutual attention: look at us kissing. Look at us touching. Pictures or it didn't happen. The next day I find myself tagged on my new profile kissing a female friend, pressed underneath her, hair and sweat and sideboob, giggling at something just off-camera. I detag, but for some reason I leave it up, mistaking the profile archive for the online equivalent of a personal photo album, as so many of us did in the early days. That was before we understood that giving anyone a picture of your breasts, whether a lover or a listed corporation, gives them power over you; before we learned that we had to take care and cover up in cyberspace just like we do in meatspace, in the nominally "real" world.

Four years later, I'm in a conference hall with sensible shoes and a glass of juice, chatting nervously to an editor who has just given me a job as a political blogger, the magazine's youngest by far. I have won prizes and irritated politicians; suddenly everyone wants to talk to me. Including a bored-looking man in an overstuffed Marks and Spencer's suit, one of the jaundiced breed of lifelong political wonks who begin to look middle-aged at around twenty-two and spend the next thirty years gradually expanding on a diet of other people's principles. He asks if he can speak to me alone.

The wonk tells me that a gossip site has pictures of me, and unless I'm nice to him, unless I "handle the situation," he's going to use them. Pictures of me at college with my boobs out, kissing another girl—shock, horror, same-sex snogging! Do I remember the picture? I do now. Yes. Well, I'd better watch out, because there are a lot of people who think I ought to be taken down a peg.

The man who sent this message is the sort of scum that rises to the surface of the cybersphere out of our deep and roiling instincts to hurt and shame other people, those who believe that the only true democracy is the democracy of hating. He is the blogger the government fears, the one with dirt on everyone, the one who hates liberals and anyone who dares to have principles in public almost but not quite as much as he hates women.

Particularly young women, or pretty women. Half the traffic to his site is driven by revealing or demeaning pictures of female journalists, politicians and public figures, close-ups on breasts and bottoms, fuelling comment threads full of one-handed rape fantasies where any and every woman in a position of influence can be "taken down a peg." He says he's going to put my breasts on the Internet.

He wants me to know he has power over me.

In the few years I have spent as a young woman with a sizeable online following, I have learned just what a fearful thing it still is to be female in public life, how much resilience and stamina it takes to weather the inevitable attacks. One of the most common insults flung at women who speak or write in public is "attention seeking" — a classic way of silencing us, particularly if we are political.

The fact that "attention seeking" is still considered a slur says much about the role of women in public life, on every scale. From the moment we can speak, young women are ordered not to do so. Little girls who talk too much, who demand the respect they have earned, are "attention seeking," and that's very bad. Little boys who do the same are "confident" or "engaging." Men in public life, whether they are celebrities or politicians, rock stars or radio DJs, actors, activists or academics, are almost never accused of being "attention seeking," with the possible exception of Bono.[7] For a man to seek attention is no crime: attention is men's due. Women, however, are supposed to be silent. We are not accorded the same right to speak. We are still little girls demanding "attention," and we should learn our place.

The notion that women should be seen and not heard is not confined to the Internet. The popular dead-tree press has always profited from objectifying some women and judging others. Readers are invited to pass judgment upon women's beauty, upon their sexual behavior, their fitness or unfitness as mothers, the shape of their bodies, the wobbliness of their thighs and their ability to snap back into a size six swimsuit two days after giving birth, and that judgment is the reader's reward for skimming lazily over whatever propaganda the red-tops[8] are peddling that day in the guise of news. . . .

It is in this climate, in this news economy of misogyny, this society where the male gaze is monetized as never before, that the worst thing any woman or girl can be is "attention seeking." Women are supposed to be looked at, but never listened to. We should be seen, but not heard — and God forbid we actually try to direct that attention or appear to enjoy it. If we raise our voices, we are "attention seeking," and a woman who wants attention, never mind respect, cannot be tolerated. If you're a woman and somebody calls you "attention seeking," that's a sure way to tell you've made an impact. It's yet another slur that should be a source of pride.

25

---

[7]**Bono:** Paul David Hewson (b. 1960), an Irish musician, songwriter, businessman, and lead singer of the rock group U2. [Eds.]

[8]**red-tops:** Common name for tabloid newspapers in England that specialize in sensational crime stories and entertainment gossip. [Eds.]

Patriarchal Surveillance

We cannot perfectly control our online selves any more than we can control the contours of our flesh. Bodies, like data, are leaky. Out of the mess of bodies and blood and bones and pixels and dreams and books and hopes we create this mess of reality we call a self, we make it and remake it. But obtaining a naked or next-to-naked picture of another person gives you power over them.

In this age of images, the right to request no photos is a sign of truly intimidating social status, of money, power or both, and women, especially young women, almost never have that right. We don't have it in the privacy of our own homes, among friends, in our beds, with our lovers. Especially not with our lovers. In the retail corridor at the New Jersey Porn Expo, shoved in between stall after stall of tacky sex merchandise, was one unobtrusive stand selling hidden cameras, "for personal security."

The stallholder was cagey about why there was such a market for concealable recording gear of the type that could be easily stashed out of sight in, say, a bedroom. Some of our customers are just extremely keen on security, he insisted. Watch out for that blinking light, the panopticon[9] eye flashing at the edge of sight.

The surrender of that power can be hugely sensual when it is done with consent—or sickening when it's coerced. Not so long ago, teenage boys would demand joyless fingering or badger female schoolmates into giving them a feel of their developing breasts in order to prove themselves cool and grown-up: nowadays a titty-picture does the job twice as well. A naked picture is never an empty boast: it is proof, proof of your power over another person, and culture still tells us that power over another person is what makes a boy into a man.

Sexist trolls, stalkers, mouth-breathing bedroom misogynists: all of   30
them attack women out of a hatred, in part, for the presence of women and girls in public space, which is what cyberspace remains, for now. Those threats, however, are made infinitely more effective by public officials warning parents of young girls to keep their daughter offline if they don't want them harassed, groomed or "sexualized," a term that seems to refer to the magical process whereby preteen girls catch a glimpse of some airbrushed boobs on a pop-up ad and are transformed into wanton cybersluts, never to be reclaimed for Jesus.

The message is remarkably similar, in fact, to the lectures one imagines young girls receiving before contraception, legal abortion and the relative relaxation of religious propriety: your sins will never

---

[9]**panopticon:** A type of prison designed by the eighteenth-century English philosopher Jeremy Bentham, which would allow a single guard to observe the activities of all inmates and thus control inmate behavior through the threat of surveillance. [Eds.]

be forgiven. One slip is enough to disgrace you for life. Naked on the Internet is different from being naked anywhere else, because there's always a record: or there could be. We grow up understanding that past indiscretions can never be erased. Don't let your guard down or your skirt up for an instant, or you'll be ruined: not just pictures, but words, promises, furtive late-night search histories will follow you forever, and you will always be ashamed.

Although the technology is new, the language of shame and sin around women's use of the Internet is very, very old. The answer seems to be the same as it always has been whenever there's a moral panic about women in public space: just stay away. Don't go into those new, exciting worlds: wait for the men to get there first and make it safe for you, and if that doesn't happen, stay home and read a book.

People learn to code by playing in coded space. We learn the Internet by being there, by growing there, by trial and error and risk-taking. If the future is digital, if tech skills and an easy facility with the Internet are to be as essential as they appear for building any kind of career in the twenty-first century, then what are we really saying when we tell girls and their parents that cyberspace is a dangerous place for them to be? We're saying precisely what we've said to young women for centuries: we'd love to have you here in the adult world of power and adventure, but you might get raped or harassed, so you'd better just sit back down and shut up and fix your face up pretty.

Perhaps one reason that women writers have, so far, the calmest and most comprehensive understanding of what surveillance technology really does to the human condition is that women grow up being watched. We grow up learning that someone is always looking at us and checking for misbehavior, checking that our skirts are long enough, our thighs tight enough, our grades good enough, our voices soft enough. Whether or not anyone is actually watching and checking at any particular moment is less important than the fact that they might be, and if a lapse is observed the penalties will be dire.

Patriarchal surveillance was a daily feature of the lives of women and girls for centuries before the computer in every workplace and the camera in every pocket made it that much easier. The emotional logic of state and corporate surveillance works in very much the same way: the police, our employers, even our parents with network connections may be watching only one in a thousand of our tweets, one in ten thousand of our indiscreet Facebook messages, they may only be watching one in a hundred CCTV cameras of the tens of thousands deployed around every major city, but we must always act as if we are observed and curb our behavior accordingly.

The Internet is only "public space," of course, in the way that a bar, a sidewalk or a shopping-mall are public space: ultimately, someone rich and mysterious owns that space and can kick you out if they don't like what you're doing there. Being aware of surveillance changes how you behave, how you live and love and tie your shoes and eat breakfast, what you say in public, what you read on the subway.

The first people to notice this were men and boys who had not grown up with the expectation of constantly being watched, who were horrified by the proliferation of spyware, private and state surveillance technology, data collection, CCTV cameras on every street corner, long-range police cameras making it impossible to hold a placard in the street without your face ending up on a database. In much of North America, it is now illegal to go out with a mask or bandana over your face. But this is nothing new—at least, not for women. As the journalist Madeline Ashby writes, "Apparently, it took the preponderance of closed-circuit television cameras for some men to feel the intensity of the gaze that women have almost always been under . . . It took Facebook. It took geo-location. That spirit of performativity you have about your citizenship now? That sense that someone's peering over your shoulder, watching everything you do and say and think and choose? That feeling of being observed? It's not a new facet of life in the twenty-first century. It's what it feels like for a girl."[10]

Pictures of girls are one of the Internet's major commodities. Melissa Gira Grant, writing in *Dissent* magazine, identifies the activity of self-branding, self-promotion and social work online as a new "second shift" of women's unpaid work,[11] but it's more than that. It is, in many cases, part of the work you do for your boss, making your company look good, presenting the right image; we're encouraged to imagine that those who pay us, employ us or live with us might be monitoring us at all times, watching what we do and say. Make sure your Twitter feed doesn't embarrass your boss. Make sure your mum doesn't see pictures of what you did last night. Whether or not they actually are watching doesn't matter—we'd better behave, just in case. It takes to another level the traditional pose of paranoia and anal self-retention that has for centuries been called "femininity."

One of the most popular terms for all of this is "NSFW," or "not safe for work," an abbreviation coined on chat forums to prevent people accidentally opening links to pictures of fannies or gaping sphincters if there's a chance their boss might be peering over their shoulder. Now, however, "not safe for work" has become shorthand for anything a bit risqué. It's rather appropriate, really, since if two decades of faux-feminist "empowerment" culture have had a project, it has been to make women "safe for work," rather than making work safe for women.

Women's sexual bodies are not deemed "safe for work," either literally or figuratively. We get to choose, online and offline, between the embattled paranoia of a "good woman," respectful to her seniors and to men, never openly sexual, never asking questions or talking honestly

[10]http://madelineashby.com/?p=1198.
[11]http://www.dissentmagazine.org/article/girl-geeks-and-boy-kings.

about our own experiences, or the dark, tawdry world of "bad women," where sluts who dare to have sex are humiliated and hurt. The ultimate power that men feel they hold over women is to drag them from one category to the other, and the Internet, with its boundless recording and publishing capabilities, can make this infinitely easier. . . .

Someone Is Wrong on the Internet

"There's nothing wrong with [her] a couple of hours of cunt kicking, garrotting and burying in a shallow grave wouldn't sort out."

Like many women with any sort of profile online, I'm used to messages of this sort—the violent rape and torture fantasies, the threats to my family and personal safety, the graphic e-mails with my face crudely pasted on to pictures of pornographic models performing sphincter-stretchingly implausible feats of physical endurance. This one appeared on a perfectly normal weekday on a racist, misogynist hate-site based in the UK, dedicated to trashing and threatening public figures, mostly women. "The misogyny here is truly gobsmacking [and] more than a few steps into sadism," wrote Mary Beard, a television historian who was also hounded by users of the site, Don't Start Me Off. "It would be quite enough to put many women off appearing in public, contributing to political debate, especially as all of this comes up on Google."[12]

That, of course, is the point. It doesn't matter if we're young or old, classically attractive or proudly ungroomed, writers or politicians or comedians or bloggers or simply women daring to voice our opinions on Twitter. Any woman active online runs the risk of attracting these kinds of frantic hate-jerkers, or worse. I'm not the only person who has had stalkers hunting for her address, and not so long ago I needed a security detail after several anonymous trolls threatened to turn up to a public lecture I was giving. I could go on.

It'd be nice to think that the rot of rank sexism was confined to fringe sites. The truly frightening thing, though, is that the people sending these messages are often perfectly ordinary men holding down perfectly ordinary jobs: the person who wrote the drooling little note to me above and ran the site it appeared on was an estate agent called Richard White, who lived in Sidcup, outer London, with a wife and kids, and just happened to run a hate Web site directed at women and minorities.[13] The Internet re-creates offline prejudices and changes them, twists them, makes them voyeuristic, and anonymity and physical distance makes it easier for some individuals to treat other people as less than human. . . .

[12]http://www.telegraph.co.uk/culture/tvandradio/9816860/Vile-online-misogyny-is -enough-to-put-women-off-appearing-in-public-says-Mary-Beard.html.
[13]Helen Lewis, "What It's Like to Be a Victim of Don't Start Me Off's Internet Hate Mob," *New Statesman*, 27 January 2013.

These messages are intended specifically to shame and frighten women out of engaging online, in this new and increasingly important public sphere. If we respond at all, we're crazy, hysterical overreacting bitches, censors, no better than Nazis, probably just desperate for a "real man" to fuck us, a "real man" like the men who lurk in comment threads threatening to rip our heads off and masturbate into the stumps.

The idea that this sort of hate speech is at all normal needs to end now. The Internet is public space, real space; it's increasingly where we interact socially, do our work, organize our lives and engage with politics, and violence online is real violence. The hatred of women in public spaces online is reaching epidemic levels and it's time to end the pretense that it's acceptable and inevitable.

The most common reaction, the one those of us who experience this type of abuse get most frequently, is: suck it up. Grow a thick skin. "Don't feed the trolls"—as if feeding them were the problem. The *Telegraph*'s Cristina Odone wrote that "Women in public arenas get a lot of flak—they always have. A woman who sticks her head above the parapet is asking for brickbats."[14]

Asking for it. By daring to be visibly female in public life, we're asking to be abused and harassed and frightened, and so is any person with the temerity to express herself while in possession of a pair of tits.

It's an attitude so quotidian that only when you pause to pick it apart does its true horror become apparent. I am contacted, not every day, but most weeks, by young women who want to build lives as journalists or activists but are afraid of the possible backlash. Every time I receive one of these letters, I get a lurch of guilt: should I tell them the truth? Should I tell them that sometimes I've been so racked with anxiety by the actions of trolls and stalkers that I've been afraid to leave the house, that I've had to call in the police, that there's every chance they might too? Or should I tell them to be brave, to take it on the chin, to not be frightened, because their fear, their reticence to speak, is precisely what the trolls want to see most of all?

I always hesitate over whether or not to speak about this. For one thing, I don't want to let on just how much this gets to me. Nobody does. It's what the bullies want, after all. They want evidence that you're hurting so they can feel big and hard, like Richard White in his ridiculous Twitter profile picture, which shows him with beefy arms aggressively folded and his face obscured by a cross. Nobody wants to appear weak, or frightened, or make out that they can't "take it"—after all, so few people complain. Maybe we really are just crazy bitches overreacting?

And so we stay silent as misogyny becomes normalized. We're told to shut up and accept that abuse of this vicious and targeted kind just happens and we'd better get used to it. While hatred and fear of women in traditionally male spaces, whether that be the Internet or the Houses

[14]Cristina Odone, "Mary Beard Is Clever. So How Can She Be Cross That Question Time Viewers Mocked Her Looks?," *Daily Telegraph*, 22 January 2013.

of Parliament, is nothing new, the specific, sadistic nature of online sexist and sexual harassment is unique, and uniquely accepted—and it can change.

Not all online sexism is intended to hurt women. Some of it is intended to impress other men, with hurting women as a regrettable but necessary side-effect. A great deal of misogyny has always been a matter between men, performed by men and boys to impress those they consider peers, and forums, games and blogs are no different.

When men say that casual online sexism, as separate from the personal femicidal misogyny that many women receive when they venture into online spaces men think are theirs alone, is "just banter," they really mean it.

Germaine Greer[15] once wrote that women had no idea how much men hate them.[16] Well, now we do. The Internet has a way of making hidden things visible, of collapsing contexts so that the type of banter that might once have been appropriate at a frat party exists on the same Twitter feeds where fifteen-year-olds are starting feminist campaigns. Combine that with the disinhibition provided by time-delay and anonymity and you have a recipe for the sort of gynophobic, racist and homophobic rage that women and men who are its targets often find incredibly frightening.

Parts of the Internet still behave like men-only spaces, even though they almost never are. Misogyny, as well as racism and homophobia, is played as a shibboleth, a way of marking out territory, not necessarily to keep women away, but to scare off anyone considered too easily offended, which in practice rarely includes men. It's a joke, certainly, the kind of weak, cruel joke whose humor revolves around exclusion, the kind of joke one is meant to "take" (can't you take a joke?) in the way one takes a punch. It's the way men have always spoken about women in private, and the reason it looks new is that women have never had so much instant and intimate access to those spaces before, where we could observe men speaking about us as they have for centuries when they thought we weren't watching. The power to watch men back is something the Web affords women, but men haven't quite realized that yet.

Right now, the beginning of a backlash against online misogyny is under way. Women and girls and their allies are coming together to expose gender violence online and combat structural sexism and racism offline, collecting stories on hashtags like the #Everydaysexism and #Aufshcrei and #Solidarityisforwhitewomen. Projects like this turn sexism and racism from something you have to sit and experience alone into something that can be turned back on your attackers, forcing men who really aren't as ignorant as they'd like to be to understand women's

[15]**Germaine Greer:** Australian academician, theorist, and feminist (b. 1939) best known for her 1970 book *The Female Eunuch*. [Eds.]
[16]Germaine Greer, *The Female Eunuch* (New York: Farrar, Straus & Giroux, 1970), p. 263.

experience in a new way, to understand that the stories they grew up hearing about how the world worked might not be the only stories out there. When bigotry is forced to see itself through the eyes of another, the reaction can be grotesque.

In 2012, the blogger Anita Sarkeesian launched a crowd-funding project to create a short film series, *Tropes vs. Women*,[17] which set out to explain the basic, lazy sexist plotlines of many videogames. The self-satisfied geeksphere exploded with rage; one user even created a flash-game called Beat Up Anita Sarkeesian, where users could click on her face and make blood, cuts and bruises appear. Sarkeesian faced down her abusers and made the series anyway. It was a hit.

Six months later, when feminist campaigner Caroline Criado-Perez successfully campaigned to get a woman's face featured on British banknotes, she was inundated with rape threats on social media.[18] She shared examples of the messages she received from sexist trolls over five days: "Everyone jump on the rape train > @CCriadoPerez is conductor" was one; "This Perez one just needs a good smashing up the arse and she'll be fine" was another. Criado-Perez decided to stand up and fight back, demanding that Twitter take more responsibility for abuse on its platform and starting a global conversation about the normalization of violent misogyny online. Technically, threats of rape and violence are already criminal, and many social media companies, including Twitter, already have rules against abuse and harassment. Just like in the offline world, however, there is a chasm of difference between what is technically illegal and what is tacitly accepted when it comes to violence against women, and the fight back is less about demanding new laws than ensuring existing ones are taken seriously.

Some people claim that the fight back against cybersexism is itself "censorship." Some Web site owners claim that promoting and publicizing sadistic misogyny is merely respecting the "freedom of speech" of anyone with a lonely hard-on for sick rape fantasies. That sort of whinging isn't just disingenuous, it's terrifically offensive to anyone with any idea of what online censorship actually looks like.

As I write, there is a real fight going on to keep the Internet as free as possible from government interference, a fight to free speech and information from the tyranny of state and corporate control. Without going into it too much here, the Internet is full of people who have spent their lives, risked their lives and even lost their lives in that fight. To claim that there's some sort of equivalence between the coordinated attack on net neutrality and digital freedom going on across the world and the uninterrupted misogyny of comment-thread mouth-breathers doesn't just take the biscuit, it pinches the whole packet and dribbles ugly bile-flecked crumbs into the keyboard.

[17] http://www.feministfrequency.com/2013/11/ms-male-character-tropes-vs-women/.
[18] http://www.newstatesman.com/internet/2013/08/diary-internet-trolls-twitter-rape-threats-and-putting-jane-austen-our-banknotes.

According to the current logic of online misogyny a woman's right to self-expression is less important by far than a man's right to punish her for that self-expression. What appears to upset many of these people more than anything else is the idea that any woman or girl, anywhere, might have a voice, might be successful, might be more socially powerful than they themselves are—at least, that's the message I get every time I'm told that I've got a lot to say for myself, and my silly little girl's mouth could be more usefully employed sucking one of the enormous penises that these commentators definitely all possess. In 2011 I wrote that a woman's opinion was the mini-skirt of the Internet; if she has one and dares to flaunt it in public, she is deemed to deserve any abuse that comes her way—she was asking for it.[19]

Since then, the situation appears to have deteriorated, not just for women in public life but for women in public full stop. The Internet is a many-to-many medium. It gives readers and audience-members a right to reply to those writers and politicians who, in the pre-digital age, enjoyed the freedom to expostulate and make pronouncements without having to listen to their readers or listeners beyond the odd angry letter in the paper. And that's great. I remain glad that I grew up as a journalist in the age of the Internet; I am used to writing for an audience that is responsive and engaged, to listening to constructive criticism and acknowledging it where it's appropriate. There's a world of difference, however, between the right to reply and the right to abuse, threaten and silence.

To be human is, in almost every case, to crave two things above all else: intimacy and information. The Internet offers us a superabundance of both, which is one of the reasons it sends existing power structures into a panic. Whether it's women and minorities fighting for the right to be understood as fully human, or citizens fighting for access to information they're not supposed to have, the impulse is always to censor, or to attempt to censor. It is extremely ironic, then, that when misogynist trolls are called out on their behavior, they claim that it's an attack on their "freedom of speech."

The hypocrisy is breathtaking, brain-aching. These people talk without irony of their right to free expression while doing everything in their power to hurt, humiliate and silence any woman with a voice or a platform, screeching abuse at us until we back down or shut up. They speak of censorhip but say nothing of the silencing in which they are engaged. I have even been told, with apparent sincerity, that using the "block" button on Twitter to prevent anybody who has posted threats of violence against me is actually an attack on the troll's freedom of speech—no apparent distinction being made between the right to express your views and the right to have your ugliest half-thoughts paid attention to.

[19]http://www.independent.co.uk/voices/commentators/laurie-penny-a-womans-opinion-is-the-miniskirt-of-the-internet-6256946.html.

The Internet has pressing, urgent problems with freedom of speech, and none of them have anything to do with men's right to harass and threaten women with impunity. "Imagine this is not the Internet but a public square," comments the writer Ally Fogg. "One woman stands on a soapbox and expresses an idea. She is instantly surrounded by an army of 5,000 angry people yelling the worst kind of abuse at her in an attempt to shut her up. Yes, there's a free speech issue there. But not the one you think."[20]

Freedom of speech does not include the freedom to abuse and silence others with impunity. It doesn't even include the right to be paid attention to. Imagine that that was "real life." Imagine that any woman standing up in parliament, or in a lecture theatre or in a room full of her friends to talk about her own experiences learned to anticipate violence, threats and taunting if she happened to upset the men. Actually, you don't have to imagine, because that still happens every day, even in the nominally liberated West. Everywhere, people in positions of privilege warp and misuse the idea of "free speech" to shut down and silence everyone else's right to speak freely. Freedom of speech, for so many people used to the comfort of not having to examine their lives, simply means freedom from criticism and responsibility.

In the case of cybersexism, it is deeply offensive to the many, many activists, hackers and developers who have given their time, imperiled their jobs and sometimes risked their lives to keep governments like the United States from clamping down on free Internet usage to describe women speaking about feminism online as a threat to "freedom of speech."

The whole point of the Internet is that it allows many voices to speak at once. That's what the network is. The sudden presence of women in great and vocal numbers online doesn't prevent men from using the Internet, because this isn't primary school, and nobody is actually allergic to girls.

ENGAGING THE TEXT

1. How did your first experience of the Internet compare with Penny's? Did you find life online "liberating" or "something close to freedom"? In what ways might life online be more liberating for women than for men?

2. What does Penny mean when she refers to "patriarchal surveillance" on the Internet? Why does the experience of being watched online differ for men and women?

3. Are girls still actively discouraged from exploring the Internet, as Penny suggests? Do girls need to be protected more than boys when they go online? Why or why not?

[20]http://www.newstatesman.com/blogs/internet/2012/07/what-online-harassment-looks.

4. Do you agree that hatred for women online has reached "epidemic levels" (para. 45)? What examples of online misogyny have you personally encountered or heard about? What can or should be done to combat cybersexism? (For additional examples of online misogyny and questions about Anita Sarkeesian and the Gamergate controversy, see the Visual Portfolio, pp. 283–88.)

5. **Thinking Rhetorically** Penny clearly understands that some of her readers will be hostile to criticism of the Internet or any suggestion that would curb Internet freedom. How and where does she attempt to gain the sympathy of her audience or address the concerns of her critical readers?

EXPLORING CONNECTIONS

6. To what extent do Penny's early attitudes toward the Internet confirm or challenge Sherry Turkle's portrayal of how teens experience life online (p. 236)? How would you explain any differences you note between their views?

7. How do the ideas of Charles Seife (p. 289) and danah boyd (p. 303) help to explain the persistence of misogyny in online culture?

EXTENDING THE CRITICAL CONTEXT

8. Conduct an anonymous survey of students at your college to learn more about their experiences of sexting. How many of your fellow students sent or received sexts in high school? How many still sext in college? Share your results in class and discuss whether, as Penny suggests, women are learning that there is no right to privacy in a world where men use pictures to demonstrate their power over women (para. 28).

9. As a class, set up your own LiveJournal accounts and begin keeping a daily personal blog as Penny did when she was a teen. Reserve a few minutes in class each week to agree on possible topics for weekly postings. Use this blog to augment or substitute for your class journal or writing log assignment.

LOVE ME TINDER

EMILY WITT

A generation ago, most people dated a school friend, a family acquaintance, or someone they met at work or through a social group. Nowadays, the pool of eligible dates has gone global. According to a 2013 study by the National Academy of Sciences, more than a third of all couples married between 2005 and 2013 met their mates on the Internet. First-generation online dating services like Match.com and eHarmony relied on complex surveys and questionnaires to pair up people according to computer-generated indices of compatibility. More recently, data-driven dating sites have given way to social media matchmakers like Tinder and Grindr — services that emphasize opportunity over compatibility. Today, as the following selection suggests, online dating may be changing the way we think about meeting, mating, and long-term relationships. Emily Witt is a journalist, an essayist, and a critic whose work has appeared in *GQ*, *New York* magazine, *The New Yorker Observer*, and the *London Review of Books*. She has degrees from Brown University, the Columbia University Graduate School of Journalism, and Cambridge University. Her first book, *Future Sex* (2015), offers the account of her own experiences as a woman in her mid-thirties "going to bars alone, dating online, and hooking up with strangers."

THAT FALL, HIS RELATIONSHIP of two and a half years finally ended, and Eli found himself single again. He was 27 years old, losing the vestigial greenness of his youth. He wanted to have sex with some women, and he wanted some stories to tell. He updated his dating pro-files. He compiled his photos. He experimented with taglines. He down-loaded all the apps. He knew the downsides—the perfidy of the decep-tive head shot, the seductress with the intellect of a fence post—but he played anyway. He joined every free dating service demographically available to him.

Around the same time, somewhere across town, a woman named Katherine* shut down her OkCupid account. She had approached Internet dating assertively, had checked the box that read Short-term dating and the one that read Casual sex. Then a casual encounter had turned menacing, and Katherine decided she no longer wanted to pursue sex with total strangers. But she had a problem: She liked the adventure, she had the usual human need for other humans, and she needed the convenience of meeting people online. Katherine was 37, newly single, with family obligations and a full-time job. Most of her friends were married. She needed something new.

When Katherine and Eli downloaded Tinder in October 2013, they joined millions of Americans interested in trying the fastest-growing mobile dating service in the country. Tinder does not give out statistics about the number of its users, but the app has grown from being the plaything of a few hundred Los Angeles party kids to a multinational phenomenon in less than a year. Unlike the robot yentas[1] of yore (Match.com, OkCupid, eHarmony), which outcompeted one another with claims of compatibility algorithms and secret love formulas, the only promise Tinder makes is to show you the other users in your immediate vicin-ity. Depending on your feelings for these people, you swipe them to the left (meaning no thanks) or to the right (yes, please). Two people who swipe each other to the right will match. Your matches accrue in a folder, and often that's the end of the story. Other times you start texting. The swiping phase is as lulling in its eye-glazing repetition as a casino slot machine, the chatting phase ideal for idle, noncommittal flirting. In terms of popularity, Tinder is a massive and undeniable success. Whether it works depends on your idea of working.

For Katherine, still wary from her bad encounter, Tinder offered another advantage. It uses your preexisting Facebook network and shows which friends, if any, you have in common with the person in the photo. On October 16, Eli appeared on her phone. He was cute. He could tell a joke. (His tagline made her laugh.) They had one friend in com-mon, and they both liked Louis C.K. (Who *doesn't* like Louis C.K.? Eli says later. Oh, you *also* like the most popular comedian in America?) She swiped him to the right. Eli, who says he would hook up with anybody who isn't morbidly obese or in the middle of a self-destructive drug relapse, swipes everyone to the right. A match!

---

*Obviously these people requested fake names. [Author's note. All other notes are the editors'.]

[1]**yentas:** (Yiddish) gossips, busybodies, or—as here—matchmakers.

He messaged first. Sixty-nine miles away?? he asked.   5

I'm at a wedding in New Jersey, she replied.

So, Eli said to himself, *she's lonely at a wedding in New Jersey.*

Eli: So why you on Tinder?

Katherine: To date. You?

Eli said it was an esteem thing. It had taught him that women find me more attractive than I think. Unfortunately for Katherine, he told her he didn't have a lot of time to date. He worked two jobs. They wanted different things. It therefore read as mock bravado when Eli wrote, But you ever just want to fuck please please holler at me cool??? He added his number.

Katherine waited an hour to respond. Then: Ha. And then, one minute later, I will. And: I kinda do.

Eli: Please please do. ;)   10

Katherine liked that he was younger. He was funny. He did not, like one guy, start the conversation with Don't you want to touch my abs? He said please. Eli liked that Katherine was older. Katherine wrote: You can't be psycho or I will tell [name of mutual friend]. He sympathized with that, too.

The parameters were clear. They arranged to meet.

I first signed up for Tinder in May but found it skewed too young. (I'm 32.) When I looked again in mid-October, everything had changed. I swiped through people I knew from college, people I might've recognized from the train. I saw it had gone global when a friend in England posted a Tinder-inspired poem on her Facebook page (and here are we, He and Me, our flat-screen selves rendered 3D). I started to check it regularly. The more I used it, the more I considered how much it would have helped me at other times in my life—to make friends in grad school, to meet people after moving to a new city. It seemed possible that one need never be isolated again.

In December, I flew out to Los Angeles, where Tinder is based, to visit the company's offices and meet two of its founders, Sean Rad and Justin Mateen, both 27. (The third is Jonathan Badeen, the engineer who built the app.) Rad is the chief executive officer; Mateen is chief marketing officer. They are also best friends, share a resemblance to David Schwimmer,[2] and have been known to show up for work in the same outfit. I was staying only a mile from Tinder's offices in West Hollywood, and within forty-eight hours both founders showed up on my Tinder feed. Other memorable appearances on my feed in Los Angeles included a guy holding a koala bear, a guy and his Yorkshire terrier, in matching sweaters, and a pipe-smoking dandy with a Raspu-

---

[2]**David Schwimmer:** American actor, director, producer, and comedian (b. 1966) best known for playing Ross on the television series *Friends.*

tin[3] beard, horn-rimmed glasses, and a gold ring the exact shape and size of a cicada.

Rad and Mateen are local boys. They both grew up in Beverly Hills, although they attended different private schools. They first encountered each other at 14, when Sean made a play for Justin's girlfriend. (We met because we both liked the same girl—but the girl was my *girlfriend*, says Justin.) They reconnected at USC,[4] and then both started independent companies. Justin's was a social network for celebrities. Sean's was Adly, a platform that allows companies to advertise via celebrities' social networks. He sold the majority of his stake in 2012.

I didn't want to be in the ad business, he says. He also didn't want to make things for computers. Computers are going extinct, he says. Computers are just work devices. For people his age, the primary way to interface with the technical world was through a mobile device.

Rad and Mateen have shared business ideas with each other for years, and every idea begins with a problem. The key to solving the problem that interested Tinder: I noticed that no matter who you are, you feel more comfortable approaching somebody if you know they want you to approach them, says Sean. They had both experienced the frustration of sending smoke signals through social media. There are people that want to get to know you who don't know you, so they're resorting to Facebook, explains Justin. When those advances or friendings or followings are unwanted, they say, the overtures can seem a little creepy. (Consider, for example, the long-standing mystery of the Facebook poke.) Sean was interested in the idea of the double opt-in— some establishment of mutual interest that precedes interaction.

And so Tinder entered a fossilizing industry. Most of the big players (including Match.com, Plenty of Fish, OkCupid, eHarmony, Manhunt, JDate, and Christian Mingle) established themselves before billions of humans carried miniature satellite-connected data processors in their pockets, before most people felt comfortable using their real names to seek companionship online, and before a billion people joined Facebook—before Facebook even existed. Tinder's major advantages come from exploiting each of these recent developments. The company also managed to accrue, in less than a year of existence, the only truly important asset of any dating site: millions and millions of users.

Nicole is 30, a willowy brunette with curly hair who describes herself on Tinder as Dancey, smiley, lovey, tall. Like 6 [feet] tall. Since joining Tinder last summer, she has chatted with dozens of guys but only gone on two Tinder dates. In general, she thinks Tinder is hilarious.

Sometimes she'll start Tindering while on the train and will get so distracted she'll miss her stop. She finds she sometimes falls into a

---

[3]**Rasputin:** Grigori Yefimovich Rasputin (1869–1916), Russian faith healer and mystic linked to the downfall of the Russian monarchy.
[4]**USC:** The University of Southern California.

soothing swiping rhythm where she's not really looking at the men, just calming herself with a repetitive pattern of left-right swipes. Getting a match seems to activate some primal-gratification center in her mind. She likes that it's played like a game.

I'm definitely not the type of woman who walks around thinking that everyone thinks I'm hot, Nicole tells me. She does not feel like the people who want to date her are abundant and everywhere, so when a lot of matching happens, it comes as a real boost. It makes me look at my external world in a more favorable way, she says. When she's bored, she goes on Tinder. When she wants validation, she finds it on Tinder. She uses it when she's feeling down. (Tinder gets a slight uptick in use on Sundays, that day of hangovers, boredom, and planning.) Sending screenshots of the most ridiculous photos that come up has become a source of merriment for her and her friends. There seems to be a preponderance of men posing with tigers, she says.

Actually communicating with people is another story. I do a lot of not responding, which is probably horrible, politenesswise, she says. It takes an especially dynamic person to win her over at text messaging. The usual Hi, how are you? bores her. I'm a social worker, and I talk to people all day, she says. I'm not interested in someone's How are you? question. Her two dates both persuaded her to go out by being really solid text conversationalists.

The dates were fine. They did not end in sex, unlike many of her first dates on OkCupid. Part of this was simply that expectations are so much lower on Tinder; all you know about the people in your folder is that your advances are welcome. The lack of stated purpose in each profile can lead to some confusion. In fact, many of the people I interviewed asked *me* what the site is supposed to be for. Some people, used to reading between the lines in such matters, simply assume casual sex. Not Nicole. I ask how she makes that clear, and she says she does not respond to messages that arrive at 3 A.M.

She has used the site both in New York, where she lives, and in the Bay Area, where she is from. She observes a clear difference. When she signed on in the Bay, she felt a flood of recognition: These are my people! she said. They're on Tinder here! I ask what that means, and she says, More earthy, hipstery, thirty-something folks. She had more matches. They were all so cute and looked so friendly and warm and fun. But how does she distinguish that from people in New York? She describes a typical photo of a New Yorker as a selfie taken in a fancy lounge bathroom while wearing a suit.

As a college student, cofounder Justin Mateen perfected a system of party promotion. He would strike an agreement with a club to ensure a minimum of drink sales. He would hire a performer. Then he would enlist representatives from the fraternities and sororities of USC and UCLA to recruit people, promising a free ticket for every ten tickets sold from their houses and a monetary prize if they brought one hundred partygoers. He took a cut of sales — the more money the bar made, the bigger his cut. It was a good little gig until his parents began to bother him about it: We don't want you to be a party thrower, they said.

But it helped, when Sean and Justin started Tinder, that Justin knew how to populate a party. They had disdain for traditional advertising; they wanted a new challenge. He wanted the app to catch on with the most difficult group of people—college students too young and socially active to need online dating, people who saw it as a stigmatized practice. He wanted people to join Tinder not because they saw an ad on Facebook but because they recognized its social value.

So Justin mined his contacts for models and sorority girls. Whitney Wolfe, Tinder's vice president of marketing, remembers going to the Apple store and telling the guy behind the counter about Tinder and watching his eyes pop out as he began swiping through; there may have been only 200 people, she remembers, but they were 200 of the prettiest girls you've ever seen.

In the beginning, Justin ran individual campaigns to encourage people to sign up. He would text each person personally. He targeted what he called social influencers, avoiding the awkward crowd of people probably most in need of a new way to make friends. Then he hit USC, enlisting the help of his younger brother and sister, who were students there. He launched Tinder on campus with a party for 300 USC students at his parents' house.

He shows me a photo of it from Instagram: a pool in the sunshine, shirtless partygoers, lanterns, an inflatable slide. To his mother's chagrin, he hung a giant Tinder banner from the roof. That was sixty-two weeks ago, he says, using Instagram's preferred metric of time. A year and ten weeks after the pool party, the company claims to have made a half billion matches and registers 450 million swipes a day.

Inspired in part by the path of Facebook, which launched first at 30 elite colleges, Justin turned not just to the Ivy League but to schools known for their good parties. After seeding USC, Justin and Whitney traveled to schools like SMU[5] in Dallas. Whitney might stand on a table in a fraternity and announce that there were 200 hot sorority girls on the app waiting for the men to sign up, then run to the sorority and tell them the reverse. They left a trail of stickers behind them—in the best campus bars, in the most exclusive nightclubs.

I was in a sorority, so I knew how to get into the brains of sorority girls, says Whitney, who is now 24. Justin knew how to get into the brains and the pants of sorority girls. For colleges they did not visit, Justin hired a campus representative, usually the younger sibling of someone he knew from Los Angeles, several of them scions, all of them the most social and charismatic people he could find.

My interviews with Tinder's employees took place half in their offices, half in the leather interiors of luxury cars or while descending in

[5]**SMU:** Southern Methodist University.

the elevator from brunch at Soho House[6] or waiting for the valet in the gardenia-scented drive of the Beverly Hills Hotel. Justin and Sean grew up rich and popular in a city of surface and sheen. They have none of the affectations of Hollywood executives. (They wear flannel shirts and sneakers; their shared office is littered with Nerf gun darts.) Still, their acute understanding of the metrics of social status seems a product of their environment. Sean is the homebody of the two, preferring the company of his girlfriend of six months, Alexa, who is the daughter of Michael Dell, the founder and CEO of Dell. They met on Tinder, and her friends call her Tinderella. Things get awkward at family functions when Sean opines that computers are dead.

Justin is more raffish. If he is less interested in having a serious relationship than Sean, it is because what genuinely seems to make him happiest is going out in the world, making new friends, and persuading them to download Tinder. His home, a spacious bungalow on the border of Beverly Hills and West Hollywood, feels like a barely occupied hotel. (He selected his dining-room table because it reminded him of the lobby of the Delano South Beach in Miami.)

One day he had a lunch meeting with the producers of *The Mindy Project*, which will be putting Tinder in an upcoming episode, so I rode along with him. As I listened to him chat with his art consultants over Bluetooth in his black Mercedes SUV with its Tinder sticker on the spare tire, I wondered whether L.A.'s VIP-obsessed culture had something to do with the company's exponential growth. It's difficult to imagine Tinder coming from Silicon Valley. The key to Tinder—the double opt-in—is an idea born of real-world experience (this is what you want in a bar—to know that the person you want to hit on wants you to hit on him or her) as opposed to sophisticated computer metrics. For once in the tech world, the socially gifted are leading the socially stunted.

Ben messaged me first. He was interesting, because his tagline said, Tall, dominant man seeks submissive girl. Intelligence and humor a must. He agreed to be interviewed, then added, Will still put the moves on you, obviously. Good, I thought, staring with boredom and resentment at my phone. He turned out to be a gentleman, saying he has used the service to make friends as much as he has to facilitate his BDSM fetish. I am not into BDSM, but I did feel happy when Ben kissed me and then when he text-messaged me a week later and called me darling.

I talked to a European who uses Tinder while traveling for work. I noticed when I was in the Midwest that girls were far more approachable, he said. They returned messages more. I talked to a tech consultant in Los Angeles who uses Tinder to enliven a dull or overly male social situation—like the last bachelor party he went to in Las Vegas. The guys met some women on Tinder. People coupled off. People got naked. Mayhem ensued. I asked about the women—were they, er, *from*

35

---

[6]**Soho House:** A group of private clubs drawing members primarily from the arts and media.

Las Vegas? They weren't locals, and they weren't hookers, he said. They didn't have to be: The above experience is what people are optimizing for when they're single in Vegas, he says. He said he has friends that start firing up the app as soon as they land at the airport.

One canard is that Tinder disproportionately favors the beautiful. I swiped one guy, David, to the right because his photo made me laugh. He had taken a common trope—the painfully serious selfie—and turned it into a joke.

He messaged a few days later and turned out to be the most overtly sexual person I chatted with on Tinder. Like most heterosexuals, I have spent years watching my gay friends cruise apps like Grindr with muted fascination. How easy it was for willing men to have spontaneous sex with strangers! What was wrong with women like me, equally willing and desirous, at least in theory, but in practice so finicky and inhibited? The idea of a Grindr for straight people took hold in the heterosexual imagination, becoming a sort of Holy Grail. But it never seemed to work out. Blendr has a pretty sordid feeling to it. Bang With Friends was conceived drunkenly and ended in a lawsuit.

When Tinder appeared, its mimicry of Grindr's location-based approach seemed to indicate that Grindr for straight people had finally arrived. Sean and Justin insist that that's a mischaracterization. (Married people can use it to meet tennis partners!) But like most people, I know the difference between corporate skywriting and what humans are actually like. If Mormons in Utah are using Tinder to find husbands and wives, hedonists in New York are fulfilling their dreams of a futuristic mobile-phone-sex utopia.

I have already had what I would consider some pretty inappropriate thoughts concerning you so far, wrote David. He had used the service for casual sex before. My level of knowledge when it comes to sex, the psychology behind it all and lots of fun stuff is not something I hide. He said several women have taken advantage of his comfort and confidence to use me for sex and ask me to help them experience new things.

I told him I would be interested in meeting up . . . at some point. This was genuine. He wanted to meet up that night. When I said no, he asked why. I told him I had plans with friends. He offered to pick me up from the party I was going to. I wrote, No, I'm flattered but just want to hang out with friends tonight. He suggested we meet afterward. Not tonight, I wrote. He asked what the real reason was. I was guilty of making an overture I no longer wanted to keep, and things started feeling less like flirtation than unwanted pressure. After a certain point, I knew I would not be having casual sex with David.

I don't agree with the Tinder founders, who say there isn't a straight version of Grindr because girls aren't wired that way—I know too many women who have used dating services for casual sex. Most mainstream dating companies downplay or ignore the use of their services for casual sex, the philosophy being that people who want that will find it.

If casual sex is the main selling point, however, people who don't want it will be alienated.

But sometimes one wishes the geniuses of the tech world would address certain problems even more directly. Beyond proving that users are real because they have a Facebook account, how could a dating app help a sexually adventurous woman both pursue casual encounters and reliably vet potential partners? How could it help her minimize the risk of rape?

I thought also of the party I was headed to, of the problems of creepiness that Tinder purported to solve. There's creepiness, and then there's the stigma of everyday loneliness and desire. But isn't desperation one of the animating forces of life? I hoped my friends would not wait for the double opt-in, that they would creepily ask their crushes to be their Facebook friends, that they would stare at each other, and reveal their vulnerability, and make excruciating overtures that would be met with catastrophically embarrassing rejections. I went to my party, during which David texted twice—and once the next morning, and once the day after that, and twice the following Monday.

Sarah is the kind of person whose presence on an online dating site 45 convinces everyone else that it's normal to use it. She is a native New Yorker, 28 years old, beautiful and stylish, with a job at a tech company and a large network of friends and family in the city, and she's immediately perceivable as a happy, well-rounded person. Like most people I interviewed, she has tried other dating sites—HowAboutWe, Grouper, OkCupid—but she was most drawn to Tinder because she doesn't have to provide any information. She found most people's self-presentation on OkCupid too calculated; also, you have to write so much. Tinder, she says, is just how you would go about things at a bar, and as easy as a Facebook like. You look at people, pick one who looks nice to you, then try to talk to him.

Sarah seems to prove the theory that Tinder's success has to do with its appeal to women. Rather than a total inundation with messages by strangers on OkCupid, Sarah gets to choose whom she likes. Going through potential dates does not take up all her time—she can easily cover a few dozen in a span of minutes.

She joined Tinder in the middle of September. She was about to switch jobs and was winding things down at a previous job, so she would spend tons of time playing on Tinder. She was the first person I interviewed, though not the only one, who referred to using Tinder with the verb *play*. Contrary to some opinions, Sarah found she could tell more from a person's photos than she could from a carefully thought-out Web site profile. A picture is something that's taken in the moment, she says. You can't change your smile. Her pet peeve is surfing photos. She always thinks they're some kind of fake stock photo and always says no to people who have them. She also finds it weird when a guy lists his height: I think they're lying to me.

She casts a broad net. If she feels indecisive, she swipes yes. She does not waste time trying to compose lyrical messages: Just say some bullshit. She also doesn't like prolonged messaging: Just go out or not. To do anything else is a waste of one's battery. (Tinder's location-based tech drains phone batteries.) On the casual-sex question, she's not interested. In the beginning, someone messaged her, So if you're on Tinder you're into stranger sex, when are we having stranger sex? Isn't Tinder for that? She replied, Not for me, and blocked him. It's not that she isn't into casual sex. I have people that I can use in that way if I want to, she said. I don't need to find five of them.

Sarah's first four Tinder dates were fine, but the fifth was one of those minor miracles of coincidence that sometimes manifest themselves amid the throngs of New York City. One weekend night, Sarah went to a bar and got very, very drunk. The next morning, her friends asked her about the guy whose number she got. What guy? she asked. Her memory was foggy. Her friends were appalled—only the best-looking guy in the bar! She had no memory of the event. She went on Tinder, swiping despondently. She resumed a chat she'd been having with a man whose photos were cute-ish, whom she had swiped to the right despite the presence of one weird artistic selfie that made the guy look like kind of a douchebag. They chatted with the usual banalities: Hey and How's your day? and How's your weekend? He asked for her number. She gave it to him. Then the magical moment: I have something weird to tell you, he said. He had not been sure until she gave him the proof—her number was already in his phone. It was the guy from the previous night. When I met her, they had gone out five times in two weeks.

Katherine and Eli, the older woman and the younger man, met at what he remembers as a weird, kind of fancy bar that's in some kind of labyrinth.

Despite the intensity of their texting, they did not start making out right away. Instead, they talked. They shared their recent sexual histories, their past sexual histories, their addiction problems. It seemed like a fair thing to do, says Eli. Maybe it wasn't sexy, but the theme of it was more intimate, like I need to know you better as, like, a safety thing.

They went to her place. They had sex. It was great. (Both parties confirmed this.) Then they had sex again. He left after midnight, because he had to work in the morning. That they haven't met again is more because they live inconveniently far from each other. I might not go out to Bushwick,[7] where he lives with his *roommates*, says Katherine, but I think our paths will cross again in one way or another.

I ask Eli if he is looking for a girlfriend. He says he would like a partner, sure, but that he still wants to meet people, that he's interested

---

[7]**Bushwick:** A rapidly gentrifying neighborhood in Brooklyn, New York.

in polyamory.[8] He attributes his flexibility to how he was raised, in a home where acceptance of sexual diversity was seen as the enlightened political position. I'm definitely queer, in a sense, he says. In the sense of being way more open-minded to anything.

Eli is pursuing a sexual narrative that doesn't end in closure, that doesn't bear the expectations of gendered rituals. And whether it's for sex or just for meeting people, maybe Tinder will be the app for the never-ending present, for the idea of one's life not as culminating in a happy ending but a long series of encounters, sexual or otherwise. When I watched the founders of Tinder giving interviews, every reporter they spoke with seemed to ask how many marriages had resulted. After talking to people about their experiences, I realize that to think about marriage is to completely miss the point of Tinder. The app is about the world around you, the people in your immediate vicinity, and the desires of a particular moment.

Eli really likes Tinder. He considers it to be the most honest form 55 of online dating. He loves the feeling of scoring, a high without consequences. When I met him, he had just had an encounter he called awful, but that was, in its own way, a kind of dream.

She messaged at 10 P.M. on Thanksgiving night. She was a woman with whom he had transitioned from Tinder to text messaging, but this posed a problem: He could not remember who she was, what she looked like, and worst of all, her name. He got on a train anyway. He arrived at a glossy doorman building in Lower Manhattan. She had not yet arrived home, which meant Eli called and got her voice mail, from which (with relief) he learned her identity before she arrived. It turned out she's one of the ones who are on Tinder, and I'm like, Why are you talking to me, I'm a chubby Jew, my teeth are yellow because I drink coffee, and you're very successful and pretty.

But the night went downhill from there. They undressed and kissed and got into bed together, but they didn't connect. He spent the night, though she didn't feel like having sex. She talked really fast and mentioned her intention to wean herself off Adderall. Eli felt like perhaps she was disappointed in him, that he failed to meet her expectations. He left in the morning. I ask if the encounter depressed him. He thinks for a minute, tilts his head to the side, then says no: At the end of the day, I got to see her naked.

ENGAGING THE TEXT

1. Witt suggests that services like Tinder aren't used much by college students who are "too young and socially active to need online dating" (para. 28). How common is online dating among the students at your college? In your experience, when do people generally begin to explore services like Tinder, OkCupid, Plenty of Fish,

---

[8]**polyamory:** The practice of open sexuality unlimited by gender boundaries or long-term commitments.

Grindr, or Manhunt? Why, as Witt implies, might people under the age of 24 view online dating as a "stigmatizing practice"?

2. Why do Eli, Katherine, Nicole, Sarah, and David use Tinder? What are they each looking for, and what do they get out of the experience? Why, according to Witt, does Tinder appeal to women more than traditional, questionnaire-based dating services like Match.com? Do Witt's subjects strike you as representative of contemporary young women and men, or do they seem more radical or adventurous in their tastes and desires?

3. Through the stories she relates, how does Witt portray the impact of online dating on contemporary attitudes toward love, relationships, and commitment? What evidence do you see to suggest that dating is becoming a "game" or a "high, without consequences"—or that marriage itself might become obsolete? What impact do you think dating sites like Tinder and Grindr are having on American attitudes toward casual sex and long-term relationships?

4. While Witt never directly states her own opinion of online dating in this essay, in several places she indirectly hints at her view of the practice. Where does she seem to betray her own attitude toward Tinder and the contemporary online dating scene? How would you characterize her view of online dating?

EXPLORING CONNECTIONS

5. To what extent do Witt's depictions of the values and attitudes of online daters complicate Sherry Turkle's claim that social media has "tethered" a generation of young Americans who have grown up online (p. 236)? How "tethered" do Witt's subjects seem to you, and why?

6. How might the stories Witt tells of women like Katherine and Sarah complicate June Carbone and Naomi Cahn's analysis of "marriage markets" (p. 77)? Do you think women today are less interested in traditional ideas like stability and commitment in relationships because of the impact of social media? What other factors might explain why women today are postponing or deciding against traditional marriage?

7. To what extent does Witt's discussion of Tinder support or complicate Laurie Penny's claim (p. 253) that the Internet is a relatively hostile place for women? How dangerous does Tinder seem to be for the women Witt profiles in her essay? How might Penny view Witt's hope that a dating app could "help a sexually adventurous woman both pursue casual encounters" and "minimize the risk of rape" (para. 45)?

EXTENDING THE CRITICAL CONTEXT

8. Do an anonymous survey to find out how many of the students in your class have experimented with online dating. How many of your fellow students have met people through services like Tinder, Plenty of Fish, OkCupid, Blendr, Grindr, Zoosk, JDate, or ChristianMingle? How many have developed long-term relationships through these sites? Overall, how would users rate the online dating experience?

9. Over the last decade, a number of Internet dating services have sprung up that cater to specific — and often controversial — desires and appetites, services like Grindr, AshleyMadison, EstablishedMen, and CougarLife. What does the existence of such services suggest about the impact of the Internet on attitudes toward sex and relationships? In your view, do such sites provide services that mitigate or exacerbate social problems? Why?

10. Working in groups, create your own "yenta" algorithm: make a list of the personal qualities, interests, values, or beliefs you would measure to determine if two people would make a good match. Is it more important, for example, to have similar incomes, educational levels, or interests in sports, music, and food? Do couples need to share the same political and religious beliefs or have the same racial or ethnic backgrounds? Which of these factors should count the most and which the least? Later, compare your results in class and discuss the benefits or limitations of depending on "robot yentas" to choose your mate.

VISUAL PORTFOLIO
READING IMAGES OF WIRED CULTURE

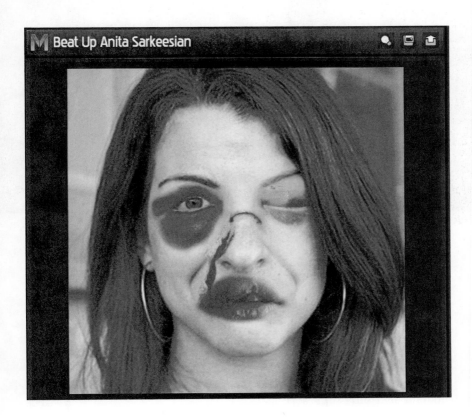

Winn McNamee / Getty Images

GodHatesFags
...therefore I abhorred them. Lev. 20:23

Follow Us On Twitter | FAQ | Contact Us | About Us

SCOTUS Opinion | Fag Marriage Amicus Brief (12-144) | Fag Marriage Amicus Brief (12-307)

Home | Pickets | Press Releases | Audio | Video | Photos | Open Letters | Reports | Blogs | Archive

Quick Links

Picket Schedule

Confessions Of Faith

Open Letter To Elect Jews

WBC Bombing

Parodies

GodSmacks

Top 10 Audio

Sermons

God's Hatred In The Bible

Downloads

Sister Sites

GodHatesIslam.com - God hates all false religious systems. That includes Islam.

GodHatesTheMedia.com - The worldwide media is in place for WBC to preach through. What they mean for evil God means for good.

SignMovies.com - Brief, fascinating videos that offer Bible-based expositions of the message of WBC.

GodHatesTheWorld.com - Country-by-country explanation of why God hates the world.

WBC pickets in Topeka, KS

WBC has engaged in 54,176 pickets in 949 cities. See our Picket Schedule. *"...make it plain upon tables..."* (Hab 2:2)

pause scrolling

Westboro Baptist Church

Since 1955, WBC has taken forth the precious from the vile, and so is as the mouth of God (Jer. 15:19). In 1991, WBC began conducting peaceful demonstrations opposing the fag lifestyle of soul-damning, nation-destroying filth.

In response, america bombed WBC, sued WBC, prosecuted WBC, burned WBC. God is now america's enemy: **6845 dead soldiers; $15.04 trillion+ national debt**. *"Arise, O LORD, in thine anger...because of the rage of mine enemies..."* (Ps 7:6)

america crossed the line on June 26, 2003, when SCOTUS ruled in Lawrence v. Texas that we must respect sodomy. SCOTUS sealed your doom on June 26, 2013, with fag marriage. WBC's gospel message is your last hope. **More about WBC.**

Written - Press Releases, Blogs, Letters...

Audio - Parodies, Hymns, Sermons...

Video - Music, News, Sign Movies...

WBC Pickets (54,176 to date)

Editors' Picks

audio top 10

Who Are You Thanking? (video news)

There are a few questions a thoughtful person might ask during such a season: What are you thankful for? Who are you thanking? And how do you show

God Still Hates Fags (sign movie)

We told you that the fag juggernaut was going to bring this world to destruction.

more

VISUAL PORTFOLIO

READING IMAGES OF WIRED CULTURE

1. What does the photo of two toddlers with smart phones on page 283 say to you? When did you get your first cell phone, and how did it change your life? When, in general, do you think children should have their own phones or access to social media, and why?

2. How common is the scene depicted in the photo on page 284 of three young women at lunch? Would you expect men at lunch to behave differently? To what extent has our growing dependence on technology hurt or improved human relationships? Do you think that there are places (restaurants, college classrooms, etc.) where access to technology should be restricted? Why, and under what circumstances?

3. The image on page 285 (top) comes from Anita Sarkeesian's *Feminist Frequency* Web site, which is devoted to analyzing representations of women in video games and gamer culture. Go online to explore the resources Sarkeesian offers on her site and in her *Tropes vs. Women in Video Games* YouTube series. What seem to be the most common stereotypes of women in video games and gamer culture? Have representations of women become less demeaning and stereotypical in recent years? In your view, do video game stereotypes pose a problem for women in the real world? Why or why not?

4. The image on page 285 (bottom) comes from a video game called "Beat Up Anita Sarkeesian" that was posted online in 2012 in response to a Kickstarter campaign to fund her *Tropes vs. Women in Video Games* YouTube series. Do some Internet research to learn more about the harassment Sarkeesian faced in response to her Web site and about the 2014 Gamergate controversy, which involved a series of misogynistic attacks on female game developers like Zoe Quinn and Brianna Wu. Working in groups, compare notes on your own online experiences. To what extent would you agree that the culture of video games and, more generally, of social media is misogynist and unwelcoming for women? What, in your view, could or should be done to address the problem?

5. What does the image on page 286 of Claudia Mitchell and Jesse Sullivan giving each other a high five say to you about the future of technology and medicine? What ethical questions does the use of "bionic" prosthetics raise? For example, would it be acceptable for amputees to be fitted with a prosthesis that gives them extraordinary powers or abilities?

6. The screen shot on page 287 shows the Internet home page of the Westboro Baptist Church in late 2014. An unaffiliated Baptist congregation, Westboro is infamous for hate speech campaigns directed against LGBT people, Jews, the Pope, the U.S. military, and liberal politicians. This site is only one of thousands of online sites that promote hate, violence, and terrorist activity. To what extent does the existence of sites like this complicate the idea that the Internet can help bridge the differences between races, cultures, and countries? Should sites like this be shut down? Why or why not?

THE LONELINESS OF THE INTERCONNECTED

CHARLES SEIFE

Most of us view the Internet as a useful tool that enriches our lives by expanding our access to information and new groups of people. Who hasn't marveled at the Internet's ability to put us instantly in touch with what's happening around the world, and who hasn't been impressed by its amazing "connectivity"? But as the author of this selection sees it, the Internet actually does the opposite. According to Charles Seife, instead of connecting us to others, the Internet isolates us in a bubble of our own making by directing us to ideas that reinforce our beliefs and people who reflect our own values and biases. Instead of exposing us to differences, the Internet actually encourages conformism and intolerance — and thus threatens basic principles that sustain a democratic society. Seife is a writer and journalist who specializes in issues related to mathematics and technology. He currently is a professor in the Arthur L. Carter Journalism Institute at New York University. His publications include *Zero: The Biography of a Dangerous Idea* (2000), which won the 2000 PEN/Martha Albrand Award for First Nonfiction, *Decoding the Universe: How the New Science of Information Is Explaining Everything in the Cosmos, from Our Brains to Black Holes* (2005), and *Virtual Unreality: The New Era of Digital Deception* (2014), the source of this selection.

> *I think it's a very firm part of human nature that if you surround yourself with like-minded people, you'll end up thinking more extreme versions of what you thought before.*
>
> —CASS SUNSTEIN

OPINIONS ARE STUBBORN THINGS. The firmest ones can weather for years a hailstorm of contrary facts, remaining nearly immutable in a flood of contrary evidence. Only slowly do they yield, eroded, bit by bit, by time as much as by the impositions of external reality.

The importance of a fact is measured not in absolute terms, but by judging it against the opinions it challenges. In the field known as information theory, the bits and bytes of an incoming message contain information only if the content is, to some degree, unexpected. If you can predict, with perfect confidence, what's inside an envelope without needing to open it, there's nothing to be gained by opening the envelope. It's the very unpredictability of the message—the fact that the reader doesn't know exactly what the letter contains—that gives the message any informational value at all. Information is that which defies expectation.

Information is not the barrage of facts that's pelting us from every direction. Information consists of those facts and messages that, in some way, shape our ideas. Information is the force that causes the erosion of our mental landscape, that undermines and reconstructs our perceptions of the world. Anything that does not affect our opinions is not information; it's noise.

As we grow and learn, the fragile and unsupported parts of our mental landscape are washed away, and we are left with some opinions that are as firm as bedrock—and just as difficult to move. And once in a great while, there is such a storm of hard, inescapable fact that it challenges to topple even one of our bedrock beliefs, and this causes a mental crisis.

In the 1950s, psychologist Leon Festinger sought to understand what happens at the crisis moment—when an immovable object of a core belief comes into conflict with the irresistible force of an undeniable contrary fact. And he did it by making an inspired choice about whom to study: an apocalyptic cult.

Festinger decided that the ideal subjects to study would be the members of a small group of people led by a housewife in a Chicago suburb. This woman, Dorothy Martin, claimed to write letters under the direction of beings from the planet Clarion. These beings told her that early in the morning on December 21, 1955, there would be a tremendous cataclysm: Chicago would be destroyed, and much of the United States would be submerged in a great flood. But all was not lost: Martin learned from her spirit guide that as the clock tolled midnight in the last few hours before the disaster, a spaceman would knock on the door and lead Martin and her followers to a saucer that would whisk them to safety.

Festinger knew that for the cult's members, the belief in this disaster and salvation was incredibly deeply held. Many of the members of the cult had made large personal sacrifices because of their faith in Mrs. Martin's prophecy; one, a respected physician, had lost his job—and become a laughingstock—when he exposed his daft beliefs to the newspapers. The members of the cult were so sure of the coming day of reckoning that they were willing to isolate themselves, give away their worldly goods, and even tear apart their clothing (to remove metal zippers and snaps that could injure them aboard the flying saucer) based upon their confidence in Mrs. Martin's writings. Only a deep, firm belief could inspire people to make such sacrifices. Yet when the spaceman failed to knock at the door, the cult members would be faced with the inescapable fact that the prophecy had been false. Here was a clear-cut case of immovable belief versus irresistible fact—and it would happen on a schedule.

For Festinger, this was a perfect case study that would help him understand what he termed "cognitive dissonance"—a situation in which a person is forced to believe two mutually incompatible ideas at the same time. In particular, it would allow him to test a somewhat counterintuitive hypothesis: that when the spaceman failed to show up, Mrs. Martin and some of her followers would become even more fervent in their beliefs. In other words, the inescapable fact that the prediction failed wouldn't merely fail to shake some of Mrs. Martin's followers from their faith—it would even strengthen their fervor.

Festinger's theory was based upon the assumption that cognitive dissonance is intensely uncomfortable for most humans. When confronted with such pain, we attempt to resolve the dissonance through whatever mechanisms we have at hand. And when the dissonance-causing-fact is as firm and unyielding as the continued existence of Chicago, there are only two basic approaches that one can take. First, a person can reshape the belief to accommodate the fact, or perhaps even discard the belief entirely. However, this would have been a very painful thing to do in this case, given how deeply held the belief was. The other alternative is to attempt to counter the weight of the oppressing fact by increasing one's conviction in the belief. Since this can't be done with facts, it's done with people. Specifically, Festinger argued that once Mrs. Martin's prophecy failed, some of the cult members would try to solve their cognitive dissonance by strengthening social bonds within the group and by attempting to gain more supporters. As Festinger puts it:

> It is unlikely that one isolated believer could withstand the kind of disconfirming evidence we have specified. If, however, the believer is a member of a group of convinced persons who can support one another, we would expect the belief to be maintained and the believers to attempt to proselytize or to persuade nonmembers that the belief is correct.[1]

It happened, more or less, as Festinger thought it would. Mrs. Martin and many of the die-hard believers weren't put off by the disconfirmation. Instead, she softened the blow by revealing new alien messages that would help explain the failed coming of the apocalypse. Even more telling, though, the group suddenly increased its attempts to proselytize—even to the point of issuing press releases to the media. The group would seek comfort by trying to increase its size.

The most potent weapon for fighting off uncomfortable facts is other people—a network of the faithful who are willing to believe with you. In the arms of fellow true believers, you can find solace from the brutal reality of disconfirmation.

10

---

[1] Leon Festinger and Henry W. Riecken, *When Prophecy Fails* (London: Pinter & Martin, 2008; first published 1956 by University of Minnesota Press), 4. [All notes are Seife's, except 2, 3, 5, 6, 11, 14, 15, 23, and 24.]

This is just as true today as it was in the 1950s. We seek shelter from the harsh information that carves away our cherished beliefs by finding other people who share our convictions. Social ties reinforce our internal mental landscape so that it can better resist a blast of unwelcome facts. But now, with the advent of the digital age, our interconnectedness has increased almost without bound. We are able to communicate with peers all around the world as easily as—more easily than—visiting our next-door neighbor. With this tremendous interconnectedness comes the ability to build many more social ties, to weave a vaster web of personal bonds than ever before. And that means that the Internet gives us much more raw social material than ever before to help us bolster our shaky prejudices and beliefs.

In a very real way, the Internet is helping us preserve our mental landscape from the weathering effects of information. We are becoming ever more resistant to the effects of uncomfortable facts—and ever more capable of treating them as mere noise.

If you've ever been to London, there's a good chance you've visited the northeast edge of Hyde Park. It's a prime tourist attraction because, if you're interested in seeing the local wildlife, you can't do better than visiting Speakers' Corner on a gray Sunday afternoon. If you choose to go, you'll almost certainly be treated to a fine display: a dozen or so men (mostly) and a few women, perched on ladders and makeshift podiums, each bellowing out their complaints and exhortations to all passersby. There are Marxists on the left, apocalyptic Christians on the right, and all variety of true believers in between, haranguing the crowd—and one another—in hopes of winning a few converts. The best (or merely the most entertaining) among them can draw crowds of fifty or a hundred people or even more; even likelier is the chance to pick up a heckler or two who will fling verbal pies in hopes of catching a speaker square in the face.

Speakers' Corner is touted as a bastion of free speech—a place where Londoners and other Britons can come and air their grievances, no matter how absurd. But it's not really the prospect of free speech that draws so many speakers to that particular corner of Hyde Park every Sunday afternoon. After all, the vast majority of speakers are able to speak freely about their beliefs in plenty of other places, both public and private, without getting hauled off to jail. What brings them to Hyde Park on Sunday is not free speech, but a free audience.

What's so valuable to the speakers is that the Sunday-afternoon ritual is likely to draw a thousand or more curious people, tourists and locals alike, all of whom mill about in hopes of finding something worth listening to for a few brief moments. It's an opportunity to speak in front of a receptive crowd of a respectable size—a size that few speakers are dynamic and interesting enough to draw on their own. It's a tremendous amount of work to build up an audience as an orator, and Speakers'

Corner is a way to reach far more people than an amateur could get any other way.

An audience used to be a precious and rare commodity. Generally, one could get it only through unusual eloquence, through power, or through money. The politician and the preacher build and wield their strength by gathering large audiences and influencing their thought. Conversely, certain offices automatically confer upon the holder massive, world-spanning audiences. The entire world hangs upon what the president or the pope has to say; before their elections, Barack Obama and Jorge Bergoglio[2] had to struggle and shout to get significant numbers of people to pay attention—and they seldom had the opportunity to garner a large audience. Money, too, buys listeners; Michael Bloomberg and Rupert Murdoch, like William Randolph Hearst and Joseph Pulitzer[3] before them, realized that nothing's better for reaching people than owning a media empire.

What opportunities were there for the rest of us? Barring an accident of fate that brings us into the public eye—as a witness or a victim or a bit player in a drama—we had to be content with writing the occasional angry letter to the editor of our local paper or joining forces with a handful of like-minded people who felt strongly about an issue dear to us. Perhaps we might try to attract the attention of somebody with his own audience, like a congressperson or a reporter. We could speak as freely as we wanted, but it made little difference if nobody heard what we were saying.

Then came the Internet.

The audience problem had vanished. The Internet's vast interconnectivity made it possible for everyone to hear everyone else—and to be heard by everyone else. This is perhaps the most important and radical change wrought by digital information. Every single person hooked up to the Web can instantly reach every other person. Your audience is potentially the world.

Twitter is an international Speakers' Corner writ larger than anyone had ever imagined. The speech isn't quite free, but the number of people listening is vast. You can say something and, in theory, hundreds of millions of people on all seven continents are able to hear you loud and clear—if you can convince them to tune in. As with Speakers' Corner, most orators on Twitter and in other corners of the Internet ramble and rave, sharing little of interest. But there are enough virtual passersby that if you have a little eloquence and a little skill, you can soon have your voice and even your image echoing around the globe.

20

[2] **Jorge Bergoglio:** Argentinian Catholic cardinal (b. 1936) who became Pope Francis in 2013. [Eds.]

[3] **Michael Bloomberg . . . Joseph Pulitzer:** Michael Bloomberg (b. 1942), Rupert Murdoch (b. 1931), William Randolph Hearst (1863–1951), and Joseph Pulitzer (1847–1911) are considered four of the most successful and influential newspaper and media magnates in U.S. history. [Eds.]

It's sometimes stunning to see how easy it can be to become an international celebrity, if only for a short time. Even against your will.

In 2002, Canadian high school student Ghyslain Raza videotaped himself swinging a large pole around himself as if it were a kung fu weapon. Somewhat portly and terribly uncoordinated, Raza cut a ridiculous figure—as many of us soon found out. For poor Raza left the videotape where some of his fellow classmates could find it, and they uploaded it to YouTube. It soon went viral; Ghyslain, dubbed "Star Wars Kid" for his very un-Jedi-like martial-arts skills, had become an international celebrity. Within a short time, hundreds of thousands of people had watched Raza's antics. As of 2013, the video had been viewed some twenty-eight million times.[4] (By way of comparison, I'll consider myself very, very lucky if this book is read by a few hundred thousand.) Upload a cute enough video of a cat playing a piano, or do something extraordinarily foolish like shoot yourself in the leg during a gun-safety class, or create something goofy enough to tickle people's fancy—dancing hamsters or dancing babies or dancing Gangnams[5]—and there's a chance you'll get a brief adrenaline burst of fame.

The point is not that you're guaranteed to be heard among the clatter and noise of the Internet; it's that, as small and insignificant as your voice might be, it is at least possible that your voice can be perceived—and amplified—to the point that you're heard by an international audience that would make any major broadcast network proud. The mob is always there, listening, waiting to hear something interesting, and even without the power of a president or the money of a Mort Zuckerman,[6] for a short time, at least, you can have a pulpit almost as bully as what they've got. This is free speech in the truest sense. It's not just the freedom to speak out about anything; it's also the ability to be heard by everybody.

With the ability to be heard comes the ability to organize. The Internet has made it easier than ever to set up networks of like-minded people—to set up groups who have a belief or an interest in common, no matter how unusual or bizarre that interest or belief might be. Even the ideas on the very fringe of human thought—a notion that might be held by only one in a million people—might find a devoted network of several hundred or even a few thousand followers on the Internet.

For example, in 2008, the Centers for Disease Control launched an investigation into a new, horrific disease. Sufferers often feel a weird crawling or biting sensation underneath the skin, and rashes and sores soon appear. Many people afflicted with the disease report pulling thin, wormlike fibers from sores. Only a few years earlier had the ailment gotten a name: Morgellons disease.

---

[4] "raze7ds," "Star Wars Kid," YouTube.com, January 15, 2006, http://www.youtube.com /watch?v= HPPj6viIBmU.

[5] **dancing Gangnams:** A reference to thousands of homemade YouTube videos imitating the 2012 hit song "Gangnam Style" by South Korean rapper Psy. [Eds.]

[6] **Mort Zuckerman:** Canadian-born American media owner and businessman (b. 1937). [Eds.]

The name Morgellons was coined by Mary Leitao,[7] a mother who was increasingly frustrated at dermatologists' inability to find out what was wrong with her young son, who kept developing strange sores that had threads poking out of them. Using a word from an old French medical article that seemed to describe a similar ailment, Leitao gave the disease a concrete name and created a foundation to attempt to find the cause of the mysterious ailment. And a Web site.

Once that Web site was established, it became a focal point for people who felt they had similar problems. The word spread quickly, and hundreds of people with similar symptoms began contacting the foundation, as well as other authorities who might be able to help, such as the Mayo Clinic and the Centers for Disease Control. By 2007—just three years after the first report of Morgellons—the CDC received about twelve hundred reports of Morgellons, triggering the inquiry.[8] This was quite remarkable, given that the disease doesn't really exist.

Morgellons appears to be a variant of a fairly well-known condition called "delusional parasitosis"—the false conviction that you've got bugs crawling under your skin. It's not uncommon in people who are taking cocaine or other drugs, and in those who have schizophrenia, and it can occasionally strike healthy (or healthy-seeming) people as well.

The CDC study was very gentle about dispelling the myth of Morgellons, saying only that it "shares a number of clinical and epidemiologic features"[9] with delusional parasitosis, but the message was clear enough: the disease was in the patients' minds. The fibers they found—which were analyzed by researchers—were almost all skin fragments or cotton threads that likely came from clothing. There are no bugs or strange foreign-body-producing organisms under the skin. Nevertheless, the victims clearly suffer, even if the disease has no external cause.

Despite the findings of the study, many Morgellons sufferers are unshaken in their belief that there really is something going on underneath their skin—whether it's parasites or, as a number of Morgellons theorists believe, alien DNA or self-replicating nanobots dumped by government airplanes. The deeper you delve into the Internet literature on the subject, the stranger the ideas become. And looking into these ideas, it becomes clear that the Internet is not just the repository in which these odd beliefs are archived and transmitted—it's also the medium that gives these ideas life in the first place. The fringe beliefs

[7] Elizabeth Devita-Raeburn, "The Morgellons Mystery," *Psychology Today*, March 1, 2007.

[8] Centers for Disease Control and Prevention, "Press-Briefing Transcripts: CDC to Launch Study on Unexplained Illness," January 16, 2008, http://www.cdc.gov/media/transcripts/2008/t080U6.htm.

[9] Michele L. Pearson et al., "Clinical, Epidemiologic, Histopathologic, and Molecular Features of an Unexplained Dermopathy," *PLOS One* 7, no. 1 (January 2012), e29908, doi:10.1371/journal.pone.0029908.

are birthed and nourished by the social connections that the Internet makes possible. As two Canadian psychiatrists put it:

> a belief is not considered delusional if it is accepted by other members of an individual's culture or subculture. Although this may be appropriate in the context of spiritual or religious beliefs, the scenario in which a widely held belief is accepted as plausible simply because many people ascribe to it requires a revised conceptualization in our current era. That is, Internet technology may facilitate the dissemination of bizarre beliefs on a much wider scale than ever before.[10]

Morgellons is an Internet disease. It is a delusion that likely would have died out naturally, but thanks to its rapid spread on the Internet, it took on a life of its own. Believers gathered around the banner of Morgellons, and the very size of that group convinced members that their collective delusion was, in fact, real. Soon there was a big community in which the bizarre belief—that there were unidentifiable little organisms crawling under your skin—was completely normal. The movement became strong enough that its members were able to compel the CDC to investigate their fictional disease.

It's not just Morgellons that has taken off in this way. A person's belief in any sort of fringe idea can gain strength—and become unshakable—thanks to social bonds with other true believers. Any idea, no matter how bizarre, can seem mainstream if you're able to find a handful of others who will believe along with you. And since we are all plugged in to the ultimate Speakers' Corner every hour of every day of every week, it's trivially easy to find a group of sympathetic souls. Those small groups are constantly forming and gathering strength, reinforcing the beliefs around which they're formed, no matter how outlandish.

There are the plushies (people who like to have sex with stuffed animals) and the furries (people who like to have sex while wearing animal costumes) and the object-sexuals (people who form sexual attachments to inanimate objects). There are groups devoted to exposing shape-shifting reptilian humanoids living among us, to revealing that the U.S. government brought down the twin towers on September 11, and to arguing that the IRS has no right to collect income taxes. There are fan groups devoted to time travelers, perpetual-motion-machine builders, and crackpot theorists of all varieties. It's not that these kinds of groups came into being with the Internet; anyone who's met a follower of Lyndon LaRouche[11] or a UFO nut or a moon hoaxer knows that strange, fringe ideas can catch on even in the absence of an Internet. But before the digital Web made society so interconnected, it was much harder to encounter such ideas—and it took active effort to engage

30

[10] Fidel Vila-Rodriguez and Bill MacEwen, "Delusional Parasitosis Facilitated by Web-Based Dissemination," *American Journal of Psychiatry* 165, no. 12 (December 2008), 1612, doi:10.1176/appi.ajp.2008.08081283.

[11] **Lyndon LaRouche:** Lyndon Hermyle LaRouche Jr. (b. 1922), the founder of the controversial LaRouche movement known for its caustic attacks on politicians and public figures. [Eds.]

with the communities that had fringe theories. Now even the craziest ideas are usually but a few mouse clicks away from confirmation and reinforcement by a band of fellow travelers.

It used to be that the roughest edges of people's odd beliefs would erode and crumble through simple isolation, through a lack of reinforcement with social bonds. Now isolation is nigh impossible, and those odd beliefs are sharpened and exaggerated when they are brought into the open in the company of a cozy group of like-minded individuals. In other words, the Internet is amplifying our quirks and our odd ideas. Bit by bit, it is driving us toward extremism.

The trend is reflected in the media we consume. The fragmentation of the media, especially the broadcast media, began before digital information first came into our lives. It's been almost two generations since the day when three networks held captive Americans who wanted to watch television. After a slow start, cable TV took off in the 1980s, and no longer could CBS, NBC, and ABC control the majority of television programming in the United States. In 1980, roughly 90 percent of prime-time television watchers in the United States were tuned in to one of the Big Three networks.[12] By 2005 that number had dropped to 32 percent, and it has continued to decline ever since. There are more choices out there, so the audience is spread more thinly. For TV news alone, CNN, Fox News, and MSNBC and various other spinoffs and subsidiaries provide direct competition to the evening newscasts of the major networks.

Then, when the Internet came along, people could get their news — even news in video format — in innumerable new ways. It's not surprising that the Big Three's evening news programs have lost 55 percent of their viewers in the past thirty years.[13] The surprise is that they've managed to hold on to that other 45 percent.

Back when the Big Three ruled the airwaves, the nightly news had to perform a delicate balancing act. A news program had to try to appeal to the entire television audience — it had to be, quite literally, a broad cast — if it was to compete with the other two networks that were taking the same strategy. This meant that the networks couldn't become too partisan or take an extreme position on anything, for fear of alienating its potential audience. If roughly half of the country was Republican, you'd instantly alienate half your audience if your program began to seem like it was too tilted in favor of Democrats.

Then cable and the Internet increased our choices. The Big Three kept trying to capture as big a slice of America as possible by staying centrist, but a couple of upstarts — particularly Fox News and MSNBC — realized that there was another possible strategy. Instead of trying to go

[12] Douglas Blanks Hindman and Kenneth Wiegand, "The Big Three's Prime-Time Decline: A Technological and Social Context," *Journal of Broadcasting and Electronic Media* 52, no. 1 (March 2008), 119, doi: 10.1080/08838150701820924.

[13] Emily Guskin et al., "Network News: Durability and Decline," in Pew Research Center, *The State of the News Media 2011*, http://stateofthemedia.org/2011/network-essay.

after the entire American population with a broadly targeted program that appealed to everyone, you could go with a narrowly targeted program that appealed to only a subgroup of the population. Throw in your lot with, say, die-hard Republicans and give them coverage that makes them happy; you'll alienate Democrats and won't get them as viewers, but you can more than make up for that loss by gaining a devoted Republican fan base. This is exactly what Fox News did. Few liberals would tune in to watch Bill O'Reilly[14] except out of grim amusement at how crazy the other side has become, but it's a program that makes the far right happy. MSNBC did exactly the reverse; by filling its schedule with shows that appeal to liberals, such as Keith Olbermann's[15] show, it made a play for the leftist Democrats to the exclusion of the more centrist and right-leaning folks. These networks have given up on broadcasting; instead they're narrowcasting.

The more choices a consumer has on his TV, the more thinly spread the audience will be for each TV show, just because there's more competition. The more thinly spread the audience, the more it makes sense to drop the pretense of trying to appeal to everybody and to instead attempt to corner the market on one chunk of the population; and as choices increase and audiences dwindle, the proportion of the population it makes economic sense to go after becomes smaller. In this light, MSNBC and Fox make perfect sense; they are the natural consequence of the ever-increasing competition to get our attention. Narrowcasting is gradually beating out broadcasting, and the casts will get narrower and narrower as the audience becomes harder and harder to find. In effect, as audience becomes more narrowly defined, the viewer is getting more power about what kind of news and data are served up and what kind of news and data are ignored.

The Internet is allowing narrowcasting on a scale never before dreamed of. When you go to CNN.com or BBC.com or PBS.org, the Web site is tracking which stories you read and which ones you don't. And they're using that information to make the Web site more appealing to you — you personally. Google News looks at your reading patterns and chooses to present you with news items that are likely to appeal to you based upon your location, your past reading choices, even your Web history. It's not just Google News, in fact. Google itself — the Web search engine — uses your search history and your past behavior to try to guess what kinds of links you're most likely to find useful. You might not even be conscious of it, but your online behavior is dictating what news you're exposed to, what data you're being served. In a very real sense, you are controlling which elements of the outside world you see and which you don't.

[14] **Bill O'Reilly:** American television host and writer (b. 1949) whose Fox News show *The O'Reilly Factor* appeals to conservative viewers. [Eds.]

[15] **Keith Olbermann:** American sports and political commentator (b. 1959), whose *Countdown with Keith Olbermann* television program ran on MSNBC from 2003 until 2011. [Eds.]

This is welcome news in many ways. We all have limited time to read, watch, or listen to the news, and we can't waste our entire day searching for information on the Internet. The better the media outlets and search engines are at giving us the news we want, the more efficiently we can use our time. But at the same time, there's a very big downside. We tend to shy away from data that challenges our assumptions, that erodes our preconceptions. Getting rid of our wrong ideas is a painful and difficult process, yet it's that very process that makes data truly useful. A fact becomes information when it challenges our assumptions. These challenges are the raw material that forces our ideas to evolve, our tastes to change, our minds to grow.

The more power we have over the data that comes in, the better able we are to shelter ourselves from uncomfortable truths—from facts that challenge our preconceptions and misperceptions. If you have a steady diet of items from Fox News and *The Drudge Report*, your belief that Barack Obama is not a U.S. citizen will be perfectly safe. If you believe that vaccines cause autism, frequenting *The Huffington Post* and MSNBC will likely strengthen your conviction rather than weaken it. With news and data that is tailored to our prejudices, we deprive ourselves of true information. We wind up wallowing in our own false ideas, reflected back at us by the media. The news is ceasing to be a window unto the world; it is becoming a mirror that allows us to gaze only upon our own beliefs.[16]

Couple this dynamic with the microsociety-building power of the hyper-interconnected Internet and you've got two major forces that are radicalizing us. Not only does the media fail to challenge our pre-conceptions—instead reinforcing them as media outlets try to cater to smaller audiences—but we all are able to find small groups of people who share and fortify the beliefs we have, no matter how quirky or out-right wrong they might be. Ironically, all this interconnection is isolating us. We are all becoming solipsists, trapped in worlds of our own creation.

Solipsism wouldn't be so bad but for the fact that the worlds we're creating around ourselves are not just fictions of the mind but have real, concrete consequences for other people who don't share the same delusions.

A bad idea, a wrong piece of information, a digital brain-altering virus can spread at the speed of light through the Internet and quickly find a home among a dispersed but digitally interconnected group of true believers. This group acts as a reservoir for the bad idea, allowing it to gather strength and reinfect people; as the group grows, the belief, no matter how crazy, becomes more and more solidly established among the faithful.

Morgellons is a relatively benign example; other than the believers themselves, the only people inconvenienced are physicians and

[16] Eli Pariser talks about this phenomenon in his book *The Filter Bubble*.

insurers. Not so with real diseases. Since the late 1980s, Peter Duesberg, a biologist at Berkeley, has been arguing that AIDS is not caused by a virus, but instead is the product of using recreational drugs—or of taking the anti-HIV drugs that are used to keep the virus in check. It was a dubious belief even at the time Duesberg proposed it, and it quickly failed several tests in the early 1990s and was soundly rejected by the scientific community.[17] Duesberg was pretty much banished from the better—and more widely read—scientific journals after that. In the days before the Internet, that would have almost guaranteed that he would fade into obscurity; forced to the fringe, Duesberg would rant and rave in fourth-tier journals and be ignored by the rest of the world. But by the mid-1990s the Web had come along, so Duesberg took to the Internet and quickly found a large audience. Several HIV-denialist groups coalesced on the Web, touting Duesberg's research as evidence that AIDS wasn't caused by a virus.

On October 28, 1999, Thabo Mbeki, then the president of South Africa, gave a controversial speech about AZT, the first anti-HIV drug. "Many in our country have called on the government to make the drug AZT available in our public health system,"[18] he said, but warned that "the toxicity of this drug is such that it is in fact a danger to health." It was astonishing that the president of South Africa would try to keep an anti-HIV drug out of his country, especially given that his country was ground zero for the epidemic. The incidence of HIV was skyrocketing—almost 13 percent of the population was infected by 1997[19]—and the country was crying out for drugs that might help. AZT was in wide use to prevent pregnant mothers from transmitting the virus to children. Why was Mbeki so convinced that AZT would do more harm than good? He didn't go into detail, but he hinted at where he had gotten his information: online. "To understand this matter better," he said, "I would urge the honorable members of the National Council to access the huge volume of literature on this matter available on the Internet."[20]

Physicians and AIDS researchers in South Africa—and around the world—were shocked. The South African newspaper the *Sunday Independent* described the reaction:

> Mark Lurie, a Medical Research Council senior scientist based in Mtubatuba in KwaZulu-Natal, was "flabbergasted" by Mbeki's speech.
> "Here is a drug that cuts the rate of mother-to-child transmission by 50 percent. If the president is telling us that this drug doesn't work, where is his evidence for such a statement?"

---

[17] See, for example, Richard Horton, "Will Duesberg Now Concede Defeat?" *The Lancet*, September 9, 1995, p. 656.

[18] Thabo Mbeki, Address to the National Council of Provinces, Cape Town, October 28, 1999, http://www.dfa.gov.za/docs/speeches/1999/mbek1028.htm.

[19] UNAIDS, *Report on the Global HIV/AIDS Epidemic*, June 1998, http://www.unaids.org/en/media/unaids/contentassets/dataimport/pub/report/1998/19981125_global_epidemic_report_en.pdf.

[20] Mbeki, Address to the National Council.

Mbeki's evidence seems to be the Internet, according to Tasneem Carrim, a media liaison officer for the presidency.

"The president got a thick set of documents. He went into many sites, including the World Health Organisation's one. The president goes into the Net all the time," she said.[21]

It soon became clear what sites Mbeki was visiting. The South African president had stumbled upon HIV-denialist Web sites and was soon consulting with them, and with Duesberg (whom Mbeki invited to South Africa). Mbeki was soon a true believer. He publicly questioned whether HIV caused AIDS, and engaged in political maneuvers to prevent the distribution of anti-HIV drugs—even ones donated for free. (Eventually the courts had to intervene to allow unfettered access to the lifesaving drugs.) The minister of health earned the scorn of the scientific world by extolling the virtues of beetroot, lemon, and garlic as better ways to prevent AIDS than the antiretroviral drugs her ministry was denying the sick and dying. A 2008 study in the *Journal of Acquired Immune Deficiency Syndromes* estimated that more than 300,000 people lost their lives between 2000 and 2005 because of Mbeki's obstinate refusal to allow his citizens to begin taking antiretroviral drugs.[22]

Of course, volumes and volumes of HIV-denial literature are still just a Google search away.

Three hundred thousand deaths might be the most extreme consequence of a Google search gone wrong. However, history is littered with examples of fringe beliefs—ones that the vast majority of people rejected—killing thousands upon thousands. For one, millions of people starved in the Soviet Union in part because Joseph Stalin[23] embraced the wacky anti-Darwinist ideas of Trofim Lysenko,[24] a man who believed that you could "train" crops to grow in the wrong seasons.

But comparing the Duesberg case with Lysenko's reveals just how much more potent fringe ideas become when they're digitized. Lysenko rose to power in part because he was of peasant stock, like his powerful benefactor, Stalin. And it was the fear of Stalin that allowed his ideas to grow and take hold. Scientists couldn't silence Lysenko; indeed, Lysenko silenced (and murdered) accomplished scientists who dared to say that Lysenkoism was nonsense. It's the opposite of what happened to Duesberg, who was shunted to the fringe and silenced by the scientific community. Had Duesberg lived in the time of Lysenko, his ideas would never have circulated around the United States, much less

[21] Adele Sulcas and Estelle Randall, "Mbeki Sparks Row over AIDS Drug," *Sunday Independent*, October 30, 1999, http://www.iol.co.za/news/south-africa/mbeki-sparks-row-over-aids-drug-l.17874?ot=inmsa.ArticlePrintPageLayout.ot.

[22] Pride Chigwedere et al., "Estimating the Lost Benefits of Antiretroviral Drug Use in South Africa," *Journal of Acquired Immune Deficiency Syndromes* 49, no. 4 (December 1, 2008), 410–15.

[23] **Joseph Stalin:** Born Joseph Dzhugashvili, Joseph Stalin (1878–1953) led the Soviet Union from the mid-1920s until his death. [Eds.]

[24] **Trofim Lysenko:** Soviet biologist and agronomist (1898–1976) who rejected Mendelian genetic theory. [Eds.]

affected a government halfway around the world several years after he was discredited at home.

Yet because of the digital revolution, the has-been professor who was a laughingstock of his home country's scientific community was able to have a Lysenko-like influence without the backing of a Joseph Stalin. And Duesberg's ideas will last much longer than Lysenko's. Lysenkoism essentially died with Stalin. However, even if the HIV-denialist movement dies in South Africa, Duesberg's ideas will remain visible to everyone for years and years to come, ready to spark a new outbreak.

Because of the interconnectedness of the digital world and the transmissibility of even large volumes of work, the most absurd fringe idea can reach far beyond the fevered mind of its creator. Even the craziest notions can be heard and amplified and transmitted by virtual communities. The extremes of human thought are gathering strength.

As we sink into the comfortable monotony of constant reinforcement, as we spend an increasing amount of time listening to sources of information that are tailored to strengthen our mental fictions rather than challenge them, we are slowly being turned into cranks ourselves. And those who don't succumb are often at the mercy of those who do.

ENGAGING THE TEXT

1. Seife defines information as "that which defies expectation" (para. 2). How often do you encounter facts or ideas that "undermine and reconstruct" your understanding of the world? When, for example, was the last time you recall encountering a fact or an idea that forced you to reexamine your beliefs? Why, according to Seife, do most of us prefer "noise" to genuine information?

2. How, in Seife's view, does the Internet foster the development and dissemination of "fringe beliefs" (para. 29) like those associated with Morgellons disease (para. 24) even in the face of contradictory evidence? What do you consider examples of odd or fringe beliefs that you've encountered online, and why do you think people often find such ideas interesting or attractive?

3. What costs and benefits does Seife associate with the kind of "narrowcasting" that the Internet has made possible? Why does narrowcasting threaten to "radicalize" Internet users? What examples of radicalization or radical thinking have you encountered during your own explorations of the Internet? How dangerous do they seem to you, and why?

4. To what extent would you agree with Seife's claim that the Internet is turning all of us into "solipsists, trapped in worlds of our own creation" (para. 41)? Why might widespread solipsism pose a threat in a democracy?

5. **Thinking Rhetorically** Seife concludes his examination of Internet isolation by warning that "because of the interconnectedness of the digital world" the "extremes of human thought are gathering strength" (para. 52). However, he doesn't offer any solutions to the looming crisis he identifies. How would you

describe his purpose in writing this selection? Why do you think he chose to address the problem of Internet extremism without trying to resolve it?

EXPLORING CONNECTIONS

6. How might Malcolm X's experience of learning to read (p. 161) be seen as supporting or challenging Seife's definition of information? In your view, does Malcolm X represent an example of critical thinking or solipsistic belief? Why?

7. How does Seife's exploration of online extremism challenge the optimistic portrayal of technology's influence on global relations offered by Eric Schmidt and Jared Cohen (p. 219)? As a class, discuss whether you think communication technologies like television and the Internet have enhanced our understanding of other peoples and cultures or exacerbated global tensions.

8. Drawing on the ideas of Seife and Sherry Turkle (p. 236), write a journal entry or a short essay discussing the impact of the Internet and social media on the development of independent critical thinking skills among today's teens.

EXTENDING THE CRITICAL CONTEXT

9. Working in groups, design and conduct a survey to identify the main sources of news that the students at your college consult regularly. Compare your results in class and discuss whether your research confirms or complicates Seife's claim that the news has become more of a "mirror" that reflects our own values than a "window" on the world. (para. 40).

10. Go online to sample a few Web sites associated with Internet extremism, like those linked with pro-ana groups that encourage anorexic girls to lose weight or those of white supremacist organizations like Stormwatch or Occidental Dissent. Debate in class whether such sites represent a real public danger in a democracy. What can or should be done to limit their influence?

INEQUALITY: CAN SOCIAL MEDIA RESOLVE SOCIAL DIVISIONS?

DANAH BOYD

We often assume that prejudice results from poor communication. If we all just talked more openly and honestly with each other, we'd all learn to live in harmony — or so the theory goes. As the author of this selection suggests, however, connecting doesn't necessarily lead to understanding. From her experience working with American teens, danah boyd has learned that instead of mitigating prejudice, social media use actually reinforces patterns of segregation most Americans live with in their non-virtual lives. A social media scholar, youth researcher, and media activist, boyd (b. 1977) is a principal researcher at Microsoft Research and the founder of the Data & Society Research Institute. She also serves as a visiting professor in New York University's Interactive Telecommunications Program and as a faculty affiliate at Harvard University's Berkman Center for Internet and Society. This selection comes from her 2014 book *It's Complicated: The Social Lives of Networked Teens.*

IN A SCHOOL CLASSROOM in Los Angeles, Keke sat down, crossed her arms defensively, and looked at me with suspicion. After an hour of short, emotionless responses to my questions about her daily life and online activities, I hit a nerve when I asked the black sixteen-year-old to explain how race operated in her community. I saw her fill with rage as she described how gang culture shaped her life. "We can't have a party without somebody being a Blood or somebody being a Crip[1] and then they get into it and then there's shooting. Then we can't go to my friend's house because it's on the wrong side of [the street]. You know what I'm saying? It's the Mexican side." Los Angeles gang culture forces her to think about where she goes, who she spends time with, and what she wears.

> We can't go places because of gangs. . . . We can't go to the mall, can't be a whole bunch of black people together. . . . I hate not being able to go places. I hate having to be careful what color shoes I'm wearing or what color is in my pants or what color's in my hair. . . . I just hate that. It's just not right.

When each color represents a different gang, the choice to wear red or blue goes beyond taste and fashion.

Although Keke understood the dynamics of gang culture in her community and was respected by the gang to which members of her family belonged, she despised the gangs' power. She hated the violence. And she had good reason to be angry. Only a few weeks before we met, Keke's brother had been shot and killed after crossing into the turf of a Latino gang. Keke was still in mourning.

Though almost sixty years had passed since the U.S. Supreme Court ruled that segregation of public high schools is unconstitutional, most American high schools that I encountered organized themselves around race and class through a variety of social, cultural, economic, and political forces. The borders of school districts often produce segregated schools as a byproduct of de facto neighborhood segregation. Students find themselves in particular classrooms—or on academic tracks—based on test scores, and these results often correlate with socioeconomic status. Friend groups are often racially and economically homogeneous,

---

[1]**a Blood . . . a Crip:** Rival African American gangs based in Los Angeles. [All notes are boyd's, except 1, 2, and 29.]

which translates into segregated lunchrooms and segregated online communities.

The most explicit manifestation of racial segregation was visible to me in schools like Keke's, where gangs play a central role in shaping social life. Her experiences with race and turf are common in her community. The resulting dynamics organize her neighborhood and infiltrate her school. When I first visited Keke's school, I was initially delighted by how diverse and integrated the school appeared to be. The majority of students were immigrants, and there was no dominant race or nationality. More than other schools I visited, classrooms looked like they were from a Benetton ad[2] or a United Nations gathering, with students from numerous racial backgrounds sitting side by side. Yet during lunch or between classes, the school's diversity dissolved as peers clustered along racial and ethnic lines. As Keke explained,

> This school is so segregated. It's crazy. We got Disneyland full of all the white people. . . . The hallways is full of the Indians, and the people of Middle Eastern descent. . . . The Latinos, they all lined up on this side. The blacks is by the cafeteria and the quad. Then the outcasts, like the uncool Latinos or uncool Indians. The uncool whites, they scattered.

Every teen I spoke with at Keke's school used similar labels to describe the different shared spaces where teens cluster. "Disneyland" was the section in the courtyard where white students gathered, while "Six Flags" described the part occupied by black students. When I tried to understand where these terms came from, one of Keke's classmates— a fifteen-year-old Latina named Lolo—explained, "It's just been here for, I think, generations. (Laughs) I'm sure if you're a ninth grader, you might not know until somebody tells you. But I did know 'cause my brother told me." Those same identifiers bled into nearby schools and were used when public spaces outside of school were identified. No one knew who created these labels, but they did know that these were the right terms to use. Each cohort had to learn the racial organization of the school, just as they had to learn the racial logic of their neighborhoods. They understood that flouting these implicit rules by crossing lines could have serious social and physical consequences.

Although Keke's experience of losing a family member to gang violence is uncommon, death is not that exceptional in a community where gun violence is pervasive. Gang members may know one another at school, but the tense civility they maintain in the hallways does not carry over to the streets. Teens of different races may converse politely in the classroom, but that doesn't mean they are friends on social media. Although many teens connect to everyone they know on sites like Facebook, this doesn't mean that they cross unspoken cultural boundaries.

---

[2]**Benetton ad:** In the 1980s, the Italian fashion brand Benetton launched its "United Colors of Benetton" marketing campaign, which often featured images of interracial harmony. [Eds.]

Communities where race is fraught maintain the same systems of segregation online and off.

What struck me as I talked with teens about how race and class operated in their communities was their acceptance of norms they understood to be deeply problematic. In a nearby Los Angeles school, Traviesa, a Hispanic fifteen-year-old, explained, "If it comes down to it, we have to supposedly stick with our own races. . . . That's just the unwritten code of high school nowadays." Traviesa didn't want to behave this way, but the idea of fighting expectations was simply too exhausting and costly to consider. In losing her brother, Keke knew those costs all too well, and they made her deeply angry. "We all humans," she said. "Skin shouldn't separate nobody. But that's what happens." Although part of Keke wanted to fight back against the racial dynamics that had killed her brother, she felt powerless.

As I watched teens struggle to make sense of the bigotry and racism that surrounded them in the mid- to late 2000s, the American media started discussing how the election of Barack Obama as the president of the United States marked the beginning of a "postracial" era. And because social media supposedly played a role in electing the first black U.S. president, some in the press argued that technology would bring people together, eradicate social divisions in the United States, and allow democracy to flourish around the world.[3] This utopian discourse did not reflect the very real social divisions that I watched emerge and persist in teens' lives.[4]

The Biases in Technology

Society has often heralded technology as a tool to end social divisions. In 1858, when the Atlantic Telegraph Company installed the first transatlantic cable, many imagined that this new communication device would help address incivility. As authors Charles Briggs and Augustus Maverick said of the telegraph: "This binds together by a vital cord all the nations of the earth. It is impossible that old prejudices and hostilities should longer exist, while such an instrument has been created for an exchange of thought between all the nations of the earth."[5] New communication media often inspire the hope that they can and will be used to bridge cultural divides. This hope gets projected onto new technologies in ways that suggest that the technology itself does the work of addressing cultural divisions.

---

[3] The rhetoric used by the U.S. media to suggest that social media could democratize the world took a more magnificent form in January 2011. As citizens throughout the Middle East began challenging authoritarian regimes, the media described the uprisings of the Arab Spring as being a product of social media. The news media began extolling social media as being the source of the various Middle East revolutions. This narrative has been widely critiqued, but it reveals prevalent notions of how technology can do cultural work to eradicate inequalities and injustices.

[4] In *Digitizing Race*, Lisa Nakamura has pointed out that many technological discourses, particularly those involving the digital divide, have envisioned or positioned users of color as technologically limited and/or uninvolved.

[5] Briggs and Maverick quoted in Carey, "Technology and Ideology," 160–61.

The mere existence of new technology neither creates nor magically solves cultural problems. In fact, their construction typically reinforces existing social divisions. This sometimes occurs when designers intentionally build tools in prejudicial ways. More often it happens inadvertently when creators fail to realize how their biases inform their design decisions or when the broader structural ecosystem in which a designer innovates has restrictions that produce bias as a byproduct. . . .

Companies often design, implement, and test new technologies in limited settings. Only when these products appear in the marketplace do people realize that aspects of the technology or its design result in biases that disproportionately affect certain users. For example, many image-capture technologies have historically had difficulty capturing darker-skinned people because they rely on light, which reflects better off of lighter objects. As a result, photography and film better capture white skin while transforming black skin in unexpected ways.[6] This same issue has reemerged in digital technologies like Microsoft's Kinect, an interactive gaming platform that relies on face recognition. Much to the frustration of many early adopters, the system often fails to recognize dark-skinned users.[7] In choosing to use image capture to do face recognition, the Kinect engineers built a system that is technically—and thus socially—biased in implementation. In other technologies, biases may emerge as a byproduct of the testing process. Apple's voice recognition software, Siri, has difficulty with some accents, including Scottish, Southern U.S., and Indian.[8] Siri was designed to recognize language iteratively. Because the creators tested the system primarily in-house, the system was better at recognizing those American English accents most commonly represented at Apple.

The Internet was supposed to be different from previous technologies. Technology pundits and early adopters believed that the Internet would be a great equalizer—where race and class wouldn't matter—because of the lack of visual cues available.[9] But it turns out that the techno-utopians were wrong. The same biases that configure unmediated aspects of everyday life also shape the mediated experiences people have on the Internet. Introducing their book *Race in Cyberspace,* scholars Beth Kolko, Lisa Nakamura, and Gilbert Rodman explain that "race matters in cyberspace precisely because all of us who spend time online are already shaped by the ways in which race matters offline and we can't help but bring our own knowledge, experiences, and values with us when we log on."[10]

Cultural prejudice permeates social media. Explicit prejudice bubbles up through the digital inscription of hateful epithets in comments sections and hatemongering Web sites while the social networks people form

---

[6] For a discussion of whiteness and photography, see Dyer, "Lighting for Whiteness."
[7] Sinclair, "Kinect Has Problems Recognizing Dark-Skinned Users?"
[8] Zax, "Siri, Why Can't You Understand Me?"
[9] Kendall, "Meaning and Identity in 'Cyberspace'"; Kolko, Nakamura, and Rodman, "Race in Cyberspace."
[10] Kolko, Nakamura, and Rodman, "Race in Cyberspace," 4–5.

online replicate existing social divisions. Some youth recognize the ways their experiences are constructed by and organized around cultural differences; many more unwittingly calcify existing structural categories. . . .

Racism in a Networked Age

In 1993, the *New Yorker* published a now infamous cartoon showing a big dog talking to a smaller dog in front of a computer monitor.[11] The caption reads, "On the Internet, no one knows you're a dog." Over the years, countless writers commenting on social issues have used this cartoon to illustrate how privacy and identity operate positively and negatively online. One interpretation of this cartoon is that embodied and experienced social factors—race, gender, class, ethnicity—do not necessarily transfer into the mediated world. . . .

When teens go online, they bring their friends, identities, and network with them. They also bring their attitudes toward others, their values, and their desire to position themselves in relation to others. It is rare for anyone to be truly anonymous, let alone as disconnected from embodied reality as the *New Yorker* cartoon suggests.[12] Not only do other people know who you are online; increasingly, software engineers are designing and building algorithms to observe people's practices and interests in order to model who they are within a broader system. Programmers implement systems that reveal similarity or difference, common practices or esoteric ones. What becomes visible—either through people or through algorithms—can affect how people understand social media and the world around them. How people respond to that information varies.

During the 2009 Black Entertainment Television (BET) Awards, thousands of those watching from home turned to Twitter to discuss the various celebrities at the ceremony. The volume of their commentary caused icons of the black community to appear in Twitter's "Trending Topics," a list of popular terms representing topics users are discussing on the service at any given moment. Beyoncé, Ne-Yo, Jamie Foxx, and other black celebrities all trended, along with the BET Awards themselves. The visibility of these names on the Trending Topics prompted a response from people who were not watching the award ceremony. In seeing the black names, one white teenage girl posted, "So many black people!" while a tweet from a young-looking white woman stated: "Why are all these black people on trending topics? Neyo? Beyonce? Tyra? Jamie Foxx? Is it black history month again? LOL." A white boy posted, "Wow!! too many negros in the trending topics for me. I may be done with this whole twitter thing." Teens were not the only ones making prejudicial remarks. A white woman tweeted, "Did anyone see the new trending topics? I dont think this is a very good neighborhood. Lock the

15

---

[11] Steiner, "On the Internet, Nobody Knows You're a Dog."
[12] Christopherson, "The Positive and Negative Implications of Anonymity in Internet Social Interactions."

car doors kids." These comments—and many more—provoked outrage, prompting the creation of a blog called "omgblackpeople" and a series of articles on race in Twitter.[13]

Unfortunately, what happened on the night of the BET Awards is not an isolated incident. In 2012, two athletes were expelled from the London Olympics after making racist comments on Twitter.[14] Racism is also not just an issue only on Twitter, where black Internet users are overrepresented compared with their online participation on other sites.[15] The now defunct site notaracistbut.com collected hundreds of comments from Facebook that began with "I'm not a racist, but . . ." and ended with a racist comment. For example, one Facebook status update from a teen girl that was posted to the site said, "Not to be a racist, but I'm starting to see that niggers don't possess a single ounce of intellect." While creators of sites like notaracistbut.com intend to publicly shame racists, racism remains pervasive online.

In countless online communities, from YouTube to Twitter to World of Warcraft, racism and hate speech run rampant.[16] Messages of hate get spread both by those who agree with the sentiment and also by those who critique it. After the critically acclaimed movie *The Hunger Games* came out, countless fans turned to Twitter to comment on the casting of Rue, a small girl described in the book as having "dark brown skin and eyes." Tweets like "Call me a racist but when I found out rue was black her death wasn't as sad" and "Why does rue have to be black not gonna lie kinda ruined the movie" sparked outrage among antiracists who forwarded the messages to call attention to them, thereby increasing the visibility of this hostility.[17] On one hand, calling attention to these messages shames those who contributed them. On the other, it incites a new type of hate, which continues to reinforce structural divides.

Annoyed with what she perceived to be a lack of manners among Asian and Asian American students at her school, Alexandra Wallace posted a racist tirade on YouTube mocking students of Asian descent at UCLA in March 2011. The video depicts Wallace, a white blond-haired girl, criticizing Asian students for not being considerate of others. The central message of the video focuses on her complaint that Asian students are rude because they talk on their cell phones in the library. To emphasize her point, she pretends to speak in a speech pattern that she believes sounds Asian, saying, "Ching chong ling long ting tong," in a mocking tone.

[13] The "omgblackpeople" blog was originally hosted on Tumblr, but as of 2013, it is no longer available. The content was reposted on: http://omgblackpeople.wordpress .com/. For a blog post covering the racist tweets surrounding the BET awards, see http:// www.blackweb20.com/2009/06/29/bet-awards-dominate-twitter-causes-racist-backlash/# .UVB-flv5ms8.

[14] Smith, "Twitter Update 2011."

[15] Saraceno, "Swiss Soccer Player Banned from Olympics for Racist Tweet."

[16] For an analysis of racism online, see Daniels, *Cyber Racism*; and Nakamura, "Don't Hate the Player, Hate the Game."

[17] For a write-up of racist commentary following the casting of *The Hunger Games*, see D. Stewart, "Racist Hunger Games Fans Are Very Disappointed."

The video—"Asians in the Library"—quickly attracted attention [20] and spread widely, prompting an outpouring of angry comments, reaction videos, and parodies. For example, comedic singer-songwriter Jimmy Wong produced a video in which he sang a mock love song called "Ching Chong!" in response to Wallace's video. Hundreds of videos—with millions of views—were designed to publicly shame her and others with similar racist attitudes. A college lifestyle blog dug up bikini pictures of Wallace and posted them under the title "Alexandra Wallace: Racist UCLA Student's Bikini Photos Revealed."[18] Meanwhile, Wallace—and her family—began receiving death threats, prompting her to drop out of UCLA and seek police protection. As one of her professors explained to the UCLA newspaper, "What Wallace did was hurtful and inexcusable, but the response has been far more egregious. She made a big mistake and she knows it, but they responded with greater levels of intolerance."[19]

Social media magnifies many aspects of daily life, including racism and bigotry. Some people use social media to express insensitive and hateful views, but others use the same technologies to publicly shame, and in some cases threaten, people who they feel are violating social decorum.[20] By increasing the visibility of individuals and their actions, social media doesn't simply shine a spotlight on the problematic action; it enables people to identify and harass others in a very public way. This, in turn, reinforces social divisions that plague American society.

Segregation in Everyday Life

In the United States, racism is pervasive, if not always visible. Class politics intertwine with race, adding another dimension to existing social divisions. Teens are acutely aware of the power of race and class in shaping their lives, even if they don't always have nuanced language to talk about it; furthermore, just because teens live in a culture in which racism is ever present doesn't mean that they understand how to deal with its complexities or recognize its more subtle effects. Some don't realize how a history of racism shapes what they observe. Heather, a white sixteen-year-old from Iowa, told me,

> I don't want to sound racist, but it is the black kids a lot of times that have the attitudes and are always talking back to the teachers, getting in fights around the school, starting fights around the school. I mean yeah, white kids of course get into their fights, but the black kids make theirs more public and so it's seen more often that oh, the black kids are such troublemakers.

[18] CoEd Staff, "Alexandra Wallace."
[19] Mandell, "Alexandra Wallace, UCLA Student."
[20] At times, self-appointed norm protectors seek to regulate online decorum by engaging in digital vigilantism. See Phillips and Miltner, "Internet's Vigilante Shame Army"; and Norton, "Anonymous 101."

In examining high school dynamics in the 1980s, linguist Penelope Eckert argued that schools are organized by social categories that appear on the surface to be about activities but in practice are actually about race and class.[21] I noticed this as I went through the rosters of various sports teams at a school in North Carolina. At first, when I asked students about why different sports seemed to attract students of one race exclusively, they told me that it was just what people were into. Later, one white boy sheepishly explained that he liked basketball but that, at his school, basketball was a black sport and thus not an activity that he felt comfortable doing. As a result of norms and existing networks, the sports teams in many schools I visited had become implicitly coded and culturally divided by race. Many teens are reticent to challenge the status quo.

Even in schools at which teens prided themselves on being open-minded, I found that they often ignorantly reproduced racial divisions. For example, in stereotypical fashion, teens from more privileged backgrounds would point to having friends of different races as "proof" of their openness.[22] When I asked about racial divisions in more privileged schools or in schools situated in progressive communities, I regularly heard the postracial society mantra, with teens initially telling me that race did not matter in friend groups at their school. And then we'd log in to their Facebook or MySpace page and I would find clues that their schools were quite segregated. For example, I'd find that friend networks within diverse schools would be divided by race. When I'd ask teens to explain this, they'd tell me that the divisions I was seeing were because of who was in what classes or who played what sport, not realizing that racial segregation played a role in those aspects of school life, too.

While on a work trip in Colorado, I met a group of privileged teens 25 who were in town because their parents were at the meeting I was attending. Bored with the adult conversations, I turned to the teens in a casual manner. I started talking with Kath, a white seventeen-year-old who attended an east coast private school renowned for its elite student body and its phenomenal diversity program. Our casual conversation turned to race dynamics in schools; she was a passionate, progressive teen who took the issue of race seriously. Curious to see how this played out in her community, I asked her if we could visit her Facebook page together. I offered her my computer, and she gleefully logged into her account. Given the small size of her school, I wasn't surprised that she

[21] Eckert, *Jocks and Burnouts.*

[22] The tendency for people to downplay racism by talking about how they have friends of different races is so common that it is a frame through which people look at cross-race connections. In the 2012 book *Some of My Best Friends Are Black,* Tanner Colby describes the challenges of racial integration in the United States through four different case studies. In a more comedic treatment of the same issue, comedian Baratunde Thurston dedicates an entire chapter in *How to Be Black* to "how to be the black friend." He offers entertaining advice to black readers on how they can make white people feel comfortable by taking concrete steps to be a "good" black friend.

was friends with nearly everyone from her grade and many students from other grades. I asked her to show me her photos so that we could look at the comments on them. Although her school had recruited students from diverse racial and ethnic backgrounds, most of those who had left comments on her profile were white. I pointed this out to her and asked her to bring up profiles of other students in her grade from different racial and ethnic backgrounds. In each case, the commenters were predominantly of the same broad racial or ethnic background as the profile owner. Kath was stunned and a bit embarrassed. In her head, race didn't matter at her school. But on Facebook people were spending their time interacting with people from similar racial backgrounds.

When I analyzed friending patterns on social network sites with youth, I consistently found that race mattered. In large and diverse high schools where teens didn't befriend everyone in their school, their connections alone revealed racial preference. In smaller diverse schools, the racial dynamics were more visible by seeing who commented on each other's posts or who appeared tagged together in photographs. Only when I visited schools with low levels of diversity did race not seem to matter in terms of online connections. For example, in Nebraska, I met a young Muslim woman of Middle Eastern descent in a mostly white school. She had plenty of friends online and off, and not surprisingly, all were white. Of course, this did not mean that she was living in a world where ethnic differences didn't matter. Her classmates posted many comments about Middle Eastern Muslim terrorists on Facebook with caveats about how she was different.

Birds of a feather flock together, and personal social networks tend to be homogeneous, as people are more likely to befriend others like them.[23] Sociologists refer to the practice of connecting with like-minded individuals as *homophily*. Studies have accounted for homophily in sex and gender, age, religion, education level, occupation, and social class. But nowhere is homophily more strongly visible in the United States than in the divides along racial and ethnic lines. The reasons behind the practice of homophily and the resultant social divisions are complex, rooted in a history of inequality, bigotry, oppression, and structural constraints in American life.[24]

It's easy to lament self-segregation in contemporary youth culture, but teens' choice to connect to people like them isn't necessarily born out of their personal racist beliefs. In many cases, teens reinforce homophily in order to cope with the racist society in which they live. In *Why Are All the Black Kids Sitting Together in the Cafeteria?* psychologist Beverly Tatum argues that self-segregation is a logical response to the systematized costs of racism. For teens who are facing cultural oppression and inequality, connecting along lines of race and ethnicity can

---

[23] For a discussion of homophily, including how American society is divided along racial and ethnic lines, see McPherson, Smith-Lovin, and Cook, "Birds of a Feather."

[24] See Lin, "Inequality in Social Capital."

help teens feel a sense of belonging, enhance identity development, and help them navigate systematic racism. Homophily isn't simply the product of hatred or prejudice. It is also a mechanism of safety. Seong, a seventeen-year-old from Los Angeles, echoed this sentiment when she told me, "In a way we connect more 'cause we see each other and we're like, oh." Familiarity mattered to Seong because, as a Korean immigrant, she feels isolated and confused by American norms that seem very foreign to her. She doesn't want to reject her non-Korean peers, but at times, she just wants to be surrounded by people who understand where she comes from. Still, teens' willingness to accept—and thus expect—self-segregation has problematic roots and likely contributes to ongoing racial inequality.[25]

Race-based dynamics are a fundamental part of many teens' lives—urban and suburban, rich and poor. When they go online, these fraught dynamics do not disappear. Instead, teens reproduce them. Although the technology makes it possible *in principle* to socialize with anyone online, in practice, teens connect to the people that they know and with whom they have the most in common.

MySpace vs. Facebook

In a historic small town outside Boston, I was sitting in the library of a newly formed charter school in the spring of 2007. One of the school's administrators had arranged for me to meet different students to get a sense of the school dynamics. Given what I knew about the school, I expected to meet with a diverse group of teens, but I found myself in a series of conversations with predominantly white, highly poised, academically motivated teens who were reluctant to talk about the dynamics of inequality and race at their school.

After I met a few of her peers, Kat, a white fourteen-year-old from a comfortable background, came into the library, and we started talking about the social media practices of her classmates. She made a passing remark about her friends moving from MySpace to Facebook, and I asked to discuss the reasons. Kat grew noticeably uncomfortable. She began simply, noting that "MySpace is just old now and it's boring." But then she paused, looked down at the table, and continued. "It's not really racist, but I guess you could say that. I'm not really into racism, but I think that MySpace now is more like ghetto or whatever." Her honesty startled me so I pressed to learn more. I asked her if people at her school were still using MySpace and she hesitantly said yes before stumbling over her next sentence. "The people who use MySpace—again, not in a racist way—but are usually more like ghetto and hip-hop rap lovers group." Probing a little deeper, Kat continued to stare at and fiddle with her hands as she told me that everyone who was still using

[25] Bonilla-Silva, *Racism Without Racists.*

MySpace was black, whereas all of her white peers had switched to Facebook.[26]

During the 2006–2007 school year, when MySpace was at its peak in popularity with American high school students, Facebook started to gain traction. Some teens who had never joined MySpace created accounts on Facebook. Others switched from MySpace to Facebook. Still others eschewed Facebook and adamantly stated that they preferred MySpace. The presence of two competing services would not be particularly interesting if it weren't for the makeup of the participants on each site. During that school year, as teens chose between MySpace and Facebook, race and class were salient factors in describing which teens used which service. The driving force was obvious: teens focused their attention on the site where their friends were socializing.[27] In doing so, their choices reified the race and class divisions that existed within their schools. As Anastasia, a white seventeen-year-old from New York, explained in a comment she left on my blog:

> My school is divided into the "honors kids" (I think that is self-explanatory), the "good not-so-honors kids," "wangstas" (they pretend to be tough and black but when you live in a suburb in Westchester you can't claim much hood), the "latinos/hispanics" (they tend to band together even though they could fit into any other groups) and the "emo kids" (whose lives are allllllways filled with woe). We were all in MySpace with our own little social networks but when Facebook opened its doors to high schoolers, guess who moved and guess who stayed behind. . . . The first two groups were the first to go and then the "wangstas" split with half of them on Facebook and the rest on MySpace. . . . I shifted with the rest of my school to Facebook and it became the place where the "honors kids" got together and discussed how they were procrastinating over their next AP English essay.

When I followed up with Anastasia, I learned that she felt as though it was taboo to talk about these dynamics. She stood by her comment but also told me that her sister said that she sounded racist. Although the underlying segregation of friendship networks defined who chose what site, most teens didn't use the language of race and class to describe their social network site preference. Some may have recognized that this was what was happening, but most described the division to me in terms of personal preference.

My interviews with teens included numerous descriptive taste-based judgments about each site and those who preferred them. Those who relished MySpace gushed about their ability to "pimp out" their profiles with "glitter," whereas Facebook users viewed the resultant profiles as "gaudy," "tacky," and "cluttered." Facebook fans relished the

---

[26] For a more detailed analysis of the division that emerged in the 2006–2007 school year between Facebook and MySpace, see boyd, "White Flight in Networked Publics?" Craig Watkins also documents the racialized tension between these sites in his work on youth and social media. Watkins, *The Young and the Digital.*

[27] As Siân Lincoln points out *in Youth Culture and Private Space,* teenagers use whatever platform their friends use, even if they personally prefer other platforms.

site's aesthetic minimalism, while MySpace devotees described Facebook profiles as "boring," "lame," "sterile," and "elitist." Catalina, a white fifteen-year-old from Austin, told me that Facebook is better because "Facebook just seems more clean to me." What Catalina saw as cleanliness, Indian-Pakistani seventeen-year-old Anindita from Los Angeles labeled "simple." She recognized the value of simplicity, but she preferred the "bling" of MySpace because it allowed her to express herself.

In differentiating Facebook and MySpace through taste, teens inadvertently embraced and reinforced a host of cultural factors that are rooted in the history of race and class. Taste is not simply a matter of personal preference; it is the product of cultural dynamics and social structure. In *Distinction,* philosopher Pierre Bourdieu describes how one's education and class position shape perceptions of taste and how distinctions around aesthetics and tastes are used to reinforce class in everyday life. The linguistic markers that teens use to describe Facebook and MySpace—and the values embedded in those markers—implicitly mark class and race whether teens realize it or not.

Just as most teens believe themselves to be friends with diverse groups of people, most teens give little thought to the ways in which race and class connect to taste. They judge others' tastes with little regard to how these tastes are socially constructed. Consider how Craig, a white seventeen-year-old from California, differentiated MySpace and Facebook users through a combination of social and cultural distinctions:

> The higher castes of high school moved to Facebook. It was more cultured, and less cheesy. The lower class usually were content to stick to MySpace. Any high school student who has a Facebook will tell you that MySpace users are more likely to be barely educated and obnoxious. Like Peet's is more cultured than Starbucks, and Jazz is more cultured than bubblegum pop, and like Macs are more cultured than PC's, Facebook is of a cooler caliber than MySpace.

In this 2008 blog post entitled "Myface; Spacebook," Craig distinguished between what he saw as highbrow and lowbrow cultural tastes, using consumption patterns to differentiate classes of people and describe them in terms of a hierarchy. By employing the term "caste," Craig used a multicultural metaphor with ethnic and racial connotations that runs counter to the American ideal of social mobility. In doing so, he located his peers in immutable categories defined by taste.

Not all teens are as articulate as Craig with regard to the issue of taste and class, but most recognized the cultural distinction between MySpace and Facebook and marked users according to stereotypes that they had about these sites. When Facebook became more broadly popular, teens who were early adopters of Facebook started lamenting the presence of "the MySpace people." Again, Craig described this dynamic:

> Facebook has become the exact thing it tried to destroy. Like Anikin Skywalker, who loved justice so much, and he decided to play God as Darth Vader, Facebook has lost its identity and mission. It once was

the cool, cultured thing to do, to have a Facebook, but now its the same. Girls have quizzes on their Facebooks: "Would you like to hook up with me? Yes, No" without a shred of dignity or subtlety. Again, I must scroll for 5 minutes to find the comment box on one's Facebook. The vexation of bulletins of MySpace are now replaced by those of applications. It alienated its "cultured" crowd by the addition of these trinkets.

From Craig's perspective, as Facebook became popular and mainstream, it, too, became lowbrow. The cultural distinction that existed during the 2006–2007 school year had faded, and now both sites felt "uncivilized" to Craig. He ended his post with a "desperate" plea to Google to build something "cultured."

In differentiating MySpace and Facebook as distinct cultural spaces and associating different types of people with each site, teens used technology to reinforce cultural distinctions during the time in which both sites were extraordinarily popular. These distinctions, far from being neutral, are wedded to everyday cultural markers. In constituting an "us" in opposition to "them," teens reinforce social divisions through their use of and attitudes toward social media. Even as teens espouse their tolerance toward others with respect to embodied characteristics, they judge their peers' values, choices, and tastes along axes that are rooted in those very characteristics.

The racial divide that these teens experienced as they watched their classmates choose between MySpace and Facebook during the 2006–2007 school year is one that happens time and again in technology adoption. In some cases, white teens use different technologies than teens of color. For example, Black and Latino urban youth embraced early smartphones like the Sidekick, but the device had limited traction among Asian, white, and suburban youth. In other cases, diverse populations adopt a particular tool, but practices within the service are divided along race and class lines. Such was the case in 2013 on both Facebook and Twitter, where teens' linguistic and visual conventions— as well as their choice of apps—were correlated with their race.[28]

People influence the technology practices of those around them. 40 Because of this, the diffusion of technology often has structural features that reflect existing social networks. As teens turn to social media to connect with their friends, they consistently reproduce networks that reflect both the segregated realities of everyday life and the social and economic inequalities that exist within their broader peer networks. Teens go online to hang out with their friends, and given the segregation of American society, their friends are quite likely to be of the same race, class, and cultural background.

---

[28] Black and African American individuals are overrepresented on Twitter compared to their participation online more generally. Scholars have begun analyzing a practice known colloquially as "Black Twitter," referring both to the significant presence of black users as well as how practices and norms in Twitter appear to differ across race lines. See Brock, "From the Blackhand Side"; and Florini, "Tweets, Tweeps, and Signifyin'."

Networks Matter

The fact that social media reproduces—and makes visible—existing social divisions within American society should not be surprising, but it does challenge a persistent fantasy that the Internet will dissolve and dismantle inequalities and create new opportunities to bring people together across race and class lines. In 2010, Secretary of State Hillary Rodham Clinton espoused such idealism in a speech at the Newseum[29] in which she argued: "The Internet can serve as a great equalizer. By providing people with access to knowledge and potential markets, networks can create opportunity where none exists. . . . Information networks have become a great leveler, and we should use them to help lift people out of poverty."[30] This rhetoric assumes that, because the Internet makes information more readily available to more people than ever before, access to the Internet will address historical informational and social inequities. Yet just because people have access to the Internet does not mean that they have equal access to information. Information literacy is not simply about the structural means of access but also about the experience to know where to look, the skills to interpret what's available, and the knowledge to put new pieces of information into context. In a world where information is easily available, strong personal networks and access to helpful people often matter more than access to the information itself.[31]

In a technological era defined by social media, where information flows through networks and where people curate information for their peers, who you know shapes what you know. "When social divisions get reinforced online, information inequities also get reproduced. When increased access to information produces information overload, sifting through the mounds of available information to make meaning requires time and skills. Those whose networks are vetting information and providing context are more privileged in this information landscape than those whose friends and family have little experience doing such information work.[32]

For many information needs, people turn to people around them. Sociologists have shown that social networks affect people's job prospects, health, and happiness.[33] Opportunities for social and economic support depend heavily on personal connections. Teens turn to their

---

[29]**Newseum:** An interactive journalism museum in Washington, DC. [Eds.]

[30]Clinton, "Internet Freedom."

[31]Scholars and government agencies have pointed out that technology uptake is often dependent on contextual relevance. When it comes to information and communication technologies, people are often more likely to appreciate their value when they see others use them in beneficial ways. If people's personal networks aren't using particular technologies, they often see no reason to use them. See Haddon, "Social Exclusion and Information and Communication'Technologies"; and Federal Communications Commission, *National Broadband Plan.*

[32]Hargittai, "Digital Reproduction of Inequality."

[33]For a sampling of relevant studies on social networks, see Fischer, *To Dwell Among Friends;* Granovetter, "Strength of Weak Ties"; Lin, *Social Capital;* and Wellman, *Networks in the Global Village.*

networks to learn about college opportunities. They also develop a sense of what's normative by watching those who surround them. When it comes to information and opportunity, who youth know matters. Just because teens can get access to a technology that can connect them to anyone anywhere does not mean that they have equal access to knowledge and opportunity.[34]

In his famous trilogy *The Information Age*, sociologist Manuel Castells argued that the industrial era is ending and that an information age has begun. His first volume—*The Rise of the Network Society*—makes the case for the power of networks as the organizational infrastructure of an economy based on information. Technology plays a central role in the network society that Castells recognizes is unfolding, and he documents the technological divide that put certain cities in better or worse positions to leverage the economic changes taking place. Although critics have accused Castells of technological determinism, Castells's analysis is more fruitfully understood as a critical accounting of what economic and cultural shifts are possible because of technology and why not everyone will benefit equally from these shifts.[35] In short, not everyone will benefit equally because networks—both social and technical—are neither evenly distributed nor meritocratic.

Social media does not radically rework teens' social networks. As a result, technology does not radically reconfigure inequality. The transformative potential of the Internet to restructure social networks in order to reduce structural inequality rests heavily on people's ability to leverage it to make new connections. This is not how youth use social media.

Not only are today's teens reproducing social dynamics online, but they are also heavily discouraged from building new connections that would diversify their worldviews. "Stranger danger" rhetoric doesn't just affect teens' interactions with adults; many teens are actively discouraged from developing relationships with other teens online for fear that those teens may turn out to be adults intending to harm them. Not all teens buy into this moral panic, but when teens do make connections online, they focus on engaging with people who share their interests, tastes, and cultural background. For these teens, turning to people who seem familiar allows them to feel safe, confident, and secure. They reinforce the homophilous social networks they inhabit instead of using technology to connect across lines of difference. Access to a wide range of people does not guarantee a reconfiguration of social connections.

The limited scope of teens' engagement with people from diverse backgrounds—and the pressure that they receive to not engage with strangers—is particularly costly for less privileged youth. Although everyone benefits from developing a heterogeneous social network,

---

[34] In *Invisible Users*, Jenna Burrell makes the issues of structural inequality especially visible in her study of Ghanaian youth. Although these youth have access to information technologies, the social networks in which they operate—and the norms that exist in their home communities—complicate their ability to connect successfully and meaningfully with more powerful users.

[35] Webster, *Theories of the Information Society*; Webster, "Information and Urban Change"; Garnham, *Information Society Theory as Ideology*.

privileged youth are more likely to have connections to people with more privilege and greater access to various resources, opportunities, and types of information. When information opportunities are tethered to social networks, how social relations are constructed matters for every aspect of social equality. When social divisions are reinforced—and inequities across social networks reproduced—there are material, social, and cultural consequences.

The issue of inequality gets realized when information is structured to flow only to certain groups of people. During the 2006–2007 school year—the period when teens were segmenting themselves into Facebook and MySpace—many college admissions officers also started using social media for college recruitment. They created online profiles, produced spreadable videos, and invited high school students to talk with them and student representatives. Although millions of teenagers were active exclusively on MySpace, most of the colleges tailored their recruitment efforts to Facebook. When I asked admissions officers about their decision to focus on Facebook, they invariably highlighted a lack of resources and a need to prioritize. Universally, when I pointed out that black and Latino youth were more likely to be on MySpace and that their decision was effectively targeting primarily white and Asian students, they were stunned. They had never considered the cultural consequences of their choices.

Today it's quite common for companies to turn to LinkedIn, a professional social network site, to recruit college interns and new graduates. Recruiters typically prioritize candidates who already have contacts to the company as performed through social media. Some even explicitly ask applicants to list everyone they know who already works at the company. Those who don't know anyone at the company are disadvantaged as candidates. This tends to reinforce same-ness because people's social networks are rarely diverse. This also provides an additional obstacle for underrepresented minorities, those who come from less advantaged communities, and people who generally lack social capital.

We don't live in a postracial society, and social media is not the cultural remedy that some people hoped it would become. Today's youth live in a world with real and pervasive social divisions. Those dynamics are reproduced online and have significant implications for how teens make sense of public life. People help define what's normative for their friends and contacts. And everyone's opportunities are dependent on whom they know. Having access to the information available through the Internet is not enough to address existing structural inequities and social divisions. The Internet will not inherently make the world more equal, nor will it automatically usher today's youth into a tolerant world. Instead, it lays bare existing and entrenched social divisions.

50

Bibliography

Bonilla-Silva, Eduardo. *Racism without Racists: Color-Blind Racism and the Persistence of Racial Inequality in America*. Lanham, MD: Rowman and Littlefield, 2006.

boyd, danah. "White Flight in Networked Publics? How Race and Class Shaped American Teen Engagement with MySpace and Facebook." In *Race after the Internet*, ed. Lisa Nakamura and Peter Chow-White, 203–22. New York: Routledge, 2011.

Briggs, Charles F. and Augustus Maverick. *The Story of the Telegraph and a History of the Great Atlantic Cable*. New York: Rudd and Carleton, 1858.

Brock, André. "From the Blackhand Side: Twitter as a Cultural Conversation." *Journal of Broadcasting and Electronic Media* 56 (2012): 529–49.

Burrell, Jenna. *Invisible Users: Youth in the Internet Cafes of Urban Ghana*. Cambridge, MA: MIT Press, 2012.

Christopherson, Kimberly M. "The Positive and Negative Implications of Anonymity in Internet Social Interactions: 'On The Internet, Nobody Knows You're a Dog.'" *Computers in Human Behavior* 23 (2007): 3038–56.

Clinton, Hillary Rodham. "Internet Freedom." Speech presented at the Newseum, January 21, 2010, http://www.foreignpolicy.com/articles/2010/01/21/internet_freedom.

CoEd Staff. "Alexandra Wallace: Racist UCLA Student's Bikini Photos Revealed." *CoEd Magazine*, March 14, 2011, http://www.foreignpolicy.com/articles/2011/03/14/alexandra-wallace-racist-ucla-students-bikini-photos-revealed-26-pics/.

Colby, Tanner. *Some of My Best Friends Are Black*. New York: Viking, 2012.

Daniels, Jessie. *Cyber Racism: White Supremacy Online and the New Attack on Civil Rights*. Lanham, MD: Rowman and Littlefield, 2009.

Eckert, Penelope. *Jocks and Burnouts: Social Categories and Identity in High School*. New York: Teachers College Press, 1989.

Federal Communications Commission. *The National Broadband Plan: Connecting America*. Washington, DC: Federal Communications Commission, 2010.

Fischer, Claude S. *America Calling: A Social History of the Telephone to 1940*. Berkeley: University of California Press, 1992.

Florini, Sarah. "Tweets, Tweeps, and Signifyin': Communication and Cultural Performance on 'Black Twitter.'" *Television New Media*, March 7, 2013, http://tvn.sagepub.com/content/early/2013/03/07/1527476413480247.

Haddon, Leslie. "Social Exclusion and Information and Communication Technologies: Lessons from Studies of Single Parents and the Young Elderly." *New Media and Society* 2 (2000): 387–406.

Hargittai, Eszter, "Digital Na(t)ives? Variation in Internet Skills and Uses among Members of the 'Net Generation.'" *Sociological Inquiry* 80 (2010): 92–113.

Kendall, Lori. "Meaning and Identity in 'Cyberspace': The Performance of Gender, Class, and Race." *Symbolic Interaction* 21, no. 2 (1998): 129–53.

Kolko, Beth E., Lisa Nakamura, and Gilbert B. Rodman. "Race in Cyberspace: An Introduction." In *Race in Cyberspace*, ed. Beth E. Kolko, Lisa Nakamura, and Gilbert B. Rodman, 1–14. New York: Routledge, 2000.

Lin, Nan. "Inequality in Social Capital." *Contemporary Sociology* 29, no. 6 (2000): 785–95.

Lincoln, Siân. *Youth Culture and Private Space*. London: Palgrave Macmillan, 2012.

Mandell, Nina. "Alexandra Wallace, UCLA Student Who Created Offensive Viral Video, Withdrawing from School." NYDailyNews.com, March 19, 2011, http://www.nydailynews.com/news/national/alexandra-wallace-ucla-student-created-offensive-viral-video-withdrawing-school-article-1.119105.

McPherson, Miller, Lynn Smith-Lovin, and James M. Cook. "Birds of a Feather: Homophily in Social Networks." *Annual Review of Sociology* 27 (2001): 415–44.

Nakamura, Lisa. *Digitizing Race: Visual Cultures of the Internet*. Minneapolis: University of Minnesota Press, 2008.

———. "Don't Hate the Player, Hate the Game: The Racialization of Labor in World of Warcraft." *Critical Studies in Media Communication* 26, no. 2 (2009): 128–44.

Phillips, Whitney, and Kate Miltner. "The Internet's Vigilante Shame Army." *Awl.* December 19, 2012, http://www.theawl.com/2012/12/the-internets-vigilante-shame -army.

Saraceno, Jon. "Swiss Soccer Player Banned from Olympics for Racist Tweet." *USA Today*, July 30, 2012, http://usatoday30.usatoday.com/sports/olympics/london /soccer/story/2012-07-30/swiss-athlete-banned-michel-morganella-olympics/5659 1966/1.

Sinclair, Brendan. "Kinect Has Problems Recognizing Dark-Skinned Users?" *Game-spot*, November 3, 2010, http://www.gamespot.com/articles/kinect-has-problems -recognizing-dark-skinned-users/1100-6283514/.

Smith, Catherine. "Google CEO Eric Schmidt's Most Controversial Quotes about Privacy." *Huffington Post*, November 4, 2010, http://www.huffingtonpost.com /2010/11/04/google-ceo-eric-schmidt-privacy_n_776924.html.

Steiner, Peter. "On the Internet, Nobody Knows You're a Dog." Cartoon, *New Yorker*, July 5, 1993.

Stewart, Christopher S. "Obsessed with the Internet: A Tale from China." *Wired*, January 13, 2010, http://www.wired.com/2010/01/ff_internetaddiction/.

Watkins, Craig S. *The Young and the Digital: What the Migration to Social Network Sites, Games, and Anytime, Anywhere Media Means for Our Future.* Boston: Beacon, 2009.

Webster, Frank. "Information and Urban Change: Manuel Castells." In *Manuel Castells*, vol. 2, ed. Frank Webster and Basil Dimitriou, 15–39. London: Sage, 2004.

Wellman, Barry. *Networks in the Global Village: Life in Contemporary Communities.* Boulder, CO: Westview, 1999.

Zax, David. "Siri, Why Can't You Understand Me?" Fast Company, December 7, 2011, http://www.fastcompany.com/1799374/siri-why-cant-you-understand-me.

ENGAGING THE TEXT

1. What kinds of racial, class, or cultural "neighborhoods" did the students in your high school divide into? Do you see evidence of such self-segregation among the students at your college, or does your experience suggest that we are moving beyond the need to "stick with our own races" (para. 7)? What factors beyond racism might explain the continued existence of such "neighborhoods"?

2. How, according to boyd, do students "maintain the same systems of segregation online and off" (para. 6)? How segregated are the online worlds of most teens? How segregated are the online lives of you and your fellow college students? What evidence have you seen that students of different racial and class backgrounds use different technological devices and different forms of social media?

3. Boyd claims that "cultural prejudice permeates social media" (para. 13). What examples of "hateful epithets" and "hatemongering" have you observed on social media sites? Does your own experience suggest that social media simply magnify and reinforce "divisions that plague American society" (para. 21)?

4. Why does boyd think that increased access to technology will not give all students equal access to information? In her view, how do colleges reinforce the inequities created by the uneven distribution of social and technological networks? What do you think could be done to address this inequity?

5. **Thinking Rhetorically** On her Web site (http://www.danah.org), boyd explains that she doesn't capitalize her name for a number of personal and political

reasons. She notes, for example, that "English is the only major language where 'I' is capitalized" and declares that she should have the right to "own" her name and write it as she wants, and not as dictated by the *New York Times* or some other guide to standard English. What nicknames or pseudonyms do you use on- and offline? How did you decide on using them, and why do you feel they're appropriate for the contexts you use them in? What, if any, political meaning do they have, and why?

EXPLORING CONNECTIONS

6. How might Sherry Turkle's analysis of teens' online identities and self-representations (p. 236) help explain why students tend to segregate themselves on social media? How might Turkle explain why teens sometimes express intolerant attitudes online that they would normally shun or repress in face-to-face interactions?

7. How does Charles Seife's exploration of "narrowcasting" and "solipsism" on the Internet (p. 289) help explain the racial segregation that boyd notes in teens' use of social media? Given boyd's analysis of teens' online behavior, would you expect them to be more or less vulnerable than adults to extremist Web sites, and why?

8. Review your notes on the selections by boyd, Sherry Turkle (p. 236), and Charles Seife (p. 289), and write a journal entry or paper on the Internet and narcissism. How does social networking isolate us from people who don't resemble us? To what extent does access to social media work to reduce or increase prejudice and intolerance?

EXTENDING THE CRITICAL CONTEXT

9. Inventory the diversity of your own social network sites. What percentage of your online friends are members of your own racial group, gender, or economic class? To what extent is your online life more or less inclusive than your life at school or work? Compare your findings in class and discuss whether the Internet promotes or works against intergroup contact and understanding.

GEORGE ORWELL...MEET MARK ZUCKERBERG

LORI ANDREWS

In the novel *1984*, George Orwell envisions a nightmare society where "Big Brother" controls every move his citizens make. The "Thought Police" in Orwell's dystopian masterwork keep the population under constant surveillance through the use of "telescreens," two-way televisions that report every action and conversation directly to the authorities. Today Orwell's warnings about the dangerous combination of technology and totalitarian control may seem more relevant than ever. As Lori Andrews explains in this selection, social networks and smartphones are funneling our personal information to "data aggregators," massive companies that track every aspect of our lives online, from the things we "like" — or "don't like" — to the Web sites we search and the e-mail we send our friends. The result is the creation of a virtual "double" of every American, a second online self that marketers, businesses, and employers can use when making crucial decisions about our future opportunities and choices. Andrews (b. 1953) is Distinguished Professor of Law and Director of the Institute for Science, Law, and Technology at the Illinois Institute of Technology. An internationally recognized expert on biotechnology and the legal aspects of genetic engineering, she has published ten books, including *Future Perfect: Confronting Decisions About Genetics* (2001), *Genetics: Ethics, Law and Policy* (2002), and *I Know Who You Are and I Saw What You Did: Social Networks and the Death of Privacy* (2011) the source of this selection.

ON A SUNDAY MORNING, I fire up my laptop and compose a memo to my co-counsel about a pro bono case we are considering filing against a biotechnology company. I attach it to an e-mail and send it to him, carefully writing, "Confidential—Legal Mail" in the subject line and putting a few key ideas in the text of the e-mail. Then I log on to the Southwest Airlines site, enter my credit card information, and buy a ticket for Florida. I enter a governmental Web site, run by the Florida Fish and Wildlife Conservation Commission, and type in my Social Security number to obtain a fishing license. I realize I'll be away on my sister's birthday and send her some books from Amazon. I check my e-mails and click through to a Web site that lists job openings for university professors. One is in a town I haven't heard of, so I Google it to find out if it will be urban enough for me. The town's name brings up a link to a local newspaper article about a poisoning and I save that information to my hard drive, thinking I might use it in the next mystery book I write. I read an e-mail from my doctor telling me she changed my prescription electronically and the new drug is waiting for me at my neighborhood CVS. Before leaving the house to pick it up, I log on to Facebook to contact friends in Florida and let them know when I'll arrive. Elsewhere on my Facebook page, I check my news feed and indicate I liked the movie I saw the previous night. Someone has tagged me in a Halloween photo from years ago, when I was a Yale undergrad. I am wearing a belly dancer's costume and I am with someone dressed like a bottle of Imperial Single Malt Scotch. I untag myself from the photo. If I do interview for a new job, I don't want someone to say to me, "Well, Ruth Bader Ginsburg[1] would never have shown her navel."

---

[1] **Ruth Bader Ginsburg:** Ruth Joan Bader Ginsburg (b. 1933) is an Associate Justice of the U.S. Supreme Court. [All notes are Andrews's except 1, the addendum to 7, 10, and 51.]

All in all, I feel good about the security of my morning's travels across the Web. I haven't responded to any wealthy widows seeking my legal help for their $50 million estates, nor to e-mails purportedly from friends whose wallets and passports were stolen in London. I haven't given my credit card to anyone with a sketchy foreign e-mail address who offers me an iPad for $30, nor have I opened the missive that tells me I've exceeded my e-mail limit. I've only dealt with Web sites I trust.

But every action I've taken has been surreptitiously chronicled and analyzed by data aggregators, who then sell the information to companies, including perhaps the one I am contemplating suing. And not only have I not been informed about this invasion of my privacy and security, there's almost nothing I can do about it.

That stunning fact is completely at odds with the offline world. I care deeply about the type of information I've entered. I wouldn't leave my Social Security number or my credit card number lying on my desk at work where someone could copy it—nor would I send that information on a postcard through the mail. I wouldn't broadcast my medical condition or my desire to find a new job to the world. But that information about me is bought and sold daily by corporations that deal with data aggregators.

If someone broke into my home and copied my documents, he'd be guilty of trespass and invasion of privacy. If the cops wanted to wiretap my conversation, they'd need a warrant. But without our knowledge or consent, virtually every entry we make on a social network or other Web site is surreptitiously being tracked and assessed. The information is just as sensitive. The harms are just as real. But the law is not as protective.

The guiding force behind this enormous theft of private information is behavioral advertising. The covert collection of personal information is an exploding industry, fueled in part by the lust of advertisers for personal data about people's habits and desires. "Online behavioral advertising," notes the Federal Trade Commission, "involves the tracking of consumers' online activities in order to deliver tailored advertising. The practice, which is typically invisible to consumers, allows businesses to align their ads more closely to the inferred interests of their audience."[2] But the unregulated amassing of personal information about people has also been used in ways that cause them harm.

Behavioral advertising was used by 85% of ad agencies in 2010.[3] They're drawn to it because it works—63% of ad agencies say targeted ads increased their revenue, with 30% of agencies reporting that behavioral advertising increased their revenue by $500,000 or more.

[2]Federal Trade Commission, "FTC Staff Report: Self-Regulatory Principles for Online Behavioral Advertising—Behavioral Advertising: Tracking, Targeting, & Technology," 2009 WL 361109 at 4 (February 2009).

[3]Audience Science Press Release, "State of Audience Targeting Industry Study: 50% of Advertisers Set to Boost Spending on Audience Targeting in 2011," Jan. 11, 2011, www.audiencescience.com/uk/press-room/press-releases/2011/state-audience-targeting-industry-study-50-advertisers-set-boost-spen.

In 2010, Internet advertising revenues exceeded that of newspapers by $3.2 billion.[4] During the first quarter of 2010, Internet users in the United States received 1.1 trillion display ads, which cost the ad sponsors about $2.7 billion.[5]

"It's a digital data vacuum cleaner on steroids, that's what the online ad industry has created," Jeff Chester, executive director of the Center for Digital Democracy, told *The New York Times*. "They're tracking where your mouse is on the page, what you put in your shopping cart, what you don't buy. A very sophisticated commercial surveillance system has been put in place."[6]

It's through data aggregation that Facebook makes its money. Facebook sits on a mountain of information worth a fortune. It's expected that in 2012 Facebook will be valued at $100 billion.[7] Currently the company generates most of its revenue by acting as an intermediary between advertisers and its database of users' personal information. Facebook will use information about my status, likes and dislikes, and the recent post about my travel plans to update its digital portrait of me. When an airline or outdoor clothing company pays Facebook to post an ad for traveling adults, Facebook will use its new information about me to post the ad on my Facebook page. This commercialization of my private data—the information I think I'm only posting to friends—is the reason Facebook earned an estimated $1.86 billion in 2010 from the display ads, 90% of its total revenue, and was expected to bring in $4.05 billion in advertising revenue the following year.[8]

Facebook uses its citizens' demographic information, interests, likes, friends, Web sites frequented, and even contact information as the foundation of its advertising platform. Facebook encourages users to disclose more information about themselves through "very powerful game-like mechanisms to reward disclosure," said media activist Cory Doctorow, co-editor of Boing Boing.[9] Doctorow compares Facebook's mechanisms to the famous Skinner box[10] used in psychology experiments.[11] But instead of a lab rat rewarded with a food pellet each time it pushes a lever in the box, a Facebook user is rewarded with "likes"

10

---

[4]Internet Advertising Bureau, Internet Advertising Revenue Report, 2010 Full Year Results, April 2011, www.iab.net/insights_research/947883/adrevenuereport.

[5]ComScore Press Release, "Americans Received 1 Trillion Display Ads in Q1 2010 as Online Advertising Market Rebounds from 2009 Recession," May 13, 2010, www.comscore.com/Press_Events/Press_Releases/2010/5/Americans_Received_1_Trillion_Display_Ads_in_Q1_2010_as_Online_Advertising_Market_Rebounds_from_2009_Recession.

[6]Louise Story, "F.T.C. to Review Online Ads and Privacy," *The New York Times*, Nov. 1, 2007, at C1, www.nytimes.com/2007/11/01/technology/01Privacy.html?ref=technology.

[7]Nicholas Carlson, "Facebook Expected to File for $100 Billion IPO This Year," June 13, 2011, www.businessinsider.com/facebook-ipo-could-come-in-q1-2012-after-october-filing-cnbc-reports-2011-6. [As of February 1, 2016, Facebook was valued at $328 billion.—Eds.]

[8]Stephanie Reese, "Quick Stat: Facebook to Bring in $4.05 Billion in Ad Revenues This Year," April 26, 2011, www.emarketer.com/blog/index.php/tag/facebook-ad-revenue/.

[9]Cory Doctorow, Talk at TEDx Observer, 2011, http://tedxtalks.ted.com/video/TEDx Observer-Cory-Doctorow.

[10]**Skinner box:** A laboratory apparatus designed by behavioral psychologist B.F. Skinner (1904–1990), used to test stimulus-response conditioning on animals. [Eds.]

[11]Doctorow, Talk at TEDx Observer.

and attention from friends and family each time that person posts more information.

"And this is not there because Facebook thinks that disclosing information is good for you necessarily," says Doctorow. "It's in service to a business model that cashes in on the precious material of our social lives and trades it for pennies."

But the collection and marketing of personal information are far more insidious, and profitable, than just the actions of Facebook. Mark Zuckerberg's brainchild makes up only 14.6% of the behavioral advertising market. And some of the other advertisers use tactics that make Zuckerberg's seem tame. Every single action I undertook that Sunday morning was potentially seized by a data aggregator through some means or another. In California, consumers are suing the company NebuAd, which contracted with 26 Internet service providers, including Delaware's Cable One, New York's Bresnan Communications, and Texas's CenturyTel, to install NebuAd's hardware on those Internet service providers' networks without ISP users' consent.[12] The hardware allowed NebuAd to use deep packet inspection—a mechanism to intercept and copy all the online transmissions of the ISPs' subscribers and transmit them to NebuAd's headquarters.[13] All of them.

Everything you post on a social network or other Web site is being digested, analyzed, and monetized. In essence, a second self—a virtual interpretation of you—is being created from the detritus of your life that exists on the Web. Increasingly, key decisions about you are based on that distorted image of you. Whether you get a mortgage, a kidney, a lover, or a job may be determined by your digital alter ego rather than by you.

In the late 1960s, sociologist John McKnight, then Director of the Midwest Office of the U.S. Commission on Civil Rights,[14] coined the term "redlining" to describe the failure of banks, supermarkets, insurers, and other institutions to offer their services in inner-city neighborhoods.[15] The term came from the practice of banks, which drew a red line on a map to indicate where they wouldn't invest.[16] But use of the term expanded to cover a wide array of racially discriminatory practices in general, such as not offering home loans to African Americans, even if they were wealthy or middle class.

Now the map used in redlining is not a geographic map but the map of your travels across the Web. A new term, "weblining," covers the practice of denying certain opportunities to people due to observations

---

[12]Complaint at 2, *Valentine v. NebuAd, Inc.*, No. C08-05113 TEH (N.D. Cal. Nov. 10, 2008); Karl Bode, "Infighting at ISPs over Using NebuAD," May 29, 2008, www.dslreports .com/shownews/Infighting-At-ISPs-Over-Using-NebuAD-94835; *Valentine* v. *NebuAd, Inc.*, 2011 WL 1296111 (N.D. Cal. 2011).

[13]Complaint at 2, *Valentine v. NebuAd, Inc.*, No. C08-05113 TEH (N.D. Cal. Nov. 10, 2008).

[14]John L. McKnight, Curriculum Vita, www.northwestern.edu/ipr/people/jlmvita.pdf.

[15]Shirley Sagawa and Eli Segal, *Common Interest, Common Good: Creating Value Through Business and Social Sector Partnerships* (Boston: Harvard Business Press, 2000), 30.

[16]D. Bradford Hunt, "Redlining," The Electronic Encyclopedia of Chicago, www .encyclopedia.chicagohistory.org/pages/1050.html.

about their digital selves. Sometimes redlining and weblining overlap, such as when a Web site uses zip code information from a social network or an online purchase elsewhere to deny a person an opportunity or charge him a higher interest rate.

"There's an anti-democratic nuance to all of this," says New York University sociologist Marshall Blonsky. "If I am Weblined and judged to be of minimal value, I will never have the products and services channeled to me—or the economic opportunities—that flow to others over the Net."[17]

Data aggregation is big business. The behemoth in the industry, Acxiom, has details on everything from your Social Security number and finances to your online habits.[18] Its former CEO, John Meyer, described it as "the biggest company you've never heard of."[19] Rapleaf is another data aggregator that combines online data, including usernames and social networks, and offline data from public records.[20] One of its competitors, ChoicePoint, has acquired more than 70 smaller database companies and will sell clients one file that contains an individual's credit report, motor vehicle history, police files, property records, court records, birth and death certificates, and marriage and divorce decrees.[21] Yet ChoicePoint didn't do a great job of keeping that information secure. In 2005, identity thieves who submitted false applications to ChoicePoint claiming to be small businesses were given access to ChoicePoint's database that contained financial records of more than 163,000 consumers.[22] The Federal Trade Commission attributed the security breach to a lack of proper security and record handling procedures and, as part of a settlement with ChoicePoint, required the company to implement a comprehensive information security program and to pay $10 million in civil penalties and $5 million to reimburse the consumers affected by the identity theft.[23] That same year, hackers targeted LexisNexis (an aggregator which later bought ChoicePoint for $4.1 billion in cash), and accessed the personal information of 310,000 customers.[24]

Weblining goes further than traditional redlining. Sometimes an individual's credit card limit is lowered, midcourse, based on data from

[17]Marcia Stepanek, "Weblining," April 3, 2000, www.businessweek.com/2000/00_14/b3675027.htm.

[18]David Goldman, "These Data Miners Know Everything About You," Dec. 16, 2010, http://money.cnn.com/galleries/2010/technology/1012/gallery.data_miners/index.html.

[19]Rowena Mason, "Acxiom: the Company That Knows If You Own a Cat or If You're Right-Handed," April 27, 2009, www.telegraph.co.uk/finance/newsbysector/retailand consumer/5231752/Acxiom-the-company-that-knows-If-You-own-a-cat-or-If-youre-right-handed.html.

[20]Goldman, "These Data Miners Know Everything About You."

[21]Ian Ayres, Super Crunchers (New York: Bantam Dell, 2007), 134.

[22]Complaint at 4, U.S. v. ChoicePoint, No. 06-CV-0198 (N.D. Ga. Jan. 30, 2006).

[23]Ibid at 4-6; Stipulated Final Judgment and Order for Civil Penalties, Permanent Injunction, and Other Equitable Relief, U.S. v. ChoicePoint, No. 06-CV-0198 (N.D. Ga. Feb. 10, 2006).

[24]Marcia Savage, "LexisNexis Security Breach Worse Than Thought," April 12, 2005, www.scmagazineus.com/lexisnexis-security-breach-worse-than-thought/article/31977/; Toby Anderson, "LexisNexis Owner Reed Elsevier Buys Choice-Point," Feb. 21, 2008, www.usatoday.com/money/industries/2008-02-21-reed-choicepoint_N.htm.

aggregators, even when the cardholder has done nothing wrong. Kevin Johnson, a condo owner and businessman, held an American Express card with a $10,800 limit. When he returned from his honeymoon, he found that the limit had been lowered to $3,800. The switch was not based on anything Kevin had done but on aggregate data. A letter from the company told him: "Other customers who have used their card at establishments where you recently shopped have a poor repayment history with American Express."[25]

Not only does weblining affect what opportunities are offered to you (in the form of advertisements, discounts, and credit lines), it also affects the types of information you see. When you open Yahoo! News or go to other news Web sites, you get a personalized set of articles, different from your spouse's or neighbor's. That may sound like a good thing, but you may be losing out on the big picture. With the physical version of The New York Times, you'd at least see the headlines about what was going on in the world, even if you were skimming the paper to get to the movie reviews. But world news may disappear entirely from your browser if you have indicated an interest in something else. Ever since I clicked on a story about the royal wedding, the world news stories I used to receive when I logged on to my e-mail have been replaced by celebrity breakup and fashion stories. But if we are all reading a different, narrow range of articles, how can we participate in a civic democracy?

"Ultimately, democracy works only if we citizens are capable of   20 thinking beyond our narrow self-interest. But to do so, we need a shared view of the world we cohabit," says Eli Pariser in The Filter Bubble: What the Internet Is Hiding from You. Pariser explains that the Internet initially seemed like the perfect tool for democracy. But now, he points out, "Personalization has given us something very different: a public sphere sorted and manipulated by algorithms, fragmented by design, and hostile to dialogue."[26]

Most people have no idea how much information is collected surreptitiously about them from social networks and other Web sites. When asked about behavioral advertising, only half of the participants in a 2010 study believed that it was a common practice.[27] One respondent said, "Behavioral advertising sounds like something my paranoid friend would dream up, but not something that would ever really occur in real life."

People have a misplaced trust that what they post is private: A Consumer Reports poll found that "61% of Americans are confident that

[25]Chris Cuomo, Jay Shaylor, Mary McGuirt, and Chris Francescani, "'GMA' Gets Answers: Some Credit Card Companies Financially Profiling Customers," Jan. 28, 2009, http://abcnews.go.com/GMA/GetsAnswers/Story?id=6747461.
[26]Eli Pariser, The Filter Bubble: What the Internet Is Hiding from You (New York: Penguin, 2011), 164.
[27]Aleecia M. McDonald and Lorrie F. Cranor, "Americans' Attitudes About Internet Behavioral Advertising Practices," Proceedings of the 9th Workshop on Privacy in the Electronic Society WPES, Oct. 4, 2010, 6.

what they do online is private and not shared without their permission" and that "57% incorrectly believe that companies must identify themselves and indicate why they are collecting data and whether they intend to share it with other organizations."[28]

When people realize that Web sites and advertising companies are collecting extensive information about them, many want legal change. A telephone survey found that 66% of adult Americans opposed being targeted by behavioral advertising and are troubled by the technologies used to enable it.[29] Also, 68% of Americans opposed being "followed" on the Web and 70% of Americans supported the idea of requiring hefty fines to be paid by a company that collects or uses someone's information without his or her consent. Most people—92%—believe that Web sites and advertising companies should be required to delete all information stored about an individual if requested to do so.

Your ability to protect yourself against unwanted data collection depends largely on the technique being used to acquire information. With some methods, companies use your own computer against you by instructing your Internet browser to store information on your computer's hard drive that data aggregators can use to track your movement online and build a profile of your online behaviors. Other methods tap the information as it travels from your computer to the recipient's Web site or e-mail address.

The collection of information from Web sites and social networks began modestly enough. Social networks asked you if you'd like to have your password stored. Web sites like Amazon.com began to keep track of your purchases on their sites to make recommendations and to allow you the convenience of not re-entering a password or credit card number each time you visit the site. Now tracking technologies with names like cookies, Flash cookies, web beacons, deep packet inspection, data scraping, and search queries allow advertisers to create a picture of you by noting what you look at, look up, and buy across the Internet. Sometimes this information is even linked to offline purchases and activities you engage in.

. . . I had no idea that Comcast, my Internet service provider, installed more than a hundred tracking tools.[30] Dictionary.com (one of my favorite Web sites, which I use more often than Facebook) installed 234 tracking tools on a user's computer without permission, only 11 from Dictionary.com itself and 223 from companies that track Internet

---

[28] "Consumer Reports Poll: Americans Extremely Concerned About Internet Privacy," Sep. 25, 2008, www.consumersunion.org/pub/core_telecom_and_utilities/006189.html.

[29] Joseph Turow, Jennifer King, Chris Jay Hoofnagle, Amy Bleakley, and Michael Hennessy, "Contrary to What Marketers Say, Americans Reject Tailored Advertising and Three Activities That Enable It," September 2009, at 3, www.ftc.gov/os/comments/privacy roundtable/544506-00113.pdf.

[30] Julia Angwin and Tom McGinty, "Sites Feed Personal Details to New Tracking Industry," The Wall Street Journal, July 30, 2010, at A1, http://online.wsj.com/article/SB10 001424052748703977004575393173432219064.html.

users.[31] The vast majority of these tools, according to a report by *The Wall Street Journal*, did not allow users to decline tracking. Among the 50 top sites assessed in this study by *The Wall Street Journal*, Dictionary.com "ranked highest in exposing users to potentially aggressive surveillance."

Increasingly ingenious and troubling technologies are used to learn ever more about you. Two apps on the iPhone and Android devices— Color and Shopkick—activate your phone's microphone and camera to collect background sound and light patterns from your location, be it a bar, your office, or your home. Using the same type of program that allows your iPhone to name a song based on just a few notes, Color makes assessments about your location to alert you if other people in your social network are nearby and Shopkick assesses if the store you've entered has a bargain to offer you. Silicon Valley blogger Mike Elgan points out the wealth of information marketers can collect about you through these phone apps: "Your gender, and the gender of people you talk to; your approximate age, and the ages of the people you talk to; what time you go to bed, and what time you wake up; what you watch on TV and listen to on the radio; how much of your time you spend alone, and how much with others; whether you live in a big city or a small town; what form of transportation you use to get to work."[32]...

Even the games you play and the apps you use on Facebook can collect and transmit personal information about you. In 2007, Facebook launched a platform that let software developers build applications that run on the site. By 2011, there were more than 550,000 apps, and those apps have become an industry, with social games, the biggest category of apps, having a projected revenue of $1.2 billion annually.[33] Facebook reported in 2010 that 70% of its users run at least one app each month.[34]

A 2010 investigation by *The Wall Street Journal* found that many of the most popular applications on Facebook were transmitting identifying information about users and their friends to advertisers and Internet tracking companies, which is a violation of Facebook's privacy policy.[35] *The Wall Street Journal* analyzed the ten most popular Facebook apps, including Zynga's FarmVille, with 59 million users, and Zynga's Mafia Wars, with 21.9 million users, and found that they were transmitting Facebook user IDs to data aggregators. When a data aggregator has a Facebook ID, it can access any public information on a person's

---

[31] "Tracking the Companies That Track You Online," Dave Davies's interview with Julia Angwin, *Fresh Air*, Aug. 19, 2010, www.npr.org/templates/story/story.php?storyId =129298003; Julia Angwin, "The Web's New Gold Mine: Your Secrets," *The Wall Street Journal*, July 30, 2010, at W1, http://online.wsj.com/article/SB1000142405274870394090457 5395073512989404.html.

[32] Mike Elgan, "Snooping: It's Not a Crime, It's a Feature," April 16, 2011, www .computerworld.com/s/article/print/9215853/Snooping_It_s_not_a_crime_it_s_a_feature.

[33] Jami Makan, "10 Things Facebook Won't Say," Jan. 10, 2011, www.smartmoney .com/spend/technology/10-things-facebook-wont-say-1294414171193/.

[34] Emily Steel and Geoffrey A. Fowler, "Facebook in Privacy Breach," *The Wall Street Journal*, Oct. 18, 2010, at A1, http://online.wsj.com/article/SB100014240527023047728045 75558484075236968.html.

[35] Ibid.

Facebook page (which could include the person's name, age, residence, occupation, and photos). The Zynga applications were sharing Facebook users' IDs with the Internet tracking company Rapleaf, which then added the information to its own database of Internet users for enhanced behavioral advertising.[36]

Rather than focusing on an individual's interaction with a Web site, some data aggregators use a method known as "scraping" to extract all the data that anyone has posted on a particular Web site, analyze it, and sell it. Web scrapers copy information from Web sites through specially coded software.[37] These software programs are also referred to as web robots, crawlers, spiders, or screen-scrapers. Scrapers are designed to search through the HTML code that makes up a Web site and extract desired information. If a certain Web site includes a discussion by new moms (or by people considering buying cars), the data scraper can sell that information and the people's e-mail addresses or IP addresses to advertisers who want to target ads to those types of consumers.

Web scrapers "are capable of making thousands of database searches per minute, far exceeding what a human user of a Web site could accomplish," says attorney Sean O'Reilly, who previously worked in the software industry. "Web vendors have a difficult time detecting a difference between consumers accessing this information for their own benefit and aggregators accessing the information to return to their own databases."[38]

Search engines such as Google, Yahoo!, and Bing also collect, store, and analyze information about individual users through their search queries. Search engines maintain "server logs," which, according to Google's Privacy Policy, include your "web request, Internet Protocol address, browser type, browser language, the date and time of your request and one or more cookies that may uniquely identify your browser."[39] Microsoft's search engine, Bing, adds that it also "will attempt to derive your approximate location based on your IP address."[40] Search engines use this information to optimize their search algorithms and to record an individual's preferences.[41] Though Google uses these logs for fraud prevention and to improve search results, it also analyzes the logs to generate more revenue through targeted advertising.[42] Yahoo! also uses this information to personalize advertising and page content. Yahoo! acknowledges that it also allows other companies to display ads

---

[36]Ibid.

[37]"Web Scraping Tutorial," March 7, 2009, www.codediesel.com/php/web-scraping-in-php-tutorial/. CodeDiesel is a web development journal.

[38]Sean O'Reilly, "Nominative Fair Use and Internet Aggregators: Copyright and Trademark Challenges Posed by Bots, Web Crawlers and Screen-Scraping Technologies," 19 Loyola Consumer Law Review 273 (2007).

[39]"Google Privacy FAQ," www.google.com/intl/en/privacy/faq.html#toc-terms-server-logs.

[40]"Bing Privacy Supplement," January 2011, http://privacy.microsoft.com/en-us/bing.mspx.

[41]"Google Privacy FAQ."

[42]Omer Tene, "What Google Knows: Privacy and Internet Search Engines," 2008 Utah Law Review 1433, 1454 (2008).

on its pages and those ads may "set and access cookies on your computer" that are not subject to Yahoo!'s privacy policy.[43]

In 2006, AOL made public 20 million queries entered into its search engine from 658,000 users on its Web site research@aol.com.[44] AOL's release contained all of those users' searches over a three-month period and detailed whether they clicked on a result, what the result was, and where it was in the list of results.[45] An AOL researcher, Abdur Chowdhury, explained the release of the queries as an effort to facilitate "closer collaboration between AOL and anyone with a desire to work on interesting problems."[46] But the project ended up breaching people's privacy. In some instances, people could be identified through the types of searches they undertook.

A quick look at some of the leaked AOL search logs makes it easy to imagine how damaging a search log can be when linked to a party in a criminal, civil, or divorce case.

User 11574916:
cocaine in urine
asian mail order brides
states reciprocity with florida
florida dui laws
extradition from new york to florida
mail order brides from largos
will one be extradited for a dui
cooking jobs in french quarter new orleans
will i be extradited from ny to fl on dui charge

User 336865:
sexy pregnant ladies naked
nudist
sexy feet
child rape stories
tamagotchi town.com
preteen sex stories
illegal child porn
incest stories
10 year old nude pics
preteen nude models
illegel anime porn
yu-gi-oh

User 59920:
cats skinned in fort lupton co
cats killed in fort lupton co

---

[43]"Yahoo! Privacy Policy," http://info.yahoo.com/privacy/us/yahoo/details.html.

[44]Tene, "What Google Knows: Privacy and Internet Search Engines."

[45]Michael Arrington, "AOL Proudly Releases Massive Amounts of Private Data," Aug. 6, 2006, http://techcrunch.com/2006/08/06/aol-proudly-releases-massive-amounts-of-user-search -data/.

[46]Abdur Chowdhury, E-mail sent to SIG-IRList newsletter, Aug. 3, 2006, http://sifaka .cs.uiuc.edu/xshen/aol/20060803_SIG-IRListE-mail.txt.

jonbenets autopsy photos
crime scene photos of the crawl space and duffle bag in ramseys
house
sexy bathing suits
what a neck looks like after its been strangled
pictures what a neck looks like after it was strangled
pictures of murder victims that have been strangled
pictures of murder by strangulation
knitting stitches
what jonbenet would look like today
new jersey park police
jonbenet in her casket
ransom note in the movie obsession what did it read
movie ransom notes
scouting knots
manila rope and its uses
brown paper bags cops use for evidence
rope to use to hog tie someone
body transport boulder colorado

User 1515830:
chai tea calories
calories in bananas
aftermath of incest
how to tell your family you're a victim of incest
pottery barn
curtains
surgical help for depression
oakland raiders comforter set
can you adopt after a suicide attempt
who is not allowed to adopt
i hate men
medication to enhance female desire
jobs in denver colorado
teaching positions in denver colorado
how long will the swelling last after my tummy tuck
divorce laws in ohio
free remote keyloggers
baked macaroni and cheese with sour cream
how to deal with anger
teaching jobs with the denver school system
marriage counseling tips
anti psychotic drugs[47]

Your Web searches provide data on which you can be judged, erro- 35
neously or not. If you've looked up the side effects of antidepressants,
that information might be used against you by an employer or a college
admissions officer. Your search for a divorce lawyer, advice about green

---

[47]Declan McCullagh, "AOL's Disturbing Glimpse into Users' Lives," Aug. 7, 2006,
http://news.cnet.com/AOLs-disturbing-glimpse-into-users-lives/2100-1030_3-6103098.html
#ixzzlM56yaUU2.

cards, or information about sexually transmitted diseases might also be used in ways that harm you.

Your second self on the Web is likely a distortion of your offline self. The person whose leaked AOL searches related to extradition might have been writing a mystery, rather than covering up a crime. The woman who was seeking information on AOL about incest might have been trying to help a friend, rather than dealing with her own troubled past.

When AOL released the supposedly anonymous queries, it was easy for reporters from *The New York Times* to identify Thelma Arnold as searcher 4417749 due to her searches for other Arnolds and her searches about Lilburn, Georgia.[48] After discussing her queries for 60-year-old single men, queries about her three dogs, and queries researching her friends' ailments, Thelma said, "My goodness, it's my whole personal life. I had no idea somebody was looking over my shoulder."[49]

But "in user search query logs, what you see is not always what you get," notes Omer Tene, a professor at a law school in Rishon Le Zion, Israel. Anyone who had access to Thelma Arnold's logs saw searches for "hand tremors," "nicotine effects on the body," "dry mouth," "bipolar," and "single dances in Atlanta." However, those were searches Thelma conducted for others and do not paint an accurate picture of her life or health.[50]

The attributes of your digital doppelgänger[51] may have more influence on what opportunities you receive than any of your offline characteristics. Rather than expanding opportunities for you, the targeted ads that you see may actually deny you certain benefits. You might be shown a credit card with a lower credit limit, not because of your credit history but because of your race, sex, zip code, or the types of Web sites you visit. As a consequence of weblining, the information collected by data aggregators is often sold to the public at large (through Web sites such as Spokeo) and might later hamper your efforts to get a job, qualify for a loan, adopt a child, or fight for your rights in a criminal trial.

As behavioral advertisers increasingly dictate a person's online and offline experiences, stereotyped characterizations may become self-fulfilling. Rather than reflecting reality, behavioral analysis may inevitably define it. When young people from "poor" zip codes are bombarded with advertisements for trade schools, they may be more likely than their peers to forgo college. And when women are routinely shown articles about cooking and celebrities, rather than stock market trends, they will likely disclaim any financial savvy in the future. Behavioral advertisers are drawing new redlines, refusing to grant people the tools necessary to escape the roles that society expects they play. Our digital doppelgängers are directing our futures and the future of society....

40

[48]Michael Barbaro and Tom Zeller, Jr., "A Face Is Exposed for AOL Searcher 4417749," *The New York Times*, Aug. 9, 2006, at A1, www.nytimes.com/2006/08/09/technology/09aol.html?pagewanted=all.
[49]Ibid.
[50]Tene, "What Google Knows: Privacy and Internet Search Engines."
[51]**doppelgänger:** German word for a "double" or "look-alike" of a person, often with negative or ominous characteristics. [Eds.]

ENGAGING THE TEXT

1. What kinds of information about herself does Andrews expose during the typical morning online she describes at the beginning of this selection (para. 1)? Which of the bits of information she divulges strike you as the most risky or dangerous to share online? Which, if any, seem relatively safe? Why?

2. In Andrews's view, what's wrong with data-mining companies collecting information about us online? Why does it matter if marketers and others can find out your marriage history, the gender of your friends, your favorite bars and restaurants, when you go to bed, or how you get to work?

3. Why does Andrews believe that "weblining" is potentially "undemocratic"? How might this practice limit opportunities and reinforce stereotypes? Why might weblining and behavioral advertising pose a greater threat to democracy than traditional print or television advertising?

4. Working in groups, create alternative profiles for the AOL users associated with each of the four search histories that Andrews offers. How might you explain the pattern of searches in each case? Should public safety officials have access to this kind of online information? Why or why not?

5. Drawing on all the information you post on social media sites, a week's worth of Internet searches, recent purchases, and other forms of online activity, compose a profile of your online "doppelgänger." How do you appear to the world online? If you were an online decisionmaker, would you recommend your "digital self" as a potential marriage partner, for a job or loan, or as an adoptive parent? Why or why not?

EXPLORING CONNECTIONS

6. Write a dialogue between Andrews and Sherry Turkle (p. 236) about the impact of the Internet on privacy and our ability to control our personal images. How might the online habits of the teens Turkle discusses lead to serious problems later in life because of data aggregation?

7. Compare Andrews's account of "weblining with Charles Seife's examination of Internet "solipsism" and "narrowcasting" (p. 289). Why do Internet data-mining and weblining pose a serious threat to the shared values that make democracy possible?

EXTENDING THE CRITICAL CONTEXT

8. Go online to read more about data-aggregating companies like Acxiom, Rapleaf, and ChoicePoint. How much data do such corporations gather each year, and on how many Americans? What kinds of data do they collect? How is this data used, and by whom? Based on your research, how serious a threat to privacy and individual liberty is the data-aggregating industry?

9. Visit the Web site of Acxiom or other data-mining companies to learn more about the socioeconomic categories they use to classify those they track. Who do you think you'd find in the following sampling of the seventy categories

used by Acxiom? Which would you want — and not want — to belong to? How might these classifications affect the types of information and opportunities their members encounter online? Does the use of such categories amount to a legal form of discrimination? Why or why not?

Savvy Single	Blue Collar Bunch	Dynamic Duos
Solo & Stable	Established Elite	Trucks & Trailers
Toys & Tots	Collegiate Crowd	Flush Families
Shooting Stars	Modest Means	Platinum Oldies
Humble Homes	Cash & Carriers	Rural Rovers
Resilient Renters		

10. Visit Lori Andrews's "Social Network Constitution" site on the Internet, and review the ten rights and freedoms it specifies for life online. Then take the interactive poll associated with the site. Which of the ten rights listed do you support? Which do you feel are most important for safeguarding privacy and freedom online? Which seem less important, and why? You can find the "Social Network Constitution" at www.socialnetworkconstitution .com/the-social-network-constitution.html.

PRECOGNITIVE POLICE

HENRICK KAROLISZYN

In May 2013, CIA system administrator Edward Snowden made head-lines when he began leaking thousands of classified documents to newspapers around the world indicating that the U.S. National Security

Agency had been spying on millions of American citizens since 2001. According to Snowden, through its classified PRISM program and other initiatives, the NSA had harvested information on personal e-mail and instant messaging contact lists, tracked cell phone usage records, and secretly tapped into the accounts of Yahoo! and Google users and online video gamers. Since the Snowden revelations, most Americans recognize that their online lives may be under constant surveillance. Many of us also wonder about what happens to the data that law enforcement gleans from online sources. According to the author of this selection, the answer is simple: Today we are moving beyond the age of information gathering into a new era of "predictive policing." Data-mining technologies, social networking, and the War on Terror are leading us, inevitably it seems, to a world in which government officials have the option of stopping crime before it happens. The cost, of course, is the constant erosion of our civil liberties. Henrick Karoliszyn is an award-winning journalist who specializes in issues of criminal justice. His work has appeared in the *New York Times*, the *Wall Street Journal*, and the *Washington Post*. This selection originally appeared online in *Aeon* magazine.

WHEN A TROUBLED YOUNG MAN named Adam Lanza stormed into Sandy Hook Elementary School and slaughtered 20 first-graders and six teachers in a small Connecticut suburb in December of 2012, a shroud of sorrow and confusion engulfed the United States and countries all over the world. Why were all these children murdered, and why did someone so clearly disordered have access to so many guns?

I covered the mass shooting for the *New York Daily News*, and worked fourteen-hour days interviewing victims' families, attending press conferences, and doing as much on-ground reporting as possible. The toughest part of the coverage came a week in, at the memorial for a six-year-old named Dylan Hockley. A slide show, accompanied by a rendition of Leonard Cohen's classic rock hymn *Hallelujah*, with lyrics altered to honor the boy, induced nausea, especially when I thought of all the other children killed and the families they left behind.

Following the mass murder, people in the United States began debating their easy access to assault weapons and large-capacity magazines. Yet the only change has been for the worse. There have been seventy-four reported school shootings[1] across the United States since Sandy Hook. And there are no signs of this trend stopping. Ease of gun ownership remains a way of life in the United States.

But what if there was an alternative to prevent these types of shootings, without eradicating guns? What if predictive policing—something

---

[1]According to the *Washington Times*, by October 2015 there had been 214 school shootings in U.S. schools since the Sandy Hook incident, an average of one per week. [Editors' note.]

like the "pre-crime" unit envisioned by the sci-fi author Philip K. Dick and dramatized in the film *Minority Report* (2002) — were to intercept killers before they struck? What if authorities could crunch numbers, find patterns, and act before homicidal maniacs got the chance?

The effort is already under way. Recently adopted predictive polic- [5] ing methods, in varying stages of development across the United States and around the world, have the same goal: authorities hope to anticipate crimes and act before they occur. Initial efforts work largely through computer algorithms, or formulas that analyze years of criminal reports to predict where the next crime will likely transpire.

The New York City police commissioner Bill Bratton is a firm believer in preventive crime fighting. At a recent 21st Century Leadership panel held at the 92nd Street Y community center in Manhattan, he refer- enced it as the new norm. "The mission of the police is to prevent crime and we are finally at a point in time where we can actually do that with some degree of confidence," he said . . .

Bratton pioneered a crude version of this concept in 1994, during his first run as commissioner. CompStat, as the system was called, ran statistics and analyzed district crime reports, arrest records, and other police data to follow crime trends and target criminal hot spots. After patrolling these hot spots for a year, murders had dropped by 60 per- cent. By 2003, murders were the lowest they had been since 1964.

Encouraged by that success, the New York Police Department (NYPD) in 2012 partnered with Microsoft to create a predictive policing tool that is far more advanced. The Domain Awareness System retrieves, ana- lyzes, and instantly displays information from more than 3,000 surveil- lance cameras, 911 calls, number-plate readers, and other sources. The objective is for the department to aggregate and act on the information before illegal activity takes place.

For example, let's say a suspicious car following children near a school is reported to the police. The predictive system can pull up who owns the vehicle, any arrest records related to the owner, and crimes occurring in the area. It can determine not only where the car is at the moment but, by accessing plate readers around the city, where it's been in days, weeks, and months prior. Based on "reasonable suspicion," all this data may be used to stop a crime when it is still just an idea.

The NYPD unveiled the system in August 2012, and by June 2014 [10] it made its first big hit. After tracking more than one million Facebook pages, 40,000 calls from Rikers Island jail, and hundreds of hours of video footage from building elevators, hallways, and grounds, the police raided a Harlem housing development and arrested 103 alleged gang mem- bers. It was the largest gang takedown in New York history. The gangs were accused of two homicides, nineteen nonfatal shootings, and about fifty other shooting incidents. But the aim of this mass arrest was to pre- vent a war zone from erupting in the future.

In the quest to predict and prevent crime, New York is hardly alone. In August 2013, the Chicago Police Department (CPD) established a "heat list" with an index of 400 people, thought to be criminals, fanned out across six predominantly black police districts. The CPD said that people on the list included shooting victims who refused to cooperate in prosecuting the shooter, as well as those identified as repeat offenders for violent crimes. The index was collected through an algorithm produced by an engineer at the Illinois Institute of Technology. The method involves officers visiting the homes of individuals they identify as likely perpetrators immediately after crimes occur in their neighborhoods, theoretically preventing future crimes.

In Los Angeles, the police department now uses PredPol, a predictive policing device that runs years' worth of crime reports through specialized algorithms to identify locales with a high probability of crime. It places little red boxes on maps of the city to indicate the spots, which are streamed into patrol cars. The police then monitor these 500 ft. x 500 ft. areas to stop would-be criminals. PredPol is used in a third of the geographic policing divisions, and focuses on burglary, break-ins, and car theft, which together amount to more than half of last year's estimated 104,000 crimes in Los Angeles, according to reports. In other words, it looks at the location of past crimes to predict future ones.

Dozens of other law enforcement agencies use PredPol. Police in Seattle are using it to zero in on gun violence. Atlanta police use it to forecast robberies. In Pennsylvania, police are focusing on car theft and burglaries. And in the United Kingdom, Kent police use it to predict drug crimes and robberies. They all share the common purpose of stomping out crime before it hatches.

But these early predictive systems are only the start. In years to come, many legal experts speculate, brain scans and DNA analysis could help to identify potential criminals at the young age of three. Some evidence for the approach came in 2009 in the *Proceedings of the National Academy of Sciences*: researchers from the United States and the United Kingdom tested seventy-eight male subjects for different forms of the so-called warrior gene, which codes for the enzyme monoamine oxidase A (MAOA), a gene that breaks down crucial neurotransmitters in the brain. One version of MAOA works efficiently; but another version breaks down brain chemicals only sluggishly, and has long been linked to aggression in observational and survey-based studies. Some researchers held that, in war-prone societies, up to two-thirds of individuals had the low-activity gene—versus the more typical percentage of just one-third, found in the more peaceful nations of the world.

To see if this controversial hypothesis held up in the lab, research- 15 ers asked the same seventy-eight subjects to take a second test. They were to hurt individuals they believed had stolen money from them by ordering varying amounts of painful hot sauce in their food. (In reality, the "thief" was a computer, so no person was actually hurt.) The findings yielded the first empirical proof that those with the low-activity form of the gene—the warriors among us—did indeed dish out more pain.

These findings soon found their way into criminal court: in 2009, at a trial in Tennessee, the defendant Bradley Waldroup was accused of killing his wife's friend—by shooting her eight times and slicing her head open—and then slicing his wife again and again with a machete. Yet despite the glaring evidence, he avoided a first-degree murder conviction based in part on the warrior gene defense. He had it.

In the United States and Europe, brain scans have in recent years supplemented DNA evidence to indicate criminality. In 2009, for instance, the Italian defendant Stefania Albertani was convicted of murdering her sister by force-feeding her psychotropic drugs and then burning her corpse. Some months later, she tried to kill her parents too. Yet in 2011 a court lowered her sentence from life to twenty years in prison after her attorneys showed that she carried the warrior gene and that her brain scans showed marked abnormalities in two regions—the insula, linked to aggression, and the anterior cingulate gyrus, involved in inhibition.

Could futuristic versions of such tests be conducted widely through the population at large? And would they give authorities a leg up in predicting and preventing crimes? Would vast gene banks and advanced brain scans as ubiquitous as the street-level security cameras of today isolate the human powder kegs hiding in plain sight?

In a lively symposium on neuroscience and the law sponsored by the New America Foundation in October 2012, Jeffrey Rosen, professor of law at George Washington University, posed this disturbing scenario: "I am walking down the street and a mobile brain scan looks at my brain along with a picture of a training camp in Afghanistan. If I've not been there, I'm sent happily on my way. But if I have, my brain lurches a certain way, I'm taken off the street and carted off to Guantánamo and detained indefinitely as a potential enemy combatant." Would this be permissible under current U.S. constitutional doctrine, Rosen, the moderator, asked.

That wouldn't be allowed in the United States as things stand now, said the panelist Hank Greely, a Stanford law professor. 20

"We might see that kind of technology employed in North Korea," added his copanelist Gary Marchant, professor of emerging technologies, law, and ethics at Arizona State University.

And even if advanced technologies could prevent all crime, is this the kind of world we want? Given the massive privacy hit we have already taken in the Internet age, should we let predictive policing finish the job?

It would be an especially onerous choice, given that predictive technologies can make devastating errors, indicting not [only] criminals but also the innocent and pure of heart. A major worry is how algorithms are being constructed in the first place. Crime-scene data collected by authorities could be flawed and biased to focus on lower-income neighborhoods and people of color. And just because data is in the system doesn't mean it's correct. "There's a real risk that the data that gets inputted is biased, or based on stereotype or overgeneralizations based on race and class," said Hanni Fakhoury, a staff attorney at the Electronic Frontier Foundation, a nonprofit digital civil liberties organization in San Francisco.

"It's easy to ensnare innocent people into these things. Crooks talk to noncriminals, too, and taking lots of data on some people will inevitably capture information on people who've done nothing wrong other than to know someone caught up in the criminal justice system."

In the United States, one result would be violation of Fourth Amendment rights against unreasonable searches and seizures. Let's say police get a predictive tip about an area where a burglary is slated to happen. If a patrol car begins monitoring and a cop sees a man on the stoop of his apartment complex with a knapsack, that would not normally be enough to make a stop. But with predictive policing, it may qualify as "reasonable suspicion."

Predictive policing could intensify the furor over Stop-and-Frisk, an NYPD policy in which individuals are randomly searched. The policy, which was adopted in the United Kingdom and recently called "unfair to young black men" by the Home Secretary, Theresa May, could become even more controversial when predictive policing tools focus on specific neighborhoods and the ethnic groups they contain.

Colleen Berryessa, the program manager for Stanford University's Center for Integration of Research on Genetics and Ethics (CIRGE), says that use of genomics might introduce more chaos still. As it stands, DNA swabbing is more of an art than a science, and DNA labs are rife with contamination, meaning that criminals and noncriminals alike could end up in a database, skewing our view of whom to suspect. It comes down to trusting authorities with a gauge as faulty as DNA.

Brain scans could be problematic, too. Referring to Rosen's scenario of a would-be terrorist shown an image of a training camp in Afghanistan, Greely asks: "Even if you do react as if you have seen that camp before, is it that you've seen that camp or a picture of that camp? Or does that camp look like the summer camp your parents sent you off to when you were eleven that you've never forgiven them for?" Certainly, we'd need to know a lot more than we know today before we can use the tools of neuroscience and genetics to pick off criminals in advance.

What's more, predictive policing will never get to the root of the problem. Even when perfected, it can't snuff the spark of criminal behavior in and of itself. There might be a better way — perhaps channeling all that money and effort into serious research on gun crime. Understanding the root of all the violence could be as effective as cigarette studies and seatbelt research have been in the past.

Shattered people are suffering in failing systems. Relentlessly monitoring and spying on them will not tell us why crimes occur. If the United States can spend a quarter of a trillion dollars on investigating, catching, and imprisoning people, why can't some of this monetary flow be redirected to mental health care for youth—the kind of intervention that involves therapists and activities, not cameras and swabs[?]

In fact, predictive techniques could be marshalled outside the realm of criminal justice, in childhood programs for at-risk children as young as three or four. If a child has the warrior gene, if there is a metabolic problem that means the child lashes out violently upon provocation, perhaps early medication and psychotherapy could intervene, Marchant suggests. "You look at these [murder] cases and see there is so much suffering that could have been prevented," he told the symposium on neuroscience and the law. "But the problem is, we never had any markers to show a risk. . . . [Now] we can pair those markers with treatment. We should put resources into finding these treatments and making it work."

No amount of predictive policing can avert another Sandy Hook massacre. But if we identified future criminals and helped them, instead of locking them up, the Adam Lanzas of the world might be defanged. Used correctly, the right preventive techniques could save six-year-old children such as Dylan Hockley from a *Hallelujah* chorus, and would be an investment worth our time.

ENGAGING THE TEXT

1. How, according to Karoliszyn, do current models of predictive policing work in places like New York, Chicago, and Los Angeles? What kinds of data are involved and how, exactly, are crimes "stopped" before they happen?

2. What problems does Karoliszyn see in the predictive policing methods he discusses? What difference is there, if any, between the predictive policing technologies he discusses and the kinds of nontechnological racial profiling practices that have been deemed unconstitutional?

3. How plausible do you find the idea that DNA testing and brain scanning will be used to identify potential criminals in the future? Why, according to Karoliszyn, are both of these future technologies prone to error? What other objections might be raised against the use of a person's DNA or brain scan in predicting his or her future behavior?

4. What alternatives to predictive policing does Karoliszyn offer? What issues might be raised by his suggestion that medical or psychological interventions be employed to "help" children who carry the warrior gene or other markers for antisocial behavior?

EXPLORING CONNECTIONS

5. What questions does Karoliszyn's discussion of predictive policing raise about the vision of an electronically "personalized" future presented by Eric Schmidt and Jared Cohen (p. 219)? What problems might arise in a world where the objects you interact with — including your car, home, and clothes — produce data about you that can be accessed and tracked?

6. Write a dialogue between Karoliszyn and Lori Andrews (p. 322) on the threat that data mining and predictive policing pose to individual rights and civil liberties. Given her examination of the "second self" we all leave behind on the Web, what dangers might Andrews see in the idea of predictive policing?

7. Drawing on the ideas of Karoliszyn, Sherry Turkle (p. 236), Laurie Penny (p. 253), and Lori Andrews, write a journal entry or an essay on the idea of Internet

surveillance and its impact. Later, hold an in-class debate on whether the Internet is a tool of social control or a means of personal liberation.

EXTENDING THE CRITICAL CONTEXT

8. Do some online research to learn more about predictive policing technologies that are being used in New York, Chicago, Los Angeles, San Francisco, and other U.S. cities. What specific kinds of data do these systems collect? How do they target crime before it occurs? How effective have these systems been, and what questions do they raise about public safety and civil liberties?

9. Research how recent technological innovations are changing police work today — innovations like smart phones, body cameras, automatic license plate readers, Stingray and GPS tracking devices, RFID tags, closed-circuit TV, drones, and facial recognition scanners. In class, discuss whether you think emerging technologies are making law enforcement more or less effective and accountable to the public. What problems do you see associated with police use of such technological innovations?

10. Research recent polls of American attitudes toward surveillance, privacy, and personal liberties. How do Americans appear to view the trade-off between individual rights, like the right to privacy, and personal and national security? Does your research suggest that respect for individual rights is strong or on the decline in America?

FURTHER CONNECTIONS

1. Working in groups, do additional research on the impact of the Internet and social media on adolescents. First, go online to identify a selection of scholarly articles reporting the results of studies conducted by psychologists or social science researchers. You may want to focus your efforts on a single topic, like Internet addiction, or the effect of Internet use on friendship, peer pressure, stress, depression, or sexual attitudes. After sampling a few of the most promising of these studies, share their conclusions with your group members. Later in class, debate whether the Internet should be viewed as a useful tool or as a source of serious problems for most teens.

2. Research predictions about the development of robots and artificial intelligence to learn more about how technology may shape the future. When do scientists and futurists believe that computers will

become as intelligent as humans? How is automation expected to affect the workplace in the next twenty to thirty years? What jobs, for example, are most likely to survive the robotics revolution? What will happen to society as a result?

3. Research the growth of mass surveillance in modern American society. How has government surveillance of the general population increased in response to terrorist threats and the development of new crime-fighting technologies? How have federal and local agencies used any of the following innovations to monitor the activities of U.S. citizens?

- Tracking cell phone and social media site use
- Data-mining bank and bookstore records
- Closed-circuit TV cameras
- Facial recognition systems
- GPS tracking
- DNA databases
- Surveillance drones
- RFID tagging

To what extent do you think these activities and technologies threaten the privacy and personal freedom of American citizens? Why?

4. In 2014 Facebook admitted that, along with professors from Cornell University and the University of California, it had participated in a controversial study that involved manipulating the news feeds of nearly 700,000 users. Go online to learn more about what came to be known as the "Facebook newsfeed scandal" and about Facebook's response to it. What ethical questions are raised when social media companies like Facebook or online dating services participate in social science research? To what extent should social media sites—including dating services—be free to use or market the information they collect for other purposes?

5. Go online to learn more about "transhumanism" and the human enhancement movement. What are the goals and expectations of advocates of transhumanism and human enhancement? How do they believe technologies like smart prosthetics, neural supplements, neural implants, nanotechnology, genetic engineering, and gene therapy will change human beings in the future? What are some of the ethical and moral questions raised by the desire for technological human enhancement? Do you think that it's part of our destiny as a species to become "posthuman"? Why or why not?

MONEY AND SUCCESS
The Myth of Individual Opportunity

FAST FACTS

1. The richest 0.1% (one-tenth of one percent) of American families own approximately 22% of U.S. wealth; the poorest 90% of families own only 23%.

2. Roughly 27% of blacks, 26% of Hispanics, 18% of Pacific Islanders, 13% of whites, and 11% of Asian Americans live below the official poverty line.

3. American women earn only 78 cents to the dollar earned by white men in the same full-time jobs; African American women earn only 64 cents to the dollar, and Latinas only 56 cents.

4. According to a 2015 AFL-CIO report, Walmart's CEO Douglas McMillon earns 537 times as much as an average nonsupervisory Walmart worker.

5. In no state can a worker afford a one-bedroom apartment on the minimum wage without spending more than 30% of his or her income on housing.

6. According to a 2012 study by the Economic Policy Institute, residents of 12 economically developed nations — including Denmark, Norway, Finland, Canada, Spain, and France — have a better chance of moving up the socioeconomic ladder than do residents of the United States.

Data from (1) Saez, Emmanuel, and Gabriel Zucman (October 2014), "Wealth Inequality in the United States since 1913: Evidence from Capitalized Income Tax Data," NBER Working Paper (http://gabriel-zucman.eu/uswealth/); (2) U.S. Department of Labor; (3) National Women's Law Center (April 2015), "Calculations from U.S. Census Bureau, Current Population Survey, 2014 Annual Social and Economic Supplement, Table PINC-05: Work Experience in 2013 — People 15 Years Old and Over by Total Money Earnings in 2013, Age, Race, Hispanic Origin, and Sex" (http://www.census.gov/hhes/www/cpstables/032014/perinc/pinc05_000.htm); (4) AFL-CIO Executive Paywatch, "High-Paid CEOs and the Low-Wage Economy"; (5) National Low Income Housing Coalition, 2015; (6) Economic Policy Institute (October 20, 2012), "U.S. Lags Behind Peer Countries in Mobility."

AMERICAN CULTURE IS CHANGING FAST. Digital technologies, for example, have transformed our lives over the past two decades, forcing us to rethink cultural assumptions about such issues as privacy, commerce, law enforcement, harassment, personal identity, and social relationships. At the same time, advocates for marriage equality pushed same-sex marriage from the fringe of national consciousness all the way to the historic Supreme Court decision of June 2015. Is a similarly dramatic shift in American attitudes toward economic justice and social class also possible — or has it perhaps already taken place?

The American Dream — our sense of the United States as a land of unique opportunities and individual achievement — is at the very heart of our cultural narrative; it would seem to be a defining, unshakable premise about who we are as a people and a nation. Its roots can be traced back to the earliest European explorers who crossed the Atlantic in search of legendary "New World" cities like Eldorado, where the streets were paved with gold. By the time the colonies declared their independence, the national myth of success was fully formed. Early immigrants like J. Hector St. John de Crèvecoeur, for example, extolled the freedom and opportunity to be found in this new land. Crèvecoeur's glowing descriptions of a classless society where anyone could attain success through honesty and hard work fired the imaginations of many European readers: in *Letters from an American Farmer* (1782) he wrote, "We are all animated with the spirit of an industry which is unfettered and unrestrained, because each person works for himself. . . . We have no princes, for whom we toil, starve, and bleed: we are the most perfect society now existing in the world." The promise of a land where hard work seemed to guarantee success drew poor immigrants from Europe and fueled national expansion into the western territories.

If Crèvecoeur was the most effective early advocate of the American Dream, the emerging nation's ultimate success story was Benjamin Franklin, the self-educated printer who rose from modest origins to become a renowned scientist, philosopher, and statesman. While it's clear to us that Franklin was a genius, he often attributed his success to practicing the virtues of honesty, hard work, and thrift, as in this passage from "Advice to a Young Tradesman": "Without industry and frugality nothing will do, and with them every thing. He that gets all he can honestly, and saves all he gets . . . will certainly become RICH." Although Franklin was no Puritan, his advice — including its moral dimension — was in perfect harmony with the Puritan work ethic of the earliest colonists.

This version of the American Dream survived for at least a century after Franklin. In the decades after the Civil War, Horatio Alger, a writer of pulp fiction for young boys, became America's best-selling author, publishing more than a hundred rags-to-riches tales like *Ragged Dick* (1868), *Struggling Upward* (1886), and *Bound to Rise* (1873). Alger's name has become synonymous with the notion that anyone can succeed, even to generations of Americans who have never read any of his works. Like Franklin, Alger's heroes were concerned with moral rectitude as well as financial gain: a benefactor advises Ragged Dick, "If you'll try to be somebody, and grow up into a respectable member of society, you will. You may not become rich, — it isn't everybody that becomes rich, you know, — but you can obtain a good position and be respected." In retrospect it's easy to see how limited Alger's promises really were; none of his enterprising young people were women, for example, and none were black. Contemporary scholar Harlon Dalton has analyzed the pernicious effects of the Alger myth for people of color, concluding that its blindness to racial bias "serves to maintain the racial pecking order [and] trivialize, if not erase, the social meaning of race."

The myth grew increasingly complicated in the twentieth century, as we can see in the dramatic shift from Alger's wholehearted optimism to F. Scott Fitzgerald's nuanced treatment of the American Dream in *The Great Gatsby*, which chronicles one man's attempt to gain everything the Roaring Twenties had to offer. If Alger's *Ragged Dick* is a sunny fairy tale for boys, *Gatsby* is a tragic fairy tale for the nation. One reason for *Gatsby*'s enduring power is surely that Fitzgerald captures the deep allure of the dream — ambition, wealth, the golden girl whose voice "is full of money" — while simultaneously undermining Gatsby's romantic quest with crime, infidelity, and violence, the "foul dust" that "floated in the wake of his dreams."

The myth faced its greatest challenge when the prosperity and energy of the Roaring Twenties collapsed into the Great Depression of the 1930s, but a booming postwar economy and our status as a global superpower restored many people's faith. As detailed in "What We Really Miss About the 1950s" by Stephanie Coontz, the postwar era did bring stability and economic opportunity to some Americans but meant "racism, sexism, and repression" for others (p. 25). Even in good times, the mood of the myth had changed. In the 1970s, Robert Ringer's enormously popular *Looking Out for Number One* urged readers to "forget foundationless traditions, forget the 'moral' standards others may have tried to cram down your throat . . . and, most important, think of yourself — Number One. . . . You and you alone will be responsible for your success or failure."

Ringer's strong emphasis on individual striving is just one element of the American Dream that feminist writers have more recently critiqued. In brief, the myth strikes them as "masculinist" — that is, reflecting the attitudes, behaviors, and values traditionally associated with men. Whether they are explorers, cowboys, inventors, oil barons, or presidents, our mythic heroes have most often been male; their masculine characteristics include physical prowess (Babe Ruth, Teddy Roosevelt, the Terminator, Muhammad Ali), self-sufficiency or isolation (Henry David Thoreau, the Marlboro Man, private detectives), and excellence in hunting or fighting (Buffalo Bill, Robert E. Lee, Wyatt Earp, Luke Skywalker). The myth's heavy emphasis on masculinity means that cultural values such as family, community, collaboration, and tradition end up undervalued, as do the myriad contributions of ordinary people who supported the supposedly "self-made" men.

Despite these complications, the notion of success clearly continues to haunt us: we spend millions every year reading about the rich and famous and learning how to "make a fortune in real estate with no money down." We become engrossed in status symbols, trying to live in the "right" neighborhoods and wear the "right" clothes. We follow the diets of movie stars and the fitness regimens of Olympic athletes. Trying to boost our chances at a good career and a comfortable life, we take out student loans that might take decades to pay off. The myth of success has even invaded our personal relationships: we tally Facebook friends and Twitter followers, and aspire to be as "successful" in marriage or parenthood as in business.

Unfortunately our dreams can easily turn into nightmares. Every American who hopes to "make it" also knows the fear of failure, because the myth of success inevitably implies comparison between the haves and the have-nots, the achievers and the drones, the stars and the anonymous crowd. It's also hard to square the myth with some brutal contemporary realities, including entrenched poverty, wage stagnation, a shrinking middle class, the extreme concentration of wealth in the hands of billionaires, and even modern forms of slavery. Upward mobility, a key promise of the American Dream, turns out to be no easier here than in England

and France with their well-defined class structures, and harder here than in Canada and some Scandinavian countries. Moreover, it is almost impossible for Americans to escape poverty: 95 percent of children born to poor parents will themselves be poor all their lives. Sociologist Robert Putnam, professor of public policy at Harvard, worries that the "opportunity gap" between rich and poor is so large that children may soon simply inherit their rank in a two-caste system of privileged and poor. Even for fortunate Americans, the recession that battered world economies in 2008 made maintaining the comfortable lifestyle of the middle class seem dependent less on hard work than on global economic forces like the price of crude oil and the migration of American jobs overseas.

The chapter's examination of class opens with profiles of two Americans who achieved the kind of success that keeps the American Dream alive — Walmart founder Sam Walton and music megastar Jay Z. Author George Packer summarizes how each rose to fame and fortune, acknowledging their accomplishments while hinting at a darker side of the Dream. The three subsequent readings critique the myth of individual success more directly, offering a wealth of information about social class from diverse perspectives. Barbara Ehrenreich's "Serving in Florida" investigates the daily grind of working-class life by recounting her personal experience of struggling to make ends meet on waitressing wages. Next, Gregory Mantsios's "Class in America — 2012" examines class from a broader and more theoretical perspective; citing compelling statistics, Mantsios portrays a social and economic system that serves the powerful and wealthy. In an excerpt from his book *Beyond Outrage*, former U.S. Secretary of Labor Robert Reich explains the growing gap between rich and poor, details the astonishing salaries of American CEOs, and argues passionately that the nation must change its course.

Midway through the chapter, the Visual Portfolio, "Reading Images of Individual Opportunity," explores dreams of success, the cost of failure, public protests against economic inequality, and the relationship of opportunity to race, gender, and education. Next, four scholars dissect the notion that the United States has become a "postracial" nation in their essay "From a Tangle of Pathology to a Race-Fair America." Alan Aja and his colleagues describe the structural barriers faced by people of color, including discriminatory hiring practices, racially segregated occupations, and a wealth gap that impedes self-employment and entrepreneurship among minorities. The chapter's media selection, Diana Kendall's "Framing Class, Vicarious Living, and Conspicuous Consumption," studies how TV distorts our view of economic inequalities — by treating poverty as individual misfortune, for example, rather than systematic oppression. The chapter ends with "Slavery in the Land of the Free" by Kevin Bales and Ron Soodalter, an exposé of the very antithesis of the American Dream: human trafficking and forced labor in homes, on farms, and in factories across the country.

Sources

Baida, Peter. *Poor Richard's Legacy: American Business Values from Benjamin Franklin to Donald Trump*. New York: William Morrow, 1990. Print.

Correspondents of the *New York Times*. *Class Matters*. New York: Times Books/Henry Holt, 2005. Print.

Dalton, Harlon L. *Racial Healing: Confronting the Fear Between Blacks and Whites*. New York: Doubleday, 1995. Print.

Fitzgerald, F. Scott. *The Great Gatsby*. New York: Scribner's, 1925. Print.

McNamee, Stephen J., and Robert K. Miller Jr. *The Meritocracy Myth*. New York: Rowman & Littlefield, 2004. Print.

Putnam, Robert. "*Bowling Alone* — Author Robert Putnam Takes on America's Opportunity Gap." *Forum with Michael Krasny*, National Public Radio, July 3, 2015. Web.

St. John de Crèvecoeur, J. Hector. *Letters from an American Farmer*. New York: Dolphin Books, 1961. First published in London, 1782. Print.

BEFORE READING

- Working alone or in groups, make a list of people who best represent your idea of success. (You may want to consider leaders in government, sports, entertainment, education, science, business, or other fields.) List the specific qualities or accomplishments that make these people successful. Compare notes with your classmates, then freewrite about the meaning of success: What does it mean to you? To the class as a whole?

- Write an imaginative profile of the man pictured in the frontispiece for this chapter (p. 345). For example, where was he born, what do you imagine his parents did for a living, and where was he educated? What do his clothes, his posture, his facial expression, and the limousine say about him today? Where does he live, what is his current job or profession, and how much money does he make? Compare your profile with those of classmates to see shared or divergent ideas about some of the issues explored throughout *Rereading America* — the "American Dream," certainly, but also cultural myths of family, education, gender, and ethnicity.

- Write down the job and salary you expect to have in the next 10–15 years. Share with classmates and keep the guesstimate in mind as you read this chapter, adjusting up or down as you gain new information.

SAM WALTON / JAY Z
GEORGE PACKER

You can't get much more successful than the two figures profiled in this selection. If you don't know the name Sam Walton, you are surely familiar with the Walmart empire he founded. Born into modest circumstances, "Mr. Sam" became America's richest man, leaving his heirs a fortune that grew to nearly $145 billion by 2013.[1] Jay Z's rise from a housing project in Brooklyn's Bedford-Stuyvesant neighborhood has been similarly meteoric. With twenty-one Grammy Awards, a clothing line, part ownership

[1] Josh Harkinson, "The Walmart Heirs Are Worth More Than Everyone in Your City Combined," *Mother Jones*, October 3, 2014. Web. http://www.motherjones.com/politics/2014/10/walmart-walton-heirs-net-worth-cities.

of the New Jersey Nets, and millions of Twitter followers, he and his wife Beyoncé are widely recognized as the music industry's most powerful brand. On the surface, Walton's and Jay Z's stories seem to validate the American Dream. Clearly, hard work, brains, initiative, and a bit of good luck can pay off handsomely, but — as in the profiles here — a darker motif often surfaces in American narratives of extreme wealth and fame. Most important, what do such exceptional success stories tell us about our own opportunities and aspirations? The biographical sketches below don't answer that question explicitly; rather, they prompt us to think more carefully about the myths and realities of success in America. Journalist and novelist George Packer has published in *The New Yorker* (where he is a staff writer), *The Nation, Harper's, Mother Jones, Foreign Affairs*, and other periodicals. His book *The Assassin's Gate: America in Iraq* (2005) studies the events that led to the U.S. invasion of Iraq in 2003. His profiles of Walton and Jay Z appear in *The Unwinding: An Inner History of the New America*, which won the National Book Award for Nonfiction in 2013.

Mr. Sam: Sam Walton

Sam was born in 1918 in Kingfisher, Oklahoma, right in the middle of the country. He grew up in a pretty hardscrabble time. After the Depression hit, his father, Thomas Walton, got a job repossessing farms around Missouri on behalf of Metropolitan Life Insurance Co. Sam sometimes traveled with his dad and saw how he tried to leave a little dignity to the farmers who had defaulted on their loans and were about to lose their land. No question, that was where Sam got his cautious attitude toward money. He was just plain cheap. It was the way he was brought up. Even after he became the richest man in America — and he hated it when *Forbes* put that spotlight on him in 1985, the attention caused his family a lot of extra trouble — he'd still stop to pick up a nickel off the ground. He never liked showy lifestyles. Honesty, neighborliness, hard work, and thrift — those were the bedrock values. Everyone put on their trousers one leg at a time.

"Money never has meant that much to me," he wrote near the end of his life. "If we had enough groceries, and a nice place to live, plenty of room to keep and feed my bird dogs, a place to hunt, a place to play tennis, and the means to get the kids good educations — that's rich. No question about it."

His father was never much of a success, but his mother had ambitions for their two boys, and the couple quarreled all the time. Maybe that was why Sam always needed to stay busy. He was a joiner and a competitor — Eagle Scout, quarterback and student body president at Hickman High in Columbia, Beta Theta Pi at the University of Missouri.

He learned to speak to people coming down the sidewalk before they spoke to him. He was small and wiry with a face like a good-natured bird of prey, and he always wanted to win.

Sam found out pretty young that he could sell things. He worked his way through high school and college delivering newspapers, and he won a contest selling subscriptions door-to-door. After college he went to work at a J.C. Penney store in Des Moines for seventy-five dollars a week. That was his first job in retail, and it lasted long enough for Sam to learn that if employees were called "associates," they gained a sense of pride in the company. Then came the war. He spent three years in the army, stateside because of a heart irregularity. When he got out, he was determined to get back into retail, this time for himself.

Sam wanted to buy a Federated department store franchise in 5 St. Louis, but his new wife, a wealthy Oklahoma lawyer's daughter named Helen, refused to live in a town with more than ten thousand people. So they ended up in Newport, Arkansas, population five thousand, where Sam bought a Ben Franklin variety store with help from his father-in-law. There was another store right across the street, and he would wander over and spend hours studying how the competition did things. That turned into a lifelong habit. It was in Newport that Sam got to thinking in ways that became the foundation of his success.

He was buying ladies' satin panties from the Ben Franklin supplier at $2.50 for a dozen, and selling them at three pairs for a dollar. But when he found a manufacturer's agent in New York who would sell him a dozen for two dollars, he put them out at four pairs for a dollar and had a great promotion. His profit per panty dropped by a third, but he sold three times as many. Buy low, sell cheap, high volume, fast turn. That became Sam's whole philosophy, and in five years he tripled his sales, making his the number one Ben Franklin in the six-state region.

People were cheap. They'd never pass up a rock-bottom price. It was true in the little all-white towns around Arkansas and Oklahoma and Missouri after the war. It was true everywhere all the time.

It was true in Bentonville, Arkansas, where Sam and Helen moved with their four kids in 1950 after a clever landlord took away the store in Newport. Sam opened Walton's 5&10 on the main square in Bentonville, population three thousand, and it did so well that over the next decade he and his brother Bud opened another fifteen stores. They were in the tiny backwaters that Kmart and Sears didn't bother with—Siloam Springs, Arkansas, and Coffeyville, Kansas, and St. Robert, Missouri. People were cheap, but there was higher volume in those places than the smart money in Chicago and New York knew. Sam spotted the locations in his two-seater Air Coupe, flying low over a town, scouting the roads and building patterns, then finding the right piece of empty land.

In the grip of his retail fever dream, he left his family on vacations to go check out stores in the area where they were staying. He scoured the competition and hired away their best men with offers of an investment stake in his franchises. He thought up stunts to bring in business and mislead his competitors into thinking he was a cornball. He squeezed every penny out of his suppliers. He never stopped working. He had to keep growing and growing. Nothing could get in his way.

On July 2, 1962, Sam opened his first independent discount store, in Rogers, Arkansas. Huge discounters, selling everything from name brand clothes to auto parts, were the wave of the future. He would ride it or be swept away. He was so cheap that he kept the sign to as few letters as possible: the new store was called "Wal-Mart." It promised "everyday low prices."

By 1969 he had 32 stores in four states. The next year, Sam took the company public. The Walton family owned 69 percent of the shares, and Sam was worth around $15 million. Entrepreneurship, free enterprise, risk—the only ways to improve other people's quality of life.

Throughout the 1970s, Wal-Mart doubled its sales every two years. By 1973 there were 55 stores in five states. By 1976 there were 125 stores, with sales of $340 million. Wal-Mart was spreading outward through the forgotten towns of middle America in a great circle whose center was Bentonville, laying waste to local hardware stores and pharmacies, saturating the regions it conquered so that no one else could compete, each new Wal-Mart built cookie-cutter fashion within a day's drive of company headquarters, where the distribution center was located. The stores were as big as airplane hangars, no windows, with giant parking lots paved over fields and trees, situated away from the center of town to attract sprawl. Sophisticated computers kept minute-by-minute track of every item of stock that was ordered, shipped, and sold.

By 1980 there were 276 stores, and sales passed $1 billion. Throughout the eighties Wal-Mart grew explosively, to all corners of the country and then overseas. Sam even built stores in big cities like Dallas and Houston, where there was more stealing and it was harder to come up with people of the right moral character who were willing to work there. Hillary Clinton became the first woman to join Wal-Mart's board. Her husband—the governor—and other politicians came to Bentonville to pay homage. In the middle of the decade, Sam officially became the richest man in America, worth $2.8 billion. He was as cheap as ever—he still got a five-dollar haircut in downtown Bentonville and didn't leave a tip. He and his company gave almost nothing to charity. But every year each Wal-Mart store would hand out a thousand-dollar college scholarship to a local high school senior, and somehow that bought better publicity than generous corporate philanthropy.

Sam still flew around in a twin-engine plane and visited hundreds of stores a year. He would lead the crowd of assembled associates in a boisterous chant (the idea had come to him on a trip to South Korea in the seventies):

"Give me a W!"
"W!"
"Give me an A!"
"Give me an L!"

"Give me a squiggly!" (Everyone including Sam performed a little twist.)

"Give me an M!"   20
"Give me an A!"
"Give me an R!"
"Give me a T!"
"What's that spell?"
"WAL-MART!"   25
"Who's number one?"
"The customer!"

Sam always showed up with his first name on a plastic tag, just like all his store clerks. He made a point of collecting suggestions, listening to complaints, and promising to act on them, and hourly workers felt more attended to by this friendly man than they ever did by their managers. The associates were given moral instruction and needed permission from the district manager to date one another. They would hold up their hands and repeat a pledge: "From this day forward, I solemnly promise and declare that every customer that comes within ten feet of me, I will smile, look them in the eye, and greet them, so help me Sam."

The boss became Mr. Sam, the object of a folksy personality cult. Annual meetings drew thousands of people to Arkansas and were staged as pep rallies, lit with evangelical fervor. From his spartan office in Bentonville, the chairman wrote a monthly letter that went out to his tens of thousands of employees, thanking and exhorting them. After he was diagnosed with leukemia in 1982, he assured them, "I'll be coming around— maybe more infrequently—but I'll be trying and wanting to see you. You know how much I love to visit with you all on how you're doing."

When a town in Louisiana tried to keep Wal-Mart out, fearing that   30
it would leave the main street deserted, the story stayed local. When reports surfaced that Wal-Mart workers were so badly paid, in part-time jobs without benefits, that they often depended on public assistance, Mr. Sam would talk about the hourly associate who retired with two hundred thousand dollars in her stock ownership plan, and he would claim that he was raising standards of living by lowering the cost of living. When clerks and truck drivers tried to join unions and Wal-Mart ruthlessly crushed them, firing anyone foolish enough to speak out, Mr. Sam would come around afterward and apologize to any associates who felt ill-treated, vowing to do better, and some of them said that if only Mr. Sam knew what was going on, things wouldn't be so bad. When the departure of factory jobs for overseas turned into a flood, Mr. Sam launched a Buy American campaign, winning praise from politicians and newspapers around the country, and Wal-Mart stores put up MADE IN THE U.S.A. signs over racks of clothing imported from Bangladesh, and consumers didn't stop to consider that Wal-Mart was driving American manufacturers overseas or out of business by demanding killingly low prices.

The face like a good-natured bird of prey under a blue-and-white Wal-Mart baseball cap smiled more as it aged. As long as Mr. Sam was alive, Wal-Mart was a great American story out of Bentonville.

In 1989 the cancer came back in his bones, incurable multiple myeloma. Mr. Sam tried not to slow down. At the next annual meeting, he predicted more than $100 billion in sales by the millennium. "Can we do it?" he shouted to nine thousand people in an arena at the University of Arkansas, and they shouted back, "Yes we can!" He wrote his memoirs, asking himself whether he should have spent more time with his family in his later years, or devoted himself to good works, and concluded that he would do the same exact things all over again. Partnerships had kept the money in the family, and Helen and the four children (they had all received your everyday heartland upbringing) were worth $23 billion, and eventually six of the surviving Waltons would have more money than the bottom 42 percent of Americans.

By early 1992, Mr. Sam was fading. In March, President and Mrs. Bush came to Bentonville, and Mr. Sam rose unsteadily from his wheelchair to receive the Presidential Medal of Freedom. In his final days, nothing cheered him more than a hospital visit from a local store manager who wanted to talk about sales figures. In April, just after turning seventy-four, Mr. Sam died.

And it was only after his death, after Wal-Mart's downhome founder was no longer its public face, that the country began to understand what his company had done. Over the years, America had become more like Wal-Mart. It had gotten cheap. Prices were lower, and wages were lower. There were fewer union factory jobs, and more part-time jobs as store greeters. The small towns where Mr. Sam had seen his opportunity were getting poorer, which meant that consumers there depended more and more on everyday low prices, and made every last purchase at Wal-Mart, and maybe had to work there, too. The hollowing out of the heartland was good for the company's bottom line. And in parts of the country that were getting richer, on the coasts and in some big cities, many consumers regarded Wal-Mart and its vast aisles full of crappy, if not dangerous, Chinese-made goods with horror, and instead purchased their shoes and meat in expensive boutiques as if overpaying might inoculate them against the spread of cheapness, while stores like Macy's, the bastions of a former middle-class economy, faded out, and America began to look once more like the country Mr. Sam had grown up in.

Just Business: Jay Z

Everything has to be put in context.

Shawn Corey Carter, born in '69, Marcy Houses, country of Bed-Stuy, planet of Brooklyn (New York and the universe came later). Fourth and last child of Gloria Carter, employed as a clerk; father Adnis Reeves, a preacher's son. Marcy was a fortress in brick, twenty-seven buildings, six floors each, four thousand people, living to the left of him, right of him, on top and bottom of him—parties and stress, a birthday one day, a shooting the next.

At four Shawn got on a ten-speed bike, put his foot up, and coasted sitting sideways. The whole block was amazed—"Oh God!" First feeling of fame and he liked it. Fame felt good.

Mom and Pop had a million records stacked in milk crates: Curtis Mayfield, Staples Singers, ConFunkShun, the Jackson 5, Rufus, the O'Jays . . . He loved Michael Jackson the most, and when Gloria got home from work and put on "Enjoy Yourself," Shawn sang and spun around the room, his sisters singing backup. The seventies weren't bad in Marcy, kind of an adventure for a kid. Dice games on the concrete, football in fields strewn with glass, junkies nodding off on benches— kids would dare each other to tip them over. "We were able to smuggle some of the magic of that dying civilization out in our music and use it to build a new world," he later wrote. "We found our fathers on wax and on the streets and in history."

Summer of 1978, he came upon a Marcy kid no one ever noticed before in the middle of a crowd, rhyming, throwing out couplets about anything, about the benches, the people listening, his own rhymes, how good he was, the best in New York, for half an hour, and Shawn thought: "That's some cool shit. I could *do* that." Home that night he wrote down rhymes in a spiral notebook. It filled up, rhyming took over his life, in front of the mirror every morning, on the kitchen table while he banged out a beat past bedtime, driving his sisters crazy—he could *do* that. When an older boy named Jaz-O, the best rapper in Marcy, taped their voices with a heavy-ass recorder and played them back, Shawn's sounded different from the one he heard in his head. "I saw it as an opening, a way to re-create myself and reimagine my world. After I recorded a rhyme, it gave me an unbelievable rush to play it back, to hear that voice."

> I'm the king of hip-hop
> Renewed like Reeboks
> Key in the lock
> Rhymes so provocative
> As long as I live

People in Marcy started calling him Jazzy.   40

Sixth grade, he tested off the charts—reading like a twelfth grader. School never challenged him, but he scoured the dictionary for words to use. One day, Miss Louden had the class take a field trip to her brownstone in Manhattan. The refrigerator door produced water and ice cubes. That was the first time he knew he was poor. People in the projects spent half their lives sitting on plastic chairs in dirty government offices waiting for their name to be called. Kids snapped on each other for every little sign of poverty, so they talked about getting rich by whatever means, and he got that hunger, too—no way he was going to sit in class all day. When he eventually got his hands on enough cheese to buy an off-white Lexus, "I could just feel that stink and shame of being broke lifting off of me, and it felt beautiful. The sad shit is that you never really shake it all the way off, no matter how much money you get."

That same sixth-grade year, 1980, his pop bounced. Worse than a father he never knew was a father who was around the first eleven years, teaching his boy how to walk fast through the hood and remember which bodega sold laundry detergent, whether it was owned by Puerto Ricans or Arabs, how to observe people in Times Square (what was that woman's dress size?), and then disappeared and never came back. The boy never again wanted to get attached to something and have it taken away, never wanted to feel that pain again, never let anyone else break his heart. He became guarded and cool, eyes flat, stopped smiling, harsh laugh: "Hah hah hah."

Next year, when he was twelve, his big brother stole some of his jewelry. Shawn got a gun, saw the devil in Eric's drugged eyes, closed his own and squeezed. He hit his brother in the arm and thought his own life was over, but Eric didn't go to the cops, even apologized for using when Shawn came to the hospital. Just another shooting in Marcy and there'd be more but he never again hit, never got hit. He was lucky.

Crack showed up in 1985, a few years behind rap, and it took over Marcy. Crack immediately changed everything and was irreversible—brought coke out of bathrooms and hallways into public view, turned adults into fiends, kids into hustlers, made parents fear their children. Authority was gone and the projects went crazy. Shawn Carter saw another opening.

He got in the game at fifteen. He was just following—kids went to college where college grads were everywhere, kids sold drugs where hustling was everywhere. His friend Hill lined him up with a local dealer, and they went in for what turned out to be a job interview. The dealer told them how serious the hustle was, that it required dedication and integrity. The dealer was later murdered—balls cut off and stuffed in his mouth, then he was shot in the back of the head. That was how serious the hustle was. It didn't stop Shawn. He wanted in.

He was helping his mom with the light bill. He was buying the right gear for himself, the Ewings,[1] the gold teeth, the girls. He was feeling the adrenaline rush. With a cousin of Hill's he got a piece of a dead-end street in Trenton and started taking New Jersey Transit over on weekends—pretty soon he was living there. He hid his work and weapons in baggy jeans and puffy coats, construction boots kept his feet warm on winter nights. He was all business. He put the hurt on the local competition with lower prices because he got his supply cheaper from the Peruvians in Washington Heights. The squeeze made him unpopular, and one afternoon there was a face-off in the park, guns drawn, nobody shot—

[1] *the Ewings:* Basketball shoes; in 1989 Patrick Ewing became the first pro basketball player to form his own footwear brand. [All notes are the editors'.]

it was win or go home. Another time, an arrest—his first, no charges—cost him his stash and he had to work sixty straight hours in Marcy to get his money back, staying awake eating cookies and writing rhymes on brown paper bags.

His dream was to be the rich guy in the nice car with the big gun. Scarface—"*Say hello to my little friend!*"[2] The hustle was a paranoid fever, one eye always open, "excited with crime and the lavish luxuries that just excited my mind," and he got addicted to the rush just like the fiends got addicted to what he sold. Kids who put on their orange uniform and walked past the hustlers on the corner to a job at McDonald's were suckers trying to play by the rules. They didn't have a dream, they had a check, surviving nine to five, but he wasn't trying to survive—he was trying to live it to the limit. Better die enormous on the street than live dormant in a little box called Apartment 5C. He rarely smoked weed and stayed sober when he drank—being conscious let him focus on the money. He was always about the money. Second best wasn't worth the ultimate price on the street, so he learned to compete and win as if his life depended on it.

The crack game didn't end the rap game. He would go back to Marcy for a few weeks at a time and get with Jaz-O to work on rhymes. But his months on the streets took him further and further away from the notebook, so he learned to memorize longer and longer rhymes without writing them down, and that became his method. He had one foot in rap, one foot out. His cousin B-High thought he was wasting his talent hustling and stopped speaking to him. "These rappers are hoes," his crew told him. "Some white person takes all their money." Secretly, he was afraid he might not make it in music. And the business looked like a pay cut—especially after EMI offered Jaz-O a record deal in 1988, flew him to London for a couple of months with Shawn tagging along, then cut him loose when his first single bombed.

Shawn switched over to Big Daddy Kane, a legendary Brooklyn rapper with a bus tour, and was given the mic at intermissions, rapping as Jay Z for his meals. Everyone who heard Jay was blown away by his verbal cleverness, his confidence, his speed-rhyming in that high outer-borough deadpan—so good so easy he didn't take it all that serious. When the tour was over he went back to hustling.

His crew extended their distribution chain down to Maryland and D.C. where the profit margins were high, riding Lexuses up and down I-95, moving a kilo of cocaine a week. His loyalty was to his money, but he had a fear of running the streets into his thirties, of being nothing. One day in Maryland in 1994 a rival fired three shots at him point-blank and missed—"divine intervention." After a decade of hustling he decided to see if he could make as much money selling records as he did selling rocks. 50

---

[2] *"Say hello to my little friend!"*: Famous quote from Brian De Palma's 1983 gangster pic *Scarface*, in which Al Pacino's "little friend" was an M-16A1 machine gun.

I figured, "Shit why risk myself I just write it in rhymes
And let you feel me, and if you don't like it then fine"

A Brooklyn producer named DJ Clark Kent put him with a Harlem
promoter named Damon Dash, who was skeptical until he saw Jay's Nike
Air Force 1s. But none of the labels wanted Jay Z—maybe it was too
crafty, maybe too real—so he took his hustling profits and started his
own label with Dash. They called it Roc-A-Fella, in case anyone doubted
their intentions. They were going to take over the world.

Reasonable Doubt came in 1996, twenty-six years in the making. It
was complex and sinister, dense with rhymes laid over lush samples from
the records his parents had loved in the seventies, a portrait of the rapper
as a young hustler from the next, lost generation, ready to kill and live
with regrets and sick thoughts or die trying for big money, diamonds,
Rolexes, fine champagne, fine girls, escape.

This shit is wicked on these mean streets
None of my friends speak
We're all trying to win

It didn't take over the world, but it was big. Jay Z swept the clubs
and sold tapes to corner stores until he landed a distribution deal. He
gave Marcy a voice, and the nightmare that America had locked in the
basement was suddenly playing in kids' bedrooms. They wanted to live
the American dream with a vengeance, like Scarface, like Jay Z, they
wanted to break the laws and win because only fools still thought you
could do it in an orange uniform or a cheap suit when that game was
fixed, and there could be a shortcut with a big payoff. It was paying off
for the former Shawn Carter. Everyone who knew rap understood that
Jay was going to be huge.

Music was just another hustle. He was a reluctant artist, still about
the money and not apologizing for it, but to make this hustle work over
the long run you needed art. He was as cold and focused as he'd been
on the streets—seven more records in seven more years, all platinum.
He softened the tracks and dumbed down his lyrics—more large living,
less regret—to hit a bigger audience and double the dollars. It turned
out lots of young whites could relate to *money cash hoes Gs cream Cris-
tal Lexus mackin poppin pimpin bitches grams rocks nines niggaz.* Jay Z
told rap's eternal story—"why I'm dope, doper than you"—a hundred
different ways, no two couplets alike, and the kids believed him, so they
wore what he wore, drank what he drank, and made him rich.

He launched a clothing line and it brought in more revenue than
his music company, hundreds of millions. Started his own movie studio,
got his own Reebok sneaker, distributed his own vodka, put out his own
cologne, trademarked his own shade of Jay Z Blue, cross-promoted everything. Stabbed a record producer in the VIP section of a Times Square
club in 1999 for bootlegging his fourth album and quoted Pacino in

Godfather II as he drove in the knife: "Lance, you broke my heart." Holed up in the Trump Hotel with his lawyer and crew playing guts, a three-card game that rewarded self-possession. Vowed never to lose his shit again and later copped a plea, getting away with probation.

He became a corporate rapper, an outlaw entrepreneur, wearing sneakers to the boardroom like in a Silicon Valley start-up, working in the legit world while living the hustler's dream. He retired from rapping in 2003 at Madison Square Garden (but that didn't last long) and became a music executive, president of Def Jam, the biggest label in hip-hop. He cut his old partner at Roc-A-Fella loose, taking the name with him— "It's just business," Jay Z told Damon Dash, sounding like another screen mobster. And he rhymed the point in his own words:

> I sold kilos of coke, I'm guessin I can sell CDs
> I'm not a businessman, I'm a business, man
> Let me handle my business, damn!

It was the same hustle all the way up—he was doing the same thing on the twenty-ninth floor in midtown that he'd been doing on the corner in Trenton. The mainstream embraced rap while rap copied the mainstream, and Jay Z played the game better than the suits because he'd learned it on the streets. When critics called him a sellout or materialist, he had the answer: selfishness was a rational response to the reality he faced.

Everything has to be put in context.

He did the things that top celebrities did: became a lifestyle brand, opened a sports bar chain, got sued by his workers for back wages, met Bono in a London cigar room with Quincy Jones, put his name to philanthropic causes, made the Forbes 400 (net worth 450 mil), hung out with presidents, carried on beefs with other stars, hooked up with a singer every bit as big as he was, bought her an island for her birthday, rented a wing of a maternity ward before she was due and made it their private suite, tried to trademark their baby girl's name for future use (the U.S. Patent Office refused), and released a single when Blue Ivy Carter was four days old, rapping: "My greatest creation was you . . . You don't yet know what swag is."

The more he won, the more they loved him everywhere, lived 60 through him, celebrated his money and power as their own. At concerts fans raised their hands together and flashed his Roc-A-Fella diamond logo as if they owned a piece of the deal. He was a mogul and a revolutionary, an icon and a thug (that was the perfect hustle), worshipped for getting to the top with a big fuck-you and no standing in line, still telling the world why he was dope, doper than you. And if he ever failed— when his sports bar in Vegas went bust, or his summer tournament basketball team stacked with NBA ringers lost, or his deal with Chrysler to put out a Jay Z edition Jeep Commander painted Jay Z Blue fell through—every trace of failure was hidden, as if the revelation might be fatal to his spell. He had to keep winning. Success wasn't about anything except itself.

When Jay Z bought a slice of the Nets and fronted the team's move to Brooklyn, he became the boss and the star, the black Branch Rickey.[3] Jackie Robinson with sins. When the new arena opened, he sold it out eight straight nights. In the smoky dark he told sixteen thousand fans, "I don't think it's a coincidence that this is where Jackie Robinson was the first African American to play professional sports and break the color barrier. And I don't think it's a coincidence that I was part of the group that brought the Nets here from New Jersey. You'll hear people say I only own a small percentage of the team. It doesn't matter what percentage— the story is that a black kid from a single-parent house made it from the Marcy projects about six minutes away from here. So the fact that I have any ownership in this franchise is fuckin amazing. The fact that I have any ownership in this venue is fuckin amazing. Don't let them diminish your accomplishment or dim your shine." Jay Z held up his middle finger. Sixteen thousand middle fingers answered him.

There were times when he looked around at his life and thought he was getting away with murder.

Ken Krimstein/The New Yorker Collection/The Cartoon Bank

[3]**Branch Rickey:** Brooklyn Dodgers executive (1881–1965) who signed Jackie Robinson, the first African American to play major league baseball.

ENGAGING THE TEXT

1. What specific personality traits, formative experiences, habits, and critical decisions were most important to Walton's success? What does his story signify to you about opportunity, success, and money in America? For example, how does your definition of "rich" compare to the one Walton offers in paragraph 2?

2. In paragraph 7, Packer summarizes one of Walton's operating principles: "People were cheap. . . . It was true everywhere all the time." Debate this claim with classmates, citing specific examples of contemporary shopping behavior, brands, or marketing strategies that support or challenge Walton's theory.

3. The idea of morality comes up twice in the profile of Walton, who sought employees "of the right moral character" (para.13) and whose store associates "were given moral instruction and needed permission from the district manager to date one another" (para. 28). In what kind of jobs or professions is it reasonable to expect particularly high moral standards, and how can these be defined and measured?

4. What adjectives would you use to describe Jay Z and his rise to fame and fortune? What were the keys to his success?

5. Discuss Jay Z's description of how he felt when he got a Lexus (para. 41) and his remark that the "stink and shame of being broke" never goes away entirely.

6. What roles do race and social class play in Jay Z's life, and what seems to be his attitude toward them? To what extent does Packer's profile emphasize or deemphasize race and class?

7. Consider the title of Packer's book in relation to these two profiles: To what extent do they suggest that something in American culture is unwinding, unravelling, or falling apart? Where does Packer seem to criticize Walton, Walmart, or Jay Z? In what ways do the profiles offer a glimpse of America's "inner history"?

8. **Thinking Rhetorically** How would you characterize Packer's prose style and voice in these two excerpts? For example, is his word choice ordinary or sophisticated? How long and complex are his sentences? What passages, if any, project a particular emotional tone such as admiration, disapproval, or amusement? Explain why you think Packer adopted this approach and why you find it effective or ineffective.

EXPLORING CONNECTIONS

9. In what respects does Jay Z's story echo Sam Walton's, and where does it most significantly diverge? Write a dialogue between Jay Z and Walton in which they discuss their commonalities, their differences, and the myths and realities of the American Dream.

10. Compare Walton and Jay Z to Ken Harvey, the vocational education student who said, "I Just Wanna Be Average" (p. 124). Why don't Walton and Jay Z want to be average? What positive or negative roles do you think schooling played in their ambition and ultimate success? Write a journal entry or essay about your

own level of ambition — do you seek to be the best, or average, or somewhere in between? How do you think most Americans view someone who is content with being average — or less than average — in terms of school, career, or social status?

EXTENDING THE CRITICAL CONTEXT

11. The U.S. Government Printing Office archives contain "Remarks on Presenting the Presidential Medal of Freedom to Samuel M. Walton in Bentonville, Arkansas" — delivered by President George H. W. Bush on March 17, 1992. To find this document, Google "GPO public papers of the presidents." Compare President Bush's summary of Walton's accomplishments to George Packer's account.

12. Packer's book *The Unwinding* works like a mosaic or kaleidoscope, presenting profiles of numerous Americans, including factory worker Tammy Thomas and Occupy Wall Street activist Nelini Stamp in addition to more prominent figures such as Oprah and Senator Elizabeth Warren. Read one or more additional profiles and explain how they extend Packer's examination of the "inner history" of America.

13. Research an important American of your choice, whether contemporary or historical, and write a brief profile of her or him, following Packer's method and style as closely as possible. For a group project, organize a set of profiles that explore a particular theme or group — for example, Westerners, female scientists, immigrants, or performers.

SERVING IN FLORIDA
BARBARA EHRENREICH

What's it like to live on minimum wage? As a journalist preparing to write about working-class life, Barbara Ehrenreich decided to take a series of unglamorous jobs — waitressing, housecleaning, retail sales — and to live on the meager wages these jobs paid. In this account of her experiences, Ehrenreich describes trying to make ends meet by adding a second waitressing job at "Jerry's" to her eight-hour shift at "The Hearthside," having discovered that $2.43 an hour plus tips doesn't add up as fast as her rent and other bills. The full account of Ehrenreich's "plunge into poverty" may be found in the *New York Times* best-seller *Nickel and Dimed: On (Not) Getting By in America* (2001). Barbara Ehrenreich (b. 1941) has published articles in many of America's leading magazines and newspapers and has authored more than a dozen books. Recent works include *Bright-Sided: How Positive Thinking Is Undermining America* (2009) and a memoir, *Living with a Wild God: A Nonbeliever's Search for the Truth About Everything* (2014).

PICTURE A FAT PERSON'S HELL, and I don't mean a place with no food. Instead there is everything you might eat if eating had no bodily consequences—the cheese fries, the chicken-fried steaks, the fudge-laden desserts—only here every bite must be paid for, one way or another, in human discomfort. The kitchen is a cavern, a stomach leading to the lower intestine that is the garbage and dishwashing area, from which issue bizarre smells combining the edible and the offal: creamy carrion, pizza barf, and that unique and enigmatic Jerry's[1] scent, citrus fart. The floor is slick with spills, forcing us to walk through the kitchen with tiny steps, like Susan McDougal in leg irons.[2] Sinks everywhere are clogged with scraps of lettuce, decomposing lemon wedges, water-logged toast crusts. Put your hand down on any counter and you risk being stuck to it by the film of ancient syrup spills, and this is unfortunate because hands are utensils here, used for scooping up lettuce onto the salad plates, lifting out pie slices, and even moving hash browns from one plate to another. The regulation poster in the single unisex rest room admonishes us to wash our hands thoroughly, and even offers instructions for doing so, but there is always some vital substance missing— soap, paper towels, toilet paper—and I never found all three at once. You learn to stuff your pockets with napkins before going in there, and too bad about the customers, who must eat, although they don't realize it, almost literally out of our hands.

The break room summarizes the whole situation: there is none, because there are no breaks at Jerry's. For six to eight hours in a row, you never sit except to pee. Actually, there are three folding chairs at a table immediately adjacent to the bathroom, but hardly anyone ever sits in this, the very rectum of the gastroarchitectural system. Rather, the function of the peri-toilet area is to house the ashtrays in which servers and dishwashers leave their cigarettes burning at all times, like votive candles, so they don't have to waste time lighting up again when they dash back here for a puff. Almost everyone smokes as if their pulmonary well-being depended on it—the multinational mélange of cooks; the dishwashers, who are all Czechs here; the servers, who are American natives—creating an atmosphere in which oxygen is only an occasional pollutant. My first morning at Jerry's, when the hypoglycemic shakes set in, I complain to one of my fellow servers that I don't understand how she can go so long without food. "Well, I don't understand how *you* can go so long without a cigarette," she responds in a tone of reproach. Because work is what you do for others; smoking is what you do for yourself. I don't know why the antismoking crusaders have never grasped the element of defiant self-nurturance that makes the habit so

---

[1] **Jerry's:** Not the real name of the restaurant where Ehrenreich worked; the restaurant was part of a "well-known national chain." [All notes are the editors', except 6, 9, 12, and 13.]

[2] **Susan McDougal in leg irons:** McDougal refused to testify against President Bill Clinton and Hillary Clinton before the Whitewater grand jury in 1996; she spent almost twenty-two months in various prisons and eventually received a presidential pardon in 2001.

endearing to its victims—as if, in the American workplace, the only thing people have to call their own is the tumors they are nourishing and the spare moments they devote to feeding them.

Now, the Industrial Revolution is not an easy transition, especially, in my experience, when you have to zip through it in just a couple of days. I have gone from craft work straight into the factory, from the air-conditioned morgue of the Hearthside[3] directly into the flames. Customers arrive in human waves, sometimes disgorged fifty at a time from their tour buses, puckish and whiny. Instead of two "girls" on the floor at once, there can be as many as six of us running around in our brilliant pink-and-orange Hawaiian shirts. Conversations, either with customers or with fellow employees, seldom last more than twenty seconds at a time. On my first day, in fact, I am hurt by my sister servers' coldness. My mentor for the day is a supremely competent, emotionally uninflected twenty-three-year-old, and the others, who gossip a little among themselves about the real reason someone is out sick today and the size of the bail bond someone else has had to pay, ignore me completely. On my second day, I find out why. "Well, it's good to see you again," one of them says in greeting. "Hardly anyone comes back after the first day." I feel powerfully vindicated—a survivor—but it would take a long time, probably months, before I could hope to be accepted into this sorority.

I start out with the beautiful, heroic idea of handling the two jobs at once, and for two days I almost do it: working the breakfast/lunch shift at Jerry's from 8:00 till 2:00, arriving at the Hearthside a few minutes late, at 2:10, and attempting to hold out until 10:00. In the few minutes I have between jobs, I pick up a spicy chicken sandwich at the Wendy's drive-through window, gobble it down in the car, and change from khaki slacks to black, from Hawaiian to rust-colored polo. There is a problem, though. When, during the 3:00–4:00 o'clock dead time, I finally sit down to wrap silver, my flesh seems to bond to the seat. I try to refuel with a purloined cup of clam chowder, as I've seen Gail and Joan do dozens of times, but Stu[4] catches me and hisses "No eating!" although there's not a customer around to be offended by the sight of food making contact with a server's lips. So I tell Gail I'm going to quit, and she hugs me and says she might just follow me to Jerry's herself.

But the chances of this are minuscule. She has left the flophouse and her annoying roommate and is back to living in her truck. But, guess what, she reports to me excitedly later that evening, Phillip has given her permission to park overnight in the hotel parking lot, as long as she keeps out of sight, and the parking lot should be totally safe since it's patrolled by a hotel security guard! With the Hearthside offering benefits like that, how could anyone think of leaving? This must be Phillip's theory, anyway.

5

---

[3] **Hearthside:** The other restaurant where Ehrenreich worked.
[4] **Gail, Joan, Stu:** Waitress, hostess, and assistant manager at the Hearthside restaurant. Phillip, mentioned in the subsequent paragraph, is the top manager.

He accepts my resignation with a shrug, his main concern being that I return my two polo shirts and aprons.

Gail would have triumphed at Jerry's, I'm sure, but for me it's a crash course in exhaustion management. Years ago, the kindly fry cook who trained me to waitress at a Los Angeles truck stop used to say: Never make an unnecessary trip; if you don't have to walk fast, walk slow; if you don't have to walk, stand. But at Jerry's the effort of distinguishing necessary from unnecessary and urgent from whenever would itself be too much of an energy drain. The only thing to do is to treat each shift as a one-time-only emergency: you've got fifty starving people out there, lying scattered on the battlefield, so get out there and feed them! Forget that you will have to do this again tomorrow, forget that you will have to be alert enough to dodge the drunks on the drive home tonight—just burn, burn, burn! Ideally, at some point you enter what servers call a "rhythm" and psychologists term a "flow state," where signals pass from the sense organs directly to the muscles, bypassing the cerebral cortex, and a Zen-like emptiness sets in. I'm on a 2:00–10:00 P.M. shift now, and a male server from the morning shift tells me about the time he "pulled a triple"—three shifts in a row, all the way around the clock—and then got off and had a drink and met this girl, and maybe he shouldn't tell me this, but they had sex right then and there and it was like *beautiful*.

But there's another capacity of the neuromuscular system, which is pain. I start tossing back drugstore-brand ibuprofens as if they were vitamin C, four before each shift, because an old mouse-related repetitive-stress injury in my upper back has come back to full-spasm strength, thanks to the tray carrying. In my ordinary life, this level of disability might justify a day of ice packs and stretching. Here I comfort myself with the Aleve commercial where the cute blue-collar guy asks: If you quit after working four hours, what would your boss say? And the not-so-cute blue-collar guy, who's lugging a metal beam on his back, answers: He'd fire me, that's what. But fortunately, the commercial tells us, we workers can exert the same kind of authority over our painkillers that our bosses exert over us. If Tylenol doesn't want to work for more than four hours, you just fire its ass and switch to Aleve.

True, I take occasional breaks from this life, going home now and then to catch up on e-mail and for conjugal visits (though I am careful to "pay" for everything I eat here, at $5 for a dinner, which I put in a jar), seeing *The Truman Show*[5] with friends and letting them buy my ticket. And I still have those what-am-I-doing-here moments at work, when I get so homesick for the printed word that I obsessively reread the six-page menu. But as the days go by, my old life is beginning to look exceedingly strange. The e-mails and phone messages addressed to my former self come from a distant race of people with exotic concerns and far

[5] **The Truman Show:** 1998 film (directed by Peter Weir and starring Jim Carrey) about a man who discovers his whole life is actually a TV show.

too much time on their hands. The neighborly market I used to cruise for produce now looks forbiddingly like a Manhattan yuppie emporium. And when I sit down one morning in my real home to pay bills from my past life, I am dazzled by the two- and three-figure sums owed to outfits like Club Body Tech and Amazon.com.

Management at Jerry's is generally calmer and more "professional" than at the Hearthside, with two exceptions. One is Joy, a plump, blowsy woman in her early thirties who once kindly devoted several minutes of her time to instructing me in the correct one-handed method of tray carrying but whose moods change disconcertingly from shift to shift and even within one. The other is B.J., aka B.J. the Bitch, whose contribution is to stand by the kitchen counter and yell, "Nita, your order's up, move it!" or "Barbara, didn't you see you've got another table out there? Come *on*, girl!" Among other things, she is hated for having replaced the whipped cream squirt cans with big plastic whipped-cream-filled baggies that have to be squeezed with both hands—because, reportedly, she saw or thought she saw employees trying to inhale the propellant gas from the squirt cans, in the hope that it might be nitrous oxide. On my third night, she pulls me aside abruptly and brings her face so close that it looks like she's planning to butt me with her forehead. But instead of saying "You're fired," she says, "You're doing fine." The only trouble is I'm spending time chatting with customers: "That's how they're getting you." Furthermore I am letting them "run me," which means harassment by sequential demands: you bring the catsup and they decide they want extra Thousand Island; you bring that and they announce they now need a side of fries, and so on into distraction. Finally she tells me not to take her wrong. She tries to say things in a nice way, but "you get into a mode, you know, because everything has to move so fast."[6]

I mumble thanks for the advice, feeling like I've just been stripped naked by the crazed enforcer of some ancient sumptuary law:[7] No chatting for *you*, girl. No fancy service ethic allowed for the serfs. Chatting with customers is for the good-looking young college-educated servers in the downtown carpaccio and ceviche joints, the kids who can make $70–$100 a night. What had I been thinking? My job is to move orders from tables to kitchen and then trays from kitchen to tables. Customers are in fact the major obstacle to the smooth transformation of information into food and food into money—they are, in short, the enemy. And the painful thing is that I'm beginning to see it this way myself. There are the traditional asshole types—frat boys who down multiple Buds

10

---

[6] In *Workers in a Lean World: Unions in the International Economy* (Verso, 1997), Kim Moody cites studies finding an increase in stress-related workplace injuries and illness between the mid-1980s and the early 1990s. He argues that rising stress levels reflect a new system of "management by stress" in which workers in a variety of industries are being squeezed to extract maximum productivity, to the detriment of their health. [Ehrenreich's note.]

[7] **sumptuary laws:** Laws which regulate personal behavior on moral or religious grounds.

and then make a fuss because the steaks are so emaciated and the fries so sparse—as well as the variously impaired—due to age, diabetes, or literacy issues—who require patient nutritional counseling. The worst, for some reason, are the Visible Christians—like the ten-person table, all jolly and sanctified after Sunday night service, who run me mercilessly and then leave me $1 on a $92 bill. Or the guy with the crucifixion T-shirt (someone to look up to) who complains that his baked potato is too hard and his iced tea too icy (I cheerfully fix both) and leaves no tip at all. As a general rule, people wearing crosses or WWJD? ("What Would Jesus Do?") buttons look at us disapprovingly no matter what we do, as if they were confusing waitressing with Mary Magdalene's[8] original profession.

I make friends, over time, with the other "girls" who work my shift: Nita, the tattooed twenty-something who taunts us by going around saying brightly, "Have we started making money yet?" Ellen, whose teenage son cooks on the graveyard shift and who once managed a restaurant in Massachusetts but won't try out for management here because she prefers being a "common worker" and not "ordering people around." Easygoing fiftyish Lucy, with the raucous laugh, who limps toward the end of the shift because of something that has gone wrong with her leg, the exact nature of which cannot be determined without health insurance. We talk about the usual girl things—men, children, and the sinister allure of Jerry's chocolate peanut-butter cream pie—though no one, I notice, ever brings up anything potentially expensive, like shopping or movies. As at the Hearthside, the only recreation ever referred to is partying, which requires little more than some beer, a joint, and a few close friends. Still, no one is homeless, or cops to it anyway, thanks usually to a working husband or boyfriend. All in all, we form a reliable mutual-support group: if one of us is feeling sick or overwhelmed, another one will "bev" a table or even carry trays for her. If one of us is off sneaking a cigarette or a pee, the others will do their best to conceal her absence from the enforcers of corporate rationality.[9]

[8]**Mary Magdalene:** A figure in the New Testament gospels whom popular culture has often painted as a prostitute. Contemporary scholars dispute that view, some offering characterizations of Mary as a saint, an apostle, or a rabbi. See, for example, *Mary Magdalene in Medieval Culture: Conflicted Roles*, ed. Peter V. Loewen and Robin Waugh (New York: Routledge, 2014).

[9]Until April 1998, there was no federally mandated right to bathroom breaks. According to Marc Linder and Ingrid Nygaard, authors of *Void Where Prohibited: Rest Breaks and the Right to Urinate on Company Time* (Cornell University Press, 1997), "The right to rest and void at work is not high on the list of social or political causes supported by professional or executive employees, who enjoy personal workplace liberties that millions of factory workers can only dream about.... While we were dismayed to discover that workers lacked an acknowledged right to void at work, [the workers] were amazed by outsiders' naïve belief that their employers would permit them to perform this basic bodily function when necessary.... A factory worker, not allowed a break for six-hour stretches, voided into pads worn inside her uniform; and a kindergarten teacher in a school without aides had to take all twenty children with her to the bathroom and line them up outside the stall door while she voided." [Ehrenreich's note.]

© David McLain/Aurora Photos

But my saving human connection—my oxytocin receptor, as it were—is George, the nineteen-year-old Czech dishwasher who has been in this country exactly one week. We get talking when he asks me, tortuously, how much cigarettes cost at Jerry's. I do my best to explain that they cost over a dollar more here than at a regular store and suggest that he just take one from the half-filled packs that are always lying around on the break table. But that would be unthinkable. Except for the one tiny earring signaling his allegiance to some vaguely alternative point of view, George is a perfect straight arrow—crew-cut, hardworking, and hungry for eye contact. "Czech Republic," I ask, "or Slovakia?" and he seems delighted that I know the difference. "Vaclav Havel," I try, "Velvet Revolution, Frank Zappa?" "Yes, yes, 1989," he says, and I realize that for him this is already history.

My project is to teach George English. "How are you today, George?" I say at the start of each shift. "I am good, and how are you today, Barbara?" I learn that he is not paid by Jerry's but by the "agent" who shipped him over—$5 an hour, with the agent getting the dollar or so difference between that and what Jerry's pays dishwashers. I learn also that he shares an apartment with a crowd of other Czech "dishers," as he calls them, and that he cannot sleep until one of them goes off for his shift, leaving a vacant bed. We are having one of our ESL [English as a Second Language] sessions late one afternoon when B.J. catches us at it and orders "Joseph" to take up the rubber mats on the floor near the dishwashing sinks and mop underneath. "I thought your name was George," I say loud enough for B.J. to hear as she strides off back to the counter. Is she embarrassed? Maybe a little, because she greets me back at the counter with "George, Joseph—there are so many of them!" I say nothing, neither nodding nor smiling, and for this I am punished later, when I think I am ready to go and she announces that I need to roll fifty more sets of silverware, and isn't it time I mixed up a fresh four-gallon batch of blue-cheese dressing? May you grow old in this place, B.J., is the curse I beam out at her when I am finally permitted to leave. May the syrup spills glue your feet to the floor.

I make the decision to move closer to Key West. First, because of the drive. Second and third, also because of the drive: gas is eating up $4–$5 a day, and although Jerry's is as high-volume as you can get, the tips average only 10 percent, and not just for a newbie like me. Between the base pay of $2.15 an hour and the obligation to share tips with the busboys and dishwashers, we're averaging only about $7.50 an hour. Then there is the $30 I had to spend on the regulation tan slacks worn by Jerry's servers—a setback it could take weeks to absorb. (I had combed the town's two downscale department stores hoping for something cheaper but decided in the end that these marked-down Dockers, originally $49, were more likely to survive a daily washing.) Of my fellow servers, everyone who lacks a working husband or boyfriend seems to have a second job: Nita does something at a computer eight hours a day; another welds. Without the forty-five-minute commute, I can picture myself working two jobs and still having the time to shower between them.

So I take the $500 deposit I have coming from my landlord, the $400 I have earned toward the next month's rent, plus the $200 reserved for emergencies, and use the $1,100 to pay the rent and deposit on trailer number 46 in the Overseas Trailer Park, a mile from the cluster of budget hotels that constitute Key West's version of an industrial park. Number 46 is about eight feet in width and shaped like a barbell inside, with a narrow region—because of the sink and the stove—separating the bedroom from what might optimistically be called the "living" area, with its two-person table and half-sized couch. The bathroom is so small my knees rub against the shower stall when I sit on the toilet, and you can't just leap out of the bed, you have to climb down to the foot of it in order to find a patch of floor space to stand on. Outside, I am within a few yards of a liquor store, a bar that advertises "free beer tomorrow," a convenience store, and a Burger King—but no supermarket or, alas, Laundromat. By reputation, the Overseas park is a nest of crime and crack, and I am hoping at least for some vibrant multicultural street life. But desolation rules night and day, except for a thin stream of pedestrians heading for their jobs at the Sheraton or the 7-Eleven. There are not exactly people here but what amounts to canned labor, being preserved between shifts from the heat.

In line with my reduced living conditions, a new form of ugliness arises at Jerry's. First we are confronted—via an announcement on the computers through which we input orders—with the new rule that the hotel bar, the Driftwood, is henceforth off-limits to restaurant employees.

The culprit, I learn through the grapevine, is the ultraefficient twenty-three-year-old who trained me—another trailer home dweller and a mother of three. Something had set her off one morning, so she slipped out for a nip and returned to the floor impaired. The restriction mostly hurts Ellen, whose habit it is to free her hair from its rubber band and drop by the Driftwood for a couple of Zins[10] before heading home at the end of her shift, but all of us feel the chill. Then the next day, when I go for straws, I find the dry-storage room locked. It's never been locked before; we go in and out of it all day—for napkins, jelly containers, Styrofoam cups for takeout. Vic, the portly assistant manager who opens it for me, explains that he caught one of the dishwashers attempting to steal something and, unfortunately, the miscreant will be with us until a replacement can be found—hence the locked door. I neglect to ask what he had been trying to steal but Vic tells me who he is—the kid with the buzz cut and the earring, you know, he's back there right now.

I wish I could say I rushed back and confronted George to get his side of the story. I wish I could say I stood up to Vic and insisted that George be given a translator and allowed to defend himself or announced that I'd find a lawyer who'd handle the case pro bono.[11] At the very least I should have testified as to the kid's honesty. The mystery to me is that there's not much worth stealing in the dry-storage room, at least not in any fenceable quantity: "Is Gyorgi here, and am having 200—maybe 250—catsup packets. What do you say?" My guess is that he had taken—if he had taken anything at all—some Saltines or a can of cherry pie mix and that the motive for taking it was hunger.

So why didn't I intervene? Certainly not because I was held back by the kind of moral paralysis that can mask as journalistic objectivity. On the contrary, something new—something loathsome and servile—had infected me, along with the kitchen odors that I could still sniff on my bra when I finally undressed at night. In real life I am moderately brave, but plenty of brave people shed their courage in POW camps, and maybe something similar goes on in the infinitely more congenial milieu of the low-wage American workplace. Maybe, in a month or two more at Jerry's, I might have regained my crusading spirit. Then again, in a month or two I might have turned into a different person altogether—say, the kind of person who would have turned George in.

But this is not something I was slated to find out. When my month-long plunge into poverty was almost over, I finally landed my dream job—housekeeping. I did this by walking into the personnel office of the only place I figured I might have some credibility, the hotel attached to Jerry's, and confiding urgently that I had to have a second job if I was to pay my rent and, no, it couldn't be front-desk clerk. "All *right*," the personnel lady fairly spits, "so it's *housekeeping*," and marches me back to

---

[10] **Zins:** Glasses of zinfandel wine.
[11] **pro bono:** Free of charge.

meet Millie, the housekeeping manager, a tiny, frenetic Hispanic woman who greets me as "babe" and hands me a pamphlet emphasizing the need for a positive attitude. The pay is $6.10 an hour and the hours are nine in the morning till "whenever," which I am hoping can be defined as a little before two. I don't have to ask about health insurance once I meet Carlotta, the middle-aged African American woman who will be training me. Carlie, as she tells me to call her, is missing all of her top front teeth.

On that first day of housekeeping and last day—although I don't yet know it's the last—of my life as a low-wage worker in Key West, Carlie is in a foul mood. We have been given nineteen rooms to clean, most of them "checkouts," as opposed to "stay-overs," and requiring the whole enchilada of bed stripping, vacuuming, and bathroom scrubbing. When one of the rooms that had been listed as a stay-over turns out to be a checkout, she calls Millie to complain, but of course to no avail. "So make up the motherfucker," she orders me, and I do the beds while she sloshes around the bathroom. For four hours without a break I strip and remake beds, taking about four and a half minutes per queen-sized bed, which I could get down to three if there were any reason to. We try to avoid vacuuming by picking up the larger specks by hand, but often there is nothing to do but drag the monstrous vacuum cleaner—it weighs about thirty pounds—off our cart and try to wrestle it around the floor. Sometimes Carlie hands me the squirt bottle of "Bam" (an acronym for something that begins, ominously, with "butyric"—the rest of it has been worn off the label) and lets me do the bathrooms. No service ethic challenges me here to new heights of performance. I just concentrate on removing the pubic hairs from the bathtubs, or at least the dark ones that I can see.

I had looked forward to the breaking-and-entering aspect of cleaning the stay-overs, the chance to examine the secret physical existence of strangers. But the contents of the rooms are always banal and surprisingly neat—zipped-up shaving kits, shoes lined up against the wall (there are no closets), flyers for snorkeling trips, maybe an empty wine bottle or two. It is the TV that keeps us going, from Jerry to Sally to *Hawaii Five-O* and then on to the soaps. If there's something especially arresting, like "Won't Take No for an Answer" on Jerry, we sit down on the edge of a bed and giggle for a moment, as if this were a pajama party instead of a terminally dead-end job. The soaps are the best, and Carlie turns the volume up full blast so she won't miss anything from the bathroom or while the vacuum is on. In Room 503, Marcia confronts Jeff about Lauren. In 505, Lauren taunts poor cheated-on Marcia. In 511, Helen offers Amanda $10,000 to stop seeing Eric, prompting Carlie to emerge from the bathroom to study Amanda's troubled face. "You take it, girl," she advises. "I would for sure."

The tourists' rooms that we clean and, beyond them, the far more expensively appointed interiors in the soaps begin after a while to merge.

20

We have entered a better world—a world of comfort where every day is a day off, waiting to be filled with sexual intrigue. We are only gate-crashers in this fantasy, however, forced to pay for our presence with backaches and perpetual thirst. The mirrors, and there are far too many of them in hotel rooms, contain the kind of person you would normally find pushing a shopping cart down a city street—bedraggled, dressed in a damp hotel polo shirt two sizes too large, and with sweat dribbling down her chin like drool. I am enormously relieved when Carlie announces a half-hour meal break, but my appetite fades when I see that the bag of hot dog rolls she has been carrying around on our cart is not trash salvaged from a checkout but what she has brought for her lunch.

Between the TV and the fact that I'm in no position, as a first dayer, to launch new topics of conversation, I don't learn much about Carlie except that she hurts, and in more than one way. She moves slowly about her work, muttering something about joint pain, and this is probably going to doom her, since the young immigrant housekeepers—Polish and Salvadoran—like to polish off their rooms by two in the afternoon, while she drags the work out till six. It doesn't make any sense to hurry, she observes, when you're being paid by the hour. Already, management has brought in a woman to do what sounds like time-motion studies and there's talk about switching to paying by the room.[12] She broods, too, about all the little evidences of disrespect that come her way, and not only from management. "They don't care about us," she tells me of the hotel guests; in fact, they don't notice us at all unless something gets stolen from a room—"then they're all over you." We're eating our lunch side by side in the break room when a white guy in a maintenance uniform walks by and Carlie calls out, "Hey you," in a friendly way, "what's your name?"

"Peter Pan," he says, his back already to us.

"That wasn't funny," Carlie says, turning to me. "That was no kind of answer. Why did he have to be funny like that?" I venture that he has an attitude, and she nods as if that were an acute diagnosis. "Yeah, he got a attitude all right."

"Maybe he's having a bad day," I elaborate, not because I feel any obligation to defend the white race but because her face is so twisted with hurt.

When I request permission to leave at about 3:30, another housekeeper warns me that no one has so far succeeded in combining housekeeping with serving at Jerry's: "Some kid did it once for five days, and you're no kid." With that helpful information in mind, I rush back to number 46, down four Advils (the name brand this time), shower, stooping to fit into the stall, and attempt to compose myself for the oncoming

25

[12]A few weeks after I left, I heard ads on the radio for housekeeping jobs at this hotel at the amazing rate of "up to $9 an hour." When I inquired, I found out that the hotel had indeed started paying by the room, and I suspect that Carlie, if she lasted, was still making the equivalent of $6 an hour or quite a bit less. [Ehrenreich's note]

shift. So much for what Marx termed the "reproduction of labor power," meaning the things a worker has to do just so she'll be ready to labor again. The only unforeseen obstacle to the smooth transition from job to job is that my tan Jerry's slacks, which had looked reasonably clean by 40-watt bulb last night when I hand washed my Hawaiian shirt, prove by daylight to be mottled with catsup and ranch-dressing stains. I spend most of my hour-long break between jobs attempting to remove the edible portions of the slacks with a sponge and then drying them over the hood of my car in the sun.

I can do this two-job thing, is my theory, if I can drink enough caffeine and avoid getting distracted by George's ever more obvious suffering.[13] The first few days after the alleged theft, he seemed not to understand the trouble he was in, and our chirpy little conversations had continued. But the last couple of shifts he's been listless and unshaven, and tonight he looks like the ghost we all know him to be, with dark half-moons hanging from his eyes. At one point, when I am briefly immobilized by the task of filling little paper cups with sour cream for baked potatoes, he comes over and looks as if he'd like to explore the limits of our shared vocabulary, but I am called to the floor for a table. I resolve to give him all my tips that night, and to hell with the experiment in low-wage money management. At eight, Ellen and I grab a snack together standing at the mephitic end of the kitchen counter, but I can only manage two or three mozzarella sticks, and lunch had been a mere handful of McNuggets. I am not tired at all, I assure myself, though it may be that there is simply no more "I" left to do the tiredness monitoring. What I would see if I were more alert to the situation is that the forces of destruction are already massing against me. There is only one cook on duty, a young man named Jesus ("Hay-Sue," that is), and he is new to the job. And there is Joy, who shows up to take over in the middle of the shift dressed in high heels and a long, clingy white dress and fuming as if she'd just been stood up in some cocktail bar.

Then it comes, the perfect storm. Four of my tables fill up at once. Four tables is nothing for me now, but only so long as they are obligingly staggered. As I bev table 27, tables 25, 28, and 24 are watching enviously. As I bev 25, 24 glowers because their bevs haven't even been ordered. Twenty-eight is four yuppyish types, meaning everything on the side and agonizing instructions as to the chicken Caesars. Twenty-five is a middle-aged black couple who complain, with some justice, that the iced tea isn't fresh and the tabletop is sticky. But table 24 is the meteorological event of the century: ten British tourists who seem to have made the decision to absorb the American experience entirely by mouth.

---

[13] In 1996 the number of persons holding two or more jobs averaged 7.8 million, or 6.2 percent of the work force. It was about the same rate for men and for women (6.1 versus 6.2). About two-thirds of multiple jobholders work one job full-time and the other part-time. Only a heroic minority—4 percent of men and 2 percent of women—work two full-time jobs simultaneously (John F. Stinson Jr., "New Data on Multiple Jobholding Available from the CPS," *Monthly Labor Review*, March 1997). [Ehrenreich's note]

Here everyone has at least two drinks—iced tea *and* milk shake, Michelob *and* water (with lemon slice in the water, please)—and a huge, promiscuous orgy of breakfast specials, mozz sticks, chicken strips, quesadillas, burgers with cheese and without, sides of hash browns with cheddar, with onions, with gravy, seasoned fries, plain fries, banana splits. Poor Jesus! Poor me! Because when I arrive with their first tray of food—after three prior trips just to refill bevs—Princess Di refuses to eat her chicken strips with her pancake and sausage special since, as she now reveals, the strips were meant to be an appetizer. Maybe the others would have accepted their meals, but Di, who is deep into her third Michelob, insists that everything else go back while they work on their starters. Meanwhile, the yuppies are waving me down for more decaf and the black couple looks ready to summon the NAACP.

Much of what happens next is lost in the fog of war. Jesus starts [30] going under. The little printer in front of him is spewing out orders faster than he can rip them off, much less produce the meals. A menacing restlessness rises from the tables, all of which are full. Even the invincible Ellen is ashen from stress. I take table 24 their reheated main courses, which they immediately reject as either too cold or fossilized by the microwave. When I return to the kitchen with their trays (three trays in three trips) Joy confronts me with arms akimbo: "What *is* this?" She means the food—the plates of rejected pancakes, hash browns in assorted flavors, toasts, burgers, sausages, eggs. "Uh, scrambled with cheddar," I try, "and that's—" "No," she screams in my face, "is it a traditional, a super-scramble, an eye-opener?" I pretend to study my check for a clue, but entropy has been up to its tricks, not only on the plates but in my head, and I have to admit that the original order is beyond reconstruction. "You don't know an eye-opener from a traditional?" she demands in outrage. All I know, in fact, is that my legs have lost interest in the current venture and have announced their intention to fold. I am saved by a yuppie (mercifully not one of mine) who chooses this moment to charge into the kitchen to bellow that his food is twenty-five minutes late. Joy screams at him to get the hell out of her kitchen, *please*, and then turns on Jesus in a fury, hurling an empty tray across the room for emphasis.

I leave. I don't walk out, I just leave. I don't finish my side work or pick up my credit card tips, if any, at the cash register or, of course, ask Joy's permission to go. And the surprising thing is that you *can* walk out without permission, that the door opens, that the thick tropical night air parts to let me pass, that my car is still parked where I left it. There is no vindication in this exit, no fuck-you surge of relief, just an overwhelming dank sense of failure pressing down on me and the entire parking lot. I had gone into this venture in the spirit of science, to test a mathematical proposition, but somewhere along the line, in the tunnel vision imposed by long shifts and relentless concentration, it became a test of myself, and clearly I have failed. Not only had I flamed out as a housekeeper/server, I had forgotten to give George my tips, and, for reasons perhaps best known to hardworking, generous people like Gail and Ellen, this hurts. I don't cry, but I am in a position to realize, for the first time in many years, that the tear ducts are still there and still capable of doing their job.

When I moved out of the trailer park, I gave the key to number 46 to Gail and arranged for my deposit to be transferred to her. She told me that Joan was still living in her van and that Stu had been fired from the Hearthside. According to the most up-to-date rumors, the drug he ordered from the restaurant was crack and he was caught dipping into the cash register to pay for it. I never found out what happened to George.

ENGAGING THE TEXT

1. What's the point of Ehrenreich's experiment? What do you think she was hoping to learn by stepping down the economic ladder, and what can you learn as her reader? Explain why you find her approach more or less effective than one that provides economic data and analysis.

2. Ehrenreich ordinarily lives much more comfortably than she did as a waitress, and of course she had an escape hatch from her experiment — she would not serve food or clean rooms forever and could have gone back to her usual life if necessary at any time. Explain the effect her status as a "tourist" in working-class culture has on you as a reader.

3. Write a journal entry about your worst job. How did your experience of being "nickeled and dimed" compare with Ehrenreich's? What was the worst aspect of this work experience for you? What, if anything, did you learn from this job — about work, about success, and about yourself?

4. **Thinking Rhetorically** Throughout this selection Ehrenreich seeks not merely to narrate facts but to elicit emotional responses from her readers. Explain how you react to one or more of the passages listed below and identify specific details in the text that help shape your responses:

    the opening description of Jerry's (paras. 1–2)

    the description of customers (para. 10)

    George's story (paras. 12–13, 16–18)

    the description of trailer number 46 (para. 15)

    Ehrenreich's footnotes throughout the narrative

EXPLORING CONNECTIONS

5. What, if anything, do you think Gail, Ellen, and George could do to substantially improve their material and economic well-being? What are the greatest barriers they face? What advice might Sam Walton or Jay Z (p. 350) give them, and how do you think it would be received?

6. Imagine that Gail, Ellen, or George has participated in the protest pictured on page 412 in the Visual Portfolio. Write a journal entry from their point of view about the experience of that day.

EXTENDING THE CRITICAL CONTEXT

7. Ehrenreich made $6.10 per hour as a housekeeper. Working in groups, sketch out a monthly budget based on this salary for (a) an individual, (b) a single parent with a preteen child, and (c) a family of four in which one adult is ill or has been laid off. Be sure to include money for basics like rent, utilities, food, clothing, transportation, and medical care.

8. Research the *least* promising job prospects in your community. Talk to potential employers and learn as much as you can about such issues as wages, working conditions, hours, drug screening, and healthcare, retirement, or other benefits.

9. Order a meal at whichever restaurant in your community is most like "Jerry's." Study the working conditions in the restaurant, paying special attention to the kinds of problems Ehrenreich faced on her shifts. Write up an informal journal entry from the imagined point of view of a server at the restaurant.

10. Research recent efforts to increase the state and federal minimum wage and the concept of a "sustainable" or a "living wage." What arguments are made for and against raising minimum income guarantees? How have experiments with sustainable wages in cities like San Francisco, New York, or Washington, DC, affected workers and businesses? In class, debate whether your own state should implement a sustainable wage program.

CLASS IN AMERICA — 2012

GREGORY MANTSIOS

Which of these gifts might a high school graduate in your family receive — a new dress, a $500 savings bond, or a BMW? The answer hints at your social class, a key factor in American lives that runs counter to the more comfortable notion that the United States is essentially a middle-class nation. The selection below makes it hard to deny class distinctions and their nearly universal influence on our lives. The essay juxtaposes myths and realities as Mantsios outlines four widely held beliefs about class in the United States and then systematically refutes them with statistical evidence. Even if you already recognize the importance of social class, some of the numbers the author cites are likely to surprise you. Mantsios is director of the Joseph S. Murphy Institute for Worker Education and Labor Studies at Queens College of the City University of New York; he is editor of *A New Labor Movement for the New Century* (1998). The essay reprinted below appeared in *Race, Class, and Gender in the United States: An Integrated Study*, edited by Paula S. Rothenberg (2013).

THERE WASN'T MUCH ATTENTION GIVEN to America's class divide, at least not until a band of mostly young activists decided to occupy Wall Street in the fall of 2011 and in the process capture the media spotlight, add the word "99 percenters" to our lexicon, and change the national— and in many ways, the international—discourse. While there has been recent interest in the rising level of inequality, the class divide is anything but recent and its consequences remain severely understated in the mass media. Perhaps most importantly, the point that is missed is that inequality is persistent and structural—and it manifests itself in a multitude of cultural and social ways.

Americans, in general, don't like to talk about class. Or so it would seem. We don't speak about class privileges, or class oppression, or the class nature of society. These terms are not part of our everyday vocabulary, and in most circles this language is associated with the language of the rhetorical fringe. Unlike people in most other parts of the world, we shrink from using words that classify along economic lines or that point to class distinctions: Phrases like "working class," "upper class," "capitalist class," and "ruling class" are rarely uttered by Americans.

For the most part, avoidance of class-laden vocabulary crosses class boundaries. There are few among the poor who speak of themselves as lower class; instead, they refer to their race, ethnic group, or geographic location. Workers are more likely to identify with their employer, industry, or occupational group than with other workers, or with the working class. Neither are those at the upper end of the economic spectrum likely to use the word "class."[1] In her study of thirty-eight wealthy and socially prominent women, Susan Ostrander asked participants if they considered themselves members of the upper class. One participant responded, "I hate to use the word 'class.' We are responsible, fortunate people, old families, the people who have something." Another said, "I hate [the term] upper class. It is so non-upper class to use it. I just call it 'all of us' — those who are well-born."[2]

It is not that Americans, rich or poor, aren't keenly aware of class differences—those quoted above obviously are; it is that class is usually not in the domain of public conversation. Class is not discussed or debated in public because class identity has been stripped from popular

The author wishes to thank Maya Pinto for her assistance in updating this article. © Gregory Mantsios, 2012. Reprinted by permission of the author.

[1] See Jay MacLead, *Ain't No Makin' It: Aspirations and Attainment in a Lower-Income Neighborhood* (Boulder, CO: Westview Press, 1995); Benjamin DeMott, *The Imperial Middle: Why Americans Can't Think Straight About Class* (New York: Morrow, 1990); Ira Katznelson, *City Trenches: Urban Politics and Patterning of Class in the United States* (New York: Pantheon Books, 1981); Charles W. Tucker, "A Comparative Analysis of Subjective Social Class: 1945–1963," *Social Forces*, no. 46 (June 1968): 508–14; Robert Nisbet, "The Decline and Fall of Social Class," *Pacific Sociological Review* 2 (Spring 1959): 11–17; and Oscar Glantz, "Class Consciousness and Political Solidarity," *American Sociological Review* 23 (August 1958): 375–82. [All notes are Mantsios's.]

[2] Susan Ostrander, "Upper-Class Women: Class Consciousness as Conduct and Meaning," in *Power Structure Research,* ed. G. William Domhoff (Beverly Hills, CA: Sage Publications, 1980), 78–79. Also see Stephen Birmingham, *America's Secret Aristocracy* (Boston: Little, Brown, 1987).

culture. The institutions that shape mass culture and define the parameters of public debate have avoided class issues. In politics, in primary and secondary education, and in the mass media, formulating issues in terms of class has been considered culturally unacceptable, unnecessarily combative, and even un-American.

There are, however, two notable exceptions to this phenomenon. First, it is acceptable in the United States to talk about "the middle class." Interestingly enough, the term middle class appears to be acceptable precisely because it mutes class differences. References to the middle class by politicians, for example, are designed to encompass and attract the broadest possible constituency. Not only do references to the middle class gloss over differences, but they also avoid any suggestion of conflict or injustice.

This leads us to a second exception to the class-avoidance phenomenon. We are, on occasion, presented with glimpses of the upper class and the lower class (the language used is "the wealthy" and "the poor"). In the media, these presentations are designed to satisfy some real or imagined voyeuristic need of "the ordinary person." As curiosities, the ground-level view of street life and trailer parks and the inside look at the rich and the famous serve as unique models, one to avoid and one to emulate. In either case, the two sets of lifestyles are presented as though they have no causal relation to each other: There is nothing to suggest that our economic system allows people to grow wealthy *at the expense of* those who are not.

Similarly, when politicians and social commentators draw attention to the plight of the poor, they do so in a manner that obscures the class structure and denies any sense of exploitation. Wealth and poverty are viewed as one of several natural and inevitable states of being: Differences are only differences. One may even say differences are the American way, a reflection of American social diversity.

We are left with one of two possible explanations for why Americans usually don't talk about class: Either class distinctions are not relevant to U.S. society, or we mistakenly hold a set of beliefs that obscure the reality of class differences and their impact on people's lives.

Let's look at four common, albeit contradictory, beliefs about class in America that have persisted over time.

Myth 1: We are a middle-class nation. Despite some variations in economic status, most Americans have achieved relative affluence in what is widely recognized as a consumer society.

Myth 2: Class really doesn't matter in the United States. Whatever differences do exist in economic standing, they are—for the most part—irrelevant. Our democracy provides for all regardless of economic class: Rich or poor, we are all equal in the eyes of the law.

Myth 3: We live in a land of upward mobility. The American public as a whole is steadily moving up the economic ladder and each generation propels itself to greater economic well-being.

Myth 4: Everyone has an equal chance to succeed. Success in the United States requires no more than hard work, sacrifice, and perseverance: "In America, anyone can become a billionaire; it's just a matter of being in the right place at the right time."

In trying to assess the legitimacy of these beliefs, we want to ask several important questions. Are there significant class differences among Americans? If these differences do exist, are they getting bigger or smaller? Do class differences have a significant impact on the way we live? How much upward mobility is there in the United States? Finally, does everyone in the United States really have an equal opportunity to succeed and an equal voice in our democracy?

The Economic Spectrum

For starters, let's look at difference. An examination of available data reveals that variations in economic well-being are, in fact, dramatic. Consider the following:

- The richest 20 percent of Americans hold nearly 90 percent of the total household wealth in the country. The wealthiest 1 percent of the American population holds 36 percent of the total national wealth. That is, the top 1 percent own over one-third of all the consumer durables (such as houses, cars, televisions, and computers) and financial assets (such as stocks, bonds, property, and bank savings).[3]

- There are 323,067 Americans—approximately 1 percent of the adult population—who earn more than $1 million annually.[4] There are over 1,000 billionaires in the United States today, more than 70 of them worth over $10 billion each.[5] It would take the typical American earning $49,445 (the median income in the United States)—and spending absolutely nothing at all—a total of 202,240 years (or over 2,500 lifetimes) to earn $10 billion.

Affluence and prosperity are clearly alive and well in certain segments of the U.S. population. However, this abundance is in sharp contrast to the poverty that persists in America. At the other end of the spectrum:

---

[3]Economic Policy Institute, "Wealth Holdings Remain Unequal in Good and Bad Times," *The State of Working America* (Washington, DC: Economic Policy Institute, 2011), accessed September 25, 2011, http://www.stateofworkingamerica.org/files/files/Figure %20B_wealth_dis_byclass.xlsx.

[4]The number of individuals filing tax returns that had a gross adjusted income of $1 million or more in 2008 was 323,067 ("Tax Stats at a Glance," Internal Revenue Service, U.S. Treasury Department, available at http://www.irs.gov/pub/irs-soi/10taxstatscard.pdf). The adult population (18 years and over) of the United States in 2008 was 229,945,000, according to U.S. Census figures, U.S. Census Bureau, *Current Population Survey, Annual Social and Economic Supplement 2010*, available at http://www.census.gov/compendia /statab/2012/tables/12s0007.pdf.

[5]*Forbes*, "The World's Billionaires List: United States," accessed September 25, 2011, http://www.forbes.com/wealth/billionaires#p_l_s_arank_-l__225.

- More than 15 percent of the American population—that is, 1 of every 7 people in this country—live below the official poverty line (calculated at $11,139 for an individual and $22,314 for a family of four).[6] In 2010, there were 42 million poor people in the United States—the largest number since the Census Bureau began publishing poverty statistics more than 50 years ago.[7]

- An estimated 3.5 million people—of whom nearly 1.4 million are children—are homeless.[8]

- The 2010 U.S. Census reported that more than 1 out of every 5 children under the age of 18 lives in poverty.[9]

Reality 1: The contrast between rich and poor is sharp, and with one-third of the American population living at one extreme or the other, it is difficult to argue that we live in a classless society.

While those at the bottom of the economic ladder have fared poorly relative to those at the top, so too have those in the middle—and their standing relative to the top has been declining as well.

- The middle fifth of the population holds less than 4 percent of the national *wealth.*[10]

- The share of wealth held by the middle fifth thirty years ago was 5.2 percent of the total. Today's share held by the middle sector is 23 percent less than what it was three decades ago.[11]

Reality 2: The middle class in the United States holds a very small share of the nation's wealth and that share has declined steadily.   15

The gap between rich and poor—and between the rich and the middle class—leaves the vast majority of the American population at a distinct disadvantage.

- Eighty percent of the population—that is, four out of every five Americans—is left sharing a little more than 10 percent of the nation's wealth.[12]

[6]Based on 2010 census figures. Carmen DeNavas-Walt, Bernadette D. Proctor, and Jessica C. Smith, U.S. Census Bureau, Current Population Reports, P60-239, *Income, Poverty, and Health Insurance Coverage in the United States: 2010* (Washington, DC: U.S. Government Printing Office).

[7]U.S. Census Bureau, "Poverty," available at http://www.census.gov/hhes/www/poverty/about/overview/index.html.

[8]National Coalition for the Homeless, "How Many People Experience Homelessness?" NCH Fact Sheet #2, July 2009, http://www.nationalhomeless.org/factsheets/How_Many.html?.

[9]See U.S. Census Bureau, "Poverty," available at http://www.census.gov/hhes/www/poverty/about/overview/index.html.

[10]Economic Policy Institute, *The State of Working America*, accessed September 25, 2011, http://www.stateofworkingamerica.org/files/files/Figure%20B_wealth_dis_byclass.xlsx.

[11]Edward N. Wolff, "Recent Trends in Household Wealth in the U.S." Levy Economics Institute of Bard College Working Paper no. 502, Levy Economics Institute, Annandale-on-Hudson, NY, March 2010.

[12]Economic Policy Institute, "Wealth Holdings Remain Unequal in Good and Bad Times," *The State of Working America* (Washington, DC: Economic Policy Institute, 2001), accessed September 25, 2011, http://www.stateofworkingamerica.org/files/files/Figure%20B_wealth_dis_byclass.xlsx.

- The income gap between the very rich (top 1 percent) and everyone else (the 99 percent) more than tripled over the past three decades, creating the greatest concentration of income since 1928.[13]

This level of inequality is neither inevitable nor universal. The income gap between rich and poor in a country is generally measured by a statistic called the Gini coefficient, which provides a mathematical ratio and scale that allows comparisons between countries of the world. The U.S. government's own reports using the Gini coefficient show that the United States ranked number 95 out of 134 countries studied — that is, 94 countries (including almost all the industrialized nations of the world) had a more equal distribution of income than the United States.[14]

The numbers and percentages associated with economic inequality are difficult to fully comprehend. To help his students visualize the distribution of income, the well-known economist Paul Samuelson asked them to picture an income pyramid made of children's blocks, with each layer of blocks representing $1,000. If we were to construct Samuelson's pyramid today, the peak of the pyramid would be much higher than the Eiffel Tower, yet almost all of us would be within 6 feet of the ground.[15] In other words, a small minority of families takes the lion's share of the national income, and the remaining income is distributed among the vast majority of middle-income and low-income families. Keep in mind that Samuelson's pyramid represents the distribution of income, not wealth (accumulated resources). The distribution of wealth is skewed even further. Ten billion dollars of wealth would reach more than 1,000 times the height of the Eiffel Tower.[16]

Reality 3: Middle- and lower-income earners — what many in other parts of the world would refer to as the working class — share a minuscule portion of the nation's wealth. For the most part, the real class divide in the United States is between the very wealthy and everyone else — and it is a divide that is staggering.

American Lifestyles

The late political theorist/activist Michael Harrington once commented, "America has the best-dressed poverty the world has ever known."[17] Clothing disguises much of the poverty in the United States, and this may explain, in part, the country's middle-class image. With increased mass marketing of "designer" clothing and with shifts in the nation's economy from blue-collar (and often better-paying) manufacturing jobs to white-

20

---

[13] Arloc Sherman and Chad Stone, "Income Gaps Between Very Rich and Everyone Else More Than Tripled in Last Three Decades, New Data Show," Center for Budget and Policy Studies, June 26, 2010.

[14] See the CIA report *The World Factbook*, https://www.cia.gov/library/publications/the-world-factbook/rankorder/2172rank.html.

[15] Paul Samuelson, *Economics*, 10th ed. (New York: McGraw-Hill, 1976), 84.

[16] Calculated at 1.5 inches per children's block and 1,050 feet for the height of the Eiffel Tower.

[17] Michael Harrington, *The Other America* (New York: Macmillan, 1962), 12–13.

collar and pink-collar jobs in the service sector, it is becoming increasingly difficult to distinguish class differences based on appearance.[18] The dress-down environment prevalent in the high-tech industry (what American Studies scholar Andrew Ross refers to as the "no-collar movement") has reduced superficial distinctions even further.[19]

Beneath the surface, there is another reality. Let's look at some "typical" and not-so-typical lifestyles.

American Profile

Name:	Harold S. Browning
Father:	Manufacturer, industrialist
Mother:	Prominent social figure in the community
Principal child-rearer:	Governess
Primary education:	An exclusive private school on Manhattan's Upper East Side *Note:* A small, well-respected primary school where teachers and administrators have a reputation for nurturing student creativity and for providing the finest educational preparation *Ambition:* "To become President"
Supplemental tutoring:	Tutors in French and mathematics
Summer camp:	Sleep-away camp in northern Connecticut *Note:* Camp provides instruction in the creative arts, athletics, and the natural sciences
Secondary education:	A prestigious preparatory school in Westchester County *Note:* Classmates included the sons of ambassadors, doctors, attorneys, television personalities, and well-known business leaders *Supplemental education:* Private SAT tutor *After-school activities:* Private riding lessons

---

[18] Stuart Ewen and Elizabeth Ewen, *Channels of Desire: Mass Images and the Shaping of American Consciousness* (New York: McGraw-Hill, 1982).

[19] Andrew Ross, *No-Collar: The Humane Workplace and Its Hidden Costs* (New York: Basic Books, 2002).

Ambition: "To take over my father's business"

High-school graduation gift: BMW

Family activities: Theater, recitals, museums, summer vacations in Europe, occasional winter trips to the Caribbean

Note: As members of and donors to the local art museum, the Brownings and their children attend private receptions and exhibit openings at the invitation of the museum director

Higher education: An Ivy League liberal arts college in Massachusetts

Major: Economics and political science

After-class activities: Debating club, college newspaper, swim team

Ambition: "To become a leader in business"

First full-time job (age 23): Assistant manager of operations, Browning Tool and Die, Inc. (family enterprise)

Subsequent employment: 3 years—Executive assistant to the president, Browning Tool and Die

Responsibilities included: Purchasing (materials and equipment), personnel, and distribution networks

4 years—Advertising manager, Lackheed Manufacturing (home appliances)

3 years—Director of marketing and sales, Comerex, Inc. (business machines)

Current employment (age 38): Executive vice president, SmithBond and Co. (digital instruments)

Typical daily activities: Review financial reports and computer printouts, dictate memoranda, lunch with clients, initiate conference calls, meet with assistants, plan business trips, meet with associates

Transportation to and from work: Chauffeured company limousine

Annual salary: $324,000

Ambition: "To become chief executive officer of the firm, or one like it, within the next five to ten years"

Current residence:	Eighteenth-floor condominium on Manhattan's Upper West Side, eleven rooms, including five spacious bedrooms and terrace overlooking river *Interior:* Professionally decorated and accented with elegant furnishings, valuable antiques, and expensive artwork *Note:* Building management provides doorman and elevator attendant; family employs au pair for children and maid for other domestic chores
Second residence:	Farm in northwestern Connecticut, used for weekend retreats and for horse breeding (investment/hobby) *Note:* To maintain the farm and cater to the family when they are there, the Brownings employ a part-time maid, groundskeeper, and horse breeder

Harold Browning was born into a world of nurses, maids, and governesses. His world today is one of airplanes and limousines, five-star restaurants, and luxurious living accommodations. The life and lifestyle of Harold Browning is in sharp contrast to that of Bob Farrell.

American Profile	
Name:	Bob Farrell
Father:	Machinist
Mother:	Retail clerk
Principal child-rearer:	Mother and sitter
Primary education:	A medium-size public school in Queens, New York, characterized by large class size, outmoded physical facilities, and an educational philosophy emphasizing basic skills and student discipline *Ambition:* "To become President"
Supplemental tutoring:	None
Summer camp:	YMCA day camp *Note:* Emphasis on team sports, arts and crafts

Secondary education:	Large regional high school in Queens *Note:* Classmates included the sons and daughters of carpenters, postal clerks, teachers, nurses, shopkeepers, mechanics, bus drivers, police officers, salespersons *Supplemental education:* SAT prep course offered by national chain *After-school activities:* Basketball and handball in school park *Ambition:* "To make it through college" *High-school graduation gift:* $500 savings bond
Family activities:	Family gatherings around television set, softball, an occasional trip to the movie theater, summer Sundays at the public beach
Higher education:	A two-year community college with a technical orientation *Major:* Electrical technology *After-school activities:* Employed as a part-time bagger in local supermarket *Ambition:* "To become an electrical engineer"
First full-time job (age 19):	Service-station attendant *Note:* Continued to take college classes in the evening
Subsequent employment:	Mail clerk at large insurance firm; manager trainee, large retail chain
Present employment (age 38):	Assistant sales manager, building supply firm *Typical daily activities:* Demonstrate products, write up product orders, handle customer complaints, check inventory *Transportation to and from work:* City subway *Annual salary:* $45,261 *Additional income:* $6,100 in commissions from evening and weekend work as salesman in local men's clothing store *Ambition:* "To open up my own business"
Current residence:	The Farrells own their own home in a working-class neighborhood in Queens, New York

Bob Farrell and Harold Browning live very differently: One is very privileged, the other much less so. The differences are class differences, which have a profound impact on the way they live. They are differences between playing a game of handball in the park and taking riding lessons at a private stable; watching a movie on television and going to the theater; and taking the subway to work and being driven in a limousine. More important, the difference in class determines where they live, who their friends are, how well they are educated, what they do for a living, and what they come to expect from life.

Yet, as dissimilar as their lifestyles are, Harold Browning and Bob Farrell have some things in common: they live in the same city, they work long hours, and they are highly motivated. More importantly, they are both white males.

Let's look at someone else who works long and hard and is highly motivated. This person, however, is black and female.

American Profile	
Name:	Cheryl Mitchell
Father:	Janitor
Mother:	Waitress
Principal child-rearer:	Grandmother
Primary education:	Large public school in Ocean Hill-Brownsville, Brooklyn, New York *Note:* Rote teaching of basic skills and emphasis on conveying the importance of good attendance, good manners, and good work habits; school patrolled by security guards *Ambition:* "To be a teacher"
Supplemental tutoring:	None
Summer camp:	None
Secondary education:	Large public school in Ocean Hill-Brownsville *Note*: Classmates included sons and daughters of hairdressers, groundskeepers, painters, dressmakers, dishwashers, domestics *Supplemental education:* None *After-school activities:* Domestic chores, part-time employment as babysitter and housekeeper *Ambition:* "To be a social worker" *High-school graduation gift:* new dress
Family activities:	Church-sponsored socials

Higher education:	One semester of local community college *Note*: Dropped out of school for financial reasons
First full-time job (age 17):	Counter clerk, local bakery
Subsequent employment:	File clerk with temporary-service agency, supermarket checker
Current employment (age 38):	Nurse's aide at a municipal hospital *Typical daily activities:* Make up hospital beds, clean out bedpans, weigh patients and assist them to the bathroom, take temperature readings, pass out and collect food trays, feed patients who need help, bathe patients, and change dressings *Annual salary:* $17,850 *Ambition:* "To get out of the ghetto"
Current residence:	Three-room apartment in the South Bronx, needs painting, has poor ventilation, is in a high-crime area *Note*: Cheryl Mitchell lives with her four-year-old son and her elderly mother

When we look at Cheryl Mitchell, Bob Farrell, and Harold Browning, we see three very different lifestyles. We are not looking, however, at economic extremes. Cheryl Mitchell's income as a nurse's aide puts her above the government's official poverty line.[20] Below her on the income pyramid are 42 million poverty-stricken Americans. Far from being poor, Bob Farrell has an annual income ($51,361) as an assistant sales manager that puts him above the median income level—that is, more than 50 percent of the U.S. population earns less money than Bob Farrell.[21] And while Harold Browning's income puts him in a high-income bracket, he stands only a fraction of the way up Samuelson's income pyramid. Well above him are the 323,067 Americans whose annual incomes exceed $1 million. Yet Harold Browning spends more money on his horses than Cheryl Mitchell earns in a year.

[20]Based on a poverty threshold for a three-person household in 2007 of $16,650 (DeNavas-Walt et al., p. 1).
[21]The median income in 2007 was $45,113 for men working full time, year round; $35,102 for women, and $50,233 for households (DeNavas-Walt et al., p. 6).

Reality 4: Even ignoring the extreme poles of the economic spectrum, we find enormous class differences in the lifestyles among the haves, the have-nots, and the have-littles.

Class affects more than lifestyle and material well-being. It has a significant impact on our physical and mental well-being as well. Researchers have found an inverse relationship between social class and health. Lower-class standing is correlated with higher rates of infant mortality, eye and ear disease, arthritis, physical disability, diabetes, nutritional deficiency, respiratory disease, mental illness, and heart disease.[22] In all areas of health, poor people do not share the same life chances as those in the social class above them. Furthermore, low income correlates with a lower quality of treatment for illness and disease. The results of poor health and poor treatment are borne out in the life expectancy rates within each class. Researchers have found that the higher one's class standing is, the higher one's life expectancy is. Conversely, they have also found that within each age group, the lower one's class standing, the higher the death rate; in some age groups, the figures are as much as two and three times higher.[23]

It's not just physical and mental health that is so largely determined by class. The lower a person's class standing is, the more difficult it is to secure housing; the more time is spent on the routine tasks of everyday life; the greater is the percentage of income that goes to pay for food, health care (which accounts for 23 percent of spending for low-income families)[24] and other basic necessities; and the greater is the likelihood of crime victimization.[25]

[22] U.S. Government Accountability Office, *Poverty in America: Economic Research Shows Adverse Impacts on Health Status and Other Social Conditions* (Washington, DC: U.S. Government Accountability Office, 2007), 9–16; see also E. Pamuk, D. Makuc, K. Heck, C. Reuben, and K. Lochner, *Health, United States, 1998: Socioeconomic Status and Health Chartbook* (Hyattsville, MD: National Center for Health Statistics, 1998), 145–59; Vincente Navarro, "Class, Race, and Health Care in the United States," in *Critical Perspectives in Sociology*, 2nd ed., ed. Bersh Berberoglu (Dubuque, IA: Kendall/Hunt, 1993), 148–56; Melvin Krasner, *Poverty and Health in New York City* (New York: United Hospital Fund of New York, 1989). See also U.S. Department of Health and Human Services, "Health Status of Minorities and Low Income Groups, 1985"; and Dan Hughes, Kay Johnson, Sara Rosenbaum, Elizabeth Butler, and Janet Simons, *The Health of America's Children* (The Children's Defense Fund, 1988).

[23] Pamuk et al., *Health, United States, 1998;* Kenneth Neubeck and Davita Glassberg, *Sociology: A Critical Approach* (New York: McGraw-Hill, 1996), 436–38; Aaron Antonovsky, "Social Class, Life Expectancy, and Overall Mortality," in *The Impact of Social Class* (New York: Thomas Crowell, 1972), 467–91. See also Harriet Duleep, "Measuring the Effect of Income on Adult Mortality Using Longitudinal Administrative Record Data," *Journal of Human Resources* 21, no. 2 (Spring 1986); and Paul Farmer, *Pathologies of Power: Health, Human Rights, and the New War on the Poor* (Berkeley: University of California Press, 2005).

[24] Patricia Ketsche, Sally Wallace, and Kathleen Adams, "Hidden Health Care Costs Hit Low-Income Families the Hardest," Georgia State University, September 21, 2011, http://www.gsu.edu/news/54728.html.

[25] Pamuk et al., *Health, United States, 1998,* figure 20; Dennis W. Roncek, "Dangerous Places: Crime and Residential Environment," *Social Forces* 60, no. 1 (September 1981), 74–96. See also Steven D. Levitt, "The Changing Relationship Between Income and Crime Victimization," *Economic Policy Review* 5, no. 3 (September 1999).

Class and Educational Attainment

School performance (grades and test scores) and educational attainment (level of schooling completed) also correlate strongly with economic class. Furthermore, despite some efforts to make testing fairer and schooling more accessible, current data suggest that the level of inequity is staying the same or getting worse.

In his study for the Carnegie Council on Children in 1978, Richard De Lone examined the test scores of over half a million students who took the College Board exams (SATs). His findings were consistent with earlier studies that showed a relationship between class and scores on standardized tests; his conclusion: "the higher the student's social status, the higher the probability that he or she will get higher grades."[26] Today, more than thirty years after the release of the Carnegie report, College Board surveys reveal data that are no different: test scores still correlate with family income.

In another study conducted thirty years ago, researcher William Sewell showed a positive correlation between class and overall educational achievement. In comparing the top quartile (25 percent) of his sample to the bottom quartile, he found that students from upper-class families were twice as likely to obtain training beyond high school and four times as likely to attain a postgraduate degree. Sewell concluded:

Average Combined Scores by Income (400 to 1600 scale)[27]

FAMILY INCOME	MEDIAN SCORE
More than $200,000	1721
$160,000 to $200,000	1636
$140,000 to $160,000	1619
$120,000 to $140,000	1594
$100,000 to $120,000	1580
$80,000 to $100,000	1545
$60,000 to $80,000	1503
$40,000 to $60,000	1461
$20,000 to $40,000	1398
less than $20,000	1323

These figures are based on the test results of 1,647,123 SAT takers in 2010–2011.

[26] Richard De Lone, *Small Futures* (New York: Harcourt Brace Jovanovich, 1978), 14–19.

[27] College Board, "2011 College-Bound Seniors Total Group Profile Report," available at http://professionals.collegeboard.com/profdownload/cbs2011_total_group_report.pdf.

"Socioeconomic background . . . operates independently of academic ability at every stage in the process of educational attainment."[28]

Today, the pattern persists. There are, however, two significant changes. On the one hand, the odds of getting into college have improved for the bottom quartile of the population, although they still remain relatively low compared to the top. On the other hand, the chances of completing a four-year college degree for those who are poor are extraordinarily low compared to the chances for those who are rich. Researchers estimate college completion is ten times more likely for the top 25 percent of the population than it is for the bottom 25 percent.[29]

Reality 5: From cradle to grave, class position has a significant impact on our well-being. Class accurately predicts chances for survival, educational achievement, and economic success.

Media-induced excitement over big-payoff reality shows, celebrity salaries, and multimillion-dollar lotteries suggests that we in the United States live in a "rags to riches" society. So too does news about dot-com acquisitions and initial public offerings (IPOs) that provide enormous windfalls to young company founders. But rags-to-riches stories notwithstanding, the evidence suggests that "striking it rich" is extremely rare and that class mobility in general is uncommon and becoming increasingly so.

One study showed that 79 percent of families remained in the same quintile (fifth) of income earners or moved up or down only one quintile. (Of this group, most families did not move at all.)[30] Another study showed that fewer than one in five men surpass the economic status of their fathers.[31] Several recent studies have shown that there is less class mobility in the United States than in most industrialized democracies in the world. One such study placed the United States in a virtual tie for last place.[32] Why does the United States occupy such a low position on the mobility scale? Several explanations have been offered: The gap between rich and poor in the United States is greater; the poor are poorer in the United States and have farther to go to get out of poverty; and the United States has a lower rate of unionization than other industrialized nations.

---

[28] William H. Sewell, "Inequality of Opportunity for Higher Education," *American Sociological Review* 36, no. 5 (1971): 793–809.

[29] Thomas G. Mortenson, "Family Income and Educational Attainment, 1970 to 2009," *Postsecondary Education Opportunity*, no. 221 (November 2010).

[30] Derived from David Leonhardt, "A Closer Look at Income Mobility," *New York Times*, May 14, 2005; and Katharine Bradbury and Jane Katz, "Trends in U.S. Family Income Mobility 1969–2006," Federal Reserve Bank of Boston, 2009.

[31] De Lone, *Small Futures*, 14–19. See also Daniel McMurrer, Mark Condon, and Isabel Sawhill, "Intergenerational Mobility in the United States" (Washington DC: Urban Institute, 1997), http://www.urban.org/publications/406796.html?; and Bhashkar Mazumder, "Earnings Mobility in the U.S.: A New Look at Intergenerational Inequality," Federal Reserve Bank of Chicago Working Paper no. 2001–18, March 21, 2001. doi: 10.2139/ssrn .295559.

[32] Miles Corak, "Do Poor Children Become Poor Adults? Lessons from a Cross-Country Comparison of Generational Earnings Mobility" (Bonn, Germany: IZA, 2006). Available at http://repec.iza.org/dp1993.pdf.

The bottom line is that very affluent families transmit their advantages to the next generation and poor families stay trapped.[33] For those whose annual income is in six figures, economic success is due in large part to the wealth and privileges bestowed on them at birth. Over 66 percent of the consumer units with incomes of $100,000 or more have inherited assets. Of these units, over 86 percent reported that inheritances constituted a substantial portion of their total assets.[34]

Economist Howard Wachtel likens inheritance to a series of Monopoly games in which the winner of the first game refuses to relinquish his or her cash and commercial property for the second game. "After all," argues the winner, "I accumulated my wealth and income by my own wits." With such an arrangement, it is not difficult to predict the outcome of subsequent games.[35]

Reality 6: All Americans do not have an equal opportunity to succeed, and class mobility in the United States is lower than that of the rest of the industrialized world. Inheritance laws provide built-in privileges to the offspring of the wealthy and add to the likelihood of their economic success while handicapping the chances for everyone else.

One would think that increases in worker productivity or a booming economy would reduce the level of inequality and increase class mobility. While the wages of workers *may* increase during good times—that is, relative to what they were in the past—the economic advantages of higher productivity and a booming economy go disproportionately to the wealthy, a factor that adds still further to the level of inequality. For example, during the period 2001 to 2007, the U.S. economy expanded and productivity (output per hours worked) increased by more than 15 percent. During that same period, however, the top 1 percent of U.S. households took two-thirds of the nation's income gains, their inflation-adjusted income grew more than ten times faster than the income of the bottom 90 percent, and their share of the national income reached its highest peak. At the same time, the inflation-adjusted weekly salary of the average American during that six-year economic expansion

---

[33] Jason DeParle, "Harder for Americans to Rise from Lower Rungs," *New York Times*, January 4, 2012.

[34] Howard Tuchman, *Economics of the Rich* (New York: Random House, 1973), 15. See also Greg Duncan, Ariel Kalil, Susan Mayer, Robin Tepper, and Monique Payne, "The Apple Does Not Fall Far From the Tree," in *Unequal Chances: Family Background and Economic Success*, ed. Samuel Bowles, Herbert Gintis, and Melissa Groves (Princeton, NJ: Princeton University Press, 2008), 23–79; Bhashkar Mazumder, "The Apple Falls Even Closer to the Tree Than We Thought," in Bowles et al., 80–99. For more information on inheritance, see Samuel Bowles and Herbert Gintis, "The Inheritance of Inequality," *Journal of Economic Perspectives* 16, no. 3 (Summer 2002): 2–30; and Tom Hertz, *Understanding Mobility in America*, Center for American Progress, available at http://www.american progress.org/wp-content/uploads/kf/hertz_mobility_analysis.pdf?.

[35] Howard Wachtel, *Labor and the Economy* (Orlando, FL: Academic Press, 1984), 161–162.

declined by 2.3 percent.[36] Observing similar patterns in U.S. economic history, one prominent economist described economic growth in
the United States as a "spectator sport for the majority of American families."[37] Economic decline, on the other hand, is much more "partici-
patory," with layoffs and cuts in public services hitting middle- and
lower-income families hardest—families that rely on public services
(e.g., public schools, transportation) and have fewer resources to fall back
on during difficult economic times.

Reality 7: Inequality in the United States is persistent in good times
and bad.

While most Americans rely on their wages or salaries to make ends
meet, the rich derive most of their wealth from such income-producing
assets as stocks, bonds, business equity, and non-home real estate. This
type of wealth is even more highly concentrated than wealth in general. Over 89 percent of all stocks in the United States for example, are
owned by the wealthiest 10 percent of Americans.[38] This makes the
fortunes of the wealthy (whether they are corporate executives, investment bankers, or not) closely tied to the fortunes of corporate America
and the world of finance. While defenders of capitalism and the capitalist class argue that what's good for corporate America is good for all
of America, recent economic experience has raised more doubts than
ever about this. Putting aside illegal manipulation of the financial system, the drive to maximize corporate profit has led to job destruction (as
companies seek cheaper labor in other parts of the world and transfer
investments off shore); deregulation (e.g., so environmental protections
don't inhibit corporate profit); and changes in tax policy that favor corporations (through loopholes) and those who rely on corporate profit for
their wealth (by taxing their capital gains at lower rates).

Reality 8: The privileges that accrue to the wealthy are tied to the
worlds of capital and finance—worlds whose good fortune are often the
misfortune of the rest of the population.

Government is often portrayed as the spoiler of Wall Street—and
at times it is. There are certainly examples of the government imposing
fines for environmental violations, establishing regulations that protect
consumers and workers, restrict corporate conduct, etc. But government
as the "great equalizer" often isn't what it appears to be. In 2010, for

[36] See Hannah Shaw and Chad Stone, "Incomes at the Top Rebounded in First
Full Year of Recovery, New Analysis of Tax Data Shows," Center on Budget and Policy Priorities, March 7, 2011, http://www.cbpp.org/files/3-7-12inc.pdf. Also see Andrew
Fieldhouse and Ethan Pollack, "Tenth Anniversary of the Bush-Era Tax Cuts," Economic Policy Institute, June 1, 2011, http://www.epi.org/publication/tenth_anniversary_of
_the_bush-era_tax_cuts/.

[37] Alan Blinder, quoted by Paul Krugman, in "Disparity and Despair," *U.S. News and
World Report*, March 23, 1992, 54.

[38] Derived from Edward N. Wolff, "Recent Trends in Household Wealth in the U.S."
Levy Economics Institute at Bard College, March 2010, table 9. Available at http://www
.levyinstitute.org/pubs/wp_589.pdf.

example, when the federal government concluded a fraud case against a major investment bank (Goldman Sachs), it touted the case as one of the largest settlements in U.S. history—a whopping $550 million. It turns out that $550 million was less than 4 percent of what the bank paid its executives in bonuses that year.

Similarly, changes in policy that reduce taxes are often touted as vehicles for leveling the playing field and bringing economic relief to the middle class. But at best, these do little or nothing to help middle- and low-income families. More often than not, they increase the level of inequality by providing disproportionate tax benefits to the wealthy while reducing public budgets and increasing the costs of such public services as transportation and college tuition. For example, changes in tax policy over the last five decades—especially those during the 1980s—have favored the wealthy: Federal taxes for the wealthiest 0.1 percent have fallen from 51 to 26 percent over the last fifty years, while the rate for middle income earners has risen from 14 to 16 percent.[39]

It's not just that economic resources are concentrated in the hands of a few; so too are political resources. And it is the connection between wealth and political power that allows economic inequality to persist and grow. Moreover, as the costs of political influence rise, so does the influence of the "monied" class. Running for public office has always been an expensive proposition, but it's become increasingly so: It now costs, on average, $1.4 million in campaign funds to win a seat in the House of Representatives and $7 million to win a seat in the U.S. Senate.[40] Most politicians rely on wealthy donors to finance their campaigns. Alternatively, wealthy individuals who want to make public policy often underwrite their own campaigns.* The average wealth of U.S. senators, for example, is $12.6 million.[41]

High-priced lobbyists also ensure that the interests of the wealthy and of corporate America are well represented in the halls of government. Not surprisingly, organizations that track the connection between political contributions and votes cast by public officials find a strong correlation between money and voting.[42] It's not that the power of the

45

---

*Over the course of three elections, Michael Bloomberg spent more than $261 million of his own money to become mayor of New York City. He spent $102 million in his last mayoral election alone—more than $172 per vote.

[39] The National Economic Council, "The Buffett Rule: A Basic Principle of Tax Fairness," White House, April 2012, citing Internal Revenue System Statistics of Income 2005 Public Use File, National Bureau of Economic Research TAXISM, and CEA calculations. Available at http://www.whitehouse.gov/sites/default/files/Buffett_Rule_Report _Final.pdf. Also cited in the *New York Times* editorial "Mr. Obama and the 'Buffett Rule,'" April 10, 2012. Available at http://www.nytimes.com/2012/04/ll/opinion/mr-obama-and -the-buffett-rule.html?_r=0.

[40] Campaign Finance Institute, "2010 Federal Election," accessed March 22, 2011, http://cfinst.org/federal/election2010.aspx.

[41] 2009 figures from the Center for Responsive Politics, "Average Wealth of Members of Congress," available at http://www.opensecrets.org/pfds/averages.php.

[42] See Larry Bartels, *Unequal Democracy: The Political Economy of the New Gilded Age* (Princeton, NJ: Princeton University Press, 2008), chapter 9; see also MAPLight.org (MAPLight tracks political contributions and their impact on the votes of public officials).

economic elite is absolute; it's not. The power of the wealthy is often miti-gated by social movements and by grassroots organizations that advo-cate on behalf of the poor and working class. The Occupy Wall Street movement—like movements that came before it—changed not only the public debate, but led to policy reforms as well. The power of the rich, however, remains so disproportionate that it severely undermines our democracy. Over three-quarters of a century ago, such an assault on dem-ocratic principles led Supreme Court Justice Louis Brandeis to observe, "We can have democracy in this country or we can have great wealth concentrated in the hands of a few, but we can't have both." Talking about the power elite or the ruling class may put people off, but there is no doubt that the interests of the wealthy predominate in American politics.

Reality 9: Wealth and power are closely linked. The economic elite have a grossly disproportionate amount of political power—more than enough power to ensure that the system that provides them such extraordinary privileges perpetuates itself.

Spheres of Power and Oppression

When we look at society and try to determine what it is that keeps most people down—what holds them back from realizing their potential as healthy, creative, productive individuals—we find institutional forces that are largely beyond individual control. Class domination is one of these forces. People do not choose to be poor or working class; instead, they are limited and confined by the opportunities afforded or denied them by a social and economic system. The class structure in the United States is a function of its economic system: capitalism, a system that is based on private rather than public ownership and control of commer-cial enterprises. Under capitalism, these enterprises are governed by the need to produce a profit for the owners, rather than to fulfill societal needs. Class divisions arise from the differences between those who own and control corporate enterprise and those who do not.

Racial and gender domination are other forces that hold people down. Although there are significant differences in the way capitalism, racism, and sexism affect our lives, there are also a multitude of paral-lels. And although class, race, and gender act independently of each other, they are at the same time very much interrelated.

On the one hand, issues of race and gender cut across class lines. 50 Women experience the effects of sexism whether they are well-paid professionals or poorly paid clerks. As women, they are not only sub-jected to stereotyping and sexual harassment, they face discrimination and are denied opportunities and privileges that men have. Similarly, a wealthy black man faces racial oppression, is subjected to racial slurs, and is denied opportunities because of his color. Regardless of their class standing, women and members of minority races are constantly dealing

Chances of Being Poor in America[43]

WHITE MALE/ FEMALE	WHITE FEMALE HEAD*	HISPANIC MALE/ FEMALE	HISPANIC FEMALE HEAD*	BLACK MALE/ FEMALE	BLACK FEMALE HEAD*
1 in 14	1 in 4	1 in 4	1 in 2	1 in 4	1 in 2

*Persons in families with female householder, no husband present.

with institutional forces that hold them down precisely because of their gender, the color of their skin, or both.

On the other hand, the experiences of women and minorities are differentiated along class lines. Although they are in subordinate positions vis-à-vis white men, the particular issues that confront women and people of color may be quite different, depending on their position in the class structure.

Power is incremental and class privileges can accrue to individual women and to individual members of a racial minority. While power is incremental, oppression is cumulative, and those who are poor, black, and female are often subject to all of the forces of class, race, and gender discrimination simultaneously. This cumulative situation is what is sometimes referred to as the double and triple jeopardy of women and people of color.

Furthermore, oppression in one sphere is related to the likelihood of oppression in another. If you are black and female, for example, you are much more likely to be poor or working class than you would be as a white male. Census figures show that the incidence of poverty varies greatly by race and gender.

In other words, being female and being nonwhite are attributes in our society that increase the chances of poverty and of lower-class standing.

Reality 10: Racism and sexism significantly compound the effects of class in society. 55

None of this makes for a very pretty picture of our country. Despite what we like to think about ourselves as a nation, the truth is that the qualities of our lives and the opportunities for success are highly circumscribed by our race, our gender, and the class we are born into. As individuals, we feel hurt and angry when someone is treating us unfairly; yet as a society we tolerate unconscionable injustice. A more just society will require a radical redistribution of wealth and power. We can start by reversing the current trends that polarize us as a people and adapt policies and practices that narrow the gaps in income, wealth, power, and privilege. That will only come about with pressure from below: strong organizations and mass movements advocating for a more just and equitable society.

[43] DeNavas-Walt et al., *Income, Poverty, and Health Insurance Coverage in the United States: 2010.*

ENGAGING THE TEXT

1. Reexamine the four myths Mantsios identifies (para. 9). What does he say is wrong about each myth, and what evidence does he provide to critique each? How persuasive do you find his evidence and reasoning?

2. Does the essay make a case that the wealthy are exploiting the poor? Does it simply assume this? Are there other possible interpretations of the data Mantsios provides? Explain your position, taking into account the information in "Class in America — 2012."

3. Work out a rough budget for a family of three with an annual income of $20,090, the poverty guideline for 2015. Be sure to include costs for food, clothing, housing, transportation, healthcare, and other unavoidable expenses. Do you think this is a reasonable "poverty line," or is it too high or too low?

4. Imagine that you are Harold S. Browning, Bob Farrell, or Cheryl Mitchell. Write an entry for this person's journal after a tough day on the job. Compare and contrast your entry with those written by other students.

5. In his final paragraph, Mantsios calls for "a radical redistribution of wealth and power" and "policies and practices that narrow the gaps in income, wealth, power, and privilege." What specific changes do you imagine Mantsios would like to see? What changes, if any, would you recommend?

EXPLORING CONNECTIONS

6. Working in small groups, discuss which class each of the following would belong to and how this class affiliation would shape the life chances of each:

   Gary Soto in "Looking for Work" (p. 19)

   Mike Rose in "I Just Wanna Be Average" (p. 123)

   George in "Serving in Florida" (p. 363)

   the narrator of Sherman Alexie's story "Gentrification" (p. 615)

   Alex Tizon, in the excerpt from *Big Little Man: In Search of My Asian Self* (p. 645)

7. Mantsios describes how "spheres of oppression" often overlap: for example, racial discrimination and sexism can multiply the challenges of working-class life. What do you think Mantsios would say about Jay Z's success (p. 355)? For example, what type(s) of oppression did Jay Z overcome, and how? Has Jay Z become a capitalist? Does his story prove that the American Dream at least sometimes comes true, and that oppression may be overcome?

EXTENDING THE CRITICAL CONTEXT

8. Mantsios points out that "inheritance laws provide built-in privileges to the offspring of the wealthy and add to the likelihood of their economic success while handicapping the chances for everyone else" (para. 38). Explain why you think this is or is not a serious problem. Keeping in mind the difference

between wealth and income, discuss how society might attempt to remedy this problem and what policies you would endorse.

9. Skim through a few recent issues of a financial magazine like *Forbes* or *Money*. Who is the audience for these publications? What kind of advice is offered? What kinds of products and services are advertised? What levels of income and investment are discussed?

10. Study the employment listings at an online source such as Monster.com. Roughly what percentage of the openings would you consider upper class, middle class, and lower class? On what basis do you make your distinctions? What do the available jobs suggest about the current levels of affluence in your area?

FROM BEYOND OUTRAGE

ROBERT B. REICH

If you're not worried about economic inequality, either you are very lucky or you haven't been paying attention. Robert Reich has been paying careful attention for decades, and he's not only worried — he's outraged. In his view, income inequality and a massive wealth gap are eroding the middle class and threatening the fabric of American society. In this reading selection, he outlines some of the most troubling trends and argues that our current economic system is sorely in need of reform. Robert B. Reich (b. 1946) served as Secretary of Labor in the Clinton administration and was named by *Time* magazine as one of the ten most effective cabinet secretaries of the twentieth century. He is currently Chancellor's Professor of Public Policy at the University of California, Berkeley and Senior Fellow at the Blum Center for Developing Economies. He has authored more than a dozen books and the film *Inequality for All*, a U.S. Documentary Special Jury Award winner at the 2013 Sundance Film Festival. This selection comes from his 2012 book *Beyond Outrage: What Has Gone Wrong with Our Economy and Our Democracy, and How to Fix It.*

Free Enterprise on Trial

In the late 1980s, I noticed a troubling trend. A larger and larger share of the nation's income and wealth was going to the very top—not just the top 1 percent, but the top of the top 1 percent—while other Americans were dividing up a shrinking share. I wrote up my findings, and my tentative explanation for this trend, in a book called *The Work of Nations*. Bill Clinton read the book, and after he was elected president, he asked me to be his secretary of labor. He told me he was committed to reversing the trend, and he called for more investment in education, training, infrastructure, and health care in order to make the bottom half of our population more productive. Clinton and his administration worked hard, but we were never able to implement his full agenda. The economic recovery of the middle and late 1990s was strong enough to generate twenty-two million new jobs and raise almost everyone's wages, but it did not reverse the long-term trend. The share of total income and wealth claimed by the top continued to grow, as did the political clout that accompanies such concentration. Most Americans remained unaware.

But now the nation is becoming aware. President Obama has made it one of the defining issues of his reelection campaign. The nonpartisan Congressional Budget Office has issued a major report on the widening disparities. The issue has become front-page news. For the first time since the 1930s, a broad cross section of the American public is talking about the concentration of income, wealth, and political power at the top.

Score a big one for the Occupiers. Regardless of whether you sympathize with the so-called Occupier movement that began spreading across America in the fall of 2011, or whether you believe it will become a growing political force in America, it has had a profound effect on the national conversation.

Even more startling is the change in public opinion. Not since the 1930s has a majority of Americans called for redistribution of income or wealth. But according to a *New York Times*/CBS News poll, an astounding 66 percent of Americans say the nation's wealth should be more evenly distributed. A similar majority believes the rich should pay more in taxes. According to a *Wall Street Journal*/NBC News poll, a majority of people who describe themselves as Republicans believe taxes should be increased on the rich.

I used to be called a class warrior for even raising the subject of widening inequality. Now it seems most Americans have become class warriors. Or at least class *worriers*. And many blame Republicans for stacking the deck in favor of the rich. In that *New York Times*/CBS News poll, 69 percent of respondents said Republican policies favor the rich (28 percent said the same of President Obama's policies).

The old view was that anyone could make it in America with enough guts and gumption. We believed in the self-made man (or, more recently, woman) who rose from rags to riches: inventors and entrepreneurs born into poverty, like Benjamin Franklin; generations of young men from humble beginnings who grew up to become president, like Abraham Lincoln. We loved the novellas of Horatio Alger and their more modern equivalents—stories that proved the American Dream was open to anyone who worked hard. In that old view, which was a kind of national morality play, being rich was proof of hard work, and lack of money was proof of indolence or worse.

A profound change has come over America. Guts, gumption, and hard work don't seem to pay off as they once did—or at least as they did in our national morality play. Instead, the game seems rigged in favor of people who are already rich and powerful—as well as their children. Instead of lionizing the rich, we're beginning to suspect they gained their wealth by ripping us off.

As recently as a decade ago the prevailing view was also that great wealth trickled downward—that the rich made investments in jobs and growth that benefited all of us. So even if we doubted that we ourselves would be wealthy, we assumed we'd still benefit from the fortunes made by a few. But that view, too, has lost its sheen. Americans see that nothing has trickled down. The rich have become far richer over the last three decades, but the rest of us haven't benefited. In fact, median incomes are dropping.

5

Wall Street moguls are doing better than ever—after having been bailed out by taxpayers. But the rest of us are doing worse. CEOs are hauling in more than three hundred times the pay of average workers (up from forty times the pay only three decades ago). But average workers have been losing their jobs and wages. The ratio of corporate profits to wages is higher than it's been since before the Great Depression. The chairman of Merck took home $17.9 million in 2010, as Merck laid off sixteen thousand workers and announced layoffs of twenty-eight thousand more. The CEO of Bank of America raked in $10 million, while the bank announced it was firing thirty thousand employees.

Even though the rate of unemployment has begun to fall, jobs still remain scarce, and the pay of the bottom 90 percent continues to drop, adjusted for inflation. But CEO pay is still rising through the stratosphere. Among the CEOs who took in more than $50 million in 2011 were Qualcomm's Paul Jacobs ($50.6 million), JCPenney's Ron Johnson ($51.5 million), Starbucks's Howard Schultz ($68.8 million), Tyco International's Ed Breen ($68.9 million), and Apple's Tim Cook ($378 million). The titans of Wall Street are doing even better.

The super-rich are not investing in jobs and growth. They're putting their bonanza into U.S. Treasury bills or investing it in Brazil or South Asia or anywhere else it can reap the highest return. The American economy is in trouble because so much income and wealth have been going to the top that the rest of us no longer have the purchasing power to keep the economy going. I'll get into this in greater detail shortly.

Some apologists for this extraordinary accumulation of income and wealth at the top attribute it to "risk taking" by courageous entrepreneurs. Mitt Romney[1] defines free enterprise as achieving success through "risk taking." The president of the Chamber of Commerce, Tom Donohue, explains that "this economy is about risk. If you don't take risk, you can't have success." But in fact the higher you go in today's economy, the easier it is to make a pile of money without taking any personal financial risk. The lower you go, the bigger the risks and the smaller the rewards.

Partners in private-equity firms like Romney's Bain Capital don't risk their own money. They invest other people's money and take 2 percent of it as their annual fee for managing the money regardless of how successful they are. They then pocket 20 percent of any upside gains. Partners like Romney pay taxes on only 15 percent of what they make—a lower rate than that paid by many middle-class Americans—because of a loophole that treats this income as capital gains. The ostensible reason capital gains are taxed at a much lower rate than ordinary income is to reward investors for risking their money, but private-equity managers usually don't risk a dime.

---

[1]**Mitt Romney:** Willard Mitt Romney, former governor of Massachusetts and the Republican nominee in the 2012 U.S. presidential election. [All notes are the editors'.]

In fact, rather than taking any real risks, they get government to subsidize them. Having piled the companies they purchase with debt, private-equity managers then typically issue "special dividends" that repay the original investors. Interest payments on that mountain of debt are tax deductible. In effect, government subsidizes them for using debt instead of incurring any real risk with equity. If the companies are subsequently forced into bankruptcy because they can't manage payments on all this debt, they dump their pension obligations on the Pension Benefit Guaranty Corporation (PBGC), a federal agency, which picks up the tab. If the PBGC can't meet the payments, taxpayers are left holding the bag.

It's another variation on Wall Street's playbook of maximizing personal gain and minimizing personal risk. If you screw up royally you can still walk away like royalty. Taxpayers will bail you out. Personal responsibility is completely foreign to the highest echelons of the Street. Citigroup's stock fell 44 percent in 2011, but its CEO, Vikram Pandit, got at least $5.45 million on top of a retention bonus of $16.7 million. The stock of JPMorgan Chase fell 20 percent, but its CEO, Jamie Dimon, was awarded a package worth $22.9 million.

The higher you go in corporate America as a whole, the less of a relationship there is between risk and reward. Executives whose pay is linked to the value of their firm's shares get a free ride when the stock market as a whole rises, even if they didn't lift a finger. On the other hand, to protect their wallets against any risk that their firm's share price might fall, they can place countervailing bets in derivatives markets. This sort of hedging helped the head of AIG,[2] Hank Greenberg, collect $250 million in 2008, when AIG collapsed.

Other CEOs are guaranteed huge compensation regardless of how their companies do. Robert Iger's arrangement as head of the Disney Company netted him $52.8 million in 2011 and guarantees him at least $30 million a year more through 2015—regardless of company performance. The swankiest golf courses of America are festooned with former CEOs who have almost sunk their companies but been handsomely rewarded. Gilbert Amelio headed Apple for a disastrous seventeen months while the firm lost nearly $2 billion, but he walked away with $9.2 million anyway. William D. McGuire was forced to resign as CEO of United-Health over a stock-options scandal but left with a pay package worth $286 million.

It doesn't even matter how long you're at the helm. Thomas E. Freston lasted just nine months as CEO of Viacom before being terminated with an exit package of $101 million. Scott Thompson lasted only four months as CEO of Yahoo!, but that was long enough for him to pocket

[2] **AIG:** American International Group, Inc., an American multinational insurance corporation that was bailed out by the U.S. Federal Reserve in 2008.

$7 million. His predecessor, Carol Bartz, lasted twenty months and left with an exit package of $10.4 million.

You can push your company to the brink and still make a fortune. Robert Rossiter, the former CEO of Lear, landed his company in bankruptcy, which wiped out his shareholders along with twenty thousand jobs, but he walked away from the wreckage with a $5.4 million bonus. In early 2012, the *Wall Street Journal* looked into the pay of executives at twenty-one of the largest companies that had recently gone through bankruptcy. The median compensation of those CEOs was $8.7 million—not much less than the $9.1 million median compensation of all CEOs of big companies. The reason CEOs get giant pay packages for lousy performance is that they stack their boards of directors' compensation committees with cronies who make sure they do.

Even if you commit fraud, your personal financial risk is minimal. Starting in 2009, the Securities and Exchange Commission (SEC) filed twenty-five cases against mortgage originators and securities firms. A few are still being litigated, but most have been settled. They generated almost $2 billion in penalties and other forms of monetary relief, according to the SEC. But almost none of this money came out of the pockets of CEOs or other company officials; it came out of the companies—or, more accurately, their shareholders. In the one instance in which company executives appear to have been penalized directly—a case brought against three former top officials of New Century Financial, a brazenly fraudulent lender that subsequently collapsed—the penalties were tiny compared with how much the executives pocketed. New Century's CEO had to disgorge $542,000 of his ill-gotten gains, but he took home more than $2.9 million in "incentive" pay in the two years before the company tanked.

Yet as economic risks are vanishing at the top and the rewards keep growing, the risks, as I said, are rising dramatically on almost everyone below, and the rewards keep shrinking. Full-time workers who put in decades with a company can now find themselves without a job overnight—with no parachute, no help finding another job, and no health insurance. More than 20 percent of the American workforce is now "contingent"—temporary workers, contractors, independent consultants—with no security at all.

Most families face the mounting risk of receiving giant hospital bills yet having no way to pay them. Fewer and fewer large and medium-sized companies offer their workers full health-care coverage—74 percent did in 1980; under 10 percent do today. As a result, health insurance premiums, co-payments, and deductibles are soaring.

Most people also face the increasing risk of not having enough to retire on. Three decades ago more than 80 percent of large and medium-sized firms gave their workers "defined benefit" pensions that guaranteed a fixed amount of money every month after they retired. Now it's fewer than 10 percent. Instead, the employers offer "defined contribution" plans, where the risk is on the workers. When the stock market plunges, as it did in 2008, 401(k) plans plunge along with it. Meanwhile, people at the top are socking away tens of millions for their retirements while paying little or no taxes—in effect, enjoying a huge government subsidy. By 2011, Mitt Romney's IRA was worth between $20 million and $100 million, including Bain Capital holdings in offshore havens like the Cayman Islands.

Romney is right: free enterprise is on trial. But he's wrong about the question at issue in that trial. It's not whether America will continue to reward risk taking. It's whether an economic system can survive when those at the top get giant rewards no matter how badly they screw up while the rest of us get screwed no matter how hard we work. . . .

The Broken Basic Bargain

As I write this, jobs are starting to return, and America appears to be emerging from the deepest economic downturn we've experienced since the Great Depression. But the pay of most Americans is not returning—and that is the longer-term and more disturbing story. For most of the last century, the basic bargain at the heart of the American economy was that employers paid their workers enough to buy what American employers were selling. That basic bargain created a virtuous cycle of higher living standards, more jobs, and better wages. But for the last thirty years that basic bargain has been coming apart.

In 1914, Henry Ford announced he was paying workers on his Model T assembly line $5 a day—three times what the typical factory employee earned at the time. The *Wall Street Journal* termed his action "an economic crime," but Ford knew it was a cunning business move. The higher wage turned Ford's autoworkers into customers who could afford to buy Model Ts. In two years Ford's profits more than doubled.

That was then. Now Ford Motor Company is paying its new hires about half what it paid its new employees a decade ago. Ford's newest workers earn about $14 an hour, in contrast to the $25 an hour earned by new Ford workers in 2002 (adjusted for inflation). Ford also gives today's new recruits a maximum of four weeks of paid time off a year; Ford workers used to get five weeks. And instead of receiving a guaranteed $3,000-a-month pension when they retire at age sixty, new hires must build their own "personal retirement plans," to which Ford contributes less than $2,000 a year.

It's the same story across America. At GE, new hires earn $12 to $19 an hour, versus $21 to $32 an hour earned by workers who started at GE a decade or more ago. According to the Commerce Department, employee pay is down to the smallest share of the economy since the government began collecting wage and salary figures data in 1929. Meanwhile, corporate profits now constitute the largest share of the economy since 1929.

In case you forgot, 1929 was the year of the crash that ushered in the Great Depression. In the years leading up to that crash, most employers forgot Henry Ford's example. The wages of most American workers remained stagnant. The gains of economic growth went mainly into corporate profits and into the pockets of the very rich. American families maintained their standard of living by going deeper into debt. In 1929 the debt bubble popped.

Sound familiar? It should. The same thing happened in the years leading up to the crash of 2008. And more recent data show the trends continuing. In other words, we still haven't learned the essential lesson of the two big economic crashes of the last seventy-five years: when the economy becomes too lopsided—disproportionately benefiting corporate owners and top executives vis-à-vis average workers—it tips over.

The real reason the American economy tanked in 2008, and why we're still struggling to recover, is that the basic bargain has been broken. The big economic news isn't the slow return of jobs. It's the continuing drop in pay. Most of the jobs we've gained since the Great Recession pay less than the jobs lost during it. An analysis from the National Employment Law Project shows that the biggest losses were in jobs paying between $19.05 and $31.40 an hour; the biggest increases have been in jobs paying an average of $9.03 to $12.91 an hour.

For several years now, conservative economists have blamed high unemployment on the purported fact that many Americans have priced themselves out of the global/high-tech jobs market. So if we want more jobs, they say, we'll need to accept lower wages and benefits. That's exactly what Americans have been doing. More and more Americans are retaining their jobs by settling for lower pay or going without cost-of-living increases. Or they've lost a higher-paying job and have taken one that pays less. Or they've joined the great army of contingent workers, self-employed "consultants," temps, and contract workers— without health-care benefits, pensions, job security, or decent wages.

All told, the decade starting in 2001 was the worst decade for American workers in a century. According to Commerce Department data, private sector wage gains even lagged behind wage gains during the decade of the Great Depression (4 percent between 2001 and 2011, adjusted for inflation, versus 5 percent from 1929 to 1939). Conservatives say that's still not enough, which is why unions have to be busted—and why Republican governors and legislators are trying to pass so-called right-to-work laws banning employment contracts requiring employees to join a union and pay union dues. Without such a requirement there's no reason for any particular worker to join a union, because he can get the bargaining advantages of unionization without paying for them— which in turn destroys unions, exactly the point. In 2012, Indiana enacted the nation's first right-to-work law in more than a decade and the first ever in the heavily unionized upper Midwest.

The current attack on public sector workers logically follows. As the pay and benefits of workers in the private sector continue to drop, Republicans claim public sector workers now take home more generous pay and benefits packages than private sector workers. It's not true on the wage side if you control for level of education, but it wasn't even true on the benefits side until private sector benefits fell off a cliff. Meanwhile, all across America, public sector workers are being "furloughed," which is a nice word for not collecting any pay for weeks at a time.

It's no great feat to create lots of lousy jobs. A few years ago the 35 Republican congresswoman Michele Bachmann remarked that if the minimum wage were repealed, "we could potentially virtually wipe out unemployment completely because we would be able to offer jobs at whatever level." If you accept her logic, why stop there? After all, slavery was a full-employment system.

Conservative economists have it wrong. The underlying problem isn't that most Americans have priced themselves out of the global/high-tech labor market. It's that most Americans are receiving a smaller share of the American pie. This not only is bad for the majority but also hobbles the economy. Lower incomes mean less overall demand for goods and services, which translates into lower wages in the future. The basic bargain once recognized that average workers are also consumers and that their paychecks keep the economy going. We can't have a full-fledged recovery and we can't sustain a healthy economy until that bargain is restored.

"If we don't decide what we're worth, who will?"

ENGAGING THE TEXT

1. Reich is interested in how people engage with economic issues, writing that "the so-called Occupier movement that began spreading across America in the fall of 2011 . . . has had a profound effect on the national conversation" (para. 3). What evidence do you see — in daily conversations, news reports, blog postings, political speeches, or protests — to suggest that economic justice has become an important topic on the national agenda?

2. Reich describes the fading myth of the self-made man and the failure of "trickle-down" economics and suggests that many Americans now view the world of money and success as a rigged game. Explain why you agree or disagree with this characterization of American attitudes. How do you think most Americans feel about CEO salaries and the wealth gap between rich and poor?

3. Describe the "basic bargain" that Reich says has been broken and discuss whether you see examples of the broken bargain in your family or community. Then consider the jobs you've held and the career paths you are considering. Do you think some kind of basic bargain still exists, and if so, what are the terms of the bargain today?

4. **Thinking Rhetorically** Reich, who served as a cabinet member in the Clinton administration, makes no effort to hide his political affiliations. Which passages in the reading are most clearly politically partisan, and how do these affect your evaluation of Reich's analysis? What changes could Reich make in tone or approach if he wanted to address a larger, more politically diverse audience?

EXPLORING CONNECTIONS

5. Among the CEOs whose salaries Reich considers outrageous is Jamie Dimon, the JPMorgan Chase CEO who "was awarded a package worth $22.9 million" (para. 15) despite his company's plunging stock price. Describe how you think Reich and Dimon would each interpret the Visual Portfolio photo of the police in front of the JPMorgan Chase & Co. building (p. 411).

6. In "Class in America — 2012" by Gregory Mantsios (p. 377), "Harold S. Browning" earns $324,000 per year as an executive vice president of a digital instruments company; his ambition is to become a CEO. Imagine that since 2012 Browning has become one of America's top two hundred CEOs and thus brings home more than $22 million per year. What would Browning's profile look like now that he's making seventy times as much money? Discuss whether CEO incomes should be limited and what the "maximum wage" should be.

EXTENDING THE CRITICAL CONTEXT

7. Write a movie review of Reich's 2013 film *Inequality for All*, assessing the clarity of the film's argument and the persuasiveness of its reasoning and evidence.

8. Do additional research on the wealth gap. What evidence supports the claim that the gap between the income (annual wages and bonuses) and the wealth

(the value of all assets minus debts) of the classes is growing? What do experts say about the future of the wealth gap? What policy changes or programs do economists propose for reducing further concentration of wealth? What do you think we should do about this issue, and why?

9. Reich reports that Hank Greenberg (Maurice R. Greenberg) collected $250 million in 2008 despite the collapse of his company, AIG (para. 16). Research the lawsuit Greenberg filed against the U.S. Federal Reserve, in which he sought up to $40 billion in compensation for AIG shareholders. (Judge Thomas C. Wheeler of the U.S. Court of Federal Claims ruled on the case in June of 2015.) Report on what you learned and explain how this affects your assessment of Reich's position.

VISUAL PORTFOLIO
READING IMAGES OF INDIVIDUAL OPPORTUNITY

Reuters / Lucy Nicholson / Landov

AP Photo/John Minchillo

Spencer Platt / Getty Images

Lonely Planet Images / Getty Images

VISUAL PORTFOLIO

READING IMAGES OF INDIVIDUAL OPPORTUNITY

1. In the photograph of a man repairing novelty items during vocational training (p. 409), what else is going on? What is the man thinking? What is his relationship to his work, to the toys, and to his coworkers? What do you make of the slogan on his T-shirt, "Freedom by any means necessary"?

2. Who are the men waiting for work on page 410, and what life histories do you imagine have brought them to this place? What kinds of work are they are hoping for? Could you find a scene like this in or near your community, and if so, what kind of wages would such workers earn? Which worker do you think is most likely to get hired, and why?

3. What are the police officers doing in front of the JPMorgan Chase & Co. building on page 411? What is happening outside the building, inside the building, and at the entryway? Analyze specific elements of the photo including the company name, the street address, the people on the second floor looking out, and the facial expressions and body language of the officers.

4. On April 15, 2015, protesters staged a "die-in" at a McDonald's in New York City, demanding a $15 per hour minimum wage (p. 412). Why do you think this was called a "die-in"? Under what circumstances might you join such a demonstration as a low-wage worker or a sympathizer? Explain why you agree or disagree with the most prominent placard in the photo — "You exploit people across the globe for profit."

5. Any photo of a child sleeping in a car is likely to be unsettling, but what makes the image on page 413 particularly powerful? What do parents, community, schools, or government agencies "owe" the boy to give him a chance to escape poverty?

FROM A TANGLE OF PATHOLOGY TO A RACE-FAIR AMERICA

ALAN AJA, DANIEL BUSTILLO, WILLIAM DARITY JR., AND DARRICK HAMILTON

Some Americans saw the election of President Barack Obama as a sign that the nation had entered a new postracial era in which the problems of racism and discrimination had been largely solved. This essay challenges that view by analyzing how race and money are intertwined in contemporary America. The authors point to continuing patterns of bias in hiring practices and unemployment rates and present dramatic data on the "racial wealth gap" between blacks and whites. Arguing that deep-rooted structural problems continue to hold back African Americans, they propose two new federal policies to support a "race-fair" America. Alan Aja is professor of Puerto Rican and Latino studies at Brooklyn College. Daniel Bustillo is a doctoral student in the School of Social Work at Columbia University. William Darity Jr. is professor of economics and the Samuel DuBois Cook Professor of Public Policy at Duke University's Sanford School of Public Policy. Darrick Hamilton is professor of economics and urban policy at The New School's Milano School of International Affairs, Management, and Urban Policy. The essay appeared in *Dissent: A Quarterly of Politics and Culture* (2014).

WHEN PRESIDENT LYNDON JOHNSON gave his June 4, 1965, commencement address at Howard University, he invoked a symbolic language that would both seize the political moment and serve as a foundation for subsequent policy. The Civil Rights Act had passed only a year earlier, and Johnson, noting that it is "not enough just to open the gates of opportunity," told the black graduating class that America needed "not just equality as a right and a theory but equality as a fact and as a result." This call for "results" was a precursor to Johnson's Executive Order 11246, a mandate for the enforcement of positive antidiscrimination measures in preferred positions of society, or "affirmative action."

But later in the speech, Johnson moved away from his point of departure, abruptly arguing that "perhaps most important—its influence radiating to every part of life—is the breakdown of the Negro family structure." This "rhetorical sleight of hand," as sociologist Stephen Steinberg aptly calls it, would reverberate in public discussion for years to come. By defining the central problem facing the black community as not the deep-seated structures that perpetuate racism but rather deficiencies internal to blacks themselves, the focus of policy would become the rehabilitation of the black family.

The roots of this ideology can be traced to Oscar Lewis's[1] notion of a "culture of poverty" and the 1965 Moynihan Report,[2] in which black families were characterized as being caught up in a "tangle of pathology." The contemporary version of this thesis is the "postracial" narrative in which America has largely transcended its racial divides. The narrative of grand racial progress is coupled with the claim that whatever racial disparities remain are overwhelmingly the result of actions (or inactions) on the part of subaltern[3] groups themselves. If blacks (and other subaltern communities, including Native Americans, Mexicans, Filipinos, Puerto Ricans, and Vietnamese) simply would reverse their self-sabotaging attitudes and behaviors, this argument goes, full equality could be achieved. Herein lies much of the rationale for austerity policies.[4] If behavioral modification is the central issue, why fund government agencies and programs, which, at best, misallocate resources to irresponsible individuals and, at worst, create dependencies that further fuel irresponsible behavior?

Post-racialists often confirm their perspective by pointing to black and minority appointments to the nation's elite positions, including the election of Barack Obama to the highest office in the land. Indeed, the president himself often perpetuates this "postracial" trope. In his speech marking the fiftieth anniversary of the March on Washington for Jobs and Freedom, Obama described how "legitimate grievances" had "tipped into excuse-making" and "the transformative message of unity and brotherhood was drowned out by the language of recrimination." "And what had once been a call for equality of opportunity," he continued, "the chance for all Americans to work hard and get ahead, was too often framed as a mere desire for government support, as if we had no agency in our own liberation, as if poverty was an excuse for not raising your child and the bigotry of others was reason to give up on yourself."

The president's rhetoric on race is consistent with the following premises:

5

1. The civil rights era has virtually ended structural barriers to black equality; remaining barriers are due to the legacy of past discrimination, the residual effects of concentrated poverty, and black folks' own behaviors. After all, virtually all groups of Americans have faced some form of discrimination but managed to "get ahead" anyway.

[1] **Oscar Lewis:** American anthropologist (1914–1970) who theorized that poor and marginalized groups may create a self-perpetuating subculture of poverty, "especially because of what happens to the worldview, aspirations, and character of the children who grow up in it." [All notes are the editors'.]

[2] **Moynihan Report:** "The Negro Family: The Case for National Action," a controversial report by sociologist and Assistant Secretary of Labor (later U.S. Senator) Daniel Patrick Moynihan that pointed to the relative scarcity of traditional nuclear families in black communities as a primary cause of African American poverty.

[3] **subaltern:** Outside the dominant power structure.

[4] **austerity policies:** Government policies that would reduce spending on programs like Head Start, Aid to Families with Dependent Children, Temporary Assistance for Needy Families, and the Supplemental Nutrition Assistance Program (food stamps).

2. Blacks need to cease making particularistic claims on America and begin, in the president's words, to "[bind] our grievances to the larger aspirations of all Americans."

3. Blacks need to recognize their own complicity in the continuation of racial inequality, as well as their own responsibility for directly changing their disparate position.

But if structural factors are largely artifacts of the past, what explains the marked and persistent racial gaps in employment and wealth? Is discrimination genuinely of only marginal importance in America today? Has America really transcended the racial divide, and can the enormous racial wealth gap be explained on the basis of dysfunctional behaviors?

The Racial Employment Gap

In marked contrast to incremental gains in relative educational attainment and income, the racial gap in mass long-term unemployment continues to remain intolerably high, with black Americans bearing a disproportionate burden. In the spring of 2014 the black unemployment rate was estimated at 12.0 percent, compared to 5.8 percent for whites. This continues a structural trend where the black rate remains roughly twice as high as the white rate. In fact, over the past forty years there has been only one year, 2000, in which the black unemployment rate has been below 8.0 percent. In contrast, there have only been four years in which the white rate has reached that level. Blacks are in a perpetual state of employment crisis.

At every rung of the educational ladder, the black unemployment rate is twice the white rate. In 2012 the unemployment rate for whites with less than a high school diploma was 11.4 percent, but for blacks with the same educational level the rate was 20.4 percent. Most telling as an indication of ongoing discrimination in U.S. labor markets is that the unemployment rate for adult white high school dropouts (11.4 percent) was less than the rate for blacks with some college education or an associate's degree (11.6 percent).

Field experiments of employment audits provide powerful evidence that employer discrimination remains a plausible explanation for racial labor market disparity. Economists Marianne Bertrand and Sendhil Mullainathan found a 50 percent higher callback rate for résumés with "white-sounding names" than for comparable résumés with "African American–sounding names." Even more telling, the "better"-quality résumés with African American–sounding names received fewer callbacks than "lower"-quality résumés with white-sounding names.

Princeton sociologist Devah Pager conducted another employment study in Milwaukee, Wisconsin, that revealed the difficulties for stigmatized populations in finding a job. Wisconsin has outlawed employer use of criminal background checks for most jobs, yet among young males of comparable race, experience, and education, audit testers with a criminal record received half as many employment callbacks as testers without a record. Nonetheless, race was found to be even more stigmatizing than incarceration. White testers with criminal records had a slightly higher callback rate than black testers without criminal records.

Racial disparities persist even for those employed. Nearly 87 percent of U.S. occupations can be classified as racially segregated even after accounting for educational differences. Black males experience the most severe underrepresentation in construction, extraction, and maintenance occupations.[5] These occupations tend to require low educational credentials but offer relatively high wages. At the other extreme, service occupations have the highest concentrations of black males; these are also low-credentialed occupations but, in contrast to construction, tend to offer relatively low pay. This distinction is noteworthy given the widely held view that the lack of "soft skills" on the part of blacks is a major factor in explaining their labor market difficulties.

The "soft skills" explanation fits neatly within the "post-racial" narrative. For example, Harvard sociologist William Julius Wilson argues that employers in service industries fail to hire black men because they "lack the soft skills that their jobs require: the tendency to maintain eye contact, the ability to carry on polite and friendly conversations with consumers, the inclination to smile and be responsive to consumer requests." Yet the hard fact remains that blacks are "crowded in" to the service sector, which typically requires customer and coworker interactions, and "crowded out" of the construction sector, which primarily involves not soft skills but working with materials and machinery. This contradicts the notion that soft-skills differentials explain the racial labor market disparity.

The Racial Wealth Gap

Wealth is of paramount importance as a pool of resources, beyond income, that individuals or families can use as a sustained mechanism for provision of support for their offspring. Wealth represents long-term resource accumulation and provides the economic security to take risks, shield against financial loss, and cope with emergencies.

Wealth is also the economic indicator in which blacks and whites are farthest apart. Prior to the Great Recession, white households had a median net worth of approximately $135,000 and black households a median net worth of a little over $12,000. Thus, the typical black family had less than 9 cents for every dollar in wealth of the typical white family. According to the Pew Hispanic Center, this gap nearly doubled after the Great Recession, with the typical black family having about a nickel for every dollar in wealth held by the typical white family; in 2009 the typical black household had less than $6,000 in net worth.

Regardless of age, household structure, education, occupation, or income, black families typically have less than a quarter of the wealth

15

---

[5] **extraction . . . occupations:** Industries that extract resources from the natural environment, such as mining, oil drilling, and timber harvesting.

of otherwise comparable white families. Perhaps even more disturbing, the median wealth of black families whose head graduated from college is less than the median wealth of white families whose head dropped out of high school, and high-earning married black households typically have less wealth than low-earning married white households.

Wealth provides, perhaps, the best evidence to dispel the myth of a postracial society. It also provides the best evidence to dispel the parallel and reinforcing myth that the vestiges of racial inequality are the result of poor choices on the part of blacks themselves. The conventional wisdom explains the persistence of this massive racial wealth gap across all levels of income by invoking allegedly poor savings behavior or inferior portfolio management on the part of blacks. For example, when asked at an April 2009 lecture at Morehouse College about the racial wealth gap, then Federal Reserve Chair Ben Bernanke attributed the gap to a lack of "financial literacy" on the part of blacks, particularly with respect to savings behavior.

But greater financial literacy will do next to nothing to close the racial wealth gap in the absence of finances to manage; nor does it provide insulation against heavy hits to one's investment portfolio. The massive loss in wealth experienced by shareholders on Wall Street in 2008 was not due to their financial illiteracy; it was due to the stock market crash. Most of the individuals defrauded in Bernie Madoff's pyramid scheme could hardly be described as "financially illiterate." Presumably, all Americans may benefit from improved knowledge about management of their personal financial resources, but racial differences in knowledge about management of personal financial resources do not explain the racial gulf in wealth. Maury Gittleman and Ed Wolff reinforced this in an analysis of data predating the mortgage market crisis that finds no significant racial advantage in asset appreciation rates for white families with positive assets after controlling for household income. They also find no meaningful difference in savings by race after controlling for household income—a conclusion that economists as ideologically disparate as Milton Friedman and Marcus Alexis (a founding member of Black Enterprise's Board of Economists) have reached.

Most of the racial wealth gap is explained by inheritances, bequests, and intrafamily transfers—transfers largely based on the economic position of the family into which an individual is born. Indeed, inheritances and intrafamily transfers are far more important considerations in explaining the racial wealth gap than education, income, and household structure. Moreover, intrafamilial shifts of resources are transfers made on a nonmerit basis. The continued structural barriers that inhibit blacks from amassing resources and making intergenerational transfers provide strong opposition to the postracial narrative. Past, present, and prospective racial exploitation and discrimination provide a sounder basis for understanding the vast material disparities between blacks and whites in the United States. There is a long history of structural impediments to black wealth accumulation. Beginning with the period of chattel slavery, when blacks were literally the property of white slave owners, and continuing through the use of restrictive covenants, redlining, general housing and lending discrimination—policies that generated a white asset-based middle class—and the foreclosure crisis (which was characterized by predation and racially disparate impacts), blacks have faced structural barriers to wealth accumulation.

The Racial Self-Employment Gap

Substantial attention has been given to black business development as a means of closing the racial wealth gap. This confuses cause and effect: the racial wealth gap would have to be closed as a prelude to closing the racial self-employment gap. Business formation, success, and survival depend heavily on the initial level of financial capital available to the entrepreneur, and black firms start with much less initial capital than white firms. Policy has often reinforced this initial disadvantage. [Sociologist] Tamara Nopper has documented specific changes in Small Business Administration policy—such as more aggregate targeting of women and other minority groups, and a shift to private-sector lenders with more stringent collateral and credit requirements—that accounted for a substantial reduction in loans directed to black business. Nopper also noted that the tendency for ethnic banks to service co-ethnics coupled with a relative paucity of black-owned banks and undercapitalization of these banks negatively affected black business access to finance. For example, in 2008 the Federal Deposit Insurance Corporation identified a total of ninety-six Asian- and Pacific Islander–owned banks with a total of $53 billion in assets in contrast to only forty-four black-owned banks with $7.5 billion in assets. The business success of certain immigrant groups relative to blacks is a consequence of greater initial wealth upon entry into the United States, the selectivity of immigration, and the support of the Small Business Administration, rather than a "deficient" entrepreneurial spirit or cultural orientation toward business among blacks.

What Can Be Done?

The most parsimonious policy approach would be carefully targeted race-based policies. However, if such policies are becoming politically unfeasible, then we need bold policies that lead to economic security, mobility, and sustainability for all Americans, or what john a. powell[6] has labeled "targeted universalism." 20

Child Trust Accounts (Baby Bonds). These accounts are designed to provide an opportunity for asset development for all newborns regardless of the financial position in which they are born. The baby bonds would set up trusts for all newborns with an average account of $20,000 that progressively

[6]**john a. powell:** Professor of law, African American studies, and ethnic studies at UC Berkeley and executive director of the Haas Institute for a Fair and Inclusive Society.

rise to $60,000 for babies born into the poorest families. The accounts would be federally managed and grow at a federally guaranteed annual interest rate of 1.5–2 percent to be accessed when the child becomes an adult and used for asset-enhancing endeavors, such as purchasing a home or starting a new business. With approximately four million infants born each year, and an average endowment of around $20,000, we estimate the cost of the program to be $80 billion. In relative proportional costs, this would constitute only 2.2 percent of 2012 federal expenditures.

These accounts could be paid for by a more equitable allocation of what the federal government already spends on asset development. A 2010 report by the Corporation for Enterprise Development and the Annie E. Casey Foundation estimates that the federal government allocated $400 billion of its 2009 budget in the form of tax subsidies and savings to promote asset-development policies, with more than half of the benefits going to the top 5 percent of earners—those with incomes higher than $160,000. In contrast, the bottom 60 percent of taxpayers received only 4 percent of the benefits. If the federal asset-promotion budget were allocated in a more progressive manner, federal policies could be transformative for low-income Americans. For example, repealing the mortgage interest deduction—which primarily benefits middle- and upper-income households—would be an important first step in creating a tax code that is fairer for all and treats renters and homeowners alike.

A Federal Job Guarantee. This would provide economic security, mobility, and sustainability for all Americans, while also addressing the longstanding pattern of racial inequality in employment. We estimate that the average cost per job directly created by the employment corps—including salary, benefits, training, and equipment—would be $50,000, with the total compensation package amounting to $750 billion, which is less than the first $787 billion stimulus package[7] and considerably less than the first phase of the bailout of the investment banks[8] estimated at $1.3 trillion. The net expenses of the job-guarantee program would be reduced because of a wide array of cost savings from other social programs; in 2011 alone, federal antipoverty programs (Medicaid, unemployment insurance, and so on) cost approximately $746 billion.

While liberal leaders, whether they be Lyndon Johnson or Barack Obama, may rhetorically acknowledge the legacies of racism, they often support policies that are based on conservative notions of a culture of poverty. Policies that emphasize deficient norms, values, and behaviors on the part of blacks and other subaltern groups amount to what William Ryan categorized over forty years ago as simply "blaming the victim." These include efforts to encourage small business development without first addressing the racial maldistribution of wealth and the current White

[7] **stimulus package:** The American Recovery and Investment Act of 2009, signed into law to stimulate the economy as the Great Recession began.

[8] **bailout of the investment banks:** The Emergency Economic Stabilization Act of 2008 and the Troubled Asset Relief Program created by that act.

House initiative, "My Brother's Keeper," which is aimed at transforming the motivation and behaviors of "defective" black male youths to make them more "employable" without addressing their lack of job opportunities and labor market discrimination. Addressing the racial employment and wealth gaps will require not paternalistic policy, but policies providing access to jobs and asset building for all Americans.

ENGAGING THE TEXT

1. Review the three premises of "postracialism" in paragraph 5. How has reading this article influenced your ideas about each of these premises? What specific ideas or information in the article challenged or reinforced your existing beliefs?

2. Do you agree that President Obama's words in paragraph 4 are indeed consistent with the three premises of postracialism the authors articulate? Why or why not?

3. At the end of their article, the authors propose two policy initiatives — "Child Trust Accounts" and a "Federal Job Guarantee" — to move the United States closer to racial equality. What do you think would be the impact of these initiatives? What arguments could be made against them, and how might those arguments be addressed?

4. In paragraphs 11–12, the authors try to discredit the notion that a lack of "soft skills" limits blacks' opportunities in the labor market. How important do you think soft skills are for workers? What soft skills should CEOs be required to have? To what extent might "soft skills" be a cover term that obscures deeper issues such as racial discrimination, gender bias, or preferences for a particular dialect or accent?

5. **Thinking Rhetorically** What is the thesis of this article? Is it implied or directly stated? Using the article's subheadings as cues, outline the organization of the article and assess the strength of the evidence in each section.

EXPLORING CONNECTIONS

6. Read or review the profiles of Sam Walton and Jay Z that open this chapter (p. 350). Which elements of Jay Z's biography fit the "tangle of black pathology" stereotype, and which don't? To what extent does Jay Z's success indicate progress toward a "race-fair" America? Finally, how might Aja and his coauthors analyze Walton's biography in terms of employment, self-employment, and the racial wealth gap?

7. Read or review "Aunt Ida Pieces a Quilt" by Melvin Dixon (p. 41). Imagine Aunt Ida as she might have been in 1965, when the Moynihan Report (para. 3) appeared; write a letter from Ida's point of view to Moynihan, challenging his characterization of black families as living in a "tangle of pathology."

8. In paragraph 18 the authors provide a quick snapshot of the "history of structural impediments to black wealth accumulation." Look ahead to "The Case for Reparations" by Ta-Nehisi Coates (p. 572); identify relevant examples of impediments in Coates's essay and explain how they have limited black accumulation of wealth.

9. Look at Matt Wuerker's "About That Dream" below, a cartoon built around a statistic. Working in small groups, draw and design your own cartoon that highlights one statistic from this selection, a previous reading, or the Fast Facts for this chapter.

EXTENDING THE CRITICAL CONTEXT

10. The quotations from President Obama in paragraph 4 come from "Remarks by the President at the 'Let Freedom Ring' Ceremony Commemorating the 59th Anniversary of the March on Washington," a speech delivered at the Lincoln Memorial on August 28, 2013. Find and read the full speech online. Discuss whether the quotations selected by Aja and his coauthors accurately represent the speech as a whole. For example, to what extent does the speech seem to support a "postracial trope" or valorize the American Dream, and to what extent does the president identify the kinds of structural changes that Aja and his colleagues consider necessary?

11. The authors note that "affirmative action" dates back to President Lyndon B. Johnson's Executive Order 11246 (para. 1). Research the contentious history of affirmative action over the past half century. How effective has the program been as a means of addressing racial inequities? What does the history of affirmative action suggest about the likelihood of implementing the kinds of initiatives favored by the authors?

FRAMING CLASS, VICARIOUS LIVING, AND CONSPICUOUS CONSUMPTION

DIANA KENDALL

Diana Kendall, a professor of sociology at Baylor University, has performed an extensive study of how newspapers and TV have portrayed social class in the last half-century. She concludes that the media shape public opinions about the upper, middle, working, and poverty classes by "framing" their stories and their programming in a relatively small number of patterned, predictable, and misleading ways. For example, "the media glorify the upper classes, even when they are accused of wrongdoing." In this excerpt from her award-winning book *Framing Class: Media Representations of Wealth and Poverty in America* (2005), Kendall analyzes how several common media frames communicate cultural messages about social class. Her recent books include *Members Only: Elite Clubs and the Process of Exclusion* (2008) and *Sociology in Our Times: The Essentials* (2015).

> *"The Simple Life 2"—the second season of the reality show, on which the celebutante Paris Hilton and her Best Friend Forever, the professional pop-star-daughter Nicole Richie, are set on a cross-country road trip*—once again takes the heaviest of topics and makes them as weightless as a social X-ray.[1]

THIS STATEMENT BY TELEVISION CRITIC CHOIRE SICHA, in [his] review of FOX TV's reality-based entertainment show *The Simple Life*, sums up a recurring theme of *Framing Class:* The media typically take "the heaviest of topics," such as class and social inequality, and trivialize it. Rather than providing a meaningful analysis of inequality and showing realistic portrayals of life in various social classes, the media either play class differences for laughs or sweep the issue of class under the rug so that important distinctions are rendered invisible. By ignoring class or trivializing it, the media involve themselves in a social construction of reality that rewards the affluent and penalizes the working class and the poor. In real life, Paris Hilton and Nicole Richie are among the richest young women in the world; however, in the world of *The Simple Life,* they can routinely show up somewhere in the city or the country, pretend they are needy, and rely on the kindness of strangers who have few economic resources.

The *Simple Life* is only one example of many that demonstrate how class is minimized or played for laughs by the media. [Below] I have

---

[1]Choire Sicha, "They'll Always Have Paris," *New York Times*, June 13, 2004, AR31 [emphasis added]. [All notes are Kendall's, except 26.]

provided many examples of how class is framed in the media and what messages those framing devices might convey to audiences. . . . I will look at the sociological implications of how framing contributes to our understanding of class and how it leads to vicarious living and excessive consumerism by many people. I will also discuss reasons why prospects for change in how journalists and television writers portray the various classes are limited. First, we look at two questions: How do media audiences understand and act upon popular culture images or frames? Is class understood differently today because of these frames?

Media Framing and the Performance of Class in Everyday Life

In a mass-mediated culture such as ours, the media do not simply mirror society; rather, they help to shape it and to create cultural perceptions.[2] The blurring between what is real and what is not real encourages people to emulate the upper classes and shun the working class and the poor. Television shows, magazines, and newspapers sell the idea that the only way to get ahead is to identify with the rich and powerful and to live vicariously through them. From sitcoms to reality shows, the media encourage ordinary people to believe that they may rise to fame and fortune; they too can be the next American Idol. Constantly bombarded by stories about the lifestyles of the rich and famous, viewers feel a sense of intimacy with elites, with whom they have little or no contact in their daily lives.[3] According to the social critic bell hooks, we overidentify with the wealthy, because the media socialize us to believe that people in the upper classes are better than we are. The media also suggest that we need have no allegiance to people in our own class or to those who are less fortunate.[4]

Vicarious living — watching how other individuals live rather than experiencing life for ourselves — through media representations of wealth and success is reflected in many people's reading and viewing habits and in their patterns of consumption. According to hooks, television promotes hedonistic consumerism:

> Largely through marketing and advertising, television promoted the myth of the classless society, offering on one hand images of an American dream fulfilled wherein any and everyone can become rich and on the other suggesting that the lived experience of this lack of class hierarchy was expressed by our *equal right to purchase anything we could afford.*[5]

---

[2]Tim Delaney and Allene Wilcox, "Sports and the Role of the Media," in *Values, Society and Evolution*, ed. Harry Birx and Tim Delaney, 199–215 (Auburn, NY: Legend, 2002).

[3]bell hooks [Gloria Watkins], *Where We Stand: Class Matters* (New York: Routledge, 2000), 73.

[4]hooks, *Where We Stand*, 77.

[5]hooks, *Where We Stand*, 71 [emphasis added].

As hooks suggests, equality does not exist in contemporary society, but media audiences are encouraged to view themselves as having an "equal right" to purchase items that somehow will make them equal to people above them in the social class hierarchy. However, the catch is that we must actually be able to afford these purchases. Manufacturers and the media have dealt with this problem by offering relatively cheap products marketed by wealthy celebrities. Paris Hilton, an heir to the Hilton Hotel fortune, has made millions of dollars by marketing products that give her fans a small "slice" of the good life she enjoys. Middle- and working-class people can purchase jewelry from the Paris Hilton Collection — sterling silver and Swarovski crystal jewelry ranging in price from fifteen to a hundred dollars — and have something that is "like Paris wears." For less than twenty dollars per item, admirers can purchase the Paris Hilton Wall Calendar; a "Paris the Heiress" Paper Doll Book; Hilton's autobiography, *Confessions of an Heiress;* and even her dog's story, *The Tinkerbell Hilton Diaries: My Life Tailing Paris Hilton.* But Hilton is only one of thousands of celebrities who make money by encouraging unnecessary consumerism among people who are inspired by media portrayals of the luxurious and supposedly happy lives of rich celebrities. The title of Hilton's television show, *The Simple Life,* appropriates the image of simple people, such as the working class and poor, who might live happy, meaningful lives, and transfers this image to women whose lives are anything but simple as they flaunt designer clothing and spend collectively millions of dollars on entertainment, travel, and luxuries that can be afforded only by the very wealthy.[6]

How the media frame stories about class *does* make a difference in what we think about other people and how we spend our money. Media frames constitute a mental shortcut (schema) that helps us formulate our thoughts.

The Upper Classes: Affluence and Consumerism for All

Although some media frames show the rich and famous in a negative manner, they still glorify the material possessions and lifestyles of the upper classes. Research has found that people who extensively watch television have exaggerated views of how wealthy most Americans are and what material possessions they own. Studies have also found that extensive television viewing leads to higher rates of spending and to lower savings, presumably because television stimulates consumer desires.[7]

For many years, most media framing of stories about the upper classes has been positive, ranging from *consensus framing* that depicts members of the upper class as being like everyone else, to *admiration framing* that portrays them as generous, caring individuals. The frame

[6]hooks, *Where We Stand,* 72.
[7]Juliet B. Schor, *Born to Buy: The Commercialized Child and the New Consumer Culture* (New York: Scribner, 2004).

most closely associated with rampant consumerism is *emulation framing*, which suggests that people in all classes should reward themselves with a few of the perks of the wealthy, such as buying a piece of Paris's line of jewelry. The writers of television shows such as ABC's *Life of Luxury*, E!'s *It's Good to Be* . . . [a wealthy celebrity, such as Nicole Kidman], and VH1's *The Fabulous Life* rely heavily on admiration and price-tag framing, by which the worth of a person is measured by what he or she owns and how many assistants constantly cater to that person's whims. On programs like FOX's *The O.C.* and *North Shore* and NBC's *Las Vegas*, the people with the most expensive limousines, yachts, and jet aircraft are declared the winners in life. Reality shows like *American Idol, The Billionaire, For Love or Money*, and *The Apprentice* suggest that anyone can move up the class ladder and live like the rich if he or she displays the best looks, greatest talent, or sharpest entrepreneurial skills. It is no wonder that the economist Juliet B. Schor finds that the overriding goal of children age ten to thirteen is to get rich. In response to the statement "I want to make a lot of money when I grow up," 63 percent of the children in Schor's study agreed, whereas only 7 percent disagreed.[8]

Many adults who hope to live the good life simply plunge farther into debt. Many reports show that middle- and working-class American consumers are incurring massive consumer debts as they purchase larger houses, more expensive vehicles, and many other items that are beyond their means. According to one analyst, media portrayals of excessive consumer spending and a bombardment of advertisements by credit-card companies encourage people to load up on debt.[9] With the average U.S. household now spending 13 percent of its after-tax income to *service* debts (not pay off the principal!), people with average incomes who continue to aspire to lives of luxury like those of the upper classes instead may find themselves spending their way into the "poorhouse" with members of the poverty class.

The Poor and Homeless: "Not Me!" — Negative Role Models in the Media

The sharpest contrasts in media portrayals are between depictions of people in the upper classes and depictions of people at the bottom of the class structure. At best, the poor and homeless are portrayed as deserving of our sympathy on holidays or when disaster strikes. In these situations, those in the bottom classes are depicted as being temporarily down on their luck or as working hard to get out of their current situation but in need of public assistance. At worst, however, the poor are blamed for their own problems; stereotypes of the homeless as bums, alcoholics, and drug addicts, caught in a hopeless downward spiral because of their *individual* pathological behavior, are omnipresent in the media.

[8]Schor, *Born to Buy*.
[9]Joseph Nocera, *A Piece of the Action: How the Middle Class Joined the Money Class* (New York: Simon and Schuster, 1994).

For the most part, people at the bottom of the class structure remain out of sight and out of mind for most media audiences. *Thematic framing* depicts the poor and homeless as "faceless" statistics in reports on poverty. *Episodic framing* highlights some problems of the poor but typically does not link their personal situations [and] concerns to such larger societal problems as limited educational opportunities, high rates of unemployment, and jobs that pay depressingly low wages.

The poor do not fare well on television entertainment shows, where writers typically represent them with one-dimensional, bedraggled characters standing on a street corner holding cardboard signs that read "Need money for food." When television writers tackle the issue of homelessness, they often portray the lead characters (who usually are white and relatively affluent) as helpful people, while the poor and homeless are depicted as deviants who might harm themselves or others. Hospital and crime dramas like *E.R., C.S.I.,* and *Law & Order* frequently portray the poor and homeless as "crazy," inebriated in public, or incompetent to provide key information to officials. Television reality shows like *Cops* go so far as to advertise that they provide "footage of debris from the bottom tiers of the urban social order."[10] Statements such as this say a lot about the extent to which television producers, directors, and writers view (or would have us view) the lower classes.

From a sociological perspective, framing of stories about the poor and homeless stands in stark contrast to framing of stories about those in the upper classes, and it suggests that we should distance ourselves from "those people." We are encouraged to view the poor and homeless as the *Other,* the outsider; in the media we find little commonality between our lives and the experiences of people at the bottom of the class hierarchy. As a result, it is easy for us to buy into the dominant ideological construction that views poverty as a problem of individuals, not of the society as a whole, and we may feel justified in our rejection of such people.[11]

The Working Class: Historical Relics and Jokes

The working class and the working poor do not fare much better than the poor and homeless in media representations. The working class is described as "labor," and people in this class are usually nothing more than faces in a crowd on television shows. The media portray people

[10]Karen De Coster and Brad Edmonds, "TV Nation: The Killing of American Brain Cells," Lewrockwell.com, 2004, www.lewrockwell.com/decoster/decoster78.html (accessed July 7, 2004).

[11]Judith Butler ("Performative Acts and Gender Constitution: An Essay in Phenomenology and Feminist Theory," in *Performing Feminisms: Feminist Critical Theory and Theatre,* ed. Sue-Ellen Case [Baltimore: Johns Hopkins University Press, 1990], 270) has described gender identity as performative, noting that social reality is not a given but is continually created as an illusion "through language, gesture, and all manner of symbolic social sign." In this sense, class might also be seen as performative, in that people act out their perceived class location not only in terms of their own class-related identity but in regard to how they treat other people, based on their perceived class position.

who *produce* goods and services as much less interesting than those who *excessively consume* them, and this problem can only grow worse as more of the workers who produce the products are thousands of miles away from us, in nations like China, very remote from the typical American consumer.[12]

Contemporary media coverage carries little information about the working class or its problems. Low wages, lack of benefits, and hazardous working conditions are considered boring and uninteresting topics, except on the public broadcasting networks or an occasional television "news show" such as *60 Minutes* or *20/20,* when some major case of worker abuse has recently been revealed. The most popular portrayal of the working class is *caricature framing,* which depicts people in negative ways, such as being dumb, white trash, buffoons, bigots, or slobs. Many television shows featuring working-class characters play on the idea that the clothing, manners, and speech patterns of the working class are not as good as those of the middle or upper classes. For example, working-class characters (such as Roseanne, the animated Homer Simpson, and *The King of Queens'* Doug) may compare themselves to the middle and upper classes by saying that they are not as "fancy as the rich people." Situation comedy writers have perpetuated working-class stereotypes, and now a number of reality shows, such as *The Swan* and *Extreme Makeover,* try to take "ordinary" working-class people and "improve" them through cosmetic surgery, new clothing, and different hairstyles.

Like their upper-class celebrity counterparts, so-called working-class comedians like Jeff Foxworthy have ridiculed the blue-collar lifestyle. They also have marketed products that make fun of the working class. Foxworthy's website, for example, includes figurines ("little statues for *inside* the house"), redneck cookbooks, Games Rednecks Play, and calendars that make fun of the working class generally. Although some people see these items as humorous ("where's yore sense of humor?"), the real message is that people in the lower classes lack good taste, socially acceptable manners, and above all, middle-class values. If you purchase "redneck" merchandise, you too can make fun of the working class and clearly distance yourself from it.

Middle-Class Framing and Kiddy-Consumerism

Media framing of stories about the middle class tells us that this economic group is the value center and backbone of the nation. *Middle-class values framing* focuses on the values of this class and suggests that they hold the nation together. Early television writers were aware that their shows needed to appeal to middle-class audiences, who were the targeted

---

[12]See Thomas Ginsberg, "Union Hopes to Win Over Starbucks Shop Workers," *Austin American-Statesman,* July 2, 2004, D6.

consumers for the advertisers' products, and middle-class values of honesty, integrity, and hard work were integral ingredients of early sitcoms. However, some contemporary television writers spoof the middle class and poke fun at values supposedly associated with people in this category. The writers of FOX's *Malcolm in the Middle* and *Arrested Development,* for example, focus on the dysfunctions in a fictional middle-class family, including conflicts between husband and wife, between parents and children, and between members of the family and outsiders.

Why do these shows make fun of the middle class? Because corporations that pay for the advertisements want to capture the attention of males between ages eighteen and thirty-nine, and individuals in this category are believed to enjoy laughing at the uptight customs of conventional middle-class families. In other shows, as well, advertisers realize the influence that their programs have on families. That is why they are happy to spend billions of dollars on product placements (such as a Diet Coke can sitting on a person's desk) in the shows and on ads during commercial breaks. In recent research, Schor examined why very young children buy into the consumerism culture and concluded that extensive media exposure to products was a key reason. According to Schor, "More children [in the United States] than anywhere else believe that their clothes and brands describe who they are and define their social status. American kids display more brand affinity than their counterparts anywhere else in the world; indeed, experts describe them as increasingly 'bonded to brands.'"[13]

Part of this bonding occurs through constant television watching and Internet use, as a steady stream of ads targets children and young people. Schor concludes that we face a greater problem than just excessive consumerism. A child's well-being is undermined by the consumer culture: "High consumer involvement is a significant cause of depression, anxiety, low self-esteem, and psychosomatic complaints."[14] Although no similar studies have been conducted to determine the effects of the media's emphasis on wealth and excessive consumerism among adults, it is likely that today's children will take these values with them into adulthood if our society does not first reach the breaking point with respect to consumer debt.

The issue of class in the United States is portrayed in the media not through a realistic assessment of wealth, poverty, or inequality but instead through its patterns of rampant consumerism. The general message remains, one article stated, "We pledge allegiance to the mall."[15]   20

---

[13]Schor, *Born to Buy*, 13.
[14]Schor, *Born to Buy*, 167.
[15]Louis Uchitelle, "We Pledge Allegiance to the Mall," *New York Times*, December 6, 2004, C12.

Media Framing and Our Distorted View of Inequality

Class clearly permeates media culture and influences our thinking on social inequality. How the media frame stories involving class constitutes a *socially constructed reality* that is not necessarily an accurate reflection of the United States. Because of their pervasive nature, the media have the symbolic capacity to define the world for other people. In turn, readers and viewers gain information from the media that they use to construct a picture of class and inequality—a picture that becomes, at least to them, a realistic representation of where they stand in the class structure, what they should (or should not) aspire to achieve, and whether and why they should view other people as superior, equal, or inferior to themselves.

Because of the media's power to socially construct reality, we must make an effort to find out about the objective nature of class and evaluate social inequality on our own terms. Although postmodern thinkers believe that it is impossible to distinguish between real life and the fictionalized version of reality that is presented by the media, some sociologists argue that we can learn the difference between media images of reality and the actual facts pertaining to wealth, poverty, and inequality. The more we become aware that we are not receiving "raw" information or "just" entertainment from the media, the more we are capable of rationally thinking about how we are represented in media portrayals and what we are being encouraged to do (engage in hedonistic consumerism, for example) by these depictions. The print and electronic media have become extremely adept at framing issues of class in a certain manner, but we still have the ability to develop alternative frames that better explain who we are and what our nation is truly like in regard to class divisions.

The Realities of Class

What are the realities of inequality? The truth is that the rich are getting richer and that the gulf between the rich and the poor continues to widen in the United States. Since the 1990s, the poor have been more likely to stay poor, and the affluent have been more likely to stay affluent. How do we know this? Between 1991 and 2001, the income of the top one-fifth of U.S. families increased by 31 percent; during the same period, the income of the bottom one-fifth of families increased by only 10 percent.[16] The chasm is even wider across racial and ethnic categories; African Americans and Latinos/Latinas are overrepresented among

---

[16]Carmen DeNavas-Walt and Robert W. Cleveland, "Income in the United States: 2002," *U.S. Census Bureau: Current Population Reports*, P60–221 (Washington, DC: U.S. Government Printing Office, 2003).

those in the bottom income levels. Over one-half of African American and Latino/Latina households fall within the lowest income categories.

Wealth inequality is even more pronounced. The super-rich (the top 0.5 percent of U.S. households) own 35 percent of the nation's wealth, with net assets averaging almost nine million dollars. The very rich (the next 0.5 percent of households) own about 7 percent of the nation's wealth, with net assets ranging from $1.4 million to $2.5 million. The rich (9 percent of households) own 30 percent of the wealth, with net assets of a little over four hundred thousand dollars. Meanwhile, everybody else (the bottom 90 percent of households) owns only 28 percent of the nation's wealth. Like income, wealth disparities are greatest across racial and ethnic categories. According to the Census Bureau, the net worth of the average white household in 2000 was more than ten times that of the average African American household and more than eight times that of the average Latino/Latina household. Moreover, in 2002, almost thirty-five million people lived below the official government poverty level of $18,556 for a family of four, an increase of more than one million people in poverty since 2001.[17]

The Realities of Hedonistic Consumerism

Consumerism is a normal part of life; we purchase the things that we need to live. However, hedonistic consumerism goes beyond all necessary and meaningful boundaries. As the word *hedonism* suggests, some people are so caught up in consumerism that this becomes the main reason for their existence, the primary thing that brings them happiness. Such people engage in the self-indulgent pursuit of happiness through what they buy. An example of this extreme was recently reported in the media. When Antoinette Millard was sued by American Express for an allegedly past-due account, she filed a counterclaim against American Express for having provided her with a big-spender's credit card that allowed her to run up bills of nearly a million dollars in luxury stores in New York.[18] Using the "victim defense," Millard claimed that, based on her income, the company should not have solicited her to sign up for the card. Although this appears to be a far-fetched defense (especially in

25

---

[17]Bernadette D. Proctor and Joseph Dalaker, "Poverty in the United States: 2002," *U.S. Census Bureau: Current Population Reports*, P60–222 (Washington, DC: U.S. Government Printing Office, 2003).

[18]Antoinette Millard, also known as Lisa Walker, allegedly was so caught up in hedonistic consumerism that she created a series of false identities (ranging from being a Saudi princess to being a lawyer, a model, and a wealthy divorcee) and engaged in illegal behavior (such as trying to steal $250,000 from an insurance company by reporting that certain jewelry had been stolen, when she actually had sold it). See Vanessa Grigoriadis, "Her Royal Lie-ness: The So-Called Saudi Princess Was Only One of the Many Identities Lisa Walker Tried On Like Jewelry," *New York Metro*, www.newyorkmetro.com/nymetro /news/people/columns/intelligencer/n_10418 (accessed December 18, 2004); Samuel Maull, "Antoinette Millard Countersues American Express for $2 Million for Allowing Her to Charge $951,000," creditsuit.org/credit.php/blog/comments/antoinette_millard_countersues _american_express_for_2_million_for_allowing (accessed December 18, 2004).

light of some of the facts),[19] it may be characteristic of the lopsided thinking of many people who spend much more money than they can hope to earn. Recent studies have shown that the average American household is carrying more than eight thousand dollars in credit-card debt and that (statistically speaking) every fifteen seconds a person in the United States goes bankrupt.[20] Although fixed costs (such as housing, food, and gasoline) have gone up for most families over the past thirty years, these debt-and-bankruptcy statistics in fact result from more people buying items that are beyond their means and cannot properly use anyway. Our consumer expectations for ourselves and our children have risen as the media have continued to attractively portray the "good life" and to bombard us with ads for something else that we *must* have.

Are we Americans actually interested in learning about class and inequality? Do we want to know where we really stand in the U.S. class structure? Although some people may prefer to operate in a climate of denial, media critics believe that more people are finally awakening to biases in the media, particularly when they see vast inconsistencies between media portrayals of class and their everyday lives. According to the sociologists Robert Perrucci and Earl Wysong, "It is apparent that increasing experiences with and knowledge about class-based inequalities among the nonprivileged is fostering a growing awareness of and concerns about the nature and extent of superclass interests, motives, and power in the economic and political arenas."[21] Some individuals are becoming aware of the effect that media biases can have on what they read, see, and hear. A recent Pew Research Center poll, for example, reflects that people in the working class do not unquestioningly accept media information and commentary that preponderantly support the status quo.[22]

Similarly, Perrucci and Wysong note that television can have a paradoxical effect on viewers: It can serve both as a pacifier and as a source of heightened class consciousness. Programs that focus on how much money the very wealthy have may be a source of entertainment for nonelites, but they may also produce antagonism among people who work hard and earn comparatively little, when they see people being paid so much for doing so little work (e.g., the actress who earns seventeen million dollars per film or the sports star who signs a hundred-million-dollar multiyear contract). Even more egregious are individuals who do not work at all but are born into the "right family" and inherit billions of dollars.

Although affluent audiences might prefer that the media industry work to "reinforce and disguise privileged-class interests,"[23] there is a

---

[19]Steve Lohr, "Maybe It's Not All Your Fault," *New York Times*, December 5, 2004, WR1.

[20]Lohr, "Maybe It's Not All Your Fault."

[21]Robert Perrucci and Earl Wysong, *The New Class Society*, 2nd ed. (Lanham, MD.: Rowman & Littlefield, 2003), 199.

[22]Perrucci and Wysong, *The New Class Society*.

[23]Perrucci and Wysong, *The New Class Society*, 284.

good chance that the United States will become more class conscious and that people will demand more accurate assessments of the problems we face if more middle- and working-class families see their lifestyles continue to deteriorate in the twenty-first century.

Is Change Likely? Media Realities Support the Status Quo

Will journalists and entertainment writers become more cognizant of class-related issues in news and in television shows? Will they more accurately portray those issues in the future? It is possible that the media will become more aware of class as an important subject to address, but several trends do not bode well for more accurate stories and portrayals of class. Among these are the issues of media ownership and control.

Media Ownership and Senior Management

Media ownership has become increasingly concentrated in recent decades. Massive mergers and acquisitions involving the three major television networks (ABC, CBS, and NBC) have created three media "behemoths"—Viacom, Disney, and General Electric—and the news and entertainment divisions of these networks now constitute only small elements of much larger, more highly diversified corporate structures. Today, these media giants control most of that industry, and a television network is viewed as "just another contributor to the bottom line."[24] As the media scholar Shirley Biagi states, "The central force driving the media business in America is the desire to make money. American media are businesses, vast businesses. The products of these businesses are information and entertainment. . . . But American media are, above all, profit-centered."[25]

Concentration of media ownership through chains, broadcast networks, cross-media ownership, conglomerates, and vertical integration (when one company controls several related aspects of the same business) are major limitations to change in how class is represented in the news and entertainment industry. Social analysts like Greg Mantsios[26] are pessimistic about the prospects for change, because of the upper-class-based loyalties of media corporate elites:

> It is no wonder Americans cannot think straight about class. The mass media is neither objective, balanced, independent, nor neutral. Those who own and direct the mass media are themselves part of the upper class, and neither they nor the ruling class in general have to conspire to manipulate public opinion. Their interest is in preserving the status quo, and their view of society as fair and equitable comes naturally to

[24]Committee of Concerned Journalists, "The State of the News Media 2004," www.journalism.org (accessed June 17, 2004).

[25]Shirley Biagi, *Media Impact: An Introduction to Mass Media* (Belmont, CA.: Wadsworth, 2003), 21.

[26]**Mantsios:** See "Class in America—2012" (p. 377). [Eds.]

them. But their ideology dominates our society and justifies what is in reality a perverse social order—one that perpetuates unprecedented elite privilege and power on the one hand and widespread deprivation on the other.[27]

According to Mantsios, wealthy media shareholders, corporate executives, and political leaders have a vested interest in obscuring class relations not only because these elites are primarily concerned about profits but because—being among the "haves" themselves—they do not see any reason to stir up class-related animosities. Why should they call attention to the real causes of poverty and inequality and risk the possibility of causing friction among the classes?

Media executives do not particularly care if the general public criticizes the *content* of popular culture as long as audiences do not begin to question the superstructure of media ownership and the benefits these corporations derive from corporate-friendly public policies. According to the sociologist Karen Sternheimer,

> Media conglomerates have a lot to gain by keeping us focused on the popular culture "problem," lest we decide to close some of the corporate tax loopholes to fund more social programs....In short, the news media promote media phobia because it doesn't threaten the bottom line. Calling for social programs to reduce inequality and poverty would.[28]

Although the corporate culture of the media industry may be set by shareholders and individuals in the top corporate ranks, day-to-day decisions often rest in the hands of the editor-in-chief (or a person in a similar role) at a newspaper or a television executive at a local station. Typically, the goals of these individuals reflect the profit-driven missions of their parent companies and the continual need to generate the right audiences (often young males between eighteen and thirty-five years of age) for advertisers. Television commentator Jeff Greenfield acknowledges this reality: "The most common misconception most people have about television concerns its product. To the viewer, the product is the programming. To the television executive, the product is the audience."[29] The profits of television networks and stations come from selling advertising, not from producing programs that are accurate reflections of social life.

Recent trends in the media industry—including concentration of ownership, a focus on increasing profits, and a move toward less regulation of the media by the federal government—do not offer reassurance that media representations of class (along with race, gender, age, and sexual orientation) will be of much concern to corporate shareholders or executives at the top media giants—unless, of course, this issue becomes related to the bottom line or there is public demand for change, neither

---

[27]Gregory Mantsios, "Media Magic: Making Class Invisible," in *Privilege: A Reader*, ed. Michael S. Kimmel and Abby L. Ferber, 99–109 (Boulder, CO: Westview, 2003), 108.

[28]Karen Sternheimer, *It's Not the Media: The Truth About Pop Culture's Influence on Children* (Boulder, CO: Westview, 2003), 211.

[29]Quoted in Biagi, *Media Impact*, 170.

of which seems likely. However, it does appear that there is a possibility for change among some journalists and entertainment writers.

Journalists: Constraints and Opportunities

Some analysts divide journalists into the "big time" players—reporters and journalists who are rich, having earned media salaries in the millions and by writing best-selling books (e.g., ABC's Peter Jennings)—and the "everyday" players, who are primarily known in their local or regional media markets.[30] Elite journalists in the first category typically are employed by major television networks (ABC, CBS, and NBC), popular cable news channels (such as CNN and FOX News), or major national newspapers such as the *Wall Street Journal, New York Times,* or *USA Today.* These journalists may be influential in national media agenda-setting, whereas the everyday media players, beat reporters, journalists, and middle- to upper-level managers at local newspapers or television stations at best can influence local markets.

Some of these individuals—at either level—are deeply concerned about the state of journalism in this country, as one recent Pew Research Center for the People and the Press study of 547 national and local reporters, editors, and executives found.[31] One of the major concerns among these journalists was that the economic behavior of their companies was eroding the quality of journalism in the United States. By way of example, some journalists believe that business pressures in the media industry are making the news "thinner and shallower."[32] Journalists are also concerned that the news media pay "too little attention...to complex issues."[33] However, a disturbing finding in the Pew study was that some journalists believe that news content is becoming more shallow because that is what the public *wants.* This cynical view may become a self-fulfilling prophecy that leads journalists to produce a shallower product, based on the mistaken belief that the public cannot handle anything else.[34]

Despite all this, some opportunities do exist in the local and national news for *civic journalism*—"a belief that journalism has an obligation to public life—an obligation that goes beyond just telling the news or unloading lots of facts."[35] Civic journalism is rooted in the assumption

---

[30]One study identified the "typical journalist" as "a white Protestant male who has a bachelor's degree from a public college, is married, 36 years old, earns about $31,000 a year, has worked in journalism for about 12 years, does not belong to a journalism association, and works for a medium-sized (42 journalists), group-owned daily newspaper" (Weaver and Wilhoit 1996). Of course, many journalists today are white women, people of color, non-Protestants, and individuals who are between the ages of 45 and 54 (Committee of Concerned Journalists, "The State of the News Media 2004").

[31]Pew Center for Civic Journalism, "Finding Third Places: Other Voices, Different Stories," 2004, www.pewcenter.org/doingcj/videos/thirdplaces.html (accessed July 6, 2004).

[32]Bill Kovach, Tom Rosenstiel, and Amy Mitchell, "A Crisis of Confidence: A Commentary on the Findings," Pew Research Center for the People and the Press, 2004, www.stateofthenewsmedia.org/prc.pdf (accessed July 6, 2004), 27.

[33]Kovach, Rosenstiel, and Mitchell, "A Crisis of Confidence," 29.

[34]Kovach, Rosenstiel, and Mitchell, "A Crisis of Confidence."

[35]Pew Center for Civic Journalism, "Finding Third Places."

that journalism has the ability either to empower a community or to help disable it. Based on a civic journalism perspective, a news reporter gathering information for a story has an opportunity to introduce other voices beyond those of the typical mainstream spokesperson called upon to discuss a specific issue such as the loss of jobs in a community or the growing problem of homelessness. Just as more journalists have become aware of the importance of fair and accurate representations of people based on race, gender, age, disability, and sexual orientation, it may be possible to improve media representations of class. Rather than pitting the middle class against the working class and the poor, for example, the media might frame stories in such a way as to increase people's aware- ness of their shared concerns in a nation where the upper class typically is portrayed as more important and more deserving than the average citizen.

The process of civic journalism encourages journalists to rethink their use of frames. Choosing a specific frame for a story is "the most powerful decision a journalist will make."[36] As journalists become more aware that the media are more than neutral storytelling devices, per- haps more of them will develop alternative frames that look deeply into a community of interest (which might include the class-based realities of neighborhoods) to see "how the community interacts with, interre- lates to, and potentially solves a pressing community problem." By ask- ing "What is the essence of this story?" rather than "What is the conflict value of this story?" journalists might be less intent, for example, on pit- ting the indigenous U.S. working class against more recent immigrants or confronting unionized workers with their nonunionized counterparts. Stories that stress conflict have winners and losers, victors and villains; they suggest that people must compete, rather than cooperate, across class lines.[37] An exploration of other types of framing devices might produce better results in showing how social mobility does or does not work in the U.S. stratification system—highlighting, for example, what an individual's real chances are for moving up the class ladder (as is promised in much of the jargon about the rich and famous).

Advocates of civic journalism suggest that two practices might help journalists do a better job of framing in the public interest: *public listen- ing* and *civic mapping*. Public listening refers to "the ability of journal- ists to listen with open minds and open ears; to understand what people are really saying."[38] Journalists engaged in public listening would be less interested in getting "superficial quotes or sound bites" and instead would move more deeply into the conversations that are actually taking place. Journalists would use open-ended questions in their interviews,

[36]Steve Smith, "Developing New Reflexes in Framing Stories," Pew Center for Civic Journalism, 1997, www.pewcenter.org/doingcj/civiccat/displayCivcat.php?id=97 (accessed July 3, 2004).

[37]Richard Harwood, "Framing a Story: What's It Really About?" Pew Center for Civic Journalism, 2004, www.pewcenter.org/doingcj/videos/framing.html (accessed July 3, 2004).

[38]Smith, "Developing New Reflexes in Framing Stories."

by which they could look more deeply into people's hopes, fears, and values, rather than asking closed-ended questions to which the only allowable response choices are "yes/no" or "agree/disagree" — answers that in effect quickly (and superficially) gauge an individual's opinion on a topic. When journalists use civic mapping, they seek out underlying community concerns through discussions with people. They attempt to look beneath the surface of current public discourse on an issue. Mapping helps journalists learn about the ideas, attitudes, and opinions that really exist among diverse groups of people, not just "public opinion" or politicians' views of what is happening.

By seeking out *third places* where they can find "other voices" and hear "different stories," journalists may learn more about people from diverse backgrounds and find out what they are actually thinking and experiencing.[39] A "third place" is a location where people gather and often end up talking about things that are important to them. According to the sociologist Ray Oldenburg, the third place is "a great variety of public places that host the regular, voluntary, informal, and happily anticipated gatherings of individuals beyond the realms of home and work."[40] If the first place is the home, and the second place is the work setting, then the third place includes such locations as churches, community centers, cafes, coffee shops, bookstores, bars, and other places where people informally gather. As journalists join in the conversation, they can learn what everyday people are thinking about a social issue such as tax cuts for the wealthy. They can also find out what concerns people have and what they think contributes to such problems as neighborhood deterioration.

In addition to listening to other voices and seeking out different stories in third places, journalists might look more systematically at how changes in public policies — such as in tax laws, welfare initiatives, or policies that affect publicly funded child care or public housing — might affect people in various class locations. What are the political and business pressures behind key policy decisions like these? How do policies affect the middle class? The working class? Others? For example, what part does class play in perceptions about local law enforcement agencies? How are police officers viewed in small, affluent incorporated cities that have their own police departments, as compared to low-income neighborhoods of the bigger cities? While wealthy residents in the smaller cities may view police officers as "employees" who do their bidding (such as prohibiting the "wrong kind of people" from entering their city limits at night), in some low-income sectors of larger cities the police may be viewed as "oppressors" or as "racists" who contribute to, rather than reduce, problems of lawlessness and crime in the community. Journalists who practice civic journalism might look beyond typical framing

40

[39]Pew Center for Civic Journalism, "Finding Third Places."

[40]Ray Oldenburg, *The Great Good Place: Cafés, Coffee Shops, Bookstores, Bars, Hair Salons and Other Hangouts at the Heart of a Community* (New York: Marlowe, 1999), 16.

devices to tell a more compelling story about how the intersections of race *and* class produce a unique chemistry between citizens and law enforcement officials. In this way, journalists would not be using taken-for-granted framing devices that have previously been employed to "explain" what is happening in these communities.

Given current constraints on the media, including the fact that much of the new investment in journalism today is being spent on disseminating the news rather than on collecting it,[41] there is room for only cautious optimism that some journalists will break out of the standard reflexive mode to explore the microscopic realities of class at the level where people live, and at the macroscopic level of society, where corporate and governmental elites make important decisions that affect everyone else.

Some media analysts believe that greater awareness of class-related realities in the media would strengthen the democratic process in the United States. According to Mantsios, "A mass media that did not have its own class interests in preserving the status quo would acknowledge that inordinate wealth and power undermine democracy and that a 'free market' economy can ravage a people and their communities."[42] It remains to be seen, however, whether organizations like the Project for Excellence in Journalism and the Committee of Concerned Journalists will be successful in their efforts to encourage journalists to move beyond the standard reflexive mode so that they will use new frames that more accurately reflect class-based realities.

Like journalists, many television entertainment writers could look for better ways to frame stories. However, these writers are also beleaguered by changes in the media environment, including new threats to their economic security from reality shows that typically do not employ in-house or freelance writers like continuing series do. As a result, it has become increasingly difficult for entertainment writers to stay gainfully employed, let alone bring new ideas into television entertainment.[43]

We cannot assume that most journalists and television writers are in a position to change media portrayals of class and inequality; however, in the final analysis, the responsibility rests with each of us to evaluate the media and to treat it as only one, limited, source of information and entertainment in our lives. For the sake of our children and grandchildren, we must balance the perspectives we gain from the media with our own lived experiences and use a wider sociological lens to look at what is going on around us in everyday life. Some analysts believe that the media amuse and lull audiences rather than stimulating them to think, but we must not become complacent, thinking that everything is all right as our society and world become increasingly divided between

---

[41] Committee of Concerned Journalists, "The State of the News Media 2004."
[42] Mantsios, "Media Magic," 108.
[43] "So You Wanna Be a Sitcom Writer?" soyouwanna.com, 2004, www.soyouwanna.com/site/syws/sitcom/sitcom.html (accessed July 7, 2004).

the "haves" and the "have nots."[44] If the media industry persists in retaining the same old frames for class, it will behoove each of us as readers and viewers to break out of those frames and more thoroughly explore these issues on our own.

Bibliography

Biagi, Shirley. *Media Impact: An Introduction to Mass Media,* Belmont, CA: Wadsworth, 2003.

Butler, Judith. "Performative Acts and Gender Constitution: An Essay in Phenomenology and Feminist Theory." In *Performing Feminisms: Feminist Critical Theory and Theatre.* Edited by Sue-Ellen Case. Baltimore: Johns Hopkins University Press, 1990.

Committee of Concerned Journalists. "The State of the News Media 2004." www .journalism.org (accessed June 17, 2004).

De Coster, Karen, and Brad Edmonds. Lewrockwell.com, 2003. "TV Nation: The Killing of American Brain Cells." www.lewrockwell.com/decoster/decoster78 .html (accessed July 7, 2004).

Delaney, Tim, and Allene Wilcox. "Sports and the Role of the Media." In *Values, Society and Evolution,* edited by Harry Birx and Tim Delaney, 199–215. Auburn, NY Legend, 2002.

DeNavas-Walt, Carmen, and Robert W. Cleveland. "Income in the United States: 2002." *U.S. Census Bureau: Current Population Reports,* P60–221. Washington, DC: U.S. Government Printing Office, 2003.

Ginsberg, Thomas. "Union Hopes to Win Over Starbucks Shop Workers." *Austin American-Statesman,* July 2, 2004, D6.

Grigoriadis, Vanessa. "Her Royal Lie-ness: The So-Called Saudi Princess Was Only One of the Many Identities Lisa Walker Tried On Like Jewelry." *New York Metro.* www.newyorkmetro.com/nymetro/news/people/columns/intelligencer/n _10418 (accessed December 18, 2004).

Harwood, Richard. "Framing a Story: What's It Really About?" Pew Center for Civic Journalism, 2004. www.pewcenter.org/doingcj/videos/framing.html (accessed July 3, 2004).

hooks, bell [Gloria Watkins]. *Where We Stand: Class Matters.* New York: Routledge, 2000.

Kovach, Bill, Tom Rosenstiel, and Amy Mitchell. "A Crisis of Confidence: A Commentary on the Findings." Pew Research Center for the People and the Press, 2004. www.stateofthenewsmedia.org/prc.pdf (accessed July 6, 2004).

Mantsios, Gregory. "Media Magic: Making Class Invisible." In *Privilege: A Reader,* edited by Michael S. Kimmel and Abby L. Ferber, 99–109. Boulder, CO: Westview, 2003.

Maull, Samuel. "Antoinette Millard Countersues American Express for $2 Million for Allowing Her to Charge $951,000." creditsuit.org/credit.php/blog/comments /antoinette_millard_countersues_american_express_for_2_million_for_allowing (accessed December 18, 2004).

Nocera, Joseph. *A Piece of the Action: How the Middle Class Joined the Money Class.* New York: Simon and Schuster, 1994.

Oldenburg, Ray. *The Great Good Place: Cafés, Coffee Shops, Bookstores, Bars Hair Salons and Other Hangouts at the Heart of a Community.* New York: Marlowe, 1999.

Perrucci, Robert, and Earl Wysong. *The New Class Society.* 2nd edition. Lanham, MD: Rowman & Littlefield, 2003.

[44]Sternheimer, *It's Not the Media.*

Pew Center for Civic Journalism. 2004, "Finding Third Places: Other Voices, Different Stories." www.pewcenter.org/doingcj/videos/thirdplaces.html (accessed July 6, 2004).

Proctor, Bernadette D., and Joseph Dalaker. "Poverty in the United States: 2002." *U.S. Census Bureau: Current Population Reports,* P60–22. Washington, DC: U.S. Government Printing Office, 2003.

Schor, Juliet B. *Born to Buy: The Commercialized Child and the New Consumer Culture.* New York: Scribner, 2004.

Sicha, Choire. "They'll Always Have Paris." *New York Times,* June 13, 2004, AR31, AR41.

Smith, Steve. "Developing New Reflexes in Framing Stories." Pew Center for Civic Journalism, 1997. www.pewcenter.org/doingcj/civiccat/displayCivcat.php?id=97 (accessed July 3, 2004).

"So You Wanna Be a Sitcom Writer?" soyouwanna.com, 2004. www.soyouwanna.com/site/syws/sitcom/sitcom.html (accessed July 7, 2004).

Sternheimer, Karen. *It's Not the Media: The Truth About Pop Culture's Influence on Children.* Boulder, CO: Westview, 2003.

Uchitelle, Louis. "We Pledge Allegiance to the Mall." *New York Times,* December 6, 2004, C12.

Weaver, David H., and G. Cleveland Wilhoit. *The American Journalist in the 1990s.* Mahwah, NJ: Lawrence Erlbaum, 1996.

ENGAGING THE TEXT

1. Debate Kendall's assertion that "the media do not simply mirror society; rather, they help to shape it and to create cultural perceptions" (para. 3). Do you agree with Kendall's claim that the media distort our perceptions of social inequality? Do you think that watching TV inclines Americans to run up credit card debt?

2. Review Kendall's explanation of why middle- and working-class people sometimes buy items beyond their means, particularly items associated with wealthy celebrities. Do you agree that this behavior is best understood as "vicarious living" and "unnecessary consumerism"? In small groups, brainstorm lists of purchases you think exemplify hedonistic or unnecessary consumerism. How does hedonistic consumerism appear in a college setting?

3. Kendall says the media use "thematic framing" and "episodic framing" in portraying poor Americans. Define these terms in your own words and discuss whether the media typically portray the poor as "deviant" or "other."

4. According to Kendall, how do media representations of the working class and the middle class differ? Do you see evidence of this difference in the shows she mentions or in others you are familiar with?

5. What does Kendall mean by "civic journalism" (para. 37)? Why is she pessimistic about the future of civic journalism in national news organizations? Do you see any evidence of such journalism in your local news outlets?

EXPLORING CONNECTIONS

6. Imagine what "Looking for Work" (p. 19) might look like if it were turned into a TV episode. Keeping Kendall's observations in mind, how do you think TV might frame Gary Soto's narrative about social class?

7. In her essay "Inequality: Can Social Media Resolve Social Divisions?" (p. 303) danah boyd writes that "social media reproduces — and makes visible — existing social divisions within American society" (para. 41), including divisions of class. Study the design of several social media sites such as Facebook, Instagram, Twitter, Tumblr, Pinterest, and Ello — how they look, what they promise, and what users they seem to be targeting. Do these sites seem neutral in terms of class, or do they reproduce the kinds of media bias that Kendall discusses in her essay?

8. In "The Loneliness of the Interconnected" (p. 289), Charles Seife points to the ease of finding like-minded people on the Internet and argues that the fragmentation of contemporary media allows us to live in an online world where everyone shares our point of view. In your experience, does the Internet reproduce the kind of bias that Kendall sees in mass media portrayals of the social classes? To what extent are poverty, the poor, and the working class visible in life online, and how are they presented?

9. Review the Visual Portfolio (p. 409) and discuss each image in terms of frames — both the literal framing of the photograph and the interpretive framing of the settings, events, and people pictured. To what extent do the photos endorse or challenge common media images or assumptions?

EXTENDING THE CRITICAL CONTEXT

10. Review Kendall's definitions of consensus framing, admiration framing, emulation framing, and price-tag framing. Then watch one of the TV shows she mentions in paragraph 8 or a similar current show and look for evidence of these framing devices. Discuss with classmates how prominent these frames seem to be in contemporary TV programs.

SLAVERY IN THE LAND OF THE FREE
KEVIN BALES AND RON SOODALTER

For most Americans, slavery may not seem like a serious threat to civil rights — at least not since 1865 when the Thirteenth Amendment to the Constitution abolished involuntary servitude. So it may come as a shock that slavery still thrives in today's United States. In fact, according to the authors of this selection, permanently indentured servants can be found in every American neighborhood and industry, washing our floors, building our houses, and picking the fruit and vegetables we eat. Slavery, it seems, is one of the fastest growing sectors of the national and world economies. Kevin Bales is founder of Free the Slaves, a Washington-based nonprofit organization dedicated to ending slavery around the world. He is also professor of contemporary slavery at the Wilberforce Institute for the Study of Slavery and Emancipation at the University of Hull and emeritus professor of sociology at Roehampton University in London. His publications include *Disposable People: New Slavery in the Global Economy* (1999) and *Understanding Global Slavery: A Reader* (2005). Ron Soodalter is a respected historian who serves on the board of the Abraham Lincoln Institute. He is coauthor, with Kevin Bales, of the *The Slave Next Door: Human Trafficking and Slavery in America Today* (2009), the source of this excerpt.

The Old Slavery and the New

> *The great thought of captains, owners, consignees, and others, was to make the most money they could in the shortest possible time. Human nature is the same now as then.*
>
> —FREDERICK DOUGLASS, *The New National Era*, August 17, 1871,
> recalling the Atlantic slave trade

CERTAIN THINGS WE KNOW TO BE TRUE. We know that slavery is a bad thing, perpetrated by bad people. We also know that slavery not only exists throughout the world today but flourishes. With approximately twenty-seven million people in bondage, it is thought to be the third most profitable criminal enterprise of our time, following only drugs and guns. In fact, more than twice as many people are in bondage in the world today than were taken from Africa during the entire 350 years of the Atlantic slave trade. And we know that slavery is alive and more than well in the United States, thriving in the dark, and practiced in many forms in places where you'd least expect it.

Meet Sandra Bearden. Sandra was a twenty-seven-year-old homemaker in a comfortable suburb of Laredo, Texas—a neighborhood of solid brick homes and manicured lawns. Married, the mother of a four-year-old son, she lived a perfectly normal middle-class existence. By all accounts, Sandra was a pleasant woman, the sort you'd chat with at the mall or the supermarket...the sort who might live next door. Yet she is currently serving a life sentence, convicted of multiple offenses, including human trafficking and slavery.

It started innocently enough. At first, all Sandra wanted was a maid—someone to do the housework and help with her small son—but she didn't want to pay a lot. So she drove across the border to a small, dirt-poor village near Vera Cruz, Mexico, where she was introduced to Maria and her parents. Maria was only twelve when she met Sandra Bearden. She had very little schooling and dreamed of getting an education—a dream that her parents encouraged but could do nothing to achieve. Over coffee in their small kitchen, Bearden offered Maria a job, as well as the chance to attend school, learn English, and taste the rich life of "el Norte." The work, as Bearden described it, was much like what Maria was already doing at home, and, with the promise of education and opportunity, Sandra's offer made a very enticing package. The fact that Sandra herself was Mexican born helped Maria's parents feel they could trust her, and they gave their permission. Sandra smuggled Maria across the border in her expensive car and drove her to her home in Laredo.

On arrival, Maria was dragged into hell. Sandra Bearden used violence and terror to squeeze work and obedience from the child. From early morning till midafternoon, Maria cooked, cleaned, scrubbed, and polished. If Maria dozed off from exhaustion, or when Sandra decided she wasn't working fast enough, Sandra would blast pepper spray into Maria's eyes. A broom was broken over the girl's back and a few days later, a bottle against her head. At one point, Bearden tortured the twelve-year-old by jamming a garden tool up her vagina. That was Maria's workday; her "time off" was worse.

When Maria wasn't working, Sandra would chain her to a pole in the backyard without food or water. An eight-foot concrete fence kept her hidden from neighbors. After chaining her, Sandra would sometimes force Maria to eat dog feces. Then Maria would be left alone, her arms chained behind her with a padlock, her legs chained and locked together till the next morning, when the work and torture would begin again. Through the long afternoon and night Maria would fade in and out of consciousness from dehydration, and in her hunger she would sometimes scoop dirt into her mouth. Like most slaves in America, Maria was in shock, disoriented, isolated, and dependent. To maintain control, Bearden kept Maria hungry and in pain.

About one-third of the handful of slaves freed in the United States each year come to liberty because an average person sees something he or she just can't ignore. Luckily, one of the Beardens' neighbors had to do some work on his roof, and that probably saved Maria's life. Looking down over the high concrete wall into the Bearden's backyard, the neighbor saw a small girl chained up and whimpering; he called 911.

The police found Maria chained hand and foot, covered in cuts and bruises, and suffering from dehydration and exposure. She was too weak to walk and had to be carried to freedom on a stretcher. Her skin was badly burned from days in the sun. (In Laredo, Texas, the *average* summer temperature is ninety-eight degrees.) Photos taken at the time show one of her eyes bloodied and infected and thick welts and scars on her skin where the chains had cut into her. She had not eaten in four days. The district attorney said, "This is the worst case I've ever seen, worse than any murder. It's tragic all the way around." Later, at Bearden's trial, the policeman who found Maria wept. "She was shaking and crying and had a scared look in her eyes. She was in severe pain," Officer Jay Reese testified. He explained that he had tried to remove the chains from Maria's arms with bolt cutters but couldn't. As he tried to move her arm to cut the chains, she twisted and whimpered because she was in so much pain. "I've never seen anything like it before," Reese said, and sitting in the witness box, this policeman began to cry.

It is hard to imagine, but Maria was one of the lucky slaves. In America, most slaves spend four to five years in bondage; Maria's enslavement lasted only seven months. Sandra Bearden was arrested, and the Mexican government brought Maria's parents up from Vera Cruz. Her father blamed himself for what had happened. "We made a decision that we thought would be good for our child, and look what happened. I made a mistake, truly, and this is all my fault," he said.[1] Unlike most slaveholders in America, Bearden was caught and convicted. Like most slaves, Maria got nothing, except the fare for the twelve-hour bus ride home. She had just turned thirteen.[2]

We all ask, "How could someone so abuse a child—to stake her in the sun, feed her excrement, beat her bloody.... Surely, only a monster could do this." Yet Sandra Bearden's treatment of Maria is not unusual....

---

[1] "Girl Reunited with Parents," *Laredo Morning Times,* May 17, 2001. [All notes are Bales and Soodalter's, except, 3, 6, 7, 8, 11, 17, and 29.]

[2] "Woman Sentenced to Life in Prison for Torturing 12-Year-Old Maid," *Amarillo Globe News,* October 20, 2001.

Equal Opportunity Slavery

Most Americans' idea of slavery comes right out of *Roots*[3]—the chains, 10
the whip in the overseer's hand, the crack of the auctioneer's gavel.
That was one form of bondage. The slavery plaguing America today
takes a different form, but make no mistake, it is real slavery. Where the
law sanctioned slavery in the 1800s, today it's illegal. Where antebellum masters took pride in the ownership of slaves as a sign of status,
today's human traffickers and slaveholders keep slaves hidden, making
it all the more difficult to locate victims and punish offenders. Where the
slaves in America were once primarily African and African American,
today we have "equal opportunity" slavery; modern-day slaves come in
all races, all types, and all ethnicities. We are, if anything, totally democratic when it comes to owning and abusing our fellow human beings.
All that's required is the chance of a profit and a person weak enough
and vulnerable enough to enslave.

This is capitalism at its worst, and it is supported by a dramatic alter-
ation in the basic economic equation of slavery. Where an average slave
in 1850 would have cost the equivalent of $40,000 in modern money,
today's slave can be bought for a few hundred dollars. This cheapness
makes the modern slave easily affordable, but it also makes him or her
a disposable commodity. For the slaveholder it's often cheaper to let a
slave die than it is to buy medicine to keep the slave alive. There is no
form of slavery, past or present, that isn't horrific; however, today's slavery is one of the most diabolical strains to emerge in the thousands of
years in which humans have been enslaving their fellows.

So How Many Slaves Are We Talking About?

According to a U.S. State Department study, some 14,500 to 17,500
people are trafficked into the United States from overseas and enslaved
each year.[4] They come from Africa, Asia, India, China, Latin America,
and the former Soviet states. Nor are native-born Americans immune
from slavers; many are stolen from the streets of their own cities and
towns. Some sources, including the federal government, have put out
extremely high estimates of the number of U.S. citizens—primarily children—caught in slavery. The fact is, the precise number of slaves in the
United States, whether trafficked in from other countries or enslaved
from our own population, is simply not known. Given the hidden
nature of the crime, the best numbers on offer are rough estimates. We do
know that slaves in America are found—or rather, *not* found—in nearly
all fifty states, working as commercial sex slaves, fruit pickers, construction workers, gardeners, and domestics. They work in restaurants,

[3]***Roots:*** Award-winning 1977 television mini-series on slavery in the United States. [Eds.]
[4]U.S. Department of State, *Trafficking in Persons Report,* June 2006, www.state
.gov/g/tip/rls/tiprpt/2006/.

factories, laundries, and sweatshops. Each year human trafficking and slavery in America generate millions upon millions of dollars for criminals who prey on the most vulnerable: the desperate, the uneducated, and the impoverished immigrant seeking a better life. Brutalized and held in slavery for years, those who survive face indifference, official confusion, stigma, and shame as they struggle to regain control over their stolen and deeply damaged lives.

While no one knows for sure how many people are enslaved in America, a conservative estimate would be around fifty thousand and growing. Even for those who have worked in this area for years, these numbers are staggering. More astounding is the fact that this is a crime that, as a rule, goes unpunished. This lack of punishment is reflected in a remarkable parallel in American crime rates. If we accept the government's estimates, about seventeen thousand people are trafficked into slavery in the United States in any given year; coincidentally about seventeen thousand people are murdered in the United States each year. Obviously, murder is the ultimate crime, but slavery comes a close second, especially considering the other crimes associated with it, such as rape and torture. Note that the national success rate in solving murder cases is about 70 percent; around eleven thousand murders are "cleared" each year. But according to the U.S. government's own numbers, the annual percentage of trafficking and slavery cases solved is less than 1 percent. If 14,500 to 17,500 people were newly enslaved in America in 2006, the fact is that in the same year the Department of Justice brought charges against only 111 people for human trafficking and slavery; 98 of them were convicted.[5] And those figures apply only to people trafficked from other countries; no measures exist for domestic slavery victims.

In July 2004 then-President Bush[6] talked about the rate of arrests and convictions for human trafficking in the United States: "Since 2001, we've charged 110 traffickers. That's triple the number charged in the previous three years. We're beginning to make good, substantial progress. The message is getting out: We're serious. And when we catch you, you'll find out we're serious. We're staying on the hunt." Strong words, but the unvarnished truth is, with less than 1 percent of the offenders apprehended and less than 1 percent of the victims freed, the flow of human "product" into America continues practically unchecked. . . .

---

[5]U.S. Department of Justice, *Attorney General's Annual Report to Congress on U.S. Government Activities to Combat Trafficking in Persons for Fiscal Year 2006*, May 2007, www.usdoj.gov/olp/human_trafficking.htm, 17. Other cases were brought by Immigration and Customs Enforcement.

[6]**then-President Bush:** George Walker Bush (b. 1946), 43rd president of the United States from 2001 to 2009. [Eds.]

Slaves in the Pastures of Plenty

California, Arizona, I harvest your crops,
Then it's north up to Oregon to gather your hops.
Dig the beets from your ground, cut the grapes
from your vine
To set on your table your light sparkling wine.
—WOODY GUTHRIE, "Pastures of Plenty"

A Study in Contrasts

About thirty miles due south of the Southwest Florida International   15
Airport is the town of Naples. It sits on its own bay off the Gulf of Mexico,
not far from Sanibel, Vanderbilt Beach, and the Isles of Capri. Naples
is a lovely town—a rich town—attracting wealthy retirees and men of
industry. A palm-lined walk down Fifth Avenue will take you past art
galleries offering everything from contemporary sculpture to portraits of
your pets; chic restaurants featuring a variety of ethnic and exotic cui-
sines; high-end clothing and jewelry stores; and a fair smattering of
Bentleys and Rolls Royces.

A small tour boat offers a sunset cruise of the bay. The area is rich
in animal and bird life, brightly colored flowers, and lush plants, but the
guide points out only the houses and properties, proudly ticking off for
the tourists the astronomical values of each. No number is below seven
figures, and several are higher. One empty lot, we are told, recently sold
for $18,000,000. It sits, like a missing tooth, between two massive struc-
tures of questionable taste but stunning worth. Many of these houses
serve as second, third, or fourth homes and are occupied for only a few
weeks a year.

The boats that line the pier are studies in sleekness and speed.
Long, shark-shaped Cigarettes and Scarabs,[7] with their two and three
outboards of 250 horsepower each, give the illusion of motion even at
the dock. Looming over the pier walk are elegant new apartment buildings, painted various pastel shades, as are many of the homes and shops
of Naples. There is nothing here to jar the senses. There is everywhere
an air of money and complacency.

If, however, you left the airport and drove forty minutes to the south-
east, along narrow state roads, you would enter the town of Immokalee.
You could never confuse the two.

Driving into Immokalee, you become instantly aware that this is not
a town concerned with its appearance. There is no movie theater, no out-
ward indication of social activity, except for the Seminole Casino, where
out-of-towners from Naples and Fort Myers come to gamble. Many of
the buildings of Immokalee are low, basic, carelessly maintained. Most
of the signs—many roughly hand-painted—are in Spanish, as well as a

---

[7]**Cigarettes and Scarabs:** Types of powerboats. [Eds.]

language that looks familiar, almost French, but spelled phonetically. This is Haitian Creole. In many of Immokalee's homes, English is neither spoken nor understood. The languages are Spanish, Creole, and more than a sprinkling of indigenous tongues—Quiche, Zapotec, Nahuatl, Ttzotzil, Mam, Mixtec, Kanjobal.[8]

There is a handful of restaurants—mostly Mexican—with names like la Michoacana, el Taquito, Mi Ranchita. The décor is minimalist, the food just acceptable; dining out is not a major activity in Immokalee. There are a couple of nail and hair salons, housed in tiny storefronts. One turquoise-and-yellow painted structure advertises "Mimi's Piñatas." Chickens run wild, their crowing a backdrop you stop hearing after a while, and the vultures crowd the roads outside of town in such profusion that they present a driving hazard. Many who live here walk from point to point or ride one-speed bicycles. They can't afford cars. There is not much vehicle traffic in Immokalee itself, with the exception of the trucks that haul the produce to the packinghouses and the long school-type buses that carry the workers to and from the fields.

The Price of Tomatoes

Immokalee is a migrant town—actually, "more a labor reserve than a town."[9] There are many such communities in Florida, but this is the epicenter. Immokalee—an unincorporated community—was built in the first decades of the twentieth century for the growing, picking, packing, and shipping of tomatoes and oranges. Old-timers can still remember the days when teamsters drove horse-drawn wagons from Fort Myers to haul the produce from the fields.[10] There are other crops—lemons, grapefruit, watermelon—but these are the big two, and the tomato crop is the biggest by far. The crews who work in the fields come from Mexico, from Guatemala, from Haiti. Most are young—in their early twenties—small in stature and dark skinned, both by birth and by long exposure to the sun. Many have the Mayan features of the "Indio puro."[11] There is a shyness—a reserve—shown a stranger and, usually, a smile.

Immokalee's year-round population of twenty-five thousand swells to forty thousand during the nine-month harvest season. There are surprisingly few women among Immokalee's farmworkers; around 95 percent of the workforce is male. They have left their home countries and crossed our borders into Texas, Arizona, or New Mexico—most with the help of a *coyote*, or "guide"—in the hope of finding a way to support their families, since no such opportunities exist at home. Instead, they have

[8]**Quiche, Zapotec, Nahuatl, Ttzotzil, Mam, Mixtec, Kanjobal:** Languages of native Mesoamerican tribal peoples. Laura Germino, Coalition of Immokalee Workers (CIW), interview, January 6, 2007. [Eds.]

[9]Greg Asbed, "Coalition of Immokalee Workers: '¡Golpear a Uno Es Golpear a Todos!' To Beat One of Us Is to Beat Us All," in vol. 3 of *Bringing Human Rights Home*, ed. Cynthia Soohoo, Martha F. Davis, and Catherine Albisa (New York: Praeger, 2007), 1–24.

[10]Lucas Benitez, CIW, interview, January 7, 2007.

[11]**"Indio puro":** Spanish for "pure Indian," indicating 100 percent Indian heritage. [Eds.]

found jobs that are unrelentingly hard, under the rigid control of crew leaders, for the lowest wages imaginable. Every day, often seven days a week, the workers walk through the 4:00 A.M. darkness to begin gathering at parking lots around town; here they wait for buses that will take them—at least some of them—to the fields. Some carry their lunch from home in white plastic bags, while others choose to buy their daily food in one of the several convenience stores, with names like La Fiesta #3 and La Mexicana #2, that open early to accommodate them. The prices are high, often twice what they are elsewhere; the workers have no choice.

Nor do they have much option as to where they live. The town is honeycombed with parks of broken-down trailers, enclaves of tiny huts, and depressing little apartments. The rents are staggering. A dilapidated single-wide trailer, with dented, dingy yellow corrugated siding that is separating from the frame, accommodates twelve men, who sleep on bare mattresses abutting each other on the floor. Each of them pays a rent of $50 a week. There are perhaps fifteen such trailers on a single lot. The few individuals who own most of these enclaves would qualify as slumlords in any community in America, but their tenants pay the rents and live in their hovels; again, they have no choice.

Picking tomatoes is brutal; it requires working bent over in the southern sun for hours on end, straightening only long enough to run 100 to 150 feet with a filled thirty-two-pound bucket and literally throw it up to the worker on the truck. Lunch is a hurried affair, and water breaks are few. But at least nowadays there's clean water; not so very long ago, it wasn't uncommon for pickers to be obliged to drink from the canals and ditches, taking in the bacteria and the runoff of insecticides and fertilizer along with the water. And until fairly recently, a picker ran the risk of being beaten if he stopped picking long enough to drink.[12]

The pickers are not free to decide when or how much to work; they must work however many hours and days a week the crew chief mandates or weather and conditions permit. For this, they are paid a piece rate—so much per full bucket. The going rate—which has barely changed in nearly thirty years, despite the steady rise in the cost of living—is $25 per ton of tomatoes picked. This means filling around 125 buckets of tomatoes a day just to gross $50. But to make the equivalent of minimum wage, the worker has to fill around *two hundred* buckets—or two and a half tons—of tomatoes; this often entails working twelve or thirteen hours a day, if and when the work is available.

Why aren't these workers paid the minimum wage? The term *minimum wage* is misleading; realistically, although the 2008 rate in Florida is $6.79 per hour, the worker stands no real guarantee of earning it. Conditions are against him. There are no fixed hours, and what records are kept are often doctored in favor of the crew leader and the grower. The worker is also at the mercy of the weather; the market; pestilence;

[12]Lucas Benitez, CIW, interview, January 7, 2007.

the availability of harvesting equipment; the yield due to the relative richness of a field's soil; the number of times a field has been picked; the distance from the picker to the truck; personal stamina; and, most frustrating, time lost traveling to and from the field and waiting unpaid hours on the bus for the dew to dry or the weather to change.

Because harvesting is by nature unpredictable, the picker must be available every day at around five in the morning; if it turns out there is no work that day, he's just out of luck. This precludes his ability to take a second job. And on days when the work is slack and few pickers are required, he's likely to go home with nothing in his pocket. If he gets to the field and it rains, he earns nothing. The days spent on buses to other regions when the local crops have been picked is unpaid time; and if he and his fellow workers arrive at the new fields before they are ready for picking, they're paid nothing as they wait for the crops to ripen. They are paid only when they are picking, and they are paid little at that. It is no wonder that the Department of Labor (DOL) has described farmworkers as a labor force in "significant economic distress."[13]

The only true measure of the pickers' compensation is their annual earnings: workers average $7,000 to $10,000 per year. On a good day, the best they can accomplish is to reach the poverty level, but their yearly earnings are well below it. There are no benefits—no overtime, no health care, no insurance of any kind. "You can only get sick in Immokalee," says Coalition of Immokalee Workers (CIW) co-founder Lucas Benitez, "between 8:00 A.M. and 4:00 P.M., which are the hours of the clinic." If a picker does get sick, he works nonetheless. If he becomes seriously ill or breaks a limb, not only is he without income, but he must pay his medical bills himself—more often than not an impossibility, since nearly all his money goes to food and rent, with perhaps a few dollars put aside to send home. "You wait until you are half dead to go to a doctor."[14]

Score One for the Dixiecrats

There is no point in looking to the government for help: farm labor is practically the only type of work not covered by the National Labor Relations Act of 1935, the law that protects workers, gives them the right to organize without fear of retaliation, and fixes wage, health, and safety rules. Yes, farmworkers can organize a union or strike for better pay, but they can be fired for doing so. This exclusion of farmworkers from the rights given to almost all other American workers came from the power of Deep South congressmen in 1935, when the law was passed. These Dixiecrat politicians were adamant that black field hands should never be allowed to organize. Not surprisingly, household servants were also excluded from full rights. Some DOL wage and hour rules do apply to farmworkers, but with only two wage and hours

---

[13]Greg Asbed, CIW, interview, January 8, 2007.
[14]Lucas Benitez, interview, January 7, 2007.

inspectors for the entire Southwest Florida region—which includes tens of thousands of farmworkers, as well as other types of laborers—there is little hope of help there either.[15] For years, the local inspector for that section of Florida generally spoke only English—in the midst of workers who did not—and spent more time in the grower's office than in the fields, where he might witness firsthand the treatment of the pickers. With the law on their side, the crew leaders and the growers hold all the cards.

With conditions so dismal, and the pay so low, why would anyone come to Immokalee to work? Or to nearby towns like Lake Placid, Wimauma, or LaBelle? There is simply no real choice: wherever a worker goes to pick America's crops, he meets similar conditions. With the trend toward consolidation and expansion of agribusinesses, it has become increasingly difficult to find work on the old-style family-owned farms of twenty-five years ago. Instead, the small farms are being gobbled up by huge companies. Competing with each other and with foreign suppliers, these megagrowers are themselves being caught in a cost/price squeeze. On the one hand, they face constantly rising costs of gasoline, pesticides, fertilizer, and a couple dozen other items necessary for production. On the other hand, the buyers—fast-food giants such as McDonald's, Subway, Taco Bell, and Burger King, and market corporations like Shop Rite, Wal-Mart, and Costco—are dictating the prices they are willing to pay for tomatoes and other crops. The buyers have turned their corporate backs on the small growers who supplied them faithfully for years. In the words of one worker advocate, the buyers "each have a purchasing company, looking to buy high volume at the lowest possible price. They are price *setters*, not price *takers*."[16] Rather than purchase from several smaller growers, as in the past, these megabuyers have decided to work with the largest suppliers, who can provide ready, uniform, year-round supplies of product. Only the huge agribusinesses, such as Gargiulo, Pacific, Nobles Collier, and the Six L's, can meet the demanding production requirements while weathering the rising costs and the squeeze on their profit margin. Size counts: even with the cost/price pressure they manage to make a tremendous amount of money, and they are growing exponentially.

As large as these agribusinesses are, they pale in the shadow of the companies that supply their needs—giants such as Exxon, John Deere, and Monsanto. Against these multinational corporations the growers have no bargaining power. So, with nothing to say about their escalating costs or the buyers' shrinking prices, the only way they can hold on to profits is by cutting labor costs. Their aim is to keep at gutter level the amount they pay—and for decades have paid—their workers, and they

[15]John Norris, U.S. DOL wage and hours inspector, Ft. Myers, FL, interview, March 28, 2007.
[16]Greg Asbed, CIW, interview, January 8, 2007.

do. As a 2004 Oxfam America[17] report put it, "Squeezed by the buyers of their produce, growers pass on the costs and risks imposed on them to those on the lowest rung of the supply chain: the farmworkers they employ."[18] And because these privately held Florida-based grower corporations are constantly expanding, a worker can move to North Carolina, Delaware, California, or even Puerto Rico and still be working in the same grower's fields—for the same pay, and under the same conditions. There is no refuge. While the large grower corporations compete, they have also banded together to control the labor market by forming the Florida Tomato Committee. The committee and the Florida Fruit and Vegetable Association are powerful lobbies with the state government; this is not surprising, since some of the large growers are themselves members of the Florida legislature.

This situation is not new. In her excellent history of Atlantic Coast farmworkers, Cindy Hahamovitch writes of Florida in the 1930s: "While the rest of growers' expenses rose over the course of the decade— the cost of seed, fertilizer, and equipment all went up—farm wages remained stagnant or fell, depending on the crop.... As a veteran of harvests in thirty-three states put it, 'Florida is the sorriest wages in the United States.'"[19] In those days, the workers were mostly African American and Bahamian; today they are most likely to be Latino. Otherwise little has changed, with one ugly exception.

Slavery in the Fields

As bad as most pickers have it, there is a rung on the ladder that is lower still—the *enslaved* farmworker. Antonio Martinez came from a family of five younger siblings, in Hidalgo, Mexico. His parents were sickly, and Antonio was unable to make a sufficient living to support them all. He met with a contractor—a *coyote*—who promised that he would smuggle Antonio into the United States and find him construction work in California for a fee of 16,000 pesos—about $1,700 American. Antonio told the man that he didn't have that much money, but the *coyote* assured him that he could pay it off once he started to work. Two weeks later, he was on a bus along with forty others, heading north toward the border.

When the bus arrived at a sparse border camp in the Sonora desert, the workers were separated and given to other *coyotes*. The man in charge of Antonio's group was called Chino. He led them through the desert for three days, despite having water and supplies for only one day, crossing the border to a whistle-stop called Tres Puntas. From there

---

[17]**Oxfam America:** A nonprofit organization dedicated to ending poverty, hunger, and social injustice around the world. [Eds.]

[18]Oxfam America, "Like Machines in the Fields: Workers Without Rights in American Agriculture," Report, March 2004, www.oxfamamerica.org/newsandpublications /publications/research_reports/art7011.html/OA-Like_Machines_in_the_Fields.pdf, 36.

[19]Cindy Hahamovitch, *The Fruits of Their Labor: Atlantic Coast Farmworkers and the Making of Migrant Poverty, 1870–1945* (Chapel Hill: University of North Carolina Press, 1997), 123.

they were driven to a house in Tucson, where Chino demanded additional money from them or their families, on pain of violence. Some of the others complied, but Antonio had no money to give. At this point, without money or papers, under violent threat, he realized he was trapped.

Antonio was told that instead of going to a construction site in California he would be put to work in the tomato fields of South Central Florida, at the pay rate of $150 per day. The promised amount went far toward allaying his misgivings. Chino then handed him over to a van driver, or *raitero,* called "el Chacal" — the jackal. Antonio was crowded into the back of the van along with seventeen other Mexican workers. On the long drive to Florida, the van stopped only for gasoline; the migrants in the back were told to urinate in a bottle when the need arose. Twice on their journey police stopped the van; on neither occasion did the officer question the presence of eighteen Mexicans packed like cargo in the back.

When el Chacal arrived in Florida, he drove to the camp of two labor contractors, Abel and Basilio Cuello. Here, Antonio overheard el Chacal negotiating with the Cuello brothers for the sale of the workers. El Chacal was demanding $500 apiece, whereas the Cuellos were willing to pay only $350. At this point, Antonio realized, "We were being sold like animals."[20]

Antonio's life was tightly controlled. The door of the shack in which he and the other workers slept was locked at night and was unlocked in the morning by Abel Cuello only when it was time to go to the fields. Cuello never left them alone; he stayed with them as they picked and threatened violence and death should they attempt to escape. The promised pay was whittled away to practically nothing as Cuello deducted for rent, food, water, even the cost of transportation to and from the fields. With the tiny amount left to them, the workers bought food or toiletries when taken by the bosses on rare trips to a small local grocery store.

After four months in slavery, Antonio saw his chance. While he and a few others were shopping, Cuello, on guard outside the market, dozed off, and the workers ran to the highway and escaped. The subsequent case against the Cuello trafficking operation was one of Florida's first contemporary cases of forced labor. Cuello was convicted and sentenced to prison on slavery charges.

Antonio still works with the crops — but under his own volition, and not with tomatoes. He also travels throughout the country, speaking about the slavery in America's fields and in the food we eat. He has marched in several campaigns against corporate abuse and participated in the ten-day hunger strike against Taco Bell. At one point, he taught a training session to law enforcement officers and government officials in Chiapas, Mexico, through the U.S. Department of Justice (DOJ). This

---

[20] *Dying to Leave,* dir. Chris Hilton, "Wide Angle" special, PBS, 2003.

author spoke with Antonio while he was participating in a late-2007 workers' march against Burger King, and his motivation was clear. Taking action against the offending corporations, he said, "is extremely important; there is more and more consumer participation in the struggle, and it makes the campaign that much stronger. The big companies buy so much produce that they must take responsibility for the conditions under which the people who harvest it are suffering. It infuriates me that some of these corporations are still ignoring the plight of the farmworkers.

"I just want you to know," he states, "why I'm out here today. For four and a half months, I was held in forced labor in the fields against my will, and it seemed like an eternity for me. They were watching me all the time, controlling all I did. I thought I was going to die. Thanks to God, I was able to escape, and it allowed me to become more and more aware. I'm out here learning more every day."[21] ...

"Guests" in the Fields

It's bad enough when slavery exists and the government is either unaware or unwilling to address it. But how about an ongoing federal program that makes it much too easy to bring people into the United States to be enslaved? Welcome to the "Guest Worker Program," also known as the H-2 program, after the type of visas assigned. Temporary agricultural workers from Latin America, Asia, eastern Europe, and the Caribbean are lured here by the *official guarantee* of good working conditions: so many hours a week at a fixed and acceptable wage, government-inspected living conditions, and medical benefits, including "payment for lost time from work and for any permanent injury." Guest workers are also entitled to "federally funded legal services for matters relating to their employment." According to the rules, any employer who receives DOL approval to import guest workers must compensate them for their travel expenses—the plane or bus fare and food costs incurred on the way to the promised job. Finally, the worker is guaranteed three-fourths of the total hours promised in his contract for the period of employment specified.[22] The conditions of the program also stipulate that the worker is obligated to stay with the employer who sponsored him; he cannot leave to seek a job elsewhere. Some employers adhere to the conditions of the law. But in a large number of cases, not a single one of these promises is honored because of employer abuses and government neglect.

The Guest Worker Program is not a new concept: the United States has been taking in foreign workers almost since its inception. Our attitude toward them—at least over the last hundred years—has been

---

[21] Antonio Martinez, CIW, interview, December 2, 2007.

[22] Mary Bauer, "Close to Slavery: Guestworker Programs in the United States," report, Southern Poverty Law Center, 2007, www.splcenter.org/pdf/static/SPLCguestworker.pdf, 7.

ambivalent. America welcomed them when we needed them—during the two World Wars, for example, when most of the permanent workforce was in the service—and limited or simply ousted them when we didn't. In 1943, to provide workers for the southern sugar cane fields, the government established the H-2 program. From its beginning it was characterized by inequity and brutality. As recently as 1986, cane cutters who attempted a work stoppage over poor conditions were beset by armed police with dogs, acting at the employers' behest. The incident became known as the "Dog Wars." In that same year, the H-2 program was expanded to include nonagricultural workers, but the number of mainly Asian and Latin American guest workers arriving for farm work under the program is still significant. The number of foreign workers certified by DOL as agricultural—or H-2A—laborers went from forty-eight thousand in 2005 to nearly seventy-seven thousand in 2007.[23]

The viability of a guest worker program has been endlessly debated, but one thing is clear: its lack of oversight provides a splendid opportunity for mistreatment and enslavement. In the words of Mary Bauer of the Southern Poverty Law Center, "The very structure of the program... lends itself to abuse."[24] Increasingly, employers use labor contractors to recruit guest workers for them. In this way they avoid technical responsibility for the workers, legally distancing themselves from any abuses that follow. The brokers recruit the workers in their home countries. Unrestricted by law or ethics, they make promises of work and wages that far exceed the provisions of the program—so much so that the workers go into massive debt, often in excess of $10,000, to pay the recruiter's inflated fee.

Employers often bring in more workers than they need. They exaggerate the number required, as well as the period of employment, since they know the government isn't paying attention. Employers know they can get away with not paying the three-fourths of the wages or meeting the other conditions the contract stipulates. The worker, heavily in debt and doomed to few work hours and pay fraud, is indentured even before he leaves home. When he arrives in America, he finds himself at the mercy of his employer. The promised forty-hour week turns out to be only twenty-five hours, and his looming debt becomes instantly insurmountable. Sometimes the workweek is eighty hours long, but the promised pay is withheld or radically reduced. The "free housing in good condition" can turn out to be a lightless, heatless shack with no bed or blankets, and sometimes no windows to keep out the cold, shared with twenty or thirty other workers. In some cases, he is locked in or kept under armed guard.[25] If transportation to the job is required, a travel fee is deducted from his pay. Fees are illegally charged for food and some-

[23]Mary Bauer, director of Southern Poverty Law Center's Immigrant Justice Project, interview, July 23, 2008.
[24]Bauer, "Close to Slavery," 42.
[25]Ibid., 39.

times rent, both of which are guaranteed him by law. The program also promises him worker's compensation for hospital or doctor's costs and lost wages, but the moment he gets sick or hurt on the job he finds this is a lie. Ignorant of the system and the language, he has no clue how to seek medical help, and his employer, far from being solicitous in the face of losing a laborer, pushes him to keep working.

To enforce control, the employer confiscates or destroys the guest worker's passport and visa, making him an illegal alien. In this way, he faces the threat of arrest and deportation should he attempt to leave or refuse to work. If he manages to escape and find his way to the local police, the likelihood of the authorities taking the word of an undocumented migrant worker, with little or no English, over that of an established local grower is slim to none. Without his papers, the worker is at considerably greater risk than his employer. And once he has made waves, he runs the risk of being blacklisted and destroys any chance of coming back in the future for a decent job.[26] The Carnegie Endowment for International Peace reported in 1999, "Blacklisting of H-2A workers appears to be widespread, is highly organized, and occurs at all stages of the recruitment and employment process."[27] The large North Carolina Growers Association has blatantly kept a blacklist, which in 1997 was titled "NCGA Ineligible for Rehire Report," listing over a thousand workers' names.[28]

All in all, there is little about this that doesn't fall under the definition of slavery. Workers are often kept against their will, held by the threat of violence, paid as little as their employers wish, and denied every basic right guaranteed by law. In fact, there is little to distinguish these thousands of guest workers from the crews held in slavery by Miguel Flores[29]—except for the stunning fact that this particular form of bondage occurs within a government-sponsored program. Admittedly, this scenario doesn't play itself out in every instance: many employers honor the conditions of the H-2A laws, providing the work promised at the agreed-upon wage. Nonetheless, this doesn't change the fact that because of the program's lack of oversight the result can be coercion and peonage....

Slavery in Your Face

At the very beginning of the trans-Atlantic slave trade some Africans were tricked into slavery.[30] A slave ship might sail upriver and find an isolated village; if the people didn't run away, the slaver might trade with them and invite them on board the ship. He might tell them about

[26]Ibid., 15–17.
[27]Quoted in ibid., 27.
[28]Ibid., 17.
[29]**Miguel Flores:** Operator of a large slavery ring in South Carolina in the 1990s; Flores and his partner, Sebastian Gomez, pled guilty to U.S. Department of Justice charges in 1997 and were sentenced to fifteen years each in federal prison. [Eds.]
[30]Robert J. Allison, "The Origins of African-American Culture," *Journal of Interdisciplinary History* 30 (Winter 1999): 475–81.

the land on the other side of the water where food was abundant, land was there for the taking, and everyone lived like kings. Excited about the chance to see the enormous "canoe" up close, villagers would flock aboard, and while they were being shown the lower decks, they would be captured, beaten, and chained. The trap was set with lies and sprung with violence, and the new slaves would be on their way to the fields of North America. Once sold to farmers, the slaves who survived would usually be put to work growing and gathering crops: cotton, sugar, fruit, vegetables, timber, all to supply the growing nation's demand for food, clothing, and building materials. All over the United States, in slave states and free states, families would eat the food grown and picked by slaves in the South.

Today, the same things occur. Farmworkers are being ensnared by deception and enslaved through violence. And we Americans obliviously munch away on the slave-picked fruit and vegetables we bring home from the grocery store or order in fast-food restaurants. The slaves tend to come from Asia and Central and South America instead of Africa, but they are tricked with the same sorts of lies and promises. And while the U.S. government tended to just ignore the illegal antebellum slave trade, today it swings through the bipolar reaction of prosecuting some cases while propping open the door to human trafficking through the Guest Worker Program.

The idea of putting slave-grown food in the mouths of our children should make us sick. Putting a stop to this travesty should be an immediate concern. The good news is, we know how to bring this slavery to an end—through greater public awareness, an enhanced system of government inspection, a complete overhaul of the Guest Worker Program, a governmental willingness to root out and prosecute cases of trafficking in the fields, and—most vital—a solid respect for the rights and humanity of the people whom we put to growing and harvesting our crops. But none of this will happen until we all decide that slave-picked food is just too bitter to swallow.

ENGAGING THE TEXT

1. Bales and Soodalter note that most people think of slavery in terms of plantations and the Old South. How does this selection challenge your own thinking about the institution of slavery? Where do you think you might find slaves working in your state or region?

2. According to the authors, the price of a slave has dropped dramatically since the nineteenth century. Can you think of any reasons why human beings might be cheaper—and more expendable—today than in the past?

3. Given that slavery is roughly as common as homicide in the United States, how might you explain why the authorities and the media don't treat it as an urgent civil rights or public safety issue?

Federal Bill Would Give America's Hens Bigger Cages

4. To what extent would you agree with Bales and Soodalter that modern slavery is an example of "capitalism at its worst"? In what sense is human trafficking similar to capitalism? How is capitalism different from slave trading?

5. Why, in the authors' view, is the U.S. Guest Worker Program not much better than slavery? Given their description of the program, do you think the government should continue to sponsor it? What could be done to improve the lot of guest workers?

EXPLORING CONNECTIONS

6. In "Theories and Constructs of Race" (p. 599), Linda Holtzman and Leon Sharpe describe the "grand sweeping story, or metanarrative" of race in the United States (para. 18) and identify "counterstories" or "counternarratives" as ways of challenging racism. Make a quick outline of the metanarrative of slavery in American society. Then use "Slavery in the Land of the Free" to write a counterstory.

7. How do the working conditions of employees like the waitresses described by Barbara Ehrenreich (p. 363) compare with those of the migrant fieldworkers described in this selection? To what extent are all low-wage workers "indentured to their employers"?

EXTENDING THE CRITICAL CONTEXT

8. Do some research to learn more about how widespread the problem of human trafficking is in the United States. How does the United States compare with other nations in terms of human trafficking? What types of jobs are typically involved in the American slave market? Who are the new slaves and slave masters? What is being done to address the problem of American and global slavery?

9. Research the working and living conditions of employees in the foreign megamanufacturing plants that produce consumer electronics, clothing, athletic shoes, and household goods for companies like Abercrombie & Fitch, IKEA, Kohl's, Walmart, Gap Inc., GUESS, Levi's, DKNY, Apple, Sony, Disney, and Nike. How are employees treated in these foreign megafactories? How much are they paid? How much control or choice do they have in their lives? In what ways do megafactory complexes mirror the conditions of slavery? To what extent do American consumers bear responsibility for these conditions?

FURTHER CONNECTIONS

1. How would you expect your county to compare with other counties in your state in terms of wealth? How would you expect your state to compare with other states? Research state and county data from the U.S. Census Bureau Web site (www.census.gov) and present or write up your findings. To what extent do you think you have had advantages or disadvantages because of where you were born or grew up?

2. Working in groups, discuss recent movies or television series that you associate with the spirit of the American Dream. What aspects of the Dream do you see in these films or TV shows? What do they tell us about the state of the Dream today and about contemporary attitudes toward wealth and success?

3. As an individual or a class project, make a video reflecting your vision of the American Dream.

4. This chapter of *Rereading America* has been criticized by conservatives for undermining the work ethic of American college students. Rush Limbaugh, for example, claimed that the chapter "presents America as a stacked deck," thus "robbing people of the ability to see the enormous opportunities directly in front of them." Do you agree? Write a journal entry or an essay in which you explain how these readings have influenced your attitudes toward work and success.

TRUE WOMEN
AND REAL MEN
Myths of Gender

THE RISE OF
THE WOMAN
=
THE RISE OF
THE NATION

FAST FACTS

1. Nearly two-thirds (65%) of women say that they face at least some discrimination in society today; however, a majority of men (51%) believe that women encounter little or no discrimination.

2. 60% of millennials (those born after 1980) and post-millennials (those born after 2000) say that they do not need to conform to traditional gender roles. Over two-thirds agree with the statement, "Gender does not define a person to the extent that it once did."

3. The National School Climate Survey reports that 85% of lesbian, gay, bisexual, and transgender students frequently experience harassment at school, and 51% heard homophobic remarks from teachers. 62% of those who reported incidents of harassment or assault to school staff said that nothing was done in response.

4. In 29 states you can be fired based on your sexual orientation; in 32 states, you can be fired based on your gender identity and expression.

5. In 2013, transgender women of color accounted for over half of all lesbian, gay, bisexual, and transgender homicide victims.

6. According to the U.S. Justice Department, 68% of sexual assaults remain unreported. A national survey of 440 four-year colleges found that 41% of these institutions did not conduct a single investigation of sexual assault in the previous five years.

Data from (1) Pew Research Center, 2014; (2) The Cassandra Gender Report, 2013; (3) Gay, Lesbian and Straight Education Network, 2013; (4) Human Rights Campaign: *2014 Annual Report*; (5) *Understanding Issues Facing Transgender Americans*, 2015; (6) *National Crime Victimization Survey: 2008–2012*; 2014 U.S. Senate Report, *Sexual Violence on Campus*.

COMMON SENSE TELLS US that there are obvious differences between females and males: after all, biology, not culture, determines whether you're able to bear children. But culture and cultural myths do shape the roles men and women play in our public and private relationships: we may be born female and male, but we are made women and men. Sociologists distinguish between sex and gender — between one's biological identity and the conventional patterns of behavior we learn to associate with each sex. While biological sex remains relatively stable, gendered behavior varies dramatically from one cultural group or historical period to the next.

European colonists to America adhered to a patriarchal culture — one in which men were dominant: ancestry was traced through the male line, and men were the explorers, traders, and leaders of the colonies. Women were subservient first to their fathers and then to their husbands; once married, all their property, and even their children, legally belonged to their husbands. By contrast, American Indian cultural beliefs led to very different gender roles. For example, Choctaw/Cherokee scholar Kay Givens McGowan writes that indigenous civilizations of the Southeast (Cherokee, Choctaw, Chickasaw, Muskogee, and Seminole) were matriarchal societies. Women held considerable social, economic, and political power: ancestry was traced through the mother; women farmed, controlled the distribution of crops, and often served as traders; and women held leadership positions on the Women's Council. McGowan notes that "When a woman married, she worked and bore children for her own lineage, not her husband's"; she also points out that unlike colonial women, Southeastern women "had sexual freedom . . . including the right to have sex with anyone they chose." Colonists could scarcely begin to understand native gender norms, and certainly had no interest in adopting them. When these two cultures came into conflict, the Southeastern civilizations were brutally suppressed, and patriarchy prevailed.

French aristocrat Alexis de Tocqueville noted the enduring impact of patriarchy on American gender roles when he published *Democracy in America* (1835). He recognized that democratic government would inevitably "raise woman, and make her more and more the equal of man." But Tocqueville maintained that complete equality would violate the natural order. In Europe, while revolutionary thinkers were beginning to view man and woman as "beings not only equal, but alike," he warned that "by thus attempting to make one sex equal to the other, both are degraded; and from so preposterous a medley of the works of nature, nothing could ever result but weak men and disorderly women."

In the United States, by contrast, Tocqueville saw men's and women's roles as entirely distinct and separate. Men's "natural" sphere encompassed business, politics, and labor, whereas women's was "the quiet circle of domestic employments," where, despite their intelligence, their chief duty was to be attractive and refined:

> American women never manage the outward concerns of the family, or conduct a business, or take a part in political life; nor are they, on the other hand, ever compelled to perform the rough labor of the fields, or to make any of those laborious exertions which demand the exertion of physical strength. No families are so poor as to form an exception to this rule. . . . Hence it is, that the women of America, who often exhibit a masculine strength of understanding and a manly energy, generally preserve great delicacy of personal appearance, and always retain the manners of women.

As an aristocrat and conservative, Tocqueville was uninterested in the hard physical labor routinely performed by many women, and he entirely discounted the roles played by working-class and slave women. American women, he continued, knew their place, and submitted willingly to their husbands' authority — that is, if they were virtuous:

> They hold that every association must have a head in order to accomplish its object and that the natural head of the conjugal association is man. . . . [T]hey attach a sort of pride to the voluntary surrender of their own will and make it their boast to bend themselves to the yoke, — not to shake it off. Such, at least, is the feeling expressed by the most virtuous of their sex.

According to Tocqueville, Americans considered male dominance "natural" in government as well as in marriage: "The object of democracy is to regulate and legalize the powers which are necessary, and not to subvert all power."

History is replete with examples of how the apparent "naturalness" of gender has been used to regulate political, economic, and personal relations between the sexes. Many nineteenth-century scientists argued that it was "unnatural" for women to attend college; rigorous intellectual activity, they asserted, would draw vital energy away from a woman's reproductive organs and make her sterile. According to this line of reasoning, women who sought higher education threatened the natural order by jeopardizing their ability to bear children and perpetuate the species. Arguments based on nature were likewise used to justify women's exclusion from political life. In his classic 1832 treatise on American democracy, James Fenimore Cooper remarked that women's domestic role and "necessary" subordination to men made them unsuitable for participation in public affairs. Thus, denying women the right to vote was perfectly consistent with the principles of American democracy and did "not very materially affect the principle of political equality."

Resistance to gender equality has been remarkably persistent in the United States. It took more than seventy years of hard political work by both black and white women's organizations to win the right to vote. But while feminists gained the vote for women in 1920 and the legal right to equal educational and employment opportunities in the 1970s, attitudes change even more slowly than laws. Contemporary antifeminist campaigns voice some of the same anxieties as their nineteenth-century counterparts over the "loss" of femininity and domesticity.

Women continue to suffer economic inequities based on cultural assumptions about gender. What's defined as "women's work"—nurturing, feeding, caring for family and home—is devalued and pays low wages or none at all. When women enter jobs traditionally held by men, they often encounter discrimination, harassment, or "glass ceilings" that limit their advancement. In fact, the United States ranked twentieth out of 142 countries on the World Economic Forum's 2014 Global Gender Gap Report, trailing Nicaragua (#6), Latvia (#15), and Burundi (#17). The report measures gender equality in four areas: economic participation and opportunity, educational attainment, political empowerment, and health and survival. While the United States has virtually eliminated the gender gap in education, it ranks sixty-fifth in "wage equality for similar work." And despite the growing number of women holding political positions, the United States placed fifty-fourth in political empowerment.

But men, too, pay a high price for their culturally imposed roles. Psychological research shows higher rates of depression among people of both sexes who adhere closely to traditional roles than among those who do not. Moreover, studies of men's mental and physical health suggest that social pressure to "be a man" (that is, to be emotionally controlled, powerful, and successful) can contribute to isolation, anxiety, stress, and illness, and may be partially responsible for men's shorter life spans. As sociologist Margaret Andersen observes, "Traditional gender roles limit the psychological and social possibilities for human beings."

Even our assumption that there are "naturally" only two genders is a cultural invention that fails to accommodate the diversity of human experience.

Some cultures have three or more gender categories. One of the best-known third genders is the American Indian *berdache*, or two-spirit, a role that was found in over 150 North American tribes. The two-spirit was a biological male who took the social role of a woman and did women's work (or in some cases both women's and men's work) or a biological female who adopted the identities of warrior and hunter, roles that were typically male. In general, they engaged in same-sex relationships, and in many tribes, two-spirits performed important work as healers, shamans, or "bridge-makers" between the natural and spiritual worlds. Today, Native Americans use "two-spirit" to refer to lesbian, gay, and transgender people.

Euro-American culture, by contrast, offers few socially acceptable alternative gender roles. Just as many Americans in the past considered it "unnatural" and socially destructive for women to vote or go to college, some now consider it "unnatural" and socially destructive for gays and lesbians to marry or for individuals to express a gender identity that violates conventional notions of masculinity or femininity. Cultural conflict over gender is ongoing and intense: a number of right-wing groups are fighting to reverse the Supreme Court's decision to legalize gay marriage. When the U.S. military announced that it would begin accepting transgender applicants, conservatives called the concern for trans rights "social pathology," and a prominent politician declared, "The military is not a social experiment. The purpose of the military is to kill people and break things."

This chapter focuses on cultural myths of gender and the influence they wield over human development and personal identity. The first four selections examine how dominant American culture defines female and male gender roles — and how those roles may define us. Jamaica Kincaid's "Girl," a story framed as a mother's advice to her daughter, presents a contemporary take on what it means to be raised a woman. Aaron H. Devor's "Becoming Members of Society" examines gender as a socially constructed category and discusses the psychological processes that underlie gender role acquisition. Mona El-Ghobashy, in "Quandaries of Representation," talks about the many stereotypes of Muslim women she has encountered and argues that since "each Muslim woman is an irreducible self," no one can truly claim to speak for all. Jean Kilbourne's "'Two Ways a Woman Can Get Hurt': Advertising and Violence" argues that the objectification of women in ads constitutes a form of cultural abuse.

The second half of the chapter opens with a series of conventional and unconventional images of women and men, which provides an opportunity to think about the ways that we "read" gender visually. "The Longest War" by Rebecca Solnit offers a furious exposé of the "pattern of violence against women that's broad and deep and horrific and incessantly overlooked." In "From Fly-Girls to Bitches and Hos," self-described "hip-hop feminist" Joan Morgan maintains that it's necessary to look behind the violent misogyny of many rap lyrics in order to understand and heal the pain of the African American men who compose and perform the songs. Next, Michael Kimmel's "'Bros Before Hos': The Guy Code" lays out the "rules" of masculinity that govern and at times distort the behavior and emotions of young men. The chapter concludes with "Sisterhood Is Complicated," in which Ruth Padawer explores the controversies that have erupted at Wellesley, a women's college, when transmasculine students demand recognition.

Sources

Cooper, James Fenimore. *The American Democrat*. N.p.: Minerva Press, 1969. Print.

Duberman, Amanda. "19 Countries Where the Gender Gap Is Smaller Than in the U.S." *Huffington Post*. 29 October 2014. Web.

Foss, Sonia H., Mary E. Domenico, and Karen A. Foss. *Gender Stories: Negotiating Identity in a Binary World*. Long Grove, IL: Waveland Press, 2013. Print.

French, Marilyn. *Beyond Power: On Women, Men, and Morals*. New York: Ballantine Books, 1985. Print.

Giddings, Paula. *When and Where I Enter: The Impact of Black Women on Race and Sex in America*. New York: Bantam Books, 1984. Print.

Hubbard, Ruth. *The Politics of Women's Biology*. New Brunswick, NJ: Rutgers University Press, 1990. Print.

Lorber, Judith. *Paradoxes of Gender*. New Haven and London: Yale University Press, 1994. Print.

McGowan, Kay Givens. "Weeping for the Lost Matriarchy." *Daughters of Mother Earth*. Ed. Barbara Alice Mann and Winona LaDuke. Westport, CT: Praeger, 2006. Print.

Ross, Janell. "Mike Huckabee Says the Military's Job Is to 'Kill People and Break Things.' Well, Not Quite." *The Washington Post*. 7 August 2015. Web.

Tocqueville, Alexis de. *Democracy in America*. Trans. Henry Reeve, Esq. Vol. 2. 2nd ed. Cambridge: Sever and Francis, 1863. Print.

Wilson, Alex. "How We Find Ourselves: Identity Development and Two-Spirit People." *Race, Gender, Sexuality, and Social Class*. Ed. Susan J. Ferguson. Los Angeles: Sage, 2013. Print.

BEFORE READING

- Imagine for a moment that you were born a different sex. How would your life be changed? Would any of your interests and activities differ? How about your relationships with other people? Write a journal entry describing your past, present, and possible future in this alternate identity.

- Collect and bring to class gender images taken from popular magazines and newspapers. Working in groups, make a collage of male, female, and transgender images; then compare and discuss your results. What do these media images tell you about what it means to be gendered in this culture?

- The woman in the frontispiece to this chapter is attending the 365 Empress Movement march in Baltimore; one of the organizers of the movement explained that women work for change 365 days a year, and that "Empress" signifies the value of black women. The march was held to demand an end to police violence, promote change in the community, and unify black women. Do a freewrite about the woman as you see her: What do you imagine that she does for a living? Is she a feminist? What role do you think she plays in the 365 Empress Movement — is she a leader, a follower involved with the group, or someone who heard about the march and just decided to show up? To support your views, refer to details of dress, makeup, hairstyle, body art, and attitude, as well as to what she's holding in her hands. How do you interpret the sign that she's carrying?

GIRL
JAMAICA KINCAID

Although she now lives in New England, Jamaica Kincaid (b. 1949) retains strong ties, including citizenship, to her birthplace — the island of Antigua in the West Indies. After immigrating to the United States to attend college, she ended up educating herself instead, eventually becoming a staff writer for *The New Yorker*, the author of several critically acclaimed books, and an instructor at Harvard University. About the influence of parents on children she says, "The magic is they carry so much you don't know about. They know you in a way you don't know yourself." Some of that magic is exercised in the story "Girl," which was first published in *The New Yorker* and later appeared in Kincaid's award-winning collection *At the Bottom of the River* (1983). She has written and edited many volumes of nonfiction on subjects ranging from colonialism to gardening and travel. She has published five novels: *Annie John* (1985), *Lucy* (1990), *The Autobiography of My Mother* (1996), *Mr. Potter* (2002), and *See Now Then* (2013).

WASH THE WHITE CLOTHES ON MONDAY and put them on the stone heap; wash the color clothes on Tuesday and put them on the clothesline to dry; don't walk barehead in the hot sun; cook pumpkin fritters[1] in very hot sweet oil; soak your little clothes right after you take them off; when buying cotton to make yourself a nice blouse, be sure that it doesn't have gum[2] on it, because that way it won't hold up well after a wash; soak salt fish overnight before you cook it; is it true that you sing benna[3] in Sunday school?; always eat your food in such a way that it won't turn someone else's stomach; on Sundays try to walk like a lady and not like the slut you are so bent on becoming; don't sing benna in Sunday school; you mustn't speak to wharf-rat boys, not even to give directions; don't eat fruits on the street—flies will follow you; *but I don't sing benna on Sundays at all and never in Sunday school*; this is how to sew on a button; this is how to make a buttonhole for the button you have just sewed on; this is how to hem a dress when you see the hem coming down and so to prevent yourself from looking like the slut I know you are so bent on becoming; this is how you iron your father's khaki shirt so that it doesn't have a crease; this is how you iron your father's khaki pants so that they don't have a crease; this is how you grow

---

[1]**fritters:** Small fried cakes of batter, often containing vegetables, fruit, or other fillings. [All notes are the editors'.]
[2]**gum:** Plant residue on cotton.
[3]**sing benna:** Sing popular music (not appropriate for Sunday school).

okra[4]—far from the house, because okra tree harbors red ants; when you are growing dasheen,[5] make sure it gets plenty of water or else it makes your throat itch when you are eating it; this is how you sweep a corner; this is how you sweep a whole house; this is how you sweep a yard; this is how you smile to someone you don't like too much; this is how you smile to someone you don't like at all; this is how you smile to someone you like completely; this is how you set a table for tea; this is how you set a table for dinner; this is how you set a table for dinner with an important guest; this is how you set a table for lunch; this is how you set a table for breakfast; this is how to behave in the presence of men who don't know you very well, and this way they won't recognize immediately the slut I have warned you against becoming; be sure to wash every day, even if it is with your own spit; don't squat down to play marbles—you are not a boy, you know; don't pick people's flowers— you might catch something; don't throw stones at blackbirds, because it might not be a blackbird at all; this is how to make a bread pudding; this is how to make doukona;[6] this is how to make pepper pot;[7] this is how to make a good medicine for a cold; this is how to make a good medicine to throw away a child before it even becomes a child; this is how to catch a fish; this is how to throw back a fish you don't like, and that way something bad won't fall on you; this is how to bully a man; this is how a man bullies you; this is how to love a man, and if this doesn't work there are other ways, and if they don't work don't feel too bad about giving up; this is how to spit up in the air if you feel like it, and this is how to move quick so that it doesn't fall on you; this is how to make ends meet; always squeeze bread to make sure it's fresh; *but what if the baker won't let me feel the bread?*; you mean to say that after all you are really going to be the kind of woman who the baker won't let near the bread?

ENGAGING THE TEXT

1. What are your best guesses as to the time and place of the story? Who is telling the story? What does this dialogue tell you about the relationship between the characters, their values and attitudes? What else can you surmise about these people (for instance, ages, occupation, social status)? On what evidence in the story do you base these conclusions?

2. Why does the story juxtapose advice on cooking and sewing, for example, with the repeated warning not to act like a slut?

3. Explain the meaning of the last line of the story: "you mean to say that after all you are really going to be the kind of woman who the baker won't let near the bread?"

[4]**okra:** A shrub whose pods are used in soups, stews, and gumbo.
[5]**dasheen:** The taro plant, cultivated, like the potato, for its edible tuber.
[6]**doukona:** Plantain pudding; the plantain fruit is similar to the banana.
[7]**pepper pot:** A spicy West Indian stew.

4. What does the story tell us about male-female relationships? According to the speaker, what roles are women and men expected to play? What kinds of power, if any, does the speaker suggest that women may have?

EXPLORING CONNECTIONS

5. How would Aaron H. Devor (below) interpret the behaviors and attitudes that the mother is trying to teach her daughter in this selection?

6. What does it mean to be a successful mother in "Girl"? How does this compare to being a good mother in Gary Soto's "Looking for Work" (p. 19)? Which mother do you consider more successful, and why?

EXTENDING THE CRITICAL CONTEXT

7. Write an imitation of the story. If you are a woman, record some of the advice or lessons your mother or another woman gave you; if you are a man, put down advice received from your father or from another male. Read what you have written aloud in class, alternating between male and female speakers, and discuss the results: How does parental guidance vary according to gender?

8. Write a page or two recording what the daughter might be thinking as she listens to her mother's advice; then compare notes with classmates.

BECOMING MEMBERS OF SOCIETY: LEARNING THE SOCIAL MEANINGS OF GENDER

AARON H. DEVOR

Gender is the most transparent of all social categories: we acquire gender roles so early in life and so thoroughly that it's hard to see them as the result of lessons taught and learned. Maleness and femaleness seem "natural," not the product of socialization. In this wide-ranging scholarly essay, Aaron H. Devor suggests that many of our notions of what it means to be female or male are socially constructed. He also touches on the various ways that different cultures define gender. A professor of sociology and formerly Dean of Graduate Studies at the University of Victoria in British Columbia, Devor is a member of the International Academy of Sex Research and author of *FTM: Female-to-Male Transsexuals in Society* (1997). He founded the Transgender Archives in 2012 and currently serves as its academic director. Born Holly Devor in 1951,

Devor announced in 2002 his decision to live as a man and to adopt the name Aaron H. Devor. This selection is taken from his groundbreaking book, *Gender Blending: Confronting the Limits of Duality* (1989).

The Gendered Self

The task of learning to be properly gendered members of society only begins with the establishment of gender identity. Gender identities act as cognitive filtering devices guiding people to attend to and learn gender role behaviors appropriate to their statuses. Learning to behave in accordance with one's gender identity is a lifelong process. As we move through our lives, society demands different gender performances from us and rewards, tolerates, or punishes us differently for conformity to, or digression from, social norms. As children, and later adults, learn the rules of membership in society, they come to see themselves in terms they have learned from the people around them.

Children begin to settle into a gender identity between the age of eighteen months and two years.[1] By the age of two, children usually understand that they are members of a gender grouping and can correctly identify other members of their gender.[2] By age three they have a fairly firm and consistent concept of gender. Generally, it is not until children are five to seven years old that they become convinced that they are permanent members of their gender grouping.[3]

Researchers test the establishment, depth, and tenacity of gender identity through the use of language and the concepts mediated by language. The language systems used in populations studied by most researchers in this field conceptualize gender as binary and permanent. All persons are either male or female. All males are first boys and then men; all females are first girls and then women. People are believed to be unable to change genders without sex change surgery, and those who do change sex are considered to be both disturbed and exceedingly rare.

This is by no means the only way that gender is conceived in all cultures. Many aboriginal cultures have more than two gender categories and accept the idea that, under certain circumstances, gender may be changed without changes being made to biological sex characteristics. Many North and South American native peoples had a legitimate social

---

[1] Much research has been devoted to determining when gender identity becomes solidified in the sense that a child knows itself to be unequivocally either male or female. John Money and his colleagues have proposed eighteen months of age because it is difficult or impossible to change a child's gender identity once it has been established around the age of eighteen months. Money and Ehrhardt, p. 243. [All notes are Devor's, except 12, 20, and 21.]

[2] Mary Driver Leinbach and Beverly I. Fagot, "Acquisition of Gender Labels: A Test for Toddlers," *Sex Roles* 15 (1986), pp. 655–66.

[3] Maccoby, pp. 225–29; Kohlberg and Ullian, p. 211.

category for persons who wished to live according to the gender role of another sex. Such people were sometimes revered, sometimes ignored, and occasionally scorned. Each culture had its own word to describe such persons, most commonly translated into English as "berdache." Similar institutions and linguistic concepts have also been recorded in early Siberian, Madagascan, and Polynesian societies, as well as in medieval Europe.[4]

Very young children learn their culture's social definitions of gender and gender identity at the same time that they learn what gender behaviors are appropriate for them. But they only gradually come to understand the meaning of gender in the same way as the adults of their society do. Very young children may learn the words which describe their gender and be able to apply them to themselves appropriately, but their comprehension of their meaning is often different from that used by adults. Five-year-olds, for example, may be able to accurately recognize their own gender and the genders of the people around them, but they will often make such ascriptions on the basis of role information, such as hair style, rather than physical attributes, such as genitals, even when physical cues are clearly known to them. One result of this level of understanding of gender is that children in this age group often believe that people may change their gender with a change in clothing, hair style, or activity.[5]

The characteristics most salient to young minds are the more culturally specific qualities which grow out of gender role prescriptions. In one study, young school age children, who were given dolls and asked to identify their gender, overwhelmingly identified the gender of the dolls on the basis of attributes such as hair length or clothing style, in spite of the fact that the dolls were anatomically correct. Only 17 percent of the children identified the dolls on the basis of their primary or secondary sex characteristics.[6] Children five to seven years old understand gender as a function of role rather than as a function of anatomy. Their understanding is that gender (role) is supposed to be stable but that it is possible to alter it at will. This demonstrates that although the standard social definition of gender is based on genitalia, this is not the way that young children first learn to distinguish gender. The process of learning to think about gender in an adult fashion is one prerequisite to becoming a full member of society. Thus, as children grow older, they

---

[4]See Susan Baker, "Biological Influences on Human Sex and Gender," in *Women: Sex and Sexuality*, ed. Catherine R. Stimpson and Ethel S. Person (Chicago: University of Chicago Press, 1980), p. 186; Evelyn Blackwood, "Sexuality and Gender in Certain Native American Tribes: The Case of Cross-Gender Females," *Signs* 10 (1984), pp. 27–42; Vern L. Bullough, "Transvestites in the Middle Ages," *American Journal of Sociology* 79 (1974), pp. 1381–89; J. Cl. DuBois, "Transsexualisme et Anthropologie Culturelle," *Gynecologie Pratique* 6 (1969), pp. 431–40; Donald C. Forgey, "The Institution of Berdache Among the North American Plains Indians," *Journal of Sex Research* 11 (Feb. 1975), pp. 1–15; Walter L. Williams, *The Spirit and the Flesh: Sexual Diversity in American Indian Culture* (Boston: Beacon, 1986).

[5]Maccoby, p. 255.

[6]Ibid., p. 227.

learn to think of themselves and others in terms more like those used by adults.

Children's developing concepts of themselves as individuals are necessarily bound up in their need to understand the expectations of the society of which they are a part. As they develop concepts of themselves as individuals, they do so while observing themselves as reflected in the eyes of others. Children start to understand themselves as individuals separate from others during the years that they first acquire gender identities and gender roles. As they do so, they begin to understand that others see them and respond to them as particular people. In this way they develop concepts of themselves as individuals, as an "I" (a proactive subject) simultaneously with self-images of themselves as individuals, as a "me" (a member of society, a subjective object). Children learn that they are both as they see themselves and as others see them.[7]

To some extent, children initially acquire the values of the society around them almost indiscriminately. To the degree that children absorb the generalized standards of society into their personal concept of what is correct behavior, they can be said to hold within themselves the attitude of the "generalized other."[8] This "generalized other" functions as a sort of monitoring or measuring device with which individuals may judge their own actions against those of their generalized conceptions of how members of society are expected to act. In this way members of society have available to them a guide, or an internalized observer, to turn the more private "I" into the object of public scrutiny, the "me." In this way, people can monitor their own behavioral impulses and censor actions which might earn them social disapproval or scorn. The tension created by the constant interplay of the personal "I" and the social "me" is the creature known as the "self."

But not all others are of equal significance in our lives, and therefore not all others are of equal impact on the development of the self. Any person is available to become part of one's "generalized other," but certain individuals, by virtue of the sheer volume of time spent in interaction with someone, or by virtue of the nature of particular interactions, become more significant in the shaping of people's values. These "significant others" become prominent in the formation of one's self-image and one's ideals and goals. As such they carry disproportionate weight in one's personal "generalized other."[9] Thus, children's individualistic impulses are shaped into a socially acceptable form both by particular individuals and by a more generalized pressure to conformity exerted by innumerable faceless members of society. Gender identity is one of the most central portions of that developing sense of self....

[7]George Herbert Mead, "Self," in The Social Psychology of George Herbert Mead, ed. Anselm Strauss (Chicago: Phoenix Books, 1962, 1934), pp. 212–60.

[8]G. H. Mead.

[9]Hans Gerth and C. Wright Mills, Character and Social Structure: The Psychology of Social Institutions (New York: Harcourt, Brace and World, 1953), p. 96.

Gender Role Behaviors and Attitudes

The clusters of social definitions used to identify persons by gender are collectively known as femininity and masculinity. Masculine characteristics are used to identify persons as males, while feminine ones are used as signifiers for femaleness. People use femininity or masculinity to claim and communicate their membership in their assigned, or chosen, sex or gender. Others recognize our sex or gender more on the basis of these characteristics than on the basis of sex characteristics, which are usually largely covered by clothing in daily life.

These two clusters of attributes are most commonly seen as mirror images of one another with masculinity usually characterized by dominance and aggression, and femininity by passivity and submission. A more even-handed description of the social qualities subsumed by femininity and masculinity might be to label masculinity as generally concerned with egoistic dominance and femininity as striving for cooperation or communion.[10] Characterizing femininity and masculinity in such a way does not portray the two clusters of characteristics as being in a hierarchical relationship to one another but rather as being two different approaches to the same question, that question being centrally concerned with the goals, means, and use of power. Such an alternative conception of gender roles captures the hierarchical and competitive masculine thirst for power, which can, but need not, lead to aggression, and the feminine quest for harmony and communal well-being, which can, but need not, result in passivity and dependence.

Many activities and modes of expression are recognized by most members of society as feminine. Any of these can be, and often are, displayed by persons of either gender. In some cases, cross gender behaviors are ignored by observers, and therefore do not compromise the integrity of a person's gender display. In other cases, they are labeled as inappropriate gender role behaviors. Although these behaviors are closely linked to sexual status in the minds and experiences of most people, research shows that dominant persons of either gender tend to use influence tactics and verbal styles usually associated with men and masculinity, while subordinate persons, of either gender, tend to use those considered to be the province of women.[11] Thus it seems likely that many aspects of masculinity and femininity are the result, rather than the cause, of status inequalities.

[10]Egoistic dominance is a striving for superior rewards for oneself or a competitive striving to reduce the rewards for one's competitors even if such action will not increase one's own rewards. Persons who are motivated by desires for egoistic dominance not only wish the best for themselves but also wish to diminish the advantages of others whom they may perceive as competing with them. See Maccoby, p. 217.

[11]Judith Howard, Philip Blumstein, and Pepper Schwartz, "Sex, Power, and Influence Tactics in Intimate Relationships," *Journal of Personality and Social Psychology* 51 (1986), pp. 102–9; Peter Kollock, Philip Blumstein, and Pepper Schwartz, "Sex and Power in Interaction: Conversational Privileges and Duties," *American Sociological Review* 50 (1985), pp. 34–46.

Popular conceptions of femininity and masculinity instead revolve around hierarchical appraisals of the "natural" roles of males and females. Members of both genders are believed to share many of the same human characteristics, although in different relative proportions; both males and females are popularly thought to be able to do many of the same things, but most activities are divided into suitable and unsuitable categories for each gender class. Persons who perform the activities considered appropriate for another gender will be expected to perform them poorly; if they succeed adequately, or even well, at their endeavors, they may be rewarded with ridicule or scorn for blurring the gender dividing line.

The patriarchal gender schema[12] currently in use in mainstream North American society reserves highly valued attributes for males and actively supports the high evaluation of any characteristics which might inadvertently become associated with maleness. The ideology which the schema grows out of postulates that the cultural superiority of males is a natural outgrowth of the innate predisposition of males toward aggression and dominance, which is assumed to flow inevitably from evolutionary and biological sources. Female attributes are likewise postulated to find their source in innate predispositions acquired in the evolution of the species. Feminine characteristics are thought to be intrinsic to the female facility for childbirth and breastfeeding. Hence, it is popularly believed that the social position of females is biologically mandated to be intertwined with the care of children and a "natural" dependency on men for the maintenance of mother-child units. Thus the goals of femininity and, by implication, of all biological females are presumed to revolve around heterosexuality and maternity.[13]

Femininity, according to this traditional formulation, "would result in warm and continued relationships with men, a sense of maternity, interest in caring for children, and the capacity to work productively and continuously in female occupations."[14] This recipe translates into a vast number of proscriptions and prescriptions. Warm and continued relations with men and an interest in maternity require that females be heterosexually oriented. A heterosexual orientation requires women to dress, move, speak, and act in ways that men will find attractive. As patriarchy has reserved active expressions of power as a masculine attribute, femininity must be expressed through modes of dress, movement, speech, and action which communicate weakness, dependency, ineffectualness, availability for sexual or emotional service, and sensitivity to the needs of others.

15

[12]**schema:** A mental framework, scheme, or pattern that helps us make sense of experience. [Eds.]

[13]Nancy Chodorow, *The Reproduction of Mothering: Psychoanalysis and the Reproduction of Mothering* (Berkeley: University of California Press, 1978), p. 134.

[14]Jon K. Meyer and John E. Hoopes, "The Gender Dysphoria Syndromes: A Position Statement on So-Called 'Transsexualism'," *Plastic and Reconstructive Surgery* 54 (October 1974), pp. 444–51.

Some, but not all, of these modes of interrelation also serve the demands of maternity and many female job ghettos. In many cases, though, femininity is not particularly useful in maternity or employment. Both mothers and workers often need to be strong, independent, and effectual in order to do their jobs well. Thus femininity, as a role, is best suited to satisfying a masculine vision of heterosexual attractiveness.

Body postures and demeanors which communicate subordinate status and vulnerability to trespass through a message of "no threat" make people appear to be feminine. They demonstrate subordination through a minimizing of spatial use: people appear feminine when they keep their arms closer to their bodies, their legs closer together, and their torsos and heads less vertical then do masculine-looking individuals. People also look feminine when they point their toes inward and use their hands in small or childlike gestures. Other people also tend to stand closer to people they see as feminine, often invading their personal space, while people who make frequent appeasement gestures, such as smiling, also give the appearance of femininity. Perhaps as an outgrowth of a subordinate status and the need to avoid conflict with more socially powerful people, women tend to excel over men at the ability to correctly interpret, and effectively display, nonverbal communication cues.[15]

Speech characterized by inflections, intonations, and phrases that convey nonaggression and subordinate status also make a speaker appear more feminine. Subordinate speakers who use more polite expressions and ask more questions in conversation seem more feminine. Speech characterized by sounds of higher frequencies are often interpreted by listeners as feminine, childlike, and ineffectual.[16] Feminine styles of dress likewise display subordinate status through greater restriction of the free movement of the body, greater exposure of the bare skin, and an emphasis on sexual characteristics. The more gender distinct the dress, the more this is the case.

Masculinity, like femininity, can be demonstrated through a wide variety of cues. Pleck has argued that it is commonly expressed in North American society through the attainment of some level of proficiency at some, or all, of the following four main attitudes of masculinity. Persons who display success and high status in their social group, who exhibit "a manly air of toughness, confidence, and self-reliance" and "the aura of aggression, violence, and daring," and who conscientiously avoid

---

[15]Erving Goffman, *Gender Advertisements* (New York: Harper Colophon Books, 1976); Judith A. Hall, *Non-Verbal Sex Differences: Communication Accuracy and Expressive Style* (Baltimore: Johns Hopkins University Press, 1984); Nancy M. Henley, *Body Politics: Power, Sex and Non-Verbal Communication* (Englewood Cliffs, N.J.: Prentice Hall, 1979); Marianne Wex, *"Let's Take Back Our Space": "Female" and "Male" Body Language as a Result of Patriarchal Structures* (Berlin: Frauenliteraturverlag Hermine Fees, 1979).

[16]Karen L. Adams, "Sexism and the English Language: The Linguistic Implications of Being a Woman," in *Women: A Feminist Perspective*, 3rd edition, ed. Jo Freeman (Palo Alto, Calif.: Mayfield, 1984), pp. 478–91; Hall, pp. 37, 130–37.

anything associated with femininity are seen as exuding masculinity.[17] These requirements reflect the patriarchal ideology that masculinity results from an excess of testosterone, the assumption being that androgens supply a natural impetus toward aggression, which in turn impels males toward achievement and success. This vision of masculinity also reflects the ideological stance that ideal maleness (masculinity) must remain untainted by female (feminine) pollutants.

Masculinity, then, requires of its actors that they organize themselves and their society in a hierarchical manner so as to be able to explicitly quantify the achievement of success. The achievement of high status in one's social group requires competitive and aggressive behavior from those who wish to obtain it. Competition which is motivated by a goal of individual achievement, or egoistic dominance, also requires of its participants a degree of emotional insensitivity to feelings of hurt and loss in defeated others, and a measure of emotional insularity to protect oneself from becoming vulnerable to manipulation by others. Such values lead those who subscribe to them to view feminine persons as "born losers" and to strive to eliminate any similarities to feminine people from their own personalities. In patriarchally organized societies, masculine values become the ideological structure of the society as a whole. Masculinity thus becomes "innately" valuable and femininity serves a contrapuntal function to delineate and magnify the hierarchical dominance of masculinity.

Body postures, speech patterns, and styles of dress which demonstrate and support the assumption of dominance and authority convey an impression of masculinity. Typical masculine body postures tend to be expansive and aggressive. People who hold their arms and hands in positions away from their bodies, and who stand, sit, or lie with their legs apart—thus maximizing the amount of space that they physically occupy—appear most physically masculine. Persons who communicate an air of authority or a readiness for aggression by standing erect and moving forcefully also tend to appear more masculine. Movements that are abrupt and stiff, communicating force and threat rather than flexibility and cooperation, make an actor look masculine. Masculinity can also be conveyed by stern or serious facial expressions that suggest minimal receptivity to the influence of others, a characteristic which is an important element in the attainment and maintenance of egoistic dominance.[18]

Speech and dress which likewise demonstrate or claim superior status are also seen as characteristically masculine behavior patterns. Masculine speech patterns display a tendency toward expansiveness similar to that found in masculine body postures. People who attempt

---

[17]Elizabeth Hafkin Pleck, *Domestic Tyranny: The Making of Social Policy Against Family Violence from Colonial Times to the Present* (Cambridge: Oxford University Press, 1989), p. 139.

[18]Goffman, *Gender Advertisements*; Hall; Henley; Wex.

to control the direction of conversations seem more masculine.[19] Those who tend to speak more loudly, use less polite and more assertive forms, and tend to interrupt the conversations of others more often also communicate masculinity to others. Styles of dress which emphasize the size of upper body musculature, allow freedom of movement, and encourage an illusion of physical power and a look of easy physicality all suggest masculinity. Such appearances of strength and readiness to action serve to create or enhance an aura of aggressiveness and intimidation central to an appearance of masculinity. Expansive postures and gestures combine with these qualities to insinuate that a position of secure dominance is a masculine one.

Gender role characteristics reflect the ideological contentions underlying the dominant gender schema in North American society. That schema leads us to believe that female and male behaviors are the result of socially directed hormonal instructions which specify that females will want to have children and will therefore find themselves relatively helpless and dependent on males for support and protection. The schema claims that males are innately aggressive and competitive and therefore will dominate over females. The social hegemony[20] of this ideology ensures that we are all raised to practice gender roles which will confirm this vision of the nature of the sexes. Fortunately, our training to gender roles is neither complete nor uniform. As a result, it is possible to point to multitudinous exceptions to, and variations on, these themes. Biological evidence is equivocal about the source of gender roles; psychological androgyny[21] is a widely accepted concept. It seems most likely that gender roles are the result of systematic power imbalances based on gender discrimination.[22]

Candorville

Candorville used with the permission of Darrin Bell, the Washington Post Writers Group and the Cartoonist Group. All rights reserved.

---

[19]Adams; Hall, pp. 37, 130–37.
[20]**hegemony:** System of preponderant influence, authority, or dominance. [Eds.]
[21]**androgyny:** The state of having both male and female characteristics. [Eds.]
[22]Howard, Blumstein, and Schwartz; Kollock, Blumstein, and Schwartz.

ENGAGING THE TEXT

1. Devor charges that most languages present gender as "binary and permanent" (para. 3). Has this been your own view? How does Devor challenge this idea — that is, what's the alternative to gender being binary and permanent — and how persuasive do you find his evidence?

2. How, according to Devor, do children "acquire" gender roles? What are the functions of the "generalized other" and the "significant other" in this process?

3. Explain the distinction Devor makes between the "I" and the "me" (paras. 7 and 8). Write a journal entry describing some of the differences between your own "I" and "me."

4. Using examples from Devor and from other reading or observation, list some "activities and modes of expression" (para. 12) that society considers characteristically female and characteristically male. Which are acceptable cross-gender behaviors, and which are not? Search for a "rule" that defines what types of cross-gender behaviors are tolerated.

5. Do some aspects of the traditional gender roles described by Devor seem to be changing? If so, which ones, and how?

EXPLORING CONNECTIONS

6. Drawing on Devor's discussion of gender role formation, analyze the difference between the "I" and the "me" of the girl in Jamaica Kincaid's story (p. 469).

7. How would Devor explain the humor of the cartoon on page 479? How does the conversation between Lemont and Clyde both reflect Devor's analysis of gender and update it?

8. Look at the photos in the Visual Portfolio (p. 515) and compare two of them. To what extent does each image reflect "the patriarchal gender schema" as Devor defines it?

EXTENDING THE CRITICAL CONTEXT

9. As a class, identify at least half a dozen men living today who are widely admired in American culture. To what extent do they embody the "four main attitudes of masculinity" outlined by Devor (para. 19)?

10. Write an essay or a journal entry analyzing your own gender role socialization. To what extent have you been pressured to conform to conventional roles? To what extent have you resisted them? What roles have "generalized others" and "significant others" played in shaping your identity?

QUANDARIES OF REPRESENTATION

MONA EL-GHOBASHY

In 2008, seventeen-year-old Samantha Elauf didn't know she was making history when she applied for a job at Abercrombie & Fitch. Elauf was rated highly for the position by the assistant manager who interviewed her but was ultimately turned down because she, like many Muslim women, wears a hijab, or head scarf, and thus violated the company's "Look Policy". Seven years later, Elauf won her case against Abercrombie when the U.S. Supreme Court ruled that the retailer had discriminated against her on the basis of her religion. As Mona El-Ghobashy notes in this selection, the hijab is often a source of trouble for Muslim women in American society. Born in Cairo, Egypt, El-Ghobashy graduated from Columbia University with a Ph.D. in political science. She previously taught at Barnard College and is currently a visiting scholar at Columbia's Institute for Religion, Culture, and Public Life. She has published articles in the *International Journal of Middle East Studies, American Behavioral Scientist*, and *Middle East Report* and is working on a book about contemporary Egyptian politics and popular movements. This article appeared in *Arab and Arab American Feminisms* (2011), edited by Rabab Abdulhadi, Evelyn Alsultany, and Nadine Naber.

EVER SINCE I WAS FIFTEEN, I have been trailed by curiosity. Once in tenth grade, while waiting in my high school guidance counselor's office, an elderly secretary got up from her desk and came over to where I was sitting to ask me, in a too-good-to-be-true New York accent, "Excuse me, deah, are you in religion?" Perfect strangers have been no less inquisitive about my head scarf. "Excuse me, does your family come from the Caucasus?" asked an extremely solicitous and almost apologetic fellow passenger on a New York City subway car several years ago. She seemed to slink away in embarrassment as I shook my head and smiled, and I remember thinking that her demeanor suggested an academic elated at identifying a potential research subject.

Now that I reflect on it, the subway has been an especially rich space for strangers to graft onto me their passions, queries, and memories. Once, as I sat impatiently in a delayed subway car on the way to college one late morning in the early 1990s, a young African American man abruptly took off his massive headphones and turned to me, "Excuse me, can I read you a poem?" "Okay," I ventured hesitatingly, relieved that the train car was entirely empty save for him and me and a snoring man in the far corner. He unfolded a white piece of paper and began to passionately read its typed contents, an endearing ode to Malcolm X and

Martin Luther King Jr. Then he folded the paper and carefully returned it to his pocket, explaining to me how it was wrongheaded to argue which leader was better, that both of their strategies were needed and had their place. He looked at me intently for affirmation, and I nodded smilingly. "Thank you, sister," he said, and then returned to complete absorption in the music piped through his headphones.

Once, in a subway car crammed with commuters returning home from work, an elderly Asian man got up from his seat and negotiated his way to where I sat. He leaned down to me and put his finger on the word "contrition" in the *New York Times* article he was reading. "Excuse me, can you explain to me the meaning of this word?" I was happy to oblige, as other passengers sneaked glances at us from behind their books and newspapers.

Once, on the N Train, an elderly olive-skinned man who had been eyeing me shyly gingerly volunteered that he was raised in Iran. I forced a polite smile; I was half-asleep and extremely fatigued from staying up all night to finish a paper. He said that he was Jewish, and that when he was a boy in Iran he memorized all of the Quran in school, and that his mother covered her head, "like you," making a hand gesture that framed his face to mimic a head covering. Perhaps he sensed some doubt in my eyes, perhaps he could not resist reminiscing about his childhood, but he then reached for his black wallet and carefully pulled out a remarkably well-preserved, sepia-toned photograph of a young, angelic-looking woman in a white head scarf. I leaned forward to look at the photograph, which he delicately placed in my hand. Its rippled edges were only slightly creased, and I was overcome by its beauty. He was positively beaming at me, and I beamed back at him.

Other encounters can only be described as bizarre, ranging from annoying but harmless quotidian intrusions to darker experiences that every woman faces in slightly different forms. On the extremely snowy Christmas Day of 2002, I made my way to Queens to meet my best friend who was in town for a short visit. Lost in a neighborhood suddenly made unrecognizable by mounds of snow and shuttered storefronts, I ducked into the only open store, a drugstore, to ask for directions to the café where I was to meet her. As I asked the security guard for its where-abouts, a customer standing in line a few feet away called out, "But do you know how to read? Will you be able to read the street signs?" The security guard stopped talking in midsentence, and we both turned to look at the man's smirking face in genuine puzzlement for several sec-onds, before it dawned on me that he was calling me illiterate. "You need to know how to read to figure out how to get there," he persisted. Cashiers, customers juggling their purchases and dripping umbrellas, and the security guard all turned to me, and time seemed to stand still. I sputtered, "I'm studying for a Ph.D., you bigot," and he retorted, "Yeah, well I have a law degree." I turned and sped out of the store, fighting back tears as I inhaled the bracing winter air.

My head scarf also attracts attention in Egypt, where I was born and now frequently return to conduct research and interviews. "You look like that over there, or do you wear that just when you come here?" I'm constantly asked. My interlocutors are puzzled and sometimes impressed when they learn that I look the same in Cairo and New York. Some seem to think of it as a badge of honor, though I point out that it entails absolutely no bravery to be *muhajjaba*[1] at an elite institution like Columbia in a hypercosmopolitan, novelty-friendly metropolis like New York. After September 11, 2001, almost everyone in Egypt asked worriedly, "How do they treat you over there? Is it really bad?"

I have not experienced any harassment, but instead an outpouring of touching concern from colleagues, friends, and even solicitous strangers. But many hundreds of Muslims in less rarefied circumstances have indeed had their lives turned upside down by September 11. In the immediate aftermath, the most that I had to worry about was how my students would perceive me, and whether I could maintain my composure and walk into class on September 13 to steer a discussion about an event I literally could not comprehend. Other Muslims, Sikhs, and non-Muslim Arabs contended with physical harm, verbal abuse, social ostracism, loss of livelihood, and government harassment.

Over the years, as the American government's military and political intervention in the Middle East has intensified, the curiosity of others has honed in on my supposed exceptionalism. The vast majority of Muslim women are oppressed, goes the conventional wisdom, and I seem different. It must be because I live in "the West." "You look so elegant, but would you be allowed to dress this way in Egypt?" a woman I didn't know once asked. A perfect stranger sitting next to me on a flight from Cairo to New York tried to strike up a conversation by pointedly asking, "Do you always travel alone?" Instead of puncturing the widespread American conviction that all Muslim women are so downtrodden that they cannot dress freely (or elegantly) or travel alone, I am unwittingly deployed to confirm such certainties.

I have come to expect that, after delivering a public lecture on some aspect of politics in the Middle East, someone will invariably ask me a question about women and why they are so oppressed "in the Muslim world." At one and the same time, I am turned into a sanitized "liberal Muslim woman" who speaks unaccented English but also a credible insider able to "explain" my coreligionists' deplorable treatment of women. Equally revealing are the plaudits I receive for being "strong" and "articulate," well before my interlocutor has had a chance to learn anything about my politics or preferences. I cannot help but think that such projections have much more to do with what others graft onto me than what I am and how I see myself. And so I am alternately amused and sobered by how others wish to package me.

[1] *muhajjaba*: A woman who wears a hijab, or head scarf. [Eds.]

Lest I appear to be whiny or caviling, let me concede that there is [10] a necessary amount of reduction in every quotidian transaction. Superficial cultural small talk is often serviceable in everyday conversation, particularly between strangers. Since I am identifiably Muslim because of my head scarf, it is inevitable that my appearance will become the subject of attention. As I wait to pick up clothes from the cleaner, it is entirely ordinary for the owner to make friendly conversation by referring to my head scarf and asking whether it means I come "from the Arab," which segues into a comparison of the weather in South Korea and Egypt and how New York's weather is really quite ideal because there are four distinct seasons, a discourse that ends with me claiming my cleaned clothes and the dry cleaner pleasantly wishing me a nice day.

Yet there remains a fine line between harmless everyday cultural interactions and the quandary of unwittingly being made to represent and somehow stand in for all Muslim women, everywhere, at all times. The task of representation entails negating the manifold stereotypes that stubbornly cling to Muslim women, a task I am reluctant to take on. As it was and continues to be for African American and Asian American women, the burden of deflecting stereotypes is especially acute for Muslim women at this historical juncture, buffeted as they are by unceasing attempts to "reform," "liberate," "uplift," and "empower" them by a motley crew of individuals, institutions, and national governments. As an identifiably Muslim woman, I often feel torn between countering pernicious stereotypes and resisting the mantle of representation that battling stereotypes entails.

When I am called upon to speak from a Muslim, Arab, or Muslim female "perspective," I always wonder: is there one Muslim/Arab/Muslim-female point of view? Do all Muslim women have the same positions on all issues, or even one single issue? I doubt that anyone would claim that Episcopalian or Reform Jewish or Catholic women have a single perspective, so why are millions or even thousands of Muslim women assumed to hold a uniform point of view? Muslim women are divided by national origin, generation, class status, level of religious observance, level of education, and political orientation. What is meant by statements such as "Muslim women are oppressed" or even "In general, Muslim women are unfree"? Conversely, it makes no sense to me to think that one person can be emblematic or representative of "Muslim women," even if it is done positively, as when attempting to identify a spokeswoman or "positive role model" for Muslim women, such as former Turkish prime minister Tansu Çiller or former Pakistani prime minister Benazir Bhutto or Iranian human rights lawyer and Nobel Prize laureate Shirin Ebadi.

There is a reason to be suspicious of the zeal to represent Muslim women. I have in mind the cottage industry of instant celebrities and "public speakers" eager to speak about and for "Muslim women." This sort of representational entrepreneurship is especially prevalent in the United States and countries in Europe with substantial Muslim minorities, where every few years a Muslim woman is trotted out as an exemplary role model to her "sisters." Inevitably, she is carefully packaged as a free-thinker and courageous gadfly eager to "speak the truth" to her core-ligionists.[2] Such entrepreneurs almost always adopt a lecturing, hectoring tone, speaking down to real Muslim women. They excoriate "Islam" for its oppression of women (sometimes its "Muslim men") and demand that Muslims "speak out against the fundamentalism in our midst," or some similar trope that is strategically deployed to launch lucrative careers as professional identity peddlers.

As is so common with disingenuous attempts to address "the community," the audience for such self-appointed spokeswomen is not their community but the publishers, talk-show hosts, and think tanks eager for more sordid tales of the backwardness of Muslims and the oppression of Muslim women. Far from valiantly subverting stereotypes, such manufactured missionaries are deeply invested in upholding stereotypes, confirming the comforting belief that Muslims are a benighted lot, incapable of any positive action and clinging to not a single redeeming value. So they must wait for the brave missionary to come and save them from themselves. Without the stereotype, the entrepreneurs have no traction.

Self-anointed representatives are a far cry from people with more modest and truer aspirations, those individuals who work away from the limelight, who live and work among the communities they seek to empower, who understand the sociological structures and intricate layers of inequality that ensnare Muslim and non-Muslim women alike. I cannot help but recall Virginia Woolf's cutting words, no less true today than when she published them in 1938:

> Money is not the only baser ingredient. Advertisement and publicity are also adulterers. Thus, culture mixed with personal charm, or culture mixed with advertisement and publicity, are also adulterated forms of culture. We must ask you to abjure them; not to appear on public platforms; not to lecture; not to allow your private face to be published, or details of your private life; not to avail yourself, in short, of any of the forms of brain prostitution which are so insidiously suggested by the pimps and panders of the brain-selling trade; or to accept any of those baubles and labels by which brain merit is advertised and certified — medals, honors, degrees — we must ask you to refuse them absolutely, since they are all tokens that culture has been prostituted and intellectual liberty sold into captivity.[3]

---

[2] I am thinking of such recent fictional and nonfictional confessional works as Ayaan Hitsi Ali, *The Caged Virgin: An Emancipation Proclamation for Women and Islam* (New York: Free Press, 2006); Asra Nomani, *Standing Alone in Mecca: An American Woman's Struggle for the Soul of Islam* (New York: HarperCollins, 2005); Nedjma and C. Jane Hunter, *The Almond: The Sexual Awakening of a Muslim Woman* (New York: Grove Press, 2005); and Irshad Manji, *The Trouble with Islam: A Muslim's Call for Reform in Her Faith* (New York: St. Martin's Press, 2004).

[3] Virginia Woolf, *Three Guineas* (New York: Harcourt, 1938), 94.

I do not share Woolf's suspicion of all institutions, but I wholeheartedly identify with her aversion to loud publicity seeking and self-promotion, the sort of entrepreneurship and scramble for representation now routine when it comes to "Muslim women."

Any organized attempts to reduce Muslim women, whether ones that seek to "represent" them or ones that seek to "liberate" them or both, ignore the variation in their life circumstances. Some Muslim women are indeed downtrodden; others are not. Those Muslim women who are oppressed are oppressed in different ways and for different reasons. The same goes for those Muslim women who are emancipated. A genuine concern with diagnosing and alleviating oppression must grapple with unsexy sociological facts and political dynamics that do not make for good copy or riveting confessional narratives. Serious students of gender oppression tackle the variation head-on; hawkers of Muslim women's oppression smother inconvenient facts to serve their agendas.

On a more rarefied plane, attempts to represent or speak for Muslim women by definition must mute their unique selves. Real Muslim and Arab women are extraordinarily diverse. . . . Like other human beings, they are fraught with ambiguity, contradiction, and inconsistency. I understand the need to suppress idiosyncrasy for purposes of sociological classification and policy intervention for poverty alleviation or literacy promotion, but I do not trust the zeal to flatten Muslim women's diversity by self-appointed spokeswomen and overnight do-gooders.

Each Muslim woman is an irreducible self, capable of speaking on her own behalf. When conceptualizing the self, I find myself returning again and again to Edward Said's final words in his beautiful memoir, *Out of Place*, where he ruminates on the multiple sources of the self:

> I occasionally experience myself as a cluster of flowing currents. I prefer this to the idea of a solid self, the identity to which so many attach so much significance. These currents, like the themes of one's life, flow along during the waking hours, and at their best, they require no reconciling, no harmonizing. They are "off" and may be out of place, but at least they are always in motion, in time, in place, in the form of all kinds of strange combinations moving about, not necessarily forward, sometimes against each other, contrapuntally yet without one central theme. A form of freedom, I'd like to think, even if I am far from being totally convinced that it is.[4]

ENGAGING THE TEXT

1. El-Ghobashy describes numerous encounters with strangers — on the subway in New York, on the plane from Egypt, and after her lectures. Choose two or three of these to analyze. What do the people she meets assume about

[4]Edward W. Said, *Out of Place* (New York: Vintage, 2000), 295.

© Malcolm Evans/evanscartoons.com

El-Ghobashy, and how do they (mis)interpret her head scarf? What stereotypes do they have about Muslim women in general or about Muslim women in America?

2. What distinction does El-Ghobashy make between "harmless everyday cultural interactions" and "pernicious stereotypes" (para. 11)?

3. Why is El-Ghobashy reluctant to battle the many stereotypes of Muslim women that she encounters? In what ways does her essay subvert such stereotypes?

4. Why would "publishers, talk-show hosts, and think tanks" be "eager for more sordid tales of the backwardness of Muslims and the oppression of Muslim women" (para. 14)? What personal, political, and economic motives might they have to promote such beliefs?

5. **Thinking Rhetorically** El-Ghobashy acknowledges that her privilege as an academic at an Ivy League school makes her experience atypical. How does this relative privilege affect the rhetorical choices she makes in the essay? She notes that hundreds of "other Muslims, Sikhs, and non-Muslim Arabs contended with physical harm, verbal abuse, social ostracism, loss of livelihood, and government harassment" in the wake of 9/11 (para. 7). Would her essay have more authority if she had endured some of these difficulties? Why or why not?

EXPLORING CONNECTIONS

6. In their discussion of racialization, Linda Holtzman and Leon Sharpe (p. 599) note that following 9/11 there was "widespread racialization of Muslims and people of Middle Eastern descent" (p. 601). To what extent can the stereotypes of Muslim women that El-Ghobashy describes be attributed to racialization?

7. How would each woman in the cartoon on page 487 explain her assumptions about the other? What is the cartoonist, Malcolm Evans, suggesting about male-dominated cultures? Given that the humor of this cartoon relies on stereotypes, do you think El-Ghobashy would approve of it or not, and why?

EXTENDING THE CRITICAL CONTEXT

8. According to the American Civil Liberties Union, more than two-thirds of women who wear a hijab reported that they had experienced discrimination. Do some online research to learn more about the kinds of bias Muslim women face because of their appearance. What cases have recently been litigated? What were the circumstances of each case, and what was the outcome? Write up your findings and report them to the class.

9. If you have ever consciously attempted to disprove a stereotype about a group that you're a part of, write a journal entry describing that experience. Why did you feel the need to refute the stereotype, how did you go about combating it, and what was the result of your efforts, if any?

"TWO WAYS A WOMAN CAN GET HURT": ADVERTISING AND VIOLENCE

JEAN KILBOURNE

Most of us like to think of ourselves as immune to the power of ads — we know that advertisers use sex to get our attention and that they make exaggerated claims about a product's ability to make us attractive, popular, and successful. Because we can see through these subtle or not-so-subtle messages, we assume that we're too smart to be swayed by them. But Jean Kilbourne argues that ads affect us in far more profound and potentially damaging ways. The way that ads portray bodies — especially women's bodies — as objects conditions us to see each other in dehumanizing ways, thus "normalizing" attitudes that can lead to sexual aggression. Kilbourne (b. 1946) has spent most of her professional life teaching and lecturing about the world of advertising. She has produced award-winning documentaries on images of women in ads (*Killing Us Softly, Slim Hopes*) and tobacco advertising (*Pack of Lies*). She has also been a member of the National Advisory Council on Alcohol Abuse and Alcoholism and has twice served as an adviser to the surgeon general of the United States. Currently she serves on the Massachusetts Governor's Commission on Sexual and Domestic Abuse and is a senior scholar at the Wellesley Centers for Women (WCW) at Wellesley College. Her most recent book, coauthored by Diane E. Levin, is *So Sexy So Soon: The New Sexualized Childhood and What Parents Can Do to Protect Their Kids* (2008). The following selection is taken from her 1999 book *Can't Buy My Love: How Advertising Changes the Way We Think and Feel* (formerly titled *Deadly Persuasion*).

SEX IN ADVERTISING IS MORE ABOUT DISCONNECTION and distance than connection and closeness. It is also more often about power than passion, about violence than violins. The main goal, as in pornography, is usually power over another, either by the physical dominance or preferred status of men or what is seen as the exploitative power of female beauty and female sexuality. Men conquer and women ensnare, always with the essential aid of a product. The woman is rewarded for her sexuality by the man's wealth, as in an ad for Cigarette boats in which the woman says, while lying in a man's embrace clearly after sex, "Does this mean I get a ride in your Cigarette?"

Sex in advertising is pornographic because it dehumanizes and objectifies people, especially women, and because it fetishizes products, imbues them with an erotic charge—which dooms us to disappointment since products never can fulfill our sexual desires or meet our emotional needs. The poses and postures of advertising are often borrowed from pornography, as are many of the themes, such as bondage, sadomasochism, and the sexual exploitation of children. When a beer ad uses the image of a man licking the high-heeled boot of a woman clad in leather, when bondage is used to sell neckties in the *New York Times*, perfume in *The New Yorker*, and watches on city buses, and when a college magazine promotes an S&M Ball, pornography can be considered mainstream.

Most of us know all this by now and I suppose some consider it kinky good fun. Pornography is more dangerously mainstream when its glorification of rape and violence shows up in mass media, in films and television shows, in comedy and music videos, and in advertising. Male violence is subtly encouraged by ads that encourage men to be forceful and dominant, and to value sexual intimacy more than emotional intimacy. "Do you want to be the one she tells her deep, dark secrets to?" asks a three-page ad for men's cologne. "Or do you want to be her deep, dark secret?" The last page advises men, "Don't be such a good boy." There are two identical women looking adoringly at the man in the ad, but he isn't looking at either one of them. Just what is the deep, dark secret? That he's sleeping with both of them? Clearly the way to get beautiful women is to ignore them, perhaps mistreat them.

"Two ways a woman can get hurt," says an ad for shaving gel, featuring a razor and a photo of a handsome man. My first thought is that the man is a batterer or date rapist, but the ad informs us that he is merely a "heartbreaker." The gel will protect the woman so that "while

Two Ways A Woman Can Get Hurt.

(Heartbreaker)

(Soap and water shave)

Skintimate® Shave Gel Ultra Protection formula contains 75% moisturizers, including vitamin E, to protect your legs from nicks, cuts and razor burn. So while guys may continue to be a pain, shaving most definitely won't.

SKINTIMATE® SHAVE GEL.
LOVE YOUR LEGS

guys may continue to be a pain, shaving most definitely won't." Desirable men are painful—heartbreakers at best.

Wouldn't it be wonderful if, realizing the importance of relationships in all of our lives, we could seek to learn relational skills from women and to help men develop these strengths in themselves? In fact, we so often

5

The right tie can make even the most casual evening more memorable

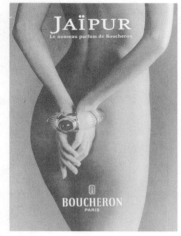

JAÏPUR

Le nouveau parfum de Boucheron

BOUCHERON
PARIS

do the opposite. The popular culture usually trivializes these abilities in women, mocks men who have real intimacy with women (it is almost always married men in ads and cartoons who are jerks), and idealizes a template for relationships between men and women that is a recipe for disaster: a template that views sex as more important than anything else, that ridicules men who are not in control of their women (who are "pussy-whipped"), and that disparages fidelity and commitment (except, of course, to brand names).

Indeed the very worst kind of man for a woman to be in an intimate relationship with, often a truly dangerous man, is the one considered most sexy and desirable in the popular culture. And the men capable of real intimacy (the ones we tell our deep, dark secrets to) constantly have their very masculinity impugned. Advertising often encourages women to be attracted to hostile and indifferent men while encouraging boys to become these men. This is especially dangerous for those of us who have suffered from "condemned isolation" in childhood: like heat-seeking missiles, we rush inevitably to mutual destruction.

Men are also encouraged to never take no for an answer. Ad after ad implies that girls and women don't really mean "no" when they say it, that women are only teasing when they resist men's advances. "NO" says an ad showing a man leaning over a woman against a wall. Is she screaming or laughing? Oh, it's an ad for deodorant and the second word, in very small print, is "sweat." Sometimes it's "all in good fun,"

as in the ad for Possession shirts and shorts featuring a man ripping the clothes off a woman who seems to be having a good time.

And sometimes it is more sinister. A perfume ad running in several teen magazines features a very young woman, with eyes blackened by makeup or perhaps something else, and the copy, "Apply generously to your neck so he can smell the scent as you shake your head 'no.'" In

other words, he'll understand that you don't really mean it and he can respond to the scent like any other animal.

Sometimes there seems to be no question but that a man should force a woman to have sex. A chilling newspaper ad for a bar in George-town features a closeup of a cocktail and the headline, "If your date won't listen to reason, try a Velvet Hammer." A vodka ad pictures a wolf hiding in a flock of sheep, a hideous grin on its face. We all know what wolves do to sheep. A campaign for Bacardi Black rum features shad-owy figures almost obliterated by darkness and captions such as "Some people embrace the night because the rules of the day do not apply."

What it doesn't say is that people who are above the rules do enormous harm to other people, as well as to themselves.

These ads are particularly troublesome, given that between one-third and three-quarters of all cases of sexual assault involve alcohol consumption by the perpetrator, the victim, or both.[1] "Make strangers your friends, and your friends a lot stranger," says one of the ads in a Cuervo campaign that uses colorful cartoon beasts and emphasizes heavy drinking. This ad is especially disturbing when we consider the role of alcohol in date rape, as is another ad in the series that says, "The night began with a bottle of Cuervo and ended with a vow of silence." Over half of all reported rapes on college campuses occur when either the victim or the assailant has been drinking.[2] Alcohol's role has different meaning for men and women, however. If a man is drunk when he commits a rape, he is considered less responsible. If a woman is drunk (or has had a drink or two or simply met the man in a bar), she is considered more responsible.

In general, females are still held responsible and hold each other responsible when sex goes wrong—when they become pregnant or are the victims of rape and sexual assault or cause a scandal. Constantly exhorted to be sexy and attractive, they discover when assaulted that that very sexiness is evidence of their guilt, their lack of "innocence." Sometimes the ads play on this by "warning" women of what might happen if they use the product. "Wear it but beware it," says a perfume ad. Beware what exactly? Victoria's Secret tempts young women with blatantly sexual ads promising that their lingerie will make them irresistible. Yet when a young woman accused William Kennedy Smith of raping her, the fact that she wore Victoria's Secret panties was used against her as an indication of her immorality. A jury acquitted Smith,

---

[1] Wilsnack, Plaud, Wilsnack, and Klassen, 1997, 262. [All notes are Kilbourne's unless otherwise indicated.]

[2] Abbey, Ross, and McDuffie, 1991. Also Martin, 1992, 230–37.

whose alleged history of violence against women was not permitted to be introduced at trial.

It is sadly not surprising that the jury was composed mostly of women. Women are especially cruel judges of other women's sexual behavior, mostly because we are so desperate to believe we are in control of what happens to us. It is too frightening to face the fact that male violence against women is irrational and commonplace. It is reassuring to believe that we can avoid it by being good girls, avoiding dark places, staying out of bars, dressing "innocently." An ad featuring two young women talking intimately at a coffee shop says, "Carla and Rachel considered themselves open-minded and non-judgmental people. Although they did agree Brenda was a tramp." These terrible judgments from other women are an important part of what keeps all women in line.

If indifference in a man is sexy, then violence is sometimes downright erotic. Not surprisingly, this attitude too shows up in advertising. "Push my buttons," says a young woman, "I'm looking for a man who can totally floor me." Her vulnerability is underscored by the fact that she is in an elevator, often a dangerous place for women. She is young, she is submissive (her eyes are downcast), she is in a dangerous place, and she is dressed provocatively. And she is literally asking for it.

"Wear it out and make it scream," says a jeans ad portraying a man sliding his hands under a woman's transparent blouse. This could be a seduction, but it could as easily be an attack. Although the ad that ran in the Czech version of *Elle* portraying three men attacking a woman seems unambiguous, the terrifying image is being used to sell jeans *to women.* So someone must think that women would find this image compelling or attractive. Why would we? Perhaps it is simply designed to get our attention, by shocking us and by arousing unconscious anxiety. Or perhaps the intent is more subtle and it is designed to play into the

fantasies of domination and even rape that some women use in order to maintain an illusion of being in control (we are the ones having the fantasies, after all, we are the directors).

A camera ad features a woman's torso wrapped in plastic, her hands 15 tied behind her back. A smiling woman in a lipstick ad has a padlocked chain around her neck. An ad for MTV shows a vulnerable young

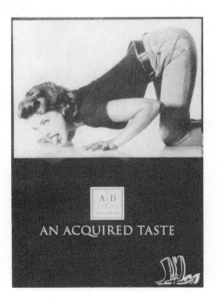

woman, her breasts exposed, and the simple copy "Bitch." A perfume ad features a man shadowboxing with what seems to be a woman.

Sometimes women are shown dead or in the process of being killed. "Great hair never dies," says an ad featuring a female corpse lying on a bed, her breasts exposed. An ad in the Italian version of *Vogue* shows a man aiming a gun at a nude woman wrapped in plastic, a leather briefcase covering her face. And an ad for Bitch skateboards, for God's sake, shows a cartoon version of a similar scene, this time clearly targeting young people. We believe we are not affected by these images, but most of us experience visceral shock when we pay conscious attention to them. Could they be any less shocking to us on an unconscious level?

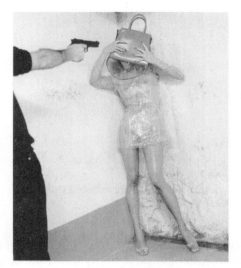

La Borsa è la Vita

Most of us become numb to these images, just as we become numb to the daily litany in the news of women being raped, battered, and killed. According to former surgeon general Antonia Novello, battery is the single greatest cause of injury to women in America, more common than automobile accidents, muggings, and stranger rapes combined, and more than one-third of women slain in this country die at the hands of husbands or boyfriends.[3] Throughout the world, the biggest problem for most women is simply surviving at home. The Global Report on Women's Human Rights concluded that "Domestic violence is a leading cause of female injury in almost every country in the world and is typically ignored by the state or only erratically punished."[4] Although usually numb to these facts on a conscious level, most women live in a state of subliminal terror, a state that, according to Mary Daly,[5] keeps us divided both from each other and from our most passionate, powerful, and creative selves.[6]

Ads don't directly cause violence, of course. But the violent images contribute to the state of terror. And objectification and disconnection create a climate in which there is widespread and increasing violence. Turning a human being into a thing, an object, is almost always the first step toward justifying violence against that person. It is very difficult, perhaps impossible, to be violent to someone we think of as an equal, someone we have empathy with, but it is very easy to abuse a thing. We see this with racism, with homophobia. The person becomes

[3]Novello, 1991. Also Blumenthal, 1995.
[4]Wright, 1995, A2.
[5]**Mary Daly:** Radical feminist scholar and author (1928–2010). [Eds.]
[6]Weil, 1999, 21.

bitch skateboards

an object and violence is inevitable. This step is already taken with women. The violence, the abuse, is partly the chilling but logical result of the objectification.

An editorial in *Advertising Age* suggests that even some advertisers are concerned about this: "Clearly it's time to wipe out sexism in beer ads; for the brewers and their agencies to wake up and join the rest of America in realizing that sexism, sexual harassment, and the cultural portrayal of women in advertising are inextricably linked."[7] Alas, this editorial was written in 1991 and nothing has changed.

It is this link with violence that makes the objectification of women a more serious issue than the objectification of men. Our economic system constantly requires the development of new markets. Not surprisingly, men's bodies are the latest territory to be exploited. Although we are growing more used to it, in the beginning the male sex object came as a surprise. In 1994 a "gender bender" television commercial in which a bevy of women office workers gather to watch a construction worker doff his shirt to quaff a Diet Coke led to so much hoopla that you'd have thought women were mugging men on Madison Avenue.[8]

There is no question that men are used as sex objects in ads now as never before. We often see nude women with fully clothed men in ads (as in art), but the reverse was unheard of, until recently. These days some ads do feature clothed and often aggressive women with nude men. And women sometimes blatantly objectify men, as in the Metroliner ad that says, "'She's reading Nietzsche,' Harris noted to himself as he walked towards the café car for a glass of cabernet. And as he passed her seat, Maureen looked up from her book and thought, 'Nice buns.'"

Although these ads are often funny, it is never a good thing for human beings to be objectified. However, there is a world of difference

[7]Brewers can help fight sexism, 1991, 28.
[8]Kilbourne, 1994, F13.

between the objectification of men and that of women. The most important difference is that there is no danger for most men, whereas objectified women are always at risk. In the Diet Coke ad, for instance, the
women are physically separated from the shirtless man. He is the one in
control. His body is powerful, not passive. Imagine a true role reversal
of this ad: a group of businessmen gather to leer at a beautiful woman
worker on her break, who removes her shirt before drinking her Diet
Coke. This scene would be frightening, not funny, as the Diet Coke ad
is. And why is the Diet Coke ad funny? Because we know it doesn't
describe any truth. However, the ads featuring images of male violence
against women do describe a truth, a truth we are all aware of, on one
level or another.

When power is unequal, when one group is oppressed and discriminated against *as a group*, when there is a context of systemic and historical
oppression, stereotypes and prejudice have different weight and meaning. As Anna Quindlen[9] said, writing about "reverse racism": "Hatred
by the powerful, the majority, has a different weight—and often very different effects—than hatred by the powerless, the minority."[10] When men
objectify women, they do so in a cultural context in which women are
constantly objectified and in which there are consequences—from economic discrimination to violence—to that objectification.

For men, though, there are no such consequences. Men's bodies
are not routinely judged and invaded. Men are not likely to be raped,
harassed, or beaten (that is to say, men presumed to be heterosexual
are not, and very few men are abused in these ways by women). How

[9]**Anna Quindlen:** Novelist and Pulitzer Prize–winning journalist who often writes
about women's issues (b. 1953). [Eds.]
[10]Quindlen, 1992, E17.

where women are women
and men are
roadkill.

harley-davidson motorclothes

many men are frightened to be alone with a woman in an elevator? How many men cross the street when a group of women approaches? Jackson Katz, who writes and lectures on male violence, often begins his workshops by asking men to describe the things they do every day to protect themselves from sexual assault. The men are surprised, puzzled, sometimes amused by the question. The women understand the question easily and have no trouble at all coming up with a list of responses. We don't list our full names in the phone directory or on our mailboxes, we try not to be alone after dark, we carry our keys in our hands when we approach our cars, we always look in the back seat before we get in, we are wary of elevators and doorways and bushes, we carry pepper sprays, whistles, Mace.

Nonetheless, the rate of sexual assault in the United States is the highest of any industrialized nation in the world.[11] According to a 1998 study by the federal government, one in five of us has been the victim of rape or attempted rape, most often before our seventeenth birthday. And more than half of us have been physically assaulted, most often by the men we live with. In fact, three of four women in the study who responded that they had been raped or assaulted as adults said the perpetrator was a current or former husband, a cohabiting partner or a date.[12] The article reporting the results of this study was buried on page twenty-three of my local newspaper, while the front page dealt with a long story about the New England Patriots football team.

A few summers ago, a Diet Pepsi commercial featured Cindy Crawford being ogled by two boys (they seemed to be about twelve years

25

[11]Blumenthal, 1995, 2.
[12]Tjaden and Thoennes, 1998.

old) as she got out of her car and bought a Pepsi from a machine. The boys made very suggestive comments, which in the end turned out to be about the Pepsi's can rather than Ms. Crawford's. There was no out-cry: the boys' behavior was acceptable and ordinary enough for a soft-drink commercial.

Again, let us imagine the reverse: a sexy man gets out of a car in the countryside and two preteen girls make suggestive comments, seem-ingly about his body, especially his buns. We would fear for them and rightly so. But the boys already have the right to ogle, to view women's bodies as property to be looked at, commented on, touched, perhaps eventually hit and raped. The boys have also learned that men ogle pri-marily to impress other men (and to affirm their heterosexuality). If any-one is in potential danger in this ad, it is the woman (regardless of the age of the boys). Men are not seen as *property* in this way by women. Indeed if a woman does whistle at a man or touches his body or even makes direct eye contact, it is still *she* who is at risk and the man who has the power.

"I always lower my eyes to see if a man is worth following," says the woman in an ad for men's pants. Although the ad is offensive to everyone, the woman is endangering only herself.

"Where women are women and men are roadkill," says an ad for motorcycle clothing featuring an angry-looking African American woman. Women are sometimes hostile and angry in ads these days, especially women of color who are often seen as angrier and more threatening than white women. But, regardless of color, we all know that women are far more likely than men to end up as roadkill—and, when it happens, they are blamed for being on the road in the first place.

Even little girls are sometimes held responsible for the violence 30 against them. In 1990 a male Canadian judge accused a three-year-old girl of being "sexually aggressive" and suspended the sentence of her molester, who was then free to return to his job of baby-sitter.[13] The deeply held belief that all women, regardless of age, are really temptresses in disguise, nymphets, sexually insatiable and seductive, conveniently transfers all blame and responsibility onto women.

All women are vulnerable in a culture in which there is such widespread objectification of women's bodies, such glorification of disconnection, so much violence against women, and such blaming of the victim. When everything and everyone is sexualized, it is the powerless who are most at risk. Young girls, of course, are especially vulnerable. In the past twenty years or so, there have been several trends in fashion and advertising that could be seen as cultural reactions to the women's movement, as perhaps unconscious fear of female power. One has been the obsession with thinness. Another has been an increase in images of violence against women. Most disturbing has been the increasing sexualization of children, especially girls. Sometimes the little girl is made up and seductively posed. Sometimes the language is suggestive. "Very cherry," says the ad featuring a sexy little African American girl who is wearing a dress with cherries all over it. A shocking ad in a gun magazine features a smiling little girl, a toddler, in a bathing suit that is tugged up suggestively in the rear. The copy beneath the photo says, "short BUTTS from FLEMING FIREARMS."[14] Other times girls are juxtaposed with grown women, as in the ad for underpants that says "You already know the feeling."

[13]Two men and a baby, 1990, 10.
[14]Herbert, 1999, WK 17.

This is not only an American phenomenon. A growing national obsession in Japan with schoolgirls dressed in uniforms is called "Loli-con," after Lolita.[15] In Tokyo hundreds of "image clubs" allow Japanese men to act out their fantasies with make-believe schoolgirls. A magazine called *V-Club* featuring pictures of naked elementary-school girls competes with another called *Anatomical Illustrations of Junior High School Girls*.[16] Masao Miyamoto, a male psychiatrist, suggests that Japanese men are turning to girls because they feel threatened by the growing sophistication of older women.[17]

In recent years, this sexualization of little girls has become even more disturbing as hints of violence enter the picture. A three-page ad for Prada clothing features a girl or very young woman with a barely pubescent body, clothed in what seem to be cotton panties and perhaps a training bra, viewed through a partially opened door. She seems surprised, startled, worried, as if she's heard a strange sound or glimpsed someone watching her. I suppose this could be a woman awaiting her lover, but it could as easily be a girl being preyed upon.

The 1996 murder of six-year-old JonBenet Ramsey[18] was a gold mine for the media, combining as it did child pornography and violence. In November of 1997 *Advertising Age* reported in an article entitled

---

[15]**Lolita:** The title character of Vladimir Nabokov's 1955 novel, Lolita is a young girl who is sexually pursued by her stepfather. [Eds.]

[16]Schoolgirls as sex toys, 1997, 2E.

[17]Ibid.

[18]**JonBenet Ramsey:** Six-year-old beauty-pageant winner who was sexually molested and murdered in her Boulder, Colorado, home in 1996. [Eds.]

"JonBenet Keeps Hold on Magazines" that the child had been on five magazine covers in October, "Enough to capture the Cover Story lead for the month. The pre-adolescent beauty queen, found slain in her home last Christmas, garnered 6.5 points. The case earned a *triple play* [italics mine] in the *National Enquirer*, and one-time appearances on *People* and *Star*."[19] Imagine describing a six-year-old child as "pre-adolescent."

Sometimes the models in ads are children, other times they just look like children. Kate Moss was twenty when she said of herself, "I look twelve."[20] She epitomized the vacant, hollow-cheeked look known as "heroin chic" that was popular in the mid-nineties. She also often looked vulnerable, abused, and exploited. In one ad she is nude in the corner of a huge sofa, cringing as if braced for an impending sexual assault. In another she is lying nude on her stomach, pliant, available, androgynous enough to appeal to all kinds of pedophiles. In a music video she is dead and bound to a chair while Johnny Cash sings "Delia's Gone."

It is not surprising that Kate Moss models for Calvin Klein, the fashion designer who specializes in breaking taboos and thereby getting himself public outrage, media coverage, and more bang for his buck. In 1995 he brought the federal government down on himself by running a campaign that may have crossed the line into child pornography.[21] Very young models (and others who just seemed young) were featured in lascivious print ads and in television commercials designed to mimic child porn. The models were awkward, self-conscious. In one commercial, a boy stands in what seems to be a finished basement. A male voiceover

[19]Johnson, 1997, 42.
[20]Leo, 1994, 27.
[21]Sloan, 1996, 27.

tells him he has a great body and asks him to take off his shirt. The boy seems embarrassed but he complies. There was a great deal of protest, which brought the issue into national consciousness but which also gave Klein the publicity and free media coverage he was looking for. He pulled the ads but, at the same time, projected that his jeans sales would almost double from $115 million to $220 million that year, partly because of the free publicity but also because the controversy made his critics seem like prudes and thus positioned Klein as the daring rebel, a very appealing image to the majority of his customers.

Having learned from this, in 1999 Klein launched a very brief advertising campaign featuring very little children frolicking in their underpants, which included a controversial billboard in Times Square.[22] Although in some ways this campaign was less offensive than the earlier one and might have gone unnoticed had the ads come from a department store catalog rather than from Calvin Klein, there was the expected protest and Klein quickly withdrew the ads, again getting a windfall of media coverage. In my opinion, the real obscenity of this campaign is the whole idea of people buying designer underwear for their little ones, especially in a country in which at least one in five children doesn't have enough to eat.

Although boys are sometimes sexualized in an overt way, they are more often portrayed as sexually precocious, as in the Pepsi commercial featuring the young boys ogling Cindy Crawford or the jeans ad portraying a very little boy looking up a woman's skirt. It may seem that I am reading too much into this ad, but imagine if the genders were reversed. We would fear for a little girl who was unzipping a man's fly

[22]Associated Press, 1999, February 18, A7.

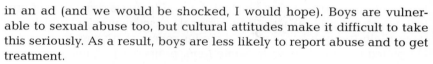

in an ad (and we would be shocked, I would hope). Boys are vulnerable to sexual abuse too, but cultural attitudes make it difficult to take this seriously. As a result, boys are less likely to report abuse and to get treatment.

Many boys grow up feeling that they are unmanly if they are not always "ready for action," capable of and interested in sex with any woman who is available. Advertising doesn't cause this attitude, of course, but it contributes to it. A Levi Strauss commercial that ran in Asia features the shock of a schoolboy who discovers that the seductive young woman who has slipped a note into the jeans of an older student is his teacher. And an ad for BIC pens pictures a young boy wearing X-ray glasses while ogling the derriere of an older woman. Again, these ads would be unthinkable if the genders were reversed. It is increasingly difficult in such a toxic environment to see children, boys or girls, as *children*.

In the past few years there has been a proliferation of sexually grotesque toys for boys, such as a Spider Man female action figure whose exaggerated breasts have antennae coming out of them and a female Spawn figure with carved skulls for breasts. Meantime even children have easy access to pornography in video games and on the World Wide Web, which includes explicit photographs of women having intercourse with groups of men, with dogs, donkeys, horses, and snakes; photographs of women being raped and tortured; some of these women made up to look like little girls.

It is hard for girls not to learn self-hatred in an environment in which there is such widespread and open contempt for women and girls. In 1997 a company called Senate distributed clothing with inside labels that included, in addition to the usual cleaning instructions, the line

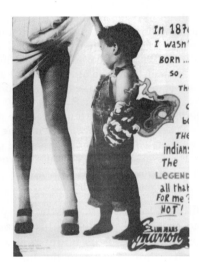

"Destroy all girls." A Senate staffer explained that he thought it was "kind of cool."[23] Given all this, it's not surprising that when boys and girls were asked in a recent study to write an essay on what it would be like to be the other gender, many boys wrote they would rather be dead. Girls had no trouble writing essays about activities, power, freedom, but boys were often stuck, could think of nothing.

It is also not surprising that, in such an environment, sexual harassment is considered normal and ordinary. According to an article in the journal *Eating Disorders*:

[23]Wire and *Times* staff reports, 1997, D1.

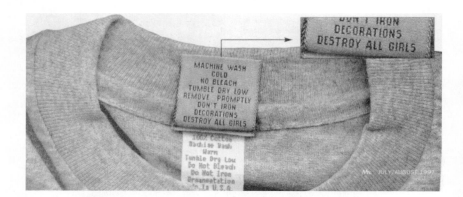

In our work with young women, we have heard countless accounts of this contempt being expressed by their male peers: the girls who do not want to walk down a certain hallway in their high school because they are afraid of being publicly rated on a scale of one to ten; the girls who are subjected to barking, grunting and mooing calls and labels of "dogs, cows, or pigs" when they pass by groups of male students; those who are teased about not measuring up to buxom, bikini-clad [models]; and the girls who are grabbed, pinched, groped, and fondled as they try to make their way through the school corridors.

Harassing words do not slide harmlessly away as the taunting sounds dissipate.... They are slowly absorbed into the child's identity and developing sense of self, becoming an essential part of who she sees herself to be. Harassment involves the use of words as weapons to inflict pain and assert power. Harassing words are meant to instill fear, heighten bodily discomfort, and diminish the sense of self.[24]

It is probably difficult for those of us who are older to understand how devastating and cruel and pervasive this harassment is, how different from the "teasing" some of us might remember from our own childhoods (not that that didn't hurt and do damage as well). A 1993 report by the American Association of University Women found that 76 percent of female students in grades eight to eleven and 56 percent of male students said they had been sexually harassed in school.[25] One high-school junior described a year of torment at her vocational school: "The boys call me slut, bitch. They call me a ten-timer, because they say I go with ten guys at the same time. I put up with it because I have no choice. The teachers say it's because the boys think I'm pretty."[26]

High school and junior high school have always been hell for those who were different in any way (gay teens have no doubt suffered the most, although "overweight" girls are a close second), but the harass-

[24]Larkin, Rice, and Russell, 1996, 5–26.
[25]Daley and Vigue, 1999, A12.
[26]Hart, 1998, A12.

ment is more extreme and more physical these days. Many young men feel they have the right to judge and touch young women and the women often feel they have no choice but to submit. One young woman recalled that "the guys at school routinely swiped their hands across girls' legs to patrol their shaving prowess and then taunt them if they were slacking off. If I were running late, I'd protect myself by faux shaving—just doing the strip between the bottom of my jeans and the top of my cotton socks."[27]

Sexual battery, as well as inappropriate sexual gesturing, touching, and fondling, is increasing not only in high schools but in elementary and middle schools as well.[28] There are reports of sexual assaults by students on other students as young as eight. A fifth-grade boy in Georgia repeatedly touched the breasts and genitals of one of his fellow students while saying, "I want to get in bed with you" and "I want to feel your boobs." Authorities did nothing, although the girl complained and her grades fell. When her parents found a suicide note she had written, they took the board of education to court.[29]

A high-school senior in an affluent suburban school in the Boston area said she has been dragged by her arms so boys could look up her skirt and that boys have rested their heads on her chest while making lewd comments. Another student in the same school was pinned down on a lunch table while a boy simulated sex on top of her. Neither student reported any of the incidents, for fear of being ostracized by their peers.[30] In another school in the Boston area, a sixteen-year-old girl, who had been digitally raped by a classmate, committed suicide.[31]

According to Nan Stein, a researcher at Wellesley College:

> Schools may in fact be training grounds for the insidious cycle of domestic violence....The school's hidden curriculum teaches young women to suffer abuse privately, that resistance is futile. When they witness harassment of others and fail to respond, they absorb a different kind of powerlessness—that they are incapable of standing up to injustice or acting in solidarity with their peers. Similarly, in schools boys receive permission, even training, to become batterers through the practice of sexual harassment.[32]

This pervasive harassment of and contempt for girls and women constitute a kind of abuse. We know that addictions for women are rooted in trauma, that girls who are sexually abused are far more likely to become addicted to one substance or another. I contend that all girls growing up in this culture are sexually abused—abused by the pornographic images of female sexuality that surround them from birth, abused by all the violence against women and girls, and abused by the constant

[27]Mackler, 1998, 56.
[28]Daley and Vigue, 1999, A1, A12.
[29]Shin, 1999, 32.
[30]Daley and Vigue, 1999, A12.
[31]Daley and Abraham, 1999, B6.
[32]Stein, 1993, 316–17.

harassment and threat of violence. Abuse is a continuum, of course, and I am by no means implying that cultural abuse is as terrible as literally being raped and assaulted. However, it hurts, it does damage, and it sets girls up for addictions and self-destructive behavior. Many girls turn to food, alcohol, cigarettes, and other drugs in a misguided attempt to cope.

As Marian Sandmaier said in *The Invisible Alcoholics: Women and Alcohol Abuse in America*, "In a culture that cuts off women from many of their own possibilities before they barely have had a chance to sense them, that pain belongs to all women. Outlets for coping may vary widely, and may be more or less addictive, more or less self-destructive. But at some level, all women know what it is to lack access to their own power, to live with a piece of themselves unclaimed."[33]

Today, every girl is endangered, not just those who have been physically and sexually abused. If girls from supportive homes with positive role models are at risk, imagine then how vulnerable are the girls who have been violated. No wonder they so often go under for good— ending up in abusive marriages, in prison, on the streets. And those who do are almost always in the grip of one addiction or another. More than half of women in prison are addicts and most are there for crimes directly related to their addiction. Many who are there for murder killed men who had been battering them for years. Almost all of the women who are homeless or in prisons and mental institutions are the victims of male violence.[34]

Male violence exists within the same cultural and sociopolitical context that contributes to addiction. Both can be fully understood only within this context, way beyond individual psychology and family dynamics. It is a context of systemic violence and oppression, including racism, classism, heterosexism, weightism, and ageism, as well as sexism, all of which are traumatizing in and of themselves. Advertising is only one part of this cultural context, but it is an important part and thus is a part of what traumatizes.

Sources

Abbey, A., Ross, L., and McDuffie, D. (1991). Alcohol's role in sexual assault. In Watson, R., ed. *Addictive behaviors in women*. Totowa, NJ: Humana Press.

Associated Press (1999, February 18). Calvin Klein retreats on ad. *Boston Globe*, A7.

Blumenthal, S. J. (1995, July). *Violence against women*. Washington, DC: Department of Health and Human Services.

Brewers can help fight sexism (1991, October 28). *Advertising Age*, 28.

Daley, B., and Vigue, D. I. (1999, February 4). Sex harassment increasing amid students, officials say. *Boston Globe*, A1, A12.

Hart, J. (1998, June 8). Northampton confronts a crime, cruelty. *Boston Globe*, A1, A12.

[33]Sandmaier, 1980, xviii.
[34]Snell, 1991.

Herbert, B. (1999, May 2). America's littlest shooters. *New York Times*, WK 17.

Johnson, J. A. (1997, November 10). JonBenet keeps hold on magazines. *Advertising Age*, 42.

Kilbourne, J. (1994, May 15). "Gender bender" ads: Same old sexism. *New York Times*, F13.

Larkin, J., Rice, C., and Russell, V. (1996, Spring). Slipping through the cracks: Sexual harassment. *Eating Disorders: The Journal of Treatment and Prevention*, vol. 4, no. 1, 5–26.

Leo, J. (1994, June 13). Selling the woman-child. *U.S. News and World Report*, 27.

Mackler, C. (1998). Memoirs of a (sorta) ex-shaver. In Edut, O., ed. (1998). *Adios, Barbie*. Seattle, WA: Seal Press, 55–61.

Martin, S. (1992). The epidemiology of alcohol-related interpersonal violence. *Alcohol, Health and Research World*, vol.16, no. 3, 230–37.

Novello, A. (1991, October 18). Quoted by Associated Press, AMA to fight wife-beating. *St. Louis Post Dispatch*, 1, 15.

Quindlen, A. (1992, June 28). All of these you are. *New York Times*, E17.

Sandmaier, M. (1980). *The invisible alcoholics: Women and alcohol abuse in America*. New York: McGraw-Hill.

Schoolgirls as sex toys. *New York Times* (1997, April 16), 2E.

Shin, A. (1999, April/May). Testing Title IX. *Ms.*, 32.

Sloan, P. (1996, July 8). Underwear ads caught in bind over sex appeal. *Advertising Age*, 27.

Snell, T. L. (1991). *Women in prison*. Washington, DC: U.S. Department of Justice.

Stein, N. (1993). No laughing matter: Sexual harassment in K-12 schools. In Buchwald, E., Fletcher, P. R., and Roth, M. (1993). *Transforming a rape culture*. Minneapolis, MN: Milkweed Editions, 311–31.

Tjaden, R., and Thoennes, N. (1998, November). *Prevalence, incidence, and consequences of violence against women: Findings from the National Violence Against Women Survey*. Washington, DC: U.S. Department of Justice.

Two men and a baby (1990, July/August). *Ms.*, 10.

Vigue, D. J., and Abraham, Y. (1999, February 7). Harassment a daily course for students. *Boston Globe*, B1, B6.

Weil, L. (1999, March). Leaps of faith. *Women's Review of Books*, 21.

Wilsnack, S. C., Plaud, J. J., Wilsnack, R. W., and Klassen, A. D. (1997). Sexuality, gender, and alcohol use. In Wilsnack, R. W., and Wilsnack, S. C., eds. *Gender and alcohol: Individual and social perspectives*. New Brunswick, N.J.: Rutgers Center of Alcohol Studies, 262.

Wire and *Times* Staff Reports (1997, May 20). Orange County skate firm's "destroy all girls" tags won't wash. *Los Angeles Times*, D1.

Wright, R. (1995, September 10). Brutality defines the lives of women around the world. *Boston Globe*, A2.

ENGAGING THE TEXT

1. What parallels does Kilbourne see between advertising and pornography? How persuasive do you find the evidence she offers? Do the photos of the ads she describes strengthen her argument? Why or why not?

2. Why is it dangerous to depict women and men as sex objects, according to Kilbourne? Why is the objectification of women *more* troubling, in her view? Do you agree?

3. How does Kilbourne explain the appeal of ads that allude to bondage, sexual aggression, and rape — particularly for female consumers? How do you respond to the ads reproduced in her essay?

4. **Thinking Rhetorically** What does Kilbourne mean when she claims that the depiction of women in advertising constitutes "cultural abuse"? How does she go about drawing connections between advertising images and social problems like sexual violence, harassment, and addiction? Which portions of her analysis do you find most and least persuasive, and why?

EXPLORING CONNECTIONS

5. Media images constitute part of the "generalized other" — the internalized sense of what is socially acceptable and unacceptable — described by Aaron H. Devor (p. 471). In addition to the violent and sexualized images Kilbourne examines, what other images or messages about gender do you encounter regularly in the media? Which ones have been most influential in the development of your "generalized other"?

6. Drawing on the essays by Kilbourne and Joan Morgan (p. 533), write an essay exploring the power of media to promote or curb violence.

EXTENDING THE CRITICAL CONTEXT

7. Kilbourne claims that popular culture idealizes dangerous, exploitative, or dysfunctional relationships between women and men. Working in small groups, discuss the romantic relationships depicted in movies you've seen recently. Does her critique seem applicable to those films? List the evidence you find for and against her argument, and compare your results with those of other groups.

8. In her analysis of two ads (the Diet Pepsi commercial featuring Cindy Crawford and the Diet Coke ad with the shirtless construction worker), Kilbourne applies a gender reversal test in order to demonstrate the existence of a double standard. Try this test yourself on a commercial or ad that relies on sexual innuendo. Write a journal entry describing the ad and explaining the results of your test.

9. Working in pairs or small groups, survey the ads in two magazines — one designed to appeal to a predominantly female audience and one aimed at a largely male audience. What differences, if any, do you see in the kinds of images and appeals advertisers use in the two magazines? How often do you see the kinds of "pornographic" ads Kilbourne discusses? Do you find any ads depicting the "relational skills" that she suggests are rarely emphasized in popular culture?

VISUAL PORTFOLIO

READING IMAGES OF GENDER

© Rafael Cardenas

Digital Vision/Getty Images

5

© Eli Reed/Magnum Photos

VISUAL PORTFOLIO

READING IMAGES OF GENDER

1. Write a brief narrative about the photo of the girl applying lipstick in the mirror (p. 515). What are the two young women doing, what are their ages, and what's their relationship? Take into consideration the details of the photograph — the framing and lighting, the facial expression of the girl with the lipstick, her sports jersey, the way she's applying the lipstick, and the position and expression of her companion. What feelings does the picture evoke?

2. Imagine that you are one of the people in the picture of the four teens on page 516, and freewrite about what is happening (or what has just happened). What are you thinking and feeling at this moment, and why? Compare your response to those of classmates: Does the gender of the "character" you adopt affect your interpretation of the image? If so, how and why?

3. Write a journal entry about the photograph of the Muslim American woman (p. 517). What do the patterns of her head scarf and keffiyeh convey about her identity? What does her jean jacket suggest? How do you read her direct gaze and expression? Share your responses in class: If you find differences of interpretation, how do you explain them?

4. The photo on page 518 is of Abby, an eight-year-old girl; the rifle that she's holding is real — a .22 caliber — although it's pink and matches her ruffled skirt. To what extent does she embody both stereotypical feminine and masculine characteristics? Do you find this picture disturbing? Why or why not?

5. On page 519, the girl on the left is Cassidy Lynn Campbell with her friend, Victoria Avalos, both male-to-female transgender people. Victoria and Cassidy helped each other come out as transgender and are close friends (you can learn more about their stories at http://time.com/135844/transgender-cassidy -lynn-campbell/). When Cassidy came out her senior year of high school, her classmates elected her homecoming queen, but her father still refers to her as his son. What does the photographer suggest about transgender identity in this photo? What do each girl's appearance, posture, and expression convey about her? Why are they holding hands?

6. How would you describe the mood or feeling the photographer has captured in the picture of the father and child (p. 520)? How do the light, the setting, the stance, and the expression of each figure contribute to this impression? Why do you think that "Masculinity" would or would not be an appropriate title for this picture?

THE LONGEST WAR
REBECCA SOLNIT

When we read about women being stoned in Afghan villages or gang-raped by men on buses in rural India, we often assume that we've made progress on issues of violence against women here in the United States. But, as Rebecca Solnit argues in this selection, nothing could be further from the truth. She once wrote that she "was a battered little kid" who "grew up in a really violent house where everything feminine and female . . . was hated."[1] It may be no surprise, then, that she feels that even in America there's a continuing "pandemic of violence by men against women." Since the 1980s, Solnit (b. 1961) has worked for human rights and environmental causes; an independent writer, historian, and activist, she has received two NEA fellowships in literature, a Guggenheim Fellowship, and a Lannan literary award for nonfiction. She is the author of seventeen books, among them *River of Shadows: Eadweard Muybridge and the Technological Wild West* (2004), which links the biography of Muybridge (who first photographed high-speed motion in the late nineteenth century) to the rise of Hollywood and Silicon Valley. The book won multiple awards, including the National Book Critics Circle Award for criticism. In 2008 she was invited to Iceland to be the first international writer in residence at the Library of Water. Solnit's *The Faraway Nearby* (2013) was nominated for a National Book Award and deals with — among other things — storytelling and the loss of her mother to Alzheimer's disease. "The Longest War" appeared in her 2014 collection of feminist essays, *Men Explain Things to Me*.

HERE IN THE UNITED STATES, where there is a reported rape every 6.2 minutes, and one in five women will be raped in her lifetime, the rape and gruesome murder of a young woman on a bus in New Delhi on December 16, 2012, was treated as an exceptional incident. The story of the sexual assault of an unconscious teenager by members of the Steubenville High School football team in Ohio was still unfolding, and gang rapes aren't that unusual here either. Take your pick: some of the twenty men who gang-raped an eleven-year-old in Cleveland, Texas, were sentenced shortly beforehand, while the instigator of the gang rape of a sixteen-year-old in Richmond, California, was sentenced in that fall of 2012 too, and four men who gang-raped a fifteen-year-

---

[1]Caitlin Donohue. "Why Can't I Be You: Rebecca Solnit." Rookiemag.com. 4 September 2014. [All notes are the editors', except 5.]

old near New Orleans were sentenced that April, though the six men who gang-raped a fourteen-year-old in Chicago that year were still at large. Not that I went out looking for incidents: they're everywhere in the news, though no one adds them up and indicates that there might actually be a pattern.

There is, however, a pattern of violence against women that's broad and deep and horrific and incessantly overlooked. Occasionally, a case involving a celebrity or lurid details in a particular case get a lot of attention in the media, but such cases are treated as anomalies, while the abundance of incidental news items about violence against women in this country, in other countries, on every continent including Antarctica, constitute a kind of background wallpaper for the news.

If you'd rather talk about bus rapes than gang rapes, there was the rape of a developmentally disabled woman on a Los Angeles bus that November and the kidnapping of an autistic sixteen-year-old on the regional transit train system in Oakland, California—she was raped repeatedly by her abductor over two days this winter—and a gang rape of multiple women on a bus in Mexico City recently, too. While I was writing this, I read that another female bus rider was kidnapped in India and gang-raped all night by the bus driver and five of his friends who must have thought what happened in New Delhi was awesome.

We have an abundance of rape and violence against women in this country and on this Earth, though it's almost never treated as a civil rights or human rights issue, or a crisis, or even a pattern. Violence doesn't have a race, a class, a religion, or a nationality, but it does have a gender.

Here I want to say one thing: though virtually all the perpetrators of such crimes are men, that doesn't mean all men are violent. Most are not. In addition, men obviously also suffer violence, largely at the hands of other men, and every violent death, every assault is terrible. Women can and do engage in intimate partner violence, but recent studies state that these acts don't often result in significant injury, let alone death; on the other hand, men murdered by their partners are often killed in self-defense, and intimate violence sends a lot of women to the hospital and the grave. But the subject here is the pandemic of violence by men against women, both intimate violence and stranger violence.

What We Don't Talk About When We Don't Talk About Gender

There's so much of it. We could talk about the assault and rape of a seventy-three-year-old in Manhattan's Central Park in September 2012, or the recent rape of a four-year-old and an eighty-three-year-old in Louisiana, or the New York City policeman who was arrested in October of 2012 for what appeared to be serious plans to kidnap, rape, cook, and eat a woman, any woman, because the hate wasn't personal (although maybe it was for the San Diego man who actually killed and cooked his wife in November and the man from New Orleans who killed, dismembered, and cooked his girlfriend in 2005).

Those are all exceptional crimes, but we could also talk about quotidian assaults, because though a rape is reported only every 6.2 minutes in this country, the estimated total is perhaps five times as high. Which means that there may be very nearly a rape a minute in the United States. It all adds up to tens of millions of rape victims. A significant portion of the women you know are survivors.

We could talk about high-school- and college-athlete rapes, or campus rapes, to which university authorities have been appallingly uninterested in responding in many cases, including that high school in Steubenville, Notre Dame University, Amherst College, and many others. We could talk about the escalating pandemic of rape, sexual assault, and sexual harassment in the U.S. military, where Secretary of Defense Leon Panetta estimated that there were nineteen thousand sexual assaults on fellow soldiers in 2010 alone and that the great majority of assailants got away with it, though four-star general Jeffrey Sinclair was indicted in September for "a slew of sex crimes against women."

Never mind workplace violence, let's go home. So many men murder their partners and former partners that we have well over a thousand homicides of that kind a year—meaning that every three years the death toll tops 9/11's casualties, though no one declares a war on this particular kind of terror. (Another way to put it: the more than 11,766 corpses from domestic-violence homicides between 9/11 and 2012 exceed the number of deaths of victims on that day *and* all American soldiers killed in the "war on terror.") If we talked about crimes like these and why they are so common, we'd have to talk about what kinds of profound change this society, or this nation, or nearly every nation needs. If we talked about it, we'd be talking about masculinity, or male roles, or maybe patriarchy, and we don't talk much about that.

Instead, we hear that American men commit murder-suicides—at the rate of about twelve a week—because the economy is bad, though they also do it when the economy is good; or that those men in India murdered the bus rider because the poor resent the rich, while other rapes in India are explained by how the rich exploit the poor; and then there are those ever-popular explanations: mental problems and intoxicants—and for jocks, head injuries. The latest spin is that lead exposure was responsible for a lot of our violence, except that both genders are exposed and one commits most of the violence. The pandemic of violence always gets explained as anything but gender, anything but what would seem to be the broadest explanatory pattern of all.

Someone wrote a piece about how white men seem to be the ones who commit mass murders in the United States and the (mostly hostile) commenters only seemed to notice the white part. It's rare that anyone says what this medical study does, even if in the driest way possible: "Being male has been identified as a risk factor for violent criminal behavior in several studies, as have exposure to tobacco smoke before birth, having antisocial parents, and belonging to a poor family."

It's not that I want to pick on men. I just think that if we noticed that women are, on the whole, radically less violent, we might be able to theorize where violence comes from and what we can do about it a lot more productively. Clearly the ready availability of guns is a huge problem for the United States, but despite this availability to everyone, murder is still a crime committed by men 90 percent of the time.

The pattern is plain as day. We could talk about this as a global problem, looking at the epidemic of assault, harassment, and rape of women in Cairo's Tahrir Square that has taken away the freedom they celebrated during the Arab Spring—and led some men there to form defense teams to help counter it—or the persecution of women in public and private in India from "Eve-teasing" to bride-burning, or "honor killings"[2] in South Asia and the Middle East, or the way that South Africa has become a global rape capital, with an estimated six hundred thousand rapes last year, or how rape has been used as a tactic and "weapon" of war in Mali, Sudan, and the Congo, as it was in the former Yugoslavia, or the pervasiveness of rape and harassment in Mexico and the femicide in Juarez,[3] or the denial of basic rights for women in Saudi Arabia and the myriad sexual assaults on immigrant domestic workers there, or the way that the Dominique Strauss-Kahn case in the United States revealed what impunity he and others had in France, and it's only for lack of space I'm leaving out Britain and Canada and Italy (with its ex-prime minister known for his orgies with the underaged),[4] Argentina and Australia and so many other countries.

Who Has the Right to Kill You?

But maybe you're tired of statistics, so let's just talk about a single incident that happened in my city while I was researching this essay in January 2013, one of many local incidents that made the local papers that month in which men assaulted women:

> A woman was stabbed after she rebuffed a man's sexual advances while she walked in San Francisco's Tenderloin neighborhood late Monday night, a police spokesman said today. The 33-year-old victim was walking down the street when a stranger approached her and propositioned her, police spokesman Officer Albie Esparza said. When

---

[2]**Eve-teasing:** street harassment of women; **bride-burning:** burning a woman alive when her family refuses to pay more for her dowry; **honor killing:** the murder of a woman by a family member for bringing "dishonor" to the family by refusing an arranged marriage, being raped, being in a relationship that the family disapproves of, or dressing "inappropriately." [Eds.]

[3]**femicide in Juarez:** In Juarez, Mexico, the disappearance and murders of women became an international sensation in the 1990s. [Eds.]

[4]**ex–prime minister . . . underaged:** Refers to Silvio Berlusconi, the seventy-six-year-old politician who was accused of paying for sex with underaged girls. [Eds.]

she rejected him, the man became very upset and slashed the victim in the face and stabbed her in the arm, Esparza said.[5]

The man, in other words, framed the situation as one in which his chosen victim had no rights and liberties, while he had the right to control and punish her. This should remind us that violence is first of all authoritarian. It begins with this premise: I have the right to control you.

Murder is the extreme version of that authoritarianism, where the murderer asserts he has the right to decide whether you live or die, the ultimate means of controlling someone. This may be true even if you are obedient, because the desire to control comes out of a rage that obedience can't assuage. Whatever fears, whatever sense of vulnerability may underlie such behavior, it also comes out of entitlement, the entitlement to inflict suffering and even death on other people. It breeds misery in the perpetrator and the victims.

As for that incident in my city, similar things happen all the time. Many versions of it happened to me when I was younger, sometimes involving death threats and often involving torrents of obscenities: a man approaches a woman with both desire and the furious expectation that the desire will likely be rebuffed. The fury and desire come in a package, all twisted together into something that always threatens to turn *eros* into *thanatos,* love into death, sometimes literally.

It's a system of control. It's why so many intimate-partner murders are of women who dared to break up with those partners. As a result, it imprisons a lot of women, and though you could say that the Tenderloin attacker on January 7, or a brutal would-be rapist near my own neighborhood on January 5, or another rapist here on January 12, or the San Franciscan who on January 6 set his girlfriend on fire for refusing to do his laundry, or the guy who was just sentenced to 370 years for some particularly violent rapes in San Francisco in late 2011, were marginal characters, rich, famous, and privileged guys do it, too.

The Japanese vice-consul in San Francisco was charged with twelve felony counts of spousal abuse and assault with a deadly weapon in September 2012, the same month that, in the same town, the ex-girlfriend of Mason Mayer (brother of Yahoo CEO Marissa Mayer) testified in court: "He ripped out my earrings, tore my eyelashes off, while spitting in my face and telling me how unlovable I am . . . I was on the ground in the fetal position, and when I tried to move, he squeezed both knees tighter into my sides to restrain me and slapped me." According to *San Francisco Chronicle* reporter Vivian Ho, she also testified that "Mayer slammed her head onto the floor repeatedly and pulled out clumps of her hair, telling her that the only way she was leaving the apartment alive was if he drove her to the Golden Gate Bridge 'where you can jump off or I will push you off.'" Mason Mayer got probation.

The summer before, an estranged husband violated his wife's restraining order against him, shooting her—and killing or wounding

---

[5] "Woman Stabbed Walking Down Tenderloin Street," KTVU, January 2013.

six other women—at her workplace in suburban Milwaukee, but since there were only four corpses the crime was largely overlooked in the media in a year with so many more spectacular mass murders in this country (and we still haven't really talked about the fact that, of sixty-two mass shootings in the United States in three decades, only one was by a woman, because when you say *lone gunman,* everyone talks about loners and guns but not about men—and by the way, nearly two-thirds of all women killed by guns are killed by their partner or ex-partner).

What's love got to do with it, asked Tina Turner, whose ex-husband Ike once said, "Yeah I hit her, but I didn't hit her more than the average guy beats his wife." A woman is beaten every nine seconds in this country. Just to be clear: not nine minutes, but nine seconds. It's the number-one cause of injury to American women; of the two million injured annually, more than half a million of those injuries require medical attention while about 145,000 require overnight hospitalizations, according to the Centers for Disease Control, and you don't want to know about the dentistry needed afterwards. Spouses are also the leading cause of death for pregnant women in the United States.

"Women worldwide ages 15 through 44 are more likely to die or be maimed because of male violence than because of cancer, malaria, war and traffic accidents combined," writes Nicholas D. Kristof, one of the few prominent figures to address the issue regularly.

The Chasm Between Our Worlds

Rape and other acts of violence, up to and including murder, as well as threats of violence, constitute the barrage some men lay down as they attempt to control some women, and fear of that violence limits most women in ways they've gotten so used to they hardly notice—and we hardly address. There are exceptions: last summer someone wrote to me to describe a college class in which the students were asked what they do to stay safe from rape. The young women described the intricate ways they stayed alert, limited their access to the world, took precautions, and essentially thought about rape all the time (while the young men in the class, he added, gaped in astonishment). The chasm between their worlds had briefly and suddenly become visible.

Mostly, however, we don't talk about it—though a graphic has been circulating on the Internet called *Ten Top Tips to End Rape,* the kind of thing young women get often enough, but this one had a subversive twist. It offered advice like this: "Carry a whistle! If you are worried you might assault someone 'by accident' you can hand it to the person you are with, so they can call for help." While funny, the piece points out something terrible: the usual guidelines in such situations put the full burden of prevention on potential victims, treating the violence as a given. There's no good reason (and many bad reasons) colleges spend more time telling women how to survive predators than telling the other half of their students not to be predators.

Threats of sexual assault now seem to take place online regularly. 25 In late 2011, British columnist Laurie Penny wrote,

> An opinion, it seems, is the short skirt of the Internet. Having one and flaunting it is somehow asking an amorphous mass of almost-entirely male keyboard-bashers to tell you how they'd like to rape, kill, and urinate on you. This week, after a particularly ugly slew of threats, I decided to make just a few of those messages public on Twitter, and the response I received was overwhelming. Many could not believe the hate I received, and many more began to share their own stories of harassment, intimidation, and abuse.

Women in the online gaming community have been harassed, threatened, and driven out. Anita Sarkeesian, a feminist media critic who documented such incidents, received support for her work, but also, in the words of a journalist, "another wave of really aggressive, you know, violent personal threats, her accounts attempted to be hacked. And one man in Ontario took the step of making an online video game where you could punch Anita's image on the screen. And if you punched it multiple times, bruises and cuts would appear on her image." The difference between these online gamers and the Taliban men who, last October, tried to murder fourteen-year-old Malala Yousafzai for speaking out about the right of Pakistani women to education is one of degree. Both are trying to silence and punish women for claiming voice, power, and the right to participate. Welcome to Manistan.

The Party for the Protection of the Rights of Rapists

It's not just public, or private, or online either. It's also embedded in our political system, and our legal system, which before feminists fought for us didn't recognize most domestic violence, or sexual harassment and stalking, or date rape, or acquaintance rape, or marital rape, and in cases of rape still often tries the victim rather than the rapist, as though only perfect maidens could be assaulted — or believed.

As we learned in the 2012 election campaign, it's also embedded in the minds and mouths of our politicians. Remember that spate of crazy pro-rape things Republican men said last summer and fall, starting with Todd Akin's notorious claim that a woman has ways of preventing pregnancy in cases of rape, a statement he made in order to deny women control over their own bodies (in the form of access to abortion after rape). After that, of course, Senate candidate Richard Mourdock claimed that rape pregnancies were "a gift from God," and soon after another Republican politician piped up to defend Akin's comment.

Happily the five publicly pro-rape Republicans in the 2012 campaign all lost their election bids. (Stephen Colbert tried to warn them that women had gotten the vote in 1920.) But it's not just a matter of the garbage they say (and the price they now pay). Congressional Republicans refused to reauthorize the Violence Against Women Act because they objected to the protection it gave immigrants, transgender women, and Native American women. (Speaking of epidemics, one of three Native American women will be raped, and on the reservations 88 percent of those rapes are by non-Native men who know tribal governments can't prosecute them. So much for rape as a crime of passion—these are crimes of calculation and opportunism.)

And they're out to gut reproductive rights—birth control as well as abortion, as they've pretty effectively done in many states over the last dozen years. What's meant by "reproductive rights," of course, is the right of women to control their own bodies. Didn't I mention earlier that violence against women is a control issue?

And though rapes are often investigated lackadaisically—there is a backlog of about four hundred thousand untested rape kits in this country—rapists who impregnate their victims have parental rights in thirty-one states. Oh, and former vice-presidential candidate and current congressman Paul Ryan (R-Manistan) is reintroducing a bill that would give states the right to ban abortions and might even conceivably allow a rapist to sue his victim for having one.

All the Things That Aren't to Blame

Of course, women are capable of all sorts of major unpleasantness, and there are violent crimes by women, but the so-called war of the sexes is extraordinarily lopsided when it comes to actual violence. Unlike the last (male) head of the International Monetary Fund, the current (female) head is not going to assault an employee at a luxury hotel; top-ranking female officers in the U.S. military, unlike their male counterparts, are not accused of any sexual assaults; and young female athletes, unlike those male football players in Steubenville, aren't likely to urinate on unconscious boys, let alone violate them and boast about it in YouTube videos and Twitter feeds.

No female bus riders in India have ganged up to sexually assault a man so badly he dies of his injuries, nor are marauding packs of women terrorizing men in Cairo's Tahrir Square, and there's just no maternal equivalent to the 11 percent of rapes that are by fathers or stepfathers. Of the people in prison in the United States, 93.5 percent are not women, and though quite a lot of the prisoners should not be there in the first place, maybe some of them should because of violence, until we think of a better way to deal with it, and them.

No major female pop star has blown the head off a young man she took home with her, as did Phil Spector. (He is now part of that 93.5 percent for the shotgun slaying of Lana Clarkson, apparently for refusing his advances.) No female action-movie star has been charged with domestic violence, because Angelina Jolie just isn't doing what Mel

Gibson and Steve McQueen did, and there aren't any celebrated female movie directors who gave a thirteen-year-old drugs before sexually assaulting that child, while she kept saying "no," as did Roman Polanski.

In Memory of Jyoti Singh

What's the matter with manhood? There's something about how masculinity is imagined, about what's praised and encouraged, about the way violence is passed on to boys that needs to be addressed. There are lovely and wonderful men out there, and one of the things that's encouraging in this round of the war against women is how many men I've seen who get it, who think it's their issue too, who stand up for us and with us in everyday life, online and in the marches from New Delhi to San Francisco this winter.

Increasingly men are becoming good allies—and there always have been some. Kindness and gentleness never had a gender, and neither did empathy. Domestic violence statistics are down significantly from earlier decades (even though they're still shockingly high), and a lot of men are at work crafting new ideas and ideals about masculinity and power.

Gay men have redefined and occasionally undermined conventional masculinity—publicly, for many decades—and often been great allies for women. Women's liberation has often been portrayed as a movement intent on encroaching upon or taking power and privilege away from men, as though in some dismal zero-sum game, only one gender at a time could be free and powerful. But we are free together or slaves together. Surely the mindset of those who think they need to win, to dominate, to punish, to reign supreme must be terrible and far from free, and giving up this unachievable pursuit would be liberatory.

There are other things I'd rather write about, but this affects everything else. The lives of half of humanity are still dogged by, drained by, and sometimes ended by this pervasive variety of violence. Think of how much more time and energy we would have to focus on other things that matter if we weren't so busy surviving. Look at it this way: one of the best journalists I know is afraid to walk home at night in our neighborhood. Should she stop working late? How many women have had to stop doing their work, or been stopped from doing it, for similar reasons? It's clear now that monumental harassment online keeps many women from speaking up and writing altogether.

One of the most exciting new political movements on Earth is the Native Canadian indigenous rights movement, with feminist and environmental overtones, called Idle No More. On December 27, shortly after the movement took off, a Native woman was kidnapped, raped, beaten, and left for dead in Thunder Bay, Ontario, by men whose remarks framed the crime as retaliation against Idle No More. Afterward, she walked four hours through the bitter cold and survived to tell her tale. Her assailants, who have threatened to do it again, are still at large.

The New Delhi rape and murder of Jyoti Singh, the twenty-three-year-old who was studying physiotherapy so that she could better herself while helping others, and the assault on her male companion (who survived) seem to have triggered the reaction that we have needed for one hundred, or one thousand, or five thousand years. May she be to women—and men—worldwide what Emmett Till,[6] murdered by white supremacists in 1955, was to African Americans and the then-nascent U.S. civil rights movement.

We have far more than eighty-seven thousand rapes in this country every year, but each of them is invariably portrayed as an isolated incident. We have dots so close they're splatters melting into a stain, but hardly anyone connects them, or names that stain. In India they did. They said that this is a civil rights issue, it's a human rights issue, it's everyone's problem, it's not isolated, and it's never going to be acceptable again. It has to change. It's your job to change it, and mine, and ours.

Sources

"Is Delhi So Different from Steubenville?," New York Times, op ed, January 13, 2013, p. SR1.

"Online Harassment Gets Real for Online Gamers." Boston: WBUR.

Wright, J. P., Dietrich, K. N., Ris, M. D., Hornung, R. W., Wessel, S. D., Lanphear, B. P. et al. (2008). "Association of Prenatal and Childhood Blood Lead Concentrations with Criminal Arrests in Early Adulthood," PLoS Med 5(5): e101. doi:10.1371/journal.pmed.0050101.

ENGAGING THE TEXT

1. What is the significance of Solnit's title, "The Longest War"? In what ways does she view violence against women as a war?

2. Solnit writes that gendered violence is "almost never treated as a civil rights or human rights issue, or a crisis, or even a pattern" (para. 4). How would violence against women be treated differently if it were considered a matter of civil or human rights? How would news or political coverage differ if it were considered a crisis? Do you agree with Solnit's assessment that violence against women follows a pattern? Why or why not?

3. Solnit contends that violence against women is "a system of control" (para. 18). How does she support this claim? Which aspects of her argument do you find most and least compelling, and why?

4. Solnit ends the essay with these words: "It has to change. It's your job to change it, and mine, and ours" (para. 41). Explain why you think her conclusion is or is not justified. What might you do to "change it"?

---

[6]**Emmett Till:** The 1955 murder of 14-year-old Emmett Till by two white men in Mississippi galvanized the civil rights movement.

5. **Thinking Rhetorically** Solnit deploys shocking statistics and horrifying stories of crimes against women to bolster her argument. Do you think she overstates her case? Do Solnit's periodic concessions to men — acknowledging that most men aren't violent (para. 5) and that many men "get it" (para. 35) — make her claims less alienating for men? Who is her intended audience in this essay?

EXPLORING CONNECTIONS

6. According to Solnit, "There's something about how masculinity is imagined, about what's praised and encouraged, about the way violence is passed on to boys that needs to be addressed" (para. 35). Write or role-play a panel discussion among Solnit, Jean Kilbourne (p. 488), Joan Morgan (p. 533), and Michael Kimmel (p. 540) in which they discuss how masculinity is imagined and how it's conveyed to boys. How should we imagine, model, or teach it differently?

7. Read or review Laurie Penny's article, "Cybersexism" (p. 253), which discusses online misogyny and violence. To what extent does Solnit agree with Penny about the causes and possible solutions to gendered violence?

8. Examine the images of Anita Sarkeesian on page 285. How do these pictures support or undercut Solnit's contention that the difference between the online gamers and the Taliban is merely "one of degree" (para. 26)?

EXTENDING THE CRITICAL CONTEXT

9. Solnit describes a "college class in which the students were asked what they do to stay safe from rape" (para. 23). Working in single-sex groups, take a few minutes to list the strategies you use to avoid sexual assault. Then compare your lists to those of other groups. If there are noticeable differences between the men's and the women's lists, how do you explain them?

10. Watch *The Hunting Ground*, a 2015 documentary that deals with campus rape and colleges' reluctance to address the issue. Then write an essay in which you evaluate the case that the film makes.

FROM FLY-GIRLS TO BITCHES AND HOS

JOAN MORGAN

As a music writer and fan of hip-hop, Joan Morgan loves the power of rap. As a feminist, she is troubled by the pervasive sexism of its lyrics. The misogyny of rap, she argues, is a symptom of crisis in the black community; it must be confronted and understood, not simply condemned, as a step toward healing the pain that it both expresses and inflicts. This passage comes from her collection of essays, *When Chickenheads Come Home to Roost: A Hip-Hop Feminist Breaks It Down* (1999). Formerly the executive editor of *Essence*, she has also written for the *Village Voice*, *Vibe*, *Ms.*, and *Spin*. She has taught at The New School, Duke University, Vanderbilt University, and Stanford University.

> *Feminist criticism, like many other forms of social analysis, is widely considered part of a hostile white culture. For a black feminist to chastise misogyny in rap publicly would be viewed as divisive and counterproductive. There is a widespread perception in the black community that public criticism of black men constitutes collaborating with a racist society....*
>
> —MICHELE WALLACE, "When Black Feminism Faces the Music, and the Music Is Rap," The *New York Times*[1]

[1]Michele Wallace, "When Black Feminism Faces the Music, and the Music Is Rap," the *New York Times*, July 29, 1990. [All notes are Morgan's.]

LORD KNOWS OUR LOVE JONES for hip-hop is understandable. Props given to rap music's artistic merits, its irrefutable impact on pop culture, its ability to be alternately beautiful, poignant, powerful, strong, irreverent, visceral, and mesmerizing—homeboy's clearly got it like that. But in between the beats, booty shaking, and hedonistic abandon, I have to wonder if there isn't something inherently unfeminist in supporting a music that repeatedly reduces me to tits and ass and encourages pimping on the regular. While it's human to occasionally fall deep into the love thang with people or situations that simply aren't good for you, feminism alerted me long ago to the dangers of romancing a misogynist (and ridiculously fine, brilliant ones with gangsta leans are no exception). Perhaps the nonbelievers were right, maybe what I'd been mistaking for love and commitment for the last twenty years was really nothing but a self-destructive obsession that made a mockery of my feminism....

I guess it all depends on how you define the f-word. My feminism places the welfare of black women and the black community on its list of priorities. It also maintains that black-on-black love is essential to the survival of both.

We have come to a point in our history, however, when black-on-black love—a love that's survived slavery, lynching, segregation, poverty, and racism—is in serious danger. The stats usher in this reality like taps before the death march: According to the U.S. Census Bureau, the number of black two-parent households has decreased from 74 percent to 48 percent since 1960. The leading cause of death among black men ages fifteen to twenty-four is homicide. The majority of them will die at the hands of other black men.[2]

Women are the unsung victims of black-on-black crime. A while back, a friend of mine, a single mother of a newborn (her "babyfather"—a brother—abdicated responsibility before their child was born) was attacked by a pit bull while walking her dog in the park. The owner (a brother) trained the animal to prey on other dogs and the flesh of his fellow community members.

A few weeks later my mom called, upset, to tell me about the murder of a family friend. She was a troubled young woman with a history of substance abuse, aggravated by her son's murder two years ago. She was found beaten and burned beyond recognition. Her murderers were not "skinheads," "The Man," or "the racist white power structure." More likely than not, they were brown men whose faces resembled her own.

Clearly, we are having a very difficult time loving one another.

Any feminism that fails to acknowledge that black folks in nineties America are living and trying to love in a war zone is useless to our struggle against sexism. Though it's often portrayed as part of the problem, rap music is essential to that struggle because it takes us straight to the battlefield.

[2]Joan Morgan, "Real Love," *Vibe*, April 1996, p. 38.

My decision to expose myself to the sexism of Dr. Dre, Ice Cube, Snoop Dogg, or the Notorious B.I.G. is really my plea to my brothers to tell me who they are. I need to know why they are so angry at me. Why is disrespecting me one of the few things that make them feel like men? What's the haps, what are you going through on the daily that's got you acting so foul?

As a black woman and a feminist I listen to the music with a willingness to see past the machismo in order to be clear about what I'm *really* dealing with. What I hear frightens me. On booming track after booming track, I hear brothers talking about spending each day high as hell on malt liquor and Chronic. Don't sleep. What passes for "40 and a blunt" good times in most of hip-hop is really alcoholism, substance abuse, and chemical dependency. When brothers can talk so cavalierly about killing each other and then reveal that they have no expectation to see their twenty-first birthday, that is straight-up depression *masquerading* as machismo.

Anyone curious about the processes and pathologies that form the psyche of the young, black, and criminal-minded needs to revisit our dearly departed Notorious B.I.G.'s first album, *Ready to Die*. Chronicling the life and times of the urban "soldier," the album is a blues-laden soul train that took us on a hustler's life journey. We boarded with the story of his birth, strategically stopped to view his dysfunctional, warring family, his first robbery, his first stint in jail, murder, drug-dealing, getting paid, partying, sexin', rap-pin', mayhem, and death. Biggie's player persona might have momentarily convinced the listener that he was livin' phat without a care in the world but other moments divulged his inner hell. The chorus of "Everyday Struggle": *I don't wanna live no more / Sometimes I see death knockin' at my front door* revealed that "Big Poppa" was also plagued with guilt, regret, and depression. The album ultimately ended with his suicide.

The seemingly impenetrable wall of sexism in rap music is really the complex mask African Americans often wear both to hide and express the pain. At the close of this millennium, hip-hop is still one of the few forums in which young black men, even surreptitiously, are allowed to express their pain.

When it comes to the struggle against sexism and our intimate relationships with black men, some of the most on-point feminist advice I've received comes from sistas like my mother, who wouldn't dream of using the term. During our battle to resolve our complicated relationships with my equally wonderful and errant father, my mother presented me with the following gem of wisdom, "One of the most important lessons you will ever learn in life and love, is that you've got to love people for what they are—not for who you would like them to be."

This is crystal clear to me when I'm listening to hip-hop. Yeah, sistas are hurt when we hear brothers calling us bitches and hos. But the real crime isn't the name-calling, it's their failure to love us—to be our brothers in the way that we commit ourselves to being their sistas. But recognize: Any man who doesn't truly love himself is incapable of loving us in the healthy way we need to be loved. It's extremely telling that men who can only see us as "bitches" and "hos" refer to themselves only as "niggas."

In the interest of our emotional health and overall sanity, black women have got to learn to love brothers realistically, and that means differentiating between who they are and who we'd like them to be. Black men are engaged in a war where the real enemies—racism and the white power structure—are masters of camouflage. They've conditioned our men to believe the enemy is brown. The effects of this have been as wicked as they've been debilitating. Being in battle with an enemy that looks just like you makes it hard to believe in the basics every human being needs. For too many black men there is no trust, no community, no family. Just self.

Since hip-hop is the mirror in which so many brothers see themselves, it's significant that one of the music's most prevalent mythologies is that black boys rarely grow into men. Instead, they remain perpetually postadolescent or die. For all the machismo and testosterone in the music, it's frighteningly clear that many brothers see themselves as powerless when it comes to facing the evils of the larger society, accepting responsibility for their lives, or the lives of their children.

So, sista friends, we gotta do what any rational, survivalist-minded person would do after finding herself in a relationship with someone whose pain makes him abusive. We've gotta continue to give up the love but *from a distance that's safe*. Emotional distance is a great enabler of unconditional love and support because it allows us to recognize that the attack, the "bitch, ho" bullshit—isn't personal but part of the illness.

And the focus of black feminists has got to change. We can't afford to keep expending energy on banal discussions of sexism in rap when sexism is only part of a huge set of problems. Continuing on our previous path is akin to demanding that a fiending, broke crackhead not rob you blind because it's *wrong* to do so.

If feminism intends to have any relevance in the lives of the majority of black women, if it intends to move past theory and become functional it has to rescue itself from the ivory towers of academia. Like it or not, hip-hop is not only the dominion of the young, black, and male, it is also the world in which young black women live and survive. A functional game plan for us, one that is going to be as helpful to Shequanna on 142nd as it is to Samantha at Sarah Lawrence, has to recognize hip-hop's ability to articulate the pain our *community* is in and use that knowledge to create a redemptive, healing space.

Notice the emphasis on "community." Hip-hop isn't only instrumental in exposing black men's pain, it brings the healing sistas need right to the surface. Sad as it may be, it's time to stop ignoring the fact that rappers meet "bitches" and "hos" daily—women who reaffirm their depiction of us on vinyl. Backstage, the road, and the 'hood are populated with women who would do anything to be with a rapper sexually for an hour if not a night. It's time to stop fronting like we don't know who rapper Jeru the Damaja was talking about when he said:

> Now a queen's a queen but a stunt's a stunt
> You can tell who's who by the things they want

Sex has long been the bartering chip that women use to gain protection, material wealth, and the vicarious benefits of power. In the black community, where women are given less access to all of the above, "trickin'" becomes a means of leveling the playing field. Denying the justifiable anger of rappers—men who couldn't get the time of day from these women before a few dollars and a record deal—isn't empowering and strategic. Turning a blind eye and scampering for moral high ground diverts our attention away from the young women who are being denied access to power and are suffering for it.

It might've been more convenient to direct our sistafied rage attention to "the sexist representation of women" in those now infamous Sir Mix-A-Lot videos, to fuss over *one* sexist rapper, but wouldn't it have been more productive to address the failing self-esteem of the 150 or so half-naked young women who were willing, unpaid participants? And what about how flip we are when it comes to using the b-word to describe each other? At some point we've all been the recipients of competitive, unsisterly, "bitchiness," particularly when vying for male attention.

Since being black and a woman makes me fluent in both isms, I sometimes use racism as an illuminating analogy. Black folks have finally gotten to the point where we recognize that we sometimes engage in oppressive behaviors that white folks have little to do with. Complexion prejudices and classism are illnesses which have their *roots* in white racism but the perpetrators are certainly black.

Similarly, sistas have to confront the ways we're complicit in our own oppression. Sad to say it, but many of the ways in which men exploit our images and sexuality in hip-hop is done with our permission and cooperation. We need to be as accountable to each other as we believe "race traitors" (i.e., one hundred or so brothers in blackface cooning in a skinhead's music video) should be to our community. To acknowledge this doesn't deny our victimization but it does raise the critical issue of whose responsibility it is to end our oppression. As a feminist, I believe it is too great a responsibility to leave to men.

A few years ago, on an airplane making its way to Montego Bay, I received another gem of girlfriend wisdom from a sixty-year-old self-declared nonfeminist. She was meeting her husband to celebrate her thirty-fifth wedding anniversary. After telling her I was twenty-seven and very much single, she looked at me and shook her head sadly. "I feel sorry for your generation. You don't know how to have relationships, especially the women." Curious, I asked her why she thought this was. "The women of your generation, you want to be right. The women of my generation, we didn't care about being right. We just wanted to win."

Too much of the discussion regarding sexism and the music focuses on being right. We feel we're *right* and the rappers are wrong. The rappers feel it's their *right* to describe their "reality" in any way they see fit. The store owners feel it's their *right* to sell whatever the consumer wants to buy. The consumer feels it's his *right* to be able to decide what he wants to listen to. We may be the "rightest" of the bunch but we sure as hell ain't doing the winning.

I believe hip-hop can help us win. Let's start by recognizing that its illuminating, informative narration and its incredible ability to articulate our collective pain is an invaluable tool when examining gender relations. The information we amass can help create a redemptive, healing space for brothers and sistas.

We're all winners when a space exists for brothers to honestly state and explore the roots of their pain and subsequently their misogyny, sans judgment. It is criminal that the only space our society provided for the late Tupac Shakur to examine the pain, confusion, drug addiction, and fear that led to his arrest and his eventual assassination was in a prison cell. How can we win if a prison cell is the only space an immensely talented but troubled young black man could dare utter these words: "Even though I'm not guilty of the charges they gave me, I'm not innocent in terms of the way I was acting. I'm just as guilty for not doing things. Not with this case but with my life. I had a job to do and I never showed up. I was so scared of this responsibility that I was running away from it."[3] We have to do better than this for our men.

And we have to do better for ourselves. We desperately need a space to lovingly address the uncomfortable issues of our failing self-esteem, the ways we sexualize and objectify ourselves, our confusion about sex and love and the unhealthy, unloving, unsisterly ways we treat each other. Commitment to developing these spaces gives our community the potential for remedies based on honest, clear diagnoses.

As I'm a black woman, I am aware that this doubles my workload—that I am definitely going to have to listen to a lot of shit I won't like—but without these candid discussions, there is little to no hope of exorcising the illness that hurts and sometimes kills us.

ENGAGING THE TEXT

1. What qualities of hip-hop music and rap artists does Morgan admire or appreciate? What fears does she have for rap's female fans and for the artists themselves? To what extent do you agree with Morgan's assessment of the misogyny, anger, and despair expressed by hip-hop?

[3]Kevin Powell, "The Vibe Q: Tupac Shakur, Ready to Live," *Vibe*, April 11, 1995, p. 52.

2. What evidence does Morgan offer that "black folks in nineties America are living and trying to love in a war zone" (para. 7)? How does she explain the causes of the violence she describes? How persuasive do you find her analysis, and why?

3. How do you interpret Morgan's call for establishing "a redemptive, healing space" (para. 18) for confronting the pain expressed by hip-hop? What kind of "space" is she talking about, and how would you go about establishing it?

4. While Morgan asserts that we need to examine the lives of rappers like Notorious B.I.G. to understand the roots of their misogyny, critics might counter that she is simply making excuses for intolerable attitudes. Write an essay explaining why you agree or disagree with Morgan's argument.

5. **Thinking Rhetorically** What audience is Morgan addressing and what persuasive strategies — of both argument and style — does she use to appeal to that audience? What do you find effective or ineffective about her approach?

EXPLORING CONNECTIONS

6. Compare Jean Kilbourne's analysis of sexism and violence in advertising (p. 488) to Morgan's discussion of the same themes in rap. What are the causes and consequences of "pornographic" depictions of women in popular culture according to each writer? Do you think Kilbourne would concur with Morgan about how we should respond to these images? Why or why not?

7. See "'Bros Before Hos': The Guy Code" (p. 540) and compare the features of Michael Kimmel's "Guy Code" to the images of masculinity portrayed by hip-hop artists.

EXTENDING THE CRITICAL CONTEXT

8. Survey the current issues of several magazines aimed at fans of rap music. What images do they present of women, men, and human relationships? How often do they reflect the themes that Morgan discusses? What other themes and patterns do you find? To what extent, if any, have the subjects and attitudes of hip-hop artists changed since the 1990s?

9. Examine the lyrics of several female rappers and compare them to those of the male rappers Morgan mentions. What similarities and differences do you find in the subjects they address and the feelings they express? If you're not a fan of rap, you may want to consult an online hip-hop dictionary for help in decoding some of the language (www.rapdict.org).

"BROS BEFORE HOS": THE GUY CODE

MICHAEL KIMMEL

According to sociologist Michael Kimmel, "guys"—young men, ages sixteen to twenty-six—represent a distinct social group. In *Guyland: The Perilous World Where Boys Become Men* (2008), he investigates the values, rites, and preoccupations of these young men. This selection from the book details the code of masculinity that guys are expected to follow. Kimmel (b. 1951) has written or edited more than a dozen books on men and masculinity as well as editing the journal *Men and Masculinities*; he teaches at the State University of New York at Stony Brook. He is also a spokesperson for the National Organization for Men Against Sexism (NOMAS) and has served as an expert witness for the U.S. Department of Justice in two key sex discrimination cases against military academies that had excluded women. His most recent work is *Angry White Men* (2013).

WHENEVER I ASK YOUNG WOMEN what they think it means to be a woman, they look at me puzzled, and say, basically, "Whatever I want." "It doesn't mean anything at all to me," says Nicole, a junior at Colby College in Maine. "I can be Mia Hamm, I can be Britney Spears, I can be Madame Curie or Madonna. Nobody can tell me what it means to be a woman anymore."

For men, the question is still meaningful—and powerful. In countless workshops on college campuses and in high-school assemblies, I've asked young men what it means to be a man. I've asked guys from every state in the nation, as well as about fifteen other countries, what sorts of phrases and words come to mind when they hear someone say, "Be a man!"[1]

The responses are rather predictable. The first thing someone usually says is "Don't cry," then other similar phrases and ideas—never show your feelings, never ask for directions, never give up, never give in, be strong, be aggressive, show no fear, show no mercy, get rich, get even, get laid, win—follow easily after that.

Here's what guys say, summarized into a set of current epigrams. Think of it as a "Real Guy's Top Ten List."

1. "Boys Don't Cry"

2. "It's Better to Be Mad Than Sad"

3. "Don't Get Mad—Get Even"

---

[1]This workshop idea was developed by Paul Kivel of the Oakland Men's Project. I am grateful to Paul for demonstrating it to my classes. [All notes are Kimmel's.]

4. "Take It Like a Man"

5. "He Who Has the Most Toys When He Dies, Wins"

6. "Just Do It," or "Ride or Die"

7. "Size Matters"

8. "I Don't Stop to Ask for Directions"

9. "Nice Guys Finish Last"

10. "It's All Good"

The unifying emotional subtext of all these aphorisms involves never showing emotions or admitting to weakness. The face you must show to the world insists that everything is going just fine, that everything is under control, that there's nothing to be concerned about (a contemporary version of Alfred E. Neuman of *MAD* magazine's "What, me worry?"). Winning is crucial, especially when the victory is over other men who have less amazing or smaller toys. Kindness is not an option, nor is compassion. Those sentiments are taboo.

This is "The Guy Code," the collection of attitudes, values, and traits that together composes what it means to be a man. These are the rules that govern behavior in Guyland, the criteria that will be used to evaluate whether any particular guy measures up. The Guy Code revisits what psychologist William Pollack called "the boy code" in his bestselling book *Real Boys*[2]—just a couple of years older and with a lot more at stake. And just as Pollack and others have explored the dynamics of boyhood so well, we now need to extend the reach of that analysis to include late adolescence and young adulthood.

In 1976, social psychologist Robert Brannon summarized the four basic rules of masculinity:[3]

1. "No Sissy Stuff!" Being a man means not being a sissy, not being perceived as weak, effeminate, or gay. Masculinity is the relentless repudiation of the feminine.

2. "Be a Big Wheel." This rule refers to the centrality of success and power in the definition of masculinity. Masculinity is measured more by wealth, power, and status than by any particular body part.

3. "Be a Sturdy Oak." What makes a man is that he is reliable in a crisis. And what makes him so reliable in a crisis is not that he is able to respond fully and appropriately to the situation at hand, but rather that he resembles an inanimate object. A rock, a pillar, a species of tree.

---

[2]See William Pollack, *Real Boys: Rescuing Our Sons from the Myths of Boyhood* (New York: Henry Holt, 1998).

[3]See Robert Brannon and Deborah David, "Introduction" to *The Forty-Nine Per Cent Majority* (Reading, MA: Addison-Wesley, 1976).

4. "Give 'em Hell." Exude an aura of daring and aggression. Live life out on the edge. Take risks. Go for it. Pay no attention to what others think.

Amazingly, these four rules have changed very little among successive generations of high-school and college-age men. James O'Neil, a developmental psychologist at the University of Connecticut, and Joseph Pleck, a social psychologist at the University of Illinois, have each been conducting studies of this normative definition of masculinity for decades. "One of the most surprising findings," O'Neil told me, "is how little these rules have changed."

Being a Man Among Men

Where do young men get these ideas? "Oh, definitely, my dad," says Mike, a twenty-year-old sophomore at Wake Forest. "He was always riding my ass, telling me I had to be tough and strong to make it in this world."

"My older brothers were always on my case," says Drew, a twenty-four-year-old University of Massachusetts grad. "They were like, always ragging on me, calling me a pussy, if I didn't want to play football or wrestle. If I just wanted to hang out and like play my Xbox, they were constantly in my face."

"It was subtle, sometimes," says Warren, a twenty-one-year-old at Towson, "and other times really out front. In school, it was the male teachers, saying stuff about how explorers or scientists were so courageous and braving the elements and all that. Then, other times, it was phys-ed class, and everyone was all over everyone else talking about 'He's so gay' and 'He's a wuss.'"

"The first thing I think of is my coach," says Don, a twenty-six-year-old former football player at Lehigh. "Any fatigue, any weakness, any sign that being hit actually hurt and he was like 'Waah! [fake crying] Widdle Donny got a boo boo. Should we kiss it guys?' He'd completely humiliate us for showing anything but complete toughness. I'm sure he thought he was building up our strength and ability to play, but it wore me out trying to pretend all the time, to suck it up and just take it."

The response was consistent: Guys hear the voices of the men in their lives—fathers, coaches, brothers, grandfathers, uncles, priests—to inform their ideas of masculinity.

This is no longer surprising to me. One of the more startling things I found when I researched the history of the idea of masculinity in America for a previous book was that men subscribe to these ideals not because they want to impress women, let alone any inner drive or desire to test themselves against some abstract standards. They do it because they want to be positively evaluated by other men. American men want to be a "man among men," an Arnold Schwarzenegger-like "man's man," not a Fabio-like "ladies' man." Masculinity is largely a "homosocial" experience: performed for, and judged by, other men.

Noted playwright David Mamet explains why women don't even enter the mix. "Women have, in men's minds, such a low place on the social ladder of this country that it's useless to define yourself in terms of a woman. What men need is men's approval." While women often become a kind of currency by which men negotiate their status with other men, women are for possessing, not for emulating.

The Gender Police

Other guys constantly watch how well we perform. Our peers are a kind of "gender police," always waiting for us to screw up so they can give us a ticket for crossing the well-drawn boundaries of manhood. As young men, we become relentless cowboys, riding the fences, checking the boundary line between masculinity and femininity, making sure that nothing slips over. The possibilities of being unmasked are everywhere. Even the most seemingly insignificant misstep can pose a threat or activate that haunting terror that we will be found out.

On the day the students in my class "Sociology of Masculinity" were scheduled to discuss homophobia, one student provided an honest and revealing anecdote. Noting that it was a beautiful day, the first day of spring after a particularly brutal Northeast winter, he decided to wear shorts to class. "I had this really nice pair of new Madras shorts," he recounted. "But then I thought to myself, these shorts have lavender and pink in them. Today's class topic is homophobia. Maybe today is not the best day to wear these shorts." Nods all around.

Our efforts to maintain a manly front cover everything we do. What we wear. How we talk. How we walk. What we eat (like the recent flap over "manwiches"—those artery-clogging massive burgers, dripping with extras). Every mannerism, every movement contains a coded gender language. What happens if you refuse or resist? What happens if you step outside the definition of masculinity? Consider the words that would be used to describe you. In workshops it generally takes less than a minute to get a list of about twenty terms that are at the tip of everyone's tongues: wimp, faggot, dork, pussy, loser, wuss, nerd, queer, homo, girl, gay, skirt, Mama's boy, pussy-whipped. This list is so effortlessly generated, so consistent, that it composes a national well from which to draw epithets and put-downs.

Ask any teenager in America what is the most common put-down in middle school or high school? The answer: "That's so gay." It's said about anything and everything—their clothes, their books, the music or TV shows they like, the sports figures they admire. "That's so gay" has become a free-floating put-down, meaning bad, dumb, stupid, wrong. It's the generic bad thing.

Listen to one of America's most observant analysts of masculinity, Eminem. Asked in an MTV interview in 2001 why he constantly used "faggot" in every one of his raps to put down other guys, Eminem told the interviewer, Kurt Loder, [20]

> The lowest degrading thing you can say to a man when you're battling him is to call him a faggot and try to take away his manhood. Call him a sissy, call him a punk. "Faggot" to me doesn't necessarily mean gay people. "Faggot" to me just means taking away your manhood.[4]

[4]Richard Kim, "A Bad Rap?" in *The Nation*, March 5, 2001, p. 5.

But does it mean homosexuality? Does it really suggest that you suspect the object of the epithet might actually be attracted to another guy? Think, for example, of how you would answer this question: If you see a man walking down the street, or meet him at a party, how do you "know" if he is homosexual? (Assume that he is not wearing a T-shirt with a big pink triangle on it, and that he's not already holding hands with another man.)

When I ask this question in classes or workshops, respondents invariably provide a standard list of stereotypically effeminate behaviors. He walks a certain way, talks a certain way, acts a certain way. He's well dressed, sensitive, and emotionally expressive. He has certain tastes in art and music—indeed, he has *any* taste in art and music! Men tend to focus on the physical attributes, women on the emotional. Women say they "suspect" a man might be gay if he's interested in what she's talking about, knows something about what she's talking about, or is sensitive and a good listener. One recently said, "I suspect he might be gay if he's looking at my eyes, and not down my blouse." Another said she suspects he might be gay if he shows no sexual interest in her, if he doesn't immediately come on to her.

Once I've established what makes a guy "suspect," I ask the men in the room if any of them would want to be thought of as gay. Rarely does a hand go up—despite the fact that this list of attributes is actually far preferable to the restrictive one that stands in the "Be a Man" box. So, what do straight men do to make sure that no one gets the wrong idea about them?

Everything that is perceived as gay goes into what we might call the Negative Playbook of Guyland. Avoid everything in it and you'll be all right. Just make sure that you walk, talk, and act in a different way from the gay stereotype; dress terribly; show no taste in art or music; show no emotions at all. Never listen to a thing a woman is saying, but express immediate and unquenchable sexual interest. Presto, you're a real man, back in the "Be a Man" box. Homophobia—the fear that people might *misperceive* you as gay—is the animating fear of American guys' masculinity. It's what lies underneath the crazy risk-taking behaviors practiced by boys of all ages, what drives the fear that other guys will see you as weak, unmanly, frightened. The single cardinal rule of manhood, the one from which all the other characteristics—wealth, power, status, strength, physicality—are derived is to offer constant proof that you are not gay.

Homophobia is even deeper than this. It's the fear *of* other men— that other men will perceive you as a failure, as a fraud. It's a fear that others will see you as weak, unmanly, frightened. This is how John Steinbeck put it in his novel *Of Mice and Men*:

> "Funny thing," [Curley's wife] said. "If I catch any one man, and he's alone, I get along fine with him. But just let two of the guys get together an' you won't talk. Jus' nothin' but mad." She dropped her fingers and put her hands on her hips. "You're all scared of each

25

other, that's what. Ever'one of you's scared the rest is goin' to get something on you."[5]

In that sense, homosexuality becomes a kind of shorthand for "unmanliness"—and the homophobia that defines and animates the daily conversations of Guyland is at least as much about masculinity as it is about sexuality.

But what would happen to a young man if he were to refuse such limiting parameters on who he is and how he's permitted to act? "It's not like I want to stay in that box," says Jeff, a first-year Cornell student at my workshop. "But as soon as you step outside it, even for a second, all the other guys are like, 'What are you, dude, a fag?' It's not very safe out there on your own. I suppose as I get older, I'll get more secure, and feel like I couldn't care less what other guys say. But now, in my fraternity, on this campus, man, I'd lose everything."

The consistency of responses is as arresting as the list is disturbing: "I would lose my friends." "Get beat up." "I'd be ostracized." "Lose my self-esteem." Some say they'd take drugs or drink. Become withdrawn, sullen, a loner, depressed. "Kill myself," says one guy. "Kill them," responds another. Everyone laughs, nervously. Some say they'd get mad. And some say they'd get even. "I dunno," replied Mike, a sophomore at Portland State University. "I'd probably pull a Columbine. I'd show them that they couldn't get away with calling me that shit."

Guys know that they risk everything—their friendships, their sense of self, maybe even their lives—if they fail to conform. Since the stakes are so enormous, young men take huge chances to prove their manhood, exposing themselves to health risks, workplace hazards, and stress-related illnesses. Here's a revealing factoid. Men ages nineteen to twenty-nine are three times less likely to wear seat belts than women the same age. Before they turn nineteen though, young men are actually *more* likely to wear seat belts. It's as if they suddenly get the idea that as long as they're driving the car, they're completely in control, and therefore safe.[6] Ninety percent of all driving offenses, excluding parking violations, are committed by men, and 93 percent of road ragers are male.[7] Safety is emasculating! So they drink too much, drive too fast, and play chicken in a multitude of dangerous venues.

The comments above provide a telling riposte to all those theories 30 of biology that claim that this definition of masculinity is "hard-wired," the result of millennia of evolutionary adaptation or the behavioral response to waves of aggression-producing testosterone, and therefore inevitable. What these theories fail to account for is the way that masculinity is coerced and policed relentlessly by other guys. If it were bio-

[5]John Steinbeck, *Of Mice and Men* (New York: Scribner's, 1937), p. 57.

[6]Eric Nagourney, "Young Men with No Attachments" in *New York Times*, January 4, 2005.

[7]Mary Blume, "The Feminist Future of the Automobile" in *International Herald Tribune*, October 8, 2004, p. 11.

logical, it would be as natural as breathing or blinking. In truth, the Guy Code fits as comfortably as a straightjacket.

Boys' Psychological Development: Where the Guy Code Begins

Masculinity is a constant test—always up for grabs, always needing to be proved. And the testing starts early. Recently, I was speaking with a young black mother, a social worker, who was concerned about a conversation she had had with her husband a few nights earlier. It seems that her husband had taken their son to the barber, which, she explained to me, is a central social institution in the African American community. As the barber prepared the boy's hair for treatment, using, apparently some heat and some painful burning chemicals, the boy began to cry. The barber turned to the boy's father and pronounced, "This boy is a wimp!" He went on, "This boy has been spending too much time with his mama! Man, you need to put your foot down. You have got to get this boy away from his mother!"

That evening the father came home, visibly shaken by the episode, and announced to his wife that from that moment on the boy would not be spending as much time with her, but instead would do more sports and other activities with him, "to make sure he doesn't become a sissy."

After telling me this story, the mother asked what I thought she should do. "Gee," I said, "I understand the pressures that dads feel to 'toughen up' their sons. But how old is your boy, anyway?"

"Three and a half," she said.

I tried to remind her, of course, that crying is the natural human response to pain, and that her son was behaving appropriately. But her story reminded me of how early this pressure starts to affect an emotionally impervious manly stoicism.

Ever since Freud, we've believed that the key to boys' development is separation, that the boy must switch his identification from mother to father in order to "become" a man. He achieves his masculinity by repudiation, dissociation, and then identification. It is a perilous path, but a necessary one, even though there is nothing inevitable about it—and nothing biological either. Throw in an overdominant mother, or an absent father, and we start worrying that the boy will not succeed in his masculine quest.

Boys learn that their connection to mother will emasculate them, turn them into Mama's Boys. And so they learn to act *as if* they have made that leap by pushing away from their mothers. Along the way they suppress all the feelings they associate with the maternal—compassion, nurturance, vulnerability, dependency. This suppression and repudiation is the origin of the Boy Code. It's what turns those happy, energetic, playful, and emotionally expressive five-year-olds into sullen, withdrawn, and despondent nine-year-olds. In the recent spate of bestselling books about boys' development, psychologists like William Pollack, James Garbarino, Michael Thompson, Dan Kindlon, and others, argue that from an early age boys are taught to refrain from crying, to suppress their emotions, never to display vulnerability. As a result, boys feel effeminate not only if they *express* their emotions, but even if they *feel* them. In their bestseller, *Raising Cain*, Kindlon and Thompson describe a "culture of cruelty" in which peers force other boys to deny their emotional needs and disguise their feelings. It's no wonder that so many boys end up feeling emotionally isolated.

These books about boys map the inner despair that comes from such emotional numbness and fear of vulnerability. Pollack calls it the "mask of masculinity," the fake front of impervious, unemotional independence, a swaggering posture that boys believe will help them to present a stoic front. "Ruffled in a manly pose," the great Irish poet William Butler Yeats put it in his poem "Coole Park" (1929), "For all his timid heart."

The ruffling starts often by age four or five, when he enters kindergarten, and it gets a second jolt when he hits adolescence. Think of the messages boys get: Stand on your own two feet! Don't cry! Don't be a sissy! As one boy in Pollack's book summarizes it: "Shut up and take it, or you'll be sorry." When I asked my nine-year-old son, Zachary, what he thought of when I said "be a man" he said that one of his friends said something about "taking it like a man. So," he explained, "I think it means acting tougher than you actually are."

Recently a colleague told me about a problem he was having. It 40 seems his seven-year-old son, James, was being bullied by another boy on his way home from school. His wife, the boy's mother, strategized with her son about how to handle such situations in the future. She suggested he find an alternate route home, tell a teacher, or perhaps even tell the boy's parents. And she offered the standard "use your words, not your fists" conflict-reducer. "How can I get my wife to stop treating James like a baby?" my colleague asked. "How will he ever learn to stand up for himself if she turns him into a wimp?"

The Boy Code leaves boys disconnected from a wide range of emotions and prohibited from sharing those feelings with others. As they grow older, they feel disconnected from adults, as well, unable to experience the guidance towards maturity that adults can bring. When they turn to anger and violence it is because these, they believe, perhaps rightly, are the only acceptable forms of emotional expression allowed them. Just as the Boy Code shuts boys down, the Guy Code reinforces those messages, suppressing what was left of boyhood exuberance and turning it into sullen indifference.

No wonder boys are more prone to depression, suicidal behavior, and various other forms of out-of-control or out-of-touch behaviors than girls are. No wonder boys drop out of school and are diagnosed as emotionally disturbed four times more often as girls, get into fights twice as often, and are six times more likely than girls to be diagnosed with Attention Deficit and Hyperactivity Disorder (ADHD).[8]

ENGAGING THE TEXT

1. What are the "rules" associated with the Guy Code, according to Kimmel? To what extent do these rules reflect your own understanding of what it means to be a man? Discuss Kimmel's assertion that "the Guy Code fits as comfortably as a straightjacket" (para. 30).

2. Outline the psychology of the Guy Code: How do boys become men, according to Kimmel, and how does their development affect their emotional lives and relationships with others?

3. Kimmel writes that "masculinity is coerced and policed relentlessly by other guys" (para. 30). Write a journal entry detailing any encounters you've observed or experienced that involve such "gender police." What happened, and how did you react at the time? Did the incident(s) have any lasting effect on your thinking or behavior? If so, how and why?

4. Kimmel argues that homophobia plays a central role in defining and reinforcing the Guy Code. What evidence do you see that young men are or are not pressured "to offer constant proof that [they] are not gay" (para. 24)?

EXPLORING CONNECTIONS

5. In what ways does Kimmel's analysis of American masculinity help to explain the violence and misogyny described by Jean Kilbourne (p. 488), Joan Morgan (p. 533), and Rebecca Solnit (p. 522)? What other factors contribute to these problems?

6. How does the image on page 542 reflect both the rewards and the costs of the Guy Code? How do you interpret the meaning and placement of the "Think again" message?

EXTENDING THE CRITICAL CONTEXT

7. Working in small groups, try to come up with a list of "rules" you associate with being a woman. As a class, debate whether a Girl Code exists, and if so, what it consists of and how it's taught and reinforced.

8. For one full day, keep track of every time you hear the word "gay" used as a pejorative term in conversation or in the media. In each case, is the speaker male or female? Who or what is he or she referring to? Is he or she joking or serious? Bring your notes to class to compare with others' observations. Do your findings bear out Kimmel's assertion that "Homophobia . . . is the animating fear of American guys' masculinity" (para. 24)?

[8]See, for example, Brad Knickerbocker, "Young and Male in America: It's Hard Being a Boy" in *Christian Science Monitor*, April 29, 1999.

SISTERHOOD IS COMPLICATED

RUTH PADAWER

Sisterhood can indeed be complicated. Originally conceived as all-female institutions, women's colleges are currently struggling with what it means to be a woman as they adapt to a new generation of transgender students. In this essay, Ruth Padawer writes about the controversies surrounding trans-men, who are demanding recognition and inclusion at Wellesley. Since 1992 Padawer has served as an adjunct professor at Columbia University Graduate School of Journalism, where she teaches reporting and writing. She also serves as a contributing writer for the *New York Times Magazine*, **where she has published feature articles on DNA testing, abortion, autism, and gender-fluid children. Her work has been featured in the** *Columbia Journalism Review*; **on the Public Broadcasting System's "Media Matters"; National Public Radio's "This American Life" and "On the Media"; and internationally in** *The Guardian*, *Haaretz Magazine*, **and** *Internazionale*. **This article appeared on October 15, 2014, in the** *New York Times Magazine*.

HUNDREDS OF YOUNG WOMEN streamed into Wellesley College on the last Monday of August, many of them trailed by parents lugging suitcases and bins filled with folded towels, decorative pillows and Costco-size jugs of laundry detergent. The banner by the campus entranceway welcoming the Class of 2018 waved in the breeze, as if beckoning the newcomers to discover all that awaited them. All around the campus stood buildings named after women: the Margaret Clapp library, the Betsy Wood Knapp media and technology center, dorms, labs, academic halls, even the parking garage. The message that anything is possible for women was also evident at a fenced-in work site, which bore the sign "Elaine Construction," after a firm named for one woman and run by another.

It was the first day of orientation, and along the picturesque paths there were cheerful upper-class student leaders providing directions and encouragement. They wore pink T-shirts stamped with this year's orientation theme: "Free to Explore" — an enticement that could be interpreted myriad ways, perhaps far more than the college intended. One of those T-shirted helpers was a junior named Timothy Boatwright. Like every other matriculating student at Wellesley, which is just west of Boston, Timothy was raised a girl and checked "female" when he applied. Though he had told his high-school friends that he was transgender, he did not reveal that on his application, in part because his mother helped him with it, and he didn't want her to know. Besides, he told me, "it seemed awkward to write an application essay for a women's college

© Martin Schoeller/AUGUST

Timothy Boatright (center), a trans man, with his Wellesley classmates.

on why you were not a woman." Like many trans students, he chose a women's college because it seemed safer physically and psychologically.

From the start, Timothy introduced himself as "masculine-of-center genderqueer." He asked everyone at Wellesley to use male pronouns and the name Timothy, which he'd chosen for himself.

For the most part, everyone respected his request. After all, he wasn't the only trans student on campus. Some two dozen other matriculating students at Wellesley don't identify as women. Of those, a half-dozen or so were trans men, people born female who identified as men, some of whom had begun taking testosterone to change their bodies. The rest said they were transgender or genderqueer, rejecting the idea of gender entirely or identifying somewhere between female and male; many, like Timothy, called themselves transmasculine. Though his gender identity differed from that of most of his classmates, he generally felt comfortable at his new school.

Last spring, as a sophomore, Timothy decided to run for a seat on the student-government cabinet, the highest position that an openly trans student had ever sought at Wellesley. The post he sought was multicultural affairs coordinator, or "MAC," responsible for promoting "a culture of diversity" among students and staff and faculty members. Along with Timothy, three women of color indicated their intent to run for the seat. But when they dropped out for various unrelated reasons before the race really began, he was alone on the ballot. An anonymous lobbying effort began on Facebook, pushing students to vote "abstain." Enough "abstains" would deny Timothy the minimum number of votes Wellesley required, forcing a new election for the seat and providing an opportunity for other candidates to come forward. The "Campaign to Abstain" argument was simple: Of all the people at a multiethnic women's college who could hold the school's "diversity" seat, the least fitting one was a *white man.*

"It wasn't about Timothy," the student behind the Abstain campaign told me: "I thought he'd do a perfectly fine job, but it just felt inappropriate to have a white man there. It's not just about that position either. Having men in elected leadership positions undermines the idea of this being a place where women are the leaders."

I asked Timothy what he thought about that argument, as we sat on a bench overlooking the tranquil lake on campus during orientation. He pointed out that he has important contributions to make to the MAC position. After all, at Wellesley, masculine-of-center students *are* cultural minorities; by numbers alone, they're about as minor as a minority can be. And yet Timothy said he felt conflicted about taking a leadership spot. "The patriarchy is alive and well," he said. "I don't want to perpetuate it."

In the nineteenth century, only men were admitted to most colleges and universities, so proponents of higher education for women had to build their own. The missions at these new schools both defied and reinforced the gender norms of the day. By offering women access to an education they'd previously been denied, the schools' very existence was radical, but most were nevertheless premised on traditional notions: College-educated women were considered more likely to be engaging wives and better mothers, who would raise informed citizens. Over time, of course, women's colleges became more committed to preparing students for careers, but even in the early 1960s, Wellesley, for example, taught students how to get groceries into the back of a station wagon without exposing their thighs.

By the late 1960s, however, gender norms were under scrutiny. Amid the growing awareness of civil rights and women's liberation, academic separation based on gender, as with race, seemed increasingly outdated. As a vast majority of women opted for coed schools, enrollment at women's colleges tumbled. The number of women's colleges dropped to fewer than 50 today from nearly 300.

In response to shifting ideas about gender, many of the remaining   10
women's colleges redefined themselves as an antidote to the sexism that feminists were increasingly identifying in society. Women's colleges argued that they offered a unique environment where every student leader was a woman, where female role models were abundant, where professors were far more likely to be women and where the message of women's empowerment pervaded academic and campus life. All that seemed to foster students' confidence. Women's colleges say their undergrads are more likely to major in fields traditionally dominated by men.

Wellesley alumnae in particular are awarded more science and engineering doctorates than female graduates of any other liberal-arts college in the nation, according to government data. Its alums have become two secretaries of state; a groundbreaking string theorist; a NASA astronaut; and Korea's first female ambassador.

As women's colleges challenged the conventions of womanhood, they drew a disproportionate number of students who identified as lesbian or bisexual. Today a small but increasing number of students at those schools identify as something other than a woman, raising the question of what it means to be a "women's college." Trans students are pushing their schools to play down the women-centric message. At Wellesley, Smith, Mount Holyoke and others, they and their many supporters have successfully lobbied to scrub all female references in student government constitutions, replacing them with gender-neutral language. At Wellesley, they have pressed administrators and fellow students to excise talk of sisterhood, arguing that that rhetoric, rather than being uplifting, excludes other gender minorities. At many schools, they have also taken leadership positions long filled by women: resident advisers on dorm floors, heads of student groups and members of college government. At Wellesley, one transmasculine student was a dorm president. At Mills College, a women's school in California, even the president of student government identifies as male.

What's a women's college to do? Trans students point out that they're doing exactly what these schools encourage: breaking gender barriers, fulfilling their deepest yearnings and forging ahead even when society tries to hold them back. But yielding to their request to dilute the focus on women would undercut the identity of a women's college. While women in coed schools generally outpace men in enrollment and performance, the equation shifts after college: Recent female graduates working full time earn far less than their male counterparts, and more experienced women are often still shut out of corporate and political leadership—all of which prompts women's-college advocates to conclude that a four-year, confidence-building workshop still has its place.

"Sisterhood is why I chose to go to Wellesley," said a physics major who graduated recently and asked not to be identified for fear she'd be denounced for her opinion. "A women's college is a place to celebrate being a woman, surrounded by women. I felt empowered by that every day. You come here thinking that every single leadership position will be held by a woman: every member of the student government, every newspaper editor, every head of the Economics Council, every head of the Society of Physics. That's an incredible thing! This is what they advertise to students. But it's no longer true. And if all that is no longer true, the intrinsic value of a women's college no longer holds."

A few schools have formulated responses to this dilemma, albeit very different ones. Hollins University, a small women's college in Virginia, established a policy several years ago stating it would confer diplomas to only women. It also said that students who have surgery or begin hormone therapy to become men—or who legally take male names—will be "helped to transfer to another institution." Mount Holyoke and Mills College, on the other hand, recently decided they will not only continue to welcome students who become trans men while at school but will also admit those who identify on their applications as trans men, noting that welcoming the former and not the latter seemed unjustifiably arbitrary.

But most women's colleges, including Wellesley, consider only female applicants. Once individuals have enrolled and announced that they are trans, the schools, more or less, leave it to the students to work out how trans classmates fit into a women's college. Two of those students hashed it out last fall after Kaden Mohamed, then a Wellesley senior who had been taking testosterone for seven months, watched a news program on WGBH-TV about the plummeting number of women's colleges. One guest was Laura Bruno, another Wellesley senior. The other guest was the president of Regis College, a women's school that went coed in 2007 to reverse its tanking enrollment. The interviewer asked Laura to describe her experience at an "all-female school" and to explain how that might be diminished "by having men there." Laura answered, "We look around and we see only women, only people like us, leading every organization on campus, contributing to every class discussion."

Kaden, a manager of the campus student cafe who knew Laura casually, was upset by her words. He emailed Laura and said her response was "extremely disrespectful." He continued: "I am not a woman. I am a trans man who is part of your graduating class, and you literally ignored my existence in your interview. . . . You had an opportunity to show people that Wellesley is a place that is complicating the meaning of being an 'all women's school,' and you chose instead to displace a bunch of your current and past Wellesley siblings."

Laura apologized, saying she hadn't meant to marginalize anyone and had actually vowed beforehand not to imply that all Wellesley students were women. But she said that under pressure, she found herself in a difficult spot: How could she maintain that women's colleges would lose something precious by including men, but at the same time argue that women's colleges should accommodate students who identify as men?

Although it may seem paradoxical, Jesse Austin said he chose to attend Wellesley because being female never felt right to him. "I figured if I was any kind of woman, I'd find it there. I knew Wellesley would have strong women. They produce a ton of strong women, strong in all sorts of ways."

When Jesse arrived on campus in the fall of 2009, his name was Sara. Eighteen years old, Sara wore form-fitting shirts and snug women's jeans, because growing up in a small, conservative town in Georgia, she learned that that's what girls were supposed to do—even though she never felt like a girl. As a child, Sara had always chosen to be male characters in pretend plays, and all her friends were boys. In middle school, those boys abandoned her because she was a social liability: not feminine enough to flirt with and not masculine enough to really be one of the guys. In high school, at the urging of well-intentioned female classmates, she started wearing her hair down instead of pulled back and began dressing like they did, even though people kept pointing out that she still acted and carried herself like a boy. "I had no idea that gender was something you could change," Jesse told me recently. "I just thought I needed to make myself fit into these fixed places: There are boys, and there are girls. I knew I didn't fit; I just didn't know what was wrong with me."

Around the middle of Sara's first year at Wellesley, she attended a presentation by trans alums, including one who was in the process of transitioning. As Sara listened, the gender dysphoria she'd always felt suddenly made sense. "It was all so clear to me," Jesse told me. "All I needed were the words." Sara spent the next two weeks scouring the Internet for videos and information on becoming a man. She learned that unlike previous generations, today's trans young adults don't consider physical transformation a prerequisite for identity. Some use hormones; some have their breasts removed in "top" surgery; some reject medical interventions altogether, as unnecessary invasions and expense. She discovered that sexual orientation is independent of gender: Some trans men are attracted to women, some to men, some to both. And she learned that trans men aren't necessarily determined to hide the fact they were raised as girls, or that they once attended a women's college.

Soon after, Sara cut her hair short and bought her first pair of men's jeans. Sara told friends she was a man. By second semester, he was using male pronouns and calling himself Jesse, the other name his mother had considered for her daughter. He also joined a tiny campus group for students who knew or suspected they were trans men. It was called Brothers, a counterweight to the otherwise ubiquitous message of sisterhood.

That summer, Jesse saw a gender therapist, and early in his sophomore year, he began injecting testosterone into his thigh every two weeks, making him one of the first students to medically transform into a man while at Wellesley. He became the administrator of Brothers. Though he felt supported, he also felt alone; all the other trans men on campus had graduated, and the other students in Brothers were not even sure they identified as men. Outside Brothers, everything at Wellesley was still sisterhood and female empowerment. Nevertheless, he said, "I thought of Wellesley as my home, my community. I felt fine there, like I totally belonged."

Jesse decided he wanted to have top surgery over winter break, and his parents agreed to pay for it. He returned for spring semester but only briefly, taking a sudden leave of absence to go home and help care for his ill father. When Jesse re-enrolled at Wellesley a year and a half later, in fall 2012, much had changed in Jesse and at school. Having been on testosterone for two years at that point, Jesse no longer looked like a woman trying to pass as a man. His voice was deep. His facial hair was thick, though he kept it trimmed to a stubble. His shoulders had become broad and muscular, his hips narrow, his arms and chest more defined.

Wellesley was different, too. By then, a whole crowd of people identified as trans—enough for two trans groups. Brothers had officially become Siblings and welcomed anyone anywhere on the gender spectrum except those who identified as women. Meanwhile, Jesse and some transmasculine students continued to meet unofficially as Brothers, though Jesse was the only one on testosterone.

Overall, campus life had a stronger trans presence than ever: At least four of the school's 70 R.A.s did not identify as women. Student organizations increasingly began meetings by asking everyone to state preferred names and pronouns. Around campus, more and more students were replacing "sisterhood" with "siblinghood" in conversation. Even the school's oldest tradition, Flower Sunday—the 138-year-old ceremony that paired each incoming student with an upper-class Big Sister to support her—had become trans-inclusive. Though the school Web site still describes Flower Sunday as "a day of sisterhood," the department that runs the event yielded to trans students' request and started referring to each participant as a Big or Little "Sister/Sibling"—or simply as Bigs and Littles.

And yet even with the increased visibility of trans students on campus, Jesse stood out. When he swiped his Wellesley ID card to get into friends' dorms, the groundskeepers would stop him and say, "You can't go in there without a woman to escort you." Residential directors who spotted him in the dorm stairwells told him the same thing. In his own dorm, parents who were visiting their daughters would stop him to ask why he was there. Because bathrooms in the dorms are not labeled "women" or "men" but rather "Wellesley only" and "non-Wellesley," students who didn't know Jesse would call him out for using the "Wellesley only" bathroom instead of the one for visitors. When he tried to explain he *was* a Wellesley student, people sometimes thought he was lying.

"Everything felt very different than it had before," he said of that semester. "I felt so distinctly male, and I felt extremely awkward. I felt like an outsider. My voice was jarring—a male voice, which is so distinct in a classroom of women—so I felt weird saying much in class. I felt much more aware of Wellesley as a women's place, even though the college was starting to change."

Once spring semester ended, Jesse withdrew. "I still think of Wellesley as a women's place, and I still think that's a wonderful idea," he said. "It just didn't encompass me anymore. I felt it was a space I shouldn't tread in."

Some female students, meanwhile, said Wellesley wasn't female enough. They complained among themselves and to the administration that sisterhood had been hijacked. "Siblinghood," they argued, lacked the warm, pro-women connotation of "sisterhood," as well as its historic resonance. Others were upset that even at a women's college, women

Clockwise from top: Jesse Austin, Alex Poon, and Kaden Mohamad, former Wellesley students.

were still expected to accommodate men, ceding attention and leadership opportunities intended for women. Still others feared the changes were a step toward coeducation. Despite all that, many were uneasy: As a marginalized group fighting for respect and clout, how could women justify marginalizing others?

"I felt for the first time that something so stable about our school was about to change, and it made me scared," said Beth, a junior that year, who asked to be identified by only her middle name because she was afraid of offending people she knew. "Changing 'sister' to 'sibling' didn't feel like it was including more people; it felt like it was taking something away from sisterhood, transforming our safe space for the sake of someone else. At the same time, I felt guilty feeling that way." Beth went to Kris Niendorf, the director of residential life, who listened sympathetically and then asked: Why does "sibling" take away from your experience? After thinking about it, Beth concluded that she was connected to her classmates not because of gender but because of their shared experiences at Wellesley. "That year was an epiphany for me. I realized that if we excluded trans students, we'd be fighting on the wrong team. We'd be on the wrong side of history."

Exactly how Wellesley will resolve the trans question is still unclear. Trans students say that aside from making sure every academic building on campus has a unisex bathroom, Wellesley has not addressed what gender fluidity means for Wellesley's identity. Last spring, Alex Poon won Wellesley's 131-year-old hoop-rolling race, an annual spirit-building competition among seniors. Alex's mother was the hoop-rolling champion of the Class of '82 and had long ago taught her daughters the ways of the hoop, on the assumption that they would one day attend her alma mater. (One of Alex's older sisters was Wellesley Class of '11; another went to Bryn Mawr.) Alex was a former Girl Scout who attended an all-girls high school. But unknown to his mother, he was using Google to search for an explanation for his confusing feelings. By the time Alex applied to Wellesley, he secretly knew he was trans but was nonetheless certain Wellesley was a good fit. For one thing, going there was a family tradition; for another, it was a place where gender could be reimagined. In his sophomore year at Wellesley, he went public with his transgender status.

On hoop-rolling day, Alex—wearing a cap backward on his buzz-cut hair—broke through the finish-line streamer. President H. Kim Bottomly took a selfie with him, each with a wide smile. A small local newspaper covered the event, noting that for the first time in the school's history, the winner was a man. And yet the page on Wellesley's Web site devoted to school traditions continues to describe the race as if it involves only women. "Back in the day, it was proclaimed that whoever won the Hoop Roll would be the first to get married. In the status-seeking 1980s, she was the first to be C.E.O. Now we just say that the winner will be the first to achieve happiness and success, whatever that means to her." But Alex isn't a her, and he told me that his happiness and success includes being recognized for what he is: a man.

That page is not the only place on the site where Wellesley markets itself as a school of only female students. Elsewhere, it crows that "all the most courageous, most provocative, most accomplished people on campus are women." The student body, it says, is "2,300 smart, singular women feeling the power of 2,300 smart, singular women together" on a campus where "our common identity, spirit and pride as Wellesley women" are celebrated. Those sorts of messages, trans students say, make them feel invisible.

"I just wish the administration would at least acknowledge our existence," said Eli Cohen, a Wellesley senior who has been taking testosterone for nearly a year. "I'd be more O.K. with 'We're not going to cater to you, because men are catered to everywhere else in life,' rather than just pretending we don't exist."

Some staff and faculty members, however, are acknowledging the trans presence. Women-and-gender-studies professors, and a handful of others, typically begin each semester asking students to indicate the names and pronouns they prefer for themselves. Kris Niendorf, director of campus and residential life, recruits trans students who want to be R.A.s., as she does with all minorities. Niendorf also initiated informational panels with trans students and alums. And before this school year began, at the urging of trans students, Niendorf required all 200 student leaders to attend a trans-sensitivity workshop focused on how to "create a more inclusive Wellesley College." For the last few years, orientation organizers have also included a trans student as one of the half-dozen upper-class students who stand before the incoming first-years and recount how they overcame a difficult personal challenge.

And yet many trans students feel that more needs to be done. They complain that too many professors assume all their students are women. Students provided numerous examples in courses across subject areas where they've been asked their viewpoint "as a woman." In a course on westerns two years ago, an essay assignment noted that western films and novels were aimed at male audiences and focused on masculinity. The professors asked students for their perspective "as a female reader or watcher"—wording that offended the three trans students in class. When a classmate pointed out the problematic wording to the professors, the instructors asked everyone instead "to explore how your own gender identity changes how you approach westerns."

At times, professors find themselves walking a fine line. Thomas Cushman, who has taught sociology at Wellesley for the last 25 years, first found out about Wellesley's trans population five years ago, after a student in one of his courses showed up at Cushman's office and introduced himself as a trans male. The student pointed out that every example Cushman gave in class referred to women, and every generic pronoun he used was female, as in "Ask your classmate if she. . . ." He told Cushman that Wellesley could no longer call itself a "women's college," given the presence of trans men, and he asked Cushman to use male pronouns and male examples more often, so trans students didn't feel excluded. Cushman said he would abide by whatever pronoun individual students requested for themselves, but he drew the line at changing his emphasis on women.

"All my life here," Cushman told me, "I've been compelled to use the female pronoun more generously to get away from the sexist 'he.' I think it's important to evoke the idea that women are part of humanity. That should be affirmed, especially after being denied for so long. Look, I teach at a women's college, so whenever I can make women's identity central to that experience, I try to do that. Being asked to change that is a bit ironic. I don't agree that this is a 'historically' women's college. It is still a women's college."

On the second day of orientation this fall, Eli Cohen arrived on campus in a muscle T and men's shorts, with a carabiner full of keys hanging from his belt loop. He was elated to be back to the place that felt most like home. It was the first time in four years that Eli had not been part of orientation—first as a newcomer and then two years as an R.A. We hung out in the Lulu Chow Wang Campus Center, known affectionately as Lulu, and watched the excited first-years flutter by, clutching their orientation schedules and their newly purchased Wellesley wear.

Just 12 days earlier, Eli underwent top surgery, which he said gave him a newfound self-assurance in his projection of manhood. It had been nine months since he started testosterone, and the effects had become particularly noticeable over the three-month summer break. His jaw line had begun to square, his limbs to thicken and the hair on his arms and legs to darken. And of course now his chest was a flat wall. As his friends caught sight of him for the first time in months, they hugged him and gushed, "You look sooo good!" 40

Though Eli secretly suspected in high school that he was a boy, it wasn't until after he arrived at Wellesley that he could imagine he might one day declare himself a man. By his second year, he had buzz-cut his hair and started wearing men's clothes. He asked his friends to call him Beckett, which is similar to his female birth name, which he asked me not to mention. His parents live only 14 miles away and dropped by for short visits. He left his girl nameplate on his dorm door. His friends understood that whenever his parents arrived, everyone was to revert to his female name and its attendant pronouns. He was an R.A. at the time and decided not to reveal his male name to his first-year students, figuring it was too complicated to explain which name to use when.

Given how guarded he had to be, being Beckett was exhausting and anxiety-inducing. Demoralized, he eventually told his pals to just use his birth name. The summer after his sophomore year, he got an internship at a Boston health center serving the L.G.B.T. community, and many of his co-workers were trans. Their confidence gave him confidence. When the Wellesley office that coordinates internships sent out an email to all interns that began, "Good morning, ladies . . . ," he emailed back to say he did not identify as a woman. The coordinator apologized and explained that all the names on her paperwork from Wellesley were female.

By summer's end, he began introducing himself as Eli, a name utterly unlike his birth name, Eli mustered the courage to tell his parents. It took a little while for his mother to accept that her only daughter was actually a son, but she came around.

When I asked Eli if trans men belonged at Wellesley, he said he felt torn. "I don't necessarily think we have a right to women's spaces. But I'm not going to transfer, because this is a place I love, a community I love. I realize that may be a little selfish. It may be a lot selfish." Where, he wondered, should Wellesley draw a line, if a line should even be drawn? At trans men? At transmasculine students? What about students who are simply questioning their gender? Shouldn't students be "free to explore" without fearing their decision will make them unwelcome?

Other trans students have struggled with these questions, too. Last December, a transmasculine Wellesley student wrote an anonymous blog post that shook the school's trans community. The student wrote to apologize for "acting in the interest of preserving a hurtful system of 45 privileging masculinity." He continued: "My feelings have changed: I do not think that trans men belong at Wellesley. . . . This doesn't mean that I think that all trans men should be kicked out of Wellesley or necessarily denied admission." He acknowledged he didn't know how Wellesley could best address the trans question, but urged fellow transmasculine classmates to "start talking, and thinking critically, about the space that we are given and occupying, and the space that we are taking from women."

The reactions were swift and strong. "A lot of trans people on campus felt emotionally unsafe," recalled Timothy, a sophomore that year. "A place that seemed welcoming suddenly wasn't. The difficulty was that because it was a trans person saying it, people who don't have enough of an understanding to appreciate the nuance of this can say, 'Well, even a trans person says there shouldn't be trans people at Wellesley, so it's O.K. for me to think the same thing, too.'"

Students and alums—queer and straight, trans and not—weighed in, sometimes in agreement but other times in anger. Some accused the blogger of speaking on behalf of women as if they were unable to speak for themselves. Others accused him of betraying transmasculine students. (He declined to comment for this article.) But other students, including several transmasculine ones, were glad he had the courage to start a public discussion about Wellesley's deeply conflicted identity. "It's a very important conversation to have," Eli said. "Why can't we have this conversation without feeling hurt or hated?"

In some ways, students are already having that conversation, though perhaps indirectly. Timothy ended up easily winning his seat on the student government last spring, capturing two-thirds of the votes. Given that 85 percent of the student body cast ballots in that race, his victory suggests most students think that transmasculine students—and transmasculine leaders—belong at Wellesley.

Another difficult conversation about trans students touches on the disproportionate attention they receive on campus. "The female-identified students somehow place more value on those students," said Rose Layton, a lesbian who said she views trans students as competitors in the campus dating scene. "They flirt with them, hook up with them. And it's not just the hetero women, but even people in the queer community. The trans men are always getting this extra bit of acknowledgment. Even though we're in a women's college, the fact is men and masculinity get more attention and more value in this social dynamic than women do."

Jesse Austin noticed the paradox when he returned to campus with a man's build and full swath of beard stubble after nearly two years on testosterone. "That was the first time in my life I was popular! People were clamoring to date me."

Trans bodies are seen as an in-between option, Timothy said. "So no matter your sexuality, a trans person becomes safe to flirt with, to explore with. But it's not really the person you're interested in, it's the novelty. For lesbians, there's the safety of 'I may be attracted to this

50

person, but they're "really" a woman, so I'm not actually bi or straight.' And for straight people, it's 'I may be attracted to a woman's body, but he's a male, so I'm not really lesbian or bi.' "

Kaden Mohamed said he felt downright objectified when he returned from summer break last year, after five months of testosterone had lowered his voice, defined his arm muscles and reshaped his torso. It was attention that he had never experienced before he transitioned. But as his body changed, students he didn't even know would run their hands over his biceps. Once at the school pub, an intoxicated Wellesley woman even grabbed his crotch and that of another trans man.

"It's this very bizarre reversal of what happens in the real world," Kaden said. "In the real world, it's women who get fetishized, catcalled, sexually harassed, grabbed. At Wellesley, it's trans men who do. If I were to go up to someone I just met and touch her body, I'd get grief from the entire Wellesley community, because they'd say it's assault — and it is. But for some reason, when it's done to trans men here, it doesn't get read the same way. It's like a free pass, that suddenly it's O.K. to talk about or touch someone's body as long as they're not a woman.". . .

On the last Friday in May, some 5,000 parents, alumnae and soon-to-be graduates streamed onto the rolling field near Severance Hall, named after Elisabeth Severance, a generous 1887 alumna. It was a gorgeous, temperate morning for Wellesley's 136th annual commencement, and once the last baccalaureate degree was conferred, the audience was asked to stand. As is the school's tradition, two graduates led an uplifting rendition of "America, the Beautiful." The lyrics, for those who needed them, were printed in the commencement program, including the chorus: "And crown thy good, with brotherhood, from sea to shining sea!"

Those words were penned by Katharine Lee Bates, an 1880 graduate of Wellesley who defied the expectations of her gender, and not just by becoming a professor, published author and famous poet. A pastor's daughter, she never married, living instead for 25 years with Katharine Coman, founder of Wellesley's economics department, with whom she was deeply in love. When a colleague described "free-flying spinsters" as a "fringe on the garment of life," Bates, then 53, answered: "I always thought the fringe had the best of it."

As parents, professors and graduates joined in the singing of Bates's most famous poem, many felt an intense pride in their connection to the graduates and this remarkable college, which has sent forth so many women who leave impressive marks on the world. As the hundreds of voices rounded the curve on "And crown thy good with . . . ," the unknowing parents continued to "brotherhood," the word that was always supposed to stand in for women too, but never really did. Wellesley women long ago learned that words matter, and for decades, this has been the point in the song when their harmonious choral singing abruptly becomes a bellow as they belt out "sisterhood," drowning out the word that long excluded them and replacing it with a demand for recognition. It's one of the most powerful moments of commencement, followed every year by cheers, applause and tears, evoked by the rush of solidarity with women throughout time, and the thrill of claiming in one of the nation's most famous songs that women matter — even if the world they're about to enter doesn't always agree.

In the last few years, a handful of graduates have changed that word once again, having decided that "sisterhood," no matter how well intended, is exclusionary, and so they instead call out "siblinghood." A few trans men find even that insufficient, and in that instant, they roar the word that represents them best: "brotherhood," not as a sexist stand-in for all humankind, but as an appeal from a tiny minority struggling to be acknowledged.

In truth, it's difficult to distinguish in the cacophony each of the words shouted atop one another. What is clear is that whatever word each person is hollering is immensely significant as a proclamation of existence, even if it's hard to make out what anyone else is saying.

ENGAGING THE TEXT

1. Why were women's colleges first established? How do women's colleges serve as "an antidote to . . . sexism" (para. 10), and how does Wellesley advertise itself to women? Is the idea of all-female institutions out of date or do they continue to fulfill an important purpose? What benefits do women today hope to gain by attending a school like Wellesley?

2. In what ways do trans students threaten to "undercut the identity" (para. 12) of women's colleges? Why do trans students sometimes "feel invisible" (para. 33) at Wellesley?

3. How has Wellesley responded to the presence of trans students on campus? Which of the university's decisions and policies seem wise and which, if any, seem inadequate or misguided? Explain.

4. According to one student, "Men and masculinity get more attention and more value" than women at Wellesley (para. 49). Does the focus on gender-neutral language, the election of trans men to leadership positions, and the "objectification" of transmasculine bodies indicate that "the patriarchy is alive and well" (para. 7) at Wellesley? Why or why not?

5. Why did Timothy Boatwright, Jesse Austin, and Alex Poon decide to attend a women's college? Did they make the right decision? How might their experience have been different had they gone to a mixed-gender school? Write an imaginative alternative history for one of the men.

EXPLORING CONNECTIONS

6. How do the views of masculinity in Aaron H. Devor's "patriarchal gender schema" (p. 476) and Michael Kimmel's "Guy Code" (p. 540) differ from those represented or expressed by the students of Wellesley?

7. Review Devor's discussion of the private "I" and the public "me" in the development of gender identity (pp. 472–74). How do the "I" and the "me" conflict at various points in the lives of Jesse Austin, Alex Poon, and Eli Cohen? How does each resolve the conflict? Write an essay comparing the experiences of two of these men.

EXTENDING THE CRITICAL CONTEXT

8. What resources for transgender or genderqueer students exist on your campus? For example, is "gender identity or expression" included in your school's antidiscrimination policy? Does your student medical center provide trans-specific services? Are gender-inclusive restrooms, locker rooms, and housing options readily available? Are there trans counselors and support groups? Do some online research to identify other types of support or accommodation that trans students need. Examine your college's Web site to see how trans-friendly or unfriendly it is. Write an essay or a journal entry detailing your findings.

FURTHER CONNECTIONS

1. Compare the rhetorical strategies and effectiveness of any two of the selections in this chapter. What is each writer's purpose and what audience is he or she addressing? To what extent and how does each author appeal to readers' reason and emotions? What kind of persona does each writer project? What kinds of evidence does each author rely on? How persuasive or compelling do you find each selection, and why?

2. Research the issue of domestic violence. How is it defined? How prevalent is domestic violence nationwide, in your state, and in your community? What are the risk factors for abusers and their victims? Investigate the resources in your community that offer assistance to victims of domestic abuse: hotlines, shelters, organizations, and government agencies that provide counseling or legal aid. Do these services focus on punishing abusers or "curing" them? Write a paper evaluating the effectiveness of different approaches to protecting victims from abusive partners.

3. Research the status of women in the field or profession you plan to pursue. Are women's salaries and compensation comparable to those of men with similar credentials and experience? What is the ratio of women to men in the field as a whole, in entry-level positions, and in executive or high-status positions? Interview at least one woman in this line of work: In what ways, if any, does she feel that her work experience has differed from a man's? Report your findings to the class.

4. Title IX, the law mandating equal funding for women's sports at publicly funded schools, has been praised for opening new opportunities for women athletes and criticized for siphoning money away from some popular men's sports. Research the impact of Title IX on athletics programs at your college or university: How has the picture of women's and men's sports changed since 1972, the year Title IX was enacted? Have women's and men's athletics attained equality at your school?

5. Some religious groups argue that laws and policies that prohibit harassment of or discrimination against homosexuals infringe on their religious freedom. Investigate a specific case in which a religious organization has made this claim. What arguments have been advanced on both sides of the case? What values and assumptions underlie these arguments? What rights and freedoms are at stake for each party in the dispute?

CREATED EQUAL
The Myth of the Melting Pot

6

Eric Gay/AP Photo

FAST FACTS

1. In 2014, for the first time in the history of the U.S. Census, a majority of American kids under five years old were children of color.

2. Multiracial births have increased from 1% in 1970 to 10% in 2013. According to the Census Bureau, the multiracial population will triple by 2060.

3. U.S.-born children of immigrants are more likely to go to college and less likely to live in poverty than the average American.

4. In 2013, the median household income of American Indian and Native Alaskans was $36,000, compared to $52,000 nationally; more Native Americans live in poverty than any other group.

5. 73% of blacks see racism as a big problem in American society, as opposed to 58% of Latinos and 44% of whites.

6. Young black men are 21 times more likely than young white men to be killed by police, according to an analysis of 2010–2012 FBI data.

Data from (1) Census Bureau 2015; (2) Pew Research Center, "Multiracial in America," 2015; (3) Center for American Progress, 2012; (4) U.S. Census, 2013 American Community Survey; (5) Pew Research Center, 2015; (6) Pro Publica 2014.

THE MYTH OF THE MELTING POT predates the drafting of the U.S. Constitution. In 1782, a year before the Peace of Paris formally ended the Revolutionary War, J. Hector St. John de Crèvecoeur envisioned the young American republic as a crucible that would forge its disparate immigrant population into a vigorous new society with a grand future:

> What, then, is the American, this new man? He is neither an European, or the descendant of an European. . . . He is an American, who leaving behind him all his ancient prejudices and manners, receives new ones from the new mode of life he has embraced, the new government he obeys, and the new rank he holds. . . . Here individuals of all nations are melted into a new race of men, whose labours and posterity will one day cause great changes in the world.

Crèvecoeur's metaphor has remained a powerful ideal for many generations of American scholars, politicians, artists, and ordinary citizens. Ralph Waldo Emerson, writing in his journal in 1845, celebrated the national vitality produced by the mingling of immigrant cultures: "In this continent — asylum of all nations, — the energy of . . . all the European tribes, — of the Africans, and of the Polynesians — will construct a new race, a new religion, a new state, a new literature." An English Jewish writer named Israel Zangwill, himself an immigrant, popularized the myth in his 1908 drama, *The Melting Pot*. In the play, the hero rhapsodizes, "Yes East and West, and North and South, the palm and the pine, the pole and the equator, the crescent and the cross — how the great Alchemist melts and fuses them with his purging flame! Here shall they all unite to build the Republic of Man and the Kingdom of God." The myth was perhaps most vividly dramatized, though, in a pageant staged by Henry Ford in the early 1920s. Decked out in the costumes of their native lands, Ford's immigrant workers sang traditional songs from their homelands as they danced their way into an enormous replica of a cast-iron pot. They then emerged from the other side wearing identical "American" business suits, waving miniature American flags, and singing "The Star-Spangled Banner."

The drama of becoming an American has deep roots: immigrants take on new identities — and a new set of cultural myths — because they want to become members of the community, equal members with all the rights, responsibilities, and opportunities of their fellow citizens. The force of the melting pot myth lies in this implied promise that all Americans are indeed "created equal." However, the myth's promises of openness, harmony, unity, and equality were deceptive from the beginning. Crèvecoeur's exclusive concern with the mingling of *European* peoples (he lists the "English, Scotch, Irish, French, Dutch, Germans, and Swedes") utterly ignored the presence of some three-quarters of a million Africans and African Americans who then lived in the United States, as well as the indigenous people who had lived on the land for thousands of years before European contact. Crèvecoeur's vision of a country embracing "all nations" clearly applied only to northern European nations. Benjamin Franklin, in a 1751 essay, was more blunt: since Africa, Asia, and most of America were inhabited by dark-skinned people, he argued, the American colonies should consciously try to increase the white population and keep out the rest: "Why increase the Sons of Africa, by Planting them in America, where we have so fair an opportunity, by excluding Blacks and Tawneys, of increasing the lovely White?" If later writers like Emerson and Zangwill saw a more inclusive cultural mix as a source of hope and renewal for the United States, others throughout this country's history have, even more than Franklin, feared that mix as a threat.

Thomas Jefferson, in his *Notes on the State of Virginia* (1785), openly expressed his anxiety about freeing the slaves. Proposing that the new state of Virginia gradually phase out slavery, he recommended that the newly emancipated slaves be sent out of the state to form separate colonies, because allowing them to remain could lead to disastrous racial conflict:

> It will probably be asked, Why not retain and incorporate the blacks into the State, and thus save the expense of supplying by importation of white settlers, the vacancies they will leave? Deep-rooted prejudices entertained by the whites; ten thousand recollections, by the blacks, of the injuries they have sustained; new provocations; the real distinctions which nature has made; and many other circumstances, will divide us into parties, and produce convulsions, which will probably never end but in the extermination of the one or the other race.

Jefferson unambiguously asserted white racial superiority as he compared the "physical and moral" characteristics of whites and blacks: "Are not the fine mixtures of red and white, the expressions of every passion by greater or less suffusions of color in the one, preferable to that eternal monotony, which reigns in the countenances, that immovable veil of black which covers the emotions of the other race?" And, in one of the more shocking passages, Jefferson claimed that blacks themselves preferred white features "as uniformly as is the preference of the Oranootan[1] for the black woman over those of his own species. The circumstance of superior beauty, is thought worthy of attention in the propagation of our horses, dogs, and other domestic animals; why not in that of man?"

Considering African Americans' intellect and capacity for the arts, Jefferson found that aside from their musical talent, "in imagination they are dull, tasteless, and anomalous." The Indians, he says,

> will often carve figures on their pipes not destitute of design and merit. They will crayon out an animal, a plant, or a country, so as to prove the existence of a germ in their minds which only wants cultivation. They astonish you with strokes of the most sublime oratory; such as prove their reason and sentiment strong, their imagination glowing and elevated. But never yet could I find that a black had uttered a thought above the level of plain narration; never saw even an elementary trait of painting or sculpture. . . . Misery is often the parent of the most affecting touches in poetry. Among the blacks is misery enough, God knows, but no poetry.

Jefferson concluded that "this unfortunate difference of color, and perhaps of faculty, is a powerful obstacle to the emancipation of these people." Comparing the black slave to the white Roman slave, he disclosed that a primary reason he favored the removal of African Americans was to prevent black and white intermarriage: "Among the Romans emancipation required but one effort. The slave, when made free, might mix with, without staining the blood of his master. But with us a second is necessary, unknown to history. When freed, he is to be removed beyond the reach of mixture."

The myth of white supremacy is a powerful American fantasy — it is the negative counterpart of the melting pot ideal: instead of the equal and harmonious blending of cultures, it proposes a racial and ethnic hierarchy based on the "natural superiority" of Anglo-Americans. Under the sway of this myth, differences become signs of inferiority, and "inferiors" are treated as childlike or even subhuman. Jefferson was far from the last politician to advocate solving the nation's racial problems by removing African Americans from its boundaries. In 1862, the Great Emancipator himself, Abraham Lincoln, called a delegation of black leaders to the White House to enlist their support in establishing a colony for African Americans in Central America. Congress had appropriated money for this project, but it was abandoned after the governments of Honduras, Nicaragua, and Costa Rica protested the plan.

The myth of white superiority has given rise to some of the most shameful passages in our national life: slavery, segregation, and lynching; the near extermination of tribal peoples and cultures; the denial of citizenship and constitutional rights to African Americans, American Indians, Chinese and Japanese immigrants; the brutal exploitation of Mexican and Asian laborers. The catalog of injustices is long and painful. The melting pot ideal itself has often masked the myth of racial and ethnic superiority. "Inferiors" are expected to "melt" into conformity with Anglo-American behavior and values. Henry Ford's pageant conveys the message that ethnic identity is best left behind — exchanged for something "better," more uniform, less threatening.

[1] **Oranootan:** Orangutan. [Eds.]

This chapter explores the interaction between these two related cultural myths: the myth of unity and the myth of difference and hierarchy. It examines how racial categories are defined and how they operate to divide us. These issues become crucial as the population of the United States grows increasingly diverse. The selections here challenge you to reconsider the fate of the melting pot myth as we enter the era of multi-ethnic, multicultural America.

The first half of the chapter focuses on the origins and lingering consequences of racism. The chapter opens with an award-winning essay, Ta-Nehisi Coates's "The Case for Reparations," that raises profound questions about the treatment of African Americans throughout the nation's history. Coates charges that white supremacy has dominated the black experience and continues to inflict damage on the bodies and psyches of black people. He calls this shameful history a "crime [that] indicts the American people themselves, at every level, and in nearly every configuration" and suggests that reparations are in order. The selection "Theories and Constructs of Race," by Linda Holtzman and Leon Sharpe, provides an academic overview of racism and offers a number of useful terms and concepts for discussing racial issues. Next comes Sherman Alexie's amusing, provocative short story, "Gentrification," in which an unnamed narrator tackles the job of removing an unsightly, smelly, perhaps rat-infested mattress from his neighbor's property. The media piece, an essay by Cheryl I. Harris and Devon W. Carbado, "Loot or Find: Fact or Frame?" examines how assumptions about race ultimately distorted media coverage of Hurricane Katrina.

The second half of the chapter offers a Visual Portfolio that gives individual faces to abstractions like race and discrimination. Here, you'll find images that challenge you to ponder the centrality of race in American culture and to rethink the ways we "read" racial identity. The readings that follow the portfolio address some of the costs associated with forsaking one's cultural or national identity in order to blend in. Alex Tizon embraces American identity obsessively in his memoir, "Land of the Giants"; Americans appear outsized to Tizon — "they were smarter, stronger, richer" than his Pilipino family. By contrast, David Treuer, in a selection from *Rez Life: An Indian's Journey Through Reservation Life*, discusses the negative consequences of forced assimilation and presents a new kind of Indian activism — the effort to restore Native languages and cultures. Finally, in "How Immigrants Become 'Other,'" Marcelo M. and Carola Suárez-Orozco argue that our immigration system is broken and explore the human costs to unauthorized immigrants — the poverty, fear, insecurity, families torn apart — that result from that brokenness.

Sources

Franklin, John Hope. *Race and History: Selected Essays, 1938–1988*. Baton Rouge: Louisiana State University Press, 1989. 321–31. Print.
Gordon, Milton M. *Assimilation in American Life: The Role of Race, Religion, and National Origins*. New York: Oxford University Press, 1964. Print.
Jefferson, Thomas. *Notes on the State of Virginia*. 1785. Print.
Njeri, Itabari. "Beyond the Melting Pot." *Los Angeles Times* 13 Jan. 1991: E1+. Print.
Pitt, Leonard. *We Americans*. 3rd ed. Vol. 2. Dubuque: Kendall/Hunt, 1987. Print.
Takaki, Ronald. "Reflections on Racial Patterns in America." In *From Different Shores: Perspectives on Race and Ethnicity in America*. Ed. Ronald Takaki. New York: Oxford University Press, 1987. 26–37. Print.

BEFORE READING

- Survey images in the popular media (newspapers, magazines, online sources, TV shows, movies, and pop music) for evidence of racial harmony or conflict. How well or poorly do these images reflect your experience of interactions with other ethnic and racial groups? Explore these questions in a journal entry, and then discuss in class.

- Investigate the language used to describe racial and ethnic group relations or interactions between members of different groups on your campus and in your community. Consult local news sources and campus publications, and keep your ears open for conversations that touch on these issues. What metaphors, euphemisms, and clichés are used to discuss group interactions? Do some freewriting about what you discover and compare notes with classmates.

- What is your emotional response to the frontispiece photo? How do you interpret the photograph's meaning? What do the woman's body language and expression suggest about her situation? What is the significance of the flag blanket? Jot down your impressions and note the visual details that support your "reading" of the picture. Then compare your responses in small groups: How much consistency or variation do you find in your interpretations?

THE CASE FOR REPARATIONS

TA-NEHISI COATES

Between 1951 and 1998, the government of West Germany paid the state of Israel and survivors of the Nazi Holocaust more than 102 billion marks — or about 62 billion in 1998 U.S. dollars — in reparation for crimes committed against the Jewish people during World War II. In 2013, the Federal Republic of Germany provided the equivalent of an additional $1 billion to care for the 56,000 remaining Holocaust survivors. Similarly, in 1988, the U.S. Congress issued a formal apology to Japanese Americans who had been detained in internment camps between 1943 and 1945 and passed legislation providing a payment of $20,000 for each internee. Eventually, nearly $2 billion was allocated to acknowledge the suffering of Japanese Americans. Why, then, hasn't a single dollar ever been given to compensate the black victims of white supremacy in the United States? Initially, Ta-Nehisi Coates (b. 1975) opposed reparations for black Americans, saying that "Blame is useless to me. Blame is for the dead."[1]

[1] "Inverse Nationalism." *The Atlantic*, 26 April 2010.

Then, as he did more research and engaged with scholars of black history, he gradually began to change his mind: "[W]e should never forget that this world was 'made.' Whiteness and blackness are not a fact of providence, but of policy — of slave codes, black codes, Jim Crow, redlining, GI Bills, housing covenants, New Deals, and mass incarcerations. I did not understand it at the time, but this way of thinking pushed me toward reparations."[2] Several years of reading and study led Coates to believe that a monstrous crime — 250 years in the making — has been committed against black people in America and that a logical response is to seek reparations. When *The Atlantic* published "The Case for Reparations" as its cover story in June 2014, the article generated more Web traffic in a single day than any story in the history of the magazine; it won the 2014 George Polk Award for Commentary as well as the Harriet Beecher Stowe Center Prize for Writing to Advance Social Justice. As a senior editor and blogger for *The Atlantic*, Coates has written extensively about race, including his 2012 cover story, "Fear of a Black President." His first book, *The Beautiful Struggle: A Memoir* (2008), is about growing up in a tough West Baltimore neighborhood; his second, *Between the World and Me* (2015), is a meditation on racism and American history addressed to his fifteen-year-old son.

And if thy brother, a Hebrew man, or a Hebrew woman, be sold unto thee, and serve thee six years; then in the seventh year thou shalt let him go free from thee. And when thou sendest him out free from thee, thou shalt not let him go away empty: thou shalt furnish him liberally out of thy flock, and out of thy floor, and out of thy winepress: of that wherewith the LORD thy God hath blessed thee thou shalt give unto him. And thou shalt remember that thou wast a bondman in the land of Egypt, and the LORD thy God redeemed thee: therefore I command thee this thing today.

—DEUTERONOMY 15: 12–15

Besides the crime which consists in violating the law, and varying from the right rule of reason, whereby a man so far becomes degenerate, and declares himself to quit the principles of human nature, and to be a noxious creature, there is commonly injury done to some person or other, and some other man receives damage by his transgression: in which case he who hath received any damage, has, besides the right of punishment common to him with other men, a particular right to seek reparation.

—JOHN LOCKE, "SECOND TREATISE"

---

[2] "How Racism Invented Race in America." *The Atlantic*, 23 June 2014.

By our unpaid labor and suffering, we have earned the right to the soil, many times over and over, and now we are determined to have it.

—ANONYMOUS, 1861

I. "So That's Just One of My Losses"

Clyde Ross was born in 1923, the seventh of 13 children, near Clarksdale, Mississippi, the home of the blues. Ross's parents owned and farmed a 40-acre tract of land, flush with cows, hogs, and mules. Ross's mother would drive to Clarksdale to do her shopping in a horse and buggy, in which she invested all the pride one might place in a Cadillac. The family owned another horse, with a red coat, which they gave to Clyde. The Ross family wanted for little, save that which all black families in the Deep South then desperately desired—the protection of the law.

In the 1920s, Jim Crow[3] Mississippi was, in all facets of society, a kleptocracy.[4] The majority of the people in the state were perpetually robbed of the vote—a hijacking engineered through the trickery of the poll tax[5] and the muscle of the lynch mob. Between 1882 and 1968, more black people were lynched in Mississippi than in any other state. "You and I know what's the best way to keep the nigger from voting," blustered Theodore Bilbo, a Mississippi senator and a proud Klansman. "You do it the night before the election."

The state's regime partnered robbery of the franchise with robbery of the purse. Many of Mississippi's black farmers lived in debt peonage, under the sway of cotton kings who were at once their landlords, their employers, and their primary merchants. Tools and necessities were advanced against the return on the crop, which was determined by the employer. When farmers were deemed to be in debt—and they often were—the negative balance was then carried over to the next season. A man or woman who protested this arrangement did so at the risk of grave injury or death. Refusing to work meant arrest under vagrancy laws and forced labor under the state's penal system.

Well into the twentieth century, black people spoke of their flight from Mississippi in much the same manner as their runagate ancestors had. In her 2010 book, *The Warmth of Other Suns*, Isabel Wilkerson tells the story of Eddie Earvin, a spinach picker who fled Mississippi in 1963, after being made to work at gunpoint. "You didn't talk about it or tell nobody," Earvin said. "You had to sneak away."

When Clyde Ross was still a child, Mississippi authorities claimed his father owed $3,000 in back taxes. The elder Ross could not read. He did not have a lawyer. He did not know anyone at the local courthouse.

5

---

[3]**Jim Crow:** Collective term for southern segregation laws. [All notes are the editors'.]
[4]**kleptocracy:** A government ruled by thieves.
[5]**poll tax:** A tax paid to register to vote. Following passage of the Fifteenth Amendment, which gave blacks voting rights, poll taxes were imposed in many states, effectively denying the vote to blacks, Native Americans, and poor people.

He could not expect the police to be impartial. Effectively, the Ross family had no way to contest the claim and no protection under the law. The authorities seized the land. They seized the buggy. They took the cows, hogs, and mules. And so for the upkeep of separate but equal, the entire Ross family was reduced to sharecropping.

This was hardly unusual. In 2001, the Associated Press published a three-part investigation into the theft of black-owned land stretching back to the antebellum period. The series documented some 406 victims and 24,000 acres of land valued at tens of millions of dollars. The land was taken through means ranging from legal chicanery to terrorism. "Some of the land taken from black families has become a country club in Virginia," the AP reported, as well as "oil fields in Mississippi" and "a baseball spring training facility in Florida."

Clyde Ross was a smart child. His teacher thought he should attend a more challenging school. There was very little support for educating black people in Mississippi. But Julius Rosenwald, a part owner of Sears, Roebuck, had begun an ambitious effort to build schools for black children throughout the South. Ross's teacher believed he should attend the local Rosenwald school. It was too far for Ross to walk and get back in time to work in the fields. Local white children had a school bus. Clyde Ross did not, and thus lost the chance to better his education.

Then, when Ross was 10 years old, a group of white men demanded his only childhood possession—the horse with the red coat. "You can't have this horse. We want it," one of the white men said. They gave Ross's father $17.

"I did everything for that horse," Ross told me. "Everything. And they took him. Put him on the racetrack. I never did know what happened to him after that, but I know they didn't bring him back. So that's just one of my losses."

The losses mounted. As sharecroppers, the Ross family saw their [10] wages treated as the landlord's slush fund.[6] Landowners were supposed to split the profits from the cotton fields with sharecroppers. But bales would often disappear during the count, or the split might be altered on a whim. If cotton was selling for 50 cents a pound, the Ross family might get 15 cents, or only five. One year Ross's mother promised to buy him a $7 suit for a summer program at their church. She ordered the suit by mail. But that year Ross's family was paid only five cents a pound for cotton. The mailman arrived with the suit. The Rosses could not pay. The suit was sent back. Clyde Ross did not go to the church program.

It was in these early years that Ross began to understand himself as an American—he did not live under the blind decree of justice, but under the heel of a regime that elevated armed robbery to a governing principle. He thought about fighting. "Just be quiet," his father told him. "Because they'll come and kill us all."

---

[6]**slush fund:** A secret stash of money used for illegal or dishonest purposes.

Clyde Ross grew. He was drafted into the Army. The draft officials offered him an exemption if he stayed home and worked. He preferred to take his chances with war. He was stationed in California. He found that he could go into stores without being bothered. He could walk the streets without being harassed. He could go into a restaurant and receive service.

Ross was shipped off to Guam. He fought in World War II to save the world from tyranny. But when he returned to Clarksdale, he found that tyranny had followed him home. This was 1947, eight years before Mississippi lynched Emmett Till and tossed his broken body into the Tallahatchie River. The Great Migration, a mass exodus of 6 million African Americans that spanned most of the 20th century, was now in its second wave. The black pilgrims did not journey north simply seeking better wages and work, or bright lights and big adventures. They were fleeing the acquisitive warlords of the South. They were seeking the protection of the law.

Clyde Ross was among them. He came to Chicago in 1947 and took a job as a taster at Campbell's Soup. He made a stable wage. He married. He had children. His paycheck was his own. No Klansmen stripped him of the vote. When he walked down the street, he did not have to move because a white man was walking past. He did not have to take off his hat or avert his gaze. His journey from peonage to full citizenship seemed near-complete. Only one item was missing—a home, that final badge of entry into the sacred order of the American middle class of the Eisenhower years.

In 1961, Ross and his wife bought a house in North Lawndale, a bustling community on Chicago's West Side. North Lawndale had long been a predominantly Jewish neighborhood, but a handful of middle-class African Americans had lived there starting in the '40s. The community was anchored by the sprawling Sears, Roebuck headquarters. North Lawndale's Jewish People's Institute actively encouraged blacks to move into the neighborhood, seeking to make it a "pilot community for interracial living." In the battle for integration then being fought around the country, North Lawndale seemed to offer promising terrain. But out in the tall grass, highwaymen, nefarious as any Clarksdale kleptocrat, were lying in wait. ¹⁵

Three months after Clyde Ross moved into his house, the boiler blew out. This would normally be a homeowner's responsibility, but in fact, Ross was not really a homeowner. His payments were made to the seller, not the bank. And Ross had not signed a normal mortgage. He'd bought "on contract": a predatory agreement that combined all the responsibilities of homeownership with all the disadvantages of renting—while offering the benefits of neither. Ross had bought his house for $27,500. The seller, not the previous homeowner but a new kind of middleman, had bought it for only $12,000 six months before selling it to Ross. In a contract sale, the seller kept the deed until the contract was paid in full—and, unlike with a normal mortgage, Ross would acquire no equity in the meantime. If he missed a single payment, he would immediately forfeit his $1,000 down payment, all his monthly payments, and the property itself.

The men who peddled contracts in North Lawndale would sell homes at inflated prices and then evict families who could not pay — taking their down payment and their monthly installments as profit. Then they'd bring in another black family, rinse, and repeat. "He loads them up with payments they can't meet," an office secretary told *The Chicago Daily News* of her boss, the speculator Lou Fushanis, in 1963. "Then he takes the property away from them. He's sold some of the buildings three or four times."

Ross had tried to get a legitimate mortgage in another neighborhood, but was told by a loan officer that there was no financing available. The truth was that there was no financing for people like Clyde Ross. From the 1930s through the 1960s, black people across the country were largely cut out of the legitimate home-mortgage market through means both legal and extralegal. Chicago whites employed every measure, from "restrictive covenants"[7] to bombings, to keep their neighborhoods segregated. . . .

Their efforts were buttressed by the federal government. In 1934, Congress created the Federal Housing Administration. The FHA insured private mortgages, causing a drop in interest rates and a decline in the size of the down payment required to buy a house. But an insured mortgage was not a possibility for Clyde Ross. The FHA had adopted a system of maps that rated neighborhoods according to their perceived stability. On the maps, green areas, rated "A," indicated "in demand" neighborhoods that, as one appraiser put it, lacked "a single foreigner or Negro." These neighborhoods were considered excellent prospects for insurance. Neighborhoods where black people lived were rated "D" and were usually considered ineligible for FHA backing. They were colored in red. Neither the percentage of black people living there nor their social class mattered. Black people were viewed as a contagion. Redlining went beyond FHA-backed loans and spread to the entire mortgage industry, which was already rife with racism, excluding black people from most legitimate means of obtaining a mortgage.

"A government offering such bounty to builders and lenders could have required compliance with a nondiscrimination policy," Charles Abrams, the urban-studies expert who helped create the New York City Housing Authority, wrote in 1955. "Instead, the FHA adopted a racial policy that could well have been culled from the Nuremberg laws."[8]

[20]

[7]**restrictive covenants:** Legally enforceable real estate contracts that prevented a particular group of people (like African Americans or Jews) from buying or occupying the property.
[9]**Nuremberg laws:** In 1935, the Nazi Party passed a series of laws that deprived German Jews of their rights as citizens. These laws represented the first step toward the wholesale murder of Jews and other "undesirables."

The devastating effects are cogently outlined by Melvin L. Oliver and Thomas M. Shapiro in their 1995 book, *Black Wealth/White Wealth*:

> Locked out of the greatest mass-based opportunity for wealth accumulation in American history, African Americans who desired and were able to afford home ownership found themselves consigned to central-city communities where their investments were affected by the "self-fulfilling prophecies" of the FHA appraisers: cut off from sources of new investment[,] their homes and communities deteriorated and lost value in comparison to those homes and communities that FHA appraisers deemed desirable.

In Chicago and across the country, whites looking to achieve the American dream could rely on a legitimate credit system backed by the government. Blacks were herded into the sights of unscrupulous lenders who took them for money and for sport. "It was like people who like to go out and shoot lions in Africa. It was the same thrill," a housing attorney told the historian Beryl Satter in her 2009 book, *Family Properties*. "The thrill of the chase and the kill."

The kill was profitable. At the time of his death, Lou Fushanis owned more than 600 properties, many of them in North Lawndale, and his estate was estimated to be worth $3 million. He'd made much of this money by exploiting the frustrated hopes of black migrants like Clyde Ross. During this period, according to one estimate, 85 percent of all black home buyers who bought in Chicago bought on contract. "If anybody who is well established in this business in Chicago doesn't earn $100,000 a year," a contract seller told *The Saturday Evening Post* in 1962, "he is loafing."

Contract sellers became rich. North Lawndale became a ghetto.

Clyde Ross still lives there. He still owns his home. He is 91, and the emblems of survival are all around him—awards for service in his community, pictures of his children in cap and gown. But when I asked him about his home in North Lawndale, I heard only anarchy.

"We were ashamed. We did not want anyone to know that we were that ignorant," Ross told me. He was sitting at his dining-room table. His glasses were as thick as his Clarksdale drawl. "I'd come out of Mississippi where there was one mess, and come up here and got in another mess. So how dumb am I? I didn't want anyone to know how dumb I was.

"When I found myself caught up in it, I said, 'How? I just left this mess. I just left no laws. And no regard. And then I come here and get cheated wide open.' I would probably want to do some harm to some people, you know, if I had been violent like some of us. I thought, 'Man, I got caught up in this stuff. I can't even take care of my kids.' I didn't have enough for my kids. You could fall through the cracks easy fighting these white people. And no law."

But fight Clyde Ross did. In 1968 he joined the newly formed Contract Buyers League—a collection of black homeowners on Chicago's South and West Sides, all of whom had been locked into the same system of predation. There was Howell Collins, whose contract called for him to pay $25,500 for a house that a speculator had bought for $14,500. There was Ruth Wells, who'd managed to pay out half her contract, expecting a mortgage, only to suddenly see an insurance bill materialize out of thin air—a requirement the seller had added without Wells's knowledge. Contract sellers used every tool at their disposal to pilfer from their clients. They scared white residents into selling low. They lied about properties' compliance with building codes, then left the buyer responsible when city inspectors arrived. They presented themselves as real-estate brokers, when in fact they were the owners. They guided their clients to lawyers who were in on the scheme.

The Contract Buyers League fought back. Members—who would eventually number more than 500—went out to the posh suburbs where the speculators lived and embarrassed them by knocking on their neighbors' doors and informing them of the details of the contract-lending trade. They refused to pay their installments, instead holding monthly payments in an escrow account. Then they brought a suit against the contract sellers, accusing them of buying properties and reselling in such a manner "to reap from members of the Negro race large and unjust profits."

In return for the "deprivations of their rights and privileges under the Thirteenth and Fourteenth Amendments," the league demanded "prayers for relief"—payback of all moneys paid on contracts and all moneys paid for structural improvement of properties, at 6 percent interest minus a "fair, non-discriminatory" rental price for time of occupation. Moreover, the league asked the court to adjudge that the defendants had "acted willfully and maliciously and that malice is the gist of this action."

Ross and the Contract Buyers League were no longer appealing to the government simply for equality. They were no longer fleeing in hopes of a better deal elsewhere. They were charging society with a crime against their community. They wanted the crime publicly ruled as such. They wanted the crime's executors declared to be offensive to society. And they wanted restitution for the great injury brought upon them by said offenders. In 1968 Clyde Ross and the Contract Buyers League were no longer simply seeking the protection of the law. They were seeking reparations.

II. "A Difference of Kind, Not Degree"

According to the most-recent statistics, North Lawndale is now on the wrong end of virtually every socioeconomic indicator. In 1930 its population was 112,000. Today it is 36,000. The halcyon talk of "interracial living" is dead. The neighborhood is 92 percent black. Its homicide rate is 45 per 100,000—triple the rate of the city as a whole. The infant-mortality rate is 14 per 1,000—more than twice the national average. Forty-three percent of the people in North Lawndale live below the poverty line— double Chicago's overall rate. Forty-five percent of all households are on food stamps—nearly three times the rate of the city at large. Sears, Roebuck left the neighborhood in 1987, taking 1,800 jobs with it. Kids in North Lawndale need not be confused about their prospects: Cook County's Juvenile Temporary Detention Center sits directly adjacent to the neighborhood.

North Lawndale is an extreme portrait of the trends that ail black Chicago. Such is the magnitude of these ailments that it can be said that blacks and whites do not inhabit the same city. The average per capita income of Chicago's white neighborhoods is almost three times that of its black neighborhoods. When the Harvard sociologist Robert J. Sampson examined incarceration rates in Chicago in his 2012 book, *Great American City*, he found that a black neighborhood with one of the highest incarceration rates (West Garfield Park) had a rate more than 40 times as high as the white neighborhood with the highest rate (Clearing). "This is a staggering differential, even for community-level comparisons," Sampson writes. "A difference of kind, not degree."

In other words, Chicago's impoverished black neighborhoods—characterized by high unemployment and households headed by single parents—are not simply poor; they are "ecologically distinct." This "is not simply the same thing as low economic status," writes Sampson. "In this pattern Chicago is not alone."

The lives of black Americans are better than they were half a century ago. The humiliation of WHITES ONLY signs [is] gone. Rates of black poverty have decreased. Black teen-pregnancy rates are at record lows— and the gap between black and white teen-pregnancy rates has shrunk significantly. But such progress rests on a shaky foundation, and fault lines are everywhere. The income gap between black and white households is roughly the same today as it was in 1970. Patrick Sharkey, a sociologist at New York University, studied children born from 1955 through 1970 and found that 4 percent of whites and 62 percent of blacks across America had been raised in poor neighborhoods. A generation later, the same study showed, virtually nothing had changed. And whereas whites born into affluent neighborhoods tended to remain in affluent neighborhoods, blacks tended to fall out of them.

This is not surprising. Black families, regardless of income, are significantly less wealthy than white families. The Pew Research Center estimates that white households are worth roughly 20 times as much as black households, and that whereas only 15 percent of whites have zero or negative wealth, more than a third of blacks do. Effectively, the black family in America is working without a safety net. When financial calamity strikes—a medical emergency, divorce, job loss—the fall is precipitous.

And just as black families of all incomes remain handicapped by a lack of wealth, so too do they remain handicapped by their restricted choice of neighborhood. Black people with upper-middle-class incomes do not generally live in upper-middle-class neighborhoods. Sharkey's research shows that black families making $100,000 typically live in the kinds of neighborhoods inhabited by white families making $30,000. "Blacks and whites inhabit such different neighborhoods," Sharkey writes, "that it is not possible to compare the economic outcomes of black and white children."

The implications are chilling. As a rule, poor black people do not work their way out of the ghetto—and those who do often face the horror of watching their children and grandchildren tumble back.

Even seeming evidence of progress withers under harsh light. In 2012 the Manhattan Institute cheerily noted that segregation had declined since the 1960s. And yet African Americans still remained—by far—the most segregated ethnic group in the country.

With segregation, with the isolation of the injured and the robbed, comes the concentration of disadvantage. An unsegregated America might see poverty, and all its effects, spread across the country with no particular bias toward skin color. Instead, the concentration of poverty has been paired with a concentration of melanin. The resulting conflagration has been devastating.

One thread of thinking in the African American community holds that these depressing numbers partially stem from cultural pathologies that can be altered through individual grit and exceptionally good behavior. (In 2011, Philadelphia Mayor Michael Nutter, responding to violence among young black males, put the blame on the family: "Too many men making too many babies they don't want to take care of, and then we end up dealing with your children." Nutter turned to those presumably fatherless babies: "Pull your pants up and buy a belt, because no one wants to see your underwear or the crack of your butt.") The thread is as old as black politics itself. It is also wrong. The kind of trenchant racism to which black people have persistently been subjected can never be defeated by making its victims more respectable. The essence of American racism is disrespect. And in the wake of the grim numbers, we see the grim inheritance.

The Contract Buyers League's suit brought by Clyde Ross and his allies took direct aim at this inheritance. The suit was rooted in Chicago's long history of segregation, which had created two housing markets—one legitimate and backed by the government, the other lawless and patrolled by predators. The suit dragged on until 1976, when the league lost a jury trial.

Securing the equal protection of the law proved hard; securing reparations proved impossible. If there were any doubts about the mood of the jury, the foreman removed them by saying, when asked about the verdict, that he hoped it would help end "the mess Earl Warren made with *Brown v. Board of Education* and all that nonsense.". . .

III. "We Inherit Our Ample Patrimony"

In 1783, the freedwoman Belinda Royall petitioned the commonwealth of Massachusetts for reparations. Belinda had been born in modern-day Ghana. She was kidnapped as a child and sold into slavery. She endured the Middle Passage[9] and 50 years of enslavement at the hands of Isaac Royall[10] and his son. But the junior Royall, a British loyalist, fled the country during the Revolution. Belinda, now free after half a century of labor, beseeched the nascent Massachusetts legislature:

> The face of your Petitioner, is now marked with the furrows of time, and her frame bending under the oppression of years, while she, by the Laws of the Land, is denied the employment of one morsel of that immense wealth, apart whereof hath been accumilated by her own industry, and the whole augmented by her servitude.
>
> WHEREFORE, casting herself at your feet if your honours, as to a body of men, formed for the extirpation of vassalage, for the reward of Virtue, and the just return of honest industry—she prays, that such allowance may be made her out of the Estate of Colonel Royall, as will prevent her, and her more infirm daughter, from misery in the greatest extreme, and scatter comfort over the short and downward path of their lives.

Belinda Royall was granted a pension of 15 pounds and 12 shillings, to be paid out of the estate of Isaac Royall—one of the earliest successful attempts to petition for reparations. At the time, black people in America had endured more than 150 years of enslavement, and the idea that they might be owed something in return was, if not the national consensus, at least not outrageous. 45

"A heavy account lies against us as a civil society for oppressions committed against people who did not injure us," wrote the Quaker John Woolman in 1769, "and that if the particular case of many individuals were fairly stated, it would appear that there was considerable due to them."

As the historian Roy E. Finkenbine has documented, at the dawn of this country, black reparations were actively considered and often effected. Quakers in New York, New England, and Baltimore went so far as to make "membership contingent upon compensating one's former slaves." In 1782, the Quaker Robert Pleasants emancipated his 78 slaves, granted them 350 acres, and later built a school on their property and provided for their education. "The doing of this justice to the injured Africans," wrote Pleasants, "would be an acceptable offering to him who 'Rules in the kingdom of men.'"

Edward Coles, a protégé of Thomas Jefferson who became a slaveholder through inheritance, took many of his slaves north and granted them a plot of land in Illinois. John Randolph, a cousin of Jefferson's, willed that all his slaves be emancipated upon his death, and that all those older than 40 be given 10 acres of land. "I give and bequeath to all my

---

[9]**Middle Passage:** The middle leg of a triangular trade route beginning and ending in Europe. Ships would leave European ports with items—such as iron, guns, and liquor—that could be traded in Africa for slaves, who would then be taken to the Americas and exchanged for sugar or cotton, which was then shipped back to Europe. Conditions on these ships were horrific: between 10 and 25 percent of the human "cargo" died en route.

[10]**Isaac Royall:** Slaves were often given the last names of their masters.

slaves their freedom," Randolph wrote, "heartily regretting that I have been the owner of one."

In his book *Forever Free*, Eric Foner recounts the story of a disgruntled planter reprimanding a freedman loafing on the job:

> Planter: "You lazy nigger, I am losing a whole day's labor by you."
> Freedman: "Massa, how many days' labor have I lost by you?"

In the 20th century, the cause of reparations was taken up by a diverse cast that included the Confederate veteran Walter R. Vaughan, who believed that reparations would be a stimulus for the South; the black activist Callie House; black-nationalist leaders like "Queen Mother" Audley Moore; and the civil-rights activist James Forman. The movement coalesced in 1987 under an umbrella organization called the National Coalition of Blacks for Reparations in America (N'COBRA). The NAACP endorsed reparations in 1993. Charles J. Ogletree Jr., a professor at Harvard Law School, has pursued reparations claims in court.

But while the people advocating reparations have changed over time, the response from the country has remained virtually the same. "They have been taught to labor," the *Chicago Tribune* editorialized in 1891. "They have been taught Christian civilization, and to speak the noble English language instead of some African gibberish. The account is square with the ex-slaves."

Not exactly. Having been enslaved for 250 years, black people were not left to their own devices. They were terrorized. In the Deep South, a second slavery ruled. In the North, legislatures, mayors, civic associations, banks, and citizens all colluded to pin black people into ghettos, where they were overcrowded, overcharged, and undereducated. Businesses discriminated against them, awarding them the worst jobs and the worst wages. Police brutalized them in the streets. And the notion that black lives, black bodies, and black wealth were rightful targets remained deeply rooted in the broader society. Now we have half-stepped away from our long centuries of despoilment, promising, "Never again." But still we are haunted. It is as though we have run up a credit-card bill and, having pledged to charge no more, remain befuddled that the balance does not disappear. The effects of that balance, interest accruing daily, are all around us.

Broach the topic of reparations today and a barrage of questions inevitably follows: Who will be paid? How much will they be paid? Who will pay? But if the practicalities, not the justice, of reparations are the true sticking point, there has for some time been the beginnings of a solution. For the past 25 years, Congressman John Conyers Jr., who represents the Detroit area, has marked every session of Congress by introducing a bill calling for a congressional study of slavery and its lingering effects as well as recommendations for "appropriate remedies."

A country curious about how reparations might actually work has an easy solution in Conyers's bill, now called HR 40, the Commission to Study Reparation Proposals for African Americans Act. We would support this bill, submit the question to study, and then assess the possible solutions. But we are not interested.

"It's because it's black folks making the claim," Nkechi Taifa, who 55 helped found N'COBRA, says. "People who talk about reparations are considered left lunatics. But all we are talking about is studying [reparations]. As John Conyers has said, we study everything. We study the water, the air. We can't even study the issue? This bill does not authorize one red cent to anyone."

That HR 40 has never—under either Democrats or Republicans—made it to the House floor suggests our concerns are rooted not in the impracticality of reparations but in something more existential. If we conclude that the conditions in North Lawndale and black America are not inexplicable but are instead precisely what you'd expect of a community that for centuries has lived in America's crosshairs, then what are we to make of the world's oldest democracy?

One cannot escape the question by hand-waving at the past, disavowing the acts of one's ancestors, nor by citing a recent date of ancestral immigration. The last slaveholder has been dead for a very long time. The last soldier to endure Valley Forge has been dead much longer. To proudly claim the veteran and disown the slaveholder is patriotism à la carte. A nation outlives its generations. We were not there when Washington crossed the Delaware, but Emanuel Gottlieb Leutze's[11] rendering has meaning to us. We were not there when Woodrow Wilson took us into World War I, but we are still paying out the pensions. If Thomas Jefferson's genius matters, then so does his taking of Sally Hemings's[12] body. If George Washington crossing the Delaware matters, so must his ruthless pursuit of the runagate Oney Judge.[13]

In 1909, President William Howard Taft told the country that "intelligent" white southerners were ready to see blacks as "useful members of the community." A week later Joseph Gordon, a black man, was lynched outside Greenwood, Mississippi. The high point of the lynching era has passed. But the memories of those robbed of their lives still live on in the lingering effects. Indeed, in America there is a strange and powerful belief that if you stab a black person 10 times, the bleeding stops and the healing begins the moment the assailant drops the knife. We believe white dominance to be a fact of the inert past, a delinquent debt that can be made to disappear if only we don't look.

---

[11]**Emanuel Gottlieb Leutze:** German-born historical and landscape painter (1816–1868), best known for his monumental *Washington Crossing the Delaware*, 1851.

[12]**Sally Hemings:** A Jefferson family slave (1773–1835), who is rumored to have borne six children to Thomas Jefferson; DNA and other evidence suggests that Jefferson was the likely father.

[13]**Oney Judge:** A slave of Martha Custis Washington, Judge (1773–1848) escaped in 1796 and fled to New Hampshire, where she met and married a free black man. George Washington made several failed attempts to return Judge to his wife. She remained a fugitive for the rest of her life, and her children, though born in New Hampshire to a free father, were legally considered "property" of the Custis estate.

There has always been another way. "It is in vain to alledge, that *our ancestors* brought them hither, and not we," Yale President Timothy Dwight said in 1810.

> We inherit our ample patrimony with all its incumbrances; and are bound to pay the debts of our ancestors. *This* debt, particularly, we are bound to discharge: and, when the righteous Judge of the Universe comes to reckon with his servants, he will rigidly exact the payment at our hands. To give them liberty, and stop here, is to entail upon them a curse.

IV. "The Ills That Slavery Frees Us From"

America begins in black plunder and white democracy, two features that are not contradictory but complementary. "The men who came together to found the independent United States, dedicated to freedom and equality, either held slaves or were willing to join hands with those who did," the historian Edmund S. Morgan wrote. "None of them felt entirely comfortable about the fact, but neither did they feel responsible for it. Most of them had inherited both their slaves and their attachment to freedom from an earlier generation, and they knew the two were not unconnected."

When enslaved Africans, plundered of their bodies, plundered of their families, and plundered of their labor, were brought to the colony of Virginia in 1619, they did not initially endure the naked racism that would engulf their progeny. Some of them were freed. Some of them intermarried. Still others escaped with the white indentured servants who had suffered as they had. Some even rebelled together, allying under Nathaniel Bacon[14] to torch Jamestown in 1676.

One hundred years later, the idea of slaves and poor whites joining forces would shock the senses, but in the early days of the English colonies, the two groups had much in common. English visitors to Virginia found that its masters "abuse their servantes with intollerable oppression and hard usage." White servants were flogged, tricked into serving beyond their contracts, and traded in much the same manner as slaves.

This "hard usage" originated in a simple fact of the New World — land was boundless but cheap labor was limited. As life spans increased in the colony, the Virginia planters found in the enslaved Africans an even more efficient source of cheap labor. Whereas indentured servants were still legal subjects of the English crown and thus entitled to certain protections, African slaves entered the colonies as aliens. Exempted

---

[14] **Nathaniel Bacon:** Bacon (1647–1676), a Virginia planter, led an armed rebellion against Governor William Berkeley; he was particularly angry at Berkeley's perceived failure to protect white settlements against Indian raids. Bacon, promising freedom to slaves and indentured servants who would join his cause, attracted a large following. In 1676, Bacon and his men captured Jamestown and burned it to the ground. Shortly thereafter, Bacon died of dysentery and the rebellion collapsed.

from the protections of the crown, they became early America's indispensable working class—fit for maximum exploitation, capable of only minimal resistance.

For the next 250 years, American law worked to reduce black people to a class of untouchables and raise all white men to the level of citizens. In 1650, Virginia mandated that "all persons except Negroes" were to carry arms. In 1664, Maryland mandated that any Englishwoman who married a slave must live as a slave of her husband's master. In 1705, the Virginia assembly passed a law allowing for the dismemberment of unruly slaves—but forbidding masters from whipping "a Christian white servant naked, without an order from a justice of the peace." In that same law, the colony mandated that "all horses, cattle, and hogs, now belonging, or that hereafter shall belong to any slave" be seized and sold off by the local church, the profits used to support "the poor of the said parish." At that time, there would have still been people alive who could remember blacks and whites joining to burn down Jamestown only 29 years before. But at the beginning of the 18th century, two primary classes were enshrined in America.

"The two great divisions of society are not the rich and poor, but white and black," John C. Calhoun, South Carolina's senior senator, declared on the Senate floor in 1848. "And all the former, the poor as well as the rich, belong to the upper class, and are respected and treated as equals." 65

In 1860, the majority of people living in South Carolina and Mississippi, almost half of those living in Georgia, and about one-third of all Southerners were on the wrong side of Calhoun's line. The state with the largest number of enslaved Americans was Virginia, where in certain counties some 70 percent of all people labored in chains. Nearly one-fourth of all white Southerners owned slaves, and upon their backs the economic basis of America—and much of the Atlantic world—was erected. In the seven cotton states, one-third of all white income was derived from slavery. By 1840, cotton produced by slave labor constituted 59 percent of the country's exports. The web of this slave society extended north to the looms of New England, and across the Atlantic to Great Britain, where it powered a great economic transformation and altered the trajectory of world history, "Whoever says Industrial Revolution," wrote the historian Eric J. Hobsbawm, "says cotton."

The wealth accorded America by slavery was not just in what the slaves pulled from the land but in the slaves themselves. "In 1860, slaves as an asset were worth more than all of America's manufacturing, all of the railroads, all of the productive capacity of the United States put together," the Yale historian David W. Blight has noted. "Slaves were the single largest, by far, financial asset of property in the entire American economy." The sale of these slaves—"in whose bodies that money congealed," writes Walter Johnson, a Harvard historian—generated even more ancillary wealth. Loans were taken out for purchase, to be repaid with interest. Insurance policies were drafted against the untimely death of a slave and the loss of potential profits. Slave sales were taxed and notarized. The vending of the black body and the sundering of the black family became an economy unto themselves, estimated to have brought in tens of millions of dollars to antebellum America. In 1860 there were more millionaires per capita in the Mississippi Valley than anywhere else in the country. . . .

Forced partings were common in the antebellum South. A slave in some parts of the region stood a 30 percent chance of being sold in his or her lifetime. Twenty-five percent of interstate trades destroyed a first marriage and half of them destroyed a nuclear family.

When the wife and children of Henry Brown, a slave in Richmond, Virginia, were to be sold away, Brown searched for a white master who might buy his wife and children to keep the family together. He failed:

> The next day, I stationed myself by the side of the road, along which the slaves, amounting to three hundred and fifty, were to pass. The purchaser of my wife was a Methodist minister, who was about starting for North Carolina. Pretty soon five waggon-loads of little children passed, and looking at the foremost one, what should I see but a little child, pointing its tiny hand towards me, exclaiming, "There's my father; I knew he would come and bid me good-bye." It was my eldest child! Soon the gang approached in which my wife was chained. I looked, and beheld her familiar face; but O, reader, that glance of agony! may God spare me ever again enduring the excruciating horror of that moment! She passed, and came near to where I stood. I seized hold of her hand, intending to bid her farewell; but words failed me; the gift of utterance had fled, and I remained speechless. I followed her for some distance, with her hand grasped in mine, as if to save her from her fate, but I could not speak, and I was obliged to turn away in silence.

In a time when telecommunications were primitive and blacks lacked freedom of movement, the parting of black families was a kind of murder. Here we find the roots of American wealth and democracy—in the for-profit destruction of the most important asset available to any people, the family. The destruction was not incidental to America's rise; it facilitated that rise. By erecting a slave society, America created the economic foundation for its great experiment in democracy. The labor strife that seeded Bacon's rebellion was suppressed. America's indispensable working class existed as property beyond the realm of politics, leaving white Americans free to trumpet their love of freedom and democratic values. Assessing antebellum democracy in Virginia, a visitor from England observed that the state's natives "can profess an unbounded love of liberty and of democracy in consequence of the mass of the people, who in other countries might become mobs, being there nearly altogether composed of their own Negro slaves."

V. The Quiet Plunder

The consequences of 250 years of enslavement, of war upon black families and black people, were profound. Like homeownership today, slave ownership was aspirational, attracting not just those who owned slaves but those who wished to. Much as homeowners today might discuss the addition of a patio or the painting of a living room, slaveholders traded tips on the best methods for breeding workers, exacting labor, and doling out punishment. Just as a homeowner today might subscribe to a magazine like *This Old House*, slaveholders had journals such as *De Bow's Review*, which recommended the best practices for wringing profits from slaves. By the dawn of the Civil War, the enslavement of black America was thought to be so foundational to the country that those who sought to end it were branded heretics worthy of death. Imagine what would happen if a president today came out in favor of taking all American homes from their owners: the reaction might well be violent.

"This country was formed for the *white*, not for the black man," John Wilkes Booth wrote, before killing Abraham Lincoln. "And looking upon *African slavery* from the same standpoint held by those noble framers of our Constitution, I for one have ever considered *it* one of the greatest blessings (both for themselves and us) that God ever bestowed upon a favored nation."

In the aftermath of the Civil War, Radical Republicans attempted to reconstruct the country upon something resembling universal equality — but they were beaten back by a campaign of "Redemption," led by White Liners, Red Shirts, and Klansmen bent on upholding a society "formed for the *white*, not for the black man." A wave of terrorism roiled the South. In his massive history *Reconstruction*, Eric Foner recounts incidents of black people being attacked for not removing their hats; for refusing to hand over a whiskey flask; for disobeying church procedures; for "using insolent language"; for disputing labor contracts; for refusing to be "tied like a slave." Sometimes the attacks were intended simply to "thin out the niggers a little."

Terrorism carried the day. Federal troops withdrew from the South in 1877. The dream of Reconstruction died. For the next century, political violence was visited upon blacks wantonly, with special treatment meted out toward black people of ambition. Black schools and churches were burned to the ground. Black voters and the political candidates who attempted to rally them were intimidated, and some were murdered. At the end of World War I, black veterans returning to their homes were assaulted for daring to wear the American uniform. The demobilization of soldiers after the war, which put white and black veterans into competition for scarce jobs, produced the Red Summer of 1919: a succession of racist pogroms against dozens of cities ranging from Longview, Texas, to Chicago to Washington, D.C. Organized white violence against blacks continued into the 1920s — in 1921 a white mob leveled Tulsa's "Black Wall Street," and in 1923 another one razed the black town of Rosewood, Florida — and virtually no one was punished.

The work of mobs was a rabid and violent rendition of prejudices 75 that extended even into the upper reaches of American government. The New Deal is today remembered as a model for what progressive government should do — cast a broad social safety net that protects the poor and the afflicted while building the middle class. When progressives wish to express their disappointment with Barack Obama, they point to the accomplishments of Franklin Roosevelt. But these progressives rarely note that Roosevelt's New Deal, much like the democracy that produced it, rested on the foundation of Jim Crow.

"The Jim Crow South," writes Ira Katznelson, a history and political-science professor at Columbia, "was the one collaborator America's democracy could not do without." The marks of that collaboration are all over the New Deal. The omnibus programs passed under the Social Security Act in 1935 were crafted in such a way as to protect the southern way of life. Old-age insurance (Social Security proper) and unemployment insurance excluded farmworkers and domestics—jobs heavily occupied by blacks. When President Roosevelt signed Social Security into law in 1935, 65 percent of African Americans nationally and between 70 and 80 percent in the South were ineligible. The NAACP protested, calling the new American safety net "a sieve with holes just big enough for the majority of Negroes to fall through."

The oft-celebrated GI Bill similarly failed black Americans, by mirroring the broader country's insistence on a racist housing policy. Though ostensibly color-blind, Title III of the bill, which aimed to give veterans access to low-interest home loans, left black veterans to tangle with white officials at their local Veterans Administration as well as with the same banks that had, for years, refused to grant mortgages to blacks. The historian Kathleen J. Frydl observes in her 2009 book, *The GI Bill*, that so many blacks were disqualified from receiving Title III benefits "that it is more accurate simply to say that blacks could not use this particular title."

In Cold War America, homeownership was seen as a means of instilling patriotism, and as a civilizing and anti-radical force. "No man who owns his own house and lot can be a Communist," claimed William Levitt, who pioneered the modern suburb with the development of the various Levittowns, his famous planned communities. "He has too much to do."

But the Levittowns were, with Levitt's willing acquiescence, segregated throughout their early years. Daisy and Bill Myers, the first black family to move into Levittown, Pennsylvania, were greeted with protests and a burning cross. A neighbor who opposed the family said that Bill Myers was "probably a nice guy, but every time I look at him I see $2,000 drop off the value of my house."

The neighbor had good reason to be afraid. Bill and Daisy Myers were from the other side of John C. Calhoun's dual society. If they moved next door, housing policy almost guaranteed that their neighbors' property values would decline.

Whereas shortly before the New Deal, a typical mortgage required a large down payment and full repayment within about 10 years, the creation of the Home Owners' Loan Corporation in 1933 and then the Federal Housing Administration the following year allowed banks to offer loans requiring no more than 10 percent down, amortized over 20 to 30 years. "Without federal intervention in the housing market, massive suburbanization would have been impossible," writes Thomas J. Sugrue, a historian at the University of Pennsylvania. "In 1930, only 30 percent of Americans owned their own homes; by 1960, more than 60 percent were home owners. Home ownership became an emblem of American citizenship."

That emblem was not to be awarded to blacks. The American real-estate industry believed segregation to be a moral principle. As late as 1950, the National Association of Real Estate Boards' code of ethics warned that "a Realtor should never be instrumental in introducing into a neighborhood . . . any race or nationality, or any individuals whose presence will clearly be detrimental to property values." A 1943 brochure specified that such potential undesirables might include madams, bootleggers, gangsters—and "a colored man of means who was giving his children a college education and thought they were entitled to live among whites."

The federal government concurred. It was the Home Owners' Loan Corporation, not a private trade association, that pioneered the practice of redlining, selectively granting loans and insisting that any property it insured be covered by a restrictive covenant—a clause in the deed forbidding the sale of the property to anyone other than whites. Millions of dollars flowed from tax coffers into segregated white neighborhoods.

"For perhaps the first time, the federal government embraced the discriminatory attitudes of the marketplace," the historian Kenneth T. Jackson wrote in his 1985 book, *Crabgrass Frontier,* a history of suburbanization. "Previously, prejudices were personalized and individualized; FHA exhorted segregation and enshrined it as public policy. Whole areas of cities were declared ineligible for loan guarantees." Redlining was not officially outlawed until 1968, by the Fair Housing Act. By then the damage was done—and reports of redlining by banks have continued.

The federal government is premised on equal fealty from all its citizens, who in return are to receive equal treatment. But as late as the mid-20th century, this bargain was not granted to black people, who repeatedly paid a higher price for citizenship and received less in return. Plunder had been the essential feature of slavery, of the society described by Calhoun. But practically a full century after the end of the Civil War and the abolition of slavery, the plunder—quiet, systemic, submerged—continued even amidst the aims and achievements of New Deal liberals. [85]

VI. Making the Second Ghetto

Today Chicago is one of the most segregated cities in the country, a fact that reflects assiduous planning. In the effort to uphold white supremacy at every level down to the neighborhood, Chicago—a city founded by the black fur trader Jean Baptiste Point du Sable—has long been a pioneer. The efforts began in earnest in 1917, when the Chicago Real Estate Board, horrified by the influx of southern blacks, lobbied to zone the entire city by race. But after the Supreme Court ruled against explicit racial zoning that year, the city was forced to pursue its agenda by more-discreet means.

Like the Home Owners' Loan Corporation, the Federal Housing Administration initially insisted on restrictive covenants, which helped bar blacks and other ethnic undesirables from receiving federally backed home loans. By the 1940s, Chicago led the nation in the use of these restrictive covenants, and about half of all residential neighborhoods in the city were effectively off-limits to blacks.

It is common today to become misty-eyed about the old black ghetto, where doctors and lawyers lived next door to meatpackers and steelwork-ers, who themselves lived next door to prostitutes and the unemployed. This segregationist nostalgia ignores the actual conditions endured by the people living there—vermin and arson, for instance—and ignores the fact that the old ghetto was premised on denying black people privi-leges enjoyed by white Americans.

In 1948, when the Supreme Court ruled that restrictive covenants, while permissible, were not enforceable by judicial action, Chicago had other weapons at the ready. The Illinois state legislature had already given Chicago's city council the right to approve—and thus to veto— any public housing in the city's wards. This came in handy in 1949, when a new federal housing act sent millions of tax dollars into Chicago and other cities around the country. Beginning in 1950, site selection for public housing proceeded entirely on the grounds of segregation. By the 1960s, the city had created with its vast housing projects what the historian Arnold R. Hirsch calls a "second ghetto," one larger than the old Black Belt but just as impermeable. More than 98 percent of all the family public-housing units built in Chicago between 1950 and the mid-1960s were built in all-black neighborhoods.

Governmental embrace of segregation was driven by the virulent racism of Chicago's white citizens. White neighborhoods vulnerable to black encroachment formed block associations for the sole purpose of enforcing segregation. They lobbied fellow whites not to sell. They lob-bied those blacks who did manage to buy to sell back. In 1949, a group of Englewood Catholics formed block associations intended to "keep up the neighborhood." Translation: keep black people out. And when civic engagement was not enough, when government failed, when private banks could no longer hold the line, Chicago turned to an old tool in the American repertoire—racial violence. "The pattern of terrorism is easily discernible," concluded a Chicago civic group in the 1940s. "It is at the seams of the black ghetto in all directions." On July 1 and 2 of 1946, a mob of thousands assembled in Chicago's Park Manor neighborhood, hoping to eject a black doctor who'd recently moved in. The mob pelted the house with rocks and set the garage on fire. The doctor moved away.

In 1947, after a few black veterans moved into the Fernwood section of Chicago, three nights of rioting broke out; gangs of whites yanked blacks off streetcars and beat them. Two years later, when a union meeting attended by blacks in Englewood triggered rumors that a home was being "sold to niggers," blacks (and whites thought to be sympathetic to them) were beaten in the streets. In 1951, thousands of whites in Cicero, 20 minutes or so west of downtown Chicago, attacked an apartment building that housed a single black family, throwing bricks and fire-bombs through the windows and setting the apartment on fire. A Cook County grand jury declined to charge the rioters—and instead indicted the family's NAACP attorney, the apartment's white owner, and the owner's attorney and rental agent, charging them with conspiring to lower property values. Two years after that, whites picketed and planted explosives in South Deering, about 30 minutes from downtown Chicago, to force blacks out.

When terrorism ultimately failed, white homeowners simply fled the neighborhood. The traditional terminology, *white flight*, implies a kind of natural expression of preference. In fact, white flight was a triumph of social engineering, orchestrated by the shared racist presumptions of America's public and private sectors. For should any nonracist white families decide that integration might not be so bad as a matter of principle or practicality, they still had to contend with the hard facts of American housing policy: When the mid-20th-century white homeowner claimed that the presence of a Bill and Daisy Myers decreased his property value, he was not merely engaging in racist dogma—he was accurately observing the impact of federal policy on market prices. Redlining destroyed the possibility of investment wherever black people lived.

Speculators in North Lawndale, and at the edge of the black ghettos, knew there was money to be made off white panic. They resorted to "block-busting"—spooking whites into selling cheap before the neighborhood became black. They would hire a black woman to walk up and down the street with a stroller. Or they'd hire someone to call a number in the neighborhood looking for "Johnny Mae." Then they'd cajole whites into selling at low prices, informing them that the more blacks who moved in, the more the value of their homes would decline, so better to sell now. With these white-fled homes in hand, speculators then turned to the masses of black people who had streamed northward as part of the Great Migration, or who were desperate to escape the ghettos; the speculators would take the houses they'd just bought cheap through block-busting and sell them to blacks on contract.

To keep up with his payments and keep his heat on, Clyde Ross took a second job at the post office and then a third job delivering pizza. His wife took a job working at Marshall Field. He had to take some of his children out of private school. He was not able to be at home to supervise his children or help them with their homework. Money and time that Ross wanted to give his children went instead to enrich white speculators.

"The problem was the money," Ross told me. "Without the money, you can't move. You can't educate your kids. You can't give them the right kind of food. Can't make the house look good. They think this neighborhood is where they supposed to be. It changes their outlook. My kids were going to the best schools in this neighborhood, and I couldn't keep them in there." . . .

Chicago, like the country at large, embraced policies that placed black America's most energetic, ambitious, and thrifty countrymen beyond the pale of society and marked them as rightful targets for legal theft. The effects reverberate beyond the families who were robbed to the community that beholds the spectacle. Don't just picture Clyde Ross working three jobs so he could hold on to his home. Think of his North Lawndale neighbors—their children, their nephews and nieces—and consider how watching this affects them. Imagine yourself as a young black child watching your elders play by all the rules only to have their possessions tossed out in the street and to have their most sacred possession—their home—taken from them. . . .

VII. Toward a New Country

Scholars have long discussed methods by which America might make reparations to those on whose labor and exclusion the country was built. In the 1970s, the Yale Law professor Boris Bittker argued in *The Case for Black Reparations* that a rough price tag for reparations could be determined by multiplying the number of African Americans in the population by the difference in white and black per capita income. That number—$34 billion in 1973, when Bittker wrote his book—could be added to a reparations program each year for a decade or two. Today Charles Ogletree, the Harvard Law School professor, argues for something broader: a program of job training and public works that takes racial justice as its mission but includes the poor of all races.

To celebrate freedom and democracy while forgetting America's origins in a slavery economy is patriotism à la carte.

Perhaps no statistic better illustrates the enduring legacy of our country's shameful history of treating black people as sub-citizens, sub-Americans, and sub-humans than the wealth gap. Reparations would seek to close this chasm. But as surely as the creation of the wealth gap required the cooperation of every aspect of the society, bridging it will require the same.

Perhaps after a serious discussion and debate—the kind that HR 40 proposes—we may find that the country can never fully repay African Americans. But we stand to discover much about ourselves in such a discussion—and that is perhaps what scares us. The idea of reparations is frightening not simply because we might lack the ability to pay. The idea of reparations threatens something much deeper—America's heritage, history, and standing in the world.

The early American economy was built on slave labor. The Capitol and the White House were built by slaves. President James K. Polk traded slaves from the Oval Office. The laments about "black pathology," the criticism of black family structures by pundits and intellectuals, ring hollow in a country whose existence was predicated on the torture of black fathers, on the rape of black mothers, on the sale of black children. An honest assessment of America's relationship to the black family reveals the country to be not its nurturer but its destroyer.

And this destruction did not end with slavery. Discriminatory laws joined the equal burden of citizenship to unequal distribution of its bounty. These laws reached their apex in the mid-20th century, when the federal government—through housing policies—engineered the wealth gap, which remains with us to this day. When we think of white supremacy, we picture COLORED ONLY signs, but we should picture pirate flags.

On some level, we have always grasped this.

"Negro poverty is not white poverty," President Johnson said in his historic civil-rights speech.

> Many of its causes and many of its cures are the same. But there are differences—deep, corrosive, obstinate differences—radiating painful roots into the community and into the family, and the nature of the individual. These differences are not racial differences. They are solely and simply the consequence of ancient brutality, past injustice, and present prejudice.

We invoke the words of Jefferson and Lincoln because they say 105 something about our legacy and our traditions. We do this because we recognize our links to the past—at least when they flatter us. But black history does not flatter American democracy; it chastens it. The popular mocking of reparations as a harebrained scheme authored by wild-eyed lefties and intellectually unserious black nationalists is fear masquerading as laughter. Black nationalists have always perceived something unmentionable about America that integrationists dare not acknowledge—that white supremacy is not merely the work of hotheaded demagogues, or a matter of false consciousness, but a force so fundamental to America that it is difficult to imagine the country without it.

And so we must imagine a new country. Reparations—by which I mean the full acceptance of our collective biography and its consequences—is the price we must pay to see ourselves squarely. The recovering alcoholic may well have to live with his illness for the rest of his life. But at least he is not living a drunken lie. Reparations beckons us to reject the intoxication of hubris and see America as it is—the work of fallible humans.

Won't reparations divide us? Not any more than we are already divided. The wealth gap merely puts a number on something we feel but cannot say—that American prosperity was ill-gotten and selective in its distribution. What is needed is an airing of family secrets, a settling with old ghosts. What is needed is a healing of the American psyche and the banishment of white guilt.

What I'm talking about is more than recompense for past injustices—more than a handout, a payoff, hush money, or a reluctant bribe. What I'm talking about is a national reckoning that would lead to spiritual renewal. Reparations would mean the end of scarfing hot dogs on the Fourth of July while denying the facts of our heritage. Reparations would mean the end of yelling "patriotism" while waving a Confederate flag. Reparations would mean a revolution of the American consciousness, a reconciling of our self-image as the great democratizer with the facts of our history. . . .

Something more than moral pressure calls America to reparations. We cannot escape our history. All of our solutions to the great problems of health care, education, housing, and economic inequality are troubled by what must go unspoken. "The reason black people are so far behind now is not because of now," Clyde Ross told me. "It's because of then." In the early 2000s, Charles Ogletree went to Tulsa, Oklahoma, to meet with the survivors of the 1921 race riot that had devastated "Black Wall Street." The past was not the past to them. "It was amazing seeing these black women and men who were crippled, blind, in wheelchairs," Ogletree told me. "I had no idea who they were and why they wanted to see me. They said, 'We want you to represent us in this lawsuit.'"

A commission authorized by the Oklahoma legislature produced a report affirming that the riot, the knowledge of which had been suppressed for years, had happened. But the lawsuit ultimately failed, in 2004. Similar suits pushed against corporations such as Aetna (which insured slaves) and Lehman Brothers (whose co-founding partner owned them) also have thus far failed. These results are dispiriting, but the crime with which reparations activists charge the country implicates more than just a few towns or corporations. The crime indicts the American people themselves, at every level, and in nearly every configuration. A crime that implicates the entire American people deserves its hearing in the legislative body that represents them. 110

John Conyers's HR 40 is the vehicle for that hearing. No one can know what would come out of such a debate. Perhaps no number can fully capture the multi-century plunder of black people in America. Perhaps the number is so large that it can't be imagined, let alone calculated and dispensed. But I believe that wrestling publicly with these questions matters as much as—if not more than—the specific answers that might be produced. An America that asks what it owes its most vulnerable citizens is improved and humane. An America that looks away is ignoring not just the sins of the past but the sins of the present and the certain sins of the future. More important than any single check cut to any African American, the payment of reparations would represent America's maturation out of the childhood myth of its innocence into a wisdom worthy of its founders.

In 2010, Jacob S. Rugh, then a doctoral candidate at Princeton, and the sociologist Douglas S. Massey published a study of the recent foreclosure crisis. Among its drivers, they found an old foe: segregation. Black home buyers—even after controlling for factors like creditworthiness—were still more likely than white home buyers to be steered toward subprime loans. Decades of racist housing policies by the American government, along with decades of racist housing practices by American businesses, had conspired to concentrate African Americans in the same neighborhoods. As in North Lawndale half a century earlier, these neighborhoods were filled with people who had been cut off from mainstream financial institutions. When subprime lenders went looking for prey, they found black people waiting like ducks in a pen.

"High levels of segregation create a natural market for subprime lending," Rugh and Massey write, "and cause riskier mortgages, and thus foreclosures, to accumulate disproportionately in racially segregated cities' minority neighborhoods."

Plunder in the past made plunder in the present efficient. The banks of America understood this. In 2005, Wells Fargo promoted a series of Wealth Building Strategies seminars. Dubbing itself "the nation's leading originator of home loans to ethnic minority customers," the bank enrolled black public figures in an ostensible effort to educate blacks on building "generational wealth." But the "wealth building" seminars were a front for wealth theft. In 2010, the Justice Department filed a discrimination suit against Wells Fargo alleging that the bank had shunted blacks into predatory loans regardless of their creditworthiness. This was not magic or coincidence or misfortune. It was racism reifying itself. According to the *New York Times*, affidavits found loan officers referring

to their black customers as "mud people" and to their subprime products as "ghetto loans."

"We just went right after them," Beth Jacobson, a former Wells Fargo 115 loan officer, told the *Times*. "Wells Fargo mortgage had an emerging-markets unit that specifically targeted black churches because it figured church leaders had a lot of influence and could convince congregants to take out subprime loans."

In 2011, Bank of America agreed to pay $355 million to settle charges of discrimination against its Countrywide unit. The following year, Wells Fargo settled its discrimination suit for more than $175 million. But the damage had been done. In 2009, half the properties in Baltimore whose owners had been granted loans by Wells Fargo between 2005 and 2008 were vacant; 71 percent of these properties were in predominantly black neighborhoods.

ENGAGING THE TEXT

1. Why does Coates devote so much time to the story of Clyde Ross? In what ways do Ross's experiences reflect the experience of black Americans more generally?

2. In part 2 of this essay ("A Difference of Kind, Not Degree") Coates paints a grim picture of black Chicago, citing statistics on homicide, infant mortality, incarceration rate, income, and household wealth. How does he use these statistics to construct his argument, and how persuasive is it? Why does Coates reject "cultural pathology" as an explanation for black poverty?

3. Coates argues that "America begins in black plunder and white democracy, two features that are not contradictory but complementary" (para. 60). How was democracy intertwined with and dependent upon slavery, according to Coates?

4. Coates asserts that "one cannot escape the question" of reparations "by hand-waving at the past, disavowing the acts of one's ancestors, nor by citing a recent date of ancestral immigration" (para. 57). How, according to Coates, do contemporary white Americans, who had little or nothing to do with slavery, still reap benefits from the historic oppression of African Americans? Why does he believe that there remains a debt to be paid?

5. In "The Case for Reparations," Coates makes only passing reference to reparations in the first two sections. He discusses the concept in detail in part 3 ("We Inherit Our Ample Patrimony"), but devotes the next four parts to the history of black exploitation and white supremacy, returning to the topic of reparations in the final section. Why does he wait so long to introduce the main subject of his essay? How does he develop the case for reparations in the four parts that never mention the idea? What would be the effect of focusing more exclusively on reparations throughout the essay?

6. **Thinking Rhetorically** Coates's language can appear extreme: He describes the "tyranny" of "the acquisitive warlords of the South" (para. 13), condemns America's 250-year "war upon black families and black people" (para. 71), and refers to the "plunder" of black bodies and labor over a dozen times. He also draws extensively

on scholarship, quoting historians, sociologists, and law professors throughout the essay. Write a paper analyzing Coates's style: Do you find his language engaging or off-putting? How does he deploy supporting evidence? Is it convincing? How might opponents of reparations object to his arguments, and how might he respond?

EXPLORING CONNECTIONS

7. Linda Holtzman and Leon Sharpe (p. 599) claim that the tendency to see "contemporary racial oppression as interpersonal and episodic gets in the way of our ability to come to grips with its fundamental nature, which is structural and systemic" (para. 5). Using specific examples from Coates, explain the distinction between individual and structural racism.

8. Write an imaginary conversation among Coates, Malcolm X (p. 161), Jay Z (p. 350), Joan Morgan (p. 533), and Cheryl I. Harris and Devon W. Carbado (p. 620) on what it means to be black in America.

9. While Coates is deliberately vague about the form that reparations should take, Alan Aja and his coauthors (p. 415) propose two concrete policies — Child Trust Accounts and a Federal Job Guarantee — to bridge the "persistent racial gaps in employment and wealth" (para. 5). How far would these policies go toward satisfying Coates's call for reparations? What would they accomplish and what would they fail to address?

10. Write an essay comparing the experiences of Clyde Ross and Antonio Martinez (in Kevin Bales and Ron Soodalter, p. 443). How are the two men exploited? What forces are arrayed against them? How do they resist? To what extent do you consider each successful or unsuccessful, and why?

11. Examine David Horsey's "American Dream Game" on page 596. How does the white character interpret the black character's slower progress toward the American Dream? What is the cartoonist suggesting about white privilege and racial blindness?

EXTENDING THE CRITICAL CONTEXT

12. Work in small groups to brainstorm a plan for reparations. Should it target blacks alone, or include "the poor of all races"? Should it pay people directly or aim for "job training and public works" (para. 97)? What kinds of public works would be most beneficial? Do some background research on the Rosewood massacre reparations, Japanese internment reparations, and German Holocaust reparations to find out who was paid, how much, and how it was distributed. Present and debate each group's ideas: Are the plans fair? Do they adequately address economic disadvantage? Would they stimulate the national soul-searching that Coates calls for?

13. In 2013, a divided Supreme Court voted 5 to 4 to strike down a key section of the Voting Rights Act of 1965. Do some online research about the case, *Shelby County v. Holder*: Why was the Voting Rights Act passed in the first place? Why

did the Court's majority rule that this section of the law was unconstitutional? Why did the dissenters disagree? How have some states changed the voting laws since this decision, and how have these changes affected minority, poor, elderly, and student voters?

14. Oscar Grant, Kendrec McDade, Yvette Smith, Eric Garner, Samuel DuBose, John Crawford, Michael Brown, Ezell Ford, Tanisha Anderson, Tamir Rice, Jerame Reid, Walter Scott, and Freddie Gray — all were unarmed blacks who were killed by police officers under questionable circumstances. How would Coates explain these cases? Research one or more of them: What led to the confrontation — were different stories told? What role, if any, did video play in the public perception of the incident? What role did the courts and the U.S. Department of Justice play? What role did social media, organized protest, and public outrage play? Was any measure of justice attained? How do you explain the outcome of the case (if an outcome has been reached)?

THEORIES AND CONSTRUCTS OF RACE
LINDA HOLTZMAN AND LEON SHARPE

At a time when 48 percent of white millennials believe that antiwhite discrimination has become as big a problem as discrimination against minority groups,[1] Linda Holtzman and Leon Sharpe provide a necessary corrective. In the following excerpt from their book *Media Messages: What Film, Television, and Popular Music Teach Us About Race, Class, Gender, and Sexual Orientation* (2nd edition, 2014), Holtzman and Sharpe offer a critical look at race, racism, and the belief that we now live in a "postracial" society. Linda Holtzman is an emeritus professor of journalism and communications at Webster University, where she taught media theory and research for twenty-five years. She has won many awards for her work as an antiracism facilitator for national social justice organizations and school districts in Illinois and Missouri. In addition, she has received grants for her work on human rights activism in the United States, Israel, and Palestine. Leon Sharpe teaches at Webster University, where he is an adjunct professor of communications. He is also founder of The Praxis Group, which has conducted workshops and training sessions for institutions and organizations nationwide, including the Coalition of Essential Schools, Focus St. Louis, and the Anti-Defamation League.

[1]DBR/MTV Bias Survey Summary, April 2014.

Key Terms

assimilation: Assimilation is the process through which newcomers (children entering a new school, families moving to a new neighborhood, and immigrants arriving in the United States) adjust to a situation by deciding how much of their old culture and habits they want to give up and how much of their new culture they want to absorb. In the context of immigration to the United States, this process includes surface and deep culture: anything from clothing, food, and language to child-rearing, dating and marriage practices, and treatment of elders in the community. Throughout U.S. history, there have been diverse waves of voluntary immigrants and refugees. Other groups have involuntarily become part of the United States through the violent conquest of their land (Mexicans, American Indians) or violent enslavement (African Americans). In order to be considered true Americans, these newcomers were expected to assimilate. The unspoken rules of assimilation were that the closer the immigrants were to existing U.S. citizens of European heritage in terms of skin color and ability to blend in, the more likely they were able to make active choices about the degree to which they wanted to reject their former culture in favor of their new culture. The more they assimilated, and the more their skin color allowed them to assimilate, the more they were entitled to the same privileges as the Europeans who came before them. Most immigrant groups of color, including Africans, Asians, and American Indians, were not entitled to citizenship until decades—sometimes a century—after newer European immigrants because the color of their skin was not considered sufficiently white. Because of this and due to the nature of racial separation in the United States, assimilation was available unequally to whites and people of color, depending on the time of their arrival to the United States.

critical race theory (CRT): An academic discipline that analyzes race in the United States through the lens of power and law. CRT is based on several core tenets, including the permanence of racism, critique of liberalism, whiteness as property, interest convergence, intersection of racism with other forms of oppression, centrality of personal experience, and use of the counternarrative as an explanatory and analytical tool.

internalized racism: The process by which people of color take in negative messages of overt and covert racism, superiority, and inferiority, and apply those messages to themselves and others in ways that are self-destructive rather than self-affirming. Internalized racism, which is always involuntary, is the direct by-product of historical and ongoing racial targeting.

internalized white supremacy: This term has begun to be used more frequently since the late twentieth century. Antiracist activists and scholars have a few different, but highly compatible concepts defining to whom the term is applicable. In general, internalized white supremacy is the assumption of white superiority in intelligence, in achievement, and in the centrality in U.S. culture by individuals who are often unaware of its powerful existence. People who internalize this dimension of white supremacy are not generally the same people whose outright racial hatred counts them among the members of the Ku Klux Klan and other racial hate groups. In fact, these people are often shocked and alarmed as they investigate this phenomenon and discover that they have been operating on the assumptions that the tenets of white superiority are "the truth." These messages strongly presume the centrality of European Americans to the individual achievement and success in the United States and to worldwide recognition in literature, science, world peace, and other fields.

meta-narrative: A comprehensive "story" of history and knowledge that unifies and simplifies the culture and value of a group or nation. When meta-narratives are applied to nations, they frequently are used to explain and justify the existing power structure.

racial discrimination: An individual act or an institutional pattern that results in the unequal treatment of members of a targeted racial group. Racial discrimination is an *action* or *behavior* that may result from conscious or unconscious *beliefs* (stereotypes) about a racial group or from predetermined *feelings* (prejudices) toward that group.

racialize: To see or describe something from a racial perspective; to emphasize race or to make something seem racial. For example, in the early twentieth century; Jews were racialized in Europe, Russia, and most of the United States. Today, in much of the United States, Judaism is regarded as a religion rather than a race. Another example occurred in the aftermath of the 9/11 terrorist attacks with the widespread racialization of Muslims and people of Middle Eastern descent.

racism: A system of institutionalized power that operates through overt or covert policies that favor white people and are biased against people of color. Racism continues to exist today in the hiring practices of some private businesses, government agencies, hospitals, universities, and so on, even where there are policies that clearly state they will not discriminate. Despite such policies, these institutions often devise strategies and engage in practices that result in the virtual elimination of people of color from their pools of potential candidates. Another commonly used approach to understanding racism is based on the comparative analysis of levels of social access—to quality education, jobs, promotions, and other opportunities—between white people and people of color.

schema: A mental model or pattern of thinking that influences the way we organize and simplify our knowledge of the world around us.

white privilege: A set of unearned advantages and opportunities created by racism that are often far more visible to people of color than they are to whites. Despite the pervasiveness of racism in the history and current structures of the United States, many white people believe that racism was eradicated by the late twentieth century and that individual achievement and success are based solely on individual intelligence, motivation, and hard work. As a result of this type of misinformation and socialization, many whites believe that all of their successes are built exclusively on their own talent, skills, merit, and hard work. In fact, in many small and large ways, whites have access to different opportunities and are treated differently than people of color, giving them an often invisible boost to this success to which people of color do not have the same access. For example, white parents rarely need to think about the danger present for their sons at a mall or on the street if they are stopped by a police officer. Ample research and statistics indicate that young African American or Latino men are far more likely to be harassed, abused, and/or arrested by police than young white men. The privilege here is that white parents generally only need to think about this danger if their son will be in an area in which there is high crime. But the danger there is potential criminals, not the police. Whites are rarely asked to speak on behalf of their whole race or justify the criminal activity or failure of other whites, while people of color are frequently asked to do all of these things. White privilege allows whites the luxury and advantage of living in a world where their personal worth, rightness, and personhood are continually validated in ways that do not apply for people of color (Olson, n.d).

white supremacy: White supremacy is typically thought of as the extremist views and actions of hate groups such as the Ku Klux Klan, White Citizens Council, and Aryan Brotherhood. This definition of white supremacy is the categorical belief and the actions based on the belief that, in every way, whites are superior to people of color. Often Jews and sometimes Catholics are also included in the category of so-called inferior people. Many of these hate groups are responsible for what we call "hate crimes," in which these "inferior" people are subjected to violence, torture, murder, and destruction of property, which are seen as justified by white supremacist individuals and organizations that believe that these "inferior" groups will destroy America if not eliminated.

There is another type of white supremacy that is more subtle, yet equally insidious in the way it pervades the minds of individuals and permeates the culture. This type assumes the dominance and superiority of white culture as reflected in the academic curricula of U.S. history and literature and science, in which the contributions of white people are more visible and valued more greatly than the contributions of people of color. In this scenario, hate and hate crimes are not central; however, white people are seen as at the center of U.S. culture. "And so you see that white centrality, especially in the way that the culture, the dominant white culture, fights for the right to tell the story, not only of America, but of the world in ways that leave white people at the center and are based on assumptions of the superiority of white people—even if as a culture we've renounced overt segregation and discrimination" (Wells 2013). By this definition, white supremacy is not always based on intent or on individual or even institutional racial hate or bigotry. However, if we look at the demographics of wealth and poverty, educational achievement and level of attainment, and job status, to name a few, we will be able to predict who is most likely to be at the top and who is most likely to be at the bottom, with race as the central factor of these predictions. Then we know that the system is infested with structural racism and the messages involve white supremacy.

Theories and Constructs of Race

The shifting meaning of race throughout U.S. history provides important clues to its definition. It is not biological, nor is it based primarily on skin color. It is not necessarily based on ethnicity nor is it based on country of origin. Rather, race is constructed socially, culturally, politically, and economically. "Various racial categories have been created or changed to meet the emerging economic and social needs of white United States culture. Racial categories artificially emphasize the relatively small external physical differences among people and leave room for the creation of false notions of mental, emotional, and intellectual differences as well" (Adams, Bell, and Griffin 1997, 83).

While race itself is fiction, the consequences of racism are a historical and contemporary fact of American life. "Racism is based on the concept of whiteness—an identity concept invented and enforced by power and violence. Whiteness is a constantly shifting boundary separating those who are entitled to have certain privileges from those whose exploitation and vulnerability to violence is justified by their not being white" (Kivel 1996, 17). The historical mutability of race is significant because of how it has been used as a marker of group identity and a means of access to privilege in this country and elsewhere. The possession of whiteness represents a valued status that confers upon its owners a set of exclusive citizenship rights (Lipsitz 1998).

The centrality of race in our society is one of the core tenets of **critical race theory (CRT)**. CRT emerged originally in the 1980s as an outgrowth of critical legal studies (Crenshaw et al. 1995; Delgado and Stefancic 2001; Taylor, Gillborn, and Ladson-Billings 2009). Over the years, CRT has expanded to other disciplines such as education. Its ideas and methodologies have also been applied in other areas of focus such as LatCrit, AsianCrit, TribalCrit, FemCrit, and QueerCrit. One of the key concepts of critical race theory is that racism is a core component of the systems and structures of power in our nation. Racial inequity is so deeply embedded in our institutional practices, so integral to our interpersonal relationships and individual attitudes, so inextricably woven into the warp and woof of everyday life, that it has become a permanent feature of the American experience. Therefore, racism, in all its manifestations, must be continuously critiqued and challenged.

Not surprisingly, foundational elements of racial inequity often go unexamined, underanalyzed, or misrepresented by the mainstream media: "Specific media frames select out limited aspects of an issue in order to make it salient for mass communication, a selectivity usually promoting a narrow reading of that issue. . . . A particular frame structures the thinking process and shapes what people see or do not see, in important societal settings" (Feagin 2009, 27). A 2007 study of print media coverage of racial disparities in health care, education, early child development, and employment determined that because racism is framed, for the most part, as being rooted in interpersonal relationships between individuals or among groups of individuals, the systemic nature of race-based power dynamics is rarely reported. In examining the explanatory frames of 140 news articles published by major outlets in eight metropolitan areas nationwide, the study found that articles

> provided clear and unambiguous accounts of how racism can exist in a number of institutions and were easy for a wide audience to identify as racist. However, the dominance of such stories reinforces the notion that racism is primarily about individual actions rather than embedded in social structures. Furthermore, overt and blatant acts of racism were framed as aberrant occurrences that were unfortunate, but did not effectively challenge the perception that the United States has largely transcended its racial past. (O'Neil 2009)

The mischaracterization of contemporary racial oppression as interpersonal and episodic gets in the way of our ability to come to grips with its fundamental nature, which is structural and systemic. Young people today have grown up and come of age during an era when *legally sanctioned* racial segregation of public facilities appears to be a thing of the past. Overt acts of racial violence, although they still occur, are less common than they were prior to the civil rights era. Youth of color and their white counterparts form friendships and interact socially across racial lines more freely today than at any other time in America's past. Yet despite the popular notion that we now live in a "postracial" society, racial injustice continues to thrive in the United States. Glaring racial disparities continue to exist in education, employment, healthcare, housing, bank lending policies, the criminal justice and penal system, household income, household net worth, and a host of other areas. Thus, what has been referred to as America's "pathology of denial" about race (Leary 2006) impedes our ability to develop systemic solutions that will lead to the dismantling of the **racialized** institutional foundations of our country. It prevents us from devising strategies that are structurally transformative.

The Social and Psychological Impact of Race

The continuous racial targeting of people of color and the privileging of whites, along with misinformation about race passed along from one generation to the next and reinforced through the media, has imbued people of all races with a distorted sense of personal and group identity. Not surprisingly, given the centuries of racial stereotyping and negative messaging directed at people of color, research indicates that a majority of white Americans continue to have strong feelings of racial bias (Banaji and Greenwald 2013, 169–188; Greenwald and Krieger 2006). Many white people in the United States are socialized to regard their race as representing not only the majority group but also the societal norm—the cultural standard and benchmark for what it means to be American. According to one writer, "For many white people, the idea that we have racial identities is difficult to come to terms with. We usually see ourselves simply as people. Whiteness, by virtue of its status as the dominant social position, is unmarked. It is relatively easy for white persons to go through life never thinking about their own racial identity. Whiteness functions as the normative ideal against which other people are categorized and judged" (Kaufman 2001).

This illusory standard of a white societal norm reinforces the notion that people of color are not merely different but also deficient. Studies indicate that, despite a decline in overt expressions of racial bigotry, a large percentage of white Americans continue to consciously or unconsciously regard white identity as positive and black identity as negative (Schmidt and Nosek 2010). The unconscious belief among whites in the superiority of their own racial group relative to blacks and other people of color is a form of *implicit bias*—learned social stereotypes that are sometimes triggered automatically in individuals without their awareness (Greenwald and Banaji 1995). There is evidence to indicate that implicit racial bias exists in children as young as six years old and endures through adulthood (Baron and Banaji 2006). Implicit bias has the capacity to influence people's judgments in regard to how they think about and treat individuals who are racially different from them even when they openly express non-prejudicial views; "to characterize the nature of an individual's prejudice correctly, one must consider both explicit racial attitudes as well as implicit, automatic biases" (Son Hing et al. 2008).

The espousing of racial openness and egalitarianism while simultaneously harboring negative racial attitudes is prevalent in contemporary society. The acting out of biased beliefs through jokes, slurs, and other racial actions and commentary is less likely to occur openly in what sociologist Joe R. Feagin refers to as the *frontstage* of public, professional, and mixed-race gatherings where a diverse range of people is present. Yet such behaviors occur quite frequently in *backstage* settings among friends and close acquaintances where whites with negative feelings toward people of color can comfortably express their beliefs without fear of being judged or marginalized socially (Feagin 2009, 184). A study analyzing more than 600 personal journals from college students throughout the nation revealed thousands of instances of racially bigoted behavior such as name-calling, inappropriate racial humor, and references to stereotypes. Although often characterized as innocent fun, such actions reinforce racial polarization and antagonism (Feagin 2009, 185–190).

In addition, the toleration of duplicitous frontstage/backstage behavior contributes to the perpetuation of an American societal norm that enables schools, employers, public service providers, real estate brokers, law enforcement agencies, and a host of other institutions to publicly embrace equal opportunity policies while privately engaging in practices that deny equal access and fair treatment to members of racially targeted groups. While many white individuals are overtly racist, millions of others benefit from institutionally sanctioned racial privilege in ways that are often invisible to them. When Linda [Holtzman] wrote earlier of her personal story, she discussed the anti-Semitism her grandparents faced in Russia and as new immigrants to the United States. But because they and their descendants would ultimately be considered white, they were allowed to find work and housing and education from which African Americans and Japanese Americans were prohibited. Without ever initiating or participating in one overtly hateful act, they benefited from racism.

Misinformation about race and identity also contributes adversely to the socialization of people of color in the United States. The myth of racial inferiority and superiority has been upheld not only by physical violence and discriminatory policies but also by the psychological violence conveyed through the stereotyping and racist messaging to which people of color, beginning early in childhood, are continuously exposed. In the interest of dominant-group hegemony, false notions of a race-based hierarchy are promulgated relentlessly through virtually every mainstream institution in our society. "Oppressed people come to embody in their very being the negations imposed on them and thus, in the reproduction of their lives, harbor a tendency to contribute to the perpetuation of their own oppression" (Outlaw 2005, 14).

People of color in America have always had to wage a battle against **internalized racism**, a condition that can cause an individual to assume self-deprecating attitudes and engage in self-destructive behaviors that reflect the traumatizing effects of racial targeting. When people are regularly subjected to the physical and psychological abuse of overt and covert racial oppression, they sometimes respond by re-enacting that abuse on themselves and other members of their racial group. When Leon [Sharpe] wrote earlier about the stories he heard his adult family members telling with such vividness and ironic humor, he was speaking of the unremitting conversations of self-empowerment and cultural affirmation that many African Americans draw upon as a source of healing strength and collective power to counteract the insidious impact of internalized racism. Such stories have been as much a part of the black resistance movement in American history as any civil rights march, economic boycott, or slave uprising.

Internalized racism, which is always involuntary, is a direct by-product of historical and ongoing racial targeting. It works in many ways. For instance, social psychologist Claude M. Steele has advanced the theory of *stereotype threat* to explain the extent to which a person's performance can be detrimentally affected by the psychological triggering of negative stereotypes assigned to one's social group identity (Steele and Aronson 1995; Steele 1997; Steele 2010). Laura Padilla has written about the manner in which many Latinos accept the negative stereotypes directed at their own group and thus question the qualifications of other Latinos who are successful. She refers to this phenomenon as *envidia* or intragroup jealousy and regards it as a clear example of how behaviors resulting from internalized racism can sabotage communities of color (Padilla 2001). Social researcher Dr. Joy DeGruy (formerly

Leary) posits the concept of intergenerational trauma resulting from what she has termed *post-traumatic slave syndrome,* a consequence of multi-generational oppression of Africans and their descendants resulting from centuries of chattel slavery followed by decades of institutionalized racism that continues to inflict emotional injury (Leary 2006). In a similar vein, social worker Maria Yellow Horse Brave Heart, through her research and clinical work examining manifestations of intergenerational trauma among Native Americans, has focused on diagnosing and treating what she identifies as *historical unresolved grief* (Brave Heart 2000). Internalized racism among people of color and implicit racial bias among whites are unhealthy psychosocial reactions to the toxic power of racial targeting. Because of their detrimental effects, they must be actively addressed and rigorously interrupted whenever possible. Nevertheless, the injury they cause can only be fully healed as racism in our society is eliminated.

The Science and Pseudoscience of Race

Is race a scientifically verifiable concept? Does racial difference actually exist among human beings? According to biologists, a race is a distinct evolutionary lineage within a species that is sharply defined by measurable genetic differences. Genetic differences between populations are necessary but not sufficient to define race (Templeton 2002). Obviously, differences exist between populations within the human species. Members of what we regard as different racial groups have visibly diverse physical characteristics (skin color, hair texture, facial features). Thus, the question becomes, do diverse human populations exhibit sufficient differences at the genetic level to constitute a scientific basis for establishing the existence of separate races within our species?

A segment of the 2003 documentary *Race: The Power of Illusion* depicts a multiethnic group of students meeting with a DNA expert. They compare their skin colors, submit blood and DNA samples, and then discuss their thoughts as to which of their classmates share the closest genetic similarity with them. Most, if not all, of them assume that the students within their own "racial" group will be the closest to them genetically. When their DNA is analyzed, the students are surprised to learn that their assumptions are wrong. The white students do not share the same genetic traits with one another, nor do the African American, Latino, or Asian students. In fact, what they all discover is that, according to the scientific evidence upon which the film is based, there is just as much genetic variation among people of the same so-called "race" as there is among people across racial populations (Gould 1981, 323; Lewontin 1970; Templeton 2002). Differences indeed exist among humans, but they are not racial.

Skin color, the most common visual cue that most of us use as a determinant of race, does not reflect extreme genetic difference, nor does it reflect a distinct evolutionary history. Diversity of skin color merely indicates the geographical adaptation of various populations as they migrated out of equatorial Africa and moved further north to regions where ultraviolet rays from the sun were less concentrated. Overexposure to certain UV rays can destroy folic acid in the body, thus having a detrimental effect on reproduction. In tropical regions, humans evolved with darker skin and large stores of melanin, which protects the body from the harmful effects of solar radiation. On the other hand, insufficient exposure to UV rays can impede the body's ability to produce vitamin D, thus preventing the absorption of calcium by the intestines. As some human populations migrated north and south into the temperate regions, their bodies gradually adapted by developing lighter skin complexions and the ability to tan so as to make optimum use of the available ultraviolet light. Difference in skin color among humans is nothing more than an indicator of the areas of the world to which one's ancestors migrated (Jablonski and Chaplin 2000; 2003). In short, there are no available data to support racial classifications or any form of social hierarchy based on racial or ethnic group membership (Cartmill 1998, 653).

So does that completely answer our question? Is race merely an optical illusion—a trick of the sun? No, it is much more complex than that. Lani Guinier writes, "If we think in categories and think about race only in one category, we conflate many different spheres of racial meaning. We fail to specify if we mean biological race, political race, historical race, or cultural race. We simplify race as a fixed category from which many people want to escape" (Guinier and Torres 2002, 4). Despite the scientific refutation of racial taxonomy as a legitimate means for biologically differentiating and categorizing diverse populations within the human species, it continues to endure as a reality in the social realm. "That race is a social construct rather than a biological fact does not minimize its impact on our lives . . . racial distinctions have powerful social meaning with profound real-world consequences" (Croteau and Hoynes 1997, 138). Most people in our society have a sense of themselves as possessing a racial identity and belonging to a racial group. Various official forms and surveys continue to have checkboxes for designating one's race. Most people harbor conscious and unconscious stereotypes and biases about other racial groups in comparison with their own. People still laugh at racial humor, people still spout racial slurs, and those racial slurs still have the capacity to sting and enrage. People still live in racially segregated communities. People are still denied jobs and promotions because of race. People are still discriminated against economically, incarcerated disproportionately, and educated less effectively because of race. People still attack and kill people because of race.

Stories and Counterstories: Decoding the Master Script

The identity and relationship dynamics of race are so pervasive in our lives today that it feels as though current notions of race have existed since the beginning of historical time. Yet that is far from true. Prior to the fifteenth century, the idea of racial divisions among humans was of minimal significance and had little impact on people's interactions with one another (Vaughan 1995). The early European aggression and hostility toward the indigenous people of Africa, Asia, and the Americas was driven by economic interests and justified primarily by a belief in the right of Christian nations such as Spain, Portugal, Great Britain, and the Netherlands to conquer any civilization and claim any land that was not under the sovereign domain of Christians.

Erecting a social construct with the epic staying power, counterrational robustness, and destructive force that has been exhibited by "race" over the centuries was not a brief or simple process. Our present-day concept of race is based on false ideas, myths, and fabrications that accumulated over the centuries to form a grand, sweeping story or **meta-narrative** to justify the exploitation of entire populations of human beings and the appropriation of their labor, land, natural resources, cultural artifacts, and intellectual property. The social construction of the American meta-narrative—the master script on race and racial hierarchy—has been formulated and upheld through an elaborate system of dehumanizing **schemas**. These racial schemas are mental models created through the telling and retelling of stories that reinforce the idea of a racial hierarchy with the white race at the top, other races beneath, and the black race at the very bottom. Such stories have been utilized to frame our history from a perspective that upholds the language, logic, and worldview of the dominant group and suppresses the language, logic, and worldviews of those who have been targeted for racial oppression.

Throughout our history, there have been an untold number of assaults on the humanness of people of color in the interest of white hegemony. These assaults prime, activate, and reinforce racial schemas and uphold the meta-narrative. They range from the creation of stereotypes and the passage of oppressive laws to the wholesale enslavement, colonization, and genocide of entire populations. In addition to attacks on life, land, and liberty, Africans, Asians, Latinos, Native Americans, and Pacific Islanders have been subject to relentless assaults on their linguistic and cultural traditions, their communal and kinship bonds, their ancestral ties, and their spiritual beliefs.

We have learned that many of the stories we have been told about race are demonstrably false. Yet if those stories go uncontested, we will accept them as truth because of the way we have been socialized. One of the strategies for challenging these stories is through the development of counterstories that refute the assumptions upon which the original stories are based. A counterstory (also referred to as a counternarrative) is a tool utilized by critical race theorists as a means of contesting the race meta-narrative. Counterstories reframe the dehumanizing schemas by revealing additional facts, examining the same facts from different perspectives, personalizing the experiences of the targeted, humanizing the voices of the oppressed, and critically analyzing the misinformation that the dominant group has heretofore represented as unimpeachable.

Let us turn our attention now to an example of how a critical counternarrative can be used to challenge a dehumanizing schema. One of the prevailing beliefs about America's past is that the indigenous people of the Western Hemisphere were primitive, uncivilized, and underdeveloped, with little or no understanding of science and technology prior to the arrival of Europeans from more sophisticated and advanced civilizations. This is a schema—a pattern of thinking that influences the way we organize and simplify our knowledge of the world around us. Let us call it the "primitive people" schema. This schema about American Indians has been repeated in various versions so often over the years that many people accept it as historical fact even though it is just a story—a story told by one group about another. The false beliefs based on this schema can be activated in our minds by a variety of stereotypical words or images, such as "redskins" or "tomahawks," which have become embedded in our popular culture. The schema is dehumanizing because it perpetuates the myth that American Indians were simple people of inferior culture and intelligence. Moreover, this "primitive people" schema contributes to the global meta-narrative of racial hierarchy by implying that, despite the brutality suffered at the hands of whites, the Indians were better off because they had the opportunity to be exposed to more "civilized" people with superior science and technology.

In reality, the notion of Native American technology as limited is grounded in Eurocentric cultural assumptions and misconceptions. If we can acknowledge that simple fact, then we can begin to craft a counternarrative that gets us closer to the truth. Native American science and technology appear to have been highly developed within the context of the Native American social, cultural, and ecological worldview. Conversely, given what we know of the adverse environmental impact that some European technology has had on the North American continent and the rest of the planet, it seems neither appropriate nor accurate to regard European technology as particularly advanced or superior. From the vantage point of twenty-first-century hindsight, the early encounters between the people of the Americas and the people of Europe could more accurately be described as the interrupted development of the technologies of one civilization in service to the overdevelopment of the technologies of another. In other words, it was a missed opportunity for mutually constructive technological synergy. Had the prevailing paradigm of the time been one of cultural reciprocity rather than cultural conquest, it is conceivable that, today, earth-dwellers of all cultures—and all species, for that matter—might be the grateful beneficiaries of the best of both technological frameworks. . . .

Summary

Students in elementary school and high school in the United States receive limited and often distorted information about our country's racial history. Most of us learned primarily about the immigrant experiences of

Europeans in the New World and only bits and pieces about the enslavement of Africans and the conquest of American Indians and Mexicans.
We have rarely learned about the immigration experiences of Puerto
Ricans, Cubans, Vietnamese, Chinese, or Japanese. Often the information that we get is limited or glossed over to eliminate elements of racial
cruelty, violence, or suppression. Sometimes the information that we get
is taught to us as African American history or Asian American history—
as if it is something completely separate from American history. At best,
perhaps we have been taught that while there are unfortunate aspects
of racism (slavery) and conquest (American Indians) in our history, there
have been many efforts to right these wrongs so that racially the United
States now has a level playing field in which people of all races have
equal life chances. Rarely is there any analysis of the connection between
individual acts of racial hatred and the institutional or structural racism in
laws or private businesses that discriminate in housing, health care, education, and employment. And seldom is there any mention of the individuals, groups, and movements that have worked to undo the policies
and effects of racism.

There are hard facts in U.S. history. There have been times when
dehumanizing a whole group of people has merged with individual acts of
hatred and with laws and policies that promote violence and oppression,
causing many, many people to die because of racism. While the omission
or revision of this part of our history may be intended to keep children
from learning such painful parts of our past, the consequences of the distortion of U.S. racial history are far-reaching. "Education as socialization
influences students simply to accept the rightness of our society. American history textbooks overtly tell us to be proud of America. The more
schooling, the more socialization, and the more likely the individual will
conclude that America is good" (Loewen 1995, 307). Education that does
not lie is not equivalent to socializing students to believe that America is
"bad" rather than "good." Rather it calls for teaching students about the
complexities of our stories and how to make inquiries and draw conclusions that allow for critical thinking and autonomous decision making.

The combination of our personal experiences, our formal education, 25
and our exposure to entertainment media constitutes our socialization
about race. If this socialization tells us that all is well racially and that
everyone has equal life chances regardless of race or ethnicity, we are
likely to see any racial problem or failure as strictly the fault of an individual. If we believe that there are no racial barriers to employment, then
we will see unemployment among people of color as lazy or slovenly. If
we believe that education is equitable for everyone, we will not be open
to discuss or vote for remedies to address defects in the educational system that have an adverse impact on students of color. The lump sum of
these distortions can be dehumanizing for everyone.

. . . Acclaimed writer and activist Audre Lorde wrote, "In our work
and in our living, we must recognize that difference is a reason for celebration and growth, rather than a reason for destruction." While our
history regarding race may be painful, we must learn it in much the same

way that Germans must learn about the Holocaust: to understand our part in it, to understand its impact on the present, to learn how to act on its contemporary implications, and to ensure that it will never happen again. Past history cannot be changed. It can only be rediscovered, reexamined, and revealed. Presenting counternarratives is an essential stage of that revelatory process. But it is only the beginning. We not only have to tell the counterstories, we have to live them. It is only through the liberatory cycle of continuous collective action, personal reflection, honest dialogue, and more action that we can transform our society, purge the toxic racist strains from the American meta-narrative, and put a process in motion that will enable future generations to write it anew.

Bibliography

Adams, Maurianne, Lee Anne Bell, and Pat Griffin, eds. 1997. *Teaching for Diversity and Social Justice: A Sourcebook.* New York: Routledge.

Banaji, Mahzarin R., and Anthony G. Greenwald. 2013. *Blindspot: Hidden Biases of Good People.* New York: Delacorte Press.

Baron, Andrew S., and Mahzarin Banaji. 2006. "The Development of Implicit Attitudes: Evidence of Race Evaluations from Ages 6 and 10 and Adulthood." *Psychological Science* 17, no. 1: 53–58.

Brave Heart, MariaYellow Horse. 2000. "Wakiksuyapi: Carrying the Historical Trauma of the Lakota." *Tulane Studies in Social Welfare* 21–22: 245–266.

Cartmill, Matt. 1998. "The Status of Race Concept in Physical Anthropology." *American Anthropologist* (New Series) 100, no. 3: 651–660.

Crenshaw, Kimberle, Neil T. Gotanda, Gary Peller, and Kendall Thomas, eds. 1995. *Critical Race Theory: The Key Writings That Formed the Movement.* New York: The New Press.

Croteau, David, and William Hoynes. 1997. *Media/Society: Industries, Images, and Audiences.* Thousand Oaks, CA: Pine Forge Press.

Delgado, Richard, and Jean Stefancic. 2001. *Critical Race Theory: An Introduction.* New York: New York University Press.

Feagin. Joe R. 2009. *The White Racial Frame: Centuries of Racial Framing and Counter-Framing.* New York: Routledge.

Gould, Stephen Jay. 1981. *The Mismeasure of Man.* New York: W. W. Norton.

Greenwald, Anthony G., and Linda H. Krieger. 2006. "Implicit Bias: Scientific Foundations." *California Law Review* 94, no. 4.

Greenwald, Anthony G., and Mahzarin Banaji. 1995. "Implicit Social Cognition: Attitudes, Self-Esteem, and Stereotypes." *Psychological Review* 1: 4–27.

Guinier, Lani, and Gerald Torres. 2002. *The Miner's Canary: Enlisting Race, Resisting Power, Transforming Democracy.* Cambridge, MA: Harvard University Press.

Jablonski, Nina G., and George Chaplin. 2000. "The Evolution of Human Skin Colorization." *Journal of Human Evolution* 39(1): 57–106.

———. 2003. "Skin Deep." *Scientific American,* 13, no. 2 (August): 72–79.

Kaufman, Cynthia. 2001. "A User's Guide to White Privilege." *Radical Philosophy Review* 4, no. 1/2: 30–38.

Kivel, Paul. 1996. *Uprooting Racism: How White People Can Work for Racial Justice.* Gabriola Island. BC: New Society.

Leary, Joy DeGruy. 2006. *Post-Traumatic Slave Syndrome: America's Legacy of Enduring Injury and Healing.* Milwaukie, OR: Uptone Press.

Lewontin, Richard C. 1970. "Further Remarks on Race and the Genetics of Intelligence." *Bulletin of the Atomic Scientists* 26(5): 23–25.

Lipsitz, George, ed. 1998. *The Possessive Investment in Whiteness: How White People Profit from Identity Politics.* Philadelphia: Temple University Press.

Loewen, James W. 1995. *Lies My Teachers Told Me: Everything Your American History Textbook Got Wrong.* New York: Touchstone.

Olson, Joan. (n.d.) "The Four Faces of Racism." Unpublished handout adapted from Cultural Bridges Training. Posted in the compilation *We're All In It Together* by North American Students of Co-operation (NASCO). http://kalamazoo.coop/sites /default/filesWe're%20all%20in%20it%20together.pdf.

O'Neil, Moira. 2009. *Invisible Structures of Opportunity: How Media Depictions of Race Trivialize Issues of Diversity and Disparity.* Washington, DC: FrameWorks Institute.

Outlaw, Lucius T. 2005. *Critical Social Theory in the Interests of Black Folks.* Lanham, MD: Rowman & Littlefield.

Padilla, Laura M. 2001. "But You're Not a Dirty Mexican": Internalized Oppression, Latinos & Law. *Texas Hispanic Journal of Law & Policy* 7: 1.

Schmidt, Kathleen, and Brian A. Nosek. 2010. "Implicit (and Explicit) Racial Attitudes Barely Changed During the Campaign and Early Presidency of Barack Obama." *Journal of Experimental Social Psychology* 46: 308–314.

Son Hing, Leanne S., Greg A. Chun-Yang, Leah K. Hamilton, and Mark P. Zanna. 2008. "A Two-Dimensional Model That Employs Explicit and Implicit Attitudes to Characterize Prejudice." *Journal of Personality and Social Psychology* 94(6): 971–987.

Steele, Claude M. 1997. "A Threat in the Air: How Stereotypes Shape Intellectual Identity and Performance." *American Psychologist* 52: 613–629.

———. 2010. *Whistling Vivaldi: And Other Clues to How Stereotypes Affect Us.* New York: W. W. Norton.

Steele, Claude M., and Joshua Aronson. 1995. "Stereotype Threat and the Intellectual Test Performance of African Americans." *Journal of Personality and Social Psychology* 69(5): 797–811.

Taylor, Edward, David Gilborn, and Gloria Ladson-Billings, eds. 2009. *Foundations of Critical Race Theory in Education.* New York: Routledge.

Templeton, Alan R. 2002. "Out of Africa Again and Again." *Nature* 416: 45–51.

Vaughan, Alden T. 1995. *Roots of American Racism: Essays on the Colonial Experience.* New York: Oxford University Press.

Wells, Kathleen. 2013. "Prof. Robert Jensen Discusses Racism, White Supremacy and White Privilege (Part 2)." *The Blog/HuffPost Black Voices.* www.huffington post.com/kathleen-wells/prof-robert-jensen-discus_b_2500184.html.

ENGAGING THE TEXT

1. What evidence do Holtzman and Sharpe offer that "race itself is a fiction" (para. 2)? What evidence do they provide that race nevertheless "continues to endure as a reality in the social realm" (para. 16)?

2. How do Holtzman and Sharpe distinguish "frontstage" from "backstage" behavior? Have you witnessed or experienced backstage behavior (racial jokes, offensive stereotypes, or racist name-calling)? Write a journal entry describing one of these incidents and detailing your response to it. Do you view such behavior as "innocent fun" or feel that it "reinforce[s] racial polarization and antagonism" (para. 8)? Why?

3. According to Holtzman and Sharpe, "Racial inequity . . . has become a permanent feature of the American experience. Therefore, racism, in all its manifestations, must be continuously critiqued and challenged" (para. 3). How would you go about challenging racism? Is the idea that racism must be "critiqued and challenged" enough, or should more be done? If so, what?

4. Holtzman and Sharpe assert that "students in elementary school and high school in the United States receive limited and often distorted information about our country's racial history" para. 23. In what ways do they claim that students are misinformed or that U.S. racial history is "glossed over"? Write a journal entry or an essay evaluating the extent to which this has been true in your experience.

5. **Thinking Rhetorically** This is an excerpt from an introductory college textbook. How do its organization, vocabulary, style, and typography identify it as such? Choose a short passage and rewrite it for a nonacademic audience. For example, how would your language and style have to change if you were writing it for your younger sister or if you were composing a blog?

EXPLORING CONNECTIONS

6. As Holtzman and Sharpe note, "Throughout our history, there have been an untold number of assaults on the humanness of people of color in the interest of white hegemony" (para. 19). Analyze how Coates's essay (p. 572) links segregation and violence against black people to the maintenance of white supremacy; focus particularly on section 5 ("The Quiet Plunder"). How persuasive is his argument?

7. How do Holtzman and Sharpe define the "primitive people" schema (para. 21)? To what extent does the image on page 640 represent this schema? In what ways does the central figure in the photo "dehumanize" American Indians? How does the photo on page 641 provide a visual "counterstory" (para. 20)?

8. How does Cheryl I. Harris and Devon W. Carbado's analysis of media coverage following Hurricane Katrina (p. 620) both illustrate and complicate Holtzman and Sharpe's discussion of media frames? What kind of counternarratives do Harris and Carbado offer in contrast to mainstream media depictions of race?

9. Use Holtzman and Sharpe's discussion of race to analyze Carmen Lugo-Lugo's classroom experience (p. 188). How does the student who asks Lugo-Lugo to cancel class reflect implicit bias and white privilege? What stereotypes of Latinas does Lugo-Lugo assume that her white students have absorbed from media images? How does her teaching of ethnic studies challenge her students' belief that we live in a "postracial" society?

10. What is the source of humor in Barry Deutsch's cartoon on page 615? What does the white woman assume about the black woman's role, and why is the black character so irritated with her?

EXTENDING THE CRITICAL CONTEXT

11. The *Journal of Blacks in Higher Education* has posted a comprehensive list of reported campus racial incidents dating from September 2011 to July 2015. Visit

the journal's Web site (www.jbhe.com/incidents) and read a half dozen of the nearly 100 summaries of the incidents; coordinate with other class members to cover different portions of the list. Jointly report your findings to the class: Do you see any patterns in the issues that are raised? How many are overtly hostile acts? How many involve students, professors, or administrators? How does the college respond? What steps might be taken to prevent similar incidents in the future?

GENTRIFICATION

SHERMAN ALEXIE

This short story packs a punch: in a scant three pages, Sherman Alexie manages to explore the racial dynamics of city life with his trademark humor. Alexie (b. 1966) grew up on the Spokane Indian Reservation in Washington State but attended a high school where, in his words, he was "the only Indian . . . except the school mascot." He has written four novels, including *Reservation Blues* (1995), which won an American Book Award; *Indian Killer* (1996); *Flight* (2007); and the semi-autobiographical young adult novel *The Absolutely True Diary of a Part-Time Indian*, which won the 2007 National Book Award for Young People's Literature. In addition, he's

produced seventeen volumes of poems and short stories, among them *War Dances* (2009), winner of the 2010 PEN/Faulkner Award for Fiction. He coauthored the script for the prize-winning film *Smoke Signals* (1998), wrote and directed *The Business of Fancydancing* (2002), and in 2014 produced a film adaptation of James Welch's classic novel *Winter in the Blood*. This selection comes from *Blasphemy: New and Selected Stories* (2012).

A MONTH AGO, MY NEXT-DOOR NEIGHBORS tossed a horribly stained mattress onto the curb in front of their house. I suppose they believed the mattress would be collected on our next regular garbage day. But the city charges thirty dollars to dispose of bulky items and you have to go online and schedule the pickup. Obviously, my neighbors had not bothered to schedule such an appointment. I'd thought the city, once they'd learned of the abandoned mattress, would have collected it anyway and automatically added the charge, plus a fine, to my neighbors' utility bill.

But four garbage collection days passed and nothing happened. The mattress, dank and dirty to begin with, had begun to mold. There were new holes in the fabric that I assumed were made by rats. We live in a large waterfront city so there are millions of rodents. It's an expected, if rather unwelcome, part of urban life. In every city in the world, there are more rats than people. But one doesn't throw a potential home for them onto the curb in front of one's house. That mattress was an apartment building for rats. Or at least a vacation home.

I'd thought to call the city and tell them about the mattress, but I doubted that I would have remained anonymous.

I am the only white man living on a block where all of my neighbors are black. Don't get me wrong. My neighbors are like any other group of neighbors I've ever had. They are the same self-appointed guardians, social directors, friendly alcoholics, paranoid assholes, overburdened parents, sullen teenagers, flirty housewives, elderly misers, amateur comedians, and hermits that exist in every neighborhood of every city in the country. They are people, not black people; and I am a person, not a white person. And that is how we relate to one another, as people. I'm not treated as the white guy on the block, at least not overtly or rudely, and I do not treat my neighbors as if they are some kind of aliens. We live as people live, aware of racial dynamics but uninterested in their applications as it applies to our neighborhood.

My next-door neighbors, an older couple with two adult sons living at home, are kind. All four of them often sit on their front porch, sharing snacks and drinks, and greeting everybody who walks past. But they'd been sitting only a few feet away from the mattress they'd so haphazardly tossed onto the curb. How could they have continued to live as if creating such a mess were normal? I wanted to ask them what they planned to do about the mattress, though I wasn't even sure of the older son's name. It's something ornately African-sounding that I hadn't quite understood when I'd first met him, and it was too late, a year later, to ask for the proper pronunciation. And that made me feel racist. If his name were something more typical, like Ron or Eddie or Vlad or Pete or Carlos or Juan, then I would have remembered it later. The simple names are easier to remember. So, in this regard, perhaps I am racist.

And, frankly, it felt racist for me to look out my front window at that abandoned mattress and wonder about the cultural norms that allowed my neighbors, so considerate otherwise, to create a health hazard. And why hadn't my other neighbors complained? Or maybe they had complained and the city had ignored the mattress because it was a black neighborhood? Who was the most racist in that situation? Was it the white man who was too terrified to confront his black neighbors on their rudeness? Was it the black folks who abandoned the mattress on their curb? Was it the black people who didn't feel the need to judge the behavior of their black neighbors? Was it the city, which let a mattress molder on the street in full view of hundreds, if not thousands, of people? Or was it all of us, black and white, passively revealing that, despite our surface friendliness, we didn't really care about one another?

In any case, after another garbage day had passed, I rented a U-Haul truck, a flatbed with enough room to carry the mattress, and parked it — hid it, really — two blocks away. I didn't want to embarrass or anger my neighbors so I set my alarm for three A.M. I didn't turn on the lights as I donned gloves, coveralls, and soft-soled shoes. Perhaps I was being over-cautious. But it was fun, too, to be on a secret mission.

I slowly opened my front door, worried the hinges might creak, and took step after careful step on the porch, avoiding the loose boards. Then I walked across my lawn rather than on the sidewalk. A dog barked. It was slightly foggy. A bat swooped near a streetlight. For a moment, I felt like I'd walked into a werewolf movie. Then I wondered what the police would do if they discovered a clean-cut white man creeping through a black neighborhood.

"Buddy," the cops would say. "You don't fit the profile of the neighborhood."

I almost laughed out loud at my joke. That would have been a stu-   10
pid way to get caught.

Then I stood next to the mattress and realized that I hadn't figured out how I was supposed to carry that heavy, awkward, water-logged thing two blocks to the truck.

Given more time, I probably could have rigged up a pulley system or a Rube Goldberg contraption that would have worked. But all I had that night was brute strength, without the brute.

I kicked the mattress a few times to flush out any rats. Then I grabbed the mattress's plastic handles — thank God they were still intact — and tried to lift the thing. It was heavier than I expected, and smelled and felt like a dead dolphin.

At first I tried to drag the mattress, but that made too much noise. Then I tried to carry it on my back, but it kept sliding from my grip. My only option was to carry the mattress on my head, like an African woman gracefully walking with a vase of water balanced on her head, except without her grace.

Of course, the mattress was too heavy and unbalanced to be carried that way for long. It kept slipping off my head onto the sidewalk. It didn't make much noise when it fell; I was more worried that my lung-burning panting would wake everybody.

It took me twenty minutes to carry that mattress to the truck and another ten to slide it into the flatbed. Then I got behind the wheel and drove to the city's waste disposal facility in the Fremont neighborhood. But it wouldn't open for another two hours so I parked on the street, lay across the seat, and fell asleep in the truck.

I was awakened by the raw noise of recycling and garbage trucks. I wiped my mouth, ran my fingers through my hair, and hoped that I wouldn't offend anybody with my breath. I also hoped that the facility workers wouldn't think that filthy mattress was mine. But I shouldn't have worried. The workers were too busy to notice one bad-breathed man with one rat-stained mattress.

They charged me forty bucks to dispose of the mattress, and it was worth it. Then I returned the truck to the U-Haul rental site and took a taxi back to my house.

I felt clean. I felt rich and modest, like an anonymous benefactor.

When I stepped out of the taxi I saw my neighbors — mother, father, and two adult sons — sitting in the usual places on their porch. They were drinking Folgers instant coffee, awful stuff they'd shared with me on many occasions.

I waved to them but they didn't wave back. I pretended they hadn't noticed me and waved again. They stared at me. They knew what I had done.

"You didn't have to do that," said the son with the African name. "We can take care of ourselves."

"I'm sorry," I said.

"You think you're better than us, don't you?"

I wanted to say that, when it came to abandoned mattresses, I was better.

"Right now, I feel worse," I said.

I knew I had done a good thing, so why did I hurt so bad? Why did I feel judged?

"You go home, white boy," the son said. "And don't you bother us anymore."

I knew the entire block would now shun me. I felt pale and lost, like an American explorer in the wilderness.

ENGAGING THE TEXT

1. What's the significance of the title, "Gentrification"? Is it serious, ironic, or both? Why?

2. How would you describe the unnamed narrator of this story? When he considers calling the city about the abandoned mattress, why is he concerned about remaining anonymous? Why does he hide the flatbed truck two blocks away from his neighbors' house? Why does he collect the mattress at 3:00 A.M. and take multiple precautions not to make any noise? Is he afraid of something? If so, what?

3. Mentioning that he is the only white man in an all-black neighborhood, the narrator explains, "We live as people live, aware of racial dynamics but uninterested in their applications as it applies to our neighborhood" (para. 4). Do you see any evidence in the story that suggests he's mistaken, self-deluded, or lying?

4. How would you respond to the series of questions that the narrator raises in paragraph 6: "Who was the most racist in that situation? Was it the white man . . . Was it the black folks . . . Was it the city . . . Or was it all of us, black and white . . . ?" Keeping in mind that the narrator may be unreliable, discuss these questions in small groups and try to come to a consensus. Report your group's conclusions to the class: If there are differences of interpretation, how do you account for them?

5. How does the narrator feel after disposing of the mattress? Why do his neighbors resent what he did, and why does he feel judged? Do you ever sympathize with the narrator? How do you interpret the final sentence of the story: "I felt pale and lost, like an American explorer in the wilderness" (para. 29)? Can you read it in more than one way? If so, how?

EXPLORING CONNECTIONS

6. To what extent does Linda Holtzman and Leon Sharpe's definition of "internalized white supremacy" in "Theories and Constructs of Race" (p. 600) apply to the narrator? Look closely at his rationale for not remembering the older son's name: "It's something ornately African-sounding. . . . If his name were something more typical, like Ron or Eddie or Vlad or Pete or Carlos or Juan, then I would have remembered it later" (para. 5). Does his admission that "perhaps" he's racist get him off the hook? Do you see any other indications in the story that the narrator may be operating out of internalized stereotypes or a sense of innate superiority?

EXTENDING THE CRITICAL CONTEXT

7. Watch the short documentary "White People" (at www.lookdifferent.org) in which the director, Jose Antonio Vargas, talks to millennials about what it means to be young and white. What's your reaction to the film? Do you identify with any of the individuals depicted in it? If so, who and why? Write a journal entry exploring these issues.

8. Vargas's style as an interviewer is deliberately nonconfrontational, in an effort to invite people to talk openly about race. What benefits and drawbacks do you see to this approach? Do you prefer Vargas's diplomacy or Ta-Nehisi Coates's (p. 572) more aggressive style of argument? Why?

LOOT OR FIND: FACT OR FRAME?

CHERYL I. HARRIS AND DEVON W. CARBADO

In 2005 Hurricane Katrina slammed into the Gulf Coast, killing more than 1,800 people and destroying thousands of homes and businesses. Hardest hit was New Orleans, where the hurricane damage was compounded by massive flooding caused by the failure of the city's levee system. Although residents were ordered to evacuate before the storm hit, many — overwhelmingly black and poor — lacked the resources to escape and were trapped for days in attics, on roofs, on freeway overpasses, and in overcrowded emergency shelters. In this article, Cheryl I. Harris and Devon W. Carbado analyze the media coverage of this disaster and the public response to the stories that emerged from the crisis in New Orleans. Both Harris and Carbado teach at UCLA's School of Law; they have written widely on constitutional issues, civil rights, gender, and critical race theory. Harris, who has also worked in the area of international human rights, served for several years as cochair for the National Conference of Black Lawyers. In 2005 she received the Distinguished Professor Award for Civil Rights Education from the ACLU Foundation of Southern California. Carbado has edited or coedited several books, including *Time on Two Crosses: The Collected Writings of Bayard Rustin* **(2003),** *Race Law Stories* **(2008),** *The Long Walk to Freedom: Runaway Slave Narratives* **(2012), and** *Acting White? Rethinking Race in Post-Racial America* **(2013). He has won multiple awards for distinguished teaching.**

Evidence of Things Seen

What do [the images on p. 621] represent? What facts do they convey? We could say that image A depicts a man who, in the aftermath of Katrina, is wading through high waters with food supplies and a big black plastic bag. We might say that image B depicts a man and woman, both wearing backpacks. They, too, are wading through high waters in the aftermath of Katrina, and the woman appears to be carrying food supplies.

This is not how these images were presented in the press. The captions that appeared with the two photos, both of which ran on Yahoo!

This chapter draws from and builds upon Cheryl I. Harris, "White Washing Race; Scapegoating Culture," *California Law Review* (2006) (book review). [All notes are Harris and Carbado's, except 8, 9, 13, 14, and 24.]

Dave Martin/AP Photo

A

Chris Graythen/Getty Images

B

news, were quite different. The caption for image A read: "A young man walks through chest-deep flood water after looting a grocery store in New Orleans." The caption for image B read: "Two residents wade through chest-deep waters after finding bread and soda from a local grocery store after Hurricane Katrina came through the area." The caption for image A, then, tells us that a crime has been committed; the caption for image B tells that a fierce, poignant struggle for survival is under way—the subjects have just found food. Image A depicts a young black man; image B shows a white man and woman.

The images and their respective captions almost immediately stirred up significant controversy. People complained that the captions accompanying the images were racially suggestive: black people "loot" and white people "find." *Boston Globe* correspondent Christina Pazzanese wondered, "I am curious how one photographer knew the food was looted by one but not the other. Were interviews conducted as they swam by?"[1]

---

[1]Cited in Aaron Kinney, "'Looting' or 'finding'?" *Salon*, September 1, 2005.

Not everyone agreed, however, that the images and captions reflected a racial problem. As one commentator put it:

> It's difficult to draw any substantiated conclusions from these photos' captions. Although they were both carried by many news outlets, they were taken by two different photographers and came from two different services, the Associated Press (AP) and the Getty Images via Agence France-Presse (AFP). Services make different stylistic standards for how they caption photographs, or the dissimilar wordings may have been due to nothing more than the preferences of different photographers and editors, or the difference might be the coincidental result of a desire to avoid repetitive wording (similar photographs from the same news services variously describe the depicted actions as "looting," "raiding," "taking," "finding" and "making off"). The viewer also isn't privy to the contexts in which the photographs were taken—it's possible that in one case the photographer actually saw his subject exiting an unattended grocery store with an armful of goods, while in the other case the photographer came upon his subjects with supplies in hand and could only make assumptions about how they obtained them.[2]

For the most part, this controversy focused on a question of fact. Did the black person really loot the goods he was carrying? Did the white man and white woman really find the food they were carrying? Indeed, the director of media relations at the Associated Press suggested that, as to image A, "he [the photographer] saw the person go into the shop and take the goods. . . . that's why he wrote 'looting' in the article."[3] In other words, the fact of the matter was that the black man in image A was a looter.

The photographer of image B, Chris Graythen, maintained,

> I wrote the caption about the two people who "found" the items. I believed in my opinion, that they did simply find them, and not "looted" them in the definition of the word. The people were swimming in chest deep water, and there were other people in the water, both white and black. I looked for the best picture. There were a million items floating in the water—we were right near a grocery store that had 5+ feet of water in it. It had no doors. The water was moving, and the stuff was floating away. These people were not ducking into a store and busting down windows to get electronics. They picked up bread and Cokes that were floating in the water. They would have floated away anyhow.[4]

To some extent, the credibility of Graythen's explanation is beside the point here. That is, the loot-or-find problem of image A and image B cannot fully be addressed with reference to the individual intent of those who either took the picture or produced the accompanying interpretive text. Indeed, it is entirely plausible that had the photos appeared without

---

[2]www.snopes.com/Katrina/photos/looters.asp.
[3]Cited in Kinney, "'Looting' or 'finding'?"
[4]Ibid.

any captions, they would have been read the same way.[5] This is because while neither "loot" nor "find" is written on either image, in the context of public disorder, the race of the subjects inscribes those meanings.

The "Color-Blind" Frame

Drawing on facts about both Hurricane Katrina and the public's response to it, this [essay] queries whether efforts to change the racial status quo and eliminate inequality should or can rely solely on facts or empiricism. There is a growing sense within the civil rights community that more empirical research is needed to persuade mainstream Americans that racism remains a problem in American society and that the elimination of racial disadvantage is not a do-it-yourself project. The idea seems to be that if only more Americans knew certain "facts" (for example, about the existence of implicit bias) they would be more inclined to support civil rights initiatives (for example, affirmative action). We agree that more empirical research is needed. Facts are important—indeed crucial—since so much of public opinion is grounded in misinformation. We simply do not think that there is a linear progression between raw empiricism and more enlightened public opinion about race and racism. Put another way, we do not believe that facts speak for themselves.

It is precisely the recognition that facts don't speak for themselves that helps to explain why scholars across academic fields and politicians across the political spectrum continue to pay significant attention to the social and cognitive processes that shape how we interpret facts. Of the variety of theories—in sociology, political science, law, anthropology, psychology, and economics—that attempt to explain these processes, most share the idea that we interpret events through frames—interpretational structures that, consciously and unconsciously, shape what we see and how we see it. In the words of one scholar, framing refers to "understanding a story you already know and saying, 'Oh yeah, that one.'"[6] As we process and make sense of an event, we take account of and simultaneously ignore facts that do not fit the frame, and sometimes we supply ones that are missing. Thus, it is sometimes said that "frames trump facts."[7]

---

[5]One study of local television news stories on crime and public opinion illustrates the strong association between criminal behavior and racial identity. Participants were shown an identical news story under three different conditions: one group witnessed a version in which the perpetrator was white; another group saw a version in which the perpetrator was black; and a third group viewed a version in which there was no picture of the perpetrator. Following the screening, the participants in the first, white-perpetrator group were less likely to recall having seen a suspect than subjects in the second, black-perpetrator group. Among those in the third group, who saw no image of the perpetrator, over 60 percent erroneously recalled seeing a perpetrator, and in 70 percent of those cases viewers identified that nonexistent image as black. See Franklin Gilliam Jr. and Shanto Iyengar, "Prime Suspects: The Influence of Local Television News on the Viewing Public," *American Journal of Political Science* 44 (2000):560.

[6]Roger Schank, "Tell Me a Story," *Narrative and Intelligence* 71 (1995).

[7]A more nuanced formulation suggests, "Like well-accepted theories that guide our interpretation of data, schemas incline us to interpret data consistent with our biases." See Jerry Kang, "Trojan Horses of Races," *Harvard Law Review* 118 (2005):1489,1515.

The most relevant and dominant frame is color blindness, or the belief [10] that race is *not* a factor in how we make sense of the world. Color blindness is a kind of metaframe that comprises three interwoven racial scripts: (1) because of *Brown v. Board of Education*[8] and the civil rights reforms it inaugurated, racism is by and large a thing of the past; (2) when racism does rear its ugly head, it is the product of misguided and irrational behavior on the part of self-declared racial bigots, who are few and far between; and (3) racial consciousness—whether in the form of affirmative action or Jim Crow[9]–like racism—should be treated with suspicion, if not rejected outright. The gradual ascendancy and eventual racial dominance of color blindness frames the facts of racial inequality (manifested, for example, in disparities in wealth and educational outcomes between blacks and whites) as a function of something other than racism. Because scientists have largely repudiated the notion of biological inferiority, color blindness frames the problem of racial disadvantage in terms of conduct. The problem is not genes but culture, not blood but behavior: were black people to engage in normatively appropriate cultural practices—work hard, attend school, avoid drugs, resist crime—they would transcend their current social status and become part of the truly advantaged. On this view, black disadvantage is both expected and deserved—a kind of natural disaster not produced by racism.

At least initially, Katrina challenged the supremacy of color blindness. The tidal wave of suffering that washed over New Orleans seemed incontrovertible evidence of the salience of race in contemporary U.S. society.[10] The simple fact that the faces of those left to fend for themselves or die were overwhelmingly black raised questions about the explanatory power of color blindness under which race is deemed irrelevant.[11] Racial suffering was everywhere. And black people were dying—prime

[8]**Brown v. Board of Education:** The 1954 landmark Supreme Court case that outlawed segregated schools. [Eds.]

[9]**Jim Crow:** System of legalized segregation that dominated the South from 1866 to the mid 1960s. Black Americans were denied access to schools, voting, and public restrooms and transportation as well as subjected to systemic racism and violence. [Eds.]

[10]We do not intend to ignore the tremendous loss suffered in the Gulf region more broadly: we focus on New Orleans because of its unique position in the national imagination, as well as its pre-Katrina racial demographics. Indeed, New Orleans was not just a city that had come to be predominantly black; it was a city that was culturally marked as black. As one noted historian has stated, "The unique culture of south Louisiana derives from black Creole culture." Quoted in "Buffetted by Katrina, City's Complex Black Community Struggles to Regroup," Associated Press, October 4, 2005, www.msnbc.com.

[11]Or fend for themselves and be punished for it. A particularly harrowing account of official indifference and hostility comes from the ordeal of two emergency room workers who had the misfortune of being in New Orleans for a conference when Hurricane Katrina struck. After their hotel in the French Quarter closed, they, along with several hundred others, collected money to hire buses for their evacuation, but the buses were prevented from entering the city. When the workers attempted to flee on foot, they were directed to wait on the interstate for rescue that never came. Neither the police nor the National Guard provided them with food or water. When the group managed to find food for themselves and set up a makeshift camp, they were repeatedly dispersed at gunpoint by the police. When they attempted to walk across the bridge into the neighboring city of Gretna, they were again turned back at gunpoint by Gretna police. See Larry Bradshaw and Lorrie Beth Slonsky, "Trapped in New Orleans," September 6, 2005, www.counterpunch.org/bradshaw09062005.html.

time live. One had to close one's eyes, or willfully blind oneself, not to see this racial disaster. Everyone, it seemed, except government officials, was riveted. And there was little disagreement that Katrina exposed shameful fissures in America's social fabric; that the precipitating event was an act of God, not the cultural pathology of the victims; and that the government's response, at least in the initial phases, was woefully inadequate. Seasoned mainstream journalists wept and railed, while ordinary Americans flooded relief organizations with money.

The tragedy of Katrina created a rupture in the racial-progress narrative that had all but erased the suffering of poor black people from the political landscape. In contrast to the pre-Katrina picture, black people were perceived to be innocent victims. Black people were perceived to have a legitimate claim on the nation-state. Black people were perceived to be deserving of government help. Katrina—or the *facts* the public observed about its effects—disrupted our tendency to *frame* black disadvantage in terms of cultural deficiency. But how did that happen? And doesn't this disruption undermine our central point about facts and frames?

Not at all. Frames are not static. Epic events like Katrina push up against and can temporarily displace them. All those people. All that suffering. This can't be America. How could we let this happen? That question—how could we let this happen?—reflected a genuine humanitarian concern for fellow human beings. Moreover, the compelling facts about Katrina raised a number of questions about racial inequality previously suppressed under color blindness. Indeed, as the humanitarian crisis peaked with the retreating floodwaters, a debate over the role of race in the disaster quickly emerged. The unrelenting spectacle of black suffering bodies demanded an explanation. Why were those New Orleans residents who remained trapped during Katrina largely black and poor? Was it, as hip-hop artist Kanye West argued, a case of presidential indifference to, or dislike of, poor black people?[12] Or was it, as Ward Connerly[13] asserted, the predictable consequence of a natural disaster that befell a city that just happened to be predominantly black? Was it, as Linda

[12]On a nationally broadcast telethon to raise money for the victims of Katrina, Kanye West departed from the scripted remarks to say, "I hate the way they portray us in the media. You see a black family: it says they are looting. You see a white family; it says they have been looking for food. And you know, it has been five days, because most of the people are black, and even for me to complain about it, I would be a hypocrite, because I have tried to turn away from the TV because it is too hard to watch. So now I am calling my business manager right now to see what is the biggest amount I can give. And just imagine if I was down there and those are my people down there." Commenting on the slow pace of the government's response, he said, "George Bush doesn't care about black people." NBC immediately cut to another star on the program and censored West's remarks from the West Coast feed of the program. It also issued the following disclaimer: "Kanye West departed from the scripted comments that were prepared for him, and his opinions in no way represent the views of the networks. It would be most unfortunate if the efforts of the artists who participated tonight and the generosity of millions of Americans who are helping those in need are overshadowed by one person's opinion." "Rapper Kanye West Accuses Bush of Racism; NBC Apologizes," *CBC Arts*, September 3, 2005, www.cbc.ca/story/arts/national/2005/09/03/Arts/kanye_west_katrina20050903.html.

[13]**Ward Connerly:** Conservative African American political activist (b. 1939). [Eds.]

Chavez[14] claimed, the result of a culture of dependency combined with local bureaucratic incompetence? Was race a factor in determining who survived and who did not?[15] Or did class provide a better explanation?[16] Finally, could we ever fully understand Katrina without meaningfully engaging the legacy of slavery?[17] These and other, similar questions were pushed into the foreground by the force of Katrina's devastation.

But the frame of color blindness did not disappear. It manifested itself in the racial divide that emerged with respect to how people answered the foregoing questions. While there is some intraracial diversity of opinion among public figures about the role of race and racism in explaining what happened, there remains a striking racial difference in how the disaster is viewed. According to public opinion polls, whites largely reject the notion that race explains the governmental disregard, while blacks assert that the fact that the victims were black and poor was a significant part of the story.[18] This difference over the difference that race makes reflects competing racial frames. Thus, while the facts of what happened in Katrina's aftermath unsettled the familiar color-blind racial script that poor black people were the authors of their own plight, those facts did not ultimately displace core ideas embedded in the color-blind frame: race is irrelevant and racism largely does not exist. Most whites

[14]**Linda Chavez:** The first Latina (b. 1947) nominated to the U.S. Cabinet, now an author and conservative political commentator. [Eds.]

[15]This was Howard Dean's view. In an address to the National Baptist Convention he stated, "As survivors are evacuated, order is restored, the water slowly begins to recede, and we sort through the rubble, we must also begin to come to terms with the ugly truth that skin color, age and economics played a deadly role in who survived and who did not." "Excerpts of DNC Chairman Howard Dean's Remarks to the National Baptist Convention of America, Inc.," U.S. Newswire, September 8, 2005, www.usnewswire.com.

[16]While some have argued that class was a more salient factor than race in explaining who was affected, we do not think that given the country's history of de jure and de facto racial subordination, race can be so neatly disaggregated from class. Particularly in the context of New Orleans—a city that was predominantly black and predominantly poor—the fact that those left on the overpasses and in the Superdome were black had everything to do with why they were poor. The point is not to reproduce another unhelpful version of the race-versus-class debate but to avoid sublimating the racial dimension of the issues raised by Katrina. Recent survey analysis suggests that race was in fact a crucial factor in explaining who was in harm's way. See "Katrina Hurts Blacks and Poor Victims Most," CNN/*USA Today*/Gallup Poll, October 25, 2005.

[17]Both the Reverend Jesse Jackson and Representative Cynthia McKinney drew a link between the events in the Gulf and slavery. In response to a question by Anderson Cooper on CNN about whether race was a determinative factor in the federal government's response to Katrina, Jackson replied, "It is at least a factor. Today I saw 5,000 African Americans on the I-10 causeway desperate, perishing, dehydrated, babies dying. It looked like Africans in the hull of a slave ship. It was so ugly and so obvious. Have we missed this catastrophe because of indifference and ineptitude or is it a combination of both? And certainly I think the issue of race as a factor will not go away from this equation." Jesse Jackson, Remarks on *360 Degrees*, CNN, September 2, 2005. In an address on the floor of the House of Representatives on September 8, 2005, Representative McKinney said, "As I saw the African Americans, mostly African-American families ripped apart, I could only think about slavery, families ripped apart, herded into what looked like concentration camps." Cynthia McKinney, "Text of Remarks Delivered on the Floor of the House on Sept. 8, 2005," reprinted in "A Few Thoughts on the State of Our Nation," September 12, 2005, www.counterpunch .org/mckinney09122005.html.

[18]"Huge Racial Divide over Katrina and Its Consequences," Report of the Pew Research Center for People and the Press, September 8, 2005, 2; available at http://people -press.org/reports/display.php3?Report ID=255.

were able to see black people as victims, but they were unwilling to link their victim status to race or racism. A more acceptable story was that black people in New Orleans suffered only because of bureaucratic inefficiencies in the wake of a natural disaster. Race simply could not be a factor. Katrina then only partially destabilized the frame of color blindness. To the extent that our starting point for thinking about race is that it does not matter, other racial frames or scripts more easily fit within the overarching frame. These frames can both explicitly invoke race and, even more powerfully, implicitly play the race card. After the initial uncertainty, what emerged in the wake of Katrina was the frame of "law and order"—a racial script that permeated the debate over the iconic photographs with which we began our essay, and over the post-Katrina relief efforts. The media were both author and reader of events in ways that both challenged and underwrote this racial frame.

A Picture Is Worth a Thousand Words

Recall Chris Graythen's response to the racial controversy concerning the images with which we began this chapter. With regard to image B, Graythen asserted that he "looked for the best picture." More specifically, Graythen searched for an image that would best narrate a particular factual story: that people were wading through water to find food. According to Graythen, both whites and blacks were finding food in the chest-high water. Unlike pre-Katrina New Orleans, this space was racially integrated. Graythen searched this racially integrated body of water for a picture that would most successfully convey the idea of people finding food (as distinct from people "ducking into a store and busting down windows to get electronics"). Graythen's "best picture"—his "Oh yeah, that one"—emerged when he saw the two white people photographed in image B. Their images best fit the caption that Graythen already had in mind, people wading through water to find food. Because people are more likely to associate blacks with looting ("ducking into a store and busting down windows to get electronics") than with finding food, Graythen's selection makes sense. Indeed, one can infer from Graythen's decision to photograph white people that it was easier to frame white people as despondent people finding food than it was to frame black people in that way. To put the point slightly differently, there would be some dissonance between the image of black people in those high waters and a caption describing people finding food. This dissonance is not about facts—whether in fact the black people were finding food; the dissonance is about frames—the racial association between black people and looting, particularly on the heels of a natural disaster or social upheaval.

Two caveats before moving on. First, nothing above is intended to suggest that Graythen's decision to photograph the two white people was racially conscious—that is, intentionally motivated by race. Frames operate both consciously and unconsciously; his selection of whites to

15

photograph (and his "natural selection" against blacks) converged with existing racial frames about criminality and perpetrators, on the one hand, and law-abidingness and victims, on the other. The two photos were perfect mirror images of each other. But only image B could convey a story of survival against adversity; image A was inconsistent with that script. The presence of a black man with a big plastic bag in the context of a natural disaster is already inscribed with meaning. In that sense, the black man in image A did not require a caption to be framed; nor did the white man and woman in image B. The stereotype of black criminality was activated by image A and the many images like it, which showed the central problem in New Orleans not to be the lack of humanitarian aid, but the lack of law and order.

The second caveat: our analysis should not be read as an argument against empiricism or a claim that facts are irrelevant. We simply mean to say that racial frames shape our perceptions of the facts. This does not mean that we are overdetermined by frames or that we are unable to escape their interpretative strictures. Rather, the point is that dependence on "just the facts" will seldom be enough to dislodge racial frames.[19] Partly this is because racial frames are installed not as the result of empiricism, but in spite of it. Consider color blindness. It is the dominant racial frame for understanding race not because of facts but because of a well-financed political project to entrench and naturalize a color-blind understanding of American race relations.[20] Accordingly, something more than facts is required to undo the racial work color blindness continues to perform; and something more than facts is required to dislodge the normativity of color blindness itself.

From Rescue to Occupation: Seeing the Invisible

> I'd rather have them here dead than alive. And at least they're not robbing you and you [don't] have to worry about feeding them.[21]
> —A RESIDENT OF ST. GABRIEL WHEN ASKED FOR HER REACTIONS TO THE DECISION TO DESIGNATE THE TOWN AS A COLLECTIVE MORGUE

[19] As Gary Blasi contends, "If we store social categories in our heads by means of prototypes or exemplars rather than statistics, then our basic cognitive mechanisms not only predispose us toward stereotypes . . . , but also limit the potentially curative effect of information that contradicts the statistical assumptions about base rates that are embedded in our stereotypes." Gary Blasi, "Advocacy Against the Stereotype," *UCLA Law Review* 49 (2002):1241, 1256–57.

[20] See Lee Cokorinos, *The Assault on Diversity* (Institute for Democracy Studies, 2002), tracing the network of conservative activists and organizations that have waged a well-funded campaign over two decades to change the corpus of civil rights laws, end affirmative action, and reframe the political discourse on race and racism.

[21] This should not suggest that she was without any compassion. She went on to say, "[The bodies] have to go somewhere. These are people's families. They have to—they still have to have dignity." It's precisely our point that one can have compassion and still see black people through racial frames. *Paula Zahn Now*, CNN, September 8, 2005.

To the extent that our discussion of the problem of racial frames has largely examined representational issues, one might reasonably ask: What are the material consequences of this problem? And how, if at all, did it injure black New Orleanians in the wake of Hurricane Katrina? The answer relates to two interconnected frames: the frame of law and order and the frame of black criminality. Working together, these frames rendered black New Orleanians dangerous, unprotectable, and unrescuable.

In the immediate aftermath of Katrina, the media pointedly criticized the slow pace at which the federal government was responding to the disaster. But the critical stance was short-lived and quickly gave way to a focus on the breakdown of law and order, a frame that activated a familiar stereotype about black criminality. While initially blacks were seen as victims of Hurricane Katrina and a failed governmental response, this victim status proved to be highly unstable. Implicit in the frame that "this can't be America" is the notion that the neglect in the wake of Katrina was a violation of the duty of care owed to all citizens of the nation. This social contract includes blacks as citizens; and indeed the claim by blacks, "We are American" — a statement vigorously asserted by those contained in the convention center[22] — responded to and relied upon that frame.[23]

As time progressed, the social currency of the image of blacks as citizens of the state to whom a duty of care is owed diminished. It rubbed uneasily against the more familiar racial framing of poor black people as lazy, undeserving, and inherently criminal. Concern over the looting of property gradually took precedence over the humanitarian question of when people might be rescued and taken off of the highways and rooftops. Thus, while armed white men were presumed to be defending their property, black men with guns constituted gangs of violent looters who had to be contained. Under this frame, the surrounding towns and parishes that constituted potential refuge for black New Orleans residents who had no means to evacuate before the storm became no-go areas because of concerns about black criminality.

A particularly stark example of this came during the CNN interview on September 8 between Christiane Amanpour[24] and the resident of St. Gabriel quoted above. The sentiment that dead blacks were better than live ones was enforced not only by local authorities who, like the Gretna police, turned people away at gunpoint, but by the National Guard and other local authorities who purportedly denied the Red Cross

[22]See Michael Ignatieff, "The Broken Contract," *New York Times*, September 25, 2005 (reporting that a woman held at the convention center asserted, "We are American" during a TV interview, demonstrating both anger and astonishment that she would have to remind Americans of that fact and that the social contract had failed).

[23]Note that this frame is simultaneously inclusionary and exclusionary. To the extent that it asserts black citizenship, it seeks to include black people within the nation-state. However, it excludes noncitizens, black as well as others, from the circle of care based on lack of formal American belonging. This is deeply problematic but it reveals the limited space within which blacks could assert legitimate claims on national empathy.

[24]**Christiane Amanpour:** Chief International Correspondent for CNN News. [Eds.]

permission to enter the city shortly after the storm because of concerns about the safety of the rescuers.[25]

These fears were grounded in what ultimately proved to be grossly exaggerated or completely unsubstantiated media accounts of violence and attacks particularly in the Superdome and the convention center.[26] The tone of these reports were hyperbolic, evoking all of the familiar racial subtexts: FOX News, for example, issued a news report the day before the Superdome was evacuated that "there were many reports of robberies, rapes, car-jackings, rioters and murder and that violent gangs are roaming the streets at night, hidden by the cover of darkness." The *Los Angeles Times* was no less sensational, reporting that National Guard troops had to take rooftop positions to scan for snipers and armed mobs as gunfire rang out.[27] These reports were taken as authoritative by police and other law enforcement officials. Indeed, even the mayor of the city, Ray Nagin, who is black, spoke of "hundreds of armed gang members" killing and raping people inside the Superdome, such that the crowd had descended to an "almost animalistic state.[28]

We are not arguing that there was no violence. There was. But the frames of black criminality and law and order overdetermined how we interpreted both the extent and nature of that violence. For example, consider how the "facts" about rape were interpreted and discussed. Recently, advocacy groups for victims of sexual assault have begun to challenge the official count of reported rapes—four—as unrealistically low. A national database newly created by the National Sexual Violence Resource Center reports more than forty sexual assaults, while another victim's rights organization has reported more than 150 post-Katrina violent crimes, of which about one-third were sexual assaults, including those committed in the homes of host families.[29] This suggests that reports of sexual assaults were underreported. Paradoxically, at the same time that reports of rape were cited to confirm stereotypes of black criminality, the black women victims of *actual* rapes suffered an

[25]See Anna Johnson, "Jackson Lashes Out at Bush over Hurricane Response, Criticizes Media for Katrina Coverage," AP Alert, September 3, 2005 (reporting that the Red Cross asserted that it could not enter New Orleans on orders from the National Guard and local authorities). A principal reason for the delay was that government officials believed that they had to prepare a complicated military operation rather than a relief effort. See "Misinformation Seen Key in Katrina Delays," UPI Top Stories, September 30, 2005.

[26]See Brian Thevenot and Gordon Russell, "Reports of Anarchy at the Superdome Overstated," *Seattle Times*, September 26, 2005 (reporting that "the vast majority of reported atrocities committed by evacuees have turned out to be false, or at least unsupported by any evidence, according to key military, law enforcement, medical and civilian officers in a position to know." See also Andrew Gumbel, "After the Storm, US Media Held to Account for Exaggerated Tales of Katrina Chaos," *Los Angeles Times*, September 28, 2005.

[27]Susannah Rosenblatt and James Rainey, "Reports of Post-Katrina Mayhem May Have Been Overblown," *Los Angeles Times*, September 27, 2005.

[28]Thevenot and Russell, "Reports of Anarchy."

[29]See "40 Rapes Reported in Hurricane Katrina, Rita Aftermath," NewOrleans Channel.com, wsdu, http://msnbc.msn.com/id/10590305; Nancy Cook Lauer, "Rape-Reporting Procedure Missing After Hurricane" Women's eNews, www.womensenews.org/article.cfm/dyn/aid/2448.

unconscionable degree of official disregard. While accounts of rape were invoked as signs of the disintegration of social order in New Orleans, some of the black women who experienced sexual violence were unable to file reports with law enforcement officials despite their efforts to do so, notwithstanding the city's ostensible mission to maintain law and order to protect victims from crime.

One of the more prominent examples of this official disregard was Charmaine Neville, a member of the family of renowned New Orleans musicians, who was raped by a roving group of men who invaded her community in the Lower Ninth Ward while she and her neighbors struggled unsuccessfully over a series of days to be evacuated and to obtain medical care.[30] Neville's searing account of what happened to her is a clear indictment of the government for its neglect: "What I want people to understand is that if we hadn't been left down there like animals that they were treating us like, all of those things would not have happened." Neville reported that her efforts to tell law enforcement officers and the National Guard of her assault were ignored. Neville's prominence and her fortuitous encounter with a member of the Catholic archdiocese in New Orleans during an interview at a local news station meant that her assault received media attention. Others did not.

Obviously, we are not excusing the conduct of the rapists or blaming that conduct on the government. Our point is simply that the overall governmental response in the aftermath of Katrina, shaped as it was by the racial frame of law and order, created conditions of possibility for rape and increased the likelihood that those rapes would be unaddressed. The sexual assaults against women—the vast majority of them black—became markers of black disorder, chaos, and the "animalistic" nature of New Orleans residents; but black women themselves could not occupy the position of victims worthy of rescue. Their injuries were only abstractions that were marshaled to make the larger point about the descent of New Orleans into a literal and figurative black hole. Black women's rape was invoked but not addressed. To borrow from Kimberle Crenshaw, their stories of rape were "voyeuristically included" in a law-and-order campaign.[31] Their specific injury—the fact that they were actually victims—was largely ignored.

The government focused its attention on violence directed against property and violence directed against the rescuers—reports of which have proven to be false or grossly embellished. While these acts of violence could fit comfortably within the frame of law and order, violence against black women's bodies could not. Images of black criminality could work concomitantly with and help to instantiate the law-and-order

[30]See Charmaine Neville, "How We Survived the Flood," transcript of interview given to New Orleans media outlets, September 5, 2005, www.counterpunch.org/neville09072005.html.

[31]Kimberle Crenshaw, "Mapping the Margins: Intersectionality, Identity Politics, and Violence Against Women of Color," *Stanford Law Review* 43 (1991): 1241, 1261.

frame that relies on black disorder; images of black women as innocent victims could do neither. The frames of law and order and black criminality influenced both the exaggeration (overreporting) and the marginalization (underreporting) of violent crimes in ways that make clear that facts don't speak for themselves.

In another example of the law-and-order and black-criminality frames at work in New Orleans, the characterization of the Superdome and the convention center as unsafe facilitated the shift from humanitarian rescue mission to military occupation and security. In part because of the perception of the severe security threat to rescuers, no food, water, or medical care was provided to the convention center until a force of a thousand soldiers and police in full battle gear was sent in to secure the center on September 2 at noon. They were able to do so in twenty minutes and encountered absolutely no resistance, though thousands of people were in the building.

Only one shooting was confirmed in the Superdome, when a soldier shot himself during a scuffle with an attacker. Though New Orleans police chief Eddie Compass reported that he and his officers had retrieved more than thirty weapons from criminals who had been shooting at the rescuers, he later modified his statement to say that this had happened to another unit, a SWAT team at the convention center. The director of the SWAT team, however, reported that his unit had heard gunshots only one time and that his team had recovered no weapons despite aggressive searches.

In retrospect, it is clear that the media both mischaracterized and exaggerated the security threat to the rescue mission. Certainly the chaos in the wake of Katrina and the breakdown of the communications network helped develop a climate in which rumors could and did flourish. Yet under similarly difficult conditions during other natural disasters and even war, reporters have adhered to basic journalistic standards. That they did not under these conditions could be explained as an isolated case of failure under extremely trying circumstances. That might very well be so. Yet, the important part of this story is not that the media failed to observe the basic rules of journalism; it is that the story they told was one people were all too ready to accept. It was a narrative that made sense within the commonly accepted racial frames of law and order and black criminality.

These frames made it difficult for us to make sense of reported 30 instances of "guys who looked like thugs, with pants hanging down around their asses," engaged in frantic efforts to get people collapsing from heat and exhaustion out of the Superdome and into a nearby makeshift medical facility. These images did not make racial sense. There was no ready-made social frame within which the image of black male rescuers could be placed. Existing outside of standard racial frames, black male rescuers present a socially unintelligible image. That we have trouble *seeing* "guys who look like thugs" as rescuers is not a problem of facts. It is a problem of frames. Indeed, the very use of the term "thug" already frames the fact of what they might be doing in a particular way.

Conclusion

Lessons from Hurricane Katrina include those about preparedness for natural disasters; coordination among local, state, and federal rescue efforts; and a nation's capacity for empathy and compassion. While it is less than clear that all of these lessons are being learned, we are at least discussing these lessons. Not so with respect to race. As a nation, we rarely talk about race and Katrina anymore. It is almost unspeakable to do so.

Yet, Katrina offers profound insights into how race operates in American society, insights into how various facts about our social life are racially interpreted through frames. As a result of racial frames, black people are both visible (as criminals) and invisible (as victims). Racial frames both capture and displace us—discursively and materially. More than shaping whether we see black people as criminal or innocent, perpetrator or victim, these frames shape whether we see black people at all. Indeed, one might reasonably ask: Where have all the black people gone, long time passing? It is not hyperbolic to say that post-Katrina black New Orleanians have become a part of an emerging social category: the disappeared. A critical lesson of Katrina is that civil rights advocacy groups need to think harder about frames, particularly when making interventions into natural disasters involving African Americans.

As Michele Landis Dauber reminds us, the template for the American social welfare system has been disaster relief, and the extent to which people are entitled to any form of government resources has always depended upon the claimants' ability to "narrat[e] their deprivation as a disaster—a sudden loss for which the claimant is not responsible."[32] In the case of Katrina, this disaster-relief conception of welfare would seem to promote an immediate national response to aid the hurricane victims. The problem for black people and for other nonwhites, however, as Dauber herself notes, is that racial minorities' claims to victim status have always been fraught "because they are highly likely to be cast as a 'disaster' for the dominant racial group.[33] Implicit in Dauber's analysis is the idea that the move to realign America's racial discourse and policy away from its current distortions must confront the complex problem of racial frames. The existence of racial frames makes it enormously difficult to incorporate "just the facts" into an argument about racism. Those facts will rarely, if ever, be able to escape completely the interpretational reach and normative appeal of racial frames about color blindness and black cultural dysfunctionality.

    [32]Michele Landis Dauber, "Fate, Responsibility, and 'Natural' Disaster Relief: Narrating the American Welfare State," *Law and Society* 33 (1999):257, 264.
    [33]Ibid., 307.

What is required is likely to be more in the nature of a social movement than a social survey. Facts will always play a crucial role, but just as the successes of the civil rights movement were born of organized struggle, so too must our efforts to shift racial frames ground themselves in a broader and more organic orientation than raw empiricism. People came to see the facts of de jure segregation differently not because new facts emerged about its harms but because new interpretations of those facts were made possible by social organization on the ground that pushed the courts toward a new consensus. We believe the same is true today.

ENGAGING THE TEXT

1. What is an interpretive frame? According to Harris and Carbado, what role did framing play in the controversy over the two photos of Hurricane Katrina victims wading through the water? What alternative explanations of the photos and their captions are mentioned in the article? Which explanation seems most plausible to you, and why?

2. Harris and Carbado identify several unspoken assumptions underlying the "metaframe" of color blindness. What are they, and how do they affect the way "color blind" people explain racial inequality? Do you agree that color blindness is a problem? Why or why not?

3. In what ways did Hurricane Katrina challenge existing racial frameworks? How did the public understanding of the disaster change over time, and what role did framing play in those evolving interpretations?

4. How were the interpretive frames of the government and media at odds with facts in the aftermath of Hurricane Katrina? How persuasive do you find Harris and Carbado's argument that "frames trump facts" (para. 9)?

5. Harris and Carbado contend that it's essential to "shift racial frames" (para. 34) in order to combat racial injustice. How would you go about trying to change the frame of color blindness? Brainstorm strategies and discuss their feasibility and likelihood of success.

EXPLORING CONNECTIONS

6. What are the "facts" in Keith Knight's cartoon on page 635? How does race cause the same gestures to be interpreted differently? What two racial frames are at work here?

7. Would Ta-Nehisi Coates (p. 572) agree or disagree with Harris and Carbado's assertion that "just the facts" are seldom enough to combat the power of racial frames? To what extent does Coates's argument rely on facts? Does he succeed in reframing the Federal Housing Administration, the New Deal, and the GI Bill? Do you think he manages to reframe reparations? Explain your response.

EXTENDING THE CRITICAL CONTEXT

8. Read news reports, editorials, blogs, or letters to the editor that address a current incident or issue that creates controversy over race (for example, charges of racial profiling, police brutality, insensitive remarks by a public figure, or "reverse discrimination"). How are the facts of the situation framed by participants, politicians, and pundits? What evidence, if any, do you see of the color-blindness frame? What other frames do you detect? Compare notes in class and discuss your observations.

9. As a class project, develop and conduct a mini-survey on color blindness on your campus. For example, you might ask participants to agree or disagree with

a series of short statements like these: "Racism is a serious problem today" or "It's better not to talk about race." Compile your results and write a paper discussing what you found and what further questions your survey raises.

10. Watch the award-winning documentary *Trouble the Water*. How does the film's depiction of Hurricane Katrina and its aftermath differ from the mainstream media accounts discussed by Harris and Carbado?

VISUAL PORTFOLIO

READING IMAGES OF THE MELTING POT

© Stephen Lam/Reuters/Landov

Reuters/Jim Bourg

Photo by Roland Charles 1992

© JC Lopez

VISUAL PORTFOLIO

READING IMAGES OF THE MELTING POT

1. Demonstrations erupted in many cities following the grand jury's decision not to indict the police officer who killed Michael Brown in Ferguson, Missouri. The photo on page 637 shows a protester in Oakland, California: Notice the sign the protester is holding, the graffiti on the dumpster, the fire burning behind him, the bottles and debris in the street. What does the picture say to you? How would you describe the protester's state of mind, and how would you support your interpretation?

2. The city of Baltimore experienced destructive rioting following Freddie Gray's death from a spinal cord injury that he sustained in police custody. Do some quick research to find out why residents were so angry. The photo on page 638 was taken the day after the conflagration; a line of police in riot gear is visible in the background. Why has the photographer focused on the hands in the fore-ground? What message does this image convey? Compare this picture to the previous one: Which photo do you find more powerful, and why?

3. Write a narrative that explains the situation pictured in the third image of the portfolio (p. 639). What is happening and what led up to this scene? Who are these people and what are their relationships? Identify specific details of setting, dress, body language, and facial expression that support your interpretation. Compare narratives and discuss the assumptions that inform the stories as well as the persuasiveness of the evidence they are based on.

4. How many different ways could you describe the ethnic or cultural identity of each of the four friends on page 640 based on the visual cues provided by the photo? What knowledge or assumptions about race, ethnicity, and culture underlie your interpretations?

5. Activists who object to the Major League Baseball team name "Cleveland Indians" and to the team's mascot, Chief Wahoo, have demonstrated on the Indians' open-ing day for twenty years. The photo on page 641 depicts a fan of the Chiefs talking to a Native American activist: Do you find the image of Chief Wahoo (visible on the fan's sweatshirt) offensive? Why or why not? How would you describe the contrast between fan and activist?

6. The photo on page 642 shows Charlene Teters, founder of the National Coalition on Racism in Sports and Media, protesting at a Washington Redskins game. Do some online research into the Native American sports controversy: Why do American Indians object to the use of native imagery and references? What do their opponents argue? How many sports teams still have Indian-related names or mascots, and why? What successes have indigenous activists achieved, and how did they prevail?

7. The image on page 643 depicts a section of the fence that divides the United States from Mexico. What sense does the picture give you of the photographer's views of immigration, the fence, the border, and the relationship between the two countries? What details of the picture itself — angle, lighting, proportion, position of the figures — suggest these views?

LAND OF THE GIANTS

ALEX TIZON

Alex Tizon was born in the Philippines and immigrated to the United States with his family when he was four. The source of this excerpt, *Big Little Man — In Search of My Asian Self*, is a memoir about growing up Pilipino surrounded by white culture. According to Tizon's Web site, the book is "the story of my struggle as an Asian boy trying to figure out how to be an Asian man. . . . I had believed, as a young man, that my deficit and my exclusion had to do with race." After graduating from the University of Oregon and earning a graduate degree in communications from Stanford, he worked as a journalist for twenty years, winning more than a dozen national awards for reporting. As a writer for the *Seattle Times*, Tizon and two colleagues won the 1997 Pulitzer Prize for Investigative Reporting. He served as Seattle bureau chief for the *Los Angeles Times* from 2003 to 2008 and was a Knight International Journalism Fellow based in Manila in 2009 and 2010. Currently, he teaches journalism at the University of Oregon.

OUR EARLY YEARS IN AMERICA were marked by relentless self-annihilation, though of course we did not see it that way at the time. Everything was done in the name of love, for the cause of fitting in, making friends, making the grade, landing the job, providing for the future, being good citizens of paradise — all so necessary and proper.

First was the abandonment of our native language and our unquestioned embrace of English, even though for my parents that abandonment meant cutting themselves off from a fluency they would never have again. Possessing a language meant possessing the world expressed in its words. Dispossessing it meant nothing less than the loss of a world and the beginning of bewilderment forever. "Language is the only homeland," said poet Czeslaw Milosz. My parents left the world that created them and now would be beginners for the rest of their lives, mumblers searching for the right word, the proper phrase that approximated what they felt inside. I wonder at the eloquence that must have lived inside them that never found a way out. How much was missed on all sides.

We left behind José Rizal[1] and picked up Mark Twain. We gave up Freddie Aguilar[2] for Frank Sinatra and the Beatles, "Bayan Ko"[3] for "The Star-Spangled Banner" and *She loves you yeah, yeah, yeah*.

---

[1] **José Rizal:** Pilipino writer, nationalist, and revolutionary (1861–1896). Rizal, considered one of the greatest heroes of the Philippines, was court-martialed for sedition and executed by the Spanish army. [All notes are the editors'.]

[2] **Freddie Aguilar:** Pilipino folk musician and activist (b. 1953).

[3] **"Bayan Ko":** "My Country," originally composed in 1928 during the struggle for Pilipino independence from the United States. Freddie Aguilar recorded a new interpretation in 1978 that became the anthem of the anti-Marcos movement.

My parents' adulation of all things white and Western and their open derision of all things brown or native or Asian was the engine of their self-annihilation. Was it purely coincidence that our first car, first house, first dog in America were white? That our culminating moment in America was a white Christmas? White was the apex of humanity, the farthest point on the evolutionary arc and therefore the closest earthly representation of ultimate truth and beauty.

I grew up hearing my parents' offhanded comments about how strong and capable the Americans were, how worthy of admiration, and conversely how weak and incapable and deserving of mockery their own countrymen were: "They can't do it on their own; they need help." I heard it in their breathless admiration for mestizos — persons of mixed European and Asian blood — how elegant and commanding they were, and the more European the better. To be called mestizo was the ultimate flattery. White spouses were prizes; mestizo babies, blessings; they represented an instant elevation, an infusion of royal blood, the promise of a more gifted life.

One late evening at the White House I was playing on the floor of my parents' bedroom closet, behind a row of shirts, when the door opened. It was my father. Instead of revealing myself, I just sat there watching him in silence, cloaked by a wall of sleeves. He changed into his house clothes and then stood at a small mirror appearing to massage his nose, running an index finger and thumb along the bridge, pinching and pulling it as if to make his nose narrower and longer. He stood there doing that for a short time and then left, shutting the door behind him. I thought it curious but did not think about it again until a few months later, when I saw him do it again as he absently watched television. He didn't know I was in the room.

"What are you doing, Papa?"

It startled him. "Nothing, son. Just massaging."

"Does your nose hurt?"

He looked at me, deciding what to say, and then he seemed to relax. "*Halika dito, anak.* Come here, son. You should do this," he said to me gently. He showed me how to use my fingers to pinch the bridge of my nose and then tug on it in a sustained pull, holding it in place for twenty seconds at a time and then repeating. "You should do this every day. If you do, your nose will become more *tangus*. Sharper. Narrower. You'll look more mestizo. Your nose is so round! And so flat! *Talagang Pilipino!* So Filipino!"

"What's wrong with flat?"

"Nothing is wrong with flat. *Pero* sharper is better. People will treat you better. They'll think you come from a better family. They'll think you're smarter and *mas guapo*, more handsome. *Talaga, anak.* This is true. See my nose? The other day a woman, a *puti*, a white, talked to me in Spanish because she thought I was from Spain. That happens to me. I massage every day. Don't you think I look Castilian?" He turned to show his profile. "*Ay anak.* My son. Believe me."

I did believe him. Just as he had believed his father when the lesson was taught to him decades earlier. These were the givens: Aquiline was better than flat. Long better than wide. Light skin better than dark. Round eyes better than *chinky*. Blue eyes better than brown. Thin lips better than full. Blond better than black. Tall better than short. Big better than small. The formula fated us to lose. We had landed on a continent of Big Everything.

One sunny afternoon, my father and I walked to a hardware store a few blocks from our house. As we were about to go inside, three American men in overalls and T-shirts walked out, filling the doorway and inadvertently blocking our path. They were enormous, all of them well over six feet tall, with beards and beefy arms and legs. My father and I stood looking up at this wall of denim and hair. The Americans appeared ready to scoot over. "Excuse us," my father said, and we moved to the side. One of the men said thanks, another snickered as they passed.

My father leaned down and whispered in my ear, *"Land of the Giants."* It was the name of a television show my family had started watching, a science-fiction series about a space crew marooned on a planet of gargantuan humans. The crew members were always being picked up by enormous hands and toyed with. The show's tagline: "Mini-people — Playthings in a World of Giant Tormentors." My family was captivated by the show. I think we related to the mini-people who in every episode were confronted by impossibly large humanoids. 15

Americans did seem to me at times like a different species, one that had evolved over generations into supreme behemoths. Kings in overalls. They were living proof of a basic law of conquest: victors ate better. The first time I sat as a guest at an American dinner table, I could scarcely believe the bounty: a whole huge potato for each of us, a separate plate of vegetables, my own steak. A separate slab of meat just for me! At home, that single slab would have fed my entire family.

The size of American bodies came to represent American capacities in everything we desired: they were smarter, stronger, richer; they lived in comfort and had the surplus to be generous. They knew the way to beauty and bounty because they were already there, filling the entryway with their meaty limbs and boulder heads and big, toothy grins like searchlights, imploring us with their booming voices to come on in. Have a seat at the table! Americans spoke a few decibels louder than we were used to.

We were small in everything. We were poor. I mean pockets-out immigrant poor. We were undernourished and scrawny, our genetics revealing not-so-distant struggles with famine and disease and war. We were inarticulate, our most deeply felt thoughts expressed in halting, heavily accented English, which might have sounded like grunts to Americans, given how frequently we heard "Excuse me?" or "Come again?" or "What?" The quizzical look on their faces as they tried to decipher the alien sounds.

My father, who was a funny, dynamic conversationalist in his own language, a man about Manila, would never be quite so funny or dynamic or quick-witted or agile or confident again. He would always be a small man in America. My mother was small, too, but it was acceptable, even desirable, for women to be small. American men found my mother attractive. She never lacked attention or employment. My father was the one most demoted in the great new land. He was supposed to be the man of the family, and he did not know which levers to pull or push, and he didn't have the luxury of a lifetime, like his children, to learn them.

I'm convinced it was because of a gnawing awareness of his limitations in the land of the giants that he was a dangerous man to belittle. [20] Gentle and gregarious in the company of friends, he was a different person in the larger world of strangers: wary, opaque, tightly coiled. My father stood all of five feet six inches and 150 pounds, every ounce of which could turn maniacal in an instant. He took offense easily and let his fists fly quickly. He was not deterred by mass. He recognized it, but became blind with fury when it trespassed on him or his family. I once watched him scold a man twice his size, an auto mechanic he thought was taking advantage of him, and threaten to leap over the counter to teach him a lesson. "You kick a man in the balls and he's not so big anymore," he once told me. Actually, he told me more than once.

My mother corroborated the stories of my father challenging other men over perceived slights, losing as many fights as he won and getting downright clobbered on a few occasions, once landing in the hospital for a week. My mother was present at some of those fights; she was the cause of at least one, in which an unfortunate young man ogled her and ended up laid out on the sidewalk.

I got another glimpse of his inner maniac once at a park in New Jersey when I was about twelve. A big red-haired kid on a bike spat on me and rode away laughing and making faces. My father followed him all the way back to where his family was picnicking and confronted the three men in the group, all Americans, one of whom was presumably the kid's father. They all appeared startled. I heard only part of the conversation that followed. "We could take care of it right now, right here," my father told the men in a low, threatening voice, his fists clenched into hard knots. He stood leaning forward, unblinking. The men averted their gaze and kept silent. On the walk back to our spot, my father said, "Tell me if that boy comes near you again." I was speechless. His mettle astonished me. But it was something more than bravery on display that day. His fury was outsized, reckless, as if something larger was at stake, and of course now I know there was.

Unlike my father, I worked hard to get along with strangers. We moved so much in those early years that I got used to strangers as companions as we passed from place to place. I learned American English, trained out whatever accent I had inherited, picked up colloquial mannerisms. I kept a confident front, not in a loudmouthed way but in a reserved, alert manner, and I got more surefooted in my interactions as I got better at English. If I had to guess, I'd say my classmates would have described me as a little shy but smart and likable. I brooded in private.

How could someone be ashamed and capable at the same time? I was fated to have a secret life.

So I worked on becoming an American, to be in some ways more American than my American friends. But I learned, eventually, that I could never reach the ideal of the beloved. And when the realization came, it seemed to land all at once, blunt force trauma, and I felt embarrassed to have been a believer.

It's one of the beautiful lies of the American Dream: that you can become anything, do anything, accomplish anything, if you want it badly enough and are willing to work for it. Limits are inventions of the timid mind. You've got to believe. All things are possible through properly channeled effort: work, work, work; harder, faster, more! Unleash your potential! Nothing is beyond your reach! Just do it! I believed it all, drank the elixir to the last drop and licked my lips for residue. I put in the time, learned to read and write and speak more capably than my friends and neighbors, followed the rules, did my homework, memorized the tics and slangs and idiosyncrasies of winners and heroes, but I could never be quite as American as they. The lie is a lie only if you fail, and I most certainly did.

When I ask myself now when this shame inside me began, I see that I inherited the beginnings of it from my father, and he from his father, going back in my imagination as far as the arrival of the Spanish ships[4] almost five hundred years ago. An ancient inherited shame. It accompanied us across the ocean. We carried it into a country that told us: not reaching the summit was no one's fault but your own. . . .

My father continued his pugnacious ways into old age. His last fistfight, which occurred when he was sixty-eight, involved a hugely obese teenager who my father believed had disrespected him. The kid, who weighed over two hundred pounds, ended the fight by lying on my father and crushing the air out of him, almost killing him. Papa had had two heart bypass surgeries and a couple of strokes by then and was by all measures frail. He could not concede weakness. In other ways, he did evolve. His gentleness with us, his children, magnified. His remorse for leaving us[5] haunted him and kept him in a perpetual state of apologizing. *I'm sorry, anak. My son. I'm so, so sorry.* He cried easily. . . .

"Do this every day," he told me.

I followed his advice. As inconspicuously as possible, I hid from the sun. I dangled from tree branches and pull-up bars to stretch my body, praying to gravity, aiming my heels toward the center of the Earth. I tried to eat beyond my appetite, and as a teenager secretly began taking protein supplements to help me grow. I rubbed oils onto my eyelids to keep them supple, to prevent the epicanthic folds from turning my eyes

---

[4]**the arrival of the Spanish ships:** Refers to Magellan's 1521 arrival in the Philippines.
[5]**His remorse for leaving us:** When Tizon was a high school student, his parents divorced; as he explains in *Big Little Man*, his father "wrote a long letter to his children, apologizing for his failure and pledging his undying love, and then left us to start another life."

chinky. And every night before falling asleep, for at least twenty seconds, I would massage my nose. The shape of your nose determined your fate. It was the symbol of your lineage, the mark that determined which gate you entered. As I got older, I got more obsessive. I began attaching a clothespin to my nose and leaving it there all night. I was already prone to nosebleeds, and sometimes the clothespin was too tight and I'd wake up with blood on my pillow. To make my lips thinner, more mestizo, I would suck them in and place masking tape over my mouth for hours at a time. Anyone who walked into my bedroom on those nights would have thought I was being held hostage. None of it worked. The mirror mocked me. The clay of my face would never change.

ENGAGING THE TEXT

1. What does Tizon mean when he writes, "Our early years in America were marked by relentless self-annihilation" (para. 1)? How does forsaking their native language affect his parents? What's the significance of his father's nose-massaging routine? Why does Tizon himself go to such lengths to try to reshape his face and body?

2. In what ways does America appear to be a land of giants? Why does Tizon's family seem "small in everything" (para. 18)?

3. How does Tizon's father change as a result of his immigration to America? What was his personality like in the Philippines, and how is he different after he comes to the United States? Why does he become "a dangerous man to belittle" (para. 20)? In what way does he evolve in old age, and how does he remain the same?

4. Why is the American Dream a "beautiful lie" in Tizon's experience? How does he attempt to reach the Dream? To what extent does he succeed, and how does he fail? How does Tizon's version of the American Dream compare to your own?

5. What is the source of Tizon's "ancient inherited shame"? Why is he able to imaginatively trace it "as far as the arrival of the Spanish ships almost five hundred years ago" (para. 26)?

EXPLORING CONNECTIONS

6. How do Tizon and his family undergo both "surface and deep culture" assimilation as defined by Holtzman and Sharpe (p. 600)? In what ways do they suffer from internalized racism? To what extent does Tizon's experience differ from that of his parents?

7. Compare Tizon's and David Treuer's (p. 651) views on the importance of language to culture and identity. To what extent do they agree? How and why do they differ? If you speak another language at home, how crucial is it to your cultural identity and sense of self?

8. Write an imaginary conversation between Tizon and the Suárez-Orozcos (p. 666) in which they discuss both the benefits and the losses associated with immigration.

EXTENDING THE CRITICAL CONTEXT

9. Research microaggressions. You might start with this Web site, which defines microaggressions, gives examples, and suggests why they could be perceived as hurtful or insulting: www.ucop.edu/academic-personnel-programs/_files /seminars/Tool_Recognizing_Microaggressions.pdf. Then browse a few articles that take issue with the whole concept. Do you think that a focus on microaggressions represents political correctness run amok, or does it address a serious concern? Why?

10. Write a journal entry describing an experience that made you question a pre-conception you had about another race, ethnicity, or nationality. What did you believe about the group before this experience, and what happened to make you question your view? Did you change as a result? If so, how and why?

FROM REZ LIFE: AN INDIAN'S JOURNEY THROUGH RESERVATION LIFE

DAVID TREUER

Out of the 300-plus native languages originally spoken in the United States, only about half remain, and many of them are dying. David Treuer (b. 1970) is acutely aware of this loss. In the following passage, he focuses on the efforts of Ojibwe language activists to revive their native language and preserve their culture. But Treuer is at heart a storyteller. In addition to pro-filing Keller Paap, the "recovering rock star" who leads the Ojibwe language immersion program, he weaves in stories about "blood quantum" the American Indian Movement of the 1960s and 1970s (the way tribal mem-bership is determined), the Carlisle school, and the Cherokee Freedmen. Treuer has won fellowships from the National Endowment for the Human-ities, the Bush Foundation, and the Guggenheim Foundation. A professor of literature and creative writing at the University of Southern California, he has produced several well-received novels; a book of essays, *Native Amer-ican Fiction: A User's Manual* (2006); and *Rez Life: An Indian's Journey Through Reservation Life* (2012), from which this selection is taken.

I AM NOT SUPPOSED TO BE ALIVE. Native Americans were supposed to die off, as endangered species do, a century ago. Our reservations aren't supposed to exist either; they were supposed to be temporary in many ways, and, under assault by the Dawes Act[1] in the nineteenth century and by termination policy during the Eisenhower era[2] in the twentieth century, they were supposed to disappear, too.

But I am not dead after all, and neither is rez life despite the coldest wishes of a republic since two centuries before I was born. We stubbornly continue to exist. There were just over 200,000 Native Americans alive at the dawn of the twentieth century; as of the 2000 census, we number more than 2 million. If you discount population growth by immigration, we are the fastest-growing segment of the U.S. population. But even as our populations are growing, something else, I fear, is dying: our cultures.

Among my fellow Indians, this is not a popular thing to say. Most of us immediately sneer at warnings of cultural death, calling the very idea further proof that "the man" is still trying to kill us, but now with attitudes and arguments rather than discrimination and guns. Any Indian caught worrying that we might indeed vanish can expect to be grouped with the self-haters. While many things go into making a culture—kinship, history, religion, place—the disappearance of our languages suggests that our cultures, in total, may not be here for much longer.

For now, many Native American languages still exist, but most of them just barely, with only a very few living speakers, all of them old. On January 21, 2008, Marie Smith Jones, the last living fluent speaker of Eyak, one of about twenty remaining Native Alaskan languages, died at the age of eighty-nine. Linguists estimate that when Europeans first came to North America, more than 300 Native American languages were spoken here. Today, there are only about 150. Of those languages, only twenty are spoken by children. Only three languages—Dakota, Dene, and Ojibwe—have a vibrant community of speakers. Within a century, if nothing is done, hardly any Native languages will remain, though the surviving ones will include my language, Ojibwe.

Cultures change, of course. Sometimes they change slowly, in response to such factors as warming temperatures, differences in food sources, or new migration patterns. At other times, cultural changes are swift—the result of colonialism, famine, migration, or war. But at some point (which no one is anxious to identify exactly), a culture ceases to be a culture and becomes an ethnicity—that is, it changes from a life system

5

---

[1]**Dawes Act:** The General Allotment Act of 1887, sponsored by Senator Henry L. Dawes of Massachusetts, divided Indian land into individual allotments; "excess" land was purchased by the government and sold to non–Indians. Individual land ownership effectively diluted tribal power. [All notes are the editors', except 5, 8, and 9.]

[2]**termination policy during the Eisenhower era:** From 1953 to 1966, over 100 tribes lost their tribal status, over a million acres of land were removed from trust, and over 33,000 native people were relocated from reservations to large cities.

that develops its own terms into one that borrows, almost completely, someone else's.

To claim that Indian cultures can continue without Indian languages only hastens our end, even if it makes us feel better about ourselves. Our cultures and our languages—as unique, identifiable, and particular entities—are linked to our sovereignty. If we allow our own wishful thinking and complacency to finish what George Armstrong Custer began, we will lose what we've managed to retain: our languages, land, laws, institutions, ceremonies, and, finally, ourselves. Cultural death matters because if the culture dies, we will have lost the chance not only to live on our own terms (something for which our ancestors fought long and hard) but also to live in our own terms.

If my language dies, our word for bear, "makwa," will disappear, and with it the understanding that "makwa" is derived from the word for box, "makak" (because black bears box themselves up, sleeping, for the winter). So too will the word for namesake, "niiyawen'enh." Every child who gets an Ojibwe name has namesakes, sometimes as many as six or eight of them. Throughout a child's life, his or her namesakes function somewhat like godparents, giving advice and help, good for a dollar to buy an Indian taco at a powwow. But they offer something more too. The term for "my body," "niiyaw" (a possessive noun: ni- = "I/mine"; -iiyaw = "body/soul"), is incorporated into the word for a namesake because the idea (contained by the word and vice versa) is that when you take part in a naming, you are giving a part of your soul, your body, to the person being named. So, to say "my namesake," niiyawen'enh, is to say "my fellow body, myself." If these words are lost, much will happen, but also very little will happen. We will be able to go to Starbucks, GameStop, Walmart, and Home Depot. We will still use Crest Whitestrips. Some of us will still do our taxes. Some of us still won't. The mechanics of life as it is lived by modern Ojibwes will remain, for the most part, unchanged. The languages we lose, when we lose them, are always replaced by other languages. And all languages can get the job of life done. But something else might be lost and there might be more to the job of life than simply living it.

At Waadookodaading Ojibwe Language Immersion School at Lac Courte Oreilles (LCO) Reservation in Wisconsin, people are doing something about this. You drive past a lot of natural beauty between Hayward and the school—a lot of maple and pine; deep, clear lakes—most of it owned by whites. At the school, in two yellow modular buildings built with tribal funds in what used to be the corner of the school parking lot, a cultural revival is occurring. On the hot day in May when I visited the school I saw silhouettes of students drawn in chalk on the wooden decking that connects the buildings. The third and fourth grades were studying solar movement as part of their science curriculum, all done in Ojibwe, and done only here. Inside, the classroom walls are covered with signs in the Ojibwe language. A smartboard, linked to the teacher's laptop, provides state-of-the-art learning opportunities.

One of the teachers who helped start the immersion program is a lanky, tall, excitable man named Keller Paap. When these teachers started the school in 2000 they had only a few students in kindergarten. Now, there are about twenty students in the program between kindergarten and fourth grade. After greeting the fourth-grade students in the classroom, Keller brings them to the music room in the main school building, where they all sing along with Keller's guitar playing to welcome the new day. They speak, sing, argue, and flirt with each other in Ojibwe at a level that eludes most adults at LCO and every other Ojibwe reservation across the United States. After the morning singing they head back to the classroom and begin working on their science unit. "Ahaw," asks Keller. "Awegonesh ge-ayaayambam da-agawaat-eyaag?" [So. What do all you need to make a shadow?]

One girl says, shyly, "Andaatewin." 10

"Mii gwayak," says Keller. "Awegonesh gaye? Giizis ina?"

"Ahaw," says a playful boy, without a hint of shame or bashfulness.

"Mii go gaye apiichaawin," says another kid, in a spurt of intuition.

This classroom is light-years ahead of most tribal language programs, which are still stuck on "bezhig, niizh, niswi," and "makwa, waabooz, waagosh" ("one, two, three" and "bear, rabbit, fox"). They aren't listing things in Ojibwe at Waadookodaading; they are thinking in Ojibwe.

Keller; his wife, Lisa LaRonge; Alex Decoteau; and the other teach- 15 ers at Waadookodaading are, together, saving Ojibwe culture. Keller Paap is one of a few activists who have devoted their lives to saving the Ojibwe language. He is an unlikely hero. Raised in a suburb of Minneapolis, college-educated, a recovering rock star (he is an accomplished guitarist), he has given up all financial security, all his other possible prospects, everything, in order to move to LCO to open an Ojibwe-language immersion school. He is a new kind of activist for a new kind of reservation community.

Indian activism used to be a tough guy's game. In the late 1960s and early 1970s the American Indian Movement (AIM) rose from urban Indian populations across the country. Cleveland, Minneapolis, Chicago, Oakland, and Los Angeles had been destinations for Indians relocated during the 1950s, and they became the seed plots for a surge of Indian activism. Relocation, a government-sponsored program, yet another switchback in the U.S. government's long road toward freeing itself of Indians and of all responsibility toward us, was a policy that sought to integrate Indians into the mainstream workforce by severing their relationship to their reservation communities. The relocation program promised jobs, education, and housing in up-and-coming American cities. Very little of this was forthcoming. Instead, Indians were crowded into ghettos, fought for work, fought for education, and suffered. It should be said that many Indians flourished in cities in the 1950s and many still flourish there today; more than half of all Indians live in urban areas.

Still, the common notion that reservations are prisons should be revised; it was the city that became a prison for many Indians. They were stuck in a city and could not get out. They hadn't the money to move back to the reservation and yet they had little reason to stay. Franklin Avenue, Gowanus Canal, Chicago's South Side—these became signifiers of rough life as important as the reservations the Indians had come from. Out of this situation, which was supposed to gradually make Indians as Indians "disappear," came AIM.

Clyde Bellecourt, Dennis Banks, George Mitchell, and Herb Powless, among others, founded AIM in 1968. Its rationale and goals were: the U.S. government has never had the interests of American Indians in mind or at heart, and any attempt to work within the system or with the system is bound to fail. Unlike the black civil rights movement, AIM had no great strength of numbers, economic capital, or visibility to use in getting its point across. The answer: bold, graphic takeovers and marches. Within seven years AIM had marched on and taken over Alcatraz Island (more accurately, a group of Bay Area Indians took over Alcatraz and some of the high-profile AIM leadership came toward the end of the takeover); the Bureau of Indian Affairs (BIA) headquarters in Washington, D.C.; Mount Rushmore; and a replica of the *Mayflower*. At each event the AIMsters dressed in cowboy boots, tight jeans, buckskin jackets, and headbands and issued passionate, even poetic, statements about the continued mistreatment of American Indians. Often, light-skinned Indians were told they couldn't belong to AIM or had to march in the back. AIM was always concerned with its image. Its activism was a kind of art—street theater that was visual and often violent and that conveyed clear messages about the mistreatment of Indians.

The most shocking and visible moment for AIM, and the moment that marked its decline, was its standoff with the federal government at the Jumping Bull Compound on the Pine Ridge Reservation in South Dakota, which left two federal agents dead. Leonard Peltier was charged with and convicted of murder and is still serving a sentence at Leavenworth. Afterward, marked by vicious infighting and infiltrated by the FBI, AIM became, in the opinion of many, aimless. And not everyone had approved of AIM in the first place. During the 1970s anger at the Red Lake Reservation chairman, Roger Jourdain, at his policies, and at embezzlement by other employees fueled riots at Red Lake. Jourdain's house was burned down and cars were shot through with bullets. AIM tried to muscle in on the unrest and was rebuffed. The traditional community of Ponemah took a stand against AIM. As Eugene Stillday recounts, a number of veterans (of World War II, Korea, and Vietnam) from Ponemah gathered at The Cut—a narrow place in the road, bordered by the lake on one side and a large swamp on the other. They barricaded the road, built sandbag bunkers, and kept constant guard, armed with deer rifles and shotguns. Carloads of AIMsters drove up the road, were stopped, and after looking at the faces of the Ponemah veterans chose to turn around and go elsewhere.

This was what passed for activism in the late 1960s and 1970s. Keller Paap, on the other hand, is an unlikely activist. He was raised in a comfortable suburb: White Bear Lake, on the north side of St. Paul. His mother is from Red Cliff Reservation in Wisconsin; his father is of German ancestry. After graduating from high school in White Bear Lake he started college, stopped, and devoted himself to becoming a rock and roller. Keller *looks* like a rock star. He's tallish (six feet and change), thin, and bony, with long black hair, wide cheekbones and lips, and long tapered fingers that were made to hold a guitar and to play it well. When someone is talking to him about the Ojibwe language, the glazed look that comes over his eyes must be the same look he had during a guitar solo. It is not difficult to imagine him wearing a bandanna, like Steven Van Zandt,[3] or the same purse-lipped expression when he is focused on his guitar. During the day the kids sometimes start spacing out during their lessons and Keller jumps up, thumbs his iPod while gushing at the kids in Ojibwe, finds Herbie Hancock's "Rockit," and gets his kids to kick off their shoes and try to do the "robot," the "scarecrow," and "the moon walk." During the early 1980s Keller spent a lot of time practicing his break-dancing moves. Later, he and his friends followed the Grateful Dead.[4]

I first met Paap in 1994 at the University of Minnesota, where he was finishing his undergraduate degree. He was a student in the Ojibwe-language class offered through the department of American Indian Studies. At the time he didn't seem all that interested in the language.

"Back then I thought it was sort of cool," he says. "I was Ojibwe, my people were from Red Cliff, and this was our language, and it felt good to study it."

That good feeling quickly became a passion.

"It all started with hanging out with Dennis Jones, the Ojibwe-language instructor at the U. I traveled around with him and recorded his mom and worked on translating her stories. And, man! The intricacy! The crazy complexity of the language totally got me. I mean, hanging out with Nancy, and Rose Tainter, and Delores Wakefield—all those elders, sitting around the kitchen table drinking Red Rose tea and talking—it felt comfortable, like it was with my uncles and cousins and relatives up at Red Cliff when I was a kid. Even more than music, even more than the guitar, the complexity and music of the language and the feeling of belonging to something totally caught me."[5]

Catch him it did. Soon after graduating he worked as a teaching assistant for the language program. He met his wife there. Lisa LaRonge is from LCO Reservation, due south of Red Cliff. Like Keller she is tall,

[3]**Steven Van Zandt:** Rock musician and actor, best known as a member of Bruce Springsteen's E Street Band.
[4]**the Grateful Dead:** Founded in 1965 in the San Francisco Bay area; one of the longest lasting rock bands with some of the most dedicated followers (Deadheads).
[5]Interview with Keller Paap, August 2009, Scattergood Lake. [Treuer's note.]

with long brown hair. Like Keller, she has gone through many incarnations before devoting herself to the language. They moved to Lisa's reservation in 1998 and, with a few others, opened an Ojibwe-language immersion school—Waadookodaading ("we help each other"). Waadookodaading has been in operation for ten years now, as one of only a few schools generating fluent speakers of the Ojibwe language. Strangely, many other Ojibwe-language activists have some kind of artistic pedigree. Leslie Harper—who along with her sister Laurie, Adrian Liberty, and elders like Johnny Mitchell founded the Niigaane Immersion program at Leech Lake—is a writer and a former Miss Indian Minneapolis. Liberty is a drummer—his band Powermad was featured in David Lynch's *Wild at Heart.*

The goal of these activists seems odd to many: in communities rife with drugs, violence, gangs, domestic abuse, suicide, and high dropout rates, Ojibwe-language immersion seems like a perverse luxury.

Odd or not, what these fighters are after is something very different from what AIM was after in the 1960s and 1970s. AIM wanted the world to stand up and take notice of the injustices we suffered and continue to suffer. By taking notice public opinion might actually sway policy. Language activists look in the other direction—instead of looking out at the government and the mainstream and trying to convince them of something, they are looking in and are trying to convince their fellow Indians of something else. As my brother has put it on a number of occasions, "The U.S. government has spent millions of dollars trying to take our language away from us. Why would we expect the government to give it back? It's up to us to give it back to ourselves."

The U.S. government did indeed spend millions of dollars and many years trying to stamp out indigenous languages, mostly through subtle discriminatory practices (such as hiring and education) but the government also used unsubtle means, the most destructive of which was the institution of Indian boarding schools. As Native American languages endured a sustained assault, Indian identity—those elusive bonds that wed self and society and that make a people—took the greatest number of hits. Many Indians see this as proof of the spiteful, harmful attitude the feds have always had toward Indians. But governments really aren't spiteful just to be spiteful. They are like animals—they do what they do out of self-interest. And for many years, Indians were a threat—a constant, powerful, very real, very physical threat—to American imperial expansion. We were, quite simply, either in the way or powerful enough to pose a threat if provoked. The process by which Indians were dealt with only sometimes took the form of war. In many other instances Indians were subjected to a process of "Americanization." In place from colonial days, Americanization was aimed at creating a uniform public body, one that shared the same values and lifestyles and put the same premium on work, saving, expansion, and accumulation of capital. However, for Indians, the late nineteenth century and the early twentieth century was a dark time, in many ways because of the boarding schools.

In 1878–1879, the U.S. government built and funded the first of twenty-six federally controlled Indian boarding schools. Carlisle Indian Industrial School, in Carlisle, Pennsylvania, came to epitomize the boarding school era, which for many Indians was one of the darkest times in our history. The idea of the boarding schools was to forcibly break the family bonds that, in the opinion of many, kept Indians from becoming civilized and part of the American public. Carlisle drew students from more than 140 different tribes. The students had their hair cut short. Their names were changed. They were forbidden to speak their Native languages. No Indian religions were allowed at the school—attendance at Christian services was compulsory. Students were beaten for speaking their languages. Many were abused. By 1902, with twenty-six schools in operation, more than 6,000 Indian children had been removed from their homes and sent hundreds of miles away from their communities. When boarding schools and the policies that supported them were finally abolished in the 1970s, hundreds of thousands of Indians had been sent there. Carlisle alone admitted more than 12,000 students by the time of its closing in 1918.

Attendance at boarding schools was not compulsory. Parents had to agree to let their children go. But their permission was often effected through coercion. Indian agents, who got bonuses for collecting children for school, threatened to withhold annuities or supplies. They blacklisted Indian families who refused to send their children along. Some parents, like my great-grandmother, could not afford to feed their children, and while their Indianness was under assault at these boarding schools at least their children would have something to eat. After the schools had been in existence for a few decades the pressure to send children away became a norm. If you wanted your children to have a chance at a job or an education you sent them away. It simply was what was done. Agents from the BIA were extremely effective at coercing families into letting their children go. . . .

Forced assimilation in the form of allotment[6] and boarding schools had terrible effects on reservation life and Indian lives. But as bad as the U.S. government has been in its treatment of Indians, sometimes Indians are as bad or even worse to one another. One really fucked-up aspect of Indian life is that, unlike any other minority, Indians have rules, based on genetics and "blood quantum," that determine whether or not someone is *officially* an Indian. . . .

"Blood quantum" is a strange way to determine who is and who is not officially Indian. And whatever impact this might have on how one feels

30

---

[6]**allotment:** Refers to the effect of the Dawes Act; individual land ownership was designed to encourage Native Americans to assimilate into American society.

about one's identity, such exclusions have direct and sometimes dire consequences. . . . There have been blood quantum laws on the books since the eighteenth century, most notably in Virginia, where it was illegal to mix with Indians and blacks. Ironically, "one drop" laws (one drop of black blood made you black) were reversed for Indians: they had to prove they had a certain fraction of Indian blood in order to qualify for enrollment and membership and to receive their treaty rights. But it wasn't until the 1930s that blood quantum became a widespread marker for racial descent, on which hung the issue of an Indian's nationality. Until then, for hundreds of years, Indian tribes had various means of including or excluding someone. Many tribes, mine among them, practiced widespread "adoptions." Indian children (and often white children) were captured or kidnapped and formally adopted into Ojibwe families to replace children and men lost in war or lost to disease. That's what happened to John Tanner in the mid-eighteenth century. He was abducted by Shawnee in the Ohio River valley when he was about ten years old, was marched into northern Ohio and Michigan, and later was sold to an Ojibwe family. He grew up among the Ojibwe, spoke our language, married an Ojibwe woman, and made his life with us. Not that it was always a happy life for him—his Shawnee captors beat him, left him for dead, smeared feces on his face, and piled other humiliations on him during his captivity. His Ojibwe family was only marginally more loving, until he proved he could hunt and provide for them. Indians from other tribes were adopted or married in and they enjoyed not only an Indian identity but the rights secured by the tribes and bands they joined.

Such fluid cultural boundaries became more rigid in the twentieth century. As part of the IRA,[7] which brought constitutional government to many tribes, the tribes could set their own blood quantum requirements for enrollment (half, one-fourth, one-sixteenth, or whatever), but only in consultation with, and with the approval of, the BIA. Since its inception, even though Indians are the fastest-growing segment of the U.S. population, official Indians in some tribes are declining. That is, many tribes are getting smaller.

Now many tribes are shrinking by their own efforts. The Mdewakanton Sioux Community has roughly 250 enrolled members. This number has remained quite static for the last twenty years—interestingly, the period when the tribe has run multibillion-dollar Mystic Lake Casino. The Mdewakanton is supposed to be a community reserved for the descendants of Dakota Indians who sided with the U.S. government during the Dakota Conflict of 1862. In payment for their support and their reluctance to join their tribesmen they were given land near present-day Shakopee, Minnesota. However, a lawsuit working its way through the courts alleges that there are more than 20,000 eligible

---

[7] **IRA:** The Indian Reorganization Act (1934) terminated the allotment system, limited the sale of American Indian lands, and granted limited tribal sovereignty.

enrollees (according to blood quantum rules on the books) living in the United States and Canada who meet the tribal enrollment criteria and can prove membership to the band at Shakopee. These descendants have appealed to the tribe and been rejected. The tribe doesn't want them and doesn't want to enroll them. In their case this is not a matter of "identity" but a matter of resources. If enrolled they would be entitled, along with the 250 officially enrolled members, to per capita payments, which would drop from $80,000 a month down to $1,000 a month. It is easy to see why the Indians in power and enrolled at Shakopee don't want to open their arms to their tribal brothers. They are as greedy as any other Americans; I can't think of many people who after a lifetime of struggle would gladly give up $1.2 million a year in exchange for the moral high ground.[8]

Who gets to be an official Indian and who is an unofficial Indian is sometimes a matter of identity and insecurity about that identity. Sometimes it is a matter of economics and greed. In both instances tribal enrollment confuses race (descent) and culture (environment). Being enrolled won't necessarily make you more culturally Indian. And not being enrolled won't make you less so. But enrollment and nonenrollment can make you more or less poor and can determine where and how you live.

One of the strangest and most fascinating instances of the question "Who is and who isn't Indian?" is the case of the Cherokee Freedmen. 35

The forced removal of Cherokee and the other four members of the Five Civilized Tribes from their lands in Georgia, Florida, Tennessee, Kentucky, and South Carolina in the 1820s and 1830s to the Indian Territories on what was known as the Trail of Tears has become a symbolic moment in American history. The Trail of Tears has come to signify American injustice, Indian-hating presidents, paternalistic Supreme Court justices, and the Indians' plight in general. It has been written about, sung about, painted, reenacted. The Trail of Tears was brutal. Of the 15,000 Indians who were forced to march to Indian Territory in the dead of winter, 4,000 died along the way—from starvation, hypothermia, typhus, or pneumonia. One can envision the long line of the downtrodden and disposed staggering through blizzards and fording icy rivers. The Cherokee and allied tribes were forced to march because they had been dispossessed. Their 5,000 black slaves were forced to march because they were the personal property of the Indians. Once they reached Oklahoma, the black slaves continued to be slaves until emancipation. During the Civil War the Cherokee Nation was divided. Some Cherokee sided with the Union, others with the Confederacy. After the Union victory the Cherokee Nation was forced to the negotiating table, largely as punishment for supporting the Confederacy, and

[8]Kevin Diaz, *Minneapolis Star Tribune*, November 10, 2009, http://www.startribune.com/politics/state/69722942.html. [Treuer's note.]

forced to sign a treaty. One stipulation of the treaty of 1866 was that former Cherokee slaves, known as Freedmen, were to be given full citizenship in the Cherokee Nation. As members of the Cherokee Nation, the Freedmen would be entitled to all the rights and benefits of Cherokee citizens, such as allotments, the right to vote in tribal elections, the right to stand for office, and receipt of annuities.

A little over 100 years later the Cherokee Nation wanted to remove the descendants of the Freedmen from the rolls and deprive them of tribal membership. This meant that these descendants—who considered themselves culturally (if not completely racially) Cherokee, who had lived and worked on Cherokee lands, who had the same values and language as the Cherokee—would no longer be eligible to vote, hold office, receive federal housing assistance, or receive whatever casino profits might come their way. One can smell divisive greed in the air again, though one senses something else, too: the Cherokee in Oklahoma have long had one of the most welcoming, inclusive, and progressive enrollment policies. Unlike the St. Croix Band of Ojibwe in Wisconsin, the Cherokee Nation requires only proof of descent from the "Dawes rolls," a list of Cherokee and other Civilized Tribe members compiled in 1893 and closed in 1907 for the purpose of allotment. The Dawes rolls had included a few categories of tribal membership: by blood; by marriage; and, specifically, Freedmen or descendants of Freedmen, and Delaware Indians adopted into the Cherokee Nation. There is no minimum blood quantum requirement. Such a policy has been a blessing and a curse to the Cherokee. With more than 250,000 enrolled members living in almost every state in the Union, they have remarkable power of presence and numbers and a much more flexible understanding than any other tribe of what it might mean to be Indian. They also suffer from encroachment and the constant threat of cultural dissolution through acculturation—many who want to be Indian claim to be Cherokee, not because they are but because it's easy. Hence the popular refrain we all hear at parties: my grandmother was a Cherokee princess. (No one seriously claims to be descended from a Hopi princess, a Dakota princess, or an Inuit princess.)

In the late 1980s the Cherokee Nation tried to disenroll the descendants of the Freedmen. The case went to federal court, which ruled in *Nero v. Cherokee Nation* that tribes had the right to determine the criteria of their own tribal membership. This ran counter to a century of policy that said tribes could determine the criteria for membership but only in "consultation" with the BIA. Many members of the Cherokee Nation were (and are) divided over the issue, and in 2006 the Cherokee Nation Judicial Appeals Tribunal maintained that the Freedmen were potentially eligible for enrollment. The Cherokee Nation put the issue to a referendum, and as a result a constitutional amendment was passed in 2007 that limited membership in the Cherokee Nation to those who were Cherokee, Shawnee, or Delaware by blood, listed on the Dawes rolls.

The wheels on the bus go round and round. The Black Congressional Caucus got involved. It saw the exclusion of the Cherokee Freedmen as an instance of exclusion based on race. As the case worked its way through the courts, Representative Diane Watson of California introduced legislation that would block $300 million in federal funding and annul all gaming compacts between the Cherokee and the state of Oklahoma until the Cherokee Nation reinstated the Freedmen. The basis for the legislation is about as potent an irony as exists in the history of Indian-white relations: the Cherokee were being punished for breaking a treaty they made in "good faith" with the United States![9]

The U.S. government and the state government of Oklahoma don't want to be too hasty or too autocratic in dealing with the Cherokee Nation—if only because the Cherokee suffered so much, before, during, and after the Trail of Tears. But haven't the Cherokee Freedmen—not just disposed, but the dehumanized *property* of the dispossessed—suffered more? In 1828, leading up to the Trail of Tears, the Cherokee had standing in U.S. courts. Their slaves did not. Tribal enrollment has been, from the beginning, a way of determining who can claim economic benefits that devolve from treaties. From the start, enrollment and Indian citizenship have been institutions created by the U.S. government as a way of limiting its responsibility toward Indians and eventually getting out of the "Indian business." But it couldn't always control the ways in which tribes sought to define themselves. Blood quantum was supposed to be a way out for the government. But this has been tricky. The Dawes rolls (and this fact seems to have been lost) were created as a means of fractionalizing collective Cherokee landholdings and opening up the Indian Territories for white settlement. When the white bureaucrats made the rolls, they listed people who looked Cherokee as Cherokee, and those who looked black (even if these were mixed black and Cherokee) as black. The Dawes rolls were based on blood, but only on how blood "looked" (and here we remember the anthropologists scratching the chests of White Earth Indians and measuring their skulls). From the beginning, the rolls were flawed and were designed to cheat Indians. One wonders: why rely on them now for any purpose? Enrollment has become a kind of signifier for Indians that says (or is believed to say) what someone's degree of Indianness is. But this is a relatively recent development. One wonders: by fighting about enrollment at all, aren't we just adopting a system of exclusion that helps the U.S. government but doesn't help us? And couldn't the Cherokee have won a little something from everyone had they thought of the problems of race, identity, and enrollment differently? After all, very few nations in the world base citizenship on race. It can be based on many things—such as language, a naturalization process, an oath, residency, or all of the above. Couldn't the Cherokee Nation say: since we were slaveholders, we have a moral debt to the descendants of the people we wrongly enslaved? Couldn't

40

[9]See http://www.time.com/time/nation/article/0,8599,1635873,00.html.

the Cherokee say: in order to pay that debt we will allow the Freedmen to remain on the rolls as citizens of the Cherokee Nation (or even limited citizens, nonvoting citizens, or whatever), though they are not racially Cherokee? This way the Cherokee would have sacrificed some autonomy and spread some resources a little thinner but would have made right a historical wrong and emerged as the moral victors in the enrollment issue.

Many Indian tribes, many reservations, are stronger than they have ever been before. Gaming has something to do with that. So do numbers. But we are not so strong that we can afford to waste our people. We are not so strong that we can keep excluding one another. But that's exactly what tribes often do. . . .

In part, impatience with the sometimes self-serving identity politics is what motivates language-immersion activists such as Keller Paap. They feel that if they are able to bring language back to the center of our sense of ourselves, all the other complicated politics of self, all the other markers of authenticity, will fall away. They feel that the government's attempt at assimilation created the destructive, diseased social fabric in which we are wrapped today. And so the work that Keller Paap, Lisa LaRonge, . . . Adrian Liberty, Leslie Harper, and others are doing to bring the Ojibwe language back is, essentially, an antiassimilationist movement. In many ways it turns around what AIM started. (One of AIM's cries was "Indian pride"—and AIMsters didn't style themselves as BIA bureaucrats with short hair and bolo ties.) The renewed interest in tribal cultures and tribal language runs against hundreds of years of government policy. . . .

For language activists, the language is the key to everything else—identity, life and lifestyle, home and homeland. Most language activists are also traditional Indians, but very modern traditional Indians, as likely to attend a ceremony as they are to have smartphones on which they record language material and Indian ceremonial music they are trying to learn. This new traditionalism is not a turning back of the clock, but a response to it; modernism (and modern, global capitalism) is a great obliterator of cultural difference and a great infuser of a new kind of class difference, and language activism is one way Indians are not only protecting themselves and their rights but also creating meaning in their lives. For Keller Paap and his family, this means tapping maple trees, ricing, hunting, collecting wild leeks, blasting Hendrix and Chris Whitley from the tinny speakers of their VW Westy van, and competing every year in the Birkebeiner cross-country ski race held in Hayward, Wisconsin. It means choosing to live their modern lives, with all those modern contradictions, in the Ojibwe language—to choose Ojibwe over English, whether for ceremony or for karaoke. . . .

If we lose our language and the culture that goes with it, I think, something more will be lost than simply a bouquet of discrete understandings about bears or namesakes, more than an opportunity to speak to my children and friends in public without anyone eavesdropping. If the language dies, we will lose something personal, a degree of understanding that resides, for most fluent speakers, on an unconscious level. We will lose our sense of ourselves and our culture. There are many aspects of culture that are extralinguistic—that is, they exist outside or in spite of language: kinship, legal systems, governance, history, personal identity. But there is very little that is extralinguistic about a story, about language itself. I think what I am trying to say is that we will lose beauty—the beauty of the particular, the beauty of the past and the intricacies of a language tailored for our space in the world. That Native American cultures are imperiled is important and not just to Indians. It is important to everyone, or should be. When we lose cultures, we lose American plurality—the productive and lovely discomfort that true difference brings.

ENGAGING THE TEXT

1. What is lost, according to Treuer, when a language dies? Why does he focus on the Ojibwe word for "namesake" (para. 7)? What connection does he see between language and culture?

2. What differences does Treuer note between the goals of the AIM activists and the language activists? Does Ojibwe-language immersion seem to you to be "a perverse luxury" (para. 25), given the serious problems of reservation life that Treuer cites? Debate in class.

3. Since attendance at Indian boarding schools wasn't compulsory, how and why did Indian agents coerce parents into sending their children to the schools?

4. What is "blood quantum," and why is it so vital to determining who is and is not Indian? How does it differ from the "one drop rule"?

5. Who were the Cherokee Freedmen? What history complicates their designation as Cherokee? Should they remain as citizens of the Cherokee Nation? Why or why not?

6. In what sense is the "new traditionalism" a response to modernism? To what extent do you agree with Treuer's claim that the preservation of Native American cultures is "important to everyone" (para. 44)?

EXPLORING CONNECTIONS

7. What does Matt Bors, the cartoonist on page 664, suggest about the historical forgetfulness of American culture, and what does the older figure in the cartoon not forget?

8. Linda Holtzman and Leon Sharpe (p. 607) discuss how racial oppression can lead to "intergenerational trauma" and "historical unresolved grief" affecting many generations of individuals. Reread Treuer's description of how students were treated at the Indian boarding schools and how their parents were coerced into allowing their children to attend. How might these experiences affect multiple generations of a family? Write a journal entry in which you imagine the impact and trace the effects of indigenous children being separated from their communities and families to be sent to the boarding schools.

9. How does John Gatto's concept of "schooling"— as opposed to education (p. 114)— apply to the Indian boarding schools? How would Treuer define real education?

EXTENDING THE CRITICAL CONTEXT

10. To see some of the language activists Treuer mentions and to hear more about their efforts to preserve the Ojibwe language, watch any or all segments of *First Speakers: Restoring the Ojibwe Language*, a special from Twin Cities Public Television: www.tpt.org/?a=productions&id=3. How does actually hearing the Ojibwe language compare to reading about it? What other differences do you detect between the video and the essay?

11. Research the language that was originally spoken by the native inhabitants of your area. Is it a living language? What efforts, if any, are being made to preserve or restore it?

12. Watch an episode or read the transcript of an episode of *We Shall Remain*, the five-part PBS series on Native American history. How does the series represent American Indians? How does this treatment compare to the treatment of Native Americans in popular films like *Windtalkers*, *Pocahontas*, or *Dances with Wolves* that are based on historical events?

HOW IMMIGRANTS BECOME "OTHER"

MARCELO M. SUÁREZ-OROZCO AND
CAROLA SUÁREZ-OROZCO

Illegal immigration is a hot-button topic. Extremists liken those who enter the United States illegally to drug-dealers and rapists, and advocate construction of a triple-layered fence on the Mexican border monitored by predator drones. Marcelo M. Suárez-Orozco and Carola Suárez-Orozco represent the flip side of this debate, presenting the human face of unauthorized immigration. Marcelo M. Suárez-Orozco is Distinguished Professor of Education and the Dean of the Graduate School of Education and Information Studies at UCLA, where his wife, Carola, is also a Professor of Education. Both are leading experts in immigration studies, having jointly won Harvard's Virginia and Warren Stone Prize for Outstanding Book on Education and Society (2007) for their *Learning a New Land: Immigrant Students in American Society*. Together and separately, they have edited a number of books on Latinos and immigration, and cowrote *Children of Immigration: The Developing Child* (2002). In 2009–2010, Marcelo M. Suárez-Orozco was a Fellow at Princeton's Institute for Advanced Study, and in 2012, he served as Special Advisor to the Chief Prosecutor at the International Criminal Court in The Hague, Netherlands. This essay originally appeared in *Arizona Firestorm: Global Immigration Realities, National Media, and Provincial Politics*, edited by Otto Santa Ana and Celeste González de Bustamante (2012).

Unauthorized Immigration

No human being can be "illegal." While there are illegal actions—running a red light or crossing an international border without the required authorization, one action should not come to define a person's existence. The terms *illegal*, *criminal*, and *alien*, often uttered in the same breath, conjure up unsavory associations.[1] Unsettling and distancing ways to label people, they have contributed to the creation of our very own caste of untouchables.

In many cases, "illegal status," or what we prefer to term unauthorized status, may not be voluntary. We prefer this term to *undocumented*

---

[1]Santa Ana, O. (2002). *Brown tide rising: Metaphoric representations of Latinos in contemporary public discourse.* Austin: University of Texas Press. [All notes are the Suárez-Orozcos', except 13.]

immigrant as many have documents or could have documents but often find themselves in a limbo state pending a formal legal outcome.

In the mid-1990s, Sonia Martinez, mother of four children, all under the age of ten, became a young widow when her husband was stricken with cancer. With a limited education and no means to support her family on a rancho in rural southern Mexico, she reluctantly left her children behind in the care of her mother and crossed the border without papers. The week after arriving Sonia took up a job as a live-in housekeeper and nanny in the Southwest. Every month she faithfully sent money home to her family. She called them every week. Each time she called, they had less and less to say to her. Lovingly, she selected presents for each of her children over the course of the year. By Christmas she would make the pilgrimage back to her rancho to see her children and, Santa-like, shower them with American gifts. But the sweet visits home were always too short and she would soon have to face the dangerous and expensive crossing back to California, relying on the help of treacherous *coyotes* (smugglers) she hired each time. After September 11, as border controls tightened, she no longer dared to make the trek back and forth. She has stayed behind the trapdoor on this side of the border and has not seen her children since then.[2]

Sonia found herself a young widow and in a post–NAFTA [North Atlantic Free Trade Agreement] Mexican economy with promised jobs that simply never materialized and in an unforgiving economy for poorly educated, unskilled, rural workers. Plentiful jobs in the Southwest economy in the mid-1990s, relatively comfortable working conditions as a live-in housekeeper and nanny in a middle-class neighborhood, and an extremely advantageous wage differential proved irresistible. Although not raising her children came at a high emotional cost, the ability to support them was its own reward.

In 1998, Hurricane Mitch devastated Honduras, leaving little in the way of work opportunities. Like many others, Gustavo Jimenez made his way north, dangerously riding atop trains through Central America and Mexico and then crossed with a hired *coyote* into Texas. He worked a series of odd jobs but found it difficult to find steady work. Then, yet another hurricane changed his fate. When Katrina devastated New Orleans in 2005, ample work opportunities opened—dirty work in horrific conditions were hard to fill over the long haul of the cleanup and reconstruction. Mr. Jimenez quickly found work: "Who but us migrants would do these hard jobs without ever taking a break? We worked day and night in jobs Americans would never do, so that the Gulf could be rebuilt." But he found that he would be treated with disdain. It left him mystified. On one hand, "I know that by coming here illegally I am

5

[2]Note that we have used a pseudonym; this case is from IS @ NYU data—see http:// steinhardt.nyu.edu/scmsAdmin/media/users/ef58/metrocenter/Online_Supplemental_Notes .pdf.

breaking the law," but he added, "I did not come to steal from anyone. I put my all in the jobs I take. And I don't see any of the Americans wanting to do this work."[3] Gustavo's story is both old and new. Unauthorized immigrants have always been called upon to do the jobs on the dark side of the American economy. The post-Katrina cleanup is a fitting example. Adding insult to injury, these workers are the target of disdain and disparagement. The stigma of the work gets attached to them—as if those doing dirty, demanding, and dangerous jobs themselves by mimesis become dirty, despised, and dispensable.

Hervé Fonkou Takoulo is a college-educated professional with a knack for stock trading in his spare time. Mr. Takoulo arrived in the United States in 1998 on a valid visa from the troubled African nation of Cameroon. He took to New York like a duck to water. He graduated with an engineering degree from the State University of New York and married a U.S. citizen hailing from California. She was the vice president of a Manhattan media advertising company. The biracial professional couple was ecstatic when President Obama spoke of his dual African and American roots. Takoulo's wife, Caroline Jamieson, "recalled that she cried when Mr. Obama said during a 2008 campaign speech, 'With a mother from Kansas and a father from Kenya'—I said, 'Oh, Hervé, even the alliteration is right—with a mother from California and a father from Cameroon, our child could do the same!'" She cried again but for a very different reason when the letter she wrote to President Obama resulted in her husband's arrest. The letter to the president "explained that Ms. Jamieson, 42, had filed a petition seeking a green card for her husband on the basis of their 2005 marriage. But before they met, Mr. Takoulo, who first arrived in the country on a temporary business visa, had applied for political asylum and had been denied it by an immigration judge in Baltimore, who ordered him deported." Surely, this president with his extensive personal experience in Africa would understand that Cameroon had a horrendous record of human rights abuses. Instead of the hoped-for presidential reprieve, the asylum seeking Obamista was met by two immigration agents, "in front of the couple's East Village apartment building. He says one agent asked him, 'Did you write a letter to President Obama?' When he acknowledged that his wife had, he was handcuffed and sent to an immigration jail in New Jersey for deportation."[4]

When she was four, Marieli's father was assassinated in front of his wife and children. Left as a widow responsible for her family, Marieli's mother reluctantly left Guatemala for the United States, as she put it, "in order to be able to feed my family." Once in California, she applied for

[3]Gustavo's quotes are to be found in Orner, P. (Ed.). (2008). *Underground America: Narratives of undocumented lives.* San Francisco, CA: McSweeney's.

[4]Bernstein, N. (2010, June 18). Plea to Obama led to an immigrant's arrest. *New York Times.*

asylum status and waited patiently for her papers to be processed. The unforgiving bureaucratic labyrinth took six years and a small fortune to complete. Only then could she begin the process of applying to reunite with her children. In the meantime, the grandmother, who had been raising the children in her absence, died. With no one to care for them and after having patiently waited for years, Marieli's mother made the drastic choice of having her children make the crossing without papers. Finally, at age eleven, after having spent more than half her childhood away from her mother, Marieli arrived in northern California after being smuggled into the country by *coyotes*. Recognizing she "owed every-thing" to her mother but at the same time angry she had been left behind for so long, the reunification with the mother she barely knew was a rocky and bittersweet one. Marieli is now an unauthorized immigrant waiting in limbo.

The Reagan-inspired U.S. wars of proxy in El Salvador, Guatemala, and Nicaragua of the 1980s resulted in systematic killings—largely of noncombatant civilians, massive displacements of people, and the begin-ning of an international exodus of biblical proportions not only to the United States but also to neighboring Latin American countries. The U.S. invasion of Iraq has made Iraqis top the list of formally admitted refu-gees in the United States in 2009. While those escaping our foreign pol-icy debacles often make it through the legal maze, thousands of others fall through every year.

The cases reveal how war and conflict drive human migration. But the heart also plays an unanticipated but powerful role. Work, war, and love are behind almost every migrant journey—authorized or unauthorized.

Many come here fully aware that they will be breaking a law by crossing without the proper documents, but in other cases accidents, mis-understandings, and an unforgiving bureaucracy can turn good faith errors into labyrinths without exit.

During his tour of duty in Iraq, Lt. Kenneth Tenebro "harbored a fear he did not share with anyone in the military. Lieutenant Tenebro worried that his wife, Wilma, back home in New York with their infant daughter, would be deported. Wilma, who like her husband was born in the Philippines, is an illegal immigrant. . . . That was our fear all the time." When he called home, "She often cried about it. . . . Like, hey, what's going to happen? Where will I leave our daughter?" The Tene-bros' story, like many others, began as a love story and an overstayed visa. They met several years ago while Wilma was on vacation in New York at the end of a job as a housekeeper on a cruise ship. Love kept her from returning to the Philippines, and ultimately she overstayed her visa. Today, the lieutenant and the wife face an unhappy choice: "Wilma is snagged on a statute, notorious among immigration lawyers, that makes it virtually impossible for her to become a legal resident without first leaving the United States and staying away for 10 years." Lt. Tenebro is not alone—thousands of U.S. soldiers facing dangerous tours of duty have the additional burden of worrying that loved ones close to them will be deported.[5]

Combined, these testimonies embody the varieties of unauthorized journeys into the United States. Synergetic "push" and "pull" factors coalesce, luring immigrants away from familiar but relatively scarce surroundings to an alluring unknown. Immigrant optimism springs eternal. While some fly in with documents and visas and simply overstay, more immigrants come undetected through the southern border. Often they hire dangerous *coyotes* (typically from Mexico or Central America) or *snakeheads* (working from as far away as China, India, or Russia). Immigrants pay a very high price for these unauthorized journeys. While the crossing from Mexico to the United States can run approximately $3,000, the costs of longer passages are substantially higher, running up to an exorbitant $30,000 per journey. Those who arrive under the long shadow of transnational smuggling syndicates often face a period of protracted indentured servitude, as they must pay back exorbitant crossing fees. Whether the journey begins in Fujian, China, or Puebla, Mexico, tough border controls have made the crossing more dangerous than ever before—on average more than a person a day dies at the southern border attempting to cross.

The Children of Unauthorized Immigrants

Unauthorized immigrants are neither from Mars nor Venus. The majority have roots in American society. While some are married to U.S. citizens, others partner with migrants already here. Nearly half of unauthorized immigrants live in households with a partner and children. The vast majority of these children—79 percent—are U.S. citizens by birth.[6] The number of U.S.-born children in mixed-status families has expanded rapidly from 2.7 million in 2003 to 4 million in 2008.[7] Adding the 1.1 million unauthorized children living in the United States (like Marieli) means that there are 5.1 million children currently living in "mixed-status" homes.[8]

Nowhere is the story of the unauthorized immigration more dystopic than for the children who grow up in the shadows of the law. On an unbearable steamy afternoon in July 2010, Carola Suárez-Orozco found herself in a somber congressional chamber testifying on behalf of the American Psychological Association in front of an ad hoc committee of the United States House of Representatives headed by Arizona's Congressman Raúl Grijalva (D-Tucson). At her side were two children—

[5]Preston, J. (2010, May 8). Worried about deploying with family in limbo. *New York Times*.

[6]Passel, J. S., & Taylor, P. (2010). Unauthorized immigrants and their U.S.-born children. Washington, DC: Pew Research Center. Retrieved from pewhispanic.org/reports /report.php?ReportID=125.

[7]Ibid.

[8]Ibid.

precocious, overly serious. A congressional photographer afterward whispered to Carola that in over twenty years on the job he had never seen such young children testify before the U.S. Congress.

> Eleven-year-old Mathew Parea was poised and collected as he spoke in the august chamber. At a tender age, he had already been active in social justice causes for several years including a four-day fast honoring the patron saint of migrant workers, César Chávez. Mathew spoke on behalf of thousands of children of migrant families. His steady voice was riveting: "I am here to tell you about my fears growing up in Arizona. Children want to be with their parents because we know that our parents love us. The laws in Arizona are just unjust and make me fear for my family. I am always worried when my family leaves the house that something might happen to them. I think about it when my dad goes to work that he might not come back or when I go to school that there might not be someone to pick me up when I get out."[9]
>
> Heidi Portugal physically appeared younger than twelve, yet she carried herself in an unsettling serious manner. Her story embodies the immigrant dream turned nightmare: "At only 10 years of age I had a sad awakening the day of February 11th. When I woke up, I found out that my mother had been arrested. . . . My biggest preoccupation was my two little brothers and sister. What was going to happen to them? And what about my little brother that my mother was breast feeding?" She went on to explain how as the eldest sister, she took on the responsibility of caring for her younger siblings, how her mother was deported, and how she has never seen her mother again. She went on, "Before, I would admire all uniformed people that protect our country . . . [but they] took away the most precious thing that children can have, our mother. With one hit, they took away my smile and my happiness."[10]

Mathew and Heidi are part of an estimated one hundred thousand citizen[11] children whose parents have been deported. They face an impossible choice no child should have to make—staying in the United States with relatives or going with their parents to a country they do not know. These youngsters are a caste of orphans of the state, citizen children who day in and day out lose "the right to have rights"[12]—for them the protections of the Fourteenth Amendment[13] are an elusive mirage. Children whose parents are detained and/or deported by Immigration and Customs Enforcement exhibit multiple behavioral changes in the aftermath of parental detention, including anxiety, frequent crying, changes in eating and sleeping patterns, withdrawal, and anger. Such behavioral

---

[9]See Testimony of Carola Suárez-Orozco before the United States House of Representatives, www.apa.org/about/gr/issues/cyf/immigration-enforcement.aspx.

[10]Ibid.

[11]Ibid.

[12]Arendt, H. (1966). *The origins of totalitarianism*. New York: Harcourt.

[13]**the Fourteenth Amendment:** Provides equal protection and due process under the law. [Eds.]

changes were documented for both short-term after the arrest as well as in the long-term at a nine-month follow-up.[14]

They also experience dramatic increases in housing instability and food insecurity—both important dimensions of basic developmental well-being. Such insecurities, while heightened for children whose parents are detained, is ongoing for children growing up in mixed-status households. These insecurities exist even though unauthorized immigrants have very high levels of employment; among men, fully 94 percent are active in the labor force (a rate substantially higher than for U.S.-born citizens—83 percent and legal immigrants—85 percent). At the same time, more than 30 percent of children growing up in unauthorized households live below the poverty line. Harvard psychologist Hiro Yoshikawa, in his detailed study of infants and their families, documents the range of penalties American-born preschool children of unauthorized parents face. First, the children's housing and economic situation was often quite fragile. Second, unauthorized parents were less likely to take advantage of a range of benefits to which their citizen children are entitled (like Temporary Assistance to Needy Families, Head Start, the Women, Infants and Children Nutritional Program, Medicaid, and others). Lastly, they had less access to extended social networks that can provide information, babysit, or lend money in a crisis.[15]

While the majority of children of unauthorized immigrants are citizen children (4 million), there are some 1.1 million children who just like Marieli have no papers. Many arrive when they are very young, others in their teen years. These children grow up in America, attending American schools, making American friends, learning English, and developing an emerging American identity. Every year approximately 65,000 young people graduate from high schools without the requisite papers either to go on to college or to legally enter the work force.

Unauthorized immigrants live in a parallel universe. Their lives are shaped by forces and habits that are unimaginable to many American citizens. Work and fear are the two constants. They lead to routines, where the fear of apprehension and deportation is an ever-present shadow in their lives. Dropping off a child to school, a casual trip to the supermarket, a train or bus ride, expose them to the threat of apprehension, deportation, and the pain of being separated from their loved ones.

Mass unauthorized immigration has become a social phenomenon with deep structural roots in American institutions. The responsibility must be shared beyond the immigrants themselves to the businesses that thrive on their labor, the middle-class families who rely on them for

[14]Chaudry, A., Pedroza, J., Castañeda, R. M., Santos, R., & Scott, M. M. (2010). *Facing our future: Children in the aftermath of immigration enforcement.* Washington, DC: Urban Institute.

[15]Yoshikawa, H. (2011). *Immigrants raising citizens: Undocumented parents and their young children.* New York: Russell Sage Foundation.

housekeeping, babysitting, landscaping, and other amenities, consumers who have come to expect their affordable produce and rapid delivery services, and all citizens who have consciously or unconsciously enabled a dysfunctional system to flourish. Above all the political class shares the bulk of the responsibility by oscillating between denial, grandstanding, and hysterical scapegoating. They have brought us demagogic, unworkable, and self-defeating policy proposals.

Broken Lines

Outcry over our broken immigration system is focused on the borderline. Frustrated and fearful, Americans ask, "Why won't these illegals get in line like everybody else?" On the surface that is a perfectly reasonable question.

The reality, however, is that there is no orderly line to join. The terrorist attacks of September 11 threw sand in an already rusty machinery of legal immigration. In countless U.S. consulates and embassies the world over and in U.S. Citizenship and Immigration Services offices all over the country, millions wait in interminable queues. New security considerations brought an already inefficient system to a near standstill.

There are nearly 3.5 million immediate family members of U.S. citizens and permanent lawful immigrants waiting overseas for their visas.[16] In U.S. consulates in Mexico alone, approximately a quarter of a million spouses and minor children of U.S. citizens and permanent lawful residents wait to legally join their immediate relatives north of the border. In the Philippines, approximately 70,000 spouses and minor children are in the same situation. The average wait in line for these countries is from four to six years for spouses and under-age children. If you are a U.S. citizen and your sister is in the Philippines, you will have to wait twenty years before she can join you. If you are a U.S. citizen and would like to sponsor your unmarried adult child in Mexico, you will wait sixteen years and spend considerable resources.

The visa allocation system for work permits is no more functional.[17] The annual quota for work visas is 140,000 per year; as this includes spouses and children, the actual number of workers is much lower. There is no systematic queue for low-skilled workers. There are a million people waiting in Mexico alone in any given year.[18] As Roxanna Bacon, the chief counsel for the United States Citizenship and Immigration Services in Washington, D.C., succinctly stated, "Our housing industry,

[16]Anderson, S. (2010). Family immigration: The long wait to immigrate. Arlington, VA: National Foundation for American Policy. Retrieved from www.nfap.com/.

[17]Anderson, S. (2009). *Employment-based green card projections point to decade-long waits*. Arlington, VA: National Foundation for American Policy. Retrieved from www.nfap.com/.

[18]U.S. State Department (2009). Annual report on immigrant visa applicants in the family sponsored and employment based preferences registered at the National Visa Center as of November 1. Annual Report on Immigrant Visas. Washington, DC: U.S. State Department.

our service industry, our gardening, landscape industry, you name it—it's been dependent for decades on Mexican labor. None of these people qualify for an employment-based visa. So when the hate mongers say, 'Why can't they wait in line? Can't they get a visa?'—there aren't any visas to get! There is no line to wait in! And that's why everyone who knows this area of law says without comprehensive immigration reform you really aren't going to solve any of these pop-up issues."[19]

Reasonable voices have been driven off stage, while demagogic venting, grandstanding, and obfuscation saturate the airwaves, the print media, the Internet, and town halls throughout the nation. Rather than offering new solutions, an amalgamation of cultural xenophobes and economic nativists has joined together to fuel the fire. Xenophobes see mass immigration, especially from Latin America, as a growing menace to the pristine tapestry of American culture that would be stained by new arrivals from the "Brown" continent. Economic nativists wring their hands: immigration presents unfair competition for ever-scarcer jobs as well as putting downward pressure on wages. For them, immigration has come to embody the globalization in all its pathologies. Immigrants are tangible representations of enormous and amorphous problems—the globalization of terror, the outsourcing of jobs, and the discomfort of being surrounded by strangers (dis)figuring the social sphere with exotic languages, cultural habits, and uncanny ways.

References

Anderson, S. (2009). *Employment-based green card projections point to decade-long waits.* Arlington, VA: National Foundation for American Policy. Retrieved from www.nfap.com/.

Anderson, S. (2010). *Family immigration: The long wait to immigrate.* Arlington, VA: National Foundation for American Policy. Retrieved from www.nfap.com/.

Arendt, H. (1966), *The origins of totalitarianism.* New York: Harcourt.

Bernstein, N. (2006, May 22). 100 years in the back door, out the front. *New York Times.* Retrieved on July 31, 2011 from www.nytimes.com/learning/teachers/featured_articles/20060522monday.html?scp=10&sq=Ari%20Zolberg&st=cse.

Bernstein, N. (2010, June 18). Plea to Obama led to an immigrant's arrest. *New York Times.*

Chaudry, A., Pedroza, J., Castañeda, R. M., Santos, R., & Scott, M. M. (2010). *Facing our future: Children in the aftermath of immigration enforcement.* Washington, DC: Urban Institute.

Orner, P. (Ed.). (2008). *Underground America: Narratives of undocumented lives.* San Francisco, CA: McSweeney's.

Passel, J. S., & Taylor, P. (2010). Unauthorized immigrants and their U.S.-born children. Washington, DC: Pew Research Center. Retrieved from pewhispanic.org/reports/report.php?ReportID=125.

Preston, J. (2010, May 8). Worried about deploying with family in limbo. *New York Times.*

Santa Ana, O. (2002). *Brown tide rising: Metaphoric representations of Latinos in contemporary public discourse.* Austin: University of Texas Press.

[19]Bacon, R. (2010, May 22). One border, many sides. *New York Times.* Retrieved on 22 February 2012 from www.nytimes.com/2010/05/23/opinion/23deavere-smith.html?sc=8&sq-Deveare-Smith&st=cse&pagewanted=1.

Yoshikawa, H. (2011), *Immigrants raising citizens: Undocumented parents and their young children.* New York: Russell Sage Foundation.

Zolberg, A. (2008). *A nation by design: Immigration policy in the fashioning of America.* Cambridge, MA: Harvard University Press.

ENGAGING THE TEXT

1. According to the Suárez-Orozcos, how do the stories of immigrants like Sonia Martinez suggest that unauthorized immigration "may not be voluntary" (para. 2)? What "push and pull factors" do these stories reflect?

2. In what ways do the children of unauthorized immigrants routinely face insecurity and deprivation? What physical, psychological, and emotional problems do U.S.-born children experience when their parents are detained or deported? How is it that "for them the protections of the Fourteenth Amendment are an elusive mirage" (para. 14)?

3. How do the Suárez-Orozcos respond to the suggestion that unauthorized immigrants "get in line like everybody else" (para. 19)? How did the terrorist attacks of 9/11 complicate legal immigration? How long do U.S. citizens' immediate family members have to wait for a visa? What further problems do people seeking work visas face?

4. If the decision were up to you, which of the immigrants named by the Suárez-Orozcos would you allow to stay in the United States legally? Would you grant green cards to all of them, some of them, or none of them? What is the rationale for your decision? Compare your response to those of your classmates and debate.

5. **Thinking Rhetorically** What emotional or logical impact do the individual immigration stories have on the essay? What effect does the first-person testimony of the children have? The Suárez-Orozcos supplement the stories with statistics and expert testimony: How does this influence their argument? How would relying exclusively on storytelling affect the essay's credibility? Do the authors succeed in convincing you that "unauthorized immigrants live in a parallel universe" (para. 17)? Why or why not?

EXPLORING CONNECTIONS

6. In Darrin Bell's cartoon on page 675, what does he imply about the long history of anti-immigrant attitudes in the United States? What does he suggest about the immigrants themselves, and why does he construct the cartoon in reverse chronological order? To what extent would he agree with the Suárez-Orozcos that in the immigration debate, "reasonable voices" have been drowned out by "cultural xenophobes and economic nativists" (para. 23)?

7. The authors do not include any agricultural workers among their portraits of immigrants. Drawing on Kevin Bales and Ron Soodalter (p. 443), write a profile of an unauthorized Haitian immigrant picking tomatoes for a large agribusiness. Where does he live and what are his working conditions? What kinds of hours does he work and for how much money? What happens if he's injured or gets sick? Why would he submit to these conditions? Why is he excluded from the rights afforded to other American workers?

EXTENDING THE CRITICAL CONTEXT

8. As a thought experiment, assume for a moment that all unauthorized immigrants have suddenly disappeared. How would "middle-class families who rely on [immigrants] for housekeeping, babysitting, [and] landscaping" (para. 18) cope with their losses? What would be the consequences for agriculture, construction, restaurants, other businesses, and the overall economy? How do you think politicians would respond to this catastrophe? Write a story in which you imagine the consequences of the disappearance.

9. In 2014, the Obama administration, in response to the increased number of families fleeing violence in Central America, announced the development of family detention centers under the control of the U.S. Immigration and Customs Enforcement Agency (ICE). The administration requested congressional funding for 6,300 spaces to accommodate the mothers and children who have entered the United States illegally. Research and write an essay on these ICE family detention centers: Who operates them? What conditions exist for the women and children housed there? Why are these centers facing legal challenges?

10. Examine the language used by news reporters, politicians, or pro- and anti-immigrant groups in discussing immigration issues. What terms are used to describe unauthorized immigrants, what metaphors are used for the number of immigrants entering the United States, and what are their implications? What racial frames underlie this language?

FURTHER CONNECTIONS

1. Research the history of the native peoples of your state. What tribal groups inhabited the area before Europeans arrived? What is known about the cultures and languages of these tribes? How much and why did the native population decrease following European contact? What alliances and treaties were made between the tribes and the newcomers as non-natives began to occupy native lands? To what extent were treaties upheld or abandoned, and why? How were local native populations affected by relocation, the establishment of reservations, the creation of Indian boarding schools, the Dawes Act, or other legislation? What role has the Bureau of Indian Affairs played in protecting or failing to protect tribal interests? What issues are of greatest concern to the tribes in your area today? Write up the results of your research and present them to the class.

2. Some states and communities have responded to the rise in illegal immigration by enacting laws or ordinances that ban any language other than English, deny government services to undocumented immigrants, and penalize citizens (such as employers, landlords, and merchants) who "assist" them. Has your state or community adopted any such regulations? Research the arguments for and against such legislation, and discuss your findings in class. Which arguments are the most compelling, and why?

3. Investigate a recent conflict between ethnic, racial, or cultural groups on your campus or in your community. Research the issue, and interview people on each side. What event triggered the conflict? How do the groups involved perceive the issue differently? What tension, prior conflict, or injustice has contributed to the conflict and to the perceptions of those affected by it? Has the conflict been resolved? If so, write a paper discussing why you feel that the resolution was appropriate or not. If the conflict is continuing, write a paper proposing how a fair resolution might be reached.

4. Contentious debates over issues like affirmative action often hinge on whether or not the debaters accept the idea of structural racism (also called systemic racism). Proponents argue that structural racism is largely responsible for persistent racial disparities in wealth, income, home ownership, education, health care, and life expectancy. What evidence and examples of systemic racism do proponents cite? How do opponents of the concept explain racial inequalities, and what supporting evidence do they offer? Argue a position: Is it necessary to address structural discrimination in order to achieve racial equality in the United States?

ACKNOWLEDGMENTS

Alan Aja, Daniel Bustillo, William Darity Jr., and Darrick Hamilton, "From a Tangle of Pathology to a Race-Fair America" from *Dissent*, Summer 2014, pp. 39–43. Copyright © 2014 by *Dissent* Magazine. All rights reserved. Reprinted with permission of the University of Pennsylvania Press.

Sherman Alexie, "Gentrification" from *Blasphemy*, copyright © 2012 by FallsApart Productions, Inc. Used by permission of Grove/Atlantic, Inc. Any third party use of this material, outside of this publication, is prohibited. Electronic rights by permission of Nancy Stauffer Associates.

Lori Andrews, "George Orwell . . . Meet Mark Zuckerberg," reprinted with the permission of The Free Press, a Division of Simon & Schuster, Inc., from *I Know Who You Are and I Saw What You Did: Social Networks and the Death of Privacy*. Copyright © 2011 by Lori Andrews. All rights reserved.

Jean Anyon, excerpt from "Social Class and the Hidden Curriculum of Work" by Jean Anyon, first published in the *Journal of Education*, Vol. 162, no. 1, Fall 1980, is reprinted by permission of Jessica A. Bird.

Kevin Bales and Ron Soodalter, selections from "The Old Slavery and the New" and "Slaves in the Pastures of Plenty" from *The Slave Next Door: Human Trafficking and Slavery in America Today*. Copyright © 2010 by the Regents of the University of California. Reprinted by permission of the publisher, the University of California Press.

Cris Beam, excerpts from *To the End of June: The Intimate Life of American Foster Care*. Copyright © 2013 by Cris Beam. Reprinted by permission of Houghton Mifflin Harcourt Publishing Company. All rights reserved.

Sarah Boxer, "Why Are All the Cartoon Mothers Dead?" first published in *The Atlantic*, July/August 2014. Copyright © 2014 The Atlantic Media Co. All rights reserved. Distributed by Tribune Content Agency, LLC. Reprinted by permission.

danah boyd, from *It's Complicated: The Social Lives of Networked Teens*. Copyright © 2014 by danah boyd. Reprinted by permission of the publisher, Yale University Press.

June Carbone and Naomi Cahn, from *Marriage Markets: How Inequality Is Remaking the American Family* (2014), pp. 1–8, 213–14. Reprinted by permission of Oxford Publishing Ltd.

Ta-Nehisi Coates, excerpts from "The Case for Reparations" first published in *The Atlantic*, May 21, 2014. Copyright © 2014 by The Atlantic Media Co. All rights reserved. Distributed by Tribune Content Agency, LLC.

Stephanie Coontz, "What We Really Miss About the 1950's" from *The Way We Really Are: Coming to Terms with America's Changing Families*. Copyright © 1997 by Stephanie Coontz. Published by Basic Books, a member of the Perseus Books Group. Reprinted by permission of Basic Books via the Copyright Clearance Center.

William Deresiewicz, "Don't Send Your Kids to the Ivy League" as published in the *New Republic*, July 21, 2014, from *Excellent Sheep: The Miseducation of the American Elite and the Way to a Meaningful Life*. Copyright © 2014 by William Deresiewicz. All rights reserved. Reprinted with the permission of The Free Press, a Division of Simon & Schuster, Inc.

Aaron H. Devor, writing as Holly Devor, "Becoming Members of Society: Learning the Meaning of Social Gender" in *Gender Blending*. Copyright © 1989 by Holly Devor. Reprinted by permission of Indiana University Press.

Melvin Dixon, "Aunt Ida Pieces a Quilt" from *Love's Instruments*. Copyright © 1995 by Melvin Dixon. Used by permission of the Estate of Melvin Dixon.

Barbara Ehrenreich. "Serving in Florida" from *Nickel and Dimed: On (Not) Getting By in America*. Copyright © 2001 by Barbara Ehrenreich. Reprinted by arrangement with Henry Holt & Company, LLC. All rights reserved.

Mona El-Ghobashy, "Quandaries of Representation" from *Arab and Arab American Feminisms: Gender, Violence, and Belonging*, ed. Rabab Abdulhadi, Evelyn Alsultany, and Nadine Naber (2011). Reprinted by permission of the publisher, Syracuse University Press.

John Taylor Gatto. "Against School." Copyright © 2003 by *Harper's* magazine. All rights reserved. Reproduced from the September issue by special permission.

Naomi Gerstel and Natalia Sarkisian, "The Color of Family Ties: Race, Class, Gender, and Extended Family Involvement" from *American Families: A Multicultural Reader*, 2nd ed., edited by Stephanie Coontz. Copyright © 2008. Reprinted by permission.

Cheryl I. Harris and Devon W. Carbado, "Loot or Find: Fact or Frame?" In *After the Storm: Black Intellectuals Explore the Meaning of Hurricane Katrina*, edited by David Dante Troutt. Copyright © 2006. Reprinted by permission of Cheryl Harris and Devon Carbado.

Linda Holtzman and Leon Sharpe, with the assistance of Joseph Farand Gardner, from "Racing in America: Fact or Fiction" from *Media Messages: What Film, Television, and Popular Music Teach Us About Race, Class, Gender, and Sexual Orientation*. Copyright © 2014 by Taylor & Francis. Republished with permission of Taylor & Francis via the Copyright Clearance Center.

Henrick Karoliszyn, "Precognitive Police" from *AEON* online, September 3, 2014. This article was originally published by Aeon Media, http://www.aeon.co, a digital magazine for ideas and culture. Follow them on Twitter at @aeonmag, https://twitter.com/aeonmag.

Diana Kendall, "Framing Class" from *Framing Class: Media Representations of Wealth and Poverty in America*. Reprinted by permission of Rowman & Littlefield Publishers via the Copyright Clearance Center.

Jean Kilbourne, Chapter 12, "Two Ways a Woman Can Get Hurt: Advertising and Violence." Reprinted with the permission of The Free Press, a Division of Simon & Schuster, Inc., from *Can't Buy My Love: How Advertising Changes the Way We Think and Feel* by Jean Kilbourne. Previously published in hardcover as *Deadly Persuasion*. Copyright © 1999 by Jean Kilbourne. All rights reserved.

Michael Kimmel, " 'Bros Before Hos': The Guy Code" from *Guyland: The Perilous World Where Boys Become Men*, pp. 44–69. Copyright © 2008 by Michael Kimmel. Reprinted by permission of HarperCollins Publishers.

Jamaica Kincaid, "Girl" from *At the Bottom of the River* by Jamaica Kincaid. Copyright © 1983 by Jamaica Kincaid. Reprinted by permission of Farrar, Straus & Giroux, LLC.

Jonathan Kozol, "Still Separate, Still Unequal" excerpted from *The Shame of the Nation: The Restoration of Apartheid Schooling in America*, copyright © 2005 by Jonathan Kozol. Used by permission of Crown Books, an imprint of the Crown Publishing Group, a division of Penguin Random House LLC. All rights reserved. Any third party use of this material, outside of this publication, is prohibited. Interested parties must apply directly to Penguin Random House LLC for permission.

Carmen R. Lugo-Lugo, "A Prostitute, a Servant, and a Customer-Service Representative: A Latina in Academia" from *Presumed Incompetent: The Intersections of Race and Class for Women in Academia*, edited by Gabriella Guitierrez y Muha et al. is reprinted by permission of the Utah State University Press.

Malcolm X, "Learning to Read" from *The Autobiography of Malcolm X* by Malcolm X as told to Alex Haley, copyright © 1964 by Alex Haley and Malcolm X. Copyright © 1965 by Alex Haley and Betty Shabazz. Used by permission of Random House, an imprint and division of Penguin Random House LLC. All rights reserved. Electronic rights used by permission of Ballantine Books, an imprint of Random House, a division of Penguin Random House LLC. All rights reserved. Any third party use of this material, outside of this publication, is prohibited. Interested parties must apply directly to Penguin Random House LLC for permission.

Gregory Mantsios, "Class in America — 2012" from *Race, Class, and Gender in the United States*, edited by Paula Rothenberg (Worth Publishers, 2013). Reprinted with permission of Gregory Mantsios.

Joan Morgan, "From Fly-Girls to Bitches and Hos" is reprinted with the permission of Simon & Schuster, Inc., from *When Chickenheads Come Home to Roost*. Copyright © 1999 by Joan Morgan. All rights reserved.

George Packer, "Mr. Sam: Sam Walton" and "Just Business: Jay-Z" from *The Unwinding*. Copyright © 2013 by George Packer. Reprinted by permission of Farrar, Straus & Giroux, LLC.

Ruth Padawer, "Sisterhood Is Complicated," from *The New York Times*, October 19, 2014. Copyright © 2014 The New York Times. All rights reserved. Used by permission and protected by the Copyright Laws of the United States. The printing, copying, redistribution, or retransmission of this Content without express written permission is prohibited.

Laurie Penny, "Cybersexism" from *Unspeakable Things: Sex, Lies, and Revolution*. Copyright © 2014 by Laurie Penny. Reprinted by permission of the publisher Bloomsbury Publishing Plc.

INDEX OF AUTHORS AND TITLES

Against School (Gatto), 114

Aja, Alan, Daniel Bustillo, William Darity Jr., and Darrick Hamilton, *From a Tangle of Pathology to a Race-Fair America*, 415

Alexie, Sherman, *Gentrification*, 615

Andrews, Lori, *George Orwell . . . Meet Mark Zuckerberg*, 322

Anyon, Jean, *Social Class and the Hidden Curriculum of Work*, 136

Aunt Ida Pieces a Quilt (Dixon), 41

Bales, Kevin, and Ron Soodalter, *Slavery in the Land of the Free*, 443

Beam, Cris, *To the End of June: The Intimate Life of American Foster Care*, 61

Becoming Members of Society: Learning the Social Meanings of Gender (Devor), 471

Beyond Outrage (Reich), 399

Boxer, Sarah, *Why Are All the Cartoon Mothers Dead?*, 86

boyd, danah, *Inequality: Can Social Media Resolve Social Divisions?*, 303

"Bros Before Hos": The Guy Code (Kimmel), 540

Bustillo, Daniel, Alan Aja, William Darity Jr., and Darrick Hamilton, *From a Tangle of Pathology to a Race-Fair America*, 415

Cahn, Naomi, and June Carbone, *Marriage Markets: How Inequality Is Remaking the American Family*, 77

Carbado, Devon W., and Cheryl I. Harris, *Loot or Find: Fact or Frame?* 620

Carbone, June, and Naomi Cahn, *Marriage Markets: How Inequality Is Remaking the American Family*, 77

Case for Reparations, The (Coates), 572

Class in America — 2012 (Mantsios), 377

Coates, Ta-Nehisi, *The Case for Reparations*, 572

Cohen, Jared, and Eric Schmidt, *Our Future Selves*, 219

Color of Family Ties, The: Race, Class, Gender, and Extended Family Involvement (Gerstel and Sarkisian), 44

Coontz, Stephanie, *What We Really Miss About the 1950s*, 25

Cybersexism (Penny), 253

Darity, William, Jr., Alan Aja, Daniel Bustillo, and Darrick Hamilton, *From a Tangle of Pathology to a Race-Fair America*, 415

Deresiewicz, William, *Don't Send Your Kids to the Ivy League*, 200

Devor, Aaron H., *Becoming Members of Society: Learning the Social Meanings of Gender*, 471

Dixon, Melvin, *Aunt Ida Pieces a Quilt*, 41

Don't Send Your Kids to the Ivy League (Deresiewicz), 200

Ehrenreich, Barbara, *Serving in Florida*, 363

El-Ghobashy, Mona, *Quandaries of Representation*, 481

Essentials of a Good Education, The (Ravitch), 105

Framing Class, Vicarious Living, and Conspicuous Consumption (Kendall), 424

From a Tangle of Pathology to a Race-Fair America (Aja, Bustillo, Darity, and Hamilton), 415

From Fly-Girls to Bitches and Hos (Morgan), 533

Gatto, John Taylor, *Against School*, 114

Gentrification (Alexie), 615

George Orwell . . . Meet Mark Zuckerberg (Andrews), 322

Gerstel, Naomi, and Natalia Sarkisian, *The Color of Family Ties: Race, Class, Gender, and Extended Family Involvement*, 44

Girl (Kincaid), 469

Growing Up Tethered (Turkle), 236

Hamilton, Darrick, Alan Aja, Daniel Bustillo, and William Darity Jr., *From a Tangle of Pathology to a Race-Fair America*, 415

Harris, Cheryl I., and Devon W. Carbado, *Loot or Find: Fact or Frame?*, 620

Holtzman, Linda, and Leon Sharpe, *Theories and Constructs of Race*, 599

How Immigrants Become "Other" (Suárez-Orozco and Suárez-Orozco), 666

"I Just Wanna Be Average" (Rose), 123

Inequality: Can Social Media Resolve Social Divisions? (boyd), 303

Karoliszyn, Henrick, *Precognitive Police*, 336

Kendall, Diana, *Framing Class, Vicarious Living, and Conspicuous Consumption*, 424

Kilbourne, Jean, *"Two Ways a Woman Can Get Hurt": Advertising and Violence*, 488

Kimmel, Michael, *"Bros Before Hos": The Guy Code*, 540

Kincaid, Jamaica, *Girl*, 469

Kozol, Jonathan, *Still Separate, Still Unequal*, 170

Land of the Giants (Tizon), 645

Learning to Read (Malcolm X), 161

Loneliness of the Interconnected, The (Seife), 289

Longest War, The (Solnit), 522

Looking for Work (Soto), 19

Loot or Find: Fact or Frame? (Harris and Carbado), 620

Love Me Tinder (Witt), 270

Lugo-Lugo, Carmen R., *A Prostitute, a Servant, and a Customer-Service Representative: A Latina in Academia*, 188

Malcolm X, *Learning to Read*, 161

Mantsios, Gregory, *Class in America—2012*, 377

Marriage Markets: How Inequality Is Remaking the American Family (Carbone and Cahn), 77

Morgan, Joan, *From Fly-Girls to Bitches and Hos*, 533

Our Future Selves (Schmidt and Cohen), 219

Packer, George, *Sam Walton / Jay Z*, 350

Padawer, Ruth, *Sisterhood Is Complicated*, 550

Penny, Laurie, *Cybersexism*, 253

Precognitive Police (Karoliszyn), 336

Prostitute, a Servant, and a Customer-Service Representative, A: A Latina in Academia (Lugo-Lugo), 188

Quandaries of Representation (El-Ghobashy), 481

Ravitch, Diane, *The Essentials of a Good Education*, 105

Reich, Robert B., *Beyond Outrage*, 399

Rez Life: An Indian's Journey Through Reservation Life (Treuer), 651

Rose, Mike, *"I Just Wanna Be Average,"* 123

Sam Walton / Jay Z (Packer), 350

Sarkisian, Natalia, and Naomi Gerstel, *The Color of Family Ties: Race, Class, Gender, and Extended Family Involvement*, 44

Schmidt, Eric, and Jared Cohen, *Our Future Selves*, 219

Seife, Charles, *The Loneliness of the Interconnected*, 289

Serving in Florida (Ehrenreich), 363

Sharpe, Leon, and Linda Holtzman, *Theories and Constructs of Race*, 599

Sisterhood Is Complicated (Padawer), 550

Slavery in the Land of the Free (Bales and Soodalter), 443

Social Class and the Hidden Curriculum of Work (Anyon), 136

Solnit, Rebecca, *The Longest War*, 522

Soodalter, Ron, and Kevin Bales, *Slavery in the Land of the Free*, 443

Soto, Gary, *Looking for Work*, 19

Still Separate, Still Unequal (Kozol), 170

Suárez-Orozco, Carola, and Marcelo M. Suárez-Orozco, *How Immigrants Become "Other,"* 666

Suárez-Orozco, Marcelo M., and Carola Suárez-Orozco, *How Immigrants Become "Other,"* 666

Theories and Constructs of Race (Holtzman and Sharpe), 599

Tizon, Alex, *Land of the Giants*, 645

To the End of June: The Intimate Life of American Foster Care (Beam), 61

Treuer, David, *Rez Life: An Indian's Journey Through Reservation Life*, 651

Turkle, Sherry, *Growing Up Tethered*, 236

"Two Ways a Woman Can Get Hurt": Advertising and Violence (Kilbourne), 488

What We Really Miss About the 1950s (Coontz), 25

Why Are All the Cartoon Mothers Dead? (Boxer), 86

Witt, Emily, *Love Me Tinder*, 270